MW01620873

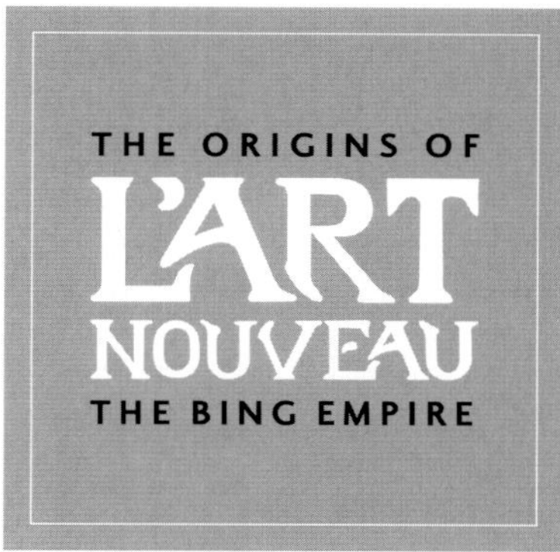
THE ORIGINS OF
L'ART
NOUVEAU
THE BING EMPIRE

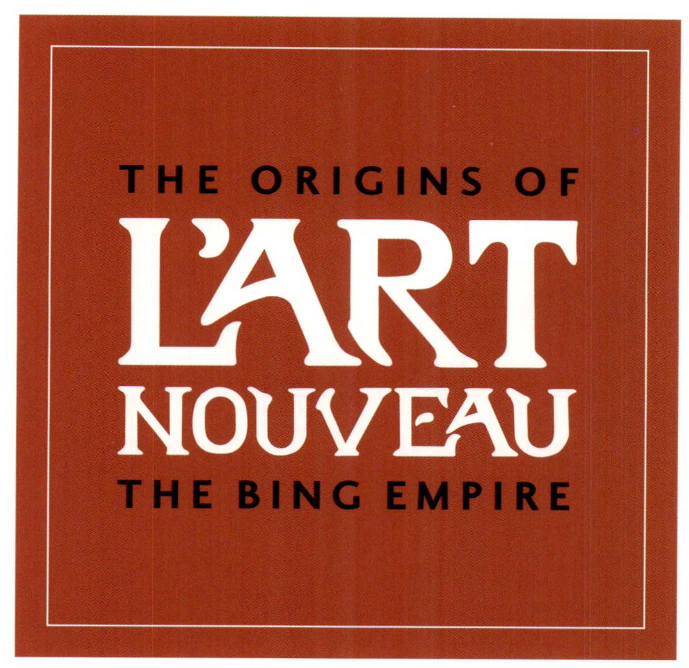

EDITED BY

GABRIEL P. WEISBERG, EDWIN BECKER

AND ÉVELYNE POSSÉMÉ

Van Gogh Museum | Musée des Arts décoratifs | Mercatorfonds

DISTRIBUTED BY Cornell University Press

This book has been published to accompany the exhibition *L'Art Nouveau: La Maison Bing*,
Van Gogh Museum, Amsterdam, 26 November 2004–27 February 2005,
Museum Villa Stuck, Munich, 17 March–31 July 2005,
CaixaForum, Barcelona, September 2005–January 2006,
Musée des Arts décoratifs, Paris, March-July 2006.

VAN GOGH MUSEUM

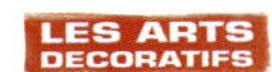

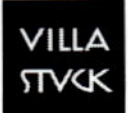

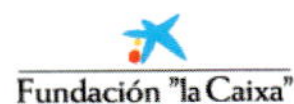

Initiative
Van Gogh Museum, Amsterdam
Musée des Arts décoratifs, Paris

Curatorial concept
Gabriel P. Weisberg
Edwin Becker
Évelyne Possémé

Selection Oriental art
Christine Shimizu

Supervising editors
Gabriel P. Weisberg
Edwin Becker
Évelyne Possémé

Authors
Edwin Becker
Rüdiger Joppien
Karine Lacquemant
Évelyne Possémé
Christine Shimizu
Philippe Thiébaut
Gabriel P. Weisberg

Biographies
Karine Lacquemant

Research assistants
Laura Gutman-Hanhivaara
Hanneke Hueber
Hervé Doucet
Hélène Andrieux
Karine Lacquemant

Research consultant
Yvonne Weisberg

Publications Coordination
Suzanne Bogman
Chloé Demey
Claire Archer

Secretary
Adrie Kok

Production
Tijdsbeeld & Pièce Montée, Ghent
Ronny Gobyn, director

Coordination
Barbara Costermans, Tijdgeest, Ghent
Petra Gunst, Tijdsbeeld & Pièce Montée, Ghent
Ann Mestdag, Mercatorfonds, Antwerp

Copyediting
Michael Raeburn, London

Translations
Wendie Shaffer and Kate Williams
First Edition Translations, Cambridge UK

Design
Griet Van Haute, Ghent

Typesetting
Griffo, Ghent

Colour separation
Kristin Van Damme, Tijdsbeeld & Pièce Montée
Die Keure, Bruges

Printing and binding
Die Keure, Bruges

Photographs
All photographs were supplied with the permission of the owners of the works reproduced. With special thanks to: Thomas Berg, Museum für Kunst und Gewerbe, Hamburg; Bildarchiv Preußischer Kulturbesitz (figs. 87–9, 280); Foto Speltdoorn (figs. 142, 151, 153, 285); Eric Fox (fig. 193); Thomas Hennocque (figs. 224–9, 232); Thomas Matyk, MAK, Vienna; Susanne Nagy, Paris, courtesy of Ms. Hilda Bénichou (figs. 183, 200, 201); Photo RMN (Arnaudet, M. Beck-Coppola, Gérard Blot, Harry Bréjat, Gendraud, Hervé Landowski, Magnoux, Jean Schormans) (figs. 8, 27, 33, 38, 45, 74, 95, 137, 145, 158, 234); Thijs Quispel; Laurent Sully-Jaulmes, Musée des Arts décoratifs, Paris

Cover
Front: Fabric with a carp swimming against the current, Japan, 19th century, Musée des Arts décoratifs, Paris
Back: Interior of L'Art Nouveau, 1895, Fonds Louis Bonnier, Institut français d'Architecture, Paris

ISBN 90 6153 572 7
D/2004/703/30

Distibuted in North America by Cornell University Press, 512 East State Street, Ithaca, New York 14850.
For further information, visit the Press website at www.cornellpress.cornell.edu.

ISBN 0-8014-4387-3

ART NOUVEAU AND SIEGFRIED BING

JOHN LEIGHTON, DIRECTOR
Van Gogh Museum, Amsterdam

BÉATRICE SALMON, DIRECTOR
Musée des Arts décoratifs, Paris

JO-ANNE BIRNIE DANZKER, DIRECTOR
Museum Villa Stuck, Munich

JOSÉ VILARASAU, PRESIDENT
Fundación 'la Caixa', Barcelona

It is surprising how few of the many exhibitions organised each year around the world, and how few publications, are dedicated to the cultural and historical significance of galleries and art dealers.[1] One might ask why. Certainly, from the nineteenth century on, art dealers have had a seminal role in the creation of artistic reputations. By commissioning artists' works, cultivating collectors, organising exhibitions and publishing catalogues about the artists they exhibited, dealers expanded, and at times created, the market for art, making art a viable commodity.

Siegfried Bing was one of these dealers. But would we remember him, and would we dedicate such a sweeping exhibition and publication to him today if his activities had been confined only to buying and selling art objects? Probably not. What makes Bing such an important and celebrated figure in the annals of art during the last quarter of the nineteenth century and the beginning of the twentieth? His name appears in most studies of *Japonisme* and of the applied arts and decorative painting in Europe at that time. In addition, the name 'Art Nouveau', which he gave to his gallery in 1895 when he transformed it into an emporium for new art, has come to define and designate an artistic movement known around the world. Even today, the term Art Nouveau is understood in all languages as commemorating the beginning of the New Style, of a modern sensibility, not only in France but also in Europe and America.[2]

What makes Bing such a fascinating topic of study is that, in addition to being a dealer, first in Japanese art, then in the applied arts, he was also a patron and supporter of the arts in effect a creative entrepreneur. Bing not only commissioned artists to produce objects for sale in his gallery, Bing also opened workshops where artists and artisans designed and manufactured objects that he hoped would fulfill his vision of a new art for a modern living environment. Bing's commitment to the applied arts worldwide, his entrepreneurship in the creation of a modern décor for the home, his international commercial contacts, and his ability to use the power of images, new typefaces and logos to communicate his ideas about a modern aesthetic, made him a pioneer in the formation of a style born out of international cooperation and artistic cross-fertilisation.

Telling Bing's story meant much more than simply looking for objects in order to assemble them in an attractive manner in a museum. Research involved perspicacity on the part of the organisers, determination in ferreting out documents that would illuminate Bing's contribution to nineteenth century art. This process took researchers to museums, archives and libraries seldom consulted in the investigation of an artist's oeuvre. The narrative that emerges is not limited to the viewing and admiration of beautifully designed objects. We learn about the commerce of art, about the design and manufacture of objects and their promotion through widely distributed advertisements in the specialised and popular press. Bing, like those who competed with him for the attention of a public that had the means to furnish their homes in the newest fashion, was a master in the use of the latest promotional techniques. What Bing had learned about commerce when he started as a dealer in Japanese art direct contacts with the primary source of supply and contacts with firms that could produce on demand for western markets led him to initiate a design aesthetic that revolutionised the consumer market for elegantly furnished households. At the latest by 1900 and the *Exposition Universelle* in Paris, Bing's logo – *Art Nouveau Bing* – was seen as a trademark for new and well-crafted objects available to an international clientele.

For the Van Gogh Museum, this exhibition extends the policy of exhibiting a wide range of aspects of art and culture of the nineteenth and early twentieth century. In the case of Bing there is an extra motivation when one thinks of the importance of Japanese art for Van Gogh and of Bing as the artist's major source of Japanese prints. A further reason was to demonstrate the connection between Japanese art and *art nouveau*: Japanese art was a fundamental source for *art nouveau*. Bing's move from Japanese art to *art nouveau* proved to be a logical evolution. Furthermore, the theme of the exhibition, which could also be titled 'Paris 1900', falls clearly in the continuum of exhibitions organised by the Van Gogh Museum around other European capitals such as Glasgow, Vienna and Prague.

With this exhibition the Museum Villa Stuck celebrates the completion of the decade-long restoration of the Villa Stuck, a nineteenth century artist's villa designed by Franz von Stuck as a *Gesamtkunstwerk*, integrating art and life. It is also the second large-scale project of the newly opened Jugendstil Museum in the Villa Stuck and follows a series of exhibitions in 2004 celebrating the accomplishments of Munich Jugendstil. The emphasis in the present exhibition on the ties between the Far East and Europe builds on other exhibitions in this museum and follows directly on a project on the relationship between the Modern in China, Japan and Europe.[3]

In Barcelona the exhibition will be presented at CaixaForum, the former Casaramona factory designed by Josep Puig i Cadafalch and considered to be one of the most important industrial buildings of Catalan *Modernisme*. The Fundación 'la Caixa', has played an important role in the recovery of *Modernisme*: for instance, opening to the public another of Puig i Cadafalch's buildings in Barcelona, Palau Macaya, in the late 70s, and refurbishing the Gran Hotel by Lluís Domènech i Montaner in Palma de Mallorca in 1992 to house the foundation's cultural centre and the collection of works by the painter Hermen Anglada Camarasa.

Another significant issue emerges at the Musée des Arts décoratifs – the co-initiator of the exhibition. Here history plays an important role. The relationship between Bing and the museum was long and intense. The Musée des Arts décoratifs possesses numerous Japanese art objects spanning all media, and is one of the largest repositories of Bing's *art nouveau* objects – all donated by Bing's son Marcel in 1908. More importantly, it was the Musée des Arts décoratifs that generously aided in the organisation of the first exhibition dedicated to Bing in 1986, mounted by The Smithsonian Traveling Exhibition Service, Washington D.C., under the curatorship of Gabriel P. Weisberg, one of the co-curators of the present exhibition. This first exhibition would not have seen the light of day without the help of the Musée des Arts décoratifs, which lent many of its treasures, or without the assistance of Yvonne Brunhammer and the staff of the Museum. The current exhibition and publication, benefiting from the earlier study but also from the expertise and dedication of the other co-curators of the exhibition, Évelyne Possémé and Edwin Becker, has presented an opportunity to provide a more complete examination of Bing's career. He now assumes his rightful place, one rarely achieved by any art dealer/entrepreneur in earlier times or since.

We are indebted to the lenders of the exhibition for enabling us, through their generous loans, to present to an international public an ambitious overview of the accomplishments of *art nouveau* in France through the eyes of its 'interpreter', Siegfried Bing.

1 Recent examples include *Theo van Gogh 1857–1891. Art Dealer, Collector and Brother of Vincent*, Amsterdam (Van Gogh Museum) & Paris (Musée d'Orsay) 1999, as well as *Gérôme & Goupil. Art and Enterprise*, Bordeaux (Musée Goupil), Pittsburgh (Frick Art and Historical Center) & New York (Dahesh Museum of Art) 2000.

2 See London & Washington 2000–1.

3 *Shanghai Modern*, Munich (Museum Villa Stuck) 2004–5.

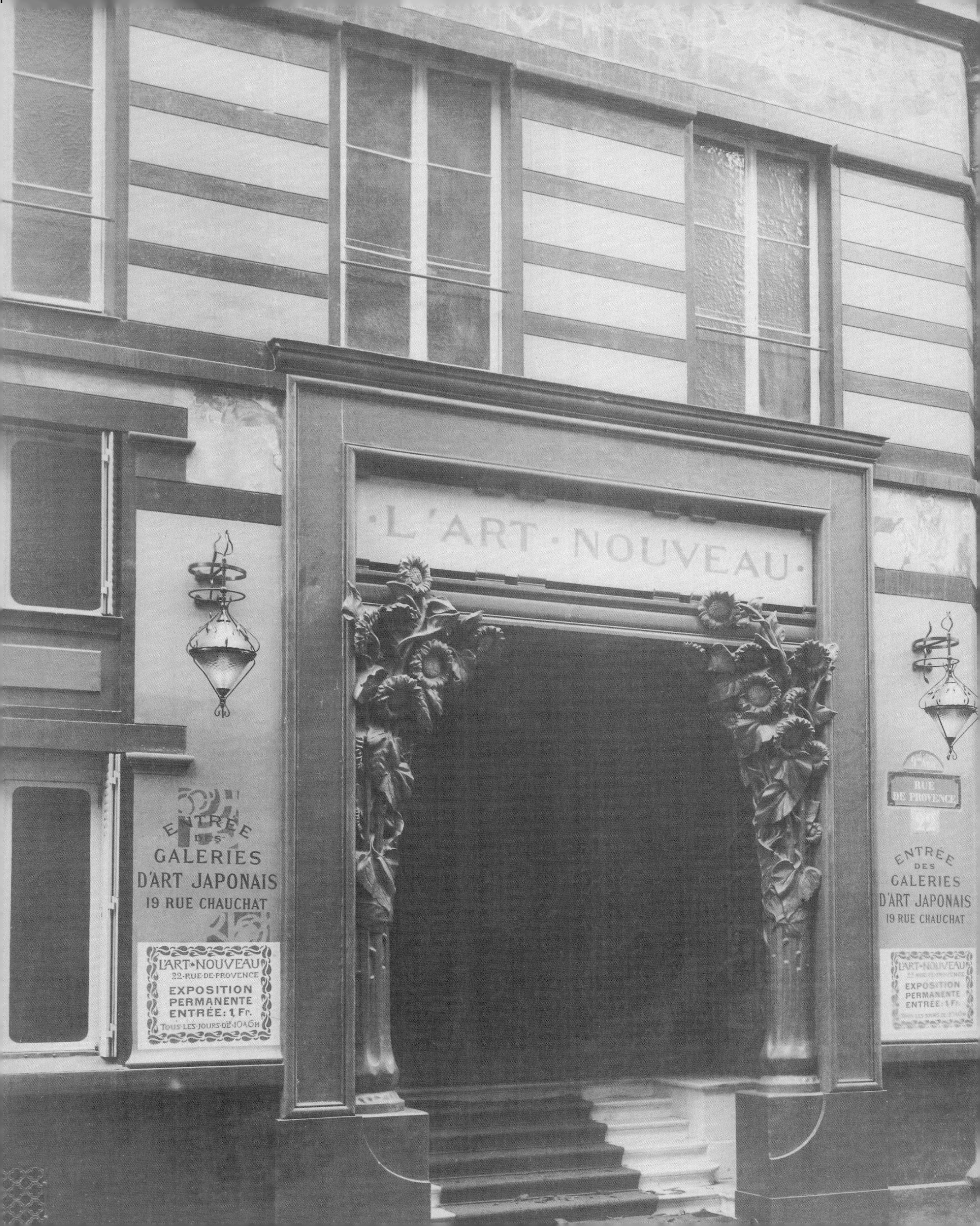
·L'ART·NOUVEAU·
ENTRÉE
DES
GALERIES
D'ART JAPONAIS
19 RUE CHAUCHAT
L'ART·NOUVEAU
22·RUE·DE·PROVENCE
EXPOSITION
PERMANENTE
ENTRÉE: 1 Fr.
TOUS·LES·JOURS·DE·10 A 6 H
RUE
DE PROVENCE
22
ENTRÉE
DES
GALERIES
D'ART JAPONAIS
19 RUE CHAUCHAT
L'ART·NOUVEAU
22·RUE·DE·PROVENCE
EXPOSITION
PERMANENTE
ENTRÉE: 1 Fr.

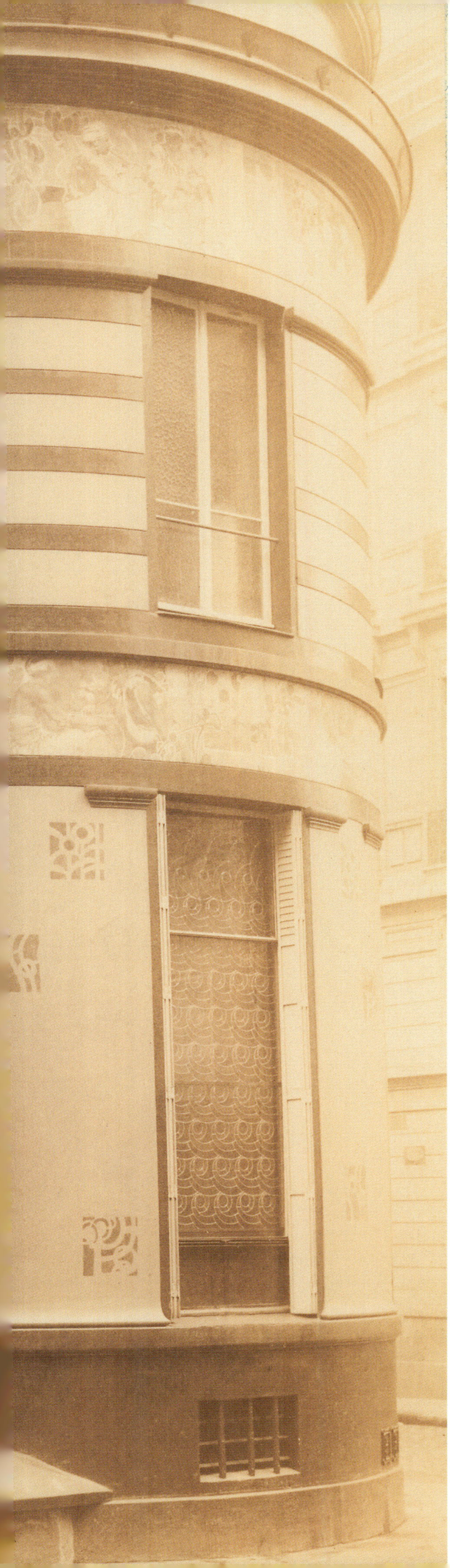

A FAMILY AFFAIR

FROM HAMBURG TO PARIS AND BEYOND

GABRIEL P. WEISBERG

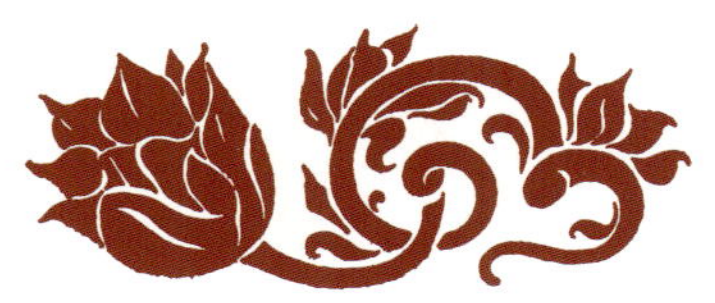

When Marcel Bing (1875–1920) asked for authorisation from the Tribunal de Commerce in April 1909 to liquidate a group of modern decorative objects remaining from the *art nouveau* emporium of his father, Siegfried Bing (1838–1905), he effectively ended a half-century-old family business.[1] The objects to be sold at auction had remained in Marcel's possession since the closing of his father's Paris shop in 1904. The official document indicates that Marcel wished to return to his and his father's earlier passion for ancient objects from the Near and Far East, thus continuing his activities as an art dealer, but not in the *art nouveau* field.[2] Yet he had held onto these objects for five years following the close of the shop, which suggests that he was reluctant to dispense with these reminders of the activity that had made the name Bing synonymous with the revival of the applied arts in France and throughout the world.

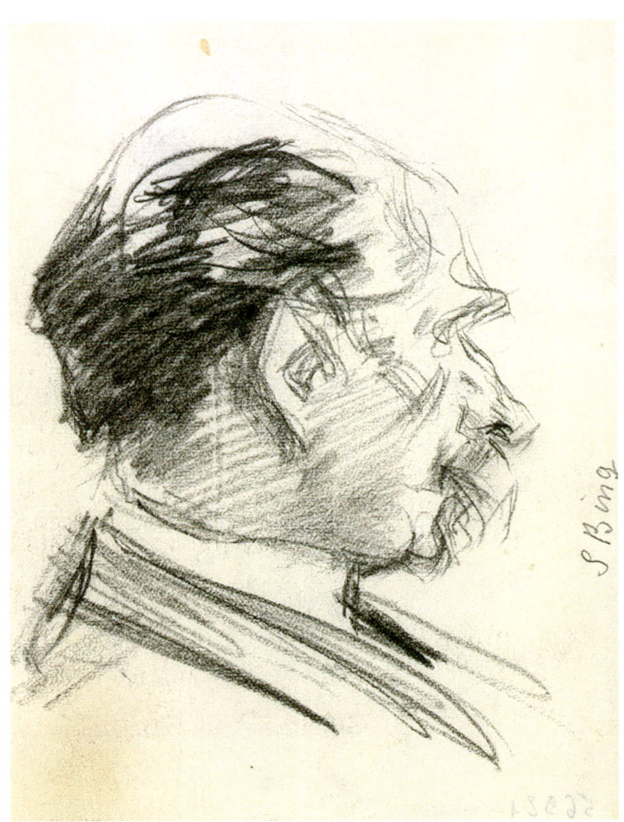

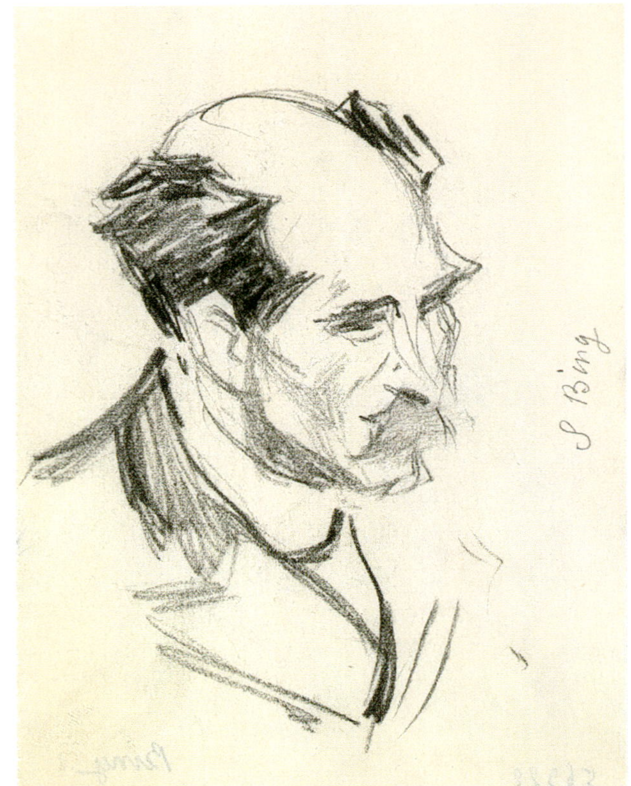

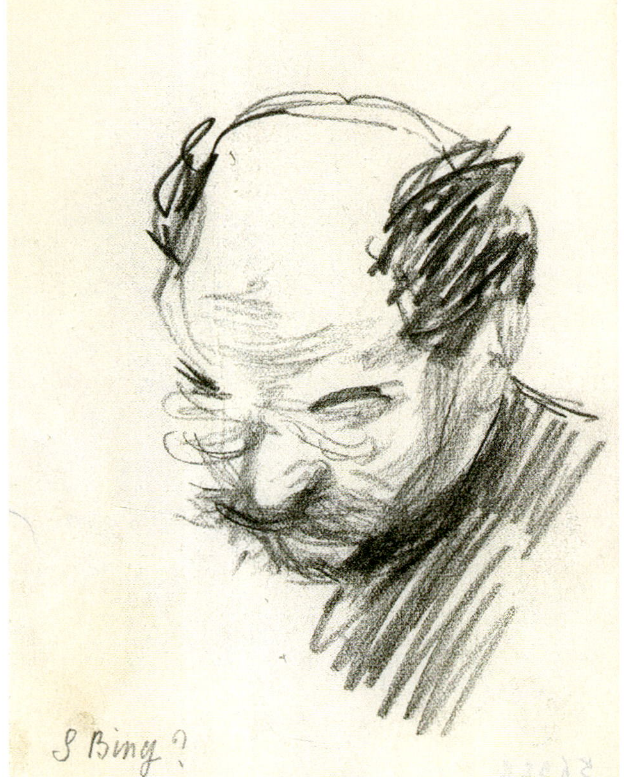

<< 1
Entrance to L'Art Nouveau at 22, rue de Provence, 1895
Fonds Louis Bonnier, Institut français d'architecture, Paris

2–4
Paul Renouard, *Portraits of Siegfried Bing*, c. 1890
Musée des Arts décoratifs (Cabinet des dessins), Paris

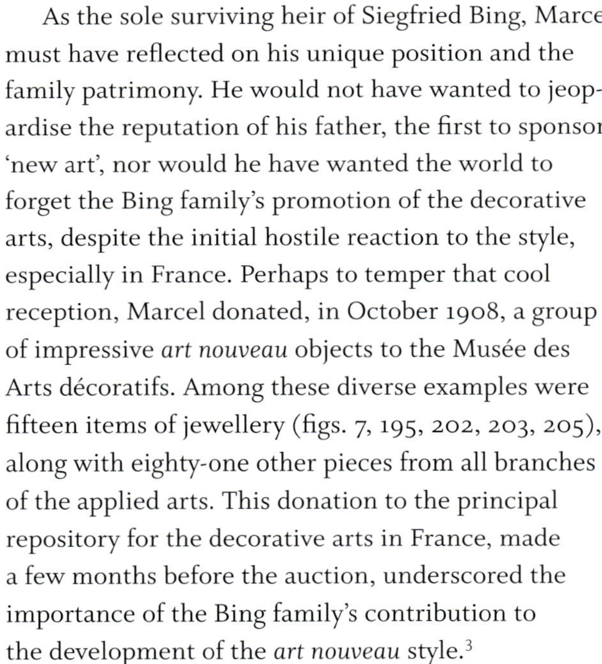

As the sole surviving heir of Siegfried Bing, Marcel must have reflected on his unique position and the family patrimony. He would not have wanted to jeopardise the reputation of his father, the first to sponsor 'new art', nor would he have wanted the world to forget the Bing family's promotion of the decorative arts, despite the initial hostile reaction to the style, especially in France. Perhaps to temper that cool reception, Marcel donated, in October 1908, a group of impressive *art nouveau* objects to the Musée des Arts décoratifs. Among these diverse examples were fifteen items of jewellery (figs. 7, 195, 202, 203, 205), along with eighty-one other pieces from all branches of the applied arts. This donation to the principal repository for the decorative arts in France, made a few months before the auction, underscored the importance of the Bing family's contribution to the development of the *art nouveau* style.[3]

The 1909 legal brief that Marcel Bing prepared for the Tribunal de Commerce is critical to the history of this new modern art, as it outlines how the family's *art nouveau* business emerged and how the gallery was modified to meet market demands. Several key dates are established in this account. 1895 is the year in which Siegfried Bing transformed his gallery into an *art nouveau* emporium, as he moved away from selling strictly Asian art objects. The document notes that, from then on, the elder Bing sold a broad range of decorative arts objects: jewellery, ceramics, furniture, paintings and sculpture. At this time, he refurbished his shop at 22, rue de Provence, in the heart of the second *arrondissement* in Paris, to allow

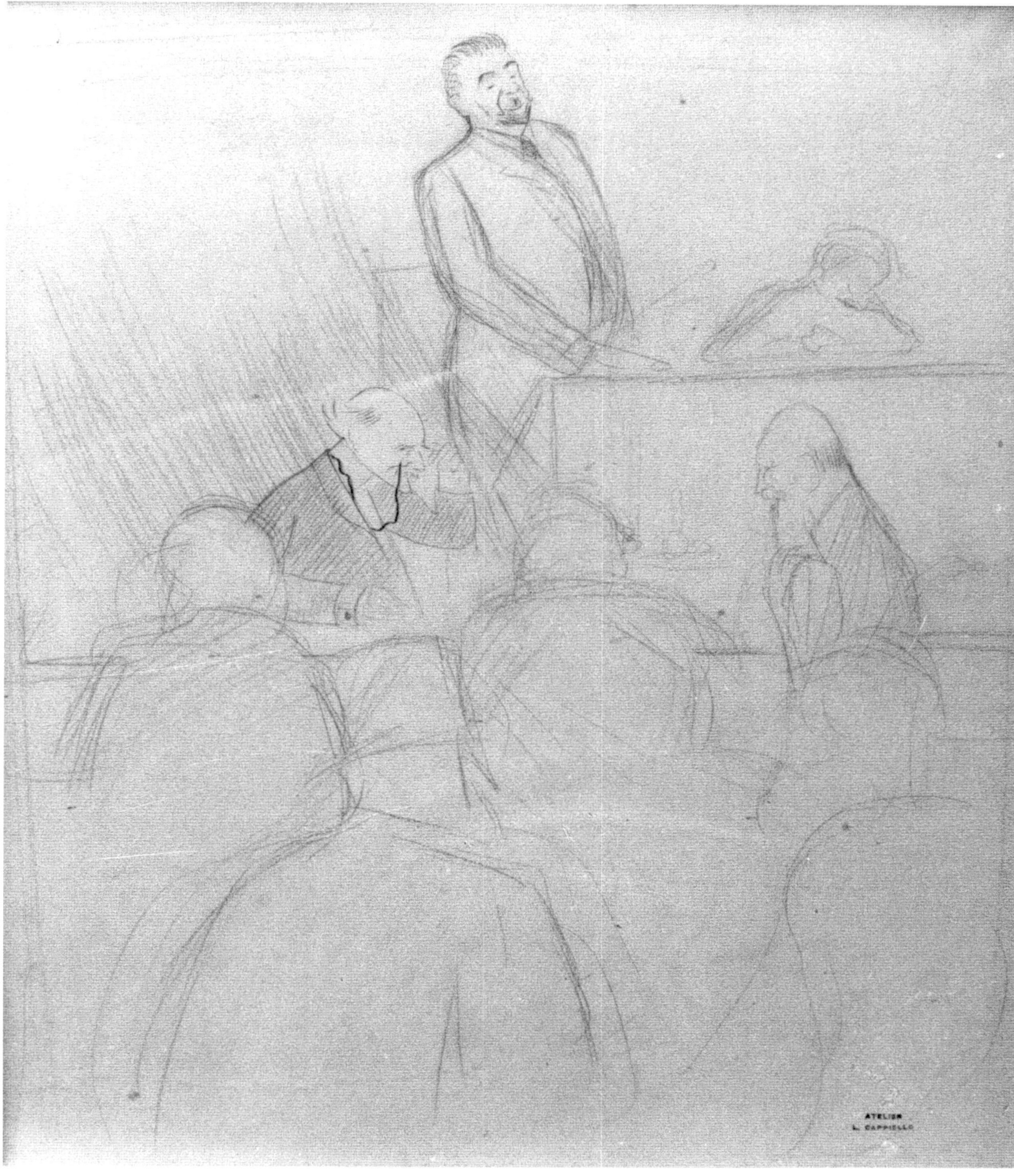

5
Leonetto Cappiello,
Siegfried Bing at an auction**, c. 1903–04**
Collection Rémy Le Fur

for the proper display and sale of these new works.[4] Nine years later, in 1904, Siegfried Bing ceased sponsoring and selling *art nouveau* objects. After closing his shop, he went to live with his son at 10, rue Saint-Georges, a location that doubled as an apartment and gallery.[5] Marcel kept a few *art nouveau* pieces of furniture to decorate his sitting room and office.[6]

While the proceeds from the 1909 auction were substantial, netting 11,920 francs, the interest in *art nouveau* was already ebbing in France. With the benefit of hindsight, we can now say that, by this year, the heyday of the style had passed. If Marcel Bing held onto a number of *art nouveau* furnishings following the sale, this was because they were part of his living environment and he was attached to them emotionally. They were, after all, not just objects to furnish his rooms, but tangible reminders of his and his father's successful and creative business venture.[7] The first years of the twentieth century were also problematic commercially as resources to buy works of art were drying up. The enthusiasm and creative dynamism that characterised the close of the nineteenth century were gone. There was a definite need for new capital to help purchase art. After the sale, Marcel moved on to concentrate on his own art trade. Yet the memory of the business he had begun with his father, their commitment to Far Eastern materials and their support of a modern style would always remain with him.

Marcel Bing apparently never again recounted any part of the story of the family business or of his personal life, despite the resounding impact he and his father had had on the history of design and on the merchandising of decorative art objects. In order to understand the Bings' transformative effect on the art world, it is essential to reexamine their origins, both in Germany and in France. How did this large and affluent Jewish family establish a far-flung commercial art empire and, in the process, nurture a design reform movement that resulted in an international style? How did the new style's sources, such as Japanese art, foster this movement and how did these contribute to the renown of this enterprising family? While these questions have been examined before, considerable new material has come to light, providing us with a better understanding of this remarkable shop and its owners, and, more broadly, of entrepreneurial patronage at the turn of the twentieth century.[8]

ORIGINS OF THE FAMILY BUSINESS

Siegfried and Marcel Bing's dealing in *objets d'art* grew out of a long tradition. In 1823, the Bing family opened an import-export business in Hamburg, Germany.[9] Moses Michael Bing (1797–1857) managed the shop, and, by 1829–30, he was joined by his younger brother, Jacob Bing (1798–1868), Siegfried Bing's father. The brothers, who were born in Frankfurt-am-Main, got along well and formed the partnership of Bing Gebrüder, which, by the early 1830s, sold a wide range of French decorative luxury items, thus increasing an awareness of French goods in Germany.[10]

At around the same time, a second branch of the family established an import-export shop in Frankfurt. Moses Salomon (later Moritz Siegfried) Bing (1799–?) founded a 'hardware and ironmongery' business in 1825 on Bornheimerstrasse, which closed in 1834. Isaac Salomon Bing (1804–1869) opened a shop in 1826 at 14, Toengesgasse, which sold French, and perhaps English, porcelain. The two eventually joined in a firm known as Bing Jun., which sold French clocks, porcelain and luxury goods to a wealthy clientele.[11] From the start, there was a concerted effort within the Bing family – between cousins both close and distant – to use the resources and know-how of its large network in order to compete in new markets in several cities, and later countries, simultaneously. By 1847, Moses Michael Bing had retired from active involvement in the Hamburg shop; he moved to Paris where he lived in Saint-Mandé on the outskirts of the city. He was replaced by Jacob Bing's brother-in-law, Joseph Samuel Renner (1804–1855). By January 1854, the latter had formed the firm of Bing et Renner. With an office in Paris and a larger one in Hamburg, the Bing empire was expanding its fortunes, when suddenly, on 15 June 1855, Joseph S. Renner died, leaving Jacob Bing as the sole owner of the Hamburg and Paris companies. The close of the 1850s also saw the Paris firm of Bing et Renner expanding in another direction: it purchased a ceramic manufactory in Saint-Genou, with the avowed purpose of producing its own porcelains for an international audience. Whether this move had been contemplated beforehand, or whether it was a means by which one of Jacob Bing's sons, Siegfried, could aid the family fortunes, is unknown. Whatever the motivation, this turn of events made it possible for a young, vigorous, imaginative member of the Bing family to make his mark on the French decorative arts scene.[12] However, in the late 1850s there was a worldwide economic depression following the end of the Crimean War, and the firms of Bing Gebrüder and Bing et Renner suffered. They were placed in 'receivership', but by 1860 they had paid all their creditors in full without having to avail themselves of bankruptcy protection.[13]

In examining the extensive archives in Hamburg, a rather detailed picture of Bing Gebrüder emerges. Between 1857 and 1860, when the Bings were working to pay off their debts, they had far-flung global business connections.[14] A sizeable list of creditors – over one hundred – shows ties with such cities as Vienna, Paris, Aachen, Venice, Samarang, Singapore, Valparaiso, Lima, Mazatlán, Caracas, Manila, Havana and Panama, among others. While the receivership documents do not reveal the type of merchandise sold, they do indicate that the company handled much more than porcelains. For example, Jacob Samuel Renner (1805–1872), the younger brother of Joseph S. Renner, a wealthy hat manufacturer in Lima, Peru, seems to have exported Peruvian goods – perhaps pottery and textiles – suggesting that the Bing family was interested

> 6
The Bing family (with Siegfried and Johanna Baer in the third row, second and third from the left, and Marcel Bing in the fourth row, left)

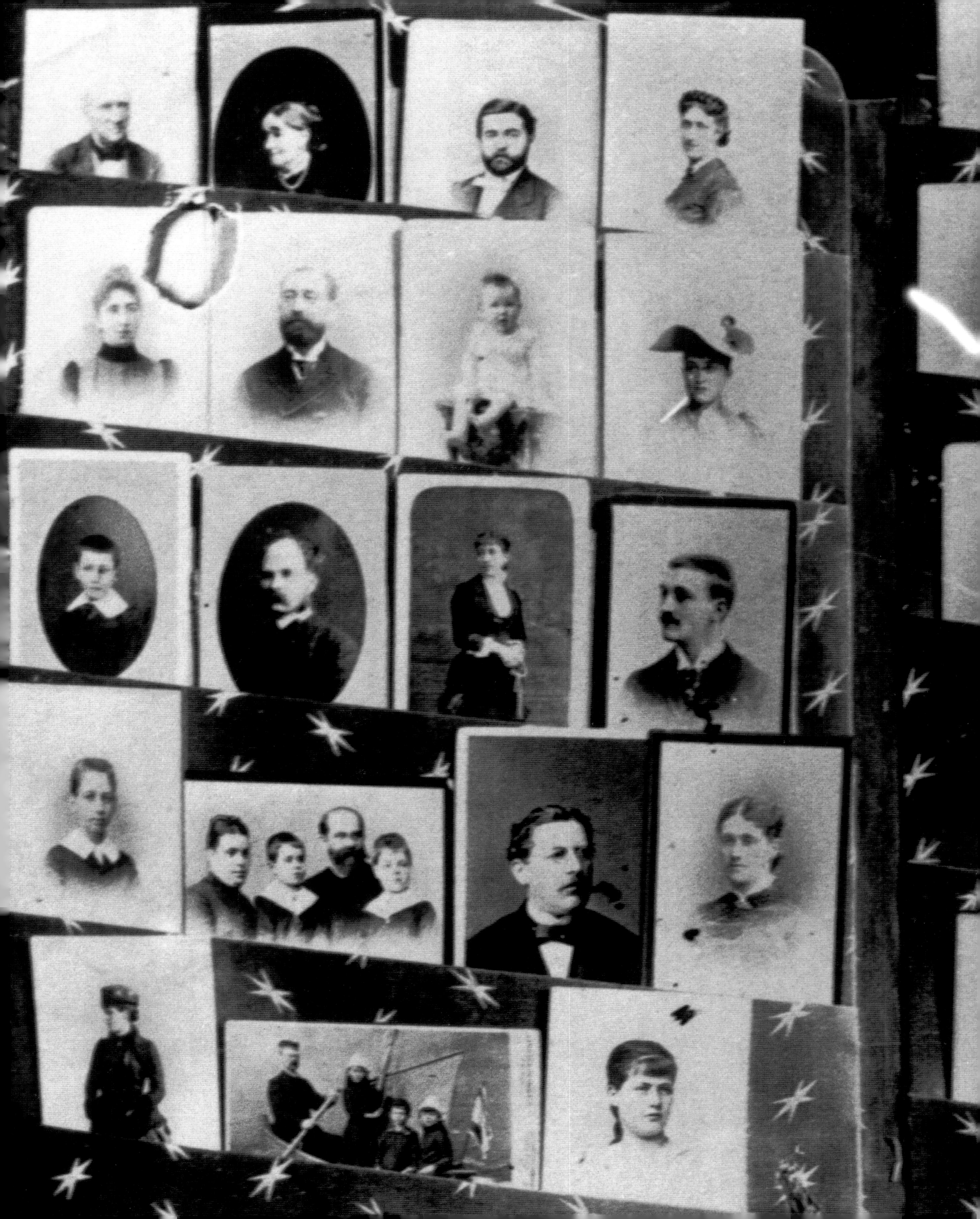

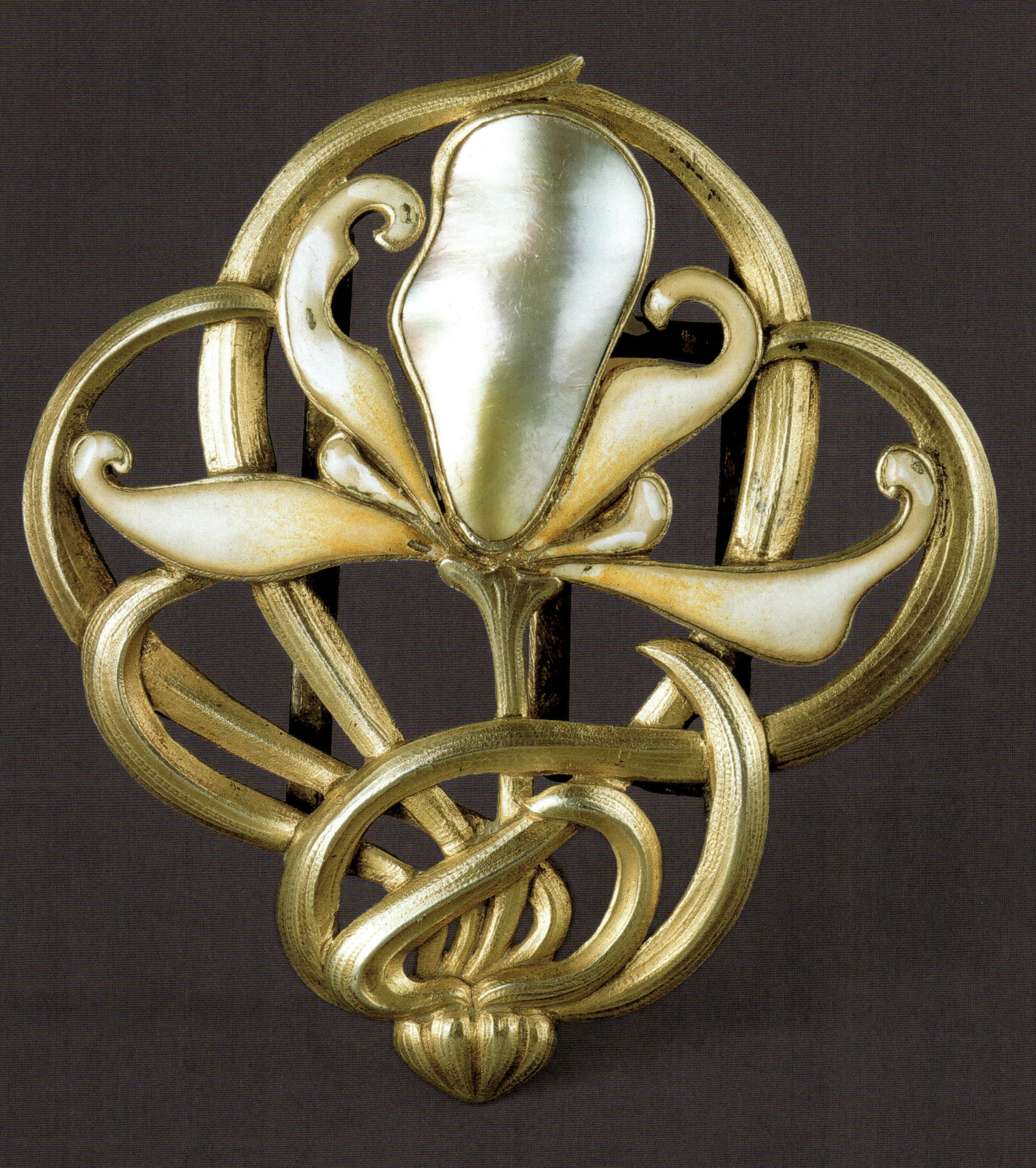

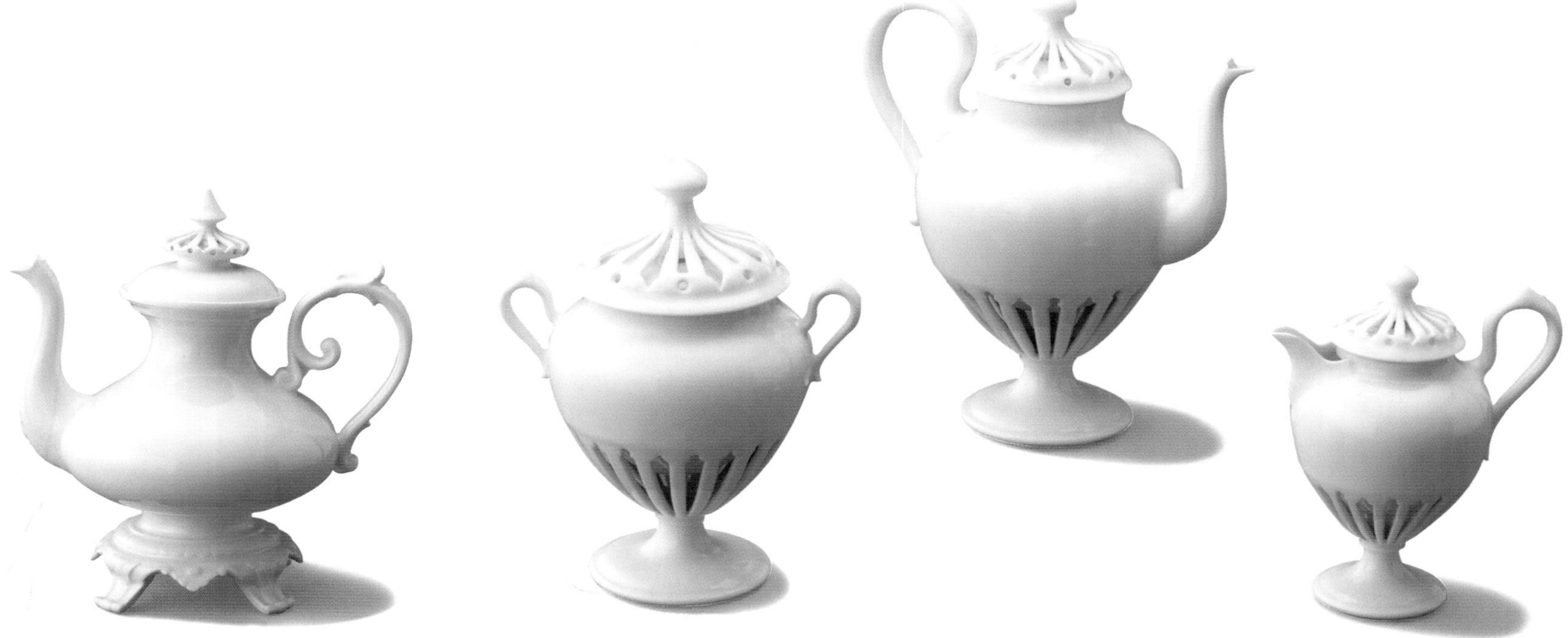

< 7
Edward Colonna, Belt buckle, c. 1900
Musée des Arts décoratifs, Paris

8
Leullier fils et Bing, Table service, 1867
Musée national Adrien Dubouché, Limoges

early on in collecting or selling exotic objects from other cultures.

SIEGFRIED BING ARRIVES IN FRANCE

Siegfried Bing came to France in 1854 to help run the business with his father. Whether or not the young man had already gained experience in the production of ceramics is unknown. He likely assisted his father manage the ceramic plant at Saint-Genou, which was losing money; by 1863 the family had sold it.[15] With Jacob Bing getting older, the death of Joseph S. Renner and the temporary reversal of the family fortune, the Bing clan decided to invest in other business ventures, specifically a second porcelain factory. In 1863, Siegfried joined with Jean-Baptiste Ernest Leullier to form the firm of Leullier fils et Bing, which manufactured ceramics to be sold in Paris and elsewhere.[16] The uniting of the already existing Leullier manufactory with capital from the Bing group was advantageous for both. The firm increased its output, winning awards for the manufacture of objects of artistic excellence during the Second Empire.[17] This era saw an increased interest in material comforts; France competed with other countries, especially England, to manufacture luxury objects of high aesthetic quality in large enough quantities to remain commercially viable.

The Leullier fils et Bing operation was quite complex for its day. The firm produced unpainted ceramic ware at plants in Esternay (Marne) and Conflans (Val-de-Marne), which was sent on to Paris to be decorated by craftsmen working, most likely, at 48, rue du faubourg Saint-Denis. Siegfried Bing's naturalisation dossier of 1876 shows him in charge of the Paris plant, indicating that he wanted to understand all aspects of ceramic production.[18] The experience of managing a shop of craftsmen early in his career proved invaluable when, at the close of the century, he organised a similar workshop system to produce, not just ceramics, but many other decorative art objects.

Bing's business acumen grew considerably during his years with Leullier. In the mid-1860s, the firm decorated porcelain table services and designed models for lamps to be produced in bronze.[19] In 1867, a porcelain table service won a major medal at the Paris World's Fair, a singular honour that was used in advertisements for the firm thereafter (fig. 8).[20] Leullier et Bing donated examples of this service to the newly founded Musée de Limoges, so that porcelain manufacturers in that city could have models of the celebrated service to study. These pieces, without any elaborate decoration, convey a sense of simple elegance. With this gesture, Bing demonstrated his belief that fine-quality decorative arts could be produced in large quantities.[21]

At the end of the 1860s, the Second Empire experienced a series of financial crises, and the Franco-Prussian War (1870–1) took its toll on daily life in France and on commercial activity. During this tumultuous period, Siegfried struggled to keep Leullier et Bing operating. He made personal sacrifices in order to keep the factory open and his employees working.[22] Bing had developed a reputation for being a skilled entrepreneur and a vigorous supporter of craftsmen at a time when his strong ties to Germany could have made him suspect to the French state.

In his 1876 naturalisation documents Bing was described as a German-born applicant for citizenship who had 'no interest in politics, who was devoted to his business and family, and [who] had no interest left in his native country having had twenty-two years of continuous residence in France'.[23] Bing was dedicated to his adopted country, even if, like many French citizens, he spent the period of the Franco-Prussian War in exile in Brussels. Upon his return after the end of the war, Bing directed his energies toward the commercial extension of the family interests and the revitalisation of an appreciation of applied arts. Central to the latter was his view that the state of the industrial arts – that is, decorative objects produced through industrial means – was flagging. To energise this aspect of artistic commercial production would require a greater awareness of new technologies, an aggressive approach to merchandising and an openness to the integration of artistic ideas of cultures outside France – namely of Japan. By wedding Japanese imagination with French tradition, Bing would eventually realise his dream of the creation of a 'new' decorative style, under the banner of 'L'Art Nouveau'.

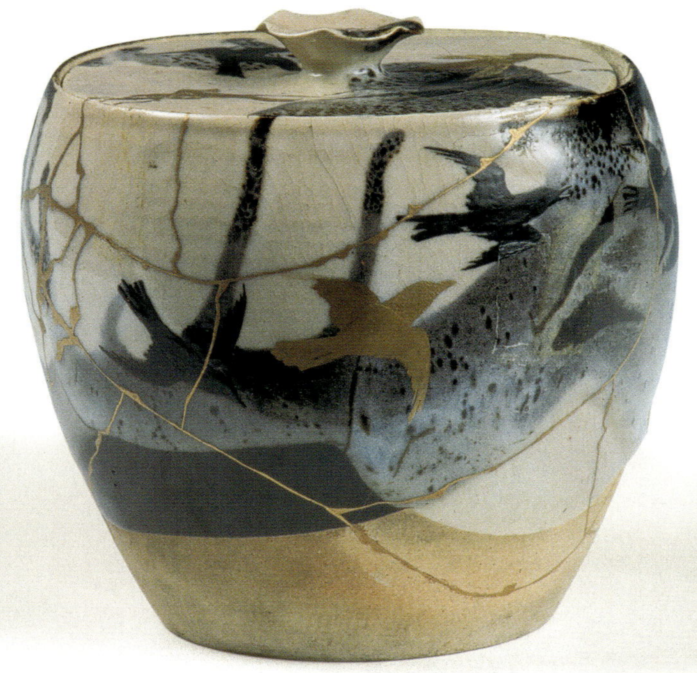

9
Water jar (mizusashi), Japan, Kyoto ware, early 19th century
Musée des Arts et Métiers, Paris

> 10–11
Combs, Japan, 19th century
Victoria and Albert Museum, London

TRADING IN JAPANESE OBJECTS

Not only was the political atmosphere in France fraught with tensions at the end of the 1860s and the early 1870s, but so was the situation of the Bing family. Jacob Bing died in 1868, ending the business under his name in Paris. Authorisation for the continuation of the firm of Bing et Renner was given to Michael Bing (1837–73), Siegfried's older brother, who also lived in the city. Meanwhile, Siegfried Bing, then working for Leullier, was considered successful enough to marry, and in July 1868 he was wedded to Johanna Baer (1847–82), a second cousin, hereby further cementing ties between Hamburg (where Johanna's family lived) and Paris.[24] (Curiously, and perhaps significantly, a branch of the Bing Gebrüder firm still continued in Hamburg; it was not liquidated until 1888.)[25] In 1873, Siegfried's brother Michael died suddenly in Paris. It was now left to Siegfried, as the only member of the Bings well positioned in France, to guide Bing et Renner.

Never lacking for new business ideas, Siegfried Bing recognised the potential of the introduction of Asian art, especially Japanese art, to the West. His interest in ceramics and his familiarity with trading

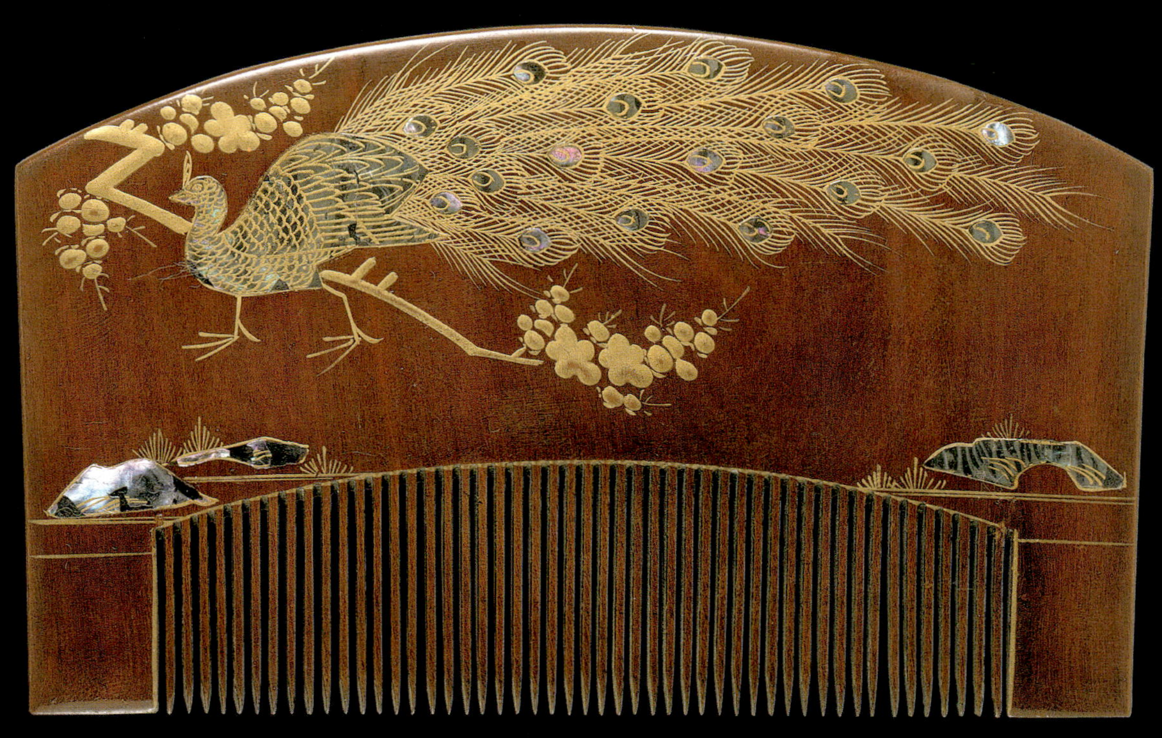

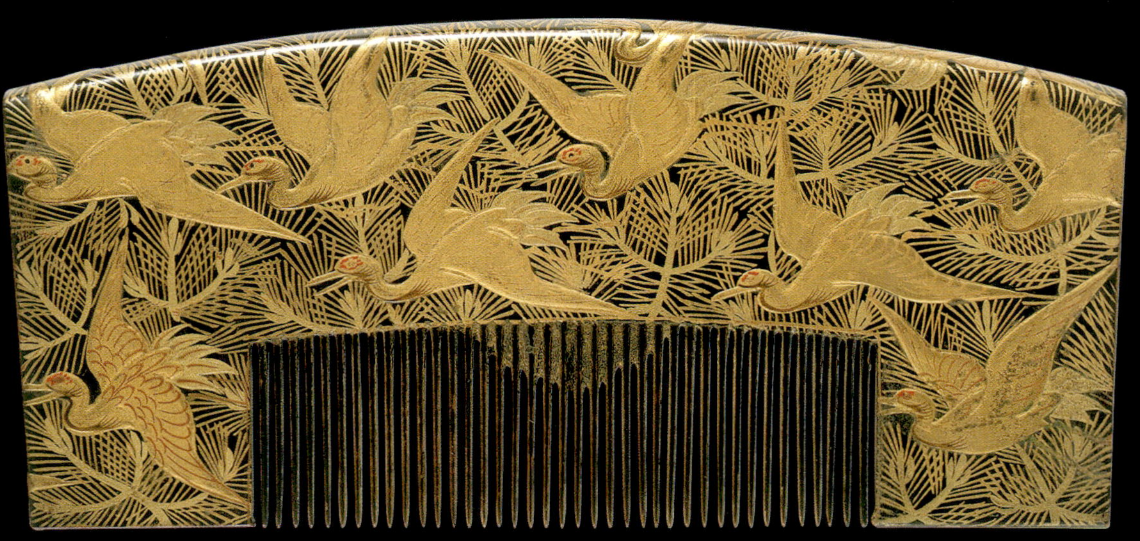

in decorative objects led him to participate in the mania for Japanese curios that swept France in the 1870s. As early as 1869, Bing contributed examples to the Union centrale des Beaux-Arts appliqués à l'industrie in Paris, where Japanese-inspired ceramics were exhibited.[26] By 1874, he was a prominent enough collector of Asian objects to be invited to join the East Asian Society in Tokyo. In 1875, as Bing was exploring his various commercial options, the firm of Leullier fils began to import art objects from Japan and China for display and sale on the rue du faubourg Saint-Denis.[27] Around this time, Bing also began moving away from the production of ceramics and toward dealing in art from the Far East. In March 1876, he sold a large collection of Asian objects at public auction at the Hôtel Drouot, netting 11,000 francs.[28] Evidently, he was developing his eye and selling groups of objects in order to purchase others that might be of greater aesthetic value. This sale is the first indication of Bing's active involvement with art from the Far East. While he remained in business with Leullier until 1881, his attention was increasingly directed toward other aspects of the art trade. By the mid-1870s, then, he seems to have made a conscious decision to combine his interest in Japanese art and his love of beautiful objects with his instinct for making a profit.

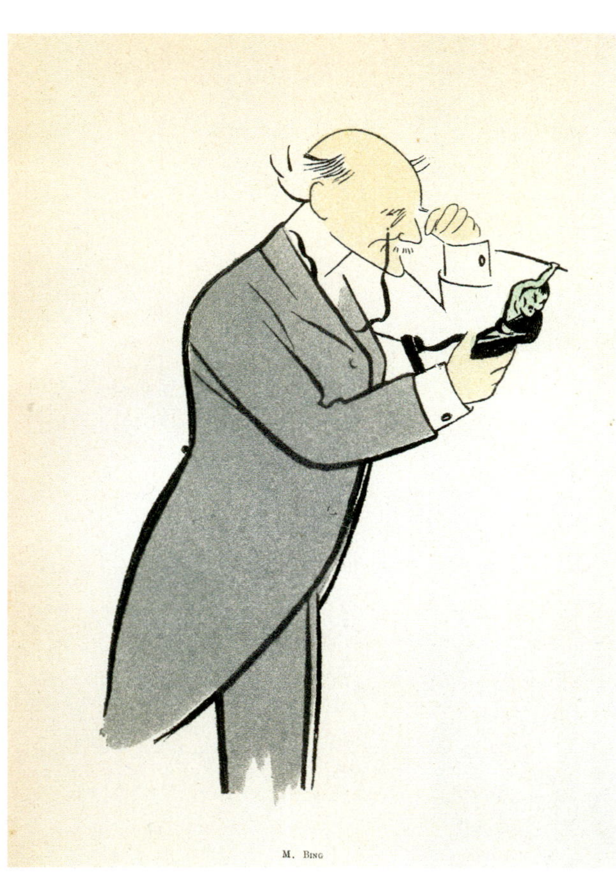

12
Leonetto Cappiello, Caricature of Bing, from *70 dessins de Cappiello*, Paris 1905

> 13
Henry Somm, *Fantaisies Japonaises*, c. 1879
Van Gogh Museum, Amsterdam

FURTHER FAMILY CONNECTIONS

As Japonisme flourished during the 1870s, Siegfried took steps to solidify his ties with Japan and obtain objects for sale in Paris. His brother-in-law Michael Martin Baer was, by 1871, established in Tokyo as Consul/Agent for the German government.[29] An effective merchant, Baer, together with Heinrich Ahrens, organised and ran a large business in Yokohama. They saw to it that German machinery was sold to the Japanese, including modern military armaments for the outfitting of boats. In return, Baer may have received Japanese art objects or, more likely, provided for the manufacture of art objects in Japan that were destined for the European market.[30] In any event, Siegfried Bing's awareness of the importance of Japan as a trading partner and a source of art objects was enhanced through contacts with his wife's family. Consequently, in the 1870s, Bing gained access to Western companies already established in Yokohama and to Japanese companies that could produce the merchandise sold in his Parisian shops.

During the late 1870s, the taste for Japonisme escalated until it reached its full flowering at the Paris World's Fair of 1878, where Japan was exceptionally well represented. Art critics in Europe, and especially in France, regarded Japan as an untouched, innocent paradise, and they represented the country in this way to the public.[31] Yet at the same time, French entrepreneurs and governmental officials were pursuing contacts in Japan, suggesting that similar trade connections had been established by them as by the Germans. France was deeply concerned about positioning itself as advantageously as other countries in order to secure favourable trade conditions. In keeping with this state of affairs, S. Bing, as he was now known, took on a partner to help with his growing interest in marketing *curiosités* from his shop at 19, rue Chauchat, close to the Hôtel Drouot.[32] This location, more than any other site in Paris, became a centre where people could see all types of merchandise from Japan; by the 1880s, S. Bing could claim to be one of the principal dealers promoting the taste, or craze, for Japonisme in France and, eventually, the world.

Bing commissioned artists such as the printmaker Henry Somm to design announcements for his new establishment. For example, Somm made an etching that could have been used as a calling card: *Fantaisies Japonaises* (fig. 13).[33] This print, which shows a young, fashionably dressed French woman entering Bing's shop, uses stereotypes of the Japonisme craze. An Asian man, dressed in a kimono, beckons the visitors to the store,

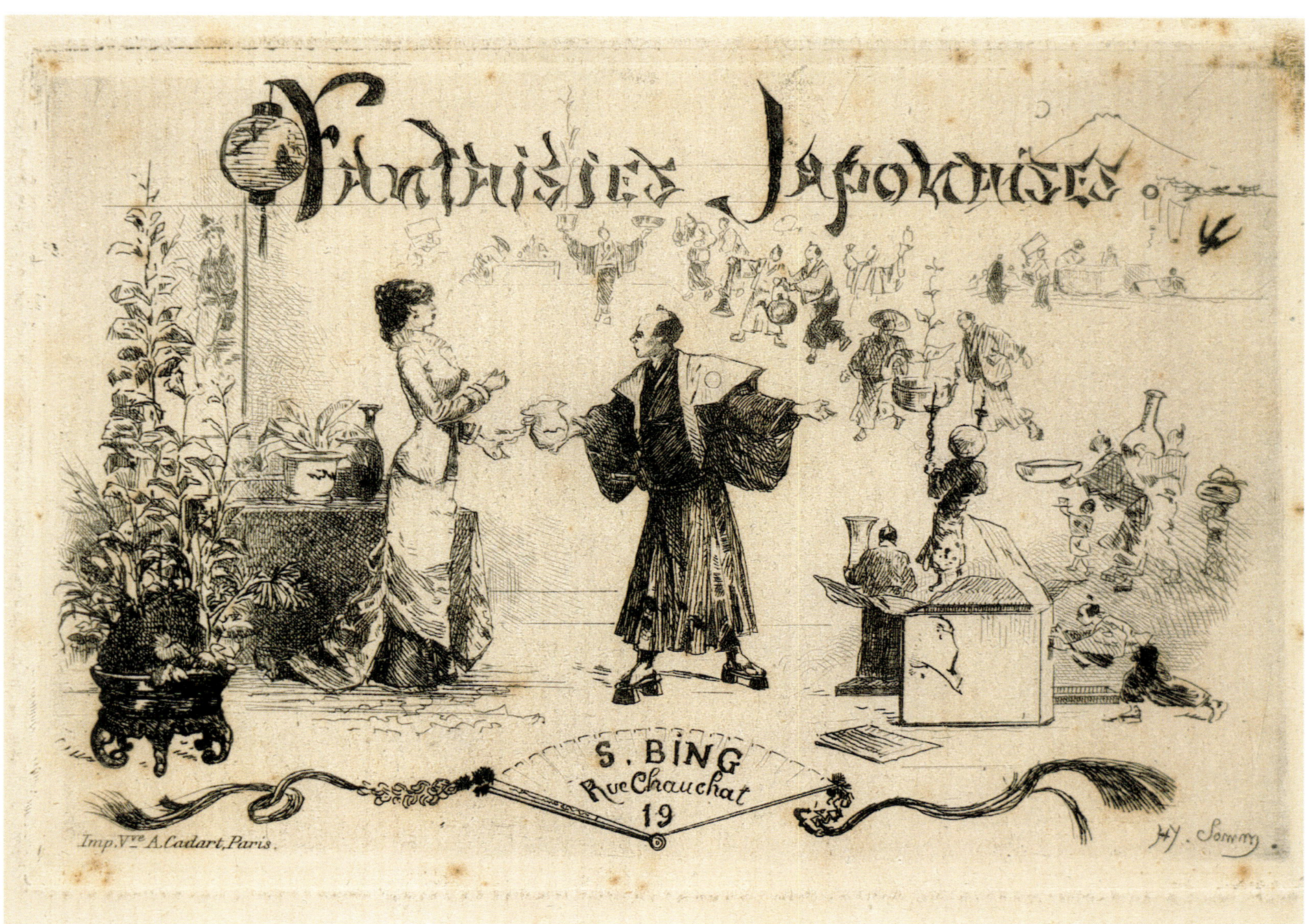

suggesting that treasures from the Far East lie within. In 1880, Bing paid for an announcement in the pages of the *Didot-Bottin* to advertise his new activities as a dealer in Japanese and Chinese curios.[34]

The growing desire to acquire art of the Far East meant that Bing had to increase his stock, and to do this he needed a new partner. Following family tradition, Bing enlisted the aid of a family member. His younger brother, August (1852–1918), came to Paris, probably by the late 1870s.[35] August became a close associate, remaining for long periods in Japan and running the Bing business from Yokohama.

Other changes in Siegfried's life occurred during the late 1870s and early 1880s. After the death of two infant sons, the birth of Marcel in 1875 was cause for joy. This youngest son was to become his closest assistant in the business. Seven years later, Johanna died. Her loss was heavy to bear, and it may have prompted Bing to devote all his energy to business, focusing on two areas: the promotion of all things Japanese and the improvement of the applied arts.

THE TRIPS TO JAPAN

Some scholars of Japonisme have assumed that Siegfried Bing travelled to Japan earlier than 1880, possibly in 1875, but there is no evidence of this.[36] A trip of 1880–81 is well documented through published comments made by Siegfried in 1888 and passenger lists published in the *Japan Weekly Mail*.[37] Siegfried apparently travelled alone, although he was joined by his brother August, who arrived in Japan in September 1881.[38] As trade with Japan increased, August travelled back and forth in 1887 and again in 1889.[39] While the exact nature of what transpired in Japan may never be known, both Siegfried and August

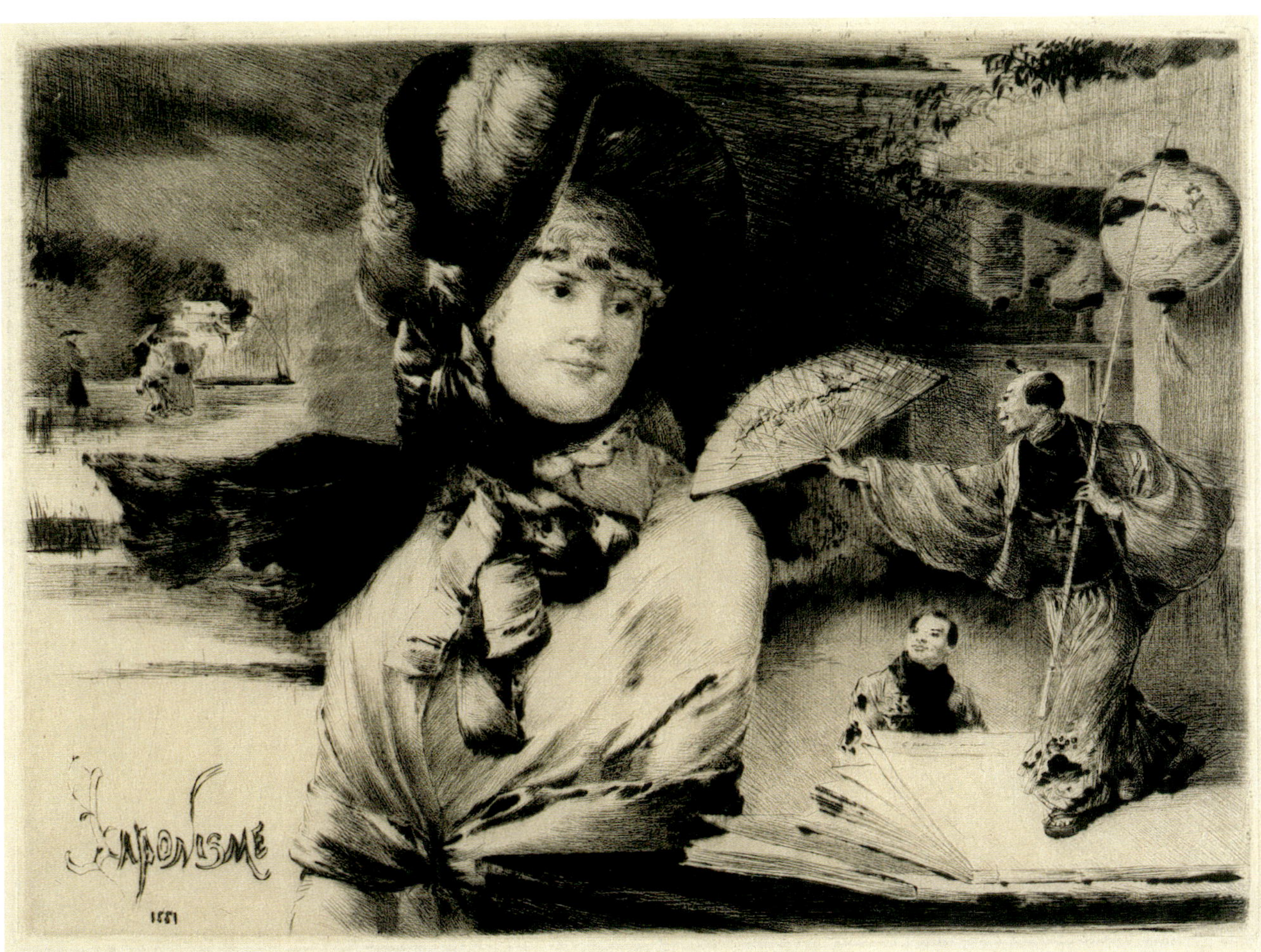

14
Henry Somm, *Japonisme*, 1881
Van Gogh Museum, Amsterdam

travelled to the Far East in the company of Winckler, who worked with H. Ahrens and Company in Yokohama, suggesting that the Bing brothers were making contacts through other German businessmen.[40] A notice in the *Tokyo Daily News* of 15 July 1880 confirms Siegfried Bing's presence in Japan: 'M. Bing is a leading French merchant and also a connoisseur of Art. He loves many kinds of art objects from our country and, most especially, the works of Shibata Zeshin. Since M. Bing wanted to meet, the employees of the Kiritsu Kôshô Kaisha [Industrial and Commercial Association of Tokyo] arranged for Bing to attend a party on the day before yesterday, that is the 13th, at the villa of Koume. [...] The German ambassador also joined this party. [...] At this gathering, M. Bing informed us that he had purchased many works by Korin from Japanese businessmen living in France. The elegant quality of these objects was appreciated by connoisseurs and all were unexpectedly sold.'[41] Bing's contact with living artists such as Shibata Zeshin indicates that he was interested not only in ancient Japanese art but in contemporary works as well. These connections influenced the choice of objects he sold in his shop and enabled him to organise special exhibitions of modern Japanese art. After Siegfried's 1880 trip and subsequent ones by August, the Far Eastern Bing business empire gained access to all types of Japanese objects, including popular curios, examples of ancient art and high quality contemporary works made expressly for Western markets.

When Siegfried returned to Paris at the end of 1881, he reorganised his business to accommodate the wide variety of Far Eastern objects. He opened three new outlets: one at 23, rue de Provence, another at 19, rue de la Paix and, finally, one at 13, rue Bleue, while maintaining his original shop at 19, rue Chauchat.[42] At 13, rue Bleue, Bing rented the ground and first floors, giving him ample space to show the contemporary works.[43] By 1881, Japonisme was at its height. This rage for all things Japanese is satirised in Henry Somm's print entitled *Japonisme* (fig. 14), in which a small Japanese man with a fan tries to get the attention of a beautiful young French woman.

To keep up with the expansion of trade with Japan, the Bing family consolidated their business by organising new partnerships. Working with his brother August and Daniel Dubuffet, Siegfried organised S. Bing et Cie., a group whose goals reached beyond that of selling works of art. Documents from the Tribunal de Commerce specify that S. Bing et Cie. was to be in charge of 'all the operations necessary for the importation of all products and raw materials from the Far East and for the exportation, principally from France, of all raw and manufactured products to the Far East'.[44] This partnership also had the ability to create 'commercial houses' in China, Japan and other locations; they could buy land, obtain concessions and carry out 'all necessary financial, commercial and industrial operations'. Bing and his partner Dubuffet thus took full advantage of the new colonial expansion of the French state into the Far East. S. Bing et Cie. was a joint-stock company whose backers included members outside the Bing family, clearly marking a watershed moment in the family's entrepreneurial activities. Essentially, this move set up Siegfried as a principal promoter of trade and investment in the Far East.

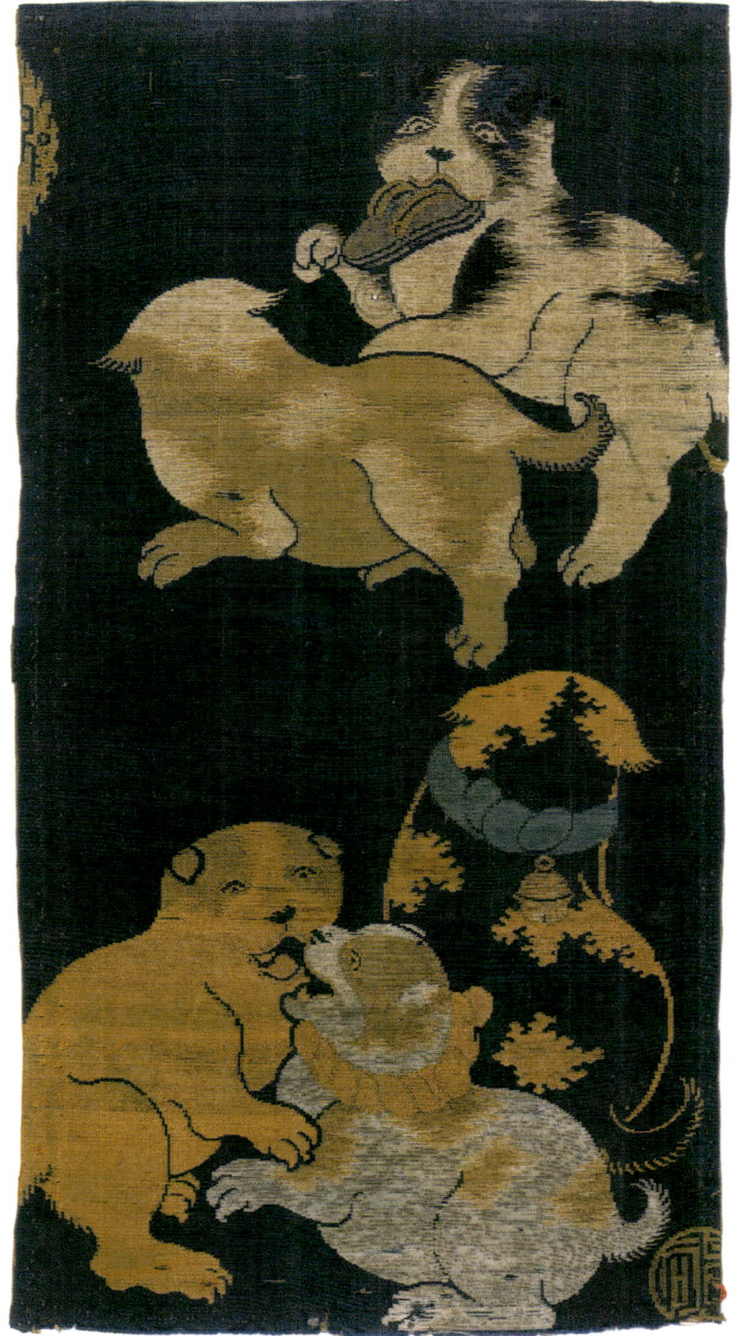

15
Fabric with puppies playing, Japan, 19th century
Musée de la Mode et du Textile, Paris

The assets that Siegfried brought to the newly organised company were his gallery at 13, rue Bleue – the site that was to become its headquarters – and an investment of 300,000 francs.[45] In return, Bing became the principal stockholder after demonstrating that his financial commitment was debt free. The legal documents also show that Siegfried was given the right to continue his business at 19, rue Chauchat and at other locations where he sold 'ancient Far Eastern objects'. However, he could only sell 'modern' art objects from the Far East if he secured them from S. Bing et Cie.; similarly, S. Bing et Cie. could only sell 'ancient' art objects if they were purchased from Siegfried Bing. In other words, Bing had devised a clever way of controlling the Far Eastern art market. Ledgers and account books were kept in order to have an accurate tally of items for each year.[46]

REINVESTING IN CAPITAL IMPROVEMENTS

At the same time that Bing et Cie. was being organised, changes occurred at Bing's adjoining properties at 19, rue Chauchat and 22, rue de Provence. Even though Siegfried did not own these properties in 1883, he was permitted to make architectural changes to his galleries in order to gain additional space for the exhibition of older Japanese works. He spent his own funds to build a glass roof over a courtyard, thus adding not only space, but light, which allowed for better viewing of the objects.[47] (As mentioned earlier, he was to renovate this gallery

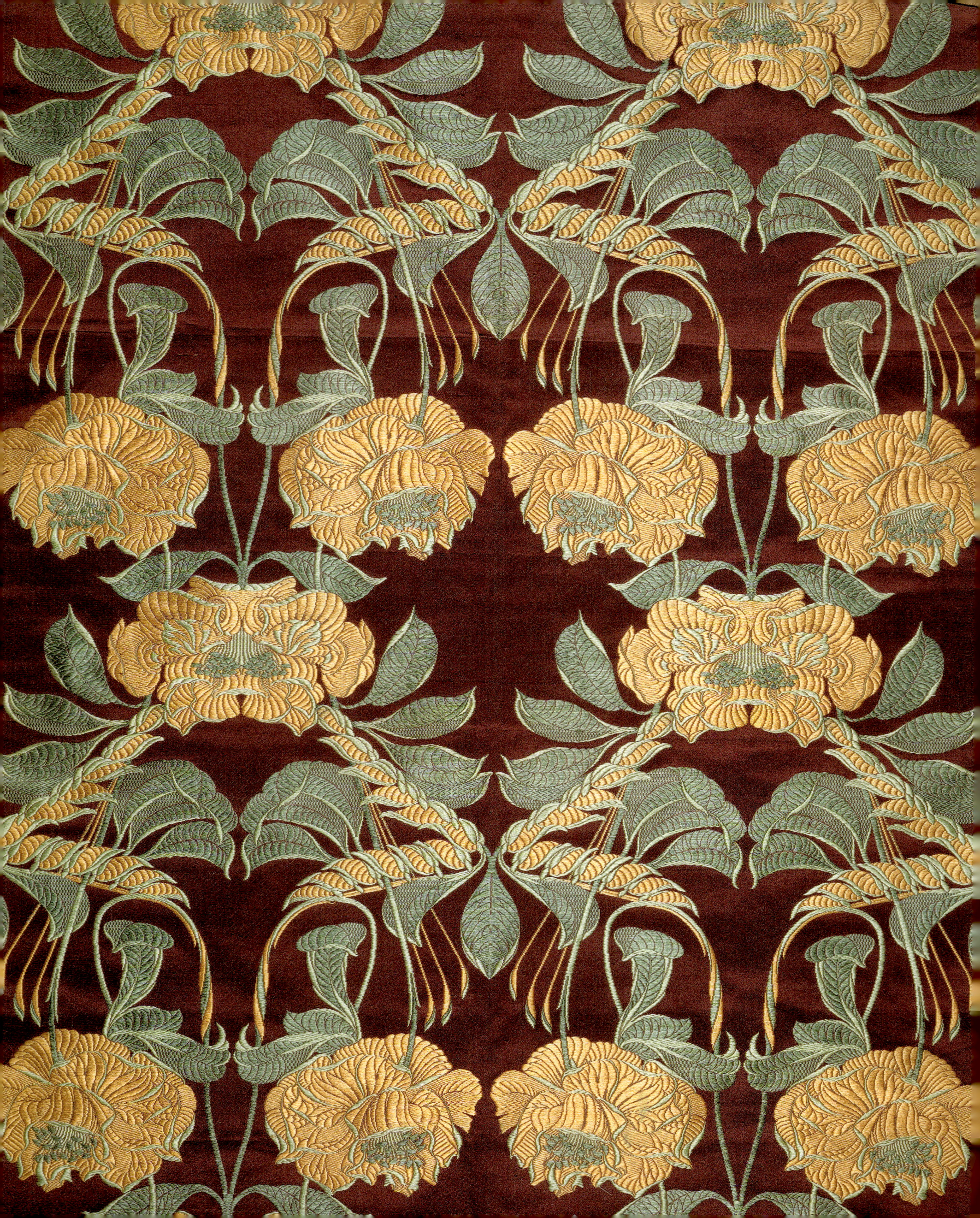

space again in 1895 to improve the display of his merchandise.) Already in 1883, Bing was taking the lead in gallery display techniques, investing his own funds to make capital improvements so that decorative art works could be better appreciated by visitors and potential clients.

While no photograph has emerged showing the new installation, a contemporary commentary provides a detailed description. At the time of the April 1884 Salon, as work was progressing on the galleries, an article appeared on Bing's 'Musée Japonais' in the Salon's illustrated catalogue, ensuring a wide, receptive audience.[48] The anonymous author commented on how workmen had not yet finished the interior and noted further that the glass display cases in various rooms made for better viewing of the smaller objects. Bing's museum of Japanese art included bronzes, lacquers, ceramics, ivories and, most likely, a few large-scale pieces of sculpture. While the Musée Oriental, founded in 1869 to great acclaim, was devoted to displaying Asian art of many countries, Bing's focus in 1884 was on Japan. With this newly refurbished gallery at 22, rue de Provence/19, rue Chauchat, Bing achieved his goal of creating a 'true decorative arts museum', where French designers could study Japanese objects.[49]

During the mid-1880s, when Siegfried found himself temporarily short of funds, he contacted various friends at museums, offering them excellent Japanese examples at reduced prices.[50] What caused a slowdown in the business is not clear, although the number of dealers selling Japanese objects had greatly increased, probably causing a glut in the market. Bing retrenched slightly, closing his shop on the rue de la Paix. At the same time, he increased his presence in Japan by opening an office in Yokohama, staffed by Daniel Dubuffet, and, in 1887, a second office in Kobe.[51] But the principal gallery remained at 19, rue Chauchat, which became known as the best location to see Japanese objects and, perhaps, to meet S. Bing himself.

STIMULATING INTEREST IN JAPAN FOR FRENCH GOODS

During the late 1880s, Bing became acutely aware that he needed to expand trade with Japan if his company was to grow, or even to remain stable. Support from the French government was critical, and, on 24 January 1887, he wrote to the French Ministry of Commerce and Industry requesting a meeting at which he hoped to lay out a plan

< 16
Georges de Feure, Fabric with peonies, c. 1899
Manufactured by Lamy et Bornet, now Maison Prelle, Lyon

17
Sword guard (tsuba), Japan, Bushû School, 19th century
Museum für Kunst und Gewerbe, Hamburg

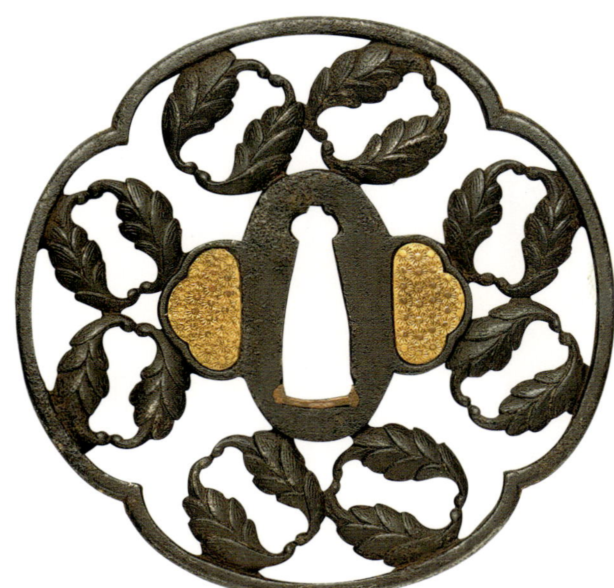

18
Sword guard (tsuba), Japan, Chôshû School, 18th century
Museum für Kunst und Gewerbe, Hamburg

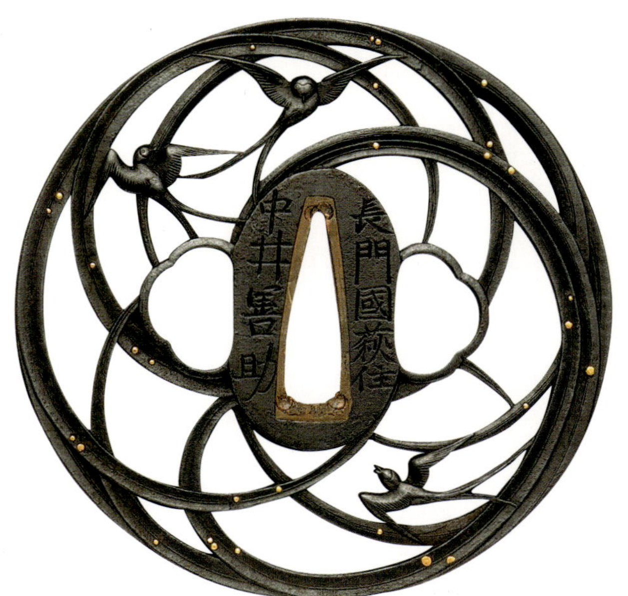

19
Nakai Zensuke Tomotsune I, Sword guard (tsuba)
Museum für Kunst und Gewerbe, Hamburg

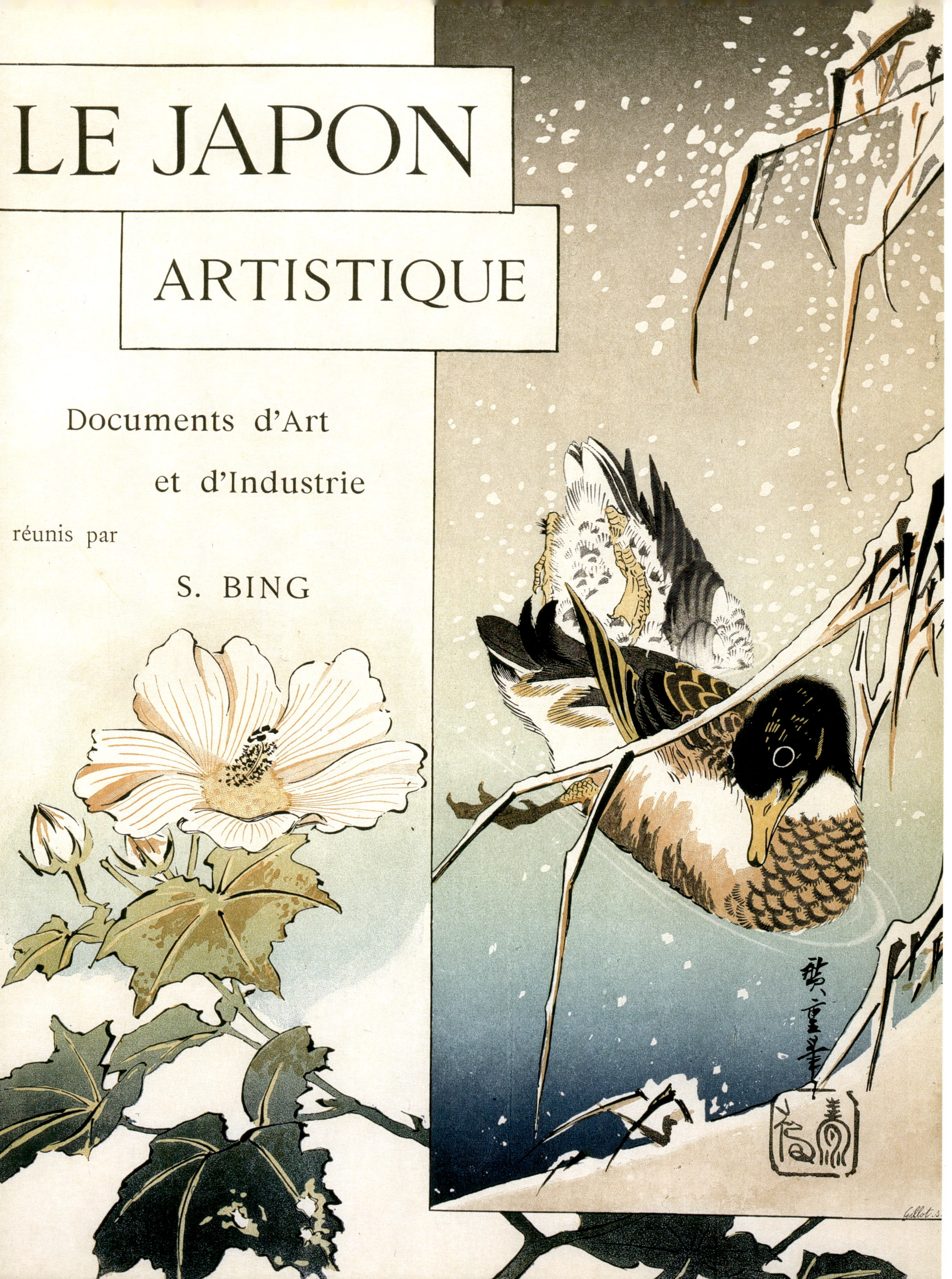
LE JAPON
ARTISTIQUE
Documents d'Art
et d'Industrie
réunis par
S. BING

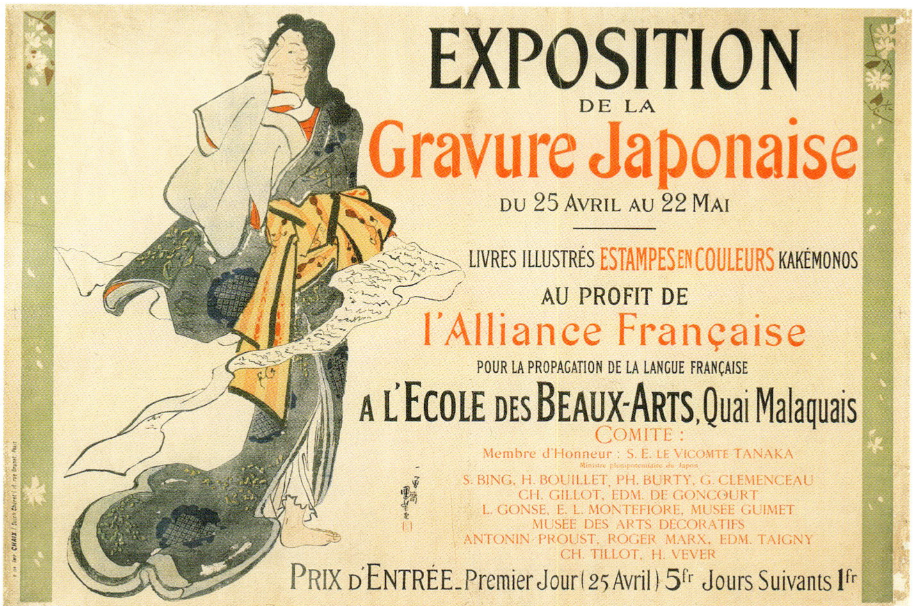

< 20
Cover of *Le Japon Artistique*, 1888, no. 1
Van Gogh Museum (Library), Amsterdam

21
Jules Chéret, Poster 'Exhibition of Japanese Prints', 1890
Musée de la Publicité, Paris

of action. At the heart of his vision for improved trade relations with Japan was the promotion of French goods in various Japanese cities. With August Bing representing several companies in Japan, French products could be made more available to the Japanese market. If the French government would apply diplomatic pressure, the Japanese might become more favourable to French products, thereby allowing France to compete more successfully with Germany and England.[52] While it is unclear if this proposition was entirely new, the fact that it came from a businessman already well established in Japan would not have been missed by French officials.

S. Bing et Cie., along with other French companies that manufactured machinery, locomotives, military equipment and so forth, took advantage of Japan's desire to modernise during the Meiji era in order to expand its trade. Much of this was accomplished with the help of the French government, just prior to the Paris World's Fair of 1889, where Japan was well represented, at a time when France was trying to increase its presence in the Far East.[53]

Accordingly, in 1888, S. Bing et Cie. opened new and larger offices in Yokohama. The business hired several Japanese staff members, who would have been recruited to improve contact between the French company and their hosts. While the exact nature of trade relations in the late 1880s between the two countries in general, and S. Bing et Cie. and Japan in particular, is unclear due to the dearth of commercial documents located, it is certain that the firm prospered. Moreover, S. Bing et Cie. became the general import-export agent for the Syndicat de l'Industrie Française au Japon, a large group of French industrialists determined to have extensive influence in Japan.[54]

Although Siegfried Bing must have been busy leading this industrialist syndicate, he remained active in the art market. He initiated a series of novel promotional activities, including the launching of the monthly magazine *Le Japon Artistique* in 1888 (fig. 20). This journal was crucial to the Japonisme movement, as readers over the world could now learn and see for themselves that Japanese objects were both beautiful, plentiful and a very sound investment.[55] Hoping to open new markets for Japanese art works, Bing organised travelling exhibitions in other countries in Europe and even in the United States. One organised with Holland in 1888 led to the National Museum of Ethnology in Leiden purchasing a number of pieces. Similarly, in 1888, Bing exhibited at the Nordiske Industri-, Landbrugs- og Kunstudstilling in Copenhagen, where Japanese examples were shown alongside applied art objects by Albert-Louis Dammouse, Ernest Chaplet, Emile Gallé and Eugène Rousseau.[56] Bing also made Japanese objects available to technical schools, and pieces were donated to the Conservatoire National des Arts et Métiers in Paris.[57] These efforts suggested to designers in France and throughout Europe that by studying Japanese decorative arts, they could break away from culturally specific, historical styles.

In 1890, on the occasion of the huge retrospective of Japanese prints held in Paris at the Ecole des Beaux-Arts (fig. 21) – an exhibition organised largely by Bing to promote the taste for *ukiyo-e* prints – Bing received the Légion d'Honneur for his sponsorship of

Japanese art.[58] This coveted award further solidified his reputation and demonstrated that the French government fully appreciated his efforts to improve trade with Japan. Today Siegfried Bing is still recognised for his entrepreneurial genius, which was, above all his other accomplishments, responsible for making Japanese art an unmistakable, integral part of artistic production in the late nineteenth century.

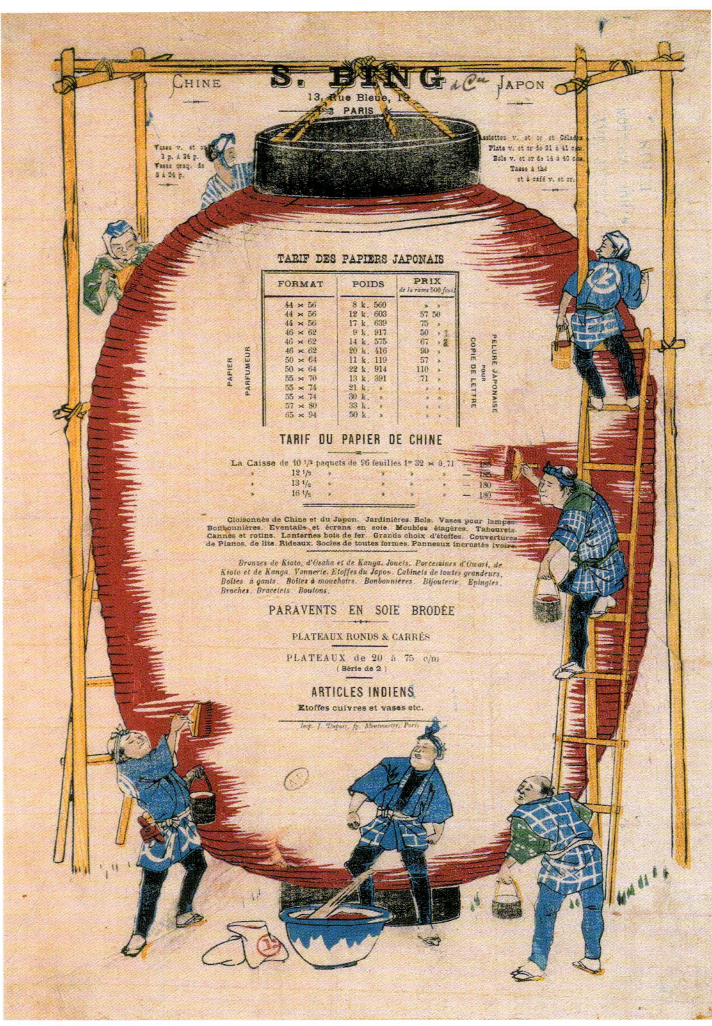

22
Advertisement 'Price list for Japanese and Chinese papers', c. 1881
Album Maciet, Bibliothèque des Arts décoratifs, Paris

> 23
Fabric with a carp swimming against the current, Japan, 19th century
Musée des Arts décoratifs, Paris

A RUPTURE IN THE FAMILY

Despite the public accolades for its promotion of Japanese art, there appears to have been private discontent within the Bing family. In 1889, August, who had worked with his brother since 1881, left Yokohama and moved to Kassel, Germany, remaining there until his death in 1918.[59] While living members of the Bing family have hinted at problems with business operations in Paris, no supporting documents have come to light. Given the complicated nature of the company and the large amount of money involved, bitterness over the new initiatives in Japan may have led to a rupture between the two brothers.[60] On the other hand, ill health may have contributed to August's decision to return to Germany, where he would be closer to family.

There is no doubt that August Bing was deeply involved in Japan and its art. On each of his trips, he took photographs and he collected Japanese as well as Chinese decorative arts, which he displayed in his home in Germany. (He later gave these to his daughter, Irene.) It is unlikely that he became a collector of Japanese art on the scale of his brother Siegfried, apparently purchasing choice Far Eastern objects primarily for the purpose of decorating his own surroundings.[61] One point is certain: after the early 1890s, August Bing is no longer mentioned in documents pertaining to S. Bing et Cie.

In December 1892, perhaps as a means of refinancing S. Bing et Cie., a new association was formed. Incorporated as Dubuffet et Cie. (Ancienne Maison Bing et Cie.), this group was made up of old and new investors. Siegfried Bing continued as a limited partner; he did not, however, manage the company as he had in the past.[62] The actual running of the business, which was to carry out the same activities as before at 13, rue Bleue, was left to Nephtalie Lévy and Daniel Dubuffet. This trading company existed until 1901.[63] When it was reformulated and new partners admitted, Siegfried Bing was no longer involved.

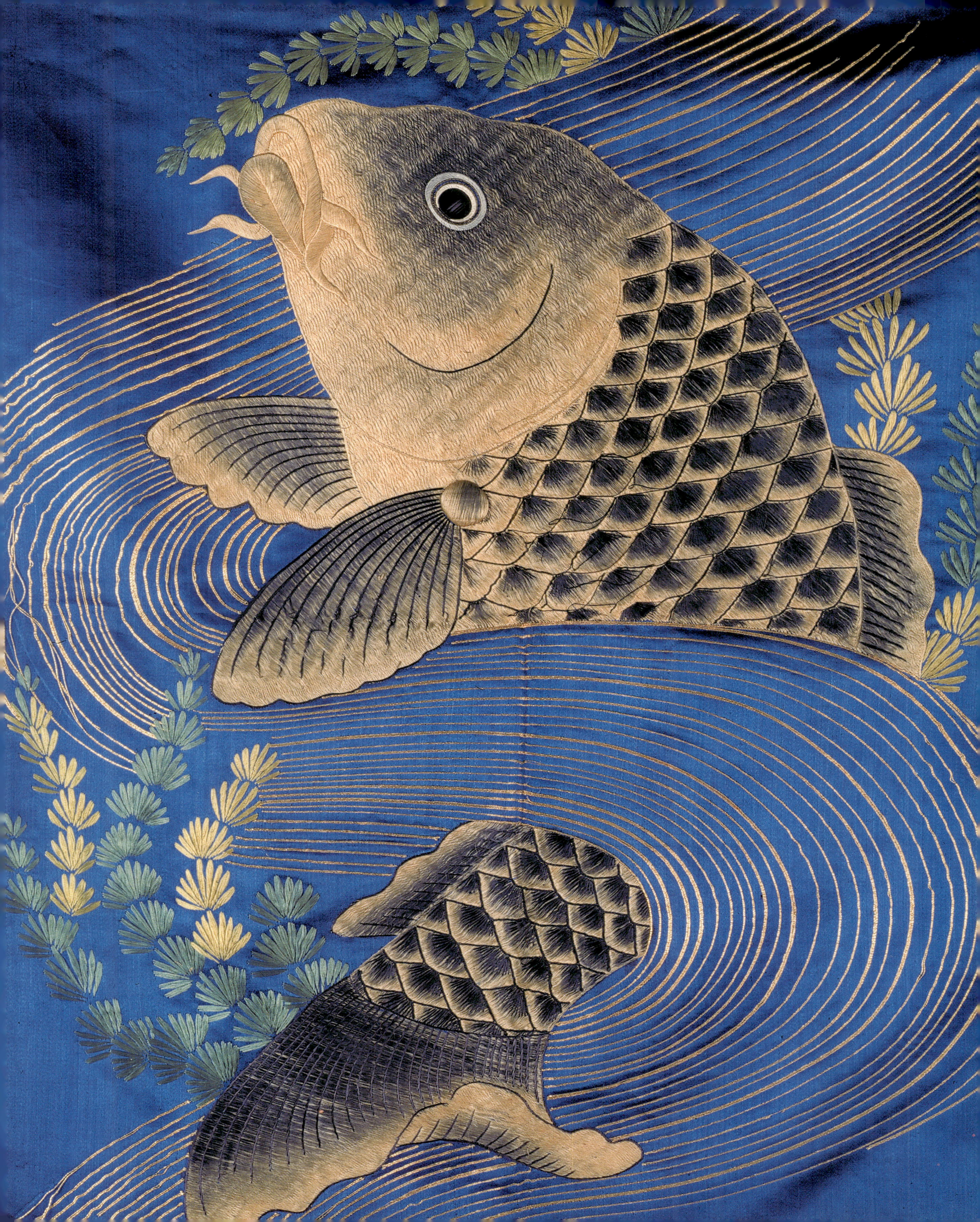

At the turn of the century, then, Bing had curtailed his formerly vigorous trading activities, presumably so that he could focus on the sale of Japanese art objects at his gallery at 19, rue Chauchat. In addition, as a distinguished connoisseur, he was often called upon to authenticate works and to appraise works when collections of Japanese art came up for sale (fig. 5). Apparently, once August Bing left the company, Siegfried replaced him with people outside the family, who assisted him with the more mundane aspects of the business. August's health improved in Kassel, whereupon he took up the latest fads, including bicycling and later driving automobiles.[64]

A NEW VENTURE IN INTERNATIONAL DESIGN

With many others now specialising in Japanese art, including Hayashi Tadamasa, a dealer with excellent contacts in Japan, Bing recognised the difficulty of maintaining his earlier level of financial engagement in the Far East. It had become far more complicated to find objects to sell in a highly competitive market. Moreover, the public's interest in things Japanese was waning, or at least shifting toward serious collectors who wanted older objects of higher quality. Part of this shift was due to Bing himself, who had promoted first-rate pieces over inexpensive curios.

Always an advocate of the improvement of the decorative arts, Bing hit on a new direction in his career. Just as work in a porcelain factory had brought him to Paris, porcelain would act as a catalyst again. After Leullier et Bing was dissolved in 1881, Siegfried remained in contact with the firm's successor, Alfred Haase, who was perhaps a distant family relative.[65] By 1900, Haase had increased his visibility as a manufacturer of porcelains by becoming actively involved in sponsoring the applied arts. With his son, René, the Haase family was linked to Siegfried Bing at the turn of the century, especially in their common interest in the production of creative porcelain pieces. René Haase, who became close to Marcel Bing, was keen to disseminate the style of *art nouveau*.[66]

At this time, Siegfried Bing continued to participate in Japanese art exhibitions in The Hague and in other countries,[67] but he also set about learning more about art activity in the United States. Earlier, in the 1880s, he had donated Asian art objects to the Metropolitan Museum of Art in New York City, and his journal, *Le Japon Artistique*, which was also published in English, was widely

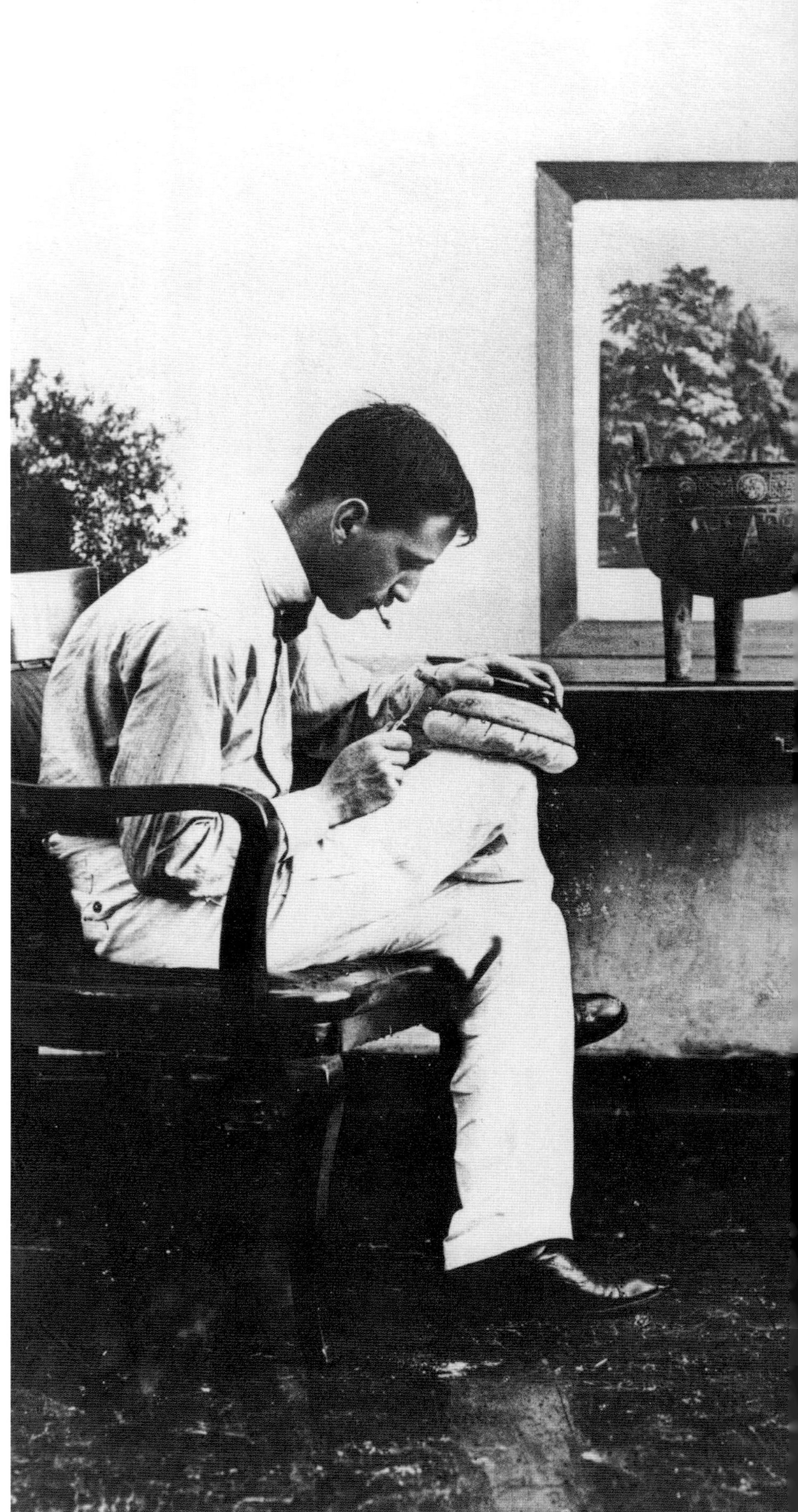

distributed in England and in the United States.[68] In 1894, following the 1893 World's Columbian Exposition in Chicago, Bing set sail for America. He wanted to judge for himself the level of dynamism and energy apparent from American decorative art works that he had seen in international exhibitions. While in the United States, Bing visited the centres of industrial arts creativity: New York, Boston, Cincinnati, Pittsburgh, among other cities. In each location, Bing took notes, which he would later use, along with studies that he had conducted prior to going to America, to produce a report: *La Culture Artistique en Amérique*. This publication would prove instrumental in Bing's promotion of the decorative arts in France, since he desired to replicate the new developments in applied arts in America in his own adopted country.

By 1895, Bing was well on his way toward dealing in *art nouveau* objects. In the 1896 *Didot-Bottin* he was listed under the rubric of 'Japoneries' and also under 'Curiosités', for his inclusion of 'L'Art Nouveau' at his galleries at 22, rue de Provence.[69] Evidently, he wanted both aspects of his commercial activities to proceed side by side. In 1900, the year that his pavilion 'L'Art Nouveau Bing' opened at the World's Fair in Paris, Siegfried still promoted his business in several areas, with his shop being recognised as one of the major attractions of the city. In that year, there were new listings in the directory that reflected Bing's new ventures in the decorative arts, under: 'ameublement', 'bronzes-objets d'art', 'céramique d'art' and 'curiosités', in addition to 'l'art nouveau'.[70] In the following years of the new century, Bing continued to advertise himself as a dealer of 'chinoiseries et japoneries', at 19, rue Chauchat, at the same time that he promoted *art nouveau* and his own line of ceramics at his shop.[71] Besides his assiduous promotion of his merchandise, he was also careful to highlight the relationship between Eastern and Western materials, which, by this time, was well understood as a principal goal of the business.

< 24
Marcel Bing working as a jeweller
Private collection, Paris

THE LAST BUSINESS YEARS OF SIEGFRIED BING

The success of the Bing empire depended largely on the close collaboration of family members. A male child was trained by his father or an older brother and eventually took over from the earlier generation. This had been the case with Siegfried Bing, and was now with Marcel, who was the only surviving heir in 1895.[72] Exactly when Marcel was introduced to the family business is not documented. However, given that Siegfried travelled alone to the United States in 1894, it must have been sometime after this date, when he was organising the Salons de l'Art Nouveau, that his son took an active role in the art trade.

From his earliest days Marcel was surrounded, both in the shop and at the Bing apartments at 9, rue Vézelay by significant art objects, which would have contributed to his appreciation of Asian art.[73] In his teens, he enrolled at the Ecole du Louvre, where he was trained in art history, including Asian art. He may have also taken courses at the Musée des Arts décoratifs.[74] Early examples of jewellery made by Marcel Bing are so rare that his emergence in 1898–9 as an experienced jeweller comes as a surprise. Since Siegfried Bing had at one time a shop next to Henri Vever, a well-known jeweller and collector of Japanese art, it is possible that Vever introduced Marcel to this art form.[75] In 1899, when Siegfried added a crafts workshop to the rear of 19, rue Chauchat, Marcel and Léon Jallot, a young designer, supervised the work of the other craftsmen with the elder Bing.[76]

In 1896, twenty-one-year-old Marcel travelled with his father to England, most likely to meet English designers, who were still working with Bing on design issues.[77] The heir to the Bing empire in France and an

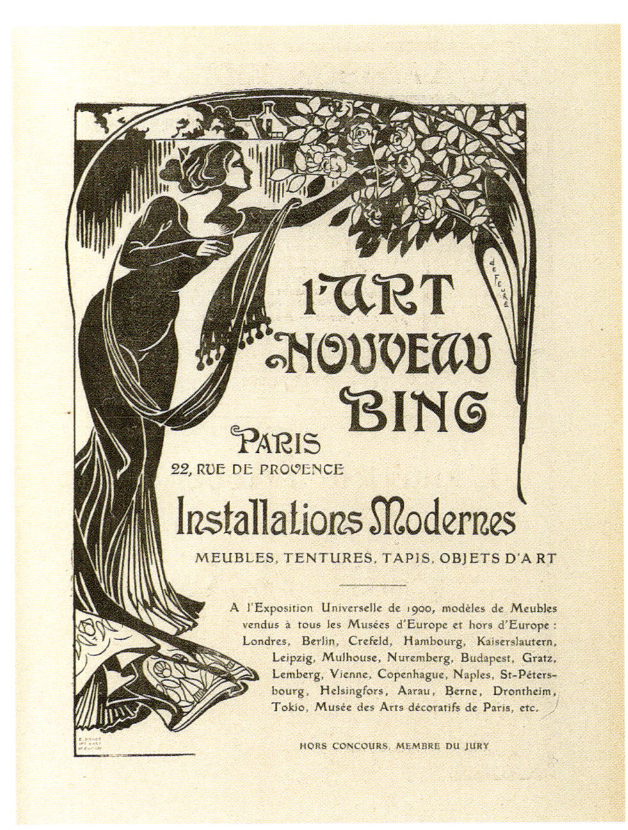

25
Georges de Feure, Advertisement for Bing's L'Art Nouveau, *Art et Décoration*, January 1902

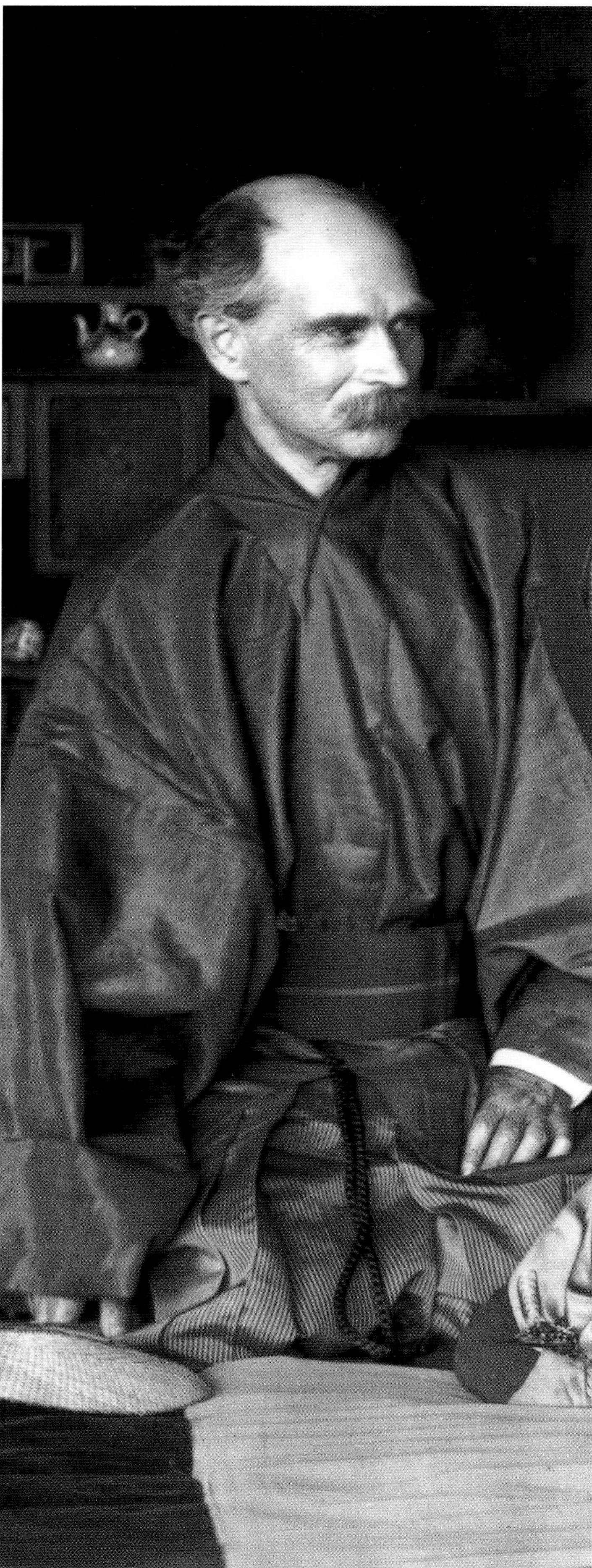

26
Siegfried Bing, 1899.
Detail of fig. 58

aspiring artist, Marcel was extremely adept at communicating with artists, and he spoke English well. In 1971 Andrée G. Duizend, a cousin, recalled Marcel as 'tall, slender, blonde with blue eyes [...] very much an artist'.[78]

While Siegfried was expanding his *art nouveau* venture, and before his retirement in 1904, Marcel gained first-hand experience in all aspects of the family business. After Siegfried died in 1905, Marcel ran the business from his apartment at 10, rue Saint-Georges. It is from that address, shortly after his father's death, that Marcel sent out notices announcing to clients that he would continue his father's work (fig. 24). A devoted son, Marcel hoped to achieve a smooth transition of the family business and to follow in the footsteps of his father.

THE LEGACY OF SIEGFRIED BING

When Siegfried died in September 1905, a long obituary appeared in the American journal *Brush and Pencil*, one of the most popular art publications of its day in the United States: '[T]he news of the death of Siegfried Bing [...] will come as a personal loss to scores of collectors in Europe and this country, who owed many of their treasures of Japanese art, and no little of their love of Oriental art, to this indefatigable dealer, who did so much to make known the transcendent qualities of the best porcelains, bronzes, lacquers, and prints of the Far East. [...] He was a typical Dealer of the old school, the friend and guide of his customers, but while keen enough at a bargain, his chief ambition was to make Oriental art felt as an influence for good upon designers.'[79] Bing's role as a dealer and promoter of Asian art was widely recognised throughout the world. Anyone who collected Japanese art also knew about his personal collection, since some of it was housed in his apartment on 9, rue Vézelay. When this group of objects was sold in May 1906,[80] Marcel Bing received over a quarter of million francs. Now a wealthy aesthete, Marcel could continue his work as an art dealer without financial worries.

After Siegfried's death, Marcel retained his father's close contacts with museums throughout Europe. He sold Egyptian and Asian antiquities to the Kaiser Friedrich Museum in Berlin in 1906 and 1908.[81] The 1906 sale also generated considerable interest among museum directors, including Justus Brinckmann of the Museum für Kunst und Gewerbe in Hamburg and Louis Sarre in Berlin, who waited anxiously to see what would be sold.[82] Some letters reveal concern about the authenticity of certain pieces, suggesting an increased level of connoisseurship since 1900.[83] Marcel Bing continued to deal in art from Asia well into the twentieth century. He operated his shop at 10, rue Saint-Georges, organising small exhibitions, publishing brochures and selling antiquities not only from the Far East, but from Persia and Egypt as well.

Marcel was not content to deal with European museums and collectors; he also pursued his father's contacts in the United States, especially Charles Lang Freer, who had been a good client of Siegfried. Several letters between Marcel Bing and Freer document the relationship even as late as 1916.[84] After World War I, the French government sent Marcel on official missions to China. During his absence, others – including René Haase – supervised the business. Haase was a longstanding employee, who became Marcel's partner. After Marcel's death in 1920, Haase took over the shop at 10, rue Saint-Georges, where he continued to sell pieces to museums such as the Louvre until 1936.[85] Among the items sold to the museum were works from the European ancient world as well as from the Far East, demonstrating the diversity of the Bing stock. In 1927, Haase held a sale at the Hôtel Drouot of Japanese prints and ceramics from China and Japan left over from the Bing inventory, netting a handsome sum.[86]

At the same time that Haase was selling antiquities to the Louvre and other European museums, he was still interested in *art nouveau*. In September 1926, he sold works by Georges de Feure, Alexandre Bigot, Emile Gallé, Adrien Dalpayrat and Edward Colonna to the Metropolitan Museum of Art in New York.[87] In addition to these sales, and just as Siegfried Bing had done earlier, Haase donated several ceramic pieces by Edward Colonna and Georges de Feure, thereby increasing the number of works in New York that could be linked to Siegfried Bing's shop.[88] Given that Marcel had seemingly sold the last of his *art nouveau* pieces in 1908, these examples must have come from Haase's own stock or personal collection. At a moment when *art nouveau* was evolving into other design styles – and had been for fifteen years – René Haase remained dedicated to seeing that Bing pieces would be preserved in the United States.

René Haase continued as a dealer until the German occupation of Paris. In May 1943, ancient art and pieces from the Far East were auctioned at the Hôtel Drouot as part of the Nazi programme to sell objects owned by Jews.[89] A catalogue for this sale was published; the reminiscences of a witness are worth citing. M. Guy Portier, son of André Portier, the expert who oversaw the cataloguing of the 1943 sale, wrote: 'I remember M. René Haase perfectly, because I pitied him so much. I met him many times, during the period when I was preparing the catalogue [...] he seemed a good man. But he was compelled, like all Jews, to wear on his coat sleeve, the yellow star. He was quite unhappy. After the catalogue was finished, I never saw him again. I never knew what happened to him. I hope he was able to save himself from the terrible hands of the Germans.'[90] The likely fate of this faithful partner of Marcel Bing was the tragic consequence of cataclysmic events. The history and significance of the Bing family and their artistic empire has remained difficult to reconstruct because so much has been lost or dispersed. However, from this sketchy outline, a story emerges of ingenuity, dedication and perseverance. By using his vast fortune in combination with imaginative entrepreneurial skills, Siegfried Bing realised his dream of introducing Japanese art to Western craftsmen in order to produce new objects for home decoration, resulting in an entirely new style that bears the name of his shop: L'Art Nouveau.

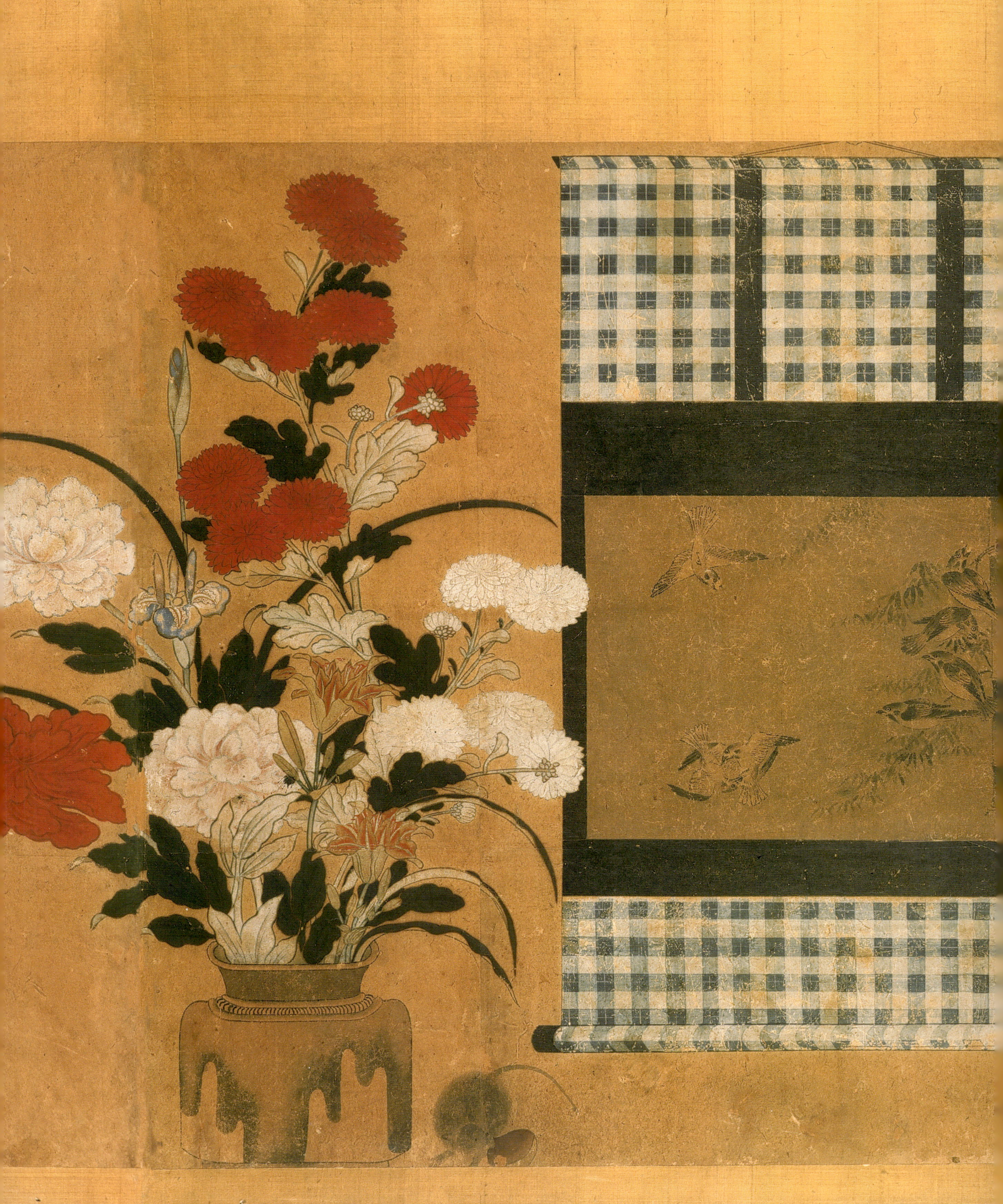

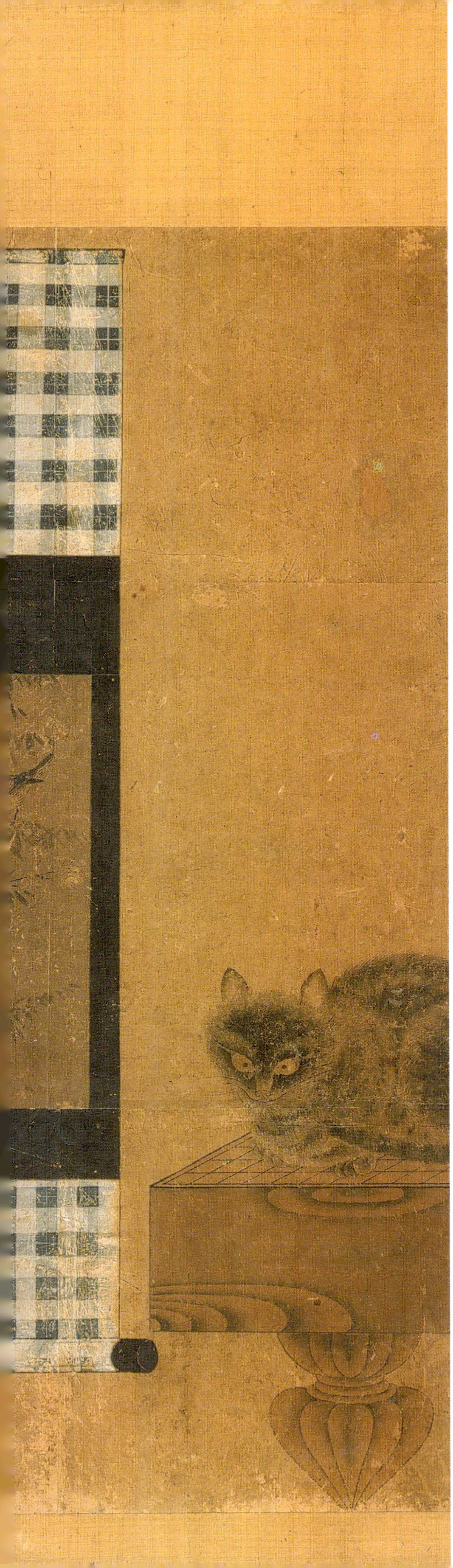

THE APPRECIATION AND STUDY OF JAPANESE ART

CHRISTINE SHIMIZU

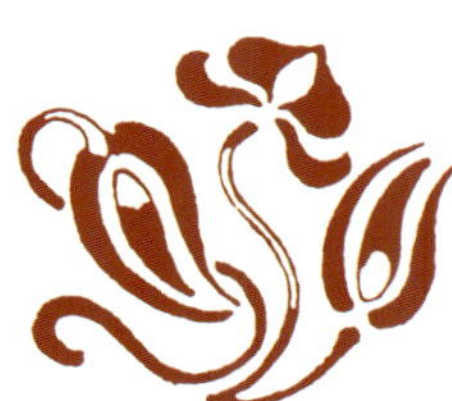

Although Siegfried Bing began to collect and sell Japanese *objets d'art* at an early date, he was following two earlier initiatives by art dealers specialising in this field. From 1878 until after the 1900 World's Fair in Paris, he dominated the market for Japanese art, his principal rivals being Wakai Kenzaburô and Hayashi Tadamasa,[1] but although he built upon the activities of previous generations who ran curio shops in Paris, in scope and number of pieces he surpassed what these earlier discoverers of Japanese art had available for sale.[2] The first generation of dealers included owners of such notable shops as *La Porte chinoise* (36, rue Vivienne), opened by Bouilliette in 1826, and, from 1862, *La Jonque chinoise* (operated by the husband and wife team of Desoye at 220, rue de Rivoli). Both stores were frequented by such well-known figures as Charles Baudelaire, Edmond de Goncourt, the art critic Philippe Burty, the painter James McNeill

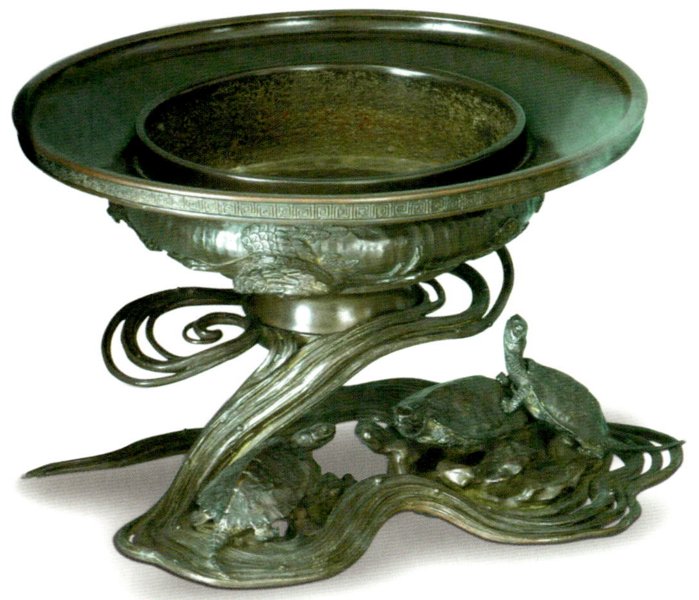

Whistler and the English critic William Michael Rossetti, who went there to satisfy their curiosity and thirst for Japanese objects.[3] Philippe Sichel (whose shop was located at 11, rue Pigalle) represented the second generation, and in 1874 he became the first art dealer to visit Japan. When he returned to France, he brought back at least five thousand pieces for his Japanese-Chinese import business, hundreds of which were sold to Edmond de Goncourt and Philippe Burty – an indication of the way private collections were extended by purchases from Paris dealers.[4] It appears to have been Burty who encouraged Bing to travel to the Far East and to buy goods for his burgeoning stores directly from Asian sources.[5] By the mid-1880s, Bing was such an adept dealer in Japanese art that he had several shops in Paris that specialised in both contemporary and ancient objects.

THE CRAZE FOR JAPANESE ART

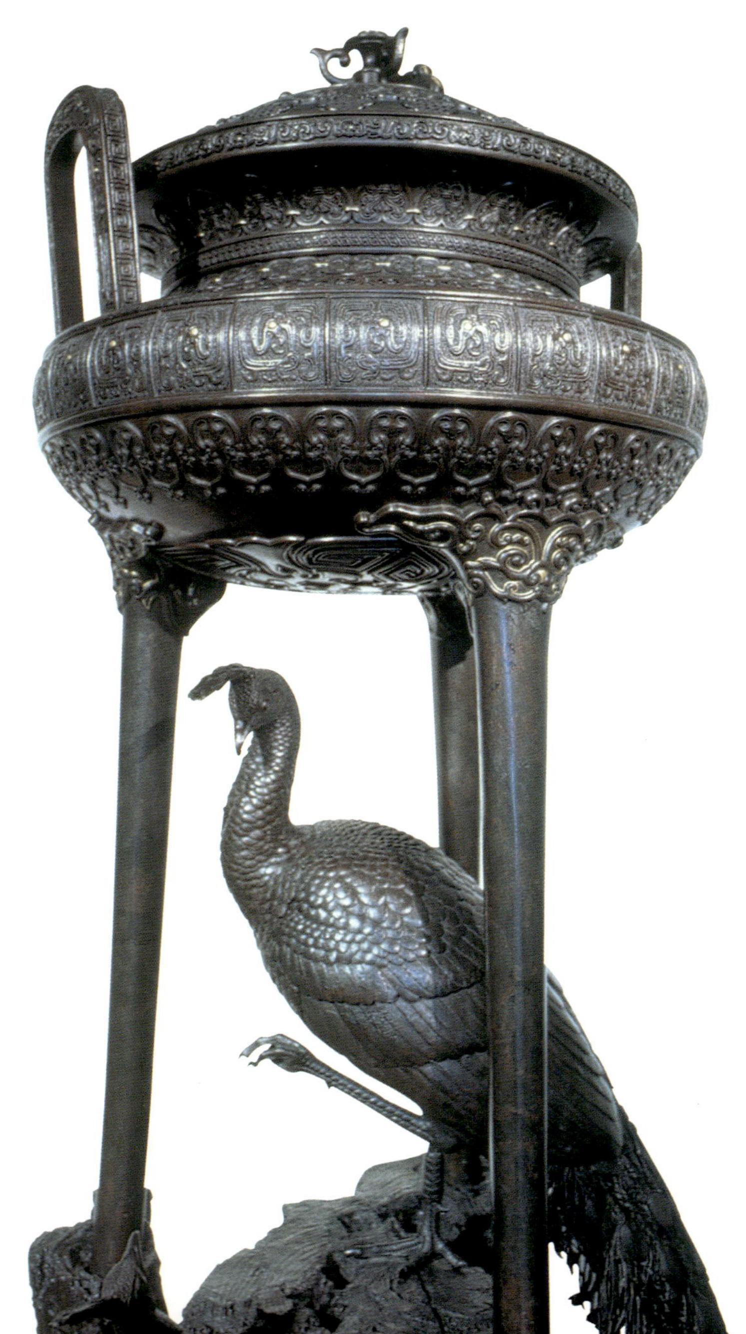

Japanese art enthusiasts unable to follow the precedent of the collector Henri Cernuschi and the art critic Théodore Duret, who travelled to Japan in 1871–2, were given the opportunity to acquire objects at the World's Fairs, which, besides showcasing Japanese techniques and aesthetics, confirmed the Japanese reputation for craftsmanship. The Paris Fair of 1867 'succeeded in creating the fashion for Japan.'[6] In addition to prints, there were two other significant areas: metalwork and ceramics. These three forms of art were especially important to Bing as he continually acquired works in these media for his own collection and to sell in his shop.

Bing's interest was reinforced by the 'Exposition Orientale' organised in September-October 1873 by Cernuschi, where he presented to the French public the bronze sculptures he had brought back from his travels in the Far East. As a result of this, French collectors for many years saw bronze as the characteristic medium of Japanese sculpture,[7] while the works that interested them most – aside from a few religious pieces[8] – were exclusively from the animal kingdom (dragons, cranes, tortoises), in accord with the current preoccupations of Western sculptors. Bing's interest in metalwork was confirmed by his sale in 1875 to the South Kensington Museum (now the Victoria and Albert Museum) in London of several bronzes. These pieces, including a cylindrical vase with wave decoration (fig. 30), a drum-shaped vase and an ascetic Buddha, were placed on public display.[9]

Bing, along with other early Japonistes, became a collector of bronzes. In 1874, he lent bronzes from his collection to the exhibition at the Union centrale in Paris, and he sold further works to the South Kensington Museum, including a bronze incense-burner in the form of a goose for £108.[10] While this was a large piece, the sale indicates that prices for Japanese bronzes had increased sharply. Bing must have understood the craze for objects of this kind and imported a number of examples, since Louis Gonse, writing in his book *L'Art Japonais* (1883), enthusiastically commented on a similar bronze: 'In M.S. Bing's private collection, I noted a large bronze goose of monumental beauty.'[11] Bing was arriving as a tastemaker; objects from his personal collection were being admired, reproduced, and commented upon.

<< 27
Anonymous, *Still Life with Cat* (two-leafed screen), Japan, beginning of the 17th century (detail of fig. 45)
Musée national des Arts asiatiques-Guimet, Paris

< 28
Jardinière, Japan, 18th century
Nordenfjeldske Kunstindustrimuseum, Trondheim

< 29
Suzuki Chôkichi, Incense-burner in form of tripod standing on root and accompanied by peacocks, Japan, c. 1877 (detail)
Victoria and Albert Museum, London

30
Cylindrical vase, Japan, 19th century
Victoria and Albert Museum, London

THE IMPACT OF PRIVATE COLLECTORS

The organisation and eventual exhibition of private art collections (either in part or in entirety) allowed Bing to play a leading role on the art scene. In this, his Japoniste colleagues, who were also doing much to promote certain aspects of the Japanese civilisation, assisted him. An early milestone occurred in 1878 and was commented upon by Raymond Koechlin, who was himself a leading collector: 'We had to wait for the [World's] Fair of 1878 before Paris gained any idea of Japanese taste. [...] From then on, Hayashi was, with Bing, the most intelligent intermediary between Japan and Paris; it was these two who revealed the real art of Japan, who moulded our taste, and whom we discover at the origin of all our fine collections.'[12]

Bing's commitment led him to open his first store, at 19, rue Chauchat, to coincide with the 1878 World's Fair. French collectors rushed to secure the pieces shown at the Fair: 'Within a very few days we saw all the entries to the Japanese section in the Champ-de-Mars snapped up by collectors for fabulous sums.'[13] From examples exhibited by the Kiritsu Kôshô Kaisha, Japan's leading industrial exporter,[14] Bing secured a huge bronze incense-burner two metres tall (fig. 29). Inlaid with gilt bronze and alloy, this highly complex piece (a tripod resting on a root accompanied by peacocks) reflects both a taste for virtuosity and an emphasis on the richly ornate.[15] It is the work of Suzuki Chôkichi, who also served as director of the metalwork department of the Kiritsu Kôshô Kaisha firm. The burner was also admired by the Director of the South Kensington Museum. Having obtained the piece for his shop, Bing sold it to the London museum for a record sum of £1,586.[16]

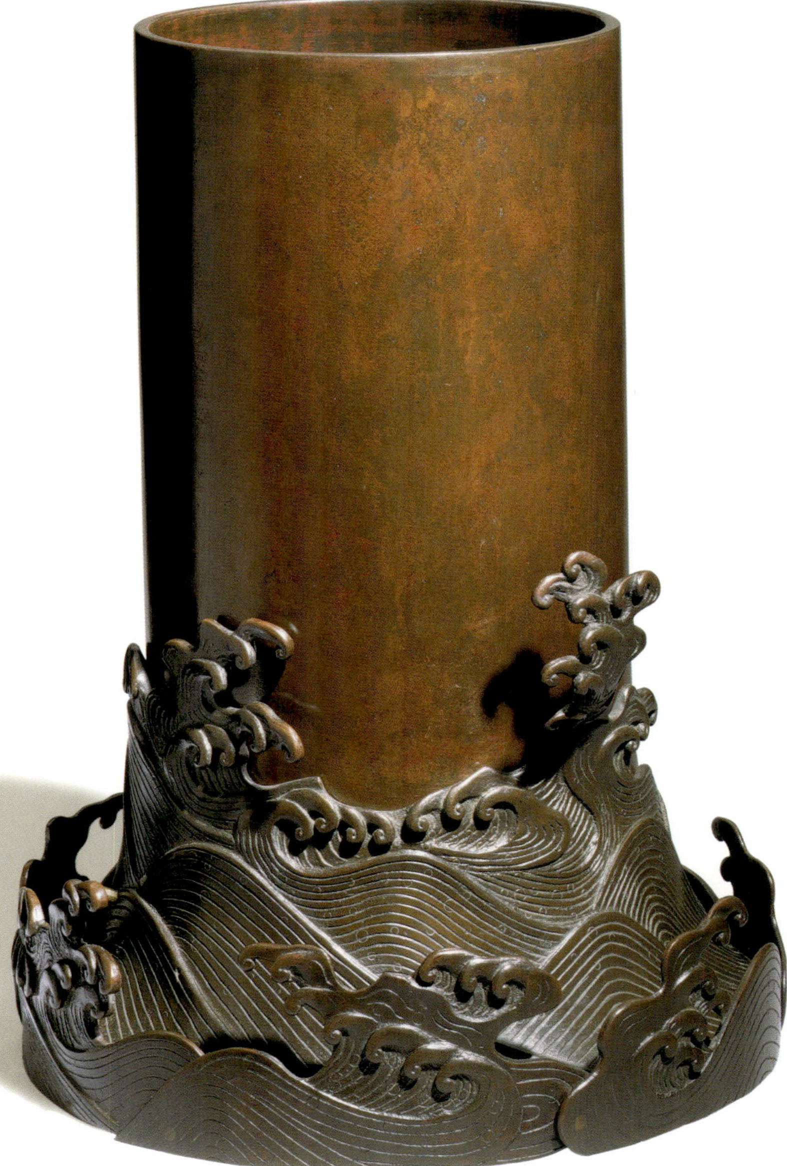

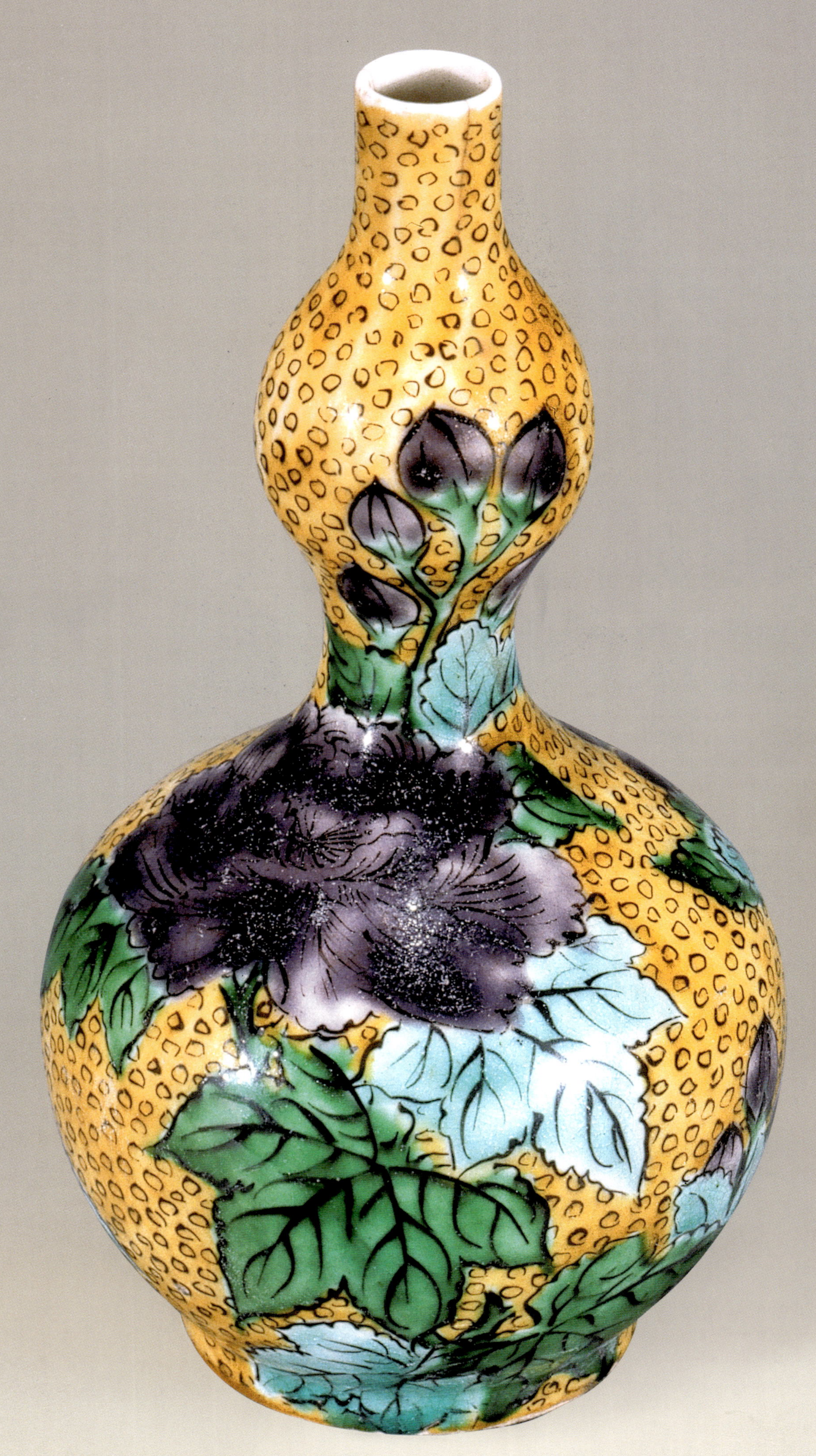

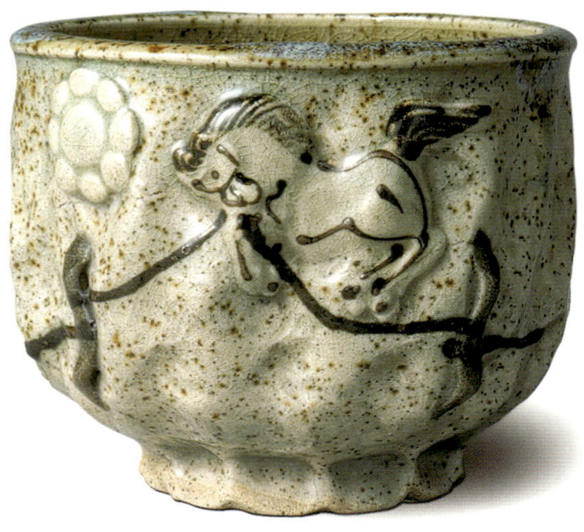

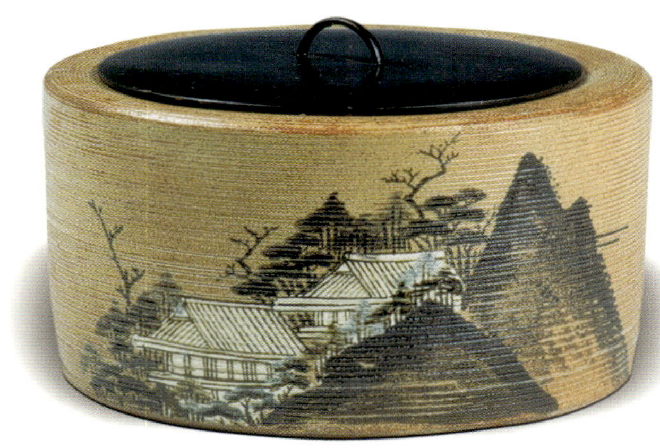

< 31
Gourd Bottle, Japan, Kutani ware, Yoshidaya kilns, 19th century
Musée des Arts décoratifs, Paris

32
Tea bowl, Japan, Soma-Ohori ware, 19th century
Musée national de Céramique, Sèvres

33
Water jar (mizusashi), Japan, early 19th century
Musée des Arts et Métiers, Paris

BING'S ROLE AS A DISSEMINATOR OF CERAMICS

Bing's involvement in spreading the appreciation of Japanese art took three forms: contribution to exhibitions and publications, the enlargement of his private collection, and his sales to collectors and museums. In spite of little knowledge of Japanese ceramics, Bing exhibited a few ceramic pieces from his collection in the Japanese pavilion at the 1878 World's Fair. However, this display was sharply criticised for a lack of specific information. Ernest Chesneau complained that the works were not classified and that the labels for the objects were inadequate: 'The collections of MM. Bing, Burty, de la Narde, de Camondo and E. Guimet are certainly unusual [...] but with the exception of Guimet's, which is of a religious character, the haphazard arrangement of the rest and the absence of logical classification, while they are of great interest to the amateur, robs them of any serious value for study.'[17] The only collections spared negative commentary were those sent by Wakai, which were 'accompanied by proper background information'. Paul Gasnault, a significant collector of ceramics, also criticised the Japanese section. Nevertheless, he recognised the quality of ceramics that came from various private collections, noting: 'Three French collectors exhibiting in the same room have saved the honour of the Japanese pavilion: MM. Vial, Bing and de la Narde. [...] Bing has a large display, and a very remarkable one, constituting one of the most complete collections we know of different types of Japanese ceramics.'[18] Some years later, Louis Gonse, writing in *L'Art Japonais*, remembered certain pieces from Bing's collection, citing 'Monkey attacking a stag', 'Appliqué vase' and 'Carp emerging from the waves' as being worthy of attention: pieces, however, which to modern eyes are hardly representative of the traditions of Old Japan and do not pre-date the 1800s.

Bing assembled a major collection of ceramics, building on his natural predilection for this medium and his own innate ability to judge saleability. He revealed a real passion, prompting a later generous comment from Gonse that light had been shed for the first time on this subject, 'due to his rigorous methods and the patient investigation that he began in Paris in 1878, continued in Japan itself, and carried on in the tireless creation of one of the finest and most interesting collections one could contemplate. [...] Today, thanks to him, we can say that the history of Japanese ceramics is established and we have a clear picture of the field.'[19] Bing never spared his energies; he also had able guides to assist him, finding support from Ninagawa Noritane and Wakai Kenzaburô. Noritane's book, the *Kwan Ko Dzu Setsu* (1876–9) provided early information on cera mics. As Burty had done, Bing acquired the book for himself, and he gave a copy in 1888 to the Conservatoire National des Arts et Métiers,[20] along with a collection of Japanese ceramics that served as models for young students to study.

Bing's interest in ceramics aroused the curiosity of other collectors. He grasped that it was ceramic pieces with dark glazes and restrained decoration that were most characteristic of Japan, quite different from the Chinese tradition that had been so much admired.[21]

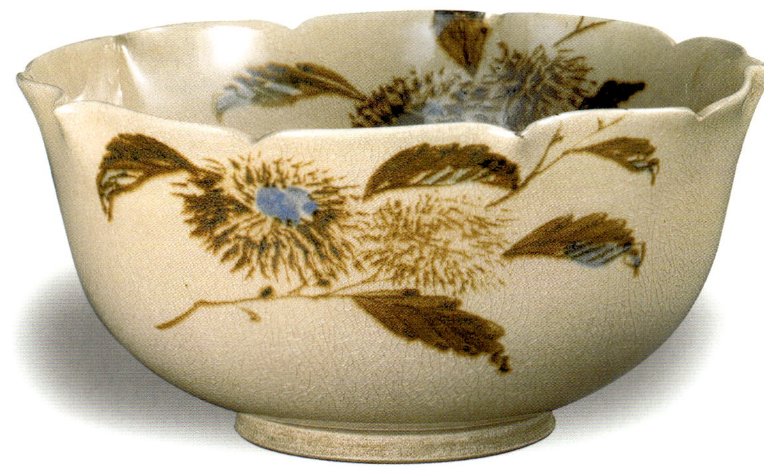

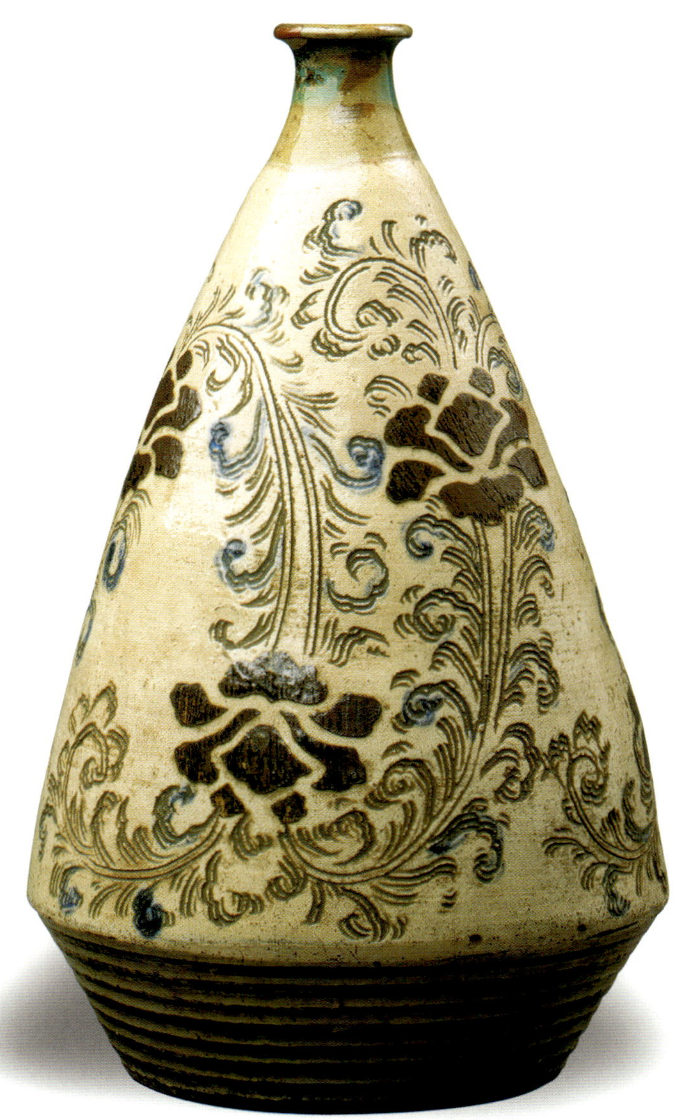

In 1883, when his close friend Louis Gonse entrusted Bing with the editing of the ceramic section of *L'Art Japonais*, Bing further commented that, 'it is through their work with natural clays, which allows much more varied glazes, decorative effects and colours, that Japanese potters have truly shown their superior and individual talents.'[22]

With his commitment to promote ceramics, Bing often found himself in direct competition with others, especially Hayashi, for sources of Japanese material that could be sold in France. Both men found their examples at the same locations. For the most part these included stoneware pieces from the Hagi, Soma, Bizen, Banko, Minpei and Seto kilns; there were others obtained in the Kyûshû region, from such sites as Yatsushiro, Takatori or Agano. Bing sold many of these pieces to museums from the mid-1870s onward. In some instances, Japanese stoneware was sold through Leullier et Bing's store (48, rue du faubourg Saint-Denis) to the national ceramic museum at Sèvres.[23] In 1886, these pieces were identified by Hayashi as coming from the Soma (c.1830), Banko, Takatori and Owari (c.1800–20) kilns (fig. 33).[24]

In April 1883, with more objects available, a huge exhibition at the Galerie Petit provided added knowledge and made a stronger statement. Comprising three thousand objects, paintings and prints from twenty-six collections, the show was organised by Gonse, who once again drew on the collections of the foremost Japonistes: Burty, Duret, Gonse, Wakai, Ephrussi, Haviland, Camondo and Bing. Critics were impressed; they called the show 'the first Japanese museum', singling Japan out from other Far Eastern countries.

The catalogue, prepared with Hayashi's help, was more scientific than earlier ones; there was a concerted effort at an accurate identification of periods and artists' signatures. Bing was strongly represented in the show with 256 objects, including Kyoto stoneware (signed Raku, Dôhachi, Mokubei, Rokubei, Eiraku, Kenzan). Other pieces were identified as coming from Bizen, Takatori and Banko; there were only thirty-three porcelain items (from Hizen and Kutani). No. 241 in the catalogue describes a bowl similar to one that Bing sold to Sèvres in 1875,[25] while 'The Carp' (no. 192) and 'Deer attacked by a monkey' (no. 144b) had previously been shown at the 1878 World's Fair.

34
Bowl, Japan, Kyoto ware, Iwakurasan kilns, end of the 17th century
Musée des Arts décoratifs, Paris

35
Sake bottle, Japan, Agano ware, Hoshô kilns, 19th century
Musée des Arts décoratifs, Paris

> 36
Brazier in form of fabulous lion's head, Japan, Bizen ware, 19th century
Musée des Arts décoratifs, Paris

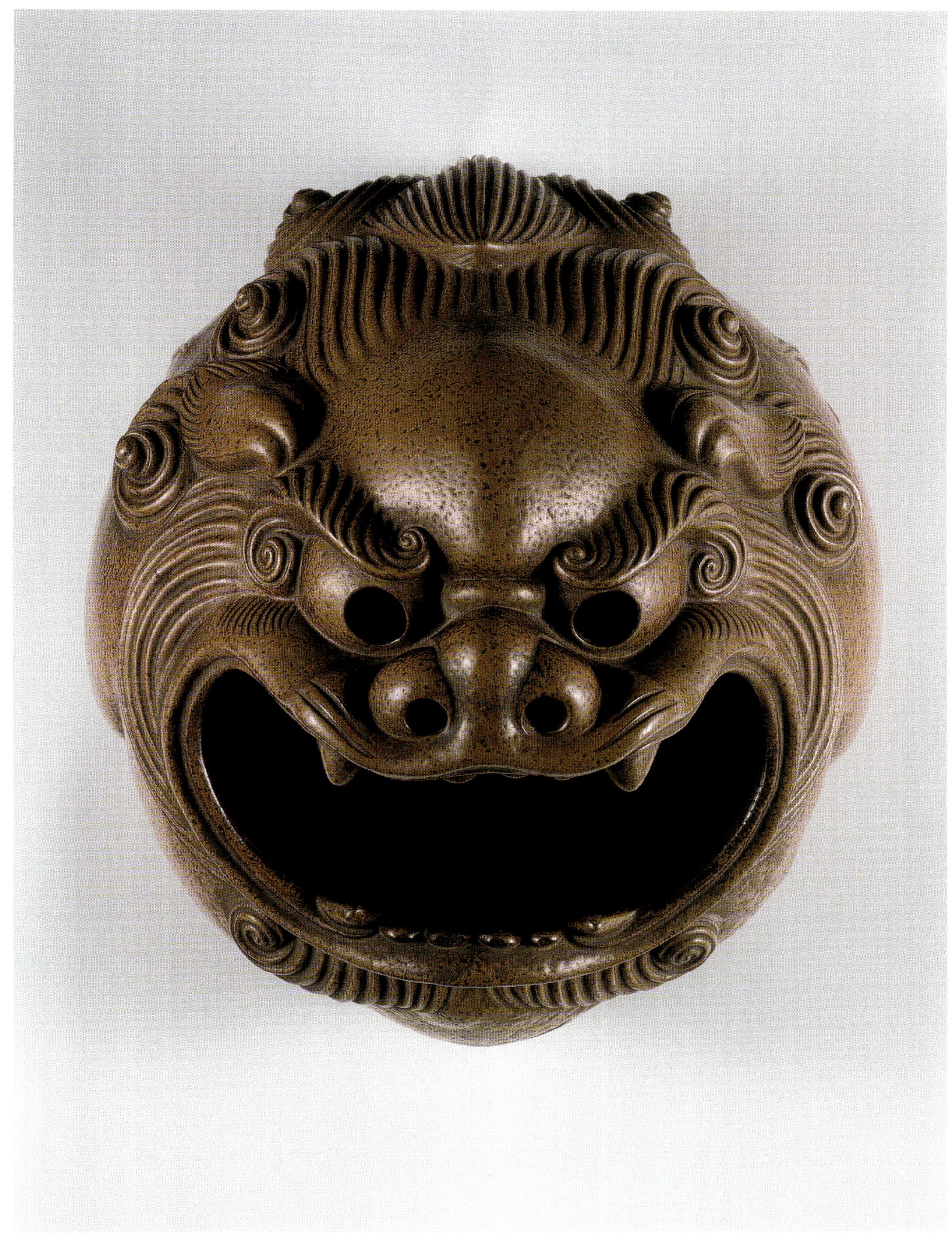

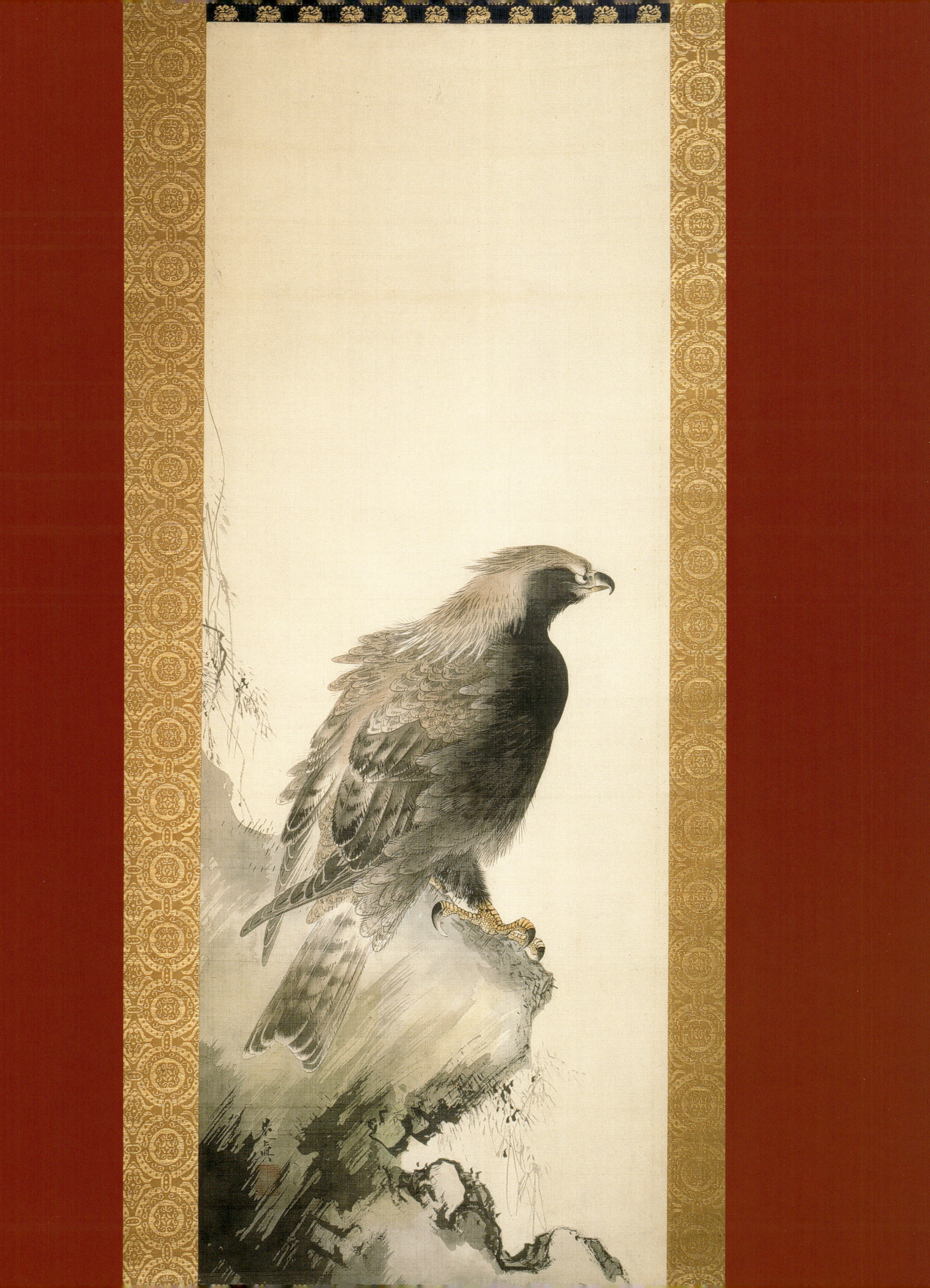

THE FASCINATION OF OTHER MEDIA

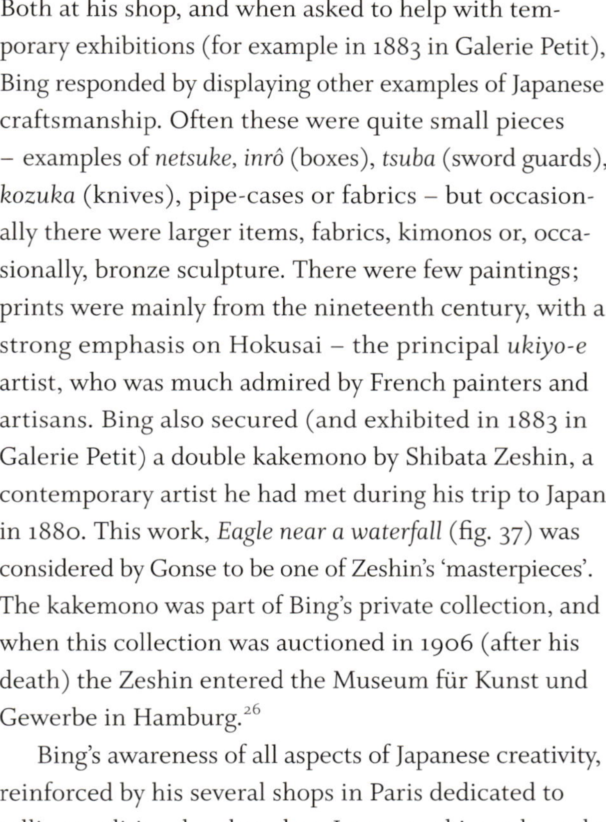

Both at his shop, and when asked to help with temporary exhibitions (for example in 1883 in Galerie Petit), Bing responded by displaying other examples of Japanese craftsmanship. Often these were quite small pieces – examples of *netsuke*, *inrô* (boxes), *tsuba* (sword guards), *kozuka* (knives), pipe-cases or fabrics – but occasionally there were larger items, fabrics, kimonos or, occasionally, bronze sculpture. There were few paintings; prints were mainly from the nineteenth century, with a strong emphasis on Hokusai – the principal *ukiyo-e* artist, who was much admired by French painters and artisans. Bing also secured (and exhibited in 1883 in Galerie Petit) a double kakemono by Shibata Zeshin, a contemporary artist he had met during his trip to Japan in 1880. This work, *Eagle near a waterfall* (fig. 37) was considered by Gonse to be one of Zeshin's 'masterpieces'. The kakemono was part of Bing's private collection, and when this collection was auctioned in 1906 (after his death) the Zeshin entered the Museum für Kunst und Gewerbe in Hamburg.[26]

Bing's awareness of all aspects of Japanese creativity, reinforced by his several shops in Paris dedicated to selling traditional and modern Japanese objects, brought an increasing number of clients to the dealer. His support of traditional Japanese artists, who were being challenged by western inroads in the Meiji period, encouraged Bing to write essays and catalogue prefaces for those Japanese artists linked to the older artistic traditions of the country. In 1883, when the first annual Salon of Japanese painters was organised in Paris, Bing was asked to write a preface to the catalogue. The show, assembled under the patronage of Wakai, a member of the conservative Ryûchikai Association (Society of the Dragon-Lake), was held to promote traditional art, a mode of painting that was coming under attack from the growing taste for Western oil painting.[27] The Salon met with little success; criticism in the Paris press considered the works shown to be 'corpses, or the mummification of painting' and failed to recognise the pieces shown as real works of art.[28] The exhibition due to take place the following year was cancelled. Some of the artists, such as Kono Bairei, Kanô Hôgai or Watanabe Seitei,had greater success in the United States, where their works were appreciated by such collectors as Ernest Fenollosa or William Sturgis Bigelow.

Another medium that attracted Bing's eye was the increasing study and appreciation of Japanese prints. In 1890, when a huge Japanese print show was held at the

< 37
Shibata Zeshin, *Eagle near a waterfall* (part of a diptych), Japan, c. 1880
Museum für Kunst und Gewerbe, Hamburg

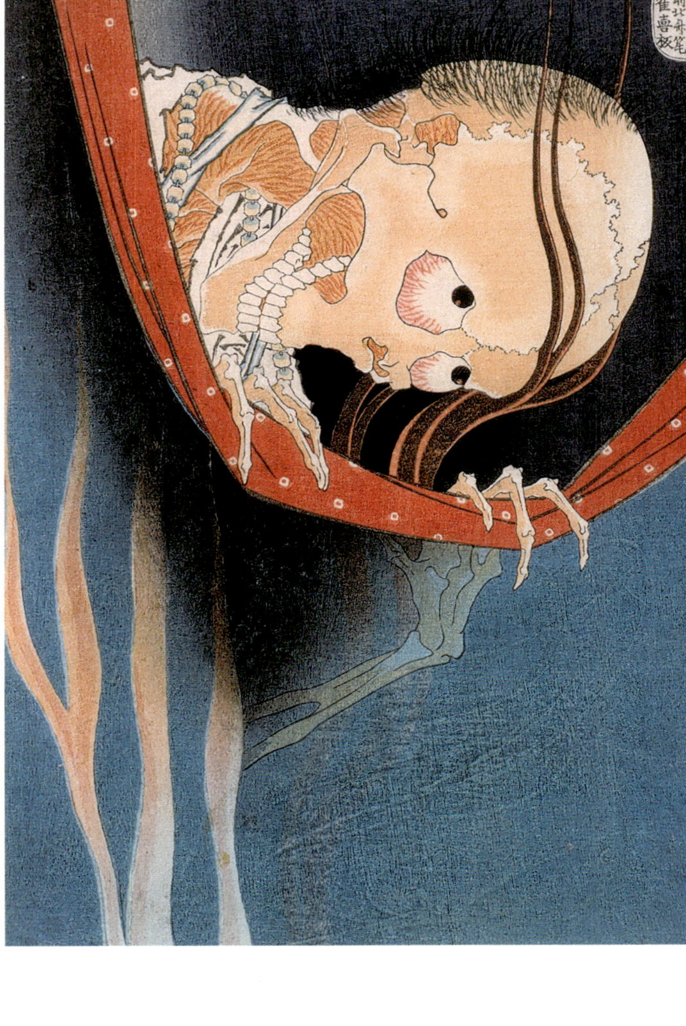

38
Katsushika Hokusai, *The Ghost of Kohada Koheiji*, from the series *One Hundred Tales*, Japan, c. 1831
Musée national des Arts asiatiques-Guimet, Paris

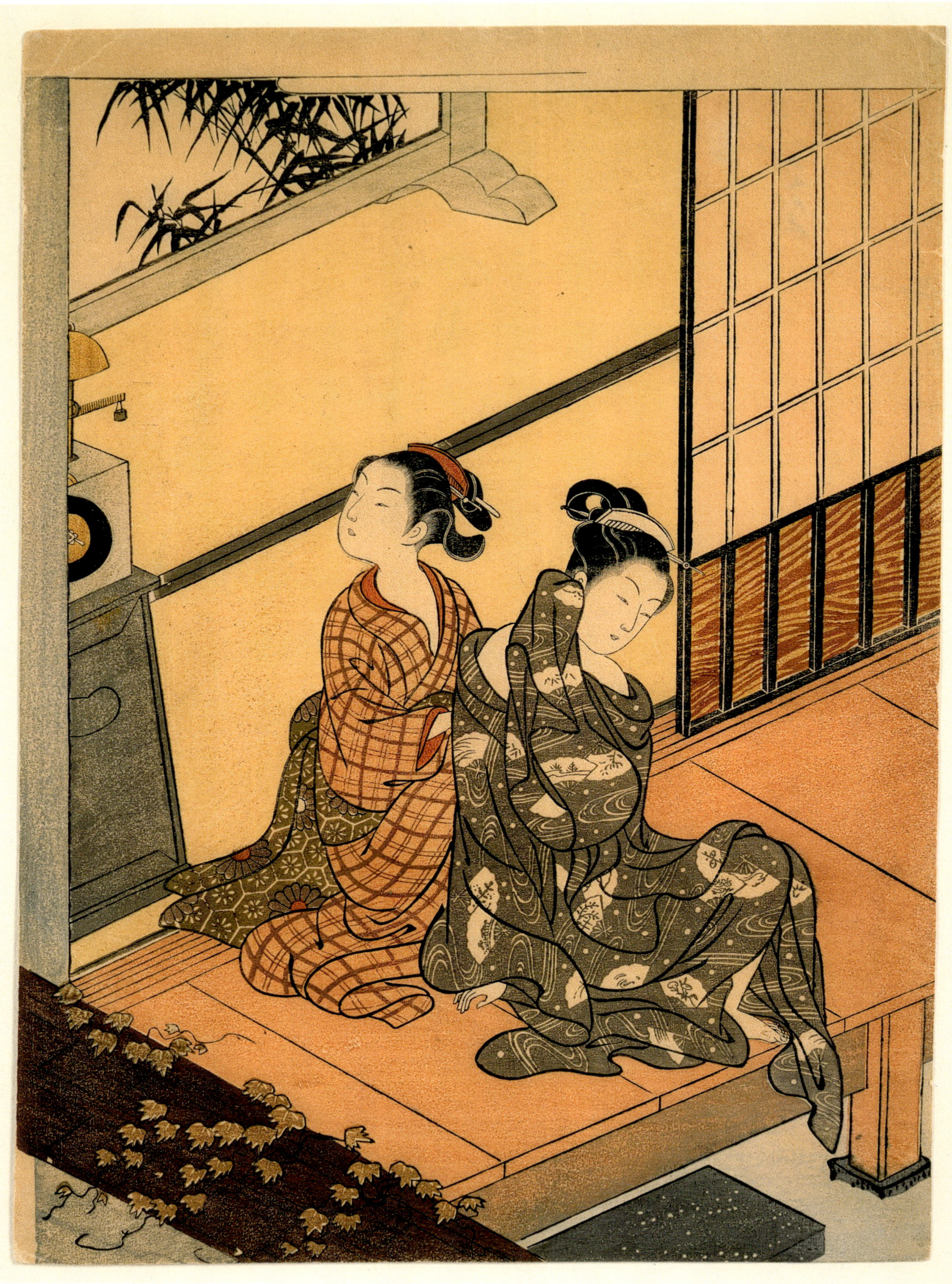

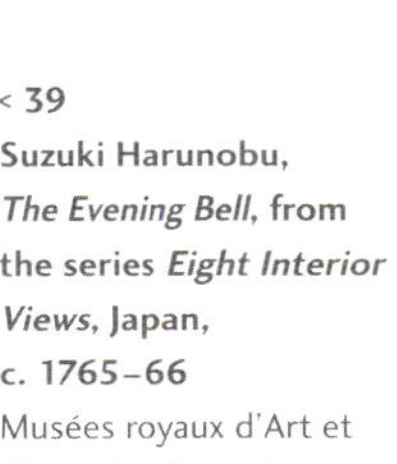

< 39
Suzuki Harunobu,
***The Evening Bell*, from the series *Eight Interior Views*, Japan, c. 1765–66**
Musées royaux d'Art et d'Histoire, Brussels

40
Kitagawa Utamaro,
***Mother and Child (Higher and Higher)*, Japan, c. 1801–04**
Musées royaux d'Art et d'Histoire, Brussels

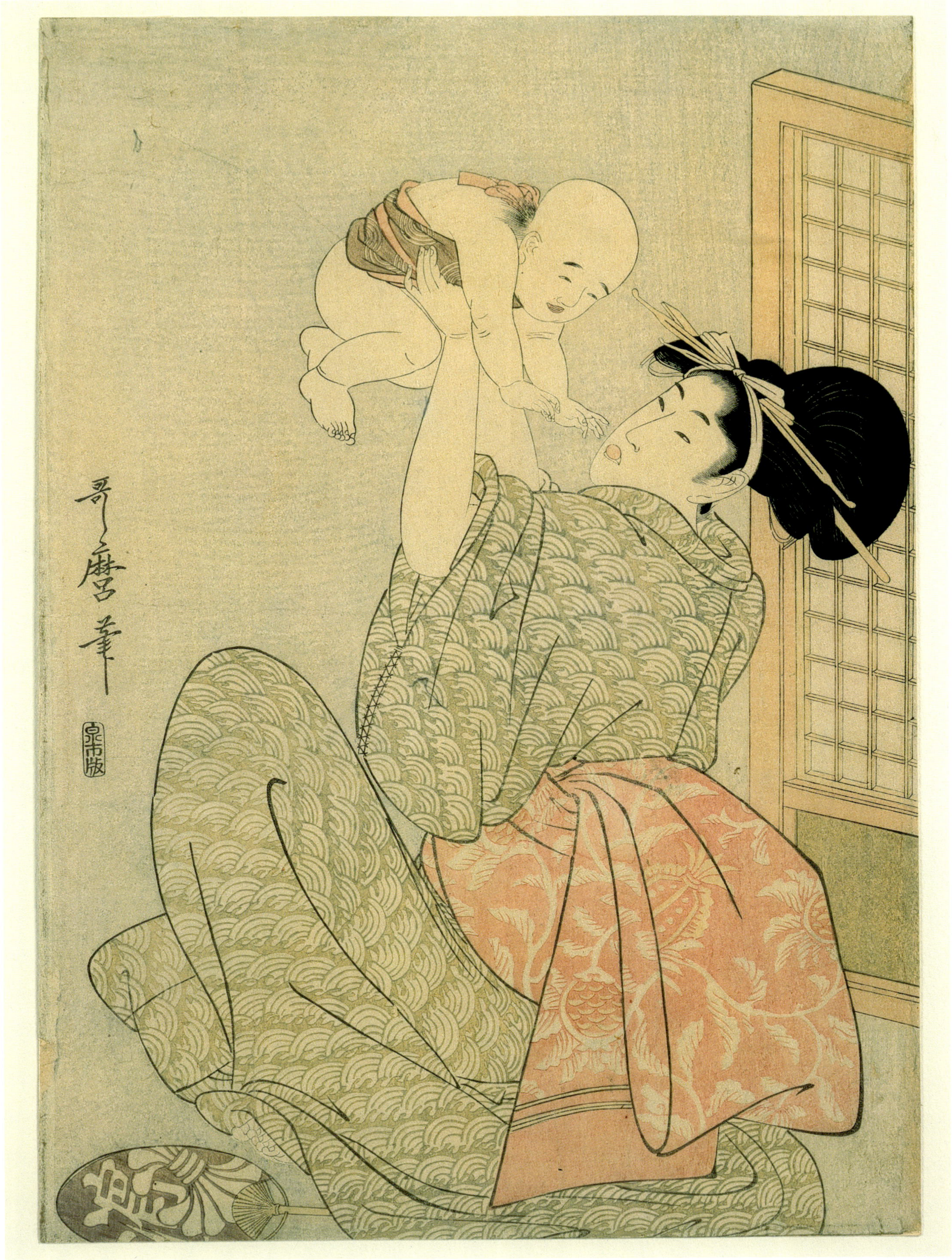

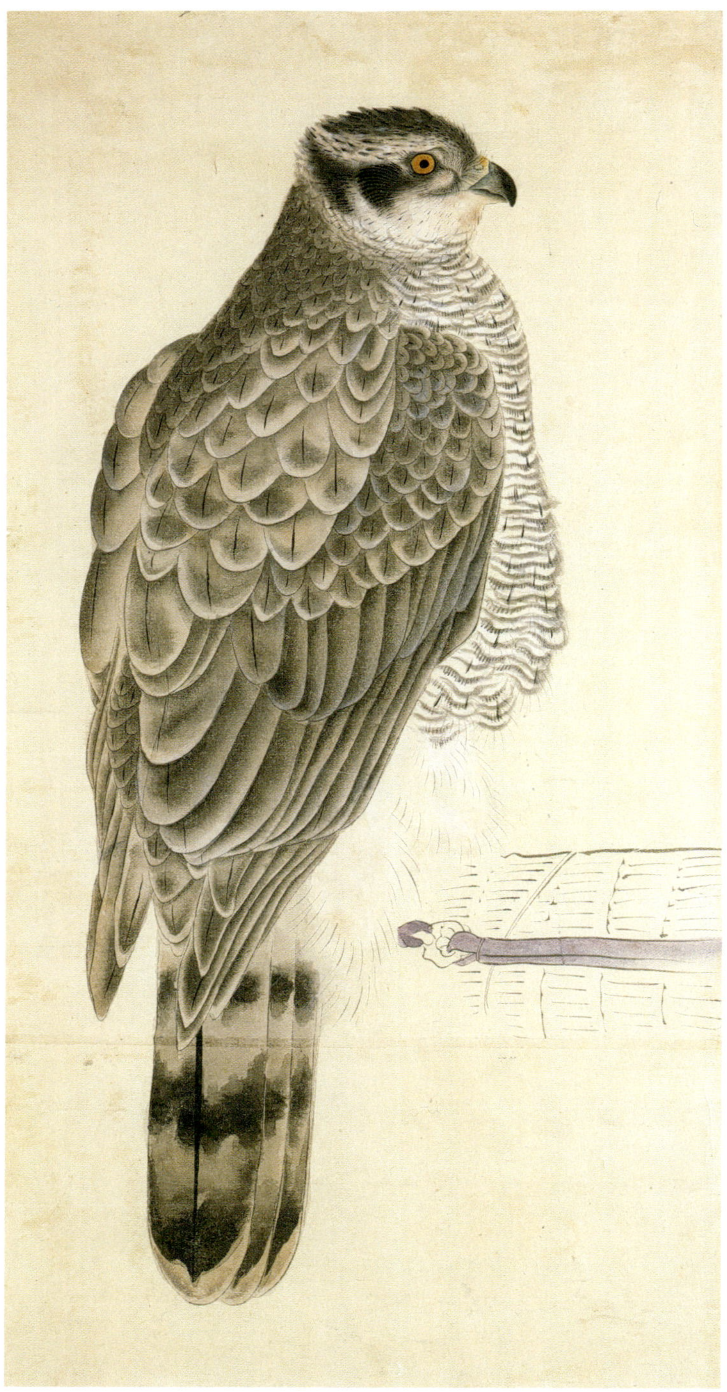

Ecole des Beaux-Arts (25 April-22 May), Bing's catalogue preface marked a high point of the craze for things Japanese. The exhibition assembled over seven hundred prints, providing an overview of the evolution of *ukiyo-e* prints from the mid-eighteenth century onwards. As a member of the organising committee, which included Burty, Gonse, Goncourt, Clemenceau and Vever, Bing saw to it that Hokusai's *Manga* was well represented in the show (figs. 44, 59). From 1858, the illustrated volumes of Hokusai's *Manga* were bought in Tokyo (then Edo) by Baron de Chassiron, and soon afterwards collectors like Théodore Duret began to acquire virtually contemporary prints by the master of landscape. But it was not until 1883 (in Galerie Petit) that Paris discovered the polychrome prints *(nishiki-e)* of the golden age: 'large compositions [...] with scenes from the lives of the women of Edo; it is impossible to describe the beauty, the harmony, the variety of the figures.'[29]

Bing, together with Gonse, was promoting an awareness of Japanese prints along with ancient Japanese art. Between 1883, the date of the publication of Gonse's book, and 1890, when the Ecole des Beaux-Arts print show opened, devotees of Japanese art began to see it as more than ethnographic material; there was now an increased awareness of its aesthetic quality. Japanese printmakers were constantly being discovered and identified. Utamaro, who had been dismissed in a few lines by Gonse in 1883, was widely praised by 1890. The recognition that there was a growing interest in these printmakers also forced Bing and Hayashi to ask their suppliers in Japan to search for as many examples as possible.[30] Both men were so successful in their dissemination of new *ukiyo-e* masters that French collectors were able to mount the large retrospective in 1890.

This exhibition was a crowning moment in Japanese print collecting in France. Gaston Migeon, curator of the Louvre, became convinced of the quality of the works and was willing to allow Japan into this temple of classic art. The catalogue was the first to establish the history of Japanese printmaking, and it demonstrated that it was a legitimate field for study, establishing the main lines of serious research that remain in place today.

However, Bing's role as a great populariser of Japanese creativity was not over. He reached out to the public through his monthly magazine *Le Japon Artistique*,[31] and by March 1892 he was moving into another area. As part of his promotional campaign Bing organised monthly Japanese dinner parties to which he invited

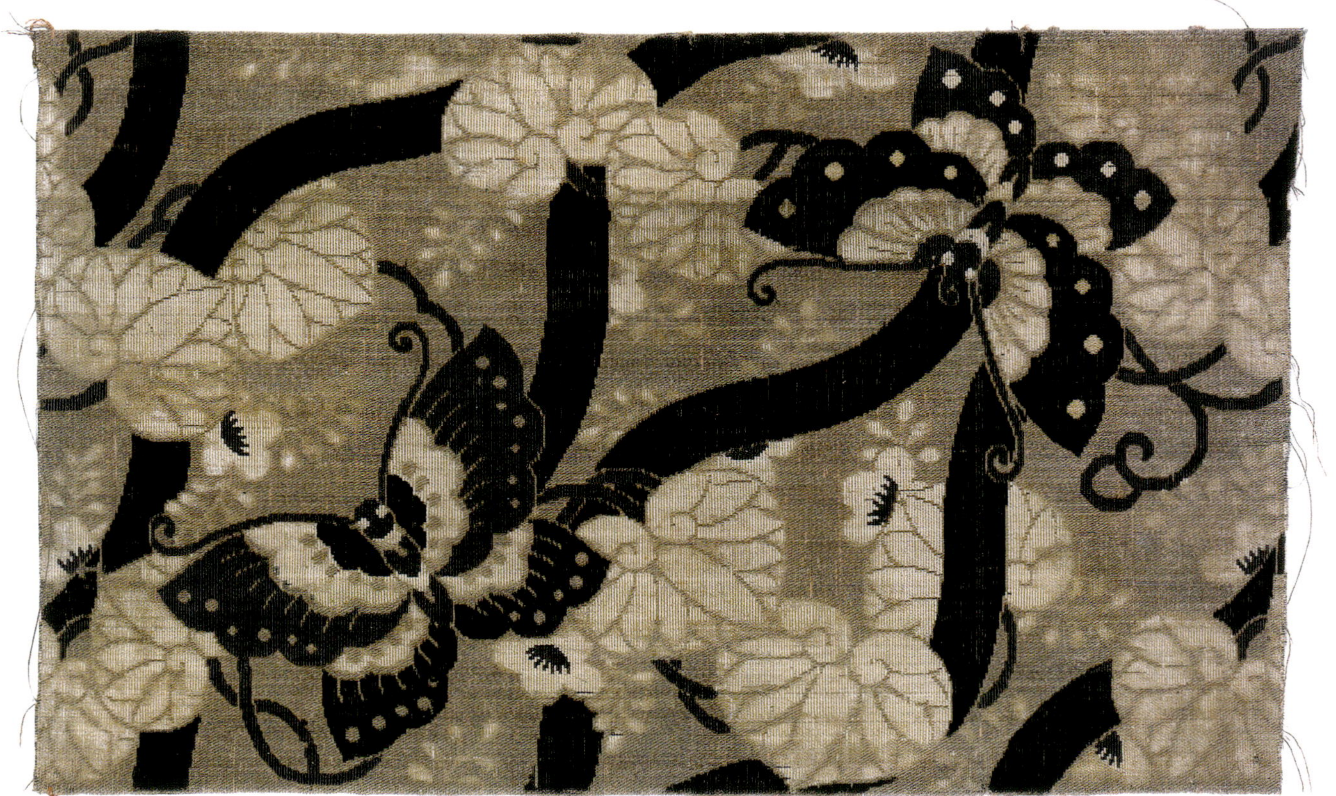

< 41
***Eagle*, from an album of drawings, Japan, 19th century**
Victoria and Albert Museum, London

42
Fabric with foliage and butterflies, Japan, 19th century
Musée de la Mode et du Textile, Paris

print collectors, where the main subject of conversation was *estampes*.[32] The rooms of his shop and his private apartment on rue Vézelay were packed with material. His house was filled with glass cabinets full of *objets d'art*; scrolls hung from the walls with amaranth coloured damask. Several generations of collectors attended these dinners. In 1904, Gaston Migeon could still recall the moment when, after meals that brought together such leading collectors as Raymond Koechlin, Henri Vever (the jeweller) and sometimes James McNeill Whistler, everyone would 'press round a large table, and the hours seemed to fly away as they leafed through big boxes of colour prints by wonderful Japanese printmakers.'[33] At an earlier moment in time, when Bing had discussions with Henry Van de Velde in the mid-1890s, the Belgian artist had also been able to go to his house to see his private collection. These were 'unforgettable moments where one handled proofs, of previously unimagined quality, from the most glorious period of Far Eastern printmaking, work by men such as Utamaro, Hokusai and Hiroshige!'[34]

Like Hayashi, Bing revealed to the West an art form that was held in low esteem in Japan; it was not appreciated there until much later. But by giving a significant place to *ukiyo-e* prints in his books and articles – to the detriment of great schools of painters – Bing transmitted an image of Japan's culture that was fraught with cultural consequences. This approach, one that had been criticised by Ernest Fenollosa when he reviewed Louis Gonse's *L'Art Japonais*, dogged the history of Japanese art for a long time in France. For numerous scholars, studying Japanese art meant simply knowing the art of printmaking and nothing more.

MUSEUMS AND BING'S SUPPORT OF JAPANESE ART

As Japanese art collections were formed, from the 1870s onwards, there was considerable interest as to what would remain intact after a collector died and what purchases would convey the spirit of the era. Some collections of Japanese art stayed together as the result of being purchased by a single museum. Examples of this are the notable collections of Anderson (of about 2,000 paintings), Fenollosa (about 5,000 items) and Gierke. These works were acquired respectively by the British Museum in London, the Museum of Fine Arts in Boston and the Berlin Museums.

The works that were either in Bing's own personal collection (kept in his apartment on rue Vézelay) or that he sold through his store – as part of his ever-changing commercial stock – were dispersed in several ways. His daily sales (for which there are no documented records) were the most obvious way of his disseminating Japanese art; the auction of his private collection in 1906

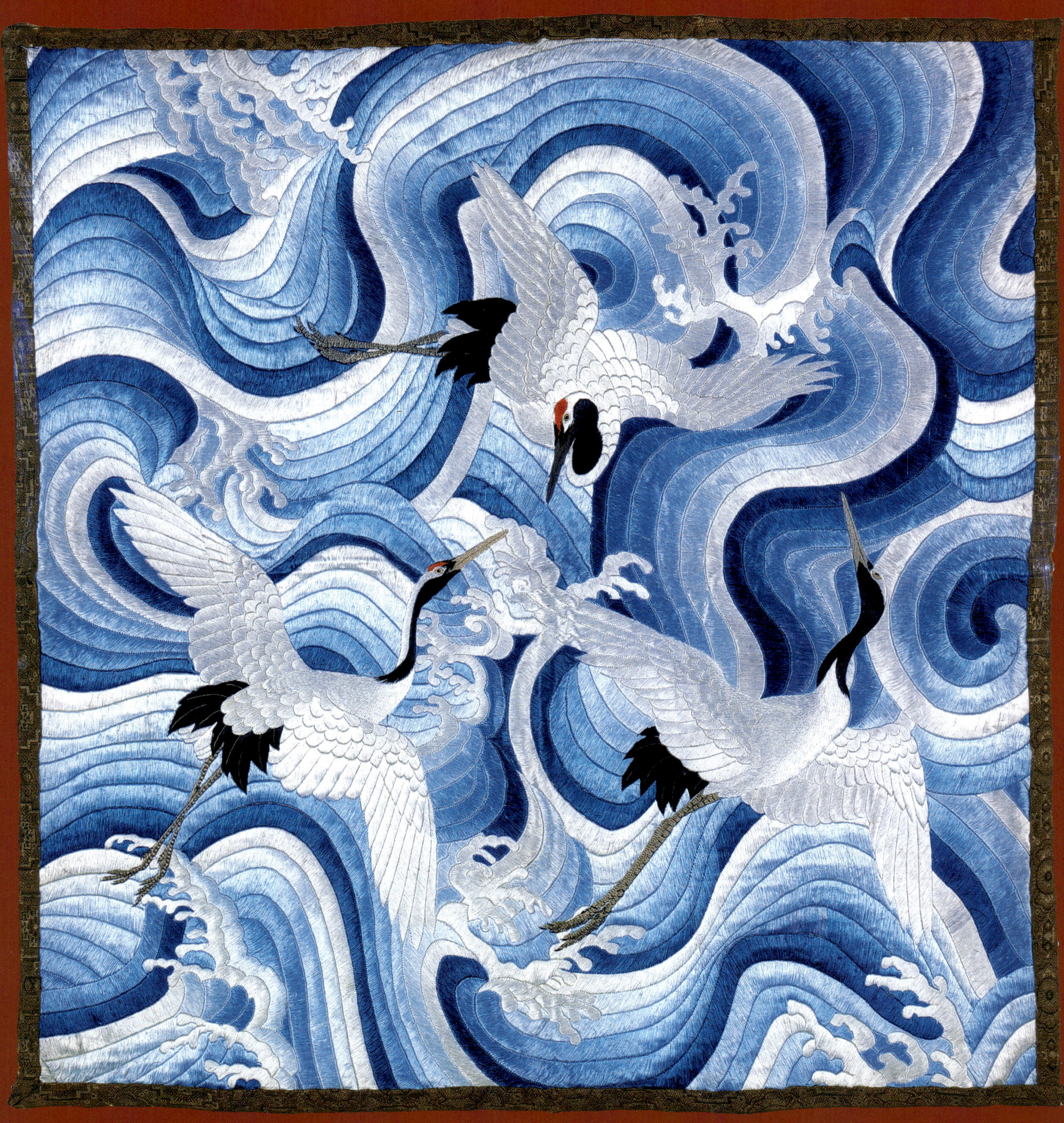

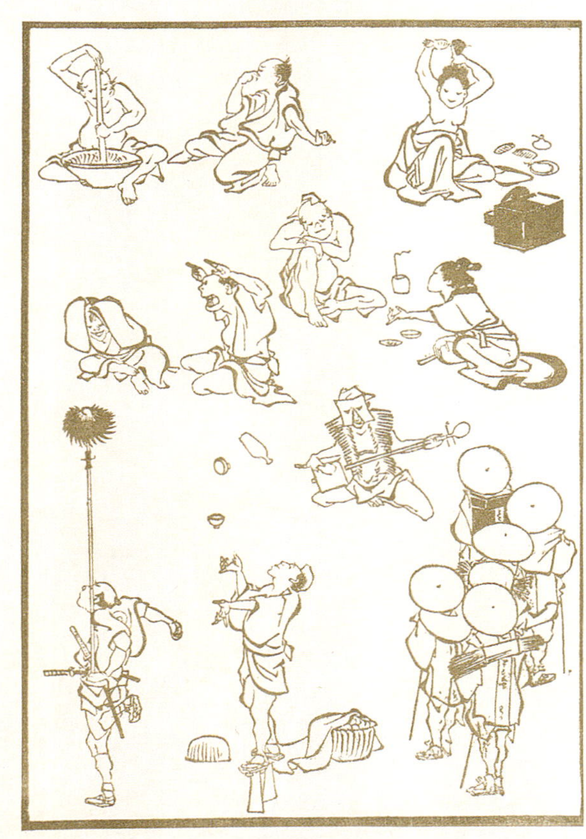

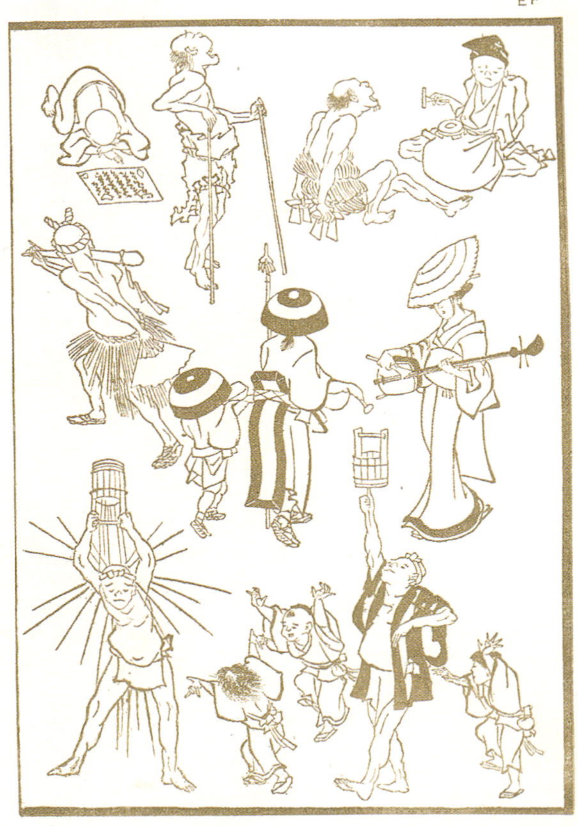

< 43
Fabric with three cranes flying over the waves, Japan, 19th century
Musée des Arts décoratifs, Paris

44
Manga images by Katsushika Hokusai from *Le Japon Artistique*, 1888, no. 8
Van Gogh Museum (Library), Amsterdam

was another; a third was the bequest of Japanese art to his family and friends in his will. There is little doubt that Bing's personal collection had, for a period of time, appeared to French connoisseurs as the epitome of Japanese art: it was seen as a yardstick by which to judge other work and other collections. Camille Mauclair, a valued art critic of the *fin-de-siècle*, remembered Bing's willingness to mould his taste when Mauclair would pay visits to study Japanese art in the 'apartment, on the rue Vézelay, piled high with millions of curios, ivories, bronzes, fabulous silks, albums of prints by Hokusai, Hiroshige, Harunobu, Utamaro'.[35]

However, Bing's taste and the specific conditions of his acquisitions meant that his collections emphasised a particular, and often partial, point of view. Once a selection of pieces had been presented to the Paris public and approved by them, French dealers in Japanese art accepted only what had already been successful and nothing else. French collections were therefore often limited to prints, *tsuba* (including numerous fakes and copies), *netsuke*, bronzes and ceramics. Paintings were often mediocre, or pale imitations of originals. Faked pieces by Hokusai arrived by the dozen; bad *ukiyo-e* paintings also appeared on the market. The finest examples of Japanese art often remained in Japan, a point noted later by Raymond Koechlin: 'Europeans received only what the Japanese wanted to send them: sometimes remarkable works, but rarely of capital importance. And, most frequently, pleasant trifles, with no artistic pretensions in the eyes of the Japanese – unless they were making them specially for the use of the barbarians in the West, as they were shrewd dealers.'[36] Sichel, by 1874, noted in his memoirs, following his trip to Japan, that unscrupulous dealers did not hesitate to consign mediocre items, forgeries and reproductions to please the European market. He added that he had discovered the source of faked ceramics and bronzes that were being sold in Europe as eighth-century wares, explaining, again, that the early dates were invented to satisfy Western demand for 'ancient' Japanese pieces.[37]

With Bing selling both ancient and modern Japanese art, the question to be asked is, was Bing involved in any of these dealings? The answer is difficult to know, because of the paucity of accurate records and an inability to reconstruct a large base of objects sold by Bing through his shop. Clearly, however, Bing was aware of the gaps and weaknesses in European collections of Japanese art; he bemoaned the fact in *Le Japon Artistique*

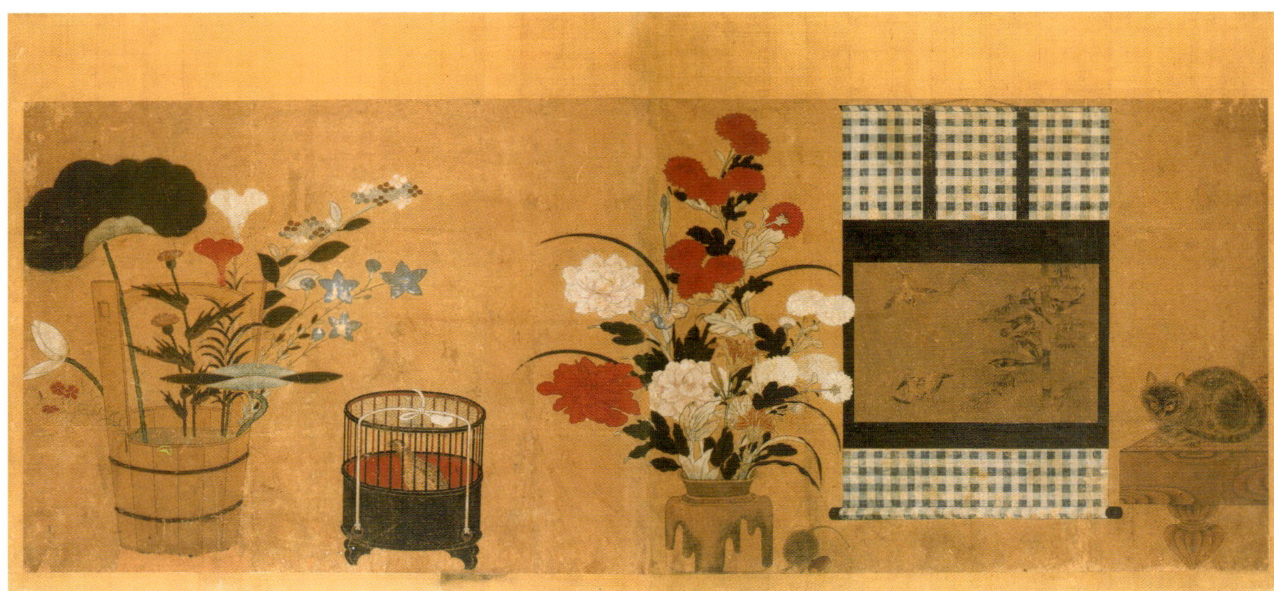

45
Anonymous, *Still Life with Cat* (two-leafed screen), Japan, beginning of the 17th century
Musée national des Arts asiatiques-Guimet, Paris

in May 1899 that Japanese religious paintings were exceedingly rare: 'Even in Japan, such works have become extremely scarce; their possession is equivalent to a fortune. It cannot be imagined that they will ever cross the oceans.'[38]

By the early 1890s, when he was moving toward the creation of *art nouveau*, Bing appears to have become aware of the fact that he was popularising a selected view of Japanese art, limited to what was sent him from Japan by his brother and others. Henry Van de Velde, a close intimate at the time, noted that Bing 'could see that this new field *[art nouveau]* offered him opportunities for the kind of prospecting his agents had been undertaking for years in the Far East without appreciable results. They had scoured Japan, China and Korea, but rarely did anything reach him worthy of his private collection, that of a museum or any major collector in Europe or the United States.'[39] While this is a telling commentary, it must also be used carefully, as Van de Velde was writing with hindsight, trying to give a stronger inflection to the turn toward *art nouveau*, which was a continuation of Bing's well-established interest in Japan. Some truth remains, however, since it was difficult to obtain major works from Japan for the European art market – something Bing only too readily understood.

What remains, then, of the myriad objects that passed through Bing's hands or through his inventories? One has to look at the catalogue of the 1906 sale of works from Bing's private collection, see what prices these works fetched, and then, by evaluating the old photographs in the sales catalogue, try to assess the importance and quality of the Bing pieces.[40] One would need to track individual items sold at this sale to their new owners to judge them against a more recent, scientific knowledge of Japanese art.

It is possible to reach a better understanding of the quality of the works Bing sold to world museums, since museum records of purchases are still in existence. Museums in Brussels, London, Paris, Copenhagen, Hamburg, Trondheim, Washington (the Freer) and New York (Metropolitan Museum of Art) secured examples directly from Bing or from collectors supplied by Bing. The South Kensington Museum, like the Museum für Kunst und Gewerbe in Hamburg, continued to acquire pieces from Bing on a regular basis.[41] In Hamburg, Justus Brinckmann, the first Director of the museum, began his Japanese collection with the assistance of Hayashi and Bing (adding textiles, *tsuba* and ceramics, figs. 17–19, 37). At the same time, in the early 1880s, Leiden purchased three sculptures from the Zôjôji Temple (1648) from Bing, as well as a 2.35 m high pagoda from the tenth year of the Tenpô era (1839).[42] A monumental standing sculpture by Jizô Bosatsu, measuring 2.26 m and dating from the fifteenth year of the Kyôhô era (1730) was also acquired in 1883.[43] In 1885, a group of twelve esoteric paintings of *The Twelve Devas (Jûni-ten)* from the Duvernet collection in Paris was purchased from Bing by Leiden for 1,800 francs. While these works were reproductions of originals probably dating from the tenth-century in the Kunôji Temple (district of Suruga in the modern prefecture of Shizuoka),[44] they acquired a higher value because they were described in Gonse's book (1883), one being accompanied by a reproduction.[45]

In Paris, Bing had dealings with several institutions: the Musée des Arts décoratifs, the Louvre and the

Conservatoire National des Arts et Métiers (1888). From 1893–4, Bing, working with Gonse, Gillot and Manzi, provided the Louvre with its first examples of Japanese art. He offered pieces from his personal collection, including prints, lacquerware and paintings.[46] Later, when Bing's collection was auctioned (1906), the Musée des Arts décoratifs and the Louvre secured other items, the former enlarging its textile holdings and the latter obtaining a wooden sculpture of a monk, a four-leafed screen with peonies and wildflowers on a silver ground – identified in the sale catalogue as by the famous painter Sôtatsu, a painted scroll showing a woman combing her hair signed by the *ukiyo-e* painter Eishi, and a Korean bottle from the Choson period.[47]

Other pieces that came from Bing entered the Louvre from private collectors: Cosson donated a Sharaku drawing[48] bought from Bing and some *inrô*; Marteau gave a Nô-mask he acquired from the Bing sale and a lacquered wooden statue of a monk.[49] Marcel Bing also made a donation to the Louvre: in 1906, in memory of his father, he gave a seventeenth-century still-life screen (figs 27, 45);[50] and in 1921, as part of his legacy, further works entered the Louvre, including a *Portrait of a Nampukuji Monk* and a *Kannon Seated on a Rock*.[51] A small round box by Ogata Kenzan, painted in iron oxide, formerly the property of Ninagawa Noritane, then Siegfried Bing, Marcel Bing and finally Raymond Koechlin, was bequeathed by Koechlin to the Louvre in 1932.[52]

All of these pieces provide a fragmentary glimpse of the diversity and aesthetic range of pieces that were once owned or sold by S. Bing. They clearly reflect the tenor of the era in which they were secured. While the objects Bing sold were not always on the masterpiece level – not until the second half of the twentieth century was the true value of Japanese art really understood in France – they do provide one measure by which to assess the collecting craze promoted by Bing and others. Without this starting point, and the genuine belief that Japanese art had real aesthetic merit, what came later could never have happened.[53] Bing's business, therefore, continued to sustain museums and the European market for Japanese art until the latter part of the twentieth century.

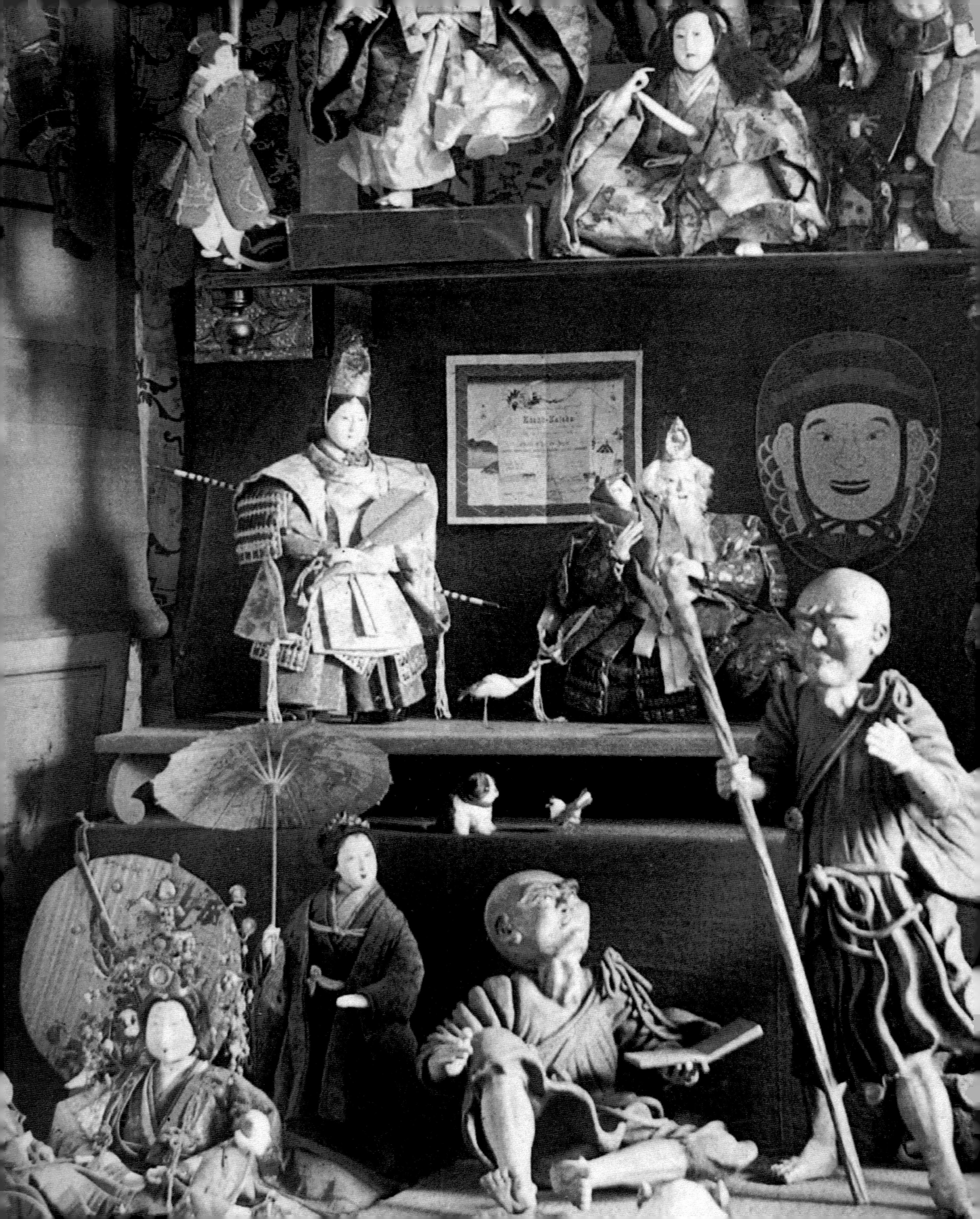

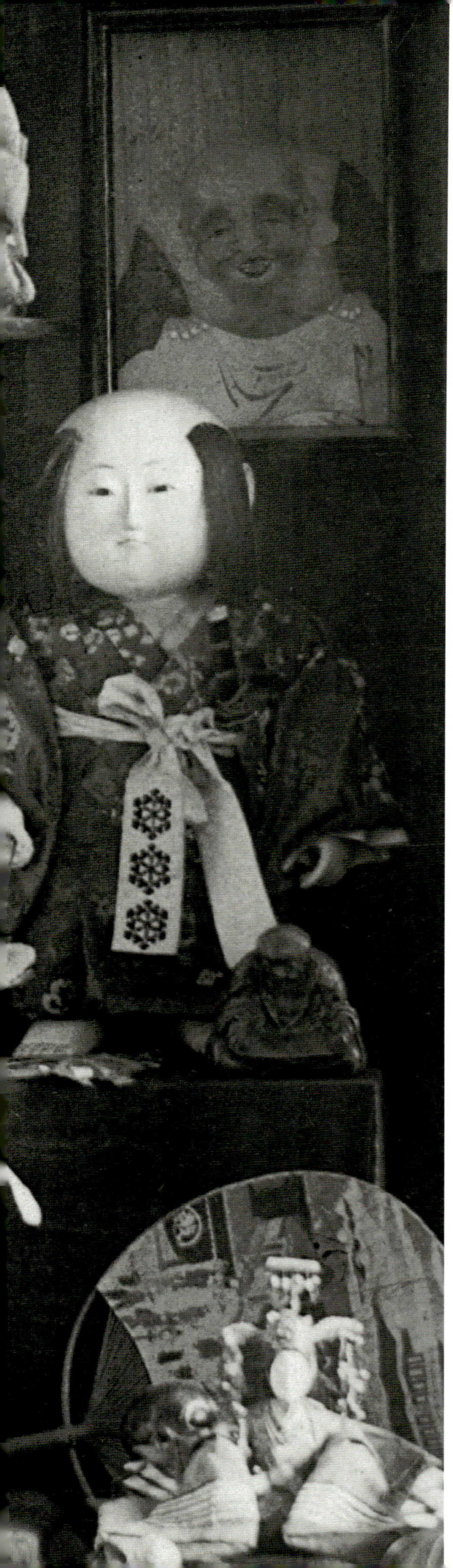

THE CREATION OF JAPONISME

GABRIEL P. WEISBERG

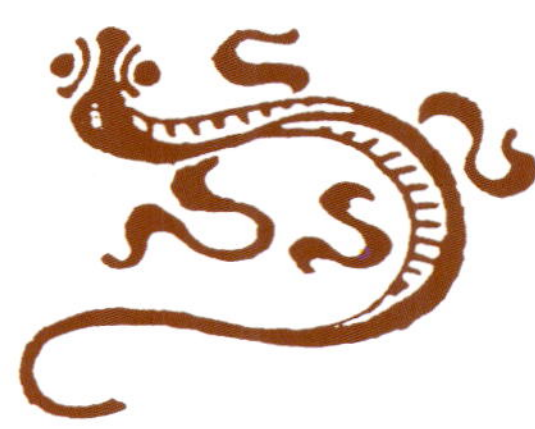

In May 1888, Siegfried Bing launched his monthly magazine *Le Japon Artistique* (figs. 20, 48, 57, 293). This venture capitalised on a craze that was sweeping the art worlds of Europe and the United States. Since the opening of trade with Japan in 1854, initiated by the American naval officer Matthew C. Perry, increasing contact occurred between this Far Eastern country and the West. By the early 1870s, French interest in Japan was reflected in the formation of several impressive private art collections of Japanese objects, including those of the writers Edmond de Goncourt and Emile Zola, the art critics Philippe Burty and Théodore Duret, and the painters James McNeill Whistler and Edgar Degas.[1] Many perceived Japanese culture and art as a fresh source of ideas that would liberate Western art from long-established, rigid conventions and lead artists toward new and imaginative forms of creativity. In 1872, Burty wrote several articles in the avant-garde magazine *La Renaissance Littéraire et Artistique*, in which he coined the term 'Japonisme'. This previously unnamed fad would become a influence in all areas of the arts over the next several decades.[2]

The Exposition Universelle (World's Fair) of 1878 marked a highpoint of Japonisme, which by then had captured the imaginations of French people across the socio-economic spectrum. Middle-class enthusiasts of Japan indulged their curiosity by purchasing trinkets such as parasols, lanterns, fans, puppets and dolls to decorate their homes (figs. 46, 61, 62),[3] while wealthy collectors could find fine-quality examples for the contemplation of traditional forms of Japanese art. For a time, it was quite easy to locate both fine art objects and inexpensive curios in the numerous shops and new 'department' stores in Paris and other European cities.

As the movement evolved, Siegfried Bing remained a central figure. While a few individuals travelled to the Far East early on – such as the art critic Théodore Duret and the dealer Auguste Sichel (who was also related to the Bing family) – none was as perspicacious as Bing. By the mid-1880s, he had several shops in Paris, each with their own line of merchandise, catering to popular and discriminating tastes. He not only sold ancient and contemporary art objects, but also established a dominant position in the market through the formation of his trading company, Bing et Cie.

Aficionados of Japonisme understood that if the style was to be more than a passing fancy and to have a lasting impact on Western culture, it had to attract a larger public beyond the present small coterie of connoisseurs.[4] Siegfried Bing's approach was to publish a magazine that would promote the art of Japan. He called it *Le Japon Artistique*.

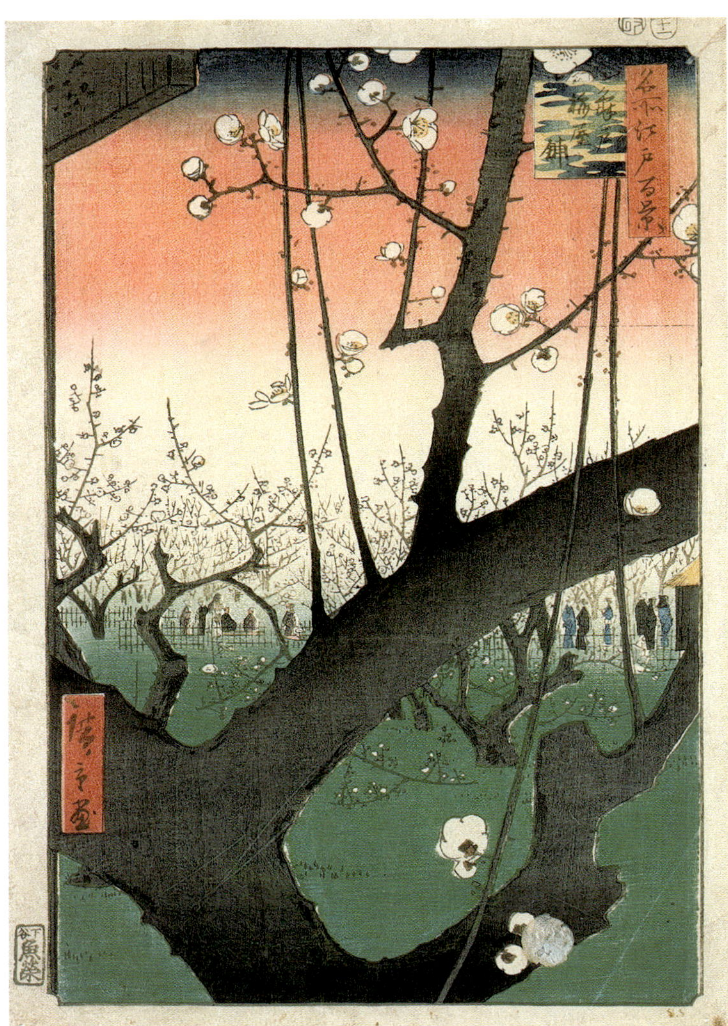

<< 46
Apartment of Jules Adeline, selection of oriental objects with Mikika doll
Bibliothèque d'Etude, Bibliothèques municipales de Rouen

47
Utagawa Hiroshige, *The Plum Tree Teahouse at Kameido*, 1857
Van Gogh Museum, Amsterdam (Vincent van Gogh Foundation)

> 48
Cover of *Le Japon Artistique*, 1889, no. 20
Van Gogh Museum (Library), Amsterdam

LE JAPON ARTISTIQUE

Philippe Burty had been the first to publish a periodical on Japanese visual culture for artists, collectors and the interested public.[5] However, only a single issue was published; it may have been too costly for Burty to produce, or perhaps it lacked the broad content necessary for commercial success. Nonetheless, Burty, who knew Bing well, since he bought objects from his shop, had planted a seed in his friend's mind. With better finances and with the interest in Japanese art at an all-time high in the mid-1880s, Bing decided to launch his own magazine. He recognised that the French market alone would not sustain an expensive journal, and, besides,

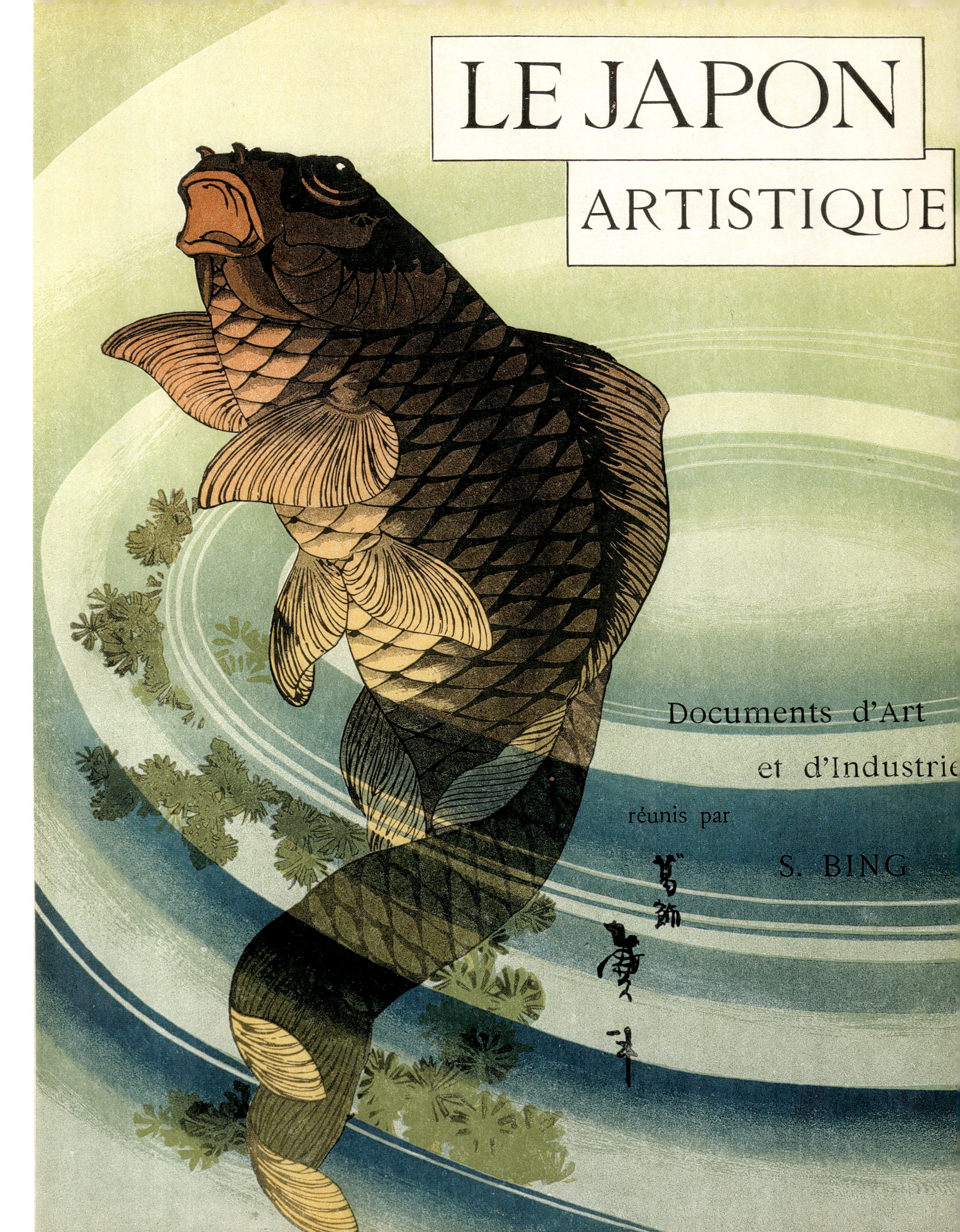
LE JAPON
ARTISTIQUE
Documents d'Art
et d'Industrie
réunis par
S. BING

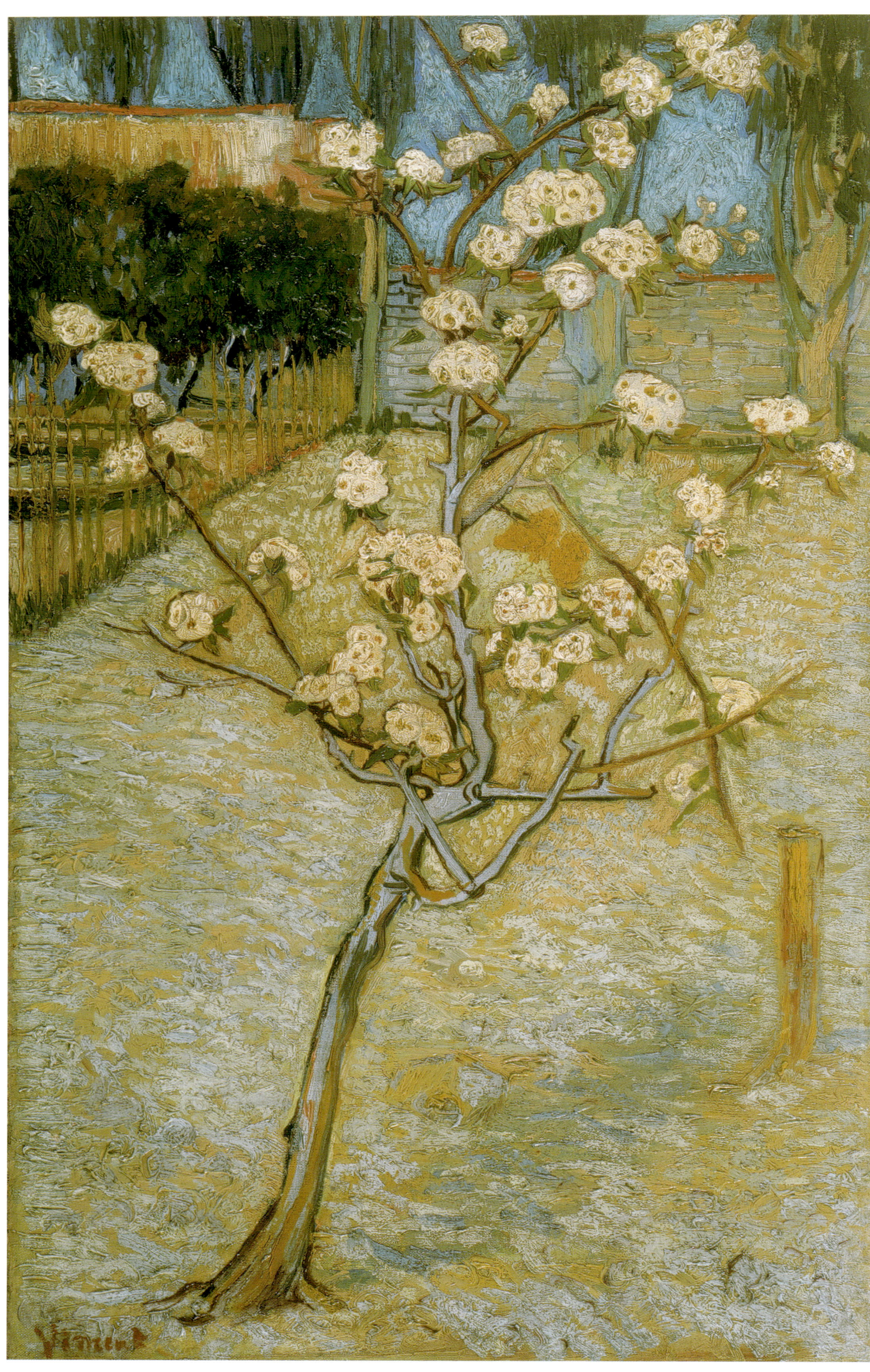

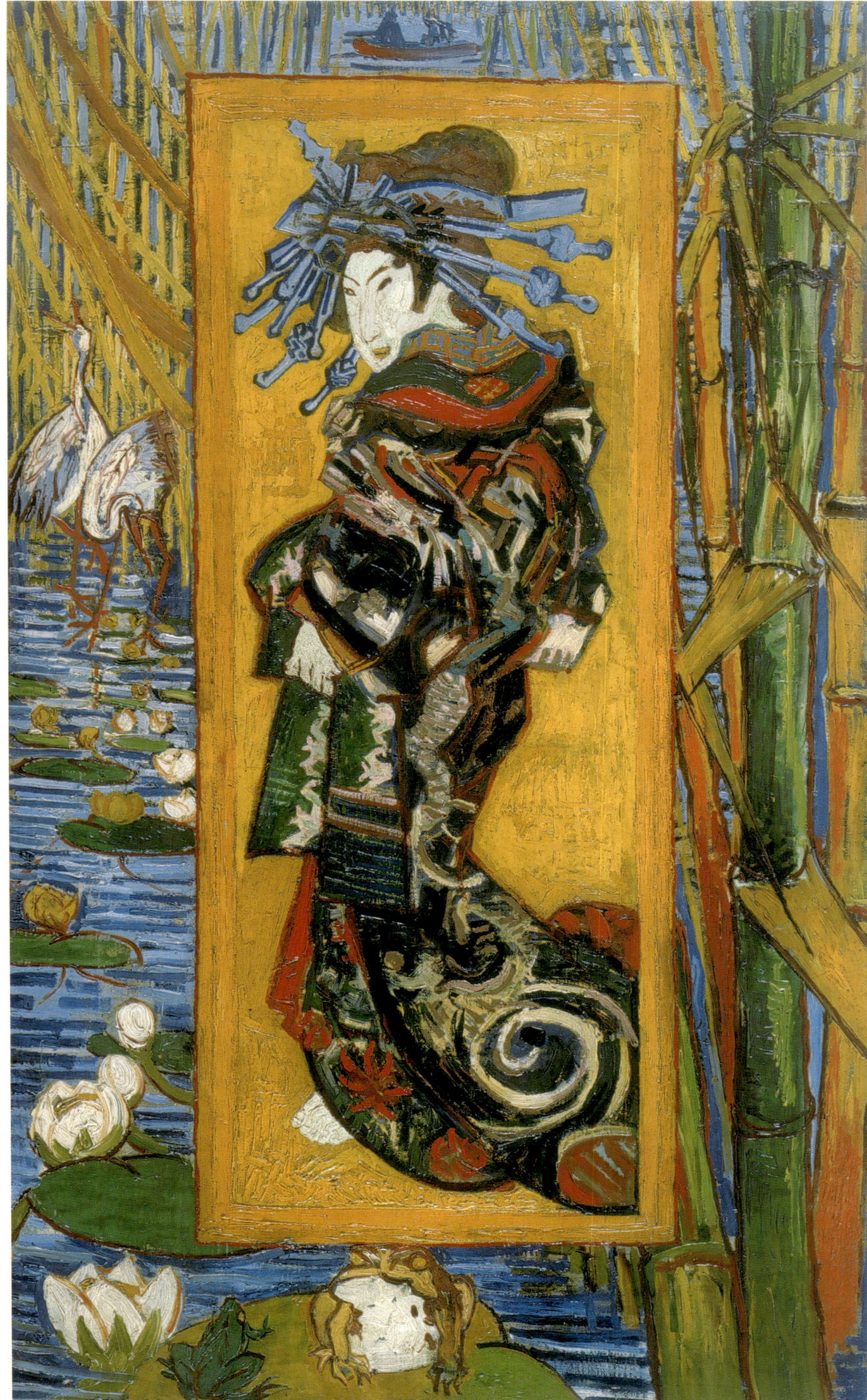

< **49**
Vincent van Gogh, *Pear Tree in Blossom*, 1888
Van Gogh Museum, Amsterdam (Vincent van Gogh Foundation)

50
Vincent van Gogh, *The Courtesan (Keisai Eisen)*, 1887
Van Gogh Museum, Amsterdam (Vincent van Gogh Foundation)

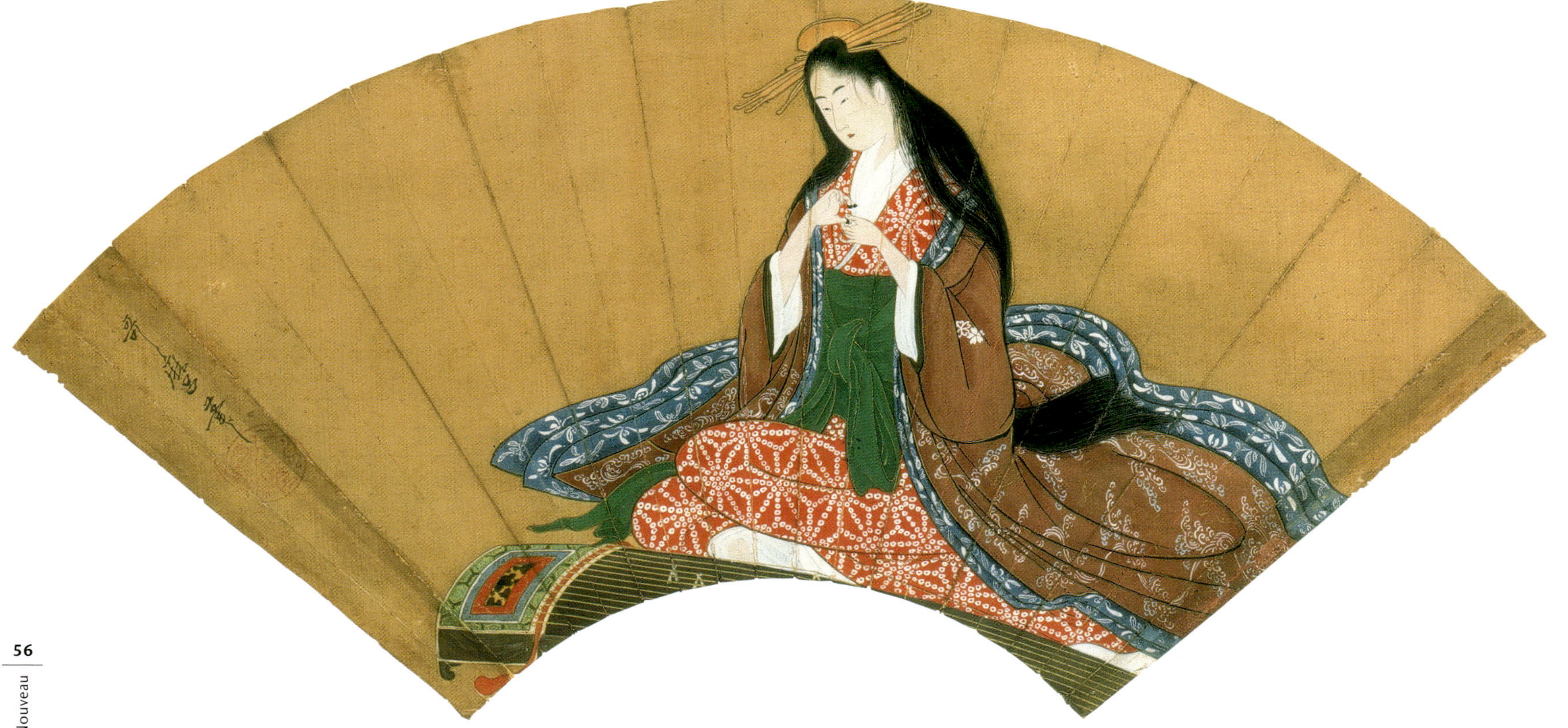

he was eager to reach lovers of Japanese art in other countries. Since England and Germany, which had burgeoning middle classes, had also been swept up in the Japonisme craze, it made sense for Bing to publish his new magazine in English and German as well.

For help with the German edition of *Le Japon Artistique*, entitled *Japanischer Formenschatz*, Bing turned to one of his oldest colleagues, Justus Brinckmann, Director of the Museum für Kunst und Gewerbe in Hamburg. Brinckmann translated the articles into German and supervised the printing in Leipzig.[6] By 1888, when the magazine first appeared, Bing had already sold a number of excellent Japanese pieces – ceramics, fabrics, prints and *inrô* (small lacquer boxes divided in compartments used to carry seals, medicines or other items) – to German clients, including Brinckmann and his museum.[7] Thus Bing already had a network of Japanese art enthusiasts who would welcome a magazine that informed them about their new treasures.[8]

Bing also produced the journal in English, under the name *Artistic Japan*. Correctly anticipating British appreciation of Japanese art for its reinvigoration of English industrial design and decorative arts, Bing had already established a connection with the South Kensington (now Victoria and Albert) Museum in London; from the mid-1870s on, Bing sold this museum a wide range of Japanese objects, from bronzes, sculptures and screens to fans and *inrô*.[9] He convinced Marcus B. Huish, director of the Fine Art Society in London, to edit the English language edition.[10] Huish, a distinguished art critic, had displayed a strong interest in Japanese art. During the course of publishing the magazine, Huish and Bing developed a close association. In January 1889, Bing took out a year's lease for the first floor of the Fine Art Society galleries in London.[11] This location in the heart of the capital enabled Bing to sell his wares, organise exhibitions of Japanese art and oversee the marketing of the magazine for British readers.

The English edition also circulated in the United States. By the end of the 1880s, Bing had a shop in New York City at 220 Fifth Avenue.[12] Here, with the assistance of the young American art dealer John Getz, who would remain in contact with him over many years, Bing could promote his art objects and his magazine at the same time. With three editions of the journal appearing monthly for four years until 1891, Siegfried Bing was easily the chief proponent of Japonisme.

Bing enlisted the support of artists, in particular Vincent van Gogh, to market Japanese art, especially Japanese prints. In July 1888, soon after the appearance of the first issue of *Le Japon Artistique*, Van Gogh commented about an exhibition at Bing's shop that displayed reproductions of illustrations included in the issue.[13] Bing guessed rightly that young artists who were devotees of Japanese art, such as Van Gogh and others from the realist and impressionist circles, would spread the word about the magazine among their friends or borrow its images for their paintings. As Van Gogh went to work for Bing as a sales representative and began to collect Japanese prints (c. 1886–7), Bing's holdings provided the core of the artist's Japanese print collection, examples of which he often referred to in his own painting (figs. 47, 49, 50).[14]

Each issue of the magazine, which measured 33 cm in height and 25 cm in width, contained one article and a series of plates, preceded by in-depth information about each one. Topics ranged from Japanese architecture to the art of the jeweller, the art of engraving to Hokusai's *Manga* or Japanese pottery. Each issue was illustrated with black-and-white engravings plus ten colour plates. Every cover sported the image of a Japanese print in colour. Each number also contained notices advertising stores that sold Japanese art, including Bing's, or new publications about Japan appropriate to the country where the magazine appeared. It is not known how many copies were printed of each issue or who subscribed to the magazine. However, documents show that it was shipped to a number of cities for distribution, including Hamburg, Leipzig, London and New York, with the central clearing-house for the periodical at the 22, rue de Provence premises in Paris.

< 51
Kitagawa Utamaro, Fan 'Courtesan playing the Koto'
Mr. John C. Weber Collection

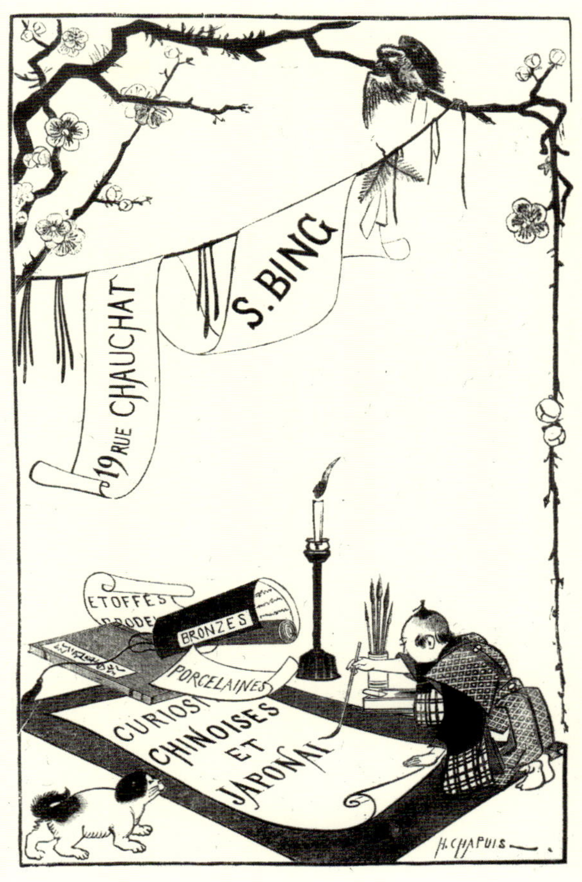

52
H. Chapuis, Advertisement for S. Bing, c. 1883, from Louis Gonse, *Catalogue de l'Exposition Rétrospective de l'Art Japonais*, Paris 1883

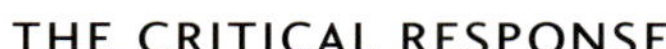

THE CRITICAL RESPONSE

In France, as in Germany and England, Bing called upon the best in the publishing trade to make the magazine a success. By using the resources of Flammarion, which published the magazine, and Charles Gillot, who helped with the reproductions, Bing allied himself with progressive businessmen who utilised the most modern processes in order to achieve the finest results in printing.[15]

Even before *Le Japon Artistique* went to press, Bing placed advertisements for it in the best-known French publications of the day to attract potential readers; among them is the one that appeared in *La Revue Illustrée* in 1887. With all of his contacts in the art world, Bing doubtless expected a favourable reaction to his venture, but, to his surprise, once the periodical reached an international audience, there was discussion about his motives for launching such a magazine. As often happened at various moments of his career, Bing found himself at the centre of controversy. The debate surrounding the publication of *Le Japon Artistique* places the magazine within the larger context of Japonisme and reveals Bing as the central figure in the movement. In the study of this artistic phenomenon, the scholar must continually weigh Bing's genuine desire to promote the arts of Japan against the financial benefits he derived from the commercial success of the movement.

In a notice published in *Le Chat Noir* on 6 May 1888, just prior to the appearance of *Le Japon Artistique*, the author and printmaker Georges Auriol observed that the taste for things Japanese had begun to lessen during the mid-1880s. Auriol, a collector of Japanese art himself, attributed this to the large number of imitations produced by Western designers and the proliferation of Japanese objects that were 'common' or made solely for Western trade consumption.[16] The fashion for inexpensive Japanese curios was waning; unless people developed more refined tastes, Japonisme might evaporate altogether. Auriol praised the forthcoming journal for its goal of teaching collectors how to appreciate the aesthetic rather than the quaint or exotic aspects of Japanese art; in short, for showing them how to become true connoisseurs. Auriol's comments in *Le Chat Noir* and Bing's answer with the first issue of the journal reveal that they were worried about the over-commercialisation of Japonisme.

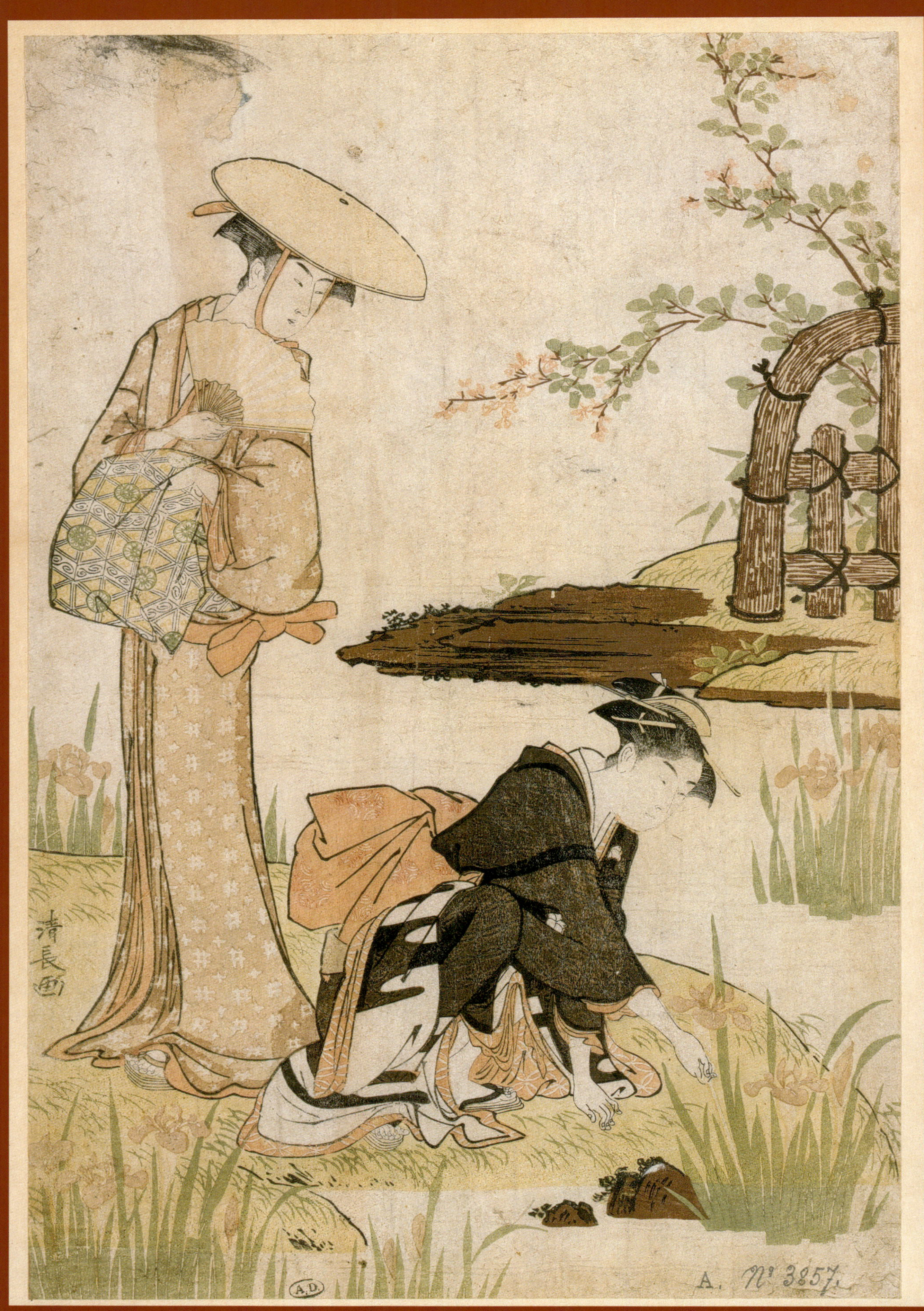
清長画
A.D.
A. Nº 3857.

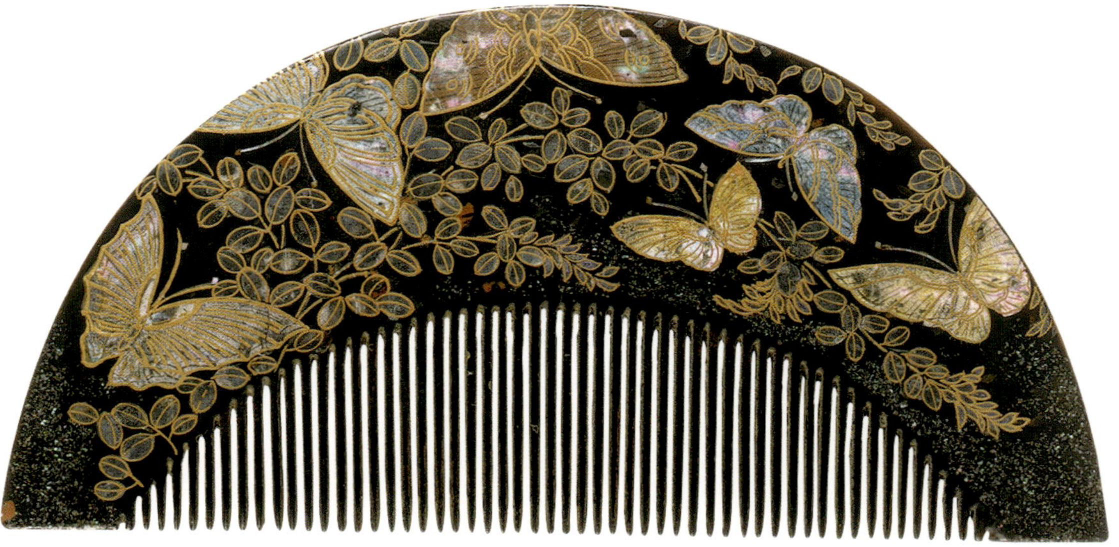

< 53
Torii Kiyonaga, *The Iris Pond*, right-hand print from a diptych
Musée des Arts décoratifs, Paris

54
Comb, Japan, 19th century
Victoria and Albert Museum, London

In sharp contrast to Auriol's appreciative notice, negative commentaries appeared in the *Japan Weekly Mail*. Published throughout the run of *Le Japon Artistique*, this periodical took exception to almost every aspect of Bing's magazine, attacking the quality of the colour plates and noting that the writing was often hyperbolic and turgid. The only positive note was the grudging recognition that the journal widened the circle of those interested in collecting good examples of Japanese art. In a particularly critical article of 1889, the *Japan Weekly Mail* accused *Le Japon Artistique* of prompting an increase in the prices that dealers asked for Japanese prints and other works of art: 'the crafty dealer [...] has pushed up prices until a single woodcut by Harunobu, Hokusai, Toyokuni, Utamaro or any of the other great masters, a woodcut that might have been bought for ten sen [the equivalent of a penny] as many years ago, now costs twenty times that amount.'[17] Although not identified by name, Bing and likely his chief competitor, Hayashi Tadamasa, the most prominent dealers of Japanese art, were implicated in this article. Those who knew how the promotion of Japanese art had evolved questioned the allegedly altruistic motives of such dealers. A subsequent statement in the same article implied that dealers had engaged in deceptive practices, for instance by selling new Japanese woodcuts made from old blocks and passing them off as originals. This accusation, coming at a time when there was renewed interest in *ukiyo-e* prints, would have cast a shadow over the purported authenticity of objects exhibited at the huge display of Japanese prints at the Ecole des Beaux-Arts in 1890.[18]

The 7 September 1889 issue of the *Japan Weekly Mail* took Bing to task for two articles on the origin of Japanese painting that he had written for *Le Japon Artistique*. This topic attracted considerable interest, since a number of Japanese paintings were entering Western private collections. Bing provided the cultural context for a variety of works, citing the influence of Japanese religion and history on their form and content. The reviewer pronounced the articles 'superficial and conjectural'. He noted: 'The writer, holding truly that the art of painting, whatever it may owe to the individual genius of its exponents, must more or less reflect, and derive its inspiration from the circumstances of the age in which it is practiced, endeavours to trace the association between the various schools of Japanese pictorial art and their national environment. Such an analysis, could it be performed exhaustively, would be in the highest degree interesting and instructive. But to perform it exhaustively demands a knowledge of Japanese annals and an appreciation of Japanese social conditions such as no foreigner possesses, and such, perhaps, as can scarcely be acquired by a foreigner from the materials available. [...] Mr. Bing touches only the hem of the garment, and we doubt if the work of weaving the whole is possible to anyone except a Japanese as deeply versed in the social and political spirit of his country as he is closely in touch with the spirit of art inspiration.'[19]

While there was perhaps some truth to this commentary, it was somewhat unfair given the scope of *Le Japon Artistique* and its intended audience. In fact, Bing rendered a valuable service to his Western readers by identifying salient areas of research and by drawing attention

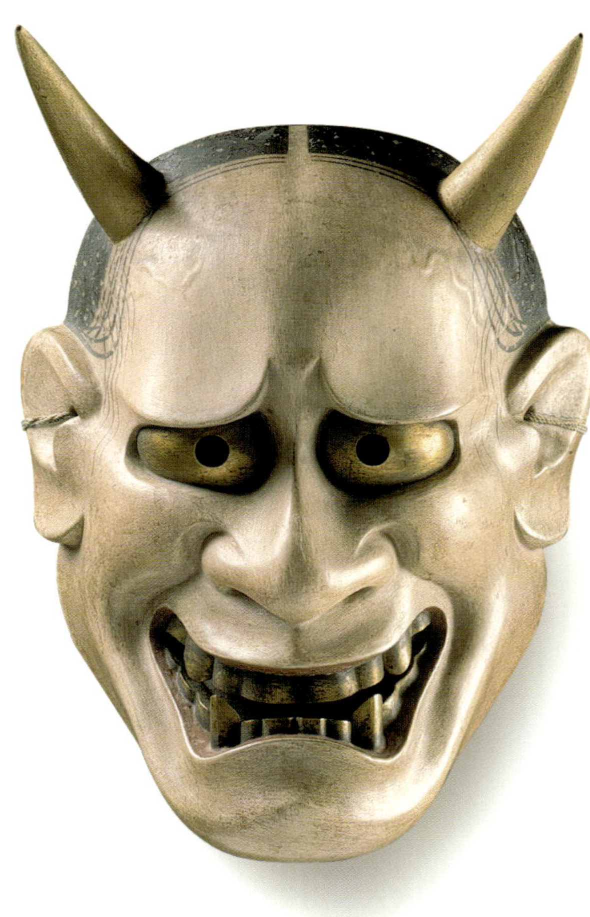

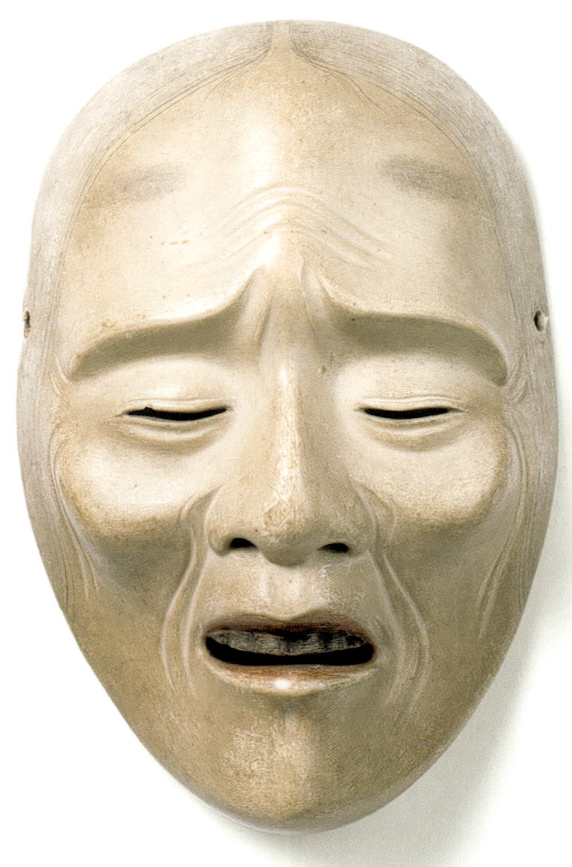

to works of art not widely known to them. He provided only the general outlines of the history of Japanese painting; there were scholarly publications that readers could consult for a more in-depth treatment of the topic.

The English press also included reviews of the journal. In June 1888, *The Academy* commented favourably on the 'attractiveness' of the first issue; the fine quality plates were seen as fully warranting the price.[20] By 1889, reviewers were calling the magazine an artistic creation in itself. The reproductions furnished models for Western craftsmen and designers, thus contributing to the spread of Japonisme. One British reviewer remarked: 'The practical benefit of such a 'graphic encyclopedia' to technical designers, and all those interested in the future of industrial art in Europe, furnishes another motive to the promoter of this enterprise. [...] It is not, however, a mere portfolio of pictures [...] for M. Bing has called the pens as well as the collections of connoisseurs to his aid.'[21]

In the United States, a notice in *The Critic* on 3 August 1889 mentioned that *Artistic Japan* could be obtained from an address on Fifth Avenue in New York City, for those who were not mail subscribers. In particular, American reviewers appreciated the way that the overall design of the magazine complemented the textual content. In December 1889, *The Critic* contained this enthusiastic appraisal: '*Artistic Japan* maintains the high degree of excellence attained in its first numbers. [...] M. Bing writes on the origin of painting gathered from history, and the writers have, evidently, had generous assistance from native Japanese experts. In each number there are a half dozen or more designs in decorative art which we cannot well imagine a good designer in any branch of ornamental industry doing without. We rank this periodical among the highest class of art journals.'[22]

MARKETING THROUGH MUSEUM SALES AND LE JAPON ARTISTIQUE

To adorn the pages of his magazine, Bing often chose art objects that were either on the art market, or objects in well-known collections of which there were similar examples on the market. What novice collector would not like to own an example of Japanese art that was close to that in a prestigious public collection?

Well before he began publishing *Le Japon Artistique*, Bing had sold Japanese art objects to museums around the world. This strategy effectively increased the numbers

55
Nô-mask of the female demon Hannya, Japan, 18th century
Victoria and Albert Museum, London

56
Nô-mask of the old woman Uba, Japan, 18th century (signed Himi Saku)
Victoria and Albert Museum, London

> 57
Poster 'Le Japon Artistique', c. 1888
Musée de la Publicité, Paris

PUBLICATION MENSUELLE

Prix du numéro : 2 francs.

LE JAPON ARTISTIQUE

Documents d'Art et d'Industrie

réunis par

S. BING

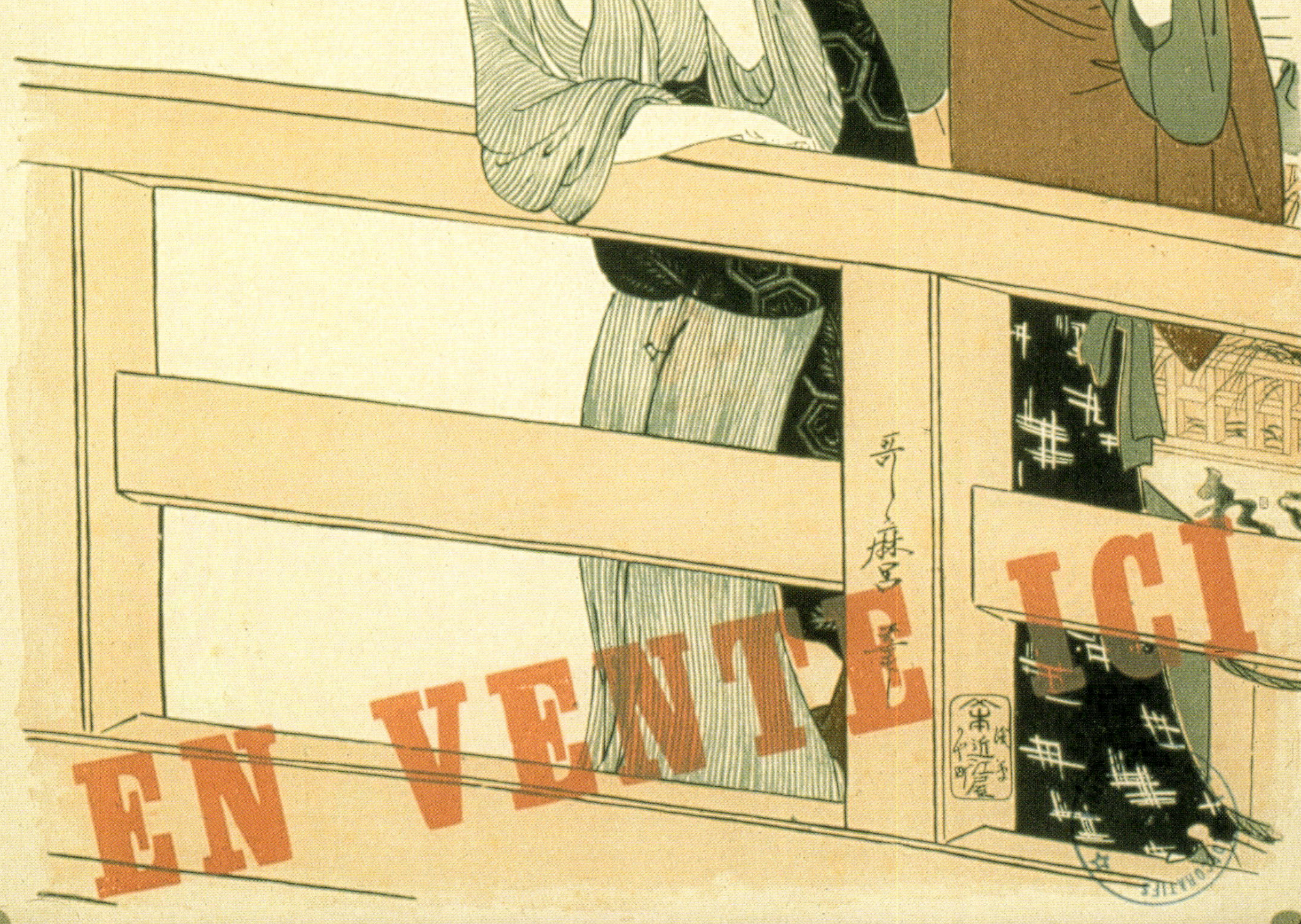

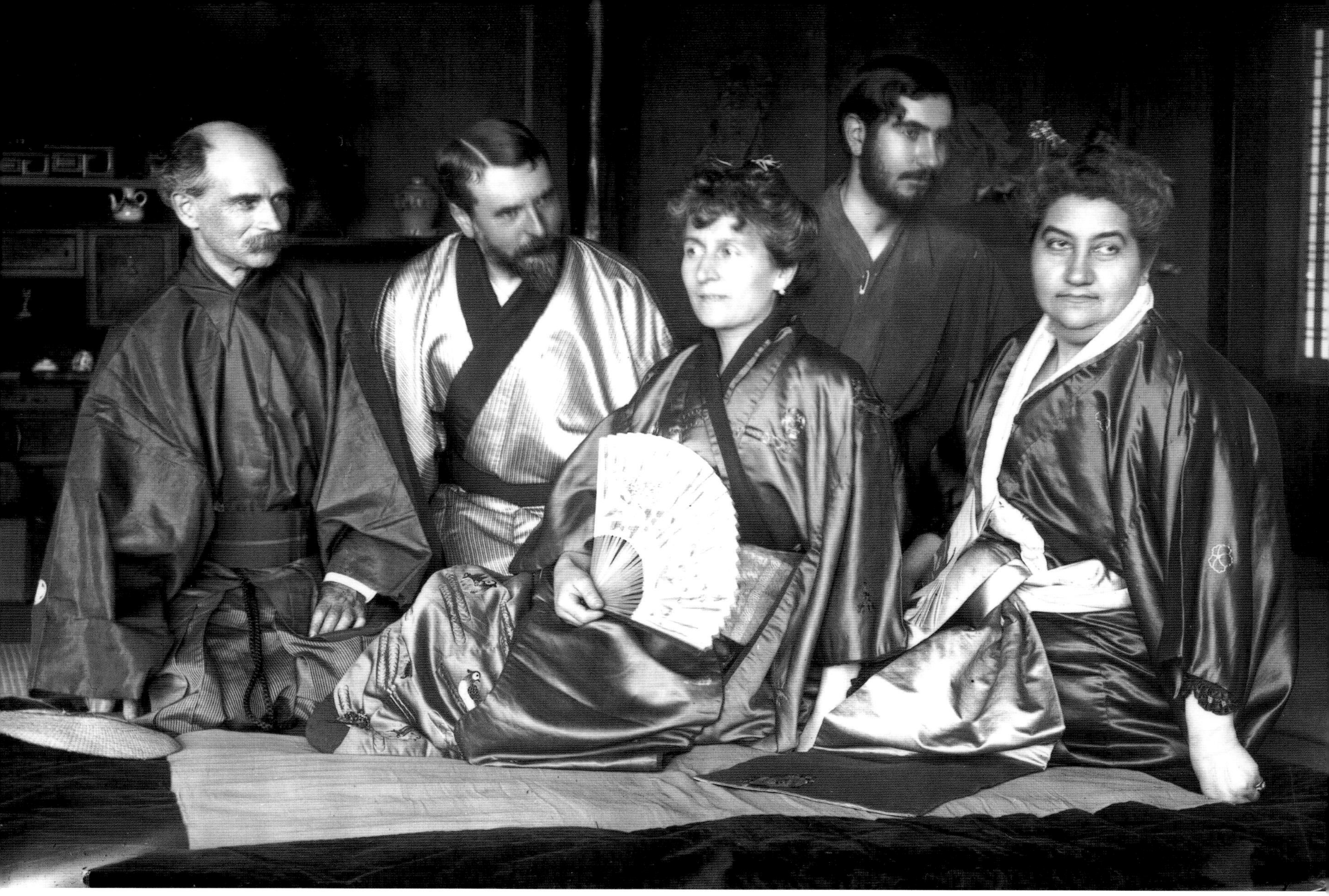

of people exposed to Japanese art, some of whom might become collectors and potential clients. Bing counted among his buyers many museums, including the Museum für Kunst und Gewerbe in Hamburg, the Musée des Arts décoratifs in Paris, and the Danske Kunstindustrimuseum in Copenhagen, all of which became major repositories of Japanese art, mostly purchased through him.

No museum started buying from Bing as early as the South Kensington Museum in London, where objects began arriving as early as 1875. The museum began acquiring Nô-masks from Bing in 1876; these expressive examples helped spread the awareness of Japanese theatre (figs. 55, 56).[23] But even though it was popularised by W. S. Gilbert and Arthur Sullivan in their production of *The Mikado* (1885), Japanese theatre remained a relatively obscure art form. To address this, Bing published articles on Japanese theatre in his journal in 1890.[24] If certain items or art forms were to have broad marketability, it was essential to educate Western readers through articles that included some historical background and an explanation of how the objects were used in Japan. For example, in 1888 Bing sold a large number of excellent Japanese combs to the South Kensington Museum for the sum of £98 (figs. 10, 11, 54).[25] These examples in lacquer were decorated with flowers, landscape elements, animals and birds, demonstrating the Japanese love of all forms of nature and the intricate ways in which Japanese designers created exquisite patterns for the most utilitarian pieces. Once the combs were sold and put on display in London, Bing called on Théodore Duret to write an article entitled 'On Combs' for *Artistic Japan*.[26]

After briefly reviewing the history of combs in his article, Duret noted that Japanese women were among the first to transform the comb into an ornamental object. Exquisitely made combs, and later hairpins, allowed for elaborate methods of dressing the hair, which became more and more complicated. The article established that combs had always been regarded as precious objects by the Japanese. Duret also demonstrated that well-known Japanese artists such as Hokusai or Utamaro gave the comb special attention in some of their prints. Most

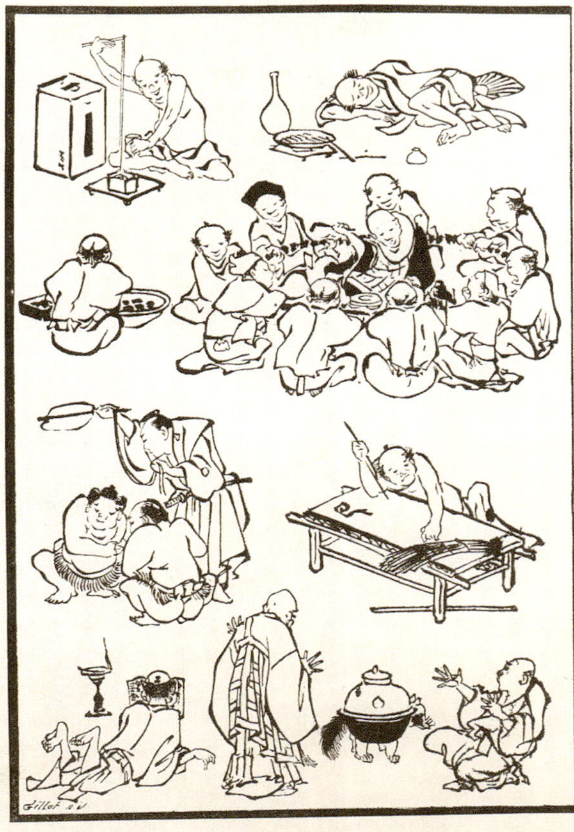

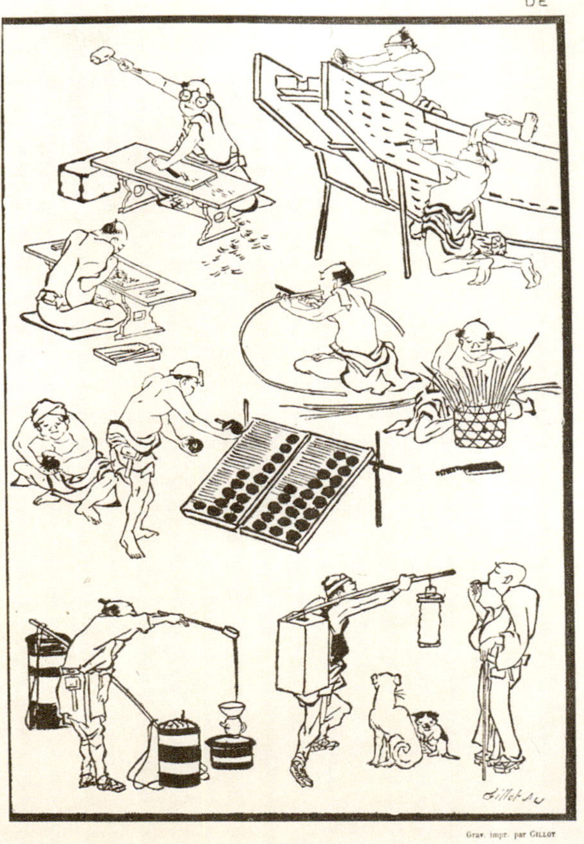

< 58
From left to right: Siegfried Bing, Louis Gonse, Mme Koechlin, Gonse's son and Mme Gonse, 1899
Krafft Archives, Collection de la Société des Amis du Vieux Reims, Musée Le Vergeur, Reims

59
Manga images by Katsushika Hokusai from *Le Japon Artistique*, 1888, no. 5
Van Gogh Museum (Library), Amsterdam

>> 60
Utagawa Kuniyoshi, *Tsukudajima* from the series *Famous Views of Tokyo*, 1833–35
Musée des Arts décoratifs, Paris

importantly, Duret emphasised to his readers that the Japanese comb was in and of itself 'an artistic work', no matter what it was made of – wood, tortoiseshell, or ivory – and that the wide range of imaginative designs used for its embellishment could serve as models for European craftsmen.

Le Japon Artistique not only piqued the public's interest in or expanded its awareness of Japanese art; the showcasing of certain objects and the dissemination of information on them created an appetite of the moment that dealers such as Bing were pleased to satisfy.

THE WRITERS

The generally favourable response to *Le Japon Artistique* resulted in part from the involvement of major European writers and collectors of Japanese art. By 1888, when the magazine appeared, the public was already familiar with books and articles by many of the authors, and their reputations helped establish the credibility of the journal, while also giving a popular inflection to Japonisme.

Among the French Japonistes who wrote for *Le Japon Artistique* were several, including Edmond de Goncourt and Philippe Burty, who had contributed to the movement in the 1860s. Goncourt in particular, with whom Bing was to engage in a bitter controversy over the publication of a book on Hokusai in the mid-1890s, used elements of Japonisme in his articles and novels.[27] He also encouraged others to collect Japanese art, and in his *Journals* noted visits to Bing's shop, where he bought pieces for his own collection. A true friendship never developed between these men, in part due to Goncourt's anti-Semitism, which was fuelled by the Dreyfus affair as well as the general attitude toward Jews at the time.[28] Philippe Burty knew Goncourt well, and the two visited each other's collections or met at Bing's to see new arrivals at the store. Burty's reputation as the leading critic of Japonisme was well known, and since both men were skilled writers and major collectors of Japanese art, it was natural that Bing would enlist them to write for *Le Japon Artistique*. When Burty died in 1890, Bing served as the expert for the sale of his vast Far Eastern holdings, once again putting his imprint on the dissemination of Japanese art.[29]

To assure the success of the periodical, Bing engaged talented writers who could succinctly explain the varied aspects of Japanese creativity. Louis Gonse, for example, editor of the *Gazette des Beaux-Arts*, had been instrumental in organising a major exhibition of Japanese

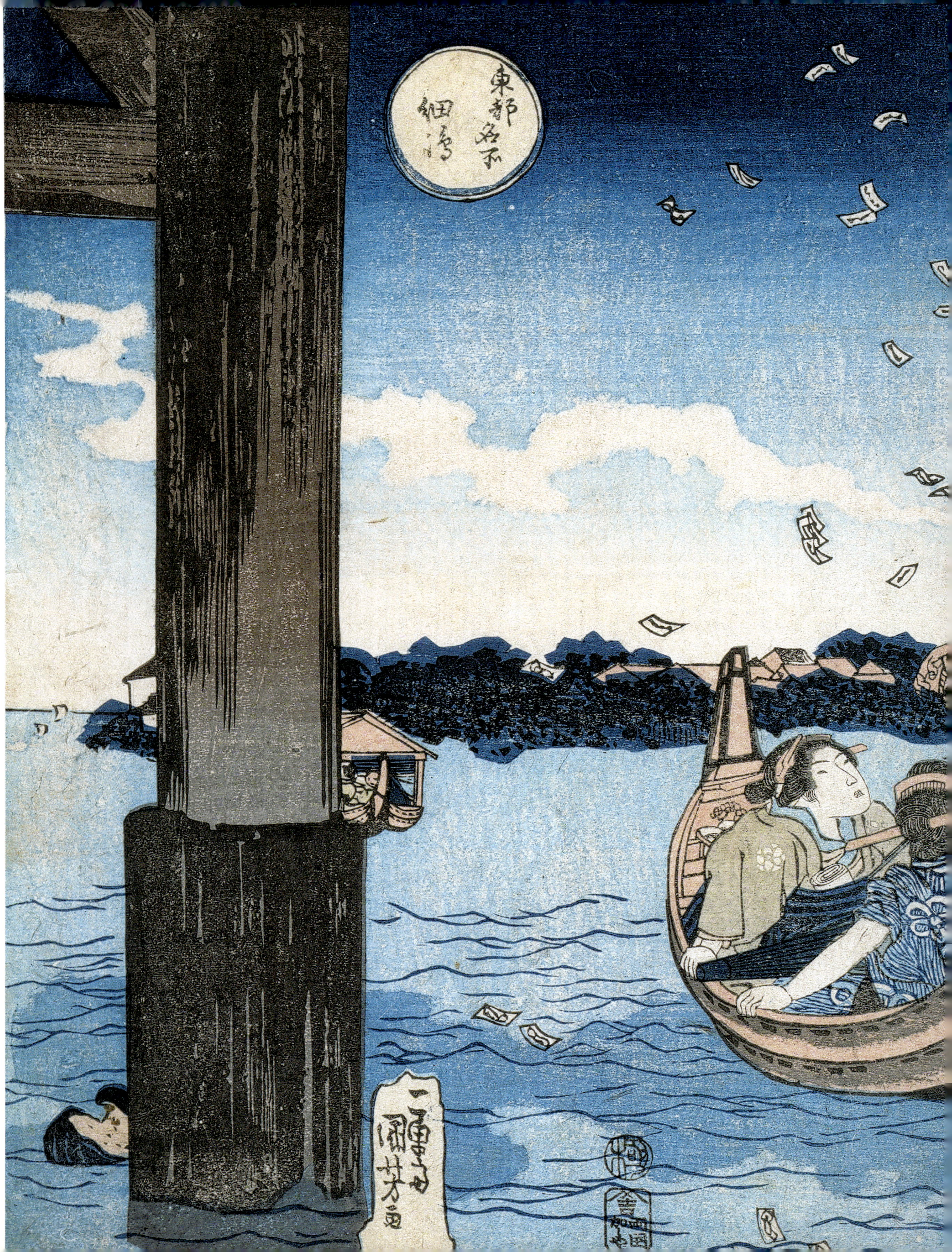

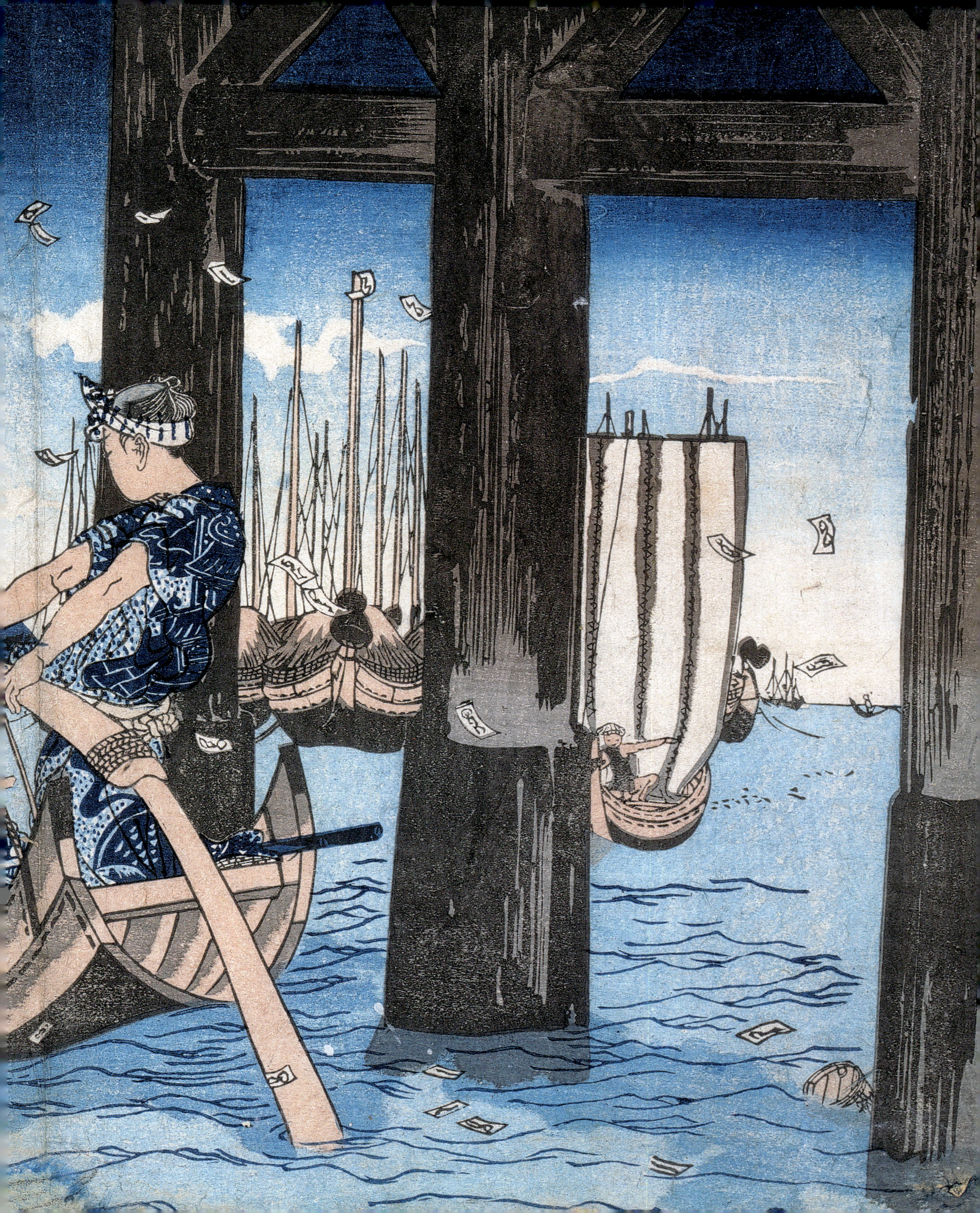

art in 1883, the same date that he wrote the first substantial book in French on Japanese art, *L'Art Japonais*.[30] Furthermore, in addition to his being knowledgeable about Japanese art, his collection provided a rich source from which pieces could be selected to highlight and illustrate in *Le Japon Artistique*. Gonse wrote one of the first major articles, entitled 'The Japanese as Decorators', which analysed this important aspect of Japanese art and touched on the positive influence of Japanese art on Western design.

A lesser-known author that Bing hired was Ary Renan, the son of Ernest Renan, the prominent historian and philosopher. The younger Renan was also a symbolist painter and a devotee of Japanese art. Bing's decision to give Renan, a member of a younger generation of aesthetes, the important assignment of writing on Hokusai – an artist about whom Bing was most passionate – cannot be underestimated.

In 1888, when Renan wrote his two articles on the Japanese printmaker, Hokusai's *Manga* – a series of albums of woodcuts – was already regarded in France as essential to the appreciation of Japanese art. These albums had strongly influenced French artists since their discovery by the printmaker Félix Bracquemond in the late 1850s. In many countries, artisans had been encouraged to study the *Manga* in order to see for themselves the Japanese fascination with depicting nature, no matter how small or common the specimen. What remained to be done was to convey the importance of the artist and his albums to a broader public.

Together, Renan's articles for the December 1888 and January 1889 issues of *Le Japon Artistique* comprised a splendid tribute to Hokusai. The author explained the reason for the printmaker's popularity in Japan and elsewhere. Renan reiterated Hokusai's love of nature, his perceptive choice of imagery, and the influence of the *Manga* (and similar albums) on contemporary Western design. Bing showed an editor's instinct for finding the right writer for an assignment and, by scheduling articles to appear at certain times, he could introduce topics that coincided with activities in the art world. Indeed, Renan's articles appeared prior to several exhibitions on Hokusai that were held in France and England in 1890.[31] Visitors would have been better informed and more eager to attend these exhibitions after reading about the artist in the journal. Bing wrote his own series of articles on Hokusai for the *Magazine of Art* in 1890–91.[32]

Other writers for the journal were part of the French art establishment. Among these was Victor Champier, a scholar and contributor to scholarly publications, who vigorously supported the movement to improve the applied arts in France during the 1890s. Bing asked Champier to write on Japanese architecture, believing that this might stimulate French architects to use Far Eastern decoration on their buildings. Two articles, which appeared as numbers 3 and 4 in the first year of the journal, commented on temple and residential architecture, providing an excellent primer on Japanese building. As always, Bing selected writers and topics with the ulterior motive of encouraging European designers to look more closely at Japanese art for inspiration.[33]

To write on jewellery design, Bing chose Lucien Falize, son of the jeweller Alexis Falize and a well-known jeweller in his own right. Falize had been incorporating Japanese motifs into small decorative pieces for years; in particular, he had revitalised the art of enamelling as a result of studying Japanese examples. He was an especially good choice for the assignment since he was regarded as a major initiator of technological advances in metal, wood and textiles, and a champion for the excellence of finely crafted objects. In his article, published in the autumn of 1888, Falize stressed the care that Japanese artists took with the smallest pieces.[34] He commented on how the crafts in Japan were changing as objects were being produced for Western markets. This shift away from traditional art forms and workshop practice in Japanese art directly resulted, of course, from the trading activities of European companies such as S. Bing et Cie. Finally, Falize emphasised the desirability of closer communication between French and Japanese artisans, an effort Siegfried Bing and his brother August made at this time by establishing a number of offices in various cities throughout Japan.

In 1889, after introducing a broad range of issues in the opening articles, Bing turned to more specialised topics. He asked William Anderson, a leading English scholar and an authority on *ukiyo-e* prints, to discuss Hiroshige, the second of the major Japanese printmakers in the view of Bing and his colleagues. This article, much as Renan's had done for Hokusai, stimulated interest in Hiroshige prior to the 1890 exhibition in Paris. Moreover, Anderson enhanced the appreciation of Japanese prints, both single sheets and albums, which could be expected to lead to further collecting.[35]

At the end of 1889 and into the following year, the journal began to address more esoteric themes. Bing approached Justus Brinckmann to write on 'The Poetic Tradition of Japanese Art', one of the most abstract contributions to date.[36] With this article, the author provided the intellectual underpinnings for what the other

> 61
Apartment of Jules Adeline, selection of oriental objects
Bibliothèque d'Etude, Bibliothèques municipales, Rouen

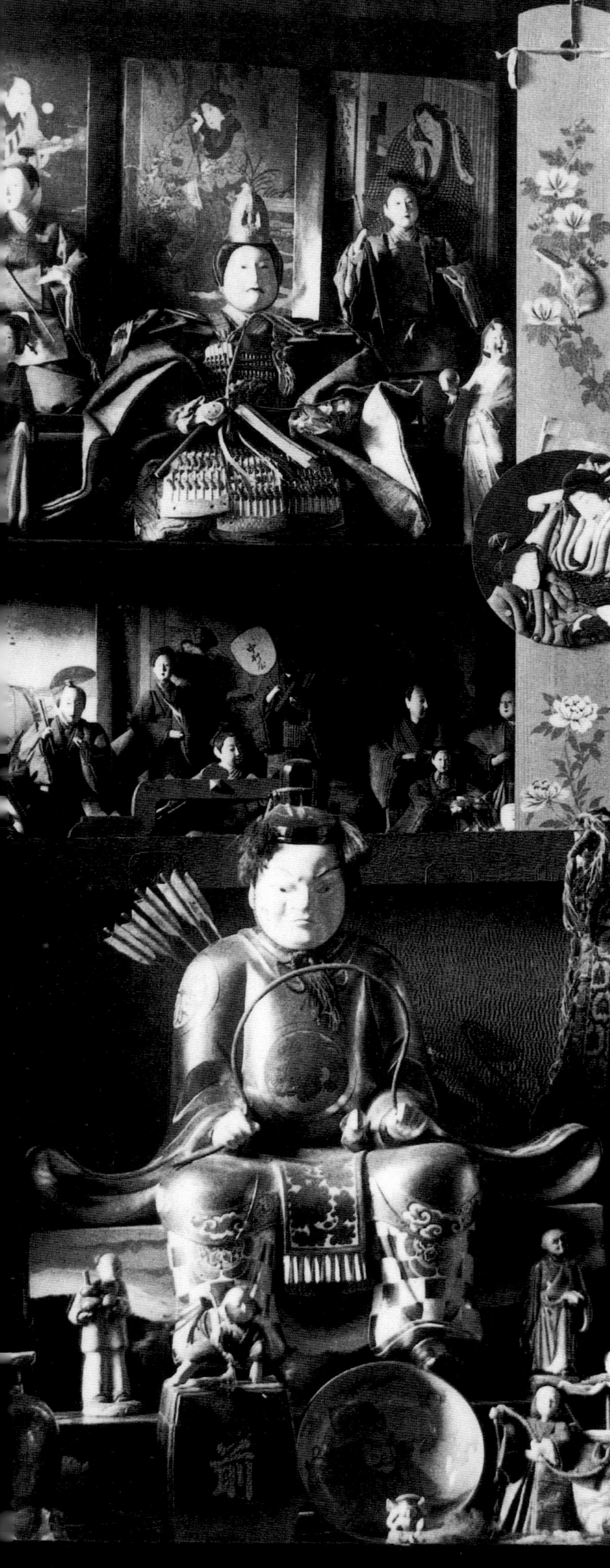

writers had advanced all along, namely that the appreciation of nature was at the core of Japanese culture and that the poetic response of its artists emphasised the harmony between the land, the people and their traditions. The choice of this topic shows that Bing aimed to reach beyond the art community to those interested in poetry, literature and Far Eastern culture. This was a radical step for an art magazine that had thus far been directed towards a fairly narrow readership.

As *Le Japon Artistique* neared the end of its four-year run, Bing backed off from this interdisciplinary direction and returned to his original purpose of holding up Japanese craftsmanship as a model for European artists working in the applied arts. The author of 'The Industrial Arts and the Manufacturers of Japan' was Arthur Lasenby Liberty, a dealer and Bing's counterpart in England, whose objects Bing would sell in Paris after he opened his shop L'Art Nouveau.[37] Liberty stressed that craftsmen in Japan worked in a stable environment that allowed them to create exquisite objects in many media. Liberty's understanding of how crafts were produced made him an ideal advocate for promoting harmony between the commercial and creative aspects of the production of decorative arts.

It is not known exactly why Bing decided to cease publication of *Le Japon Artistique*. The last several articles seemed to focus on issues that were of special interest to Bing. One of these essays, written by Marcus Huish, offered advice on building a collection of Japanese art.[38] It dealt with the selection and conservation of Japanese works, which were not limited to so-called 'high art', but also included decorative objects and popular collectibles. He emphasised the importance of studying each object closely and of looking for pieces that would fill gaps in a growing collection. Needless to say, this very practical advice for novices starting their own collections encouraged trade in Japanese art of all kinds.[39]

The thirty-sixth and final issue included an article entitled 'On the Role and Influence of the Arts of the Far East and of Japan' by the prominent art critic and fervent Japoniste Roger Marx.[40] A wide range of objects were reproduced in the article, revealing not just the variety of what Japanese artists had produced, but what was on the market. Marx suggested that *Le Japon Artistique* had achieved its goal of promoting a creative interchange between the arts of Japan and the West, a statement that could be taken as a farewell to the magazine's readers. This probably reflected Bing's own view and may be the primary reason that he ceased publication. For even if he lost money on it, with each issue published

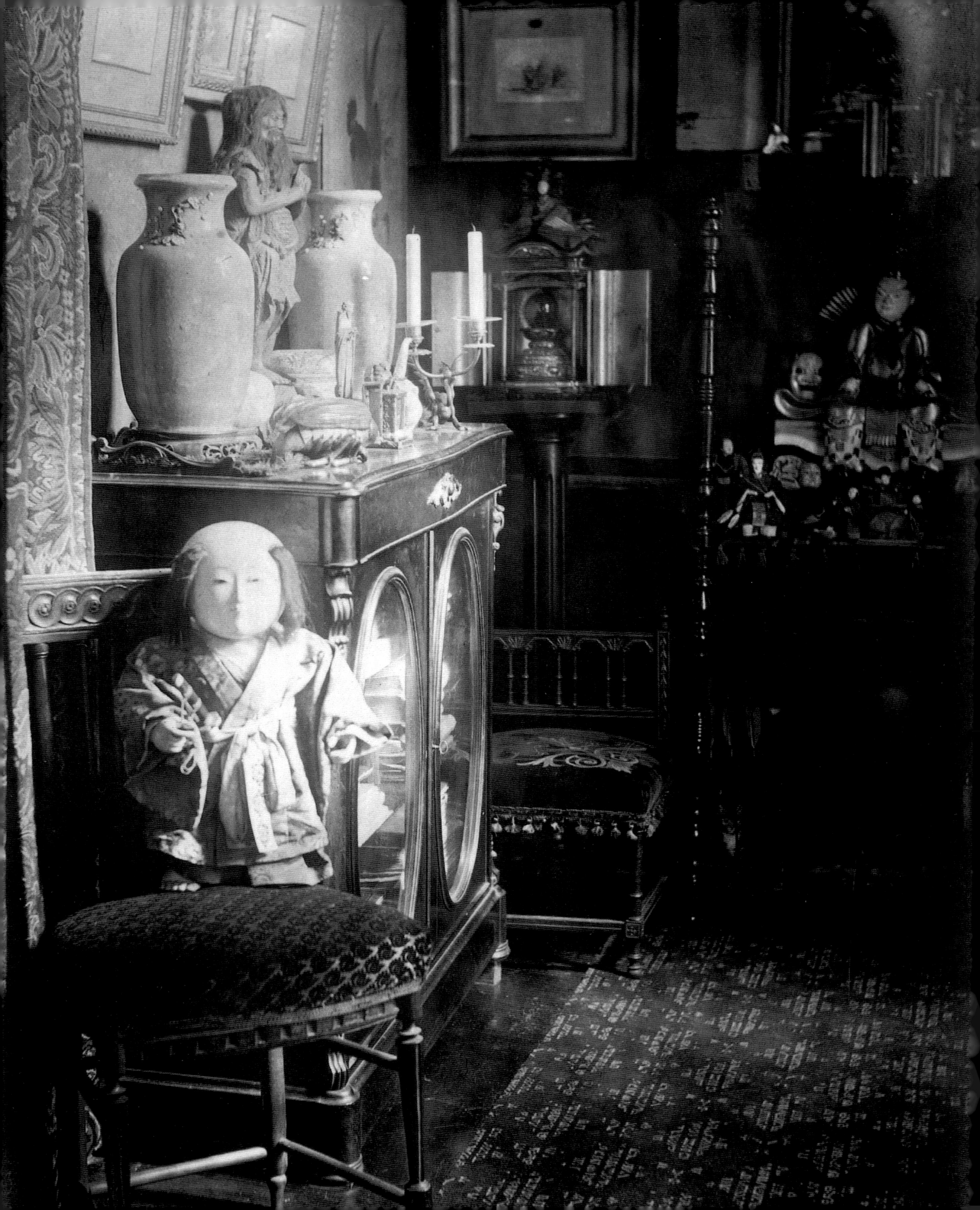

he gained further international stature. In June 1891, when the presses fell silent, there could be no doubt that he reigned as the principal dealer of Japanese art throughout Europe and the United States.

JULES ADELINE OF ROUEN AND THE SAMURAI DOLL MIKIKA

Bing sought out people with whom he could share his passion for Japanese art; if these collectors were also creative men – such as the printmaker Henry Somm, who had a sense of sardonic humour – so much the better. In Rouen, Jules Adeline, an established printmaker and book illustrator, was building a collection of Japanese objects that he eventually donated to the city museum.[41] He kept these objects, many of them dolls of various sizes, in his apartment, where they dominated his rooms with their mysterious or comical presences (figs. 46, 61, 62). A mannequin dressed in Japanese armour in his entryway guarded his home and his collection. Adeline also owned porcelain figurines, *ukiyo-e* prints by Kuniyoshi, fans and ceramic deities, which he arranged behind the armoured figure. In another corner of the apartment, Adeline and his wife had displayed larger dolls and Nô-masks, of the type that were plentiful in Parisian shops, including Bing's. On a chair, in another room, stood a very large Samurai doll nicknamed Mikika (fig. 62). As will be seen, this doll had symbolic significance for the printmaker and his friend and colleague Siegfried Bing.

In 1890, Bing gave Adeline a gift of 'theatrical figures', perhaps a large print, which suggests that by then the two men were good friends.[42] In August 1896, when Bing and his son, Marcel, stopped briefly at Berck-sur-Mer on the French coast on their way to England, Siegfried wrote a letter congratulating Adeline for having won the Légion d'Honneur.[43]

For Adeline, collecting was not only about acquiring art for its own sake; it also fulfilled a creative need. As early as 1883, he depicted the figure of Mikika in his prints. In one, the doll is standing next to an oval portrait of the printmaker amidst a group of other Japanese and Western objects. In another etching, Mikika, dressed in an elaborate kimono and holding a figurine of a Japanese woman at the end of a stick, looks as if he were alive. This large *poupée* had a commanding presence, as seen in the photographs of the period, and appears to have been more than a toy. In 1890, Adeline represented it in an etching heightened with ink, watercolour and gouache that he gave to Bing when the latter received the Légion d'Honneur

< 62
Interior of Jules Adeline's apartment with Mikika doll
Bibliothèque d'Etude, Bibliothèques municipales, Rouen

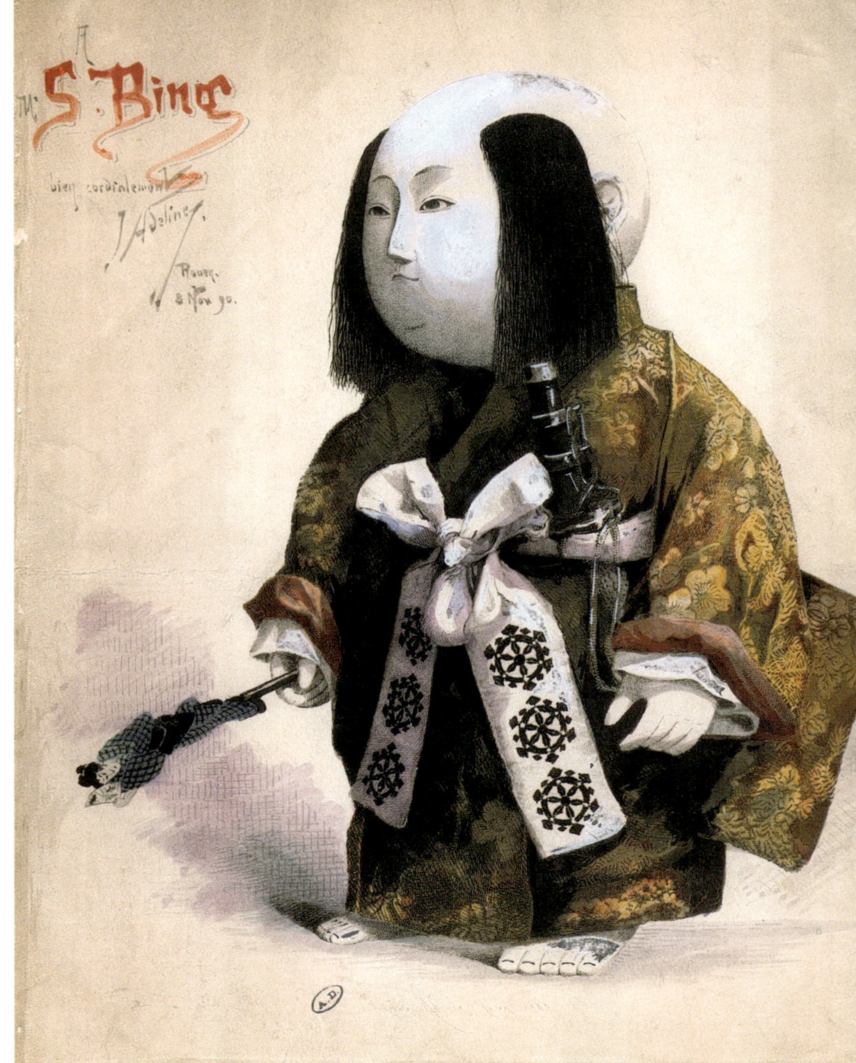

63
Jules Adeline, *Japanese Doll (Mikika)*, etching dedicated to Bing, 1890
Album Maciet, Bibliothèque des Arts décoratifs, Paris

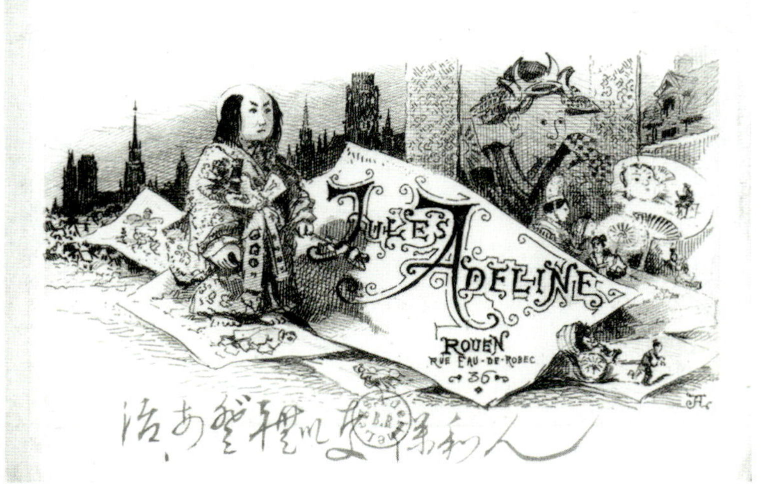

64
Jules Adeline, Visiting card, c. 1893
Bibliothèque d'Etude, Bibliothèques municipales, Rouen

for his sponsorship and dissemination of Japanese art (fig. 63). Mikika, the Samurai, clearly symbolises Bing, the tireless warrior doing battle for Japonisme.[44]

Japonisme was further romanticised in 'Mikika. Japonaiserie Rouennaise', a poem written in 1893 by Eugène Brieux.[45] Brieux used the characteristics of Adeline's doll – the round shaven head with the two long black sideburns – and the unusual name to create a light, amusing tone. The poem describes Mikika's country of origin, where it is always sunny, and colourful birds fly through the sky. He is lonely in grey Rouen, where it often rains, where people have big feet and cannot pronounce his name. The only reason he hasn't committed suicide by jumping off his shelf is because of his two fathers: the author of the poem and his owner, Adeline, who is in love with Japan and is a Japanese in exile. This humorous, fanciful poetry reflects a light-hearted side of Japonisme that first emerged in the 1860s. (Zacharie Astruc, the art critic and a friend of Edouard Manet, wrote such poems.) That this kind of poetry continued to be written for three decades until late in the century reflects its widespread popularity.

Although the receipts for Adeline's objects are lost, it is safe to assume that at least some of them came from Bing. Many of the pieces he owned reflect the comical strain in Japonisme. This would suggest that not every Japanese object sold by Bing belonged to the category of 'high art'. He responded to more popular tastes, while simultaneously selling fine art examples in his stores and acting as an expert in the sale rooms at the Hôtel Drouot. The friendship with Adeline reveals that different types of collectors came to Bing's shop and that he catered to all levels of taste.

JAPONISME AT THE FIN DE SIÈCLE

Toward the end of the century, more museums collected Japanese art not just to illustrate the cross-fertilisation in art between East and West, but also to satisfy a genuine interest in Far Eastern art for its own sake. Bing encouraged both inclinations. In October 1897, he was invited to prepare an exhibit of Japanese objects for the inauguration of the Kaiser Wilhelm Museum in Krefeld, Germany.[46] Three years later, he sent a group of objects, but they were not to the director's liking. Even though Bing had promised a broad range of pieces from all media, he had sent largely ceramics. He was asked to supplement these with additional works if the show was to go on an extended tour.[47]

What happened with the Kaiser Wilhelm show was symptomatic of the situation facing dealers in Japanese art at the end of the nineteenth century. Bing explained that good and even extraordinary objects were not as plentiful, pieces were in private collections, and he was reluctant to send the best works on tour since they could be damaged. However, the fact is that competition was keen. The flourishing of Japonisme and Bing's success in promoting both ancient and contemporary Japanese art had a rebound effect; the supply of objects began to diminish.

In his final years, Bing acted the role of elder statesman, serving on commissions that strengthened ties with the Far East. He became a founding member of the Franco-Japanese Society, where in 1901 he lectured on 'Hokusai and His Art'.[48] Bing's membership in this group led to a close friendship with Hugues Krafft, a collector and visitor to Japan, who also constructed a Japanese house, outside Paris, known as Midori-no-sato. Krafft, on many occasions, hosted dinner parties there; Bing was photographed at Midori-no-sato with M. and Mme. Gonse in 1899, wearing a kimono and enjoying one of the gatherings of Japonistes (fig. 58). He was highly sought after as an expert for many Asian art sales, and in 1900 he served on the official jury for the World's Fair charged with the selection of Japanese ceramics.[49] Thanks largely to his enthusiasm for the pottery of Miyagawa Kozan, this ceramicist received the grand prize for his porcelains.

During the opening years of the new century, even as Bing championed *art nouveau*, he maintained his involvement with Japanese art. In the spring of 1901, Bing held the Nihon-Gwakai exhibition of contemporary Japanese painting at his gallery, where the works revealed a very strong Western influence. In May 1903, Bing organised another show at his shop, 'Three Japanese Masters', featuring Hiroshige, Hokusai and Kuniyoshi, his favourite printmakers. Bing even served as an expert for a sale of bonsai trees in November 1903.[50] He was ever optimistic that new types of Japanese objects would find an audience in the West.

At age sixty-six, Bing began to realise that he could no longer keep up this furious pace. Two sales in 1904 were the last for which he acted as a consultant: the Charles Gillot sale held at the Galeries Durand-Ruel in February;[51] and the sale of Chinese and Japanese objects from the collections of John Charles Robinson (former Director of South Kensington Museum) and Ernest Hart held at the Hôtel Drouot on 9–10 June 1904.[52] He seemed determined that collections formed by old

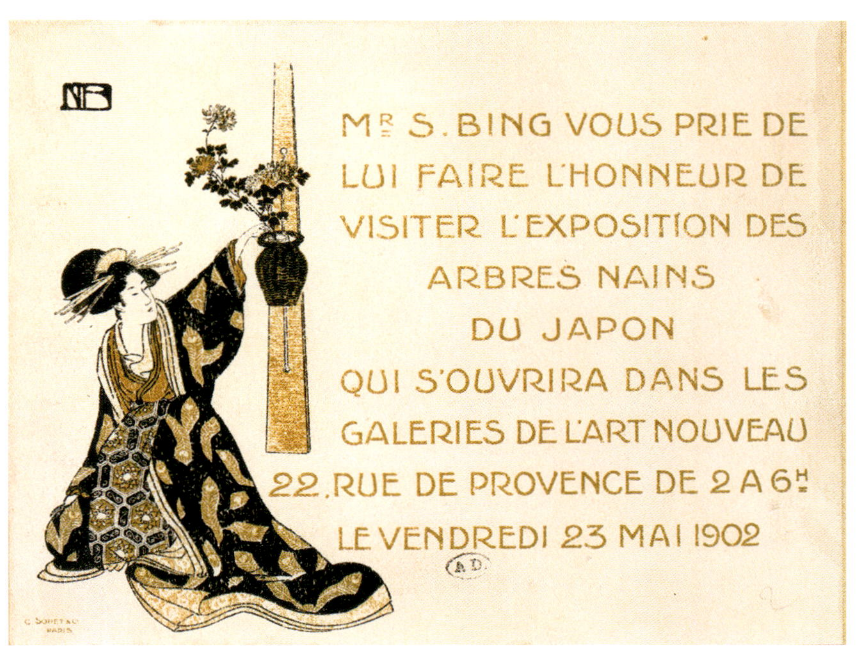

65
Advertisement 'Dwarf Trees', 1902
Album Maciet, Bibliothèque des Arts décoratifs, Paris

friends who were selling their beloved objects at the end of their lives be recognised for their artistic merit.

In late 1904, Bing closed down his gallery L'Art Nouveau at 22, rue de Provence and transferred his Asian art business to 10, rue Saint-Georges, where his son, Marcel, and Marie Nordlinger, Bing's able sales agent, assisted him.[53] Originally a jeweller in Bing's *art nouveau* workshops, the English-born Nordlinger became Bing's trusted agent, especially in dealings with Americans. In particular, she worked with Bing's wealthy client Charles L. Freer, and helped Bing expand his foothold in the American market.[54] Nordlinger's energy and acumen led Bing to send her to the United States to negotiate the sale of his *ukiyo-e* collection in 1905.[55] Even in this last year of his life, Bing was the most prominent dealer selling Japanese art, now often from his own collection. Japonisme, a small craze that had become a huge international business, would continue to be promoted by Bing's son Marcel and, after his death in 1920, by his partner, René Haase, until the German occupation of Paris in 1943. The war brought to an abrupt end the Bing empire and the design movement to which it had given birth.

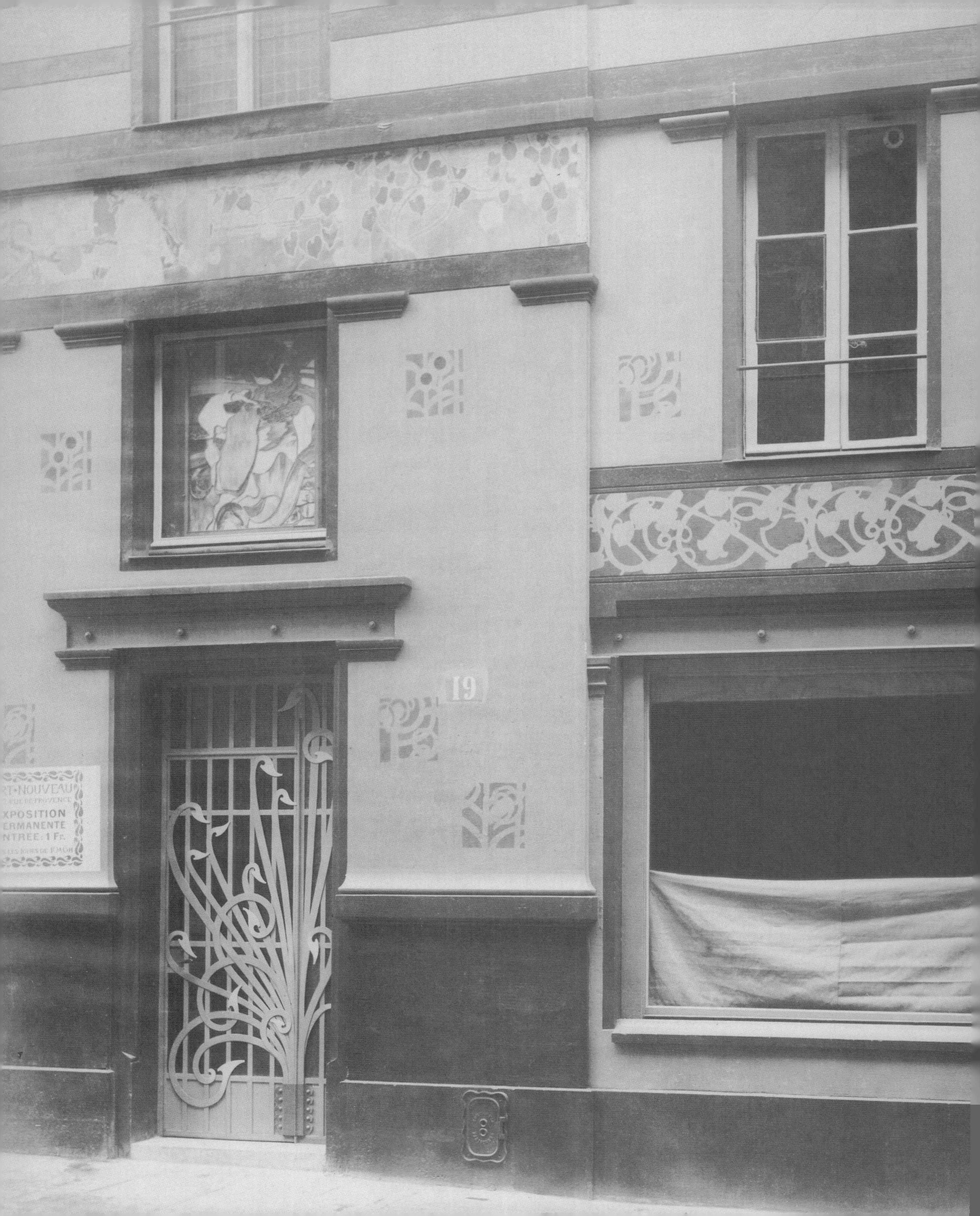
RT·NOUVEAU
XPOSITION
ERMANENTE
NTREE: 1 Fr.
19

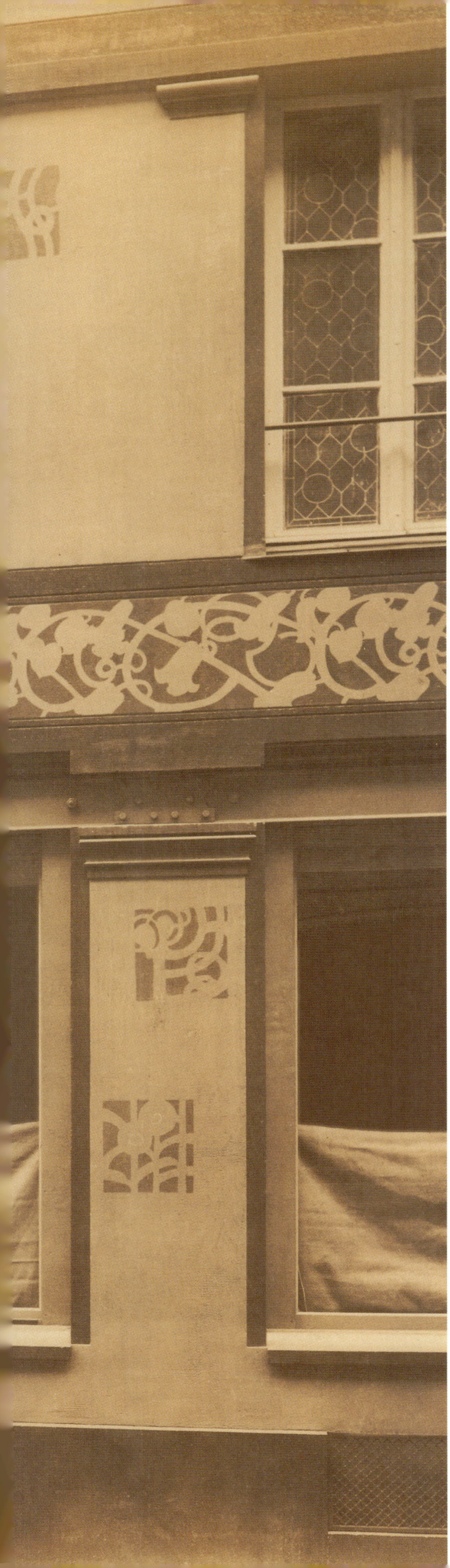

ARTS AMBASSADOR FOR EUROPE AND AMERICA

GABRIEL P. WEISBERG

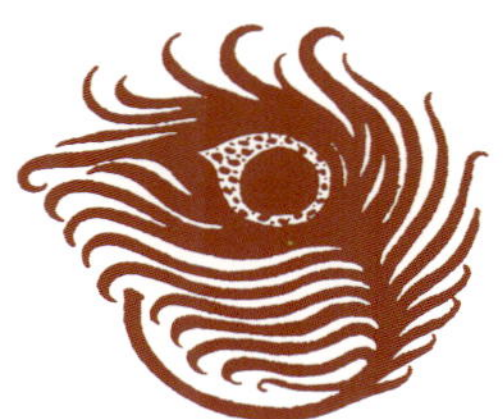

By the early 1880s, Siegfried Bing had become aware of the importance of the United States, both as a potential market for his Asian *objets d'art* business and as a place where industrial activity in the applied arts might eventually surpass that of Europe. Before long, he was seeking out contacts in America: sending objects to the new public museums, sponsoring exhibitions and sales in the major art centres of the country, and making contacts with American craftsmen. Having left the details of such arrangements to an American agent and family members during the 1880s and early 1890s, he finally came to the United States for three months in 1894 to see for himself the artistic creativity that was drawing increasing attention (and alarm) in Europe. During this short trip, he travelled to New York, Boston, Philadelphia, among other cities, organising exhibitions and auctions, as well as meeting with museum officials, art collectors and prominent designers. Upon his return to Paris, he commissioned a major series of stained-glass windows designed by avant-garde French artists and manufactured in the United States, thus sending a clear signal of his faith in American craftsmanship. In addition, he published a pamphlet entitled *La Culture artistique en Amérique*, which aimed to inform his countrymen about the state of the arts in America. Both this prestigious commission and the publication reveal Bing's support for the development of the applied arts in the United States. With America serving as a model to spur European artists to greater creativity in industrial design, Bing realised his goal of reinvigorating the arts: in short, of promoting his *art nouveau*.

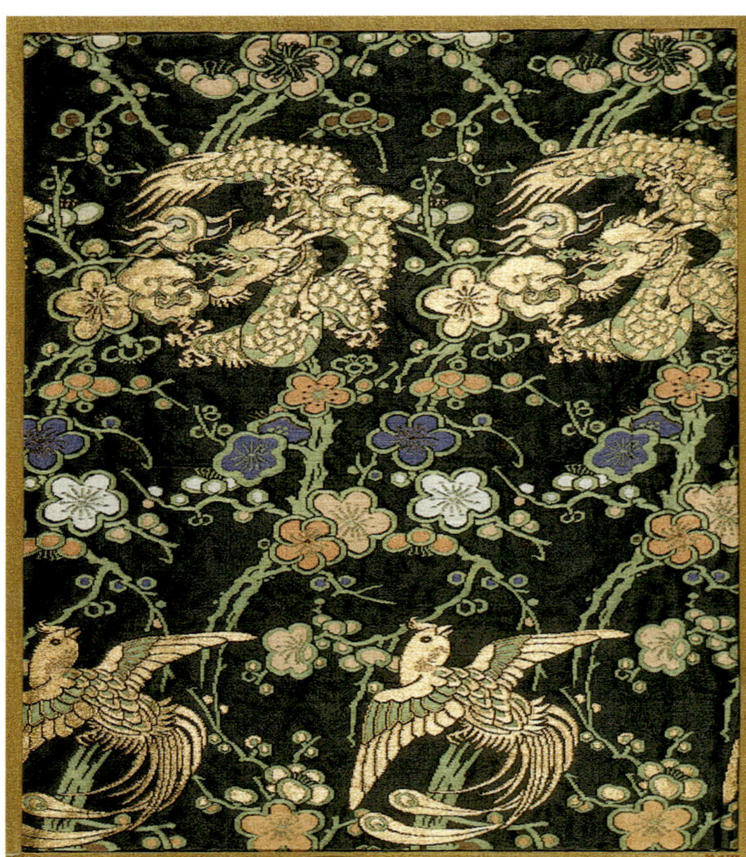

<< 66
Façade at 19, rue Chauchat, 1895 (detail of fig. 99)
Fonds Louis Bonnier, Institut français d'architecture, Paris

67–68
Silk fragments, Japan, 18th-19th century
The Metropolitan Museum of Art, New York, gift of Mr. and Mrs. H.O. Havemeyer, 1896

> 69
Ker-Xavier Roussel, *The Garden*, stained-glass window, 1895
Private collection

> 70
Ker-Xavier Roussel, *The Garden*, 1894
Carnegie Museum of Art, Pittsburgh

> 71
Edouard Vuillard, *Chestnut Trees*, c. 1894–95
Private collection

EARLY CONTACTS WITH AMERICA IN THE 1880S

Given his tendency to think globally, it was to be expected that Bing would seek out a relationship with America. Contrary to what has been assumed, his interest in the United States began well before his trip there in 1894 and the subsequent appearance in 1896 of his ground-breaking pamphlet. The dealer's earliest official association with an American arts institution is recorded in documents at the Metropolitan Museum of Art in New York. In October 1882, Bing presented the museum with 'a large vase of Chinese porcelain [...] dating from the Kienlong period'.[1] While the presentation of this gift may have been motivated in part by prospective commercial gain, it also reveals a more altruistic purpose – as already demonstrated by his generous donations to museums in Europe – of introducing Asian art to a broader public.[2] This early contact was prophetic of things to come. Once he had established a relationship with the Metropolitan, Bing relentlessly pursued his new client, sending news of available items to museum officials. He sometimes despatched family emissaries from his Paris office to New York to arrange for the sale of Japanese objects, since it was not always possible for him to travel abroad, especially as he got older.[3]

Initial contacts with America were designed to promote Bing's Asian art business. This led to shows sponsored by the dealer and to sales in galleries and auction houses, primarily in New York City, which had begun to rival Paris as a centre of artistic activity. These exhibitions and sales were advertised and reviewed in American newspapers. Bing's first Asian art sale was held in April 1887 at Moore's Art Galleries at 290 Fifth

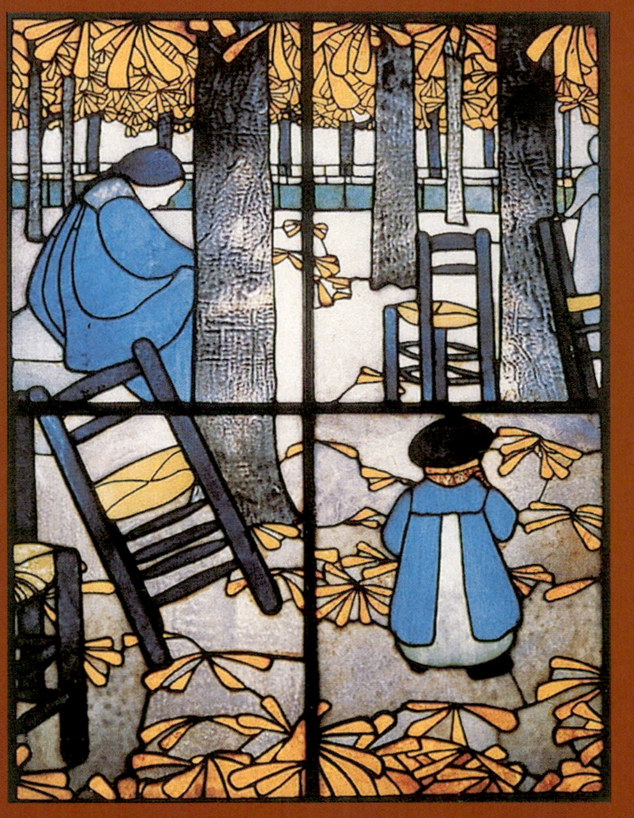
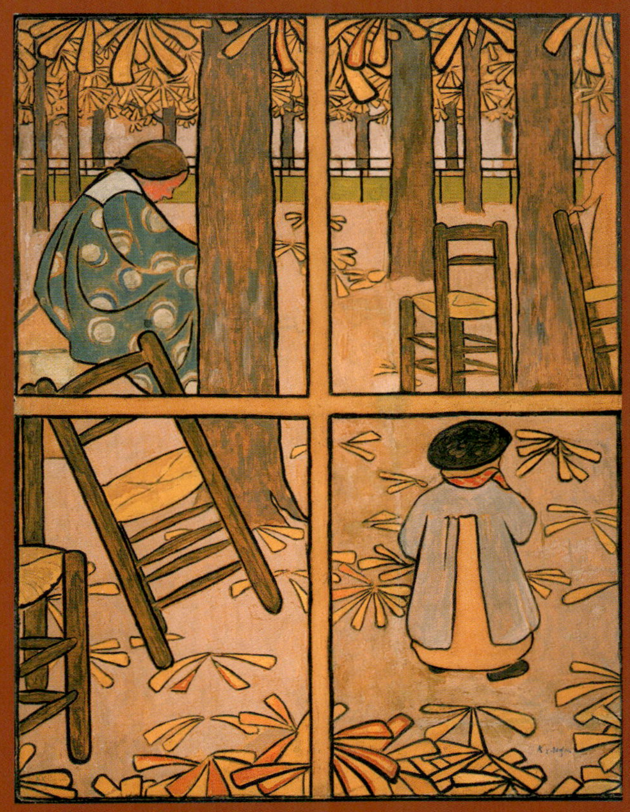
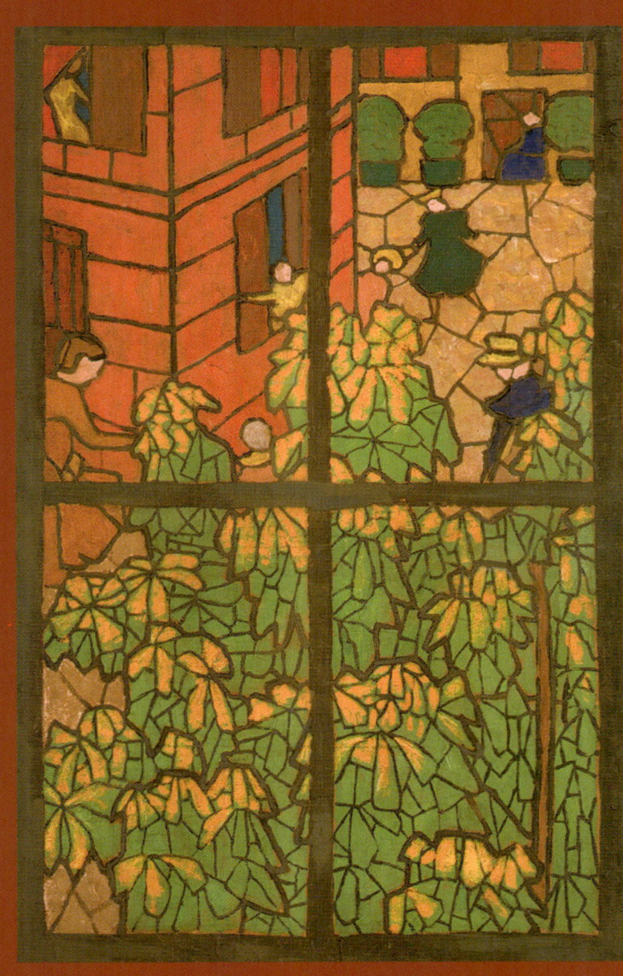

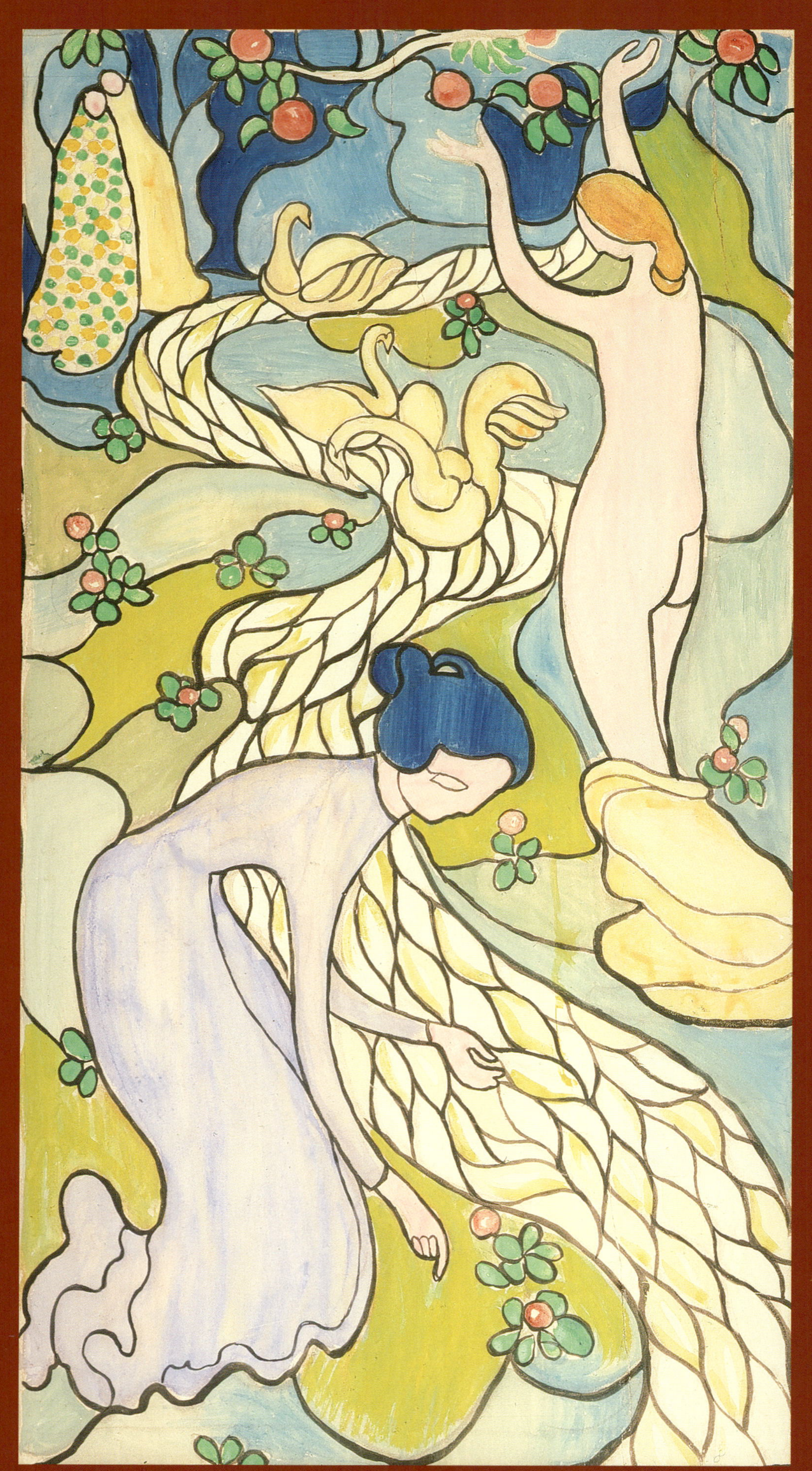

Avenue. The preliminary viewing of the pieces took place at Bing's own sales rooms at 220 Fifth Avenue, which he had probably leased that year.[4] For this sale, Bing relied on his business associate John Getz, an American dealer who had made his first trip to France in November 1886,[5] and whose own sales rooms in New York had begun to showcase Asian art. Both men worked closely together for a number of years, with Getz acting as Bing's American agent.[6]

With the 1887 sale, Bing hoped to introduce his business to American art buyers. To get the word out, he mounted a strong advertising campaign. Despite the hyperbole in the press, the objects in this sale were primarily Asian curios and contemporary objects made for the Western trade. The idea was to slowly nurture a clientele in the United States, gradually educating them to be connoisseurs, as he had in Europe.[7] The turnout for the sale was small; a reviewer for the *Art Amateur* noted that the sale was promoting the taste for Asian art and that on 'the first two days, the goods were almost given away'.[8] But Bing and Getz were patient, realising that it would take time to develop an appreciation for quality pieces.

< 72
Maurice Denis, *Women at the Stream*, 1894
Musée départemental Maurice Denis 'Le Prieuré', Saint-Germain-en-Laye

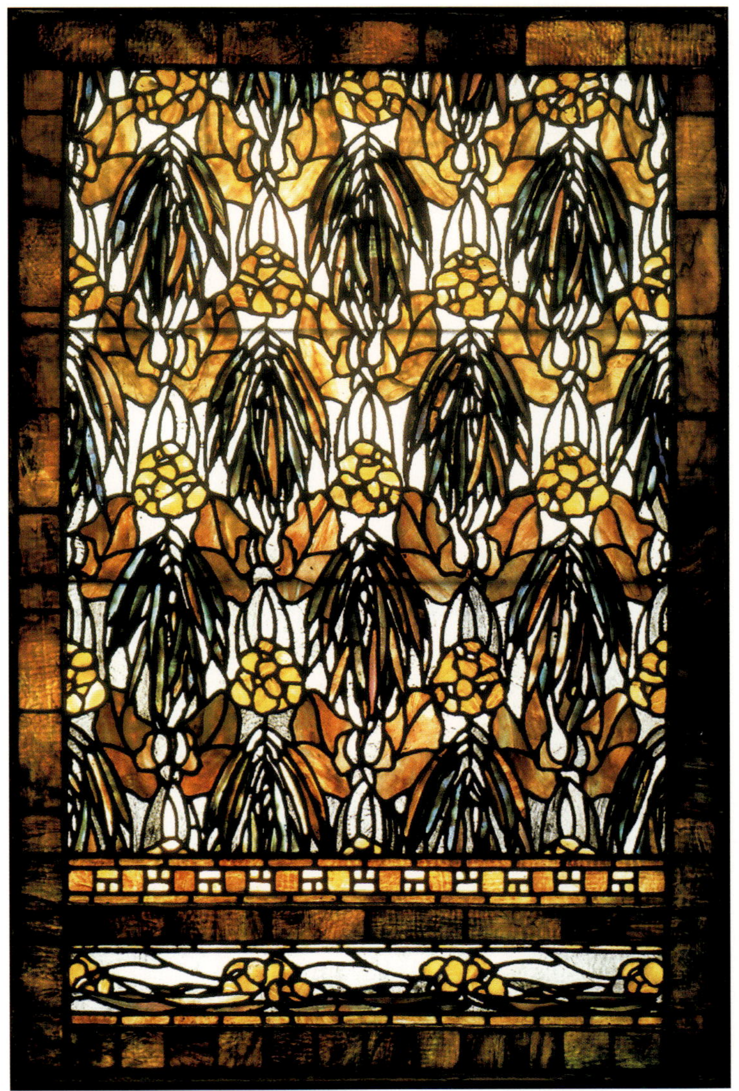

73
Louis Comfort Tiffany, Stained-glass window, 1894
Musée des Arts décoratifs, Paris

A second public sale of Asian objects took place in Philadelphia in 1888; this was also probably organised by Getz, who wrote the accompanying catalogue. In an auction at the Davis and Harvey Art Galleries on Chestnut Street, Bing marketed Chinese and Japanese porcelains, faience, pottery, bronzes, enamels, ivories, lacquers, carvings, silk, embroidery and furniture.[9] Some of these items may have been left over from the European market. No matter the offerings, Bing was well on his way to establishing a network of contacts in the major American cities. In the same year, when his journal *Artistic Japan* was launched in America, Bing held a third public auction in his own gallery in New York, in which he still had not set foot.[10] The sale lasted a week, from 21 to 27 November; 1,334 objects were sold to a broad range of clients. By the end of the decade, Bing was well known in several American cities as an influential dealer of Asian art.

TRIP TO AMERICA IN 1894

The expansion of his Asian art business was not the only reason that Bing desired ties with America. The exciting American booths at the Paris World's Fair of 1889 made French entrepreneurs and tastemakers more aware of the growing dynamism in the applied arts of

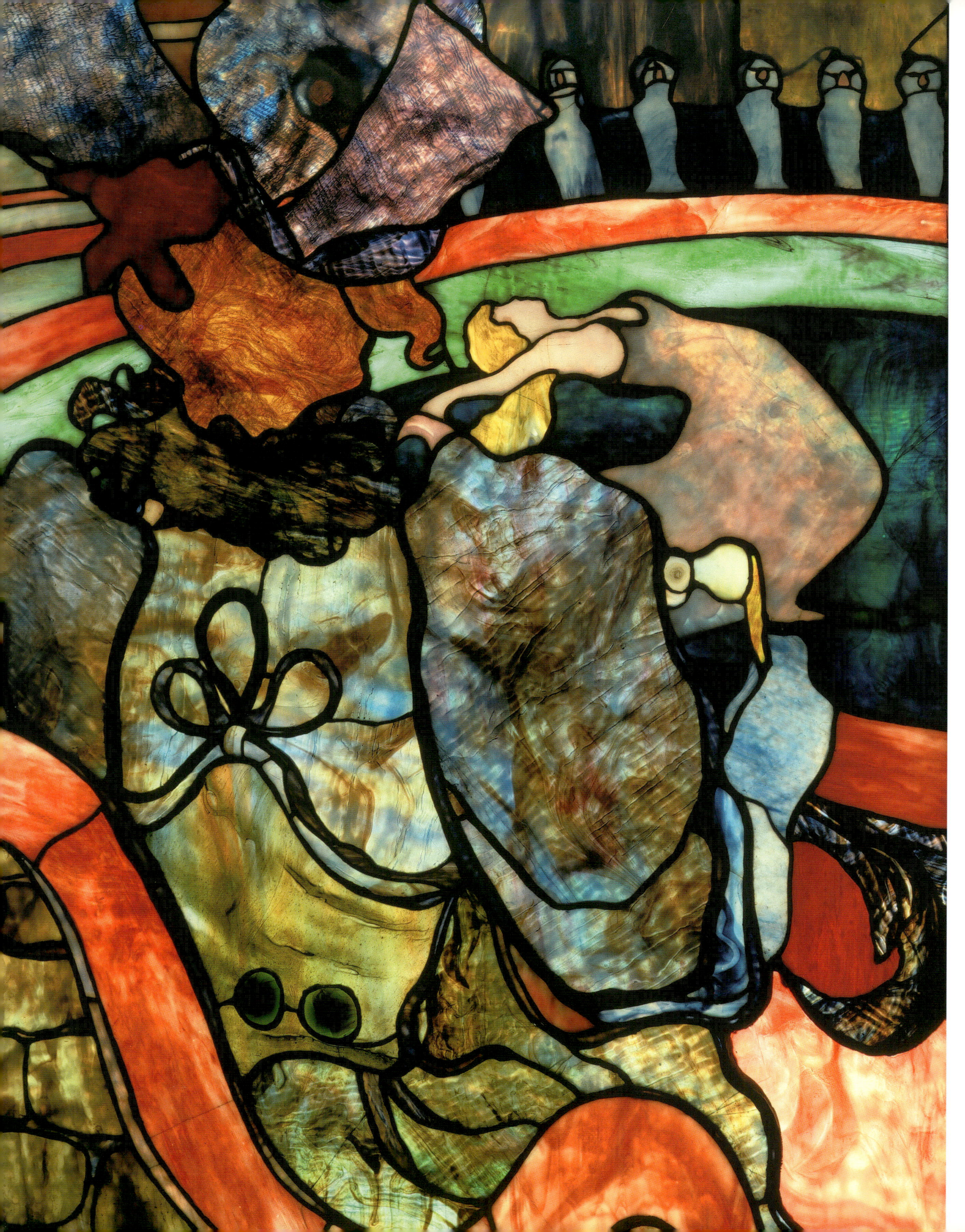

the United States.[11] Already curious about the crafts movement in America, Bing was spurred to action when he read the reviews of the 1893 Chicago World's Columbian Exposition. According to French critics who had attended the fair, France had lost its lead in the field of the decorative arts, and they admonished their countrymen to reform their methods of artistic production. Victor Champier, editor of *Art et Décoration*, was quoted in the French press: 'It is certain that we have much to do if on the occasion of our next Exposition Universelle [1900] we don't wish to see ourselves outdistanced on more than one point. French industrialists beware.'[12]

This state of affairs coincided with a shift in Bing's personal direction, as he became less interested in selling Far Eastern art and more interested in promoting Asian-inspired 'new design' in the applied arts. Thus Bing arranged to go on a mission to the United States in the winter and early spring of 1894.[13] From 12 February until he returned to France on 17 April, Bing worked on two simultaneous objectives: the further dissemination of Japanese art in America and the establishment of ties with American craftsmen and their firms. To finance the trip, he sold Japanese art during his travels.

< 74
Henri de Toulouse-Lautrec, *The Nouveau Cirque: The Female Clown and the Five Penguins (Papa Chrysanthème)*, c. 1894, stained-glass window
Musée d'Orsay, Paris

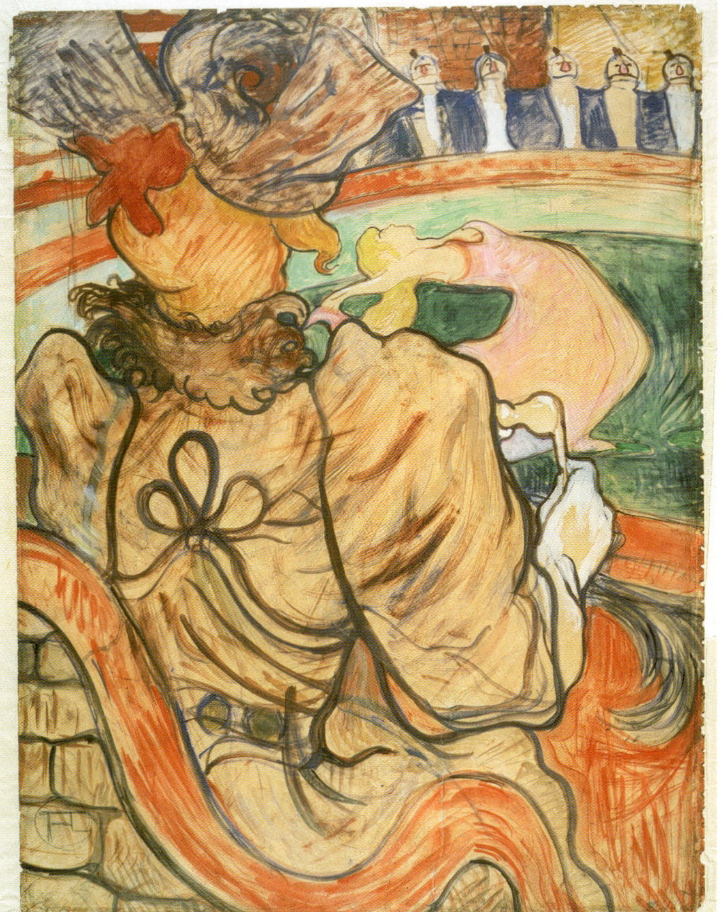

75
Henri de Toulouse-Lautrec, *The Nouveau Cirque: The Female Clown and the Five Penguins (Papa Chrysanthème)*, c. 1894
Museum of Fine Arts, Philadelphia

EXHIBITING AND SELLING ASIAN ART IN AMERICA

One of his first stops in New York was the American Art Galleries, where he made contacts with other dealers and held two auctions.[14] The first, on 23 February, attracted considerable presale publicity in the press, including the *New York Evening Post* and the *New York Daily Tribune*. This sale featured ceramics, porcelains, as well as sword-guards, *netsuke* and enamel pieces.[15] In mid-March, he presented over 290 single prints or illustrated albums, by all the principal Japanese printmakers.[16] Following upon the success of the huge exhibition in Paris in 1890 of *ukiyo-e* prints, Bing shared this art form with an American audience. The catalogue, with an introductory essay by Bing, functioned as an introduction to the history of Japanese prints and as publicity for the sale. Whether or not the prints sold in New York was unimportant, since Bing intended to take the show to several other American cities. Prints sold at one venue could be easily replaced by duplicates in another. This show also attracted attention in the press. One reviewer for *The Critic* noted that 'the exhibition of prints should be of great interest to all who care about

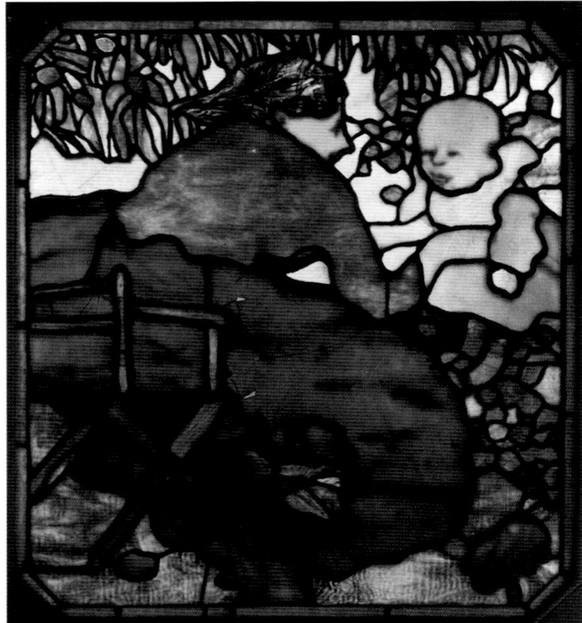

the possibilities of color-printing, for no more artistic work has ever been done [...] than that produced by the popular school of Japanese art.'[17] Other notices appeared in the *New York Evening Post* and in the *New York Daily Tribune*, whose reviewer found the show 'a remarkable collection of curious Japanese engravings [...] which are after all not easily matched in our own schools of art.'[18] Such reviews lent lustre to Bing's business enterprise and to his reputation as a promoter of *ukiyo-e* prints.

After the New York showing, Bing tried to exhibit the prints in Philadelphia at the Pennsylvania Academy of Fine Arts, as the museum was having its own show of Japanese objects. He had been invited to participate in this exhibition, but there was not enough time to send the prints for the opening; in the end, he sent only textiles. While he thus lost an opportunity to increase his visibility in Philadelphia, true to his entrepreneurial ingenuity, he quickly found another venue.

Responding to Bing's overtures, the Museum of Fine Arts in Boston agreed to exhibit the large group of prints, as well as other art objects. Arriving in Boston in early April in the company of the wealthy collector Henry O. Havemeyer of New York, Bing was warmly greeted by Ernest Fenollosa, the curator in charge of the Asian collection at the museum, and by Professor Edward Sylvester Morse, a leading Japoniste in the United States.[19] This reveals that Bing's trip was perceived by leading American figures interested in Japanese culture as a highpoint. For Bing, it enabled him to meet colleagues and study collections that were in the process of being formed. That Bing's itinerary was reported in the local papers is further evidence of the significance of the 1894 trip.[20]

Bing's Japanese print collection was soon displayed in the Museum of Fine Arts. The show completely filled all the cases in the corridor of the Japanese art department, where they were arranged by Fenollosa. The *Boston Herald* noted that the prints would be on display 'for about four weeks',[21] along with two Tanagra figurines that Bing had also loaned to the museum. In mid-April, after Bing had left the Boston area, other items from his collection or shop were added, including metalwork, suggesting that sword-guards and other such pieces were also attracting attention. Thus Bing had found in his Boston colleagues a very enthusiastic audience of professional Japonistes, who were interested in more than just prints.[22]

Bing did not have as much luck with the Metropolitan Museum of Art, although his ties with the museum remained strong. The dealer never did succeed in getting the Metropolitan to host a major exhibition of Japanese art. Having first been told that space was at a premium, Bing suggested a smaller show of textiles alone. When the museum expressed an interest in this, the textiles in Philadelphia were shipped to New York.[23] However, this exhibition failed to materialise as well. The textiles remained in storage for several years until the museum trustees sought a purchaser for them (figs. 67, 68). With Samuel P. Avery acting as middleman, Henry O. Havemeyer bought the textiles for somewhat less than the asking price and donated the entire collection to the museum.[24]

Bing's stay in the United States was brief but rewarding. Within the span of about eight weeks, he had held sales and exhibitions of Japanese art, travelled to several

76
Pierre Bonnard, *Mother and Child*, stained-glass window, 1895
Private collection

> 77
Félix Vallotton, *Parisian Women*, 1894
Private collection

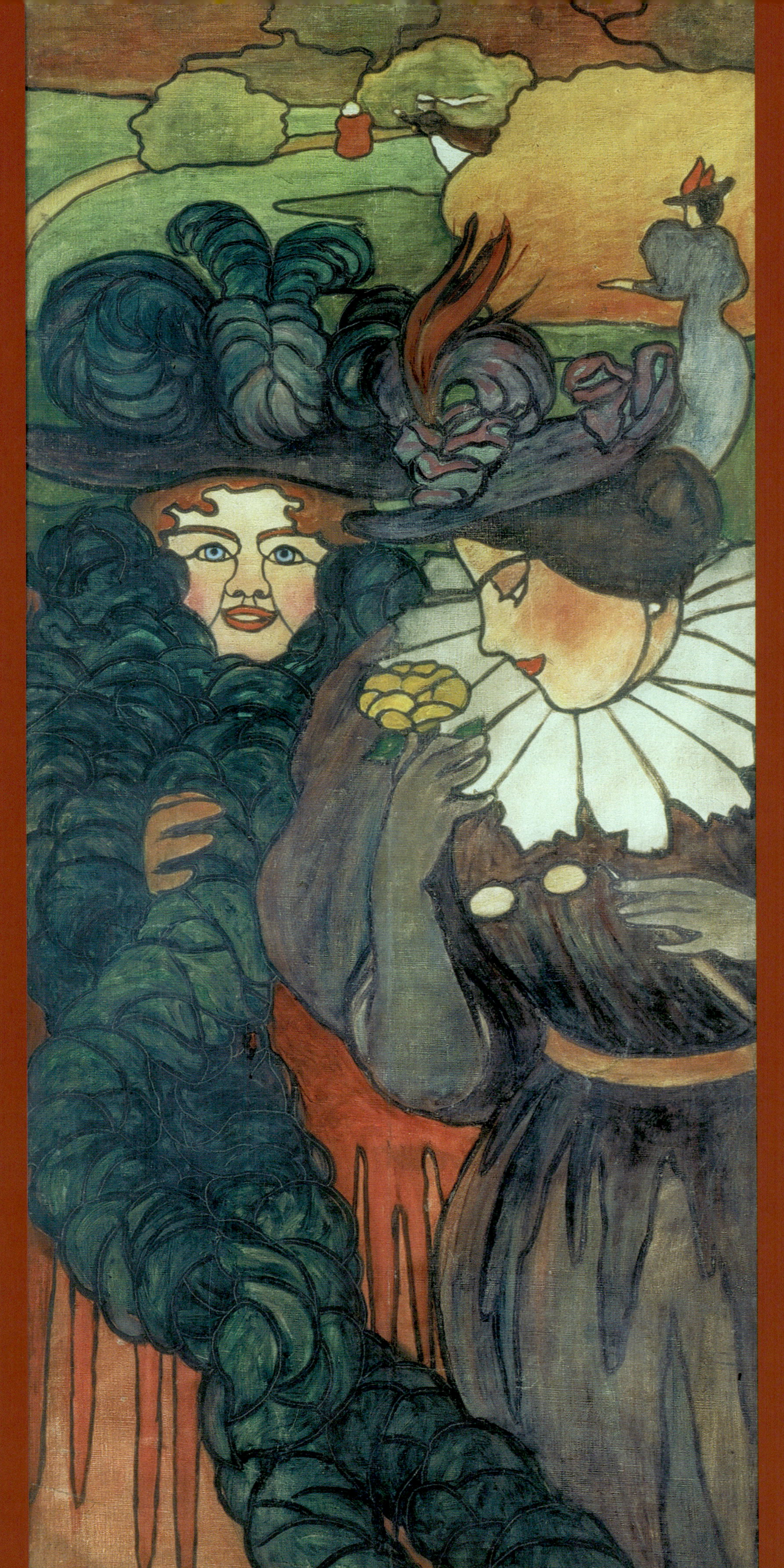

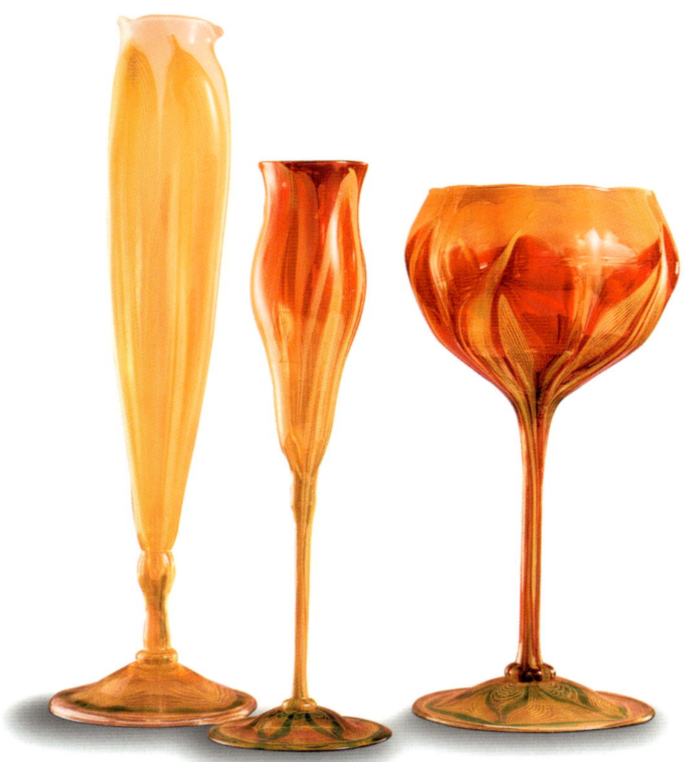

cities (possibly also Pittsburgh and Cincinnati),[25] and, as will be seen below, almost certainly met with American designers and craftsmen. He cemented commercial ties that had been made in the previous decade, further promoted Japonisme and learned first-hand about the decorative arts industry in the country. The addition of America as a profitable new market for his Japanese objects also allowed Bing to increase his resources so that he could finance his shift toward *art nouveau*. One of his major efforts in this direction involved an exciting partnership between French artists and American craftsmen.

FRENCH ARTISTS AND AMERICAN CRAFTSMEN: A STAINED-GLASS COMMISSION

While very little documentation has survived to record various meetings between Bing and American craftsmen, the circumstantial evidence is overwhelming that such meetings took place. There is, however, one prominent tastemaker and craftsman that he certainly met: Louis Comfort Tiffany, whose manufactory of stained glass was located in the Corona section of Brooklyn, New York.[26] Bing would later become Tiffany's agent for the sale of objects, marketing his wares across Europe. In May 1894, about a month after Bing's return to France, Edouard Vuillard reported to Maurice Denis that he had just seen Henri Ibels – all three members of the group known as the Nabis – who had recently had a meeting with Bing. This meeting was the beginning of a collaboration that led to the creation of stained-glass windows by ten artists, commissioned by Bing, designed by nine Frenchmen and one Swiss, manufactured in the United States, and finished in time for the Salon of the Société Nationale in Paris in April 1895.[27] Vuillard's letter mentions that Bing had returned with 'samples' of glasswork made by American craftsmen, and, with the young artists' evident approval of these, the project was underway by October. With Tiffany being the most prominent American producing high-quality stained-glass windows, it would seem impossible that these samples were not from his workshop and that he and Bing had not had discussions in New York regarding the idea of creating stained-glass windows after designs by French artists.[28]

While only a few of the windows are known today – including those by Pierre Bonnard (fig. 76) and Toulouse-Lautrec (fig. 74) – preliminary cartoons survive for other windows in the series.[29] The themes are consistent with Third Republic ideology, with their emphasis on the family, life in the city of Paris, and the theatre. Seen together, these windows would have provided a view of contemporary life as experienced by a fashionable urban elite.

The finished windows arrived in Paris in mid-April 1895.[30] Extremely pleased with the results, Bing looked forward to an enthusiastic reception by critics and public alike. When the Salon opened, however, the reviews were mixed. The most praise was reserved for the colours and the process used by Tiffany in their production. One critic in the short-lived *Revue Franco-Américaine* applauded the originality of the effort, noting that the windows were like 'a river of precious stones through which light creates unimaginable splendours'.[31] Others found the style too primitive, the designs bizarre. Others disliked the themes presented by the Nabis, finding them

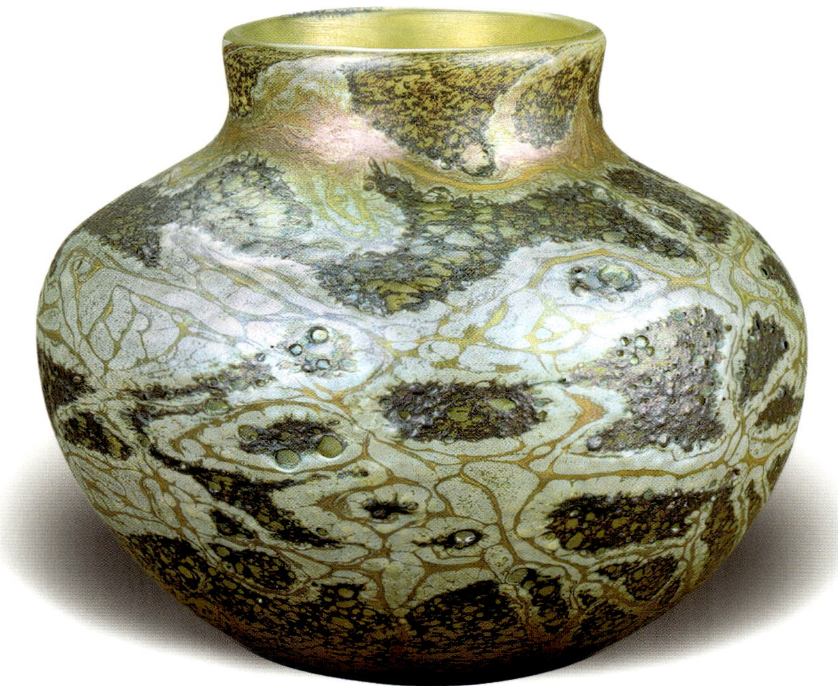

< 78
Louis Comfort Tiffany, Glasses, c. 1896
Österreichisches Museum für angewandte Kunst, Vienna

79
Louis Comfort Tiffany, Vase, c. 1898–99
Musée des Arts décoratifs, Paris

too untraditional. Such views, in fact, proved that Bing had achieved his goal, since the windows broke with the past in form and content. The same reviewer for the *Revue Franco-Américaine* recognised that the windows represented something more than successful art objects. Emphasising that the windows had been produced in New York, he wrote that they had elevated 'stained glass to a [position] of triumph at the Champ de Mars'.[32] Still another review, in the *Journal des Arts*, enthusiastically commented on the windows, especially the 'intensity of colour', which obviously made them quite original as well as objects to be studied carefully by other designers.[33] One short review also appeared in America in *Art Amateur* calling attention to the pieces that seemed like 'glass mosaics'.[34] By introducing these technical and artistic innovations to Paris, Bing confirmed that, in at least some areas of the applied arts, America had taken the lead. With actual manufactured objects as models and with his well-established connections with American firms, he challenged French designers to move forward and leave behind old traditions.

Several windows in the series merge contemporary French themes and modern technology with Japanese-inspired subject matter and style. For example, Toulouse-Lautrec based the design for his window (figs. 74, 75) on the play *Papa Chrysanthème* shown at the Nouveau Cirque in 1892, which was a Japanese fantasy similar in content to Gilbert and Sullivan's *Mikado* (1885). The artist, who was an avid theatre and cabaret spectator, borrowed motifs from the costumes and from the spectacle of an aquatic ballet. The fashionable, silhouetted young woman watching the dancers from her seat is a Japanese-inspired image, both in its subject and its two-dimensional pattern. These elements are precisely those Bing promoted in his reform of the applied arts. The windows became not only the first step toward the creation of an *art nouveau* for the home, but also showed how Japanese art could invigorate French and American design.

Following the exhibition of the windows at the 1895 April Salon of the Société Nationale des Beaux-Arts, Bing decided to include them in his first 'Salon de l'Art Nouveau', which opened in December of that year.[35] Bing installed all the windows, except for Toulouse-Lautrec's, in the lower floor of his gallery, which opened onto 22, rue de Provence. Lautrec's was set in the stairwell of the gallery on 19, rue Chauchat, where light from the outside – on a sunny day – would have shone through, creating a beautiful effect. The placement of the window was symbolic, as it announced the 'new art' with its debt to Japanese visual traditions. Even as he devoted the greater part of his attention to *art nouveau*, Bing never lost interest in Japanese art, as is clear from the number of sales and exhibitions he held in the United States. Furthermore, even after he opened the first Salon de l'Art Nouveau, he continued to exhibit and sell Japanese objects in his gallery situated at the corner of 22, rue de Provence and 19, rue Chauchat. It was, however, on rue Chauchat that one gained entrance to Bing's Japanese galleries.

On the rue Chauchat side of the gallery, remodelled by the architect Louis Bonnier, Japanese objects of all types – ceramics, bronzes, wood sculpture and *inrô* – were on view in cabinets located on the second floor of

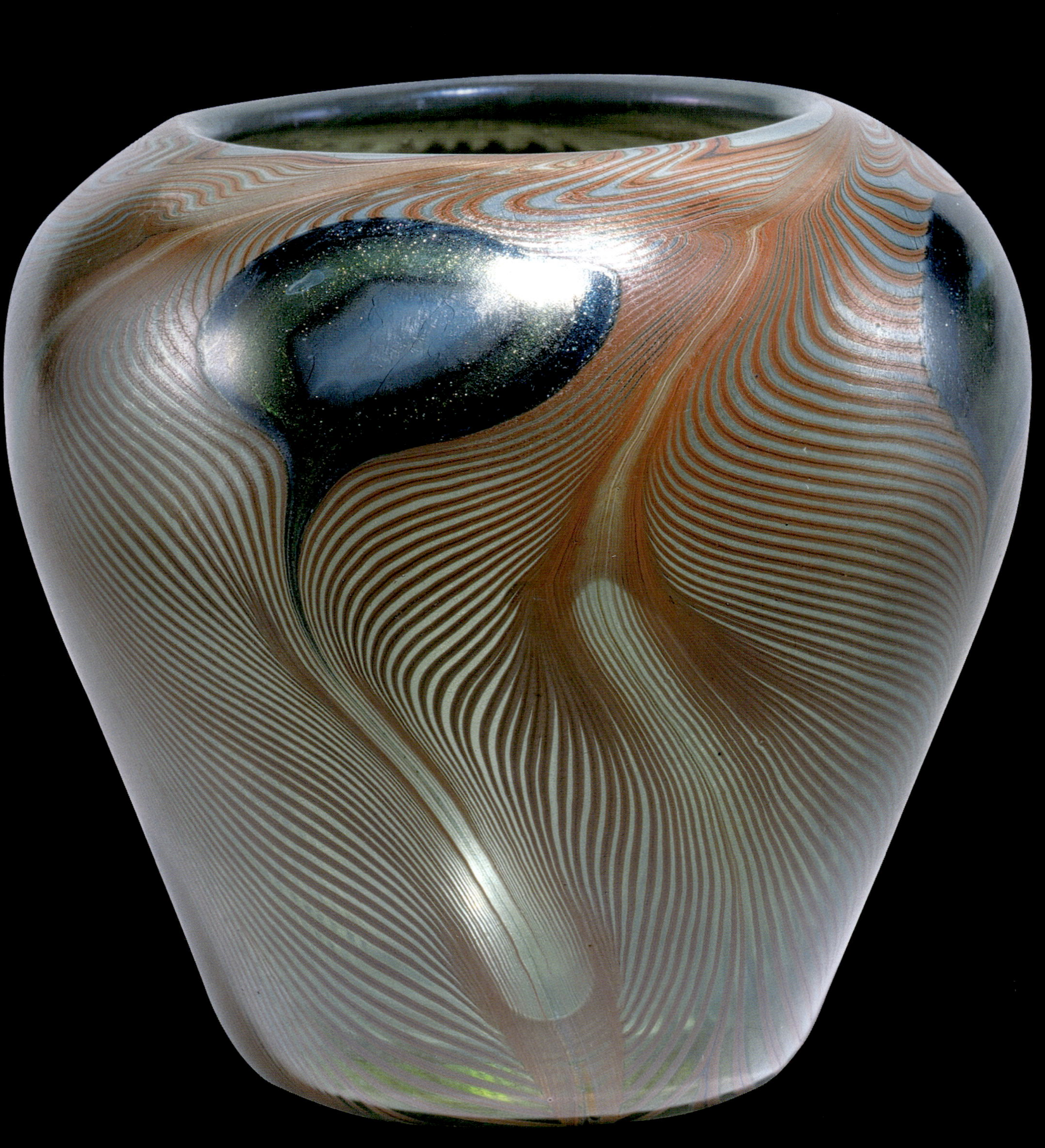

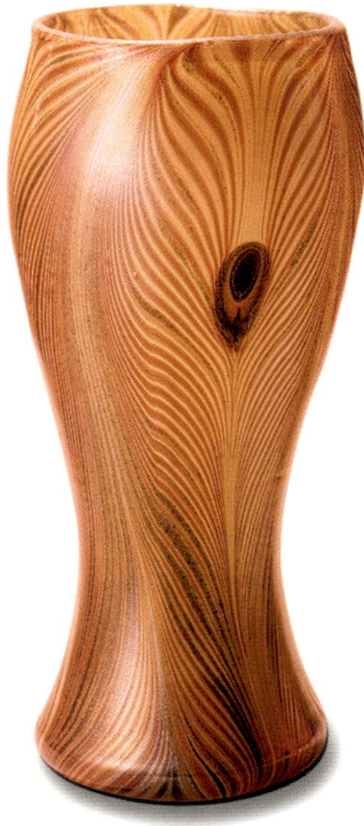

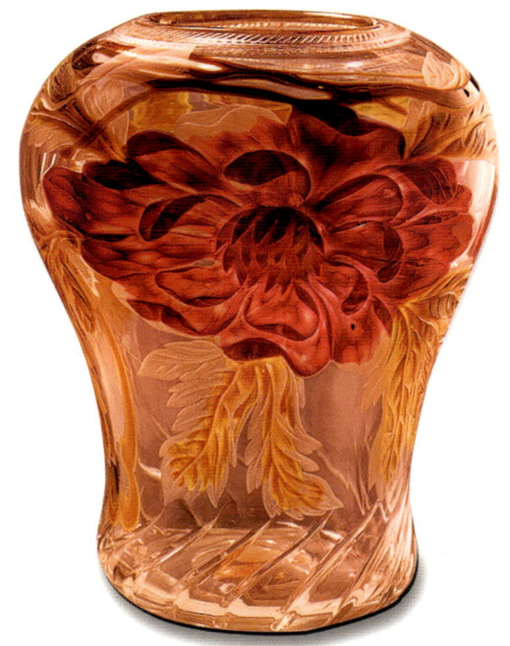

< 80
Louis Comfort Tiffany, Vase, c. 1897
Musée des Arts décoratifs, Paris

81
Louis Comfort Tiffany, Vase, c. 1897
Österreichisches Museum für angewandte Kunst, Vienna

82
Louis Comfort Tiffany, Vase, c. 1896
Österreichisches Museum für angewandte Kunst, Vienna

the gallery, which could be reached by a spiral stairway. Arranged in a circular balcony and in adjoining rooms, they took up all the space from floor to ceiling. After 1895, when Bing opened his gallery of contemporary European art, the new objects took up a much larger portion of the shop.

LA CULTURE ARTISTIQUE EN AMÉRIQUE

Among the myriad reasons that Bing had travelled to America in 1894 was a desire to write an assessment of the state of the arts in the country. Published early in 1896, either in January or February, two years after his trip and just following the opening of his Salon de l'Art Nouveau, *La Culture artistique en Amérique* has been dismissed by some as a hasty report on American creativity in the arts.[36] While admittedly not a comprehensive examination of what was necessarily a broad and detailed topic, this pamphlet does show Bing to be a perceptive art critic, as well as a passionate supporter of the development of the applied arts in the United States.

La Culture artistique en Amérique, with its sections on American painting, sculpture, architecture and the applied arts, reiterates one of Bing's basic beliefs: that all the arts should be appreciated equally. In his view, neither painting nor sculpture should be placed above the decorative or applied arts. That Bing saw all the American works included in his sample survey is unlikely; nevertheless, the fact remains that he was able to write about each area in an intelligent way, thus providing his French audience with a guide to American art. Reviews of the pamphlet in France, combined with those in the United States, suggest that its readers included European avant-garde designers and industrialists who were interested in American art and the conditions under which it was produced.

Two sections of the pamphlet, on architecture and the decorative arts, were reprinted in France in 1897, attesting to the popularity of the publication. They appeared in the *Revue Encyclopédique Larousse* under the title 'L'Architecture et les arts décoratifs en Amérique'.[37] Since few in France were aware of the larger context of American ideas, and the Third Republic was eager to stress international associations, Bing's essay made for topical, compelling reading. The broad distribution of this encyclopedia assured widespread dissemination of Bing's views.

Bing's pamphlet was discussed in American newspapers almost immediately after it appeared, strongly suggesting that an English language edition had been printed.[38] Given the author's genuine attempt to publicise and praise American art in Europe, it is perhaps surprising to find a somewhat harsh review on 21 March 1896 in the *New York Evening Post*: 'The point of view – that of a travelling foreigner in this country – has to be especially reckoned with in considering Mr. Bing's pamphlet on artistic culture in America. Judging from a prefatory epistle Mr. Bing seems to have been commissioned by the Director des Beaux-Arts to make a report on the development of art in the United States, and these hundred-odd pages are the result. One would be tempted to believe, at first, that the report might have been written without crossing the Atlantic, for the only American painters the author seems to know well are

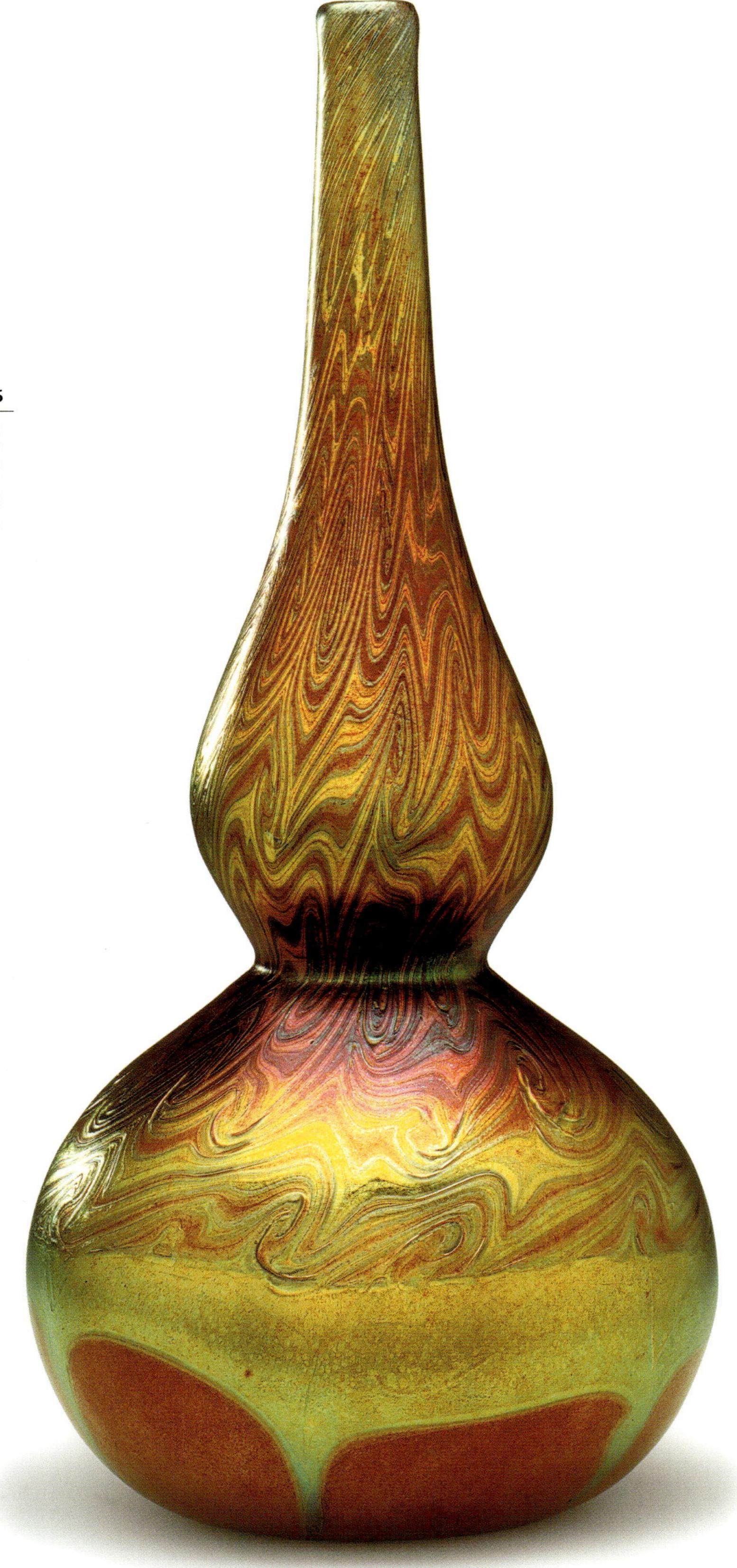

those who have taken up residence abroad. About the home-keeping talents he makes strange blunders, such as transforming J. Alden Weir into "Alden Weird," calling George Fuller a "strict imitator of the French manner" and Inness a "faithful translator of the familiar sites of his own country."'[39] The reviewer also castigated Bing for knowing little about American sculpture, and found something positive to say only about the sections on architecture and the decorative arts: 'In our architecture he finds this new thing, and the cold critic of our painting and sculpture becomes the enthusiastic admirer of those high buildings which we, in our ignorance of what we have done best worth doing, are trying to suppress by act of legislature. Of one other form of American art is M. Bing, and with more reason, a hearty admirer. But his praises of American stained glass are, however unjustly, likely to be discounted as possibly influenced by his commercial relations with a well-known firm of manufacturers.'[40] This evident swipe at Bing's commercial relationship with Tiffany reflects the reasonable but somewhat unfair view that the writings of dealers, even if they were knowledgeable, were tinged by monetary motivations. That the pamphlet was commented on at all in the widely circulated *Evening Post* reveals that it was in plain sight in New York City, at least.

A review of *La Culture artistique* appeared in the *New York Sun* about a year later, on 23 February 1897, suggesting its continuing popularity among American connoisseurs of art. Here the reviewer was more supportive, noting that the booklet was an 'appreciative and interesting report on the present conditions of American art and the outlook for its future'. Gone were the snide attacks on Bing's motivations and on his purported inability to grasp American painting and sculpture. Instead, he was praised for his involvement with American architecture and the industrial arts. Indeed, the anonymous critic wrote that Bing was 'one of the few safe judges in artistic matters living'.[41]

The lion's share of *La Culture artistique en Amérique* was devoted to the industrial arts. Noting that, in recent times, American craftsmen had achieved the same status as artists working in other areas of the visual arts, Bing singled out three designers who had helped bring this about: Samuel Colman, John LaFarge, and Louis C. Tiffany. He concurred with the enthusiastic reports of their artistic production as given by other reviewers at the moment of the Chicago Exposition in 1893. Above all, he stressed that these artists had fully integrated nature into their work, were open to incorporating new industrial processes, and were eager to banish old forms and embrace new ones.

83
Louis Comfort Tiffany, Double gourd vase, c. 1897
Museum für Kunst und Gewerbe, Hamburg

> 84
Louis Comfort Tiffany, Vase, c. 1896
Musée des Arts décoratifs, Paris

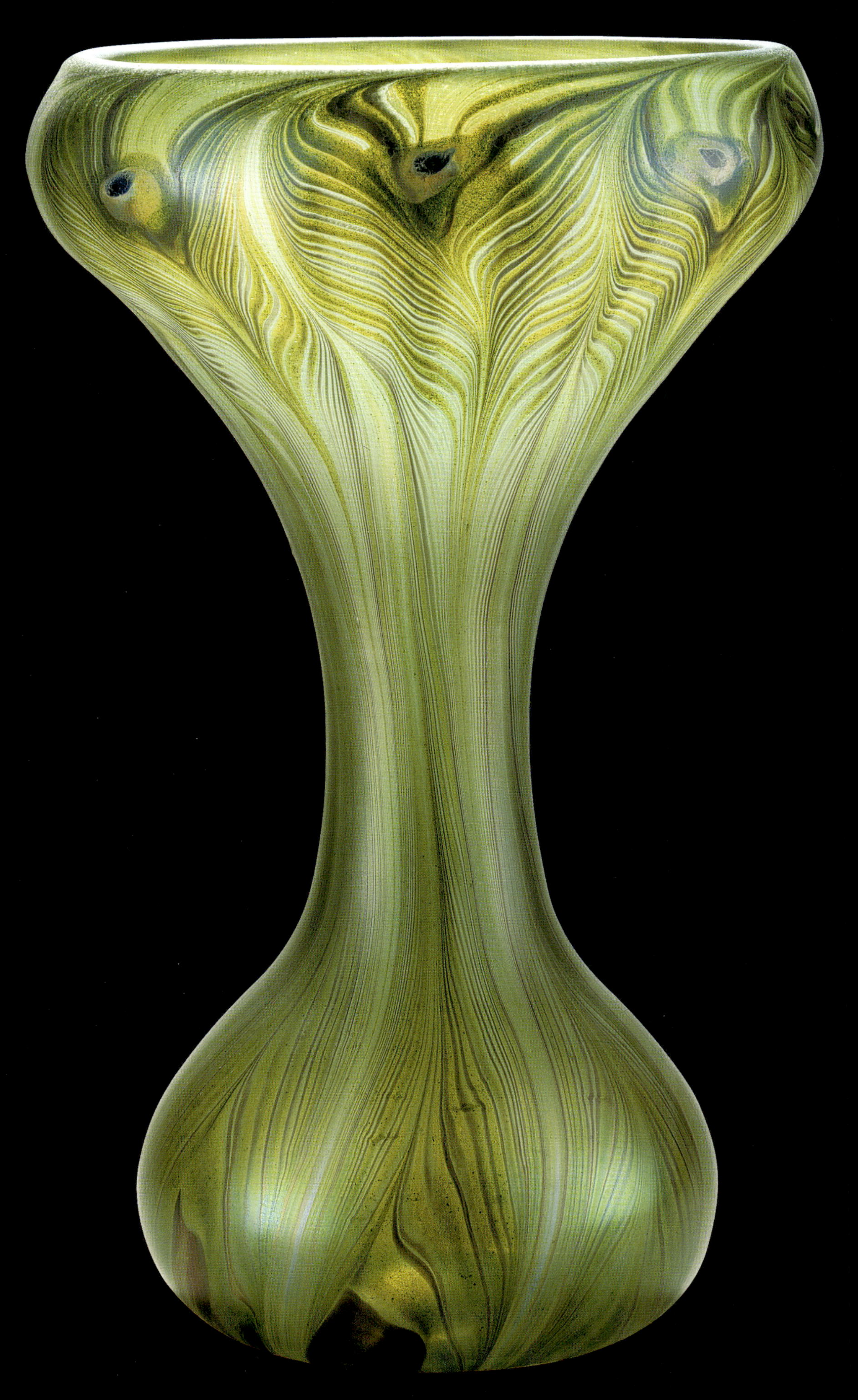

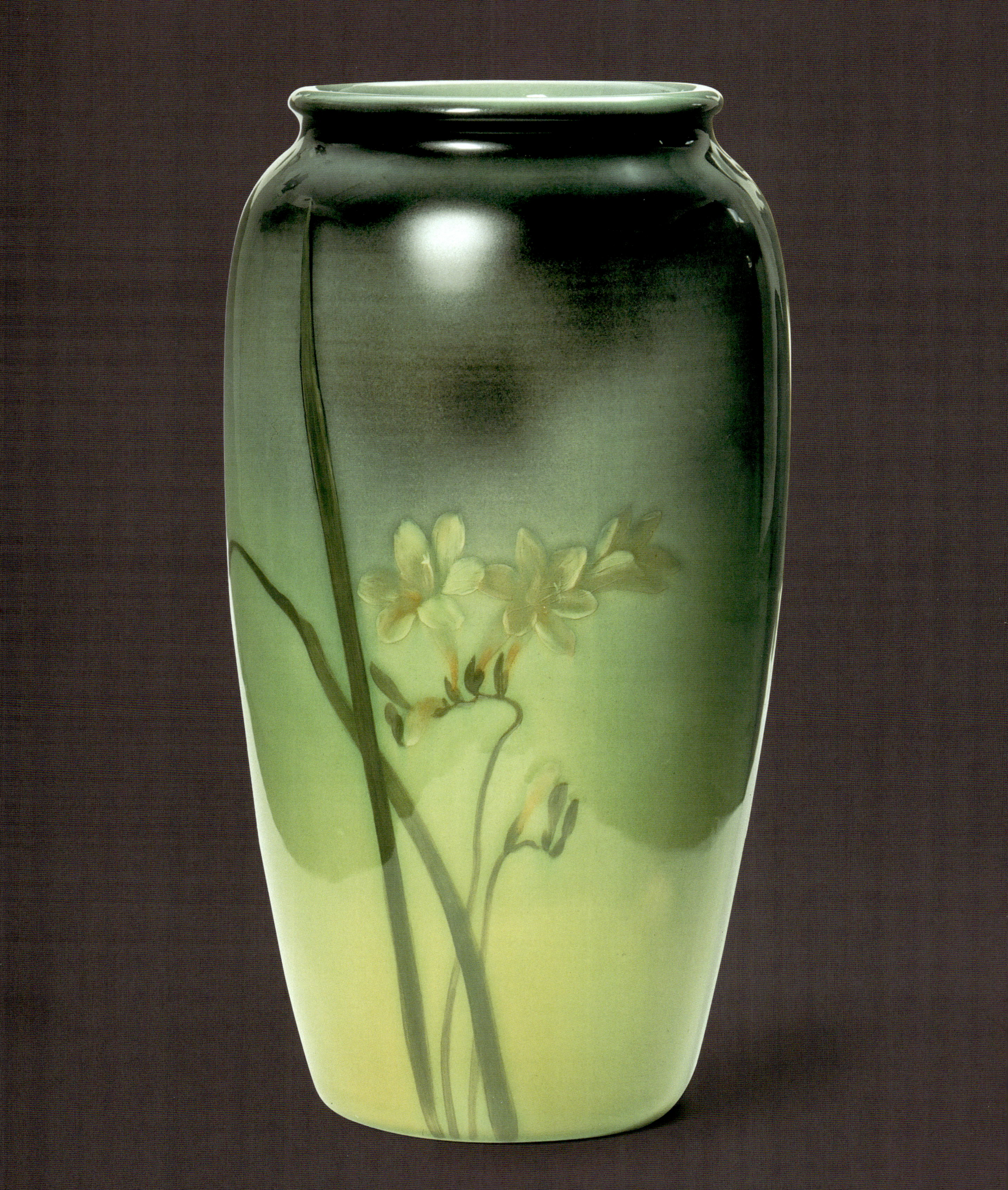

Bing reserved much of his space in the applied arts section for Louis Comfort Tiffany, with whom he seems to have spent considerable time discussing glassmaking and interior decoration.[42] Bing's visits to Tiffany's manufactory brought him into close contact with the most prominent man championing design reform in America, and this undoubtedly reinforced his desire to organise his own workshop for the creation of contemporary applied arts objects.[43]

The views espoused by Bing in *La Culture artistique en Amérique* helped further his agenda for design reform. Far from being neglected in the international press, as has been suggested by other scholars of the period, this controversial pamphlet drew the attention of critics on both sides of the Atlantic. Even the harshest American reviews acknowledged that Bing's support of American architecture and the applied arts was beneficial, while a critic in the *Nation* identified another important idea of Bing's, namely that 'a new people should produce something entirely new.'[44] Siegfried Bing, by citing America as a model, challenged French artists to generate fresh ideas that would compete with those witnessed during his trip to the United States. *La Culture artistique* became no less than an artistic manifesto inspiring an entire generation of designers and entrepreneurs.[45]

< 85
Rookwood, 'Freesias' Vase, decorated by Harriet E. Wilcox, 1900
Victoria and Albert Museum, London

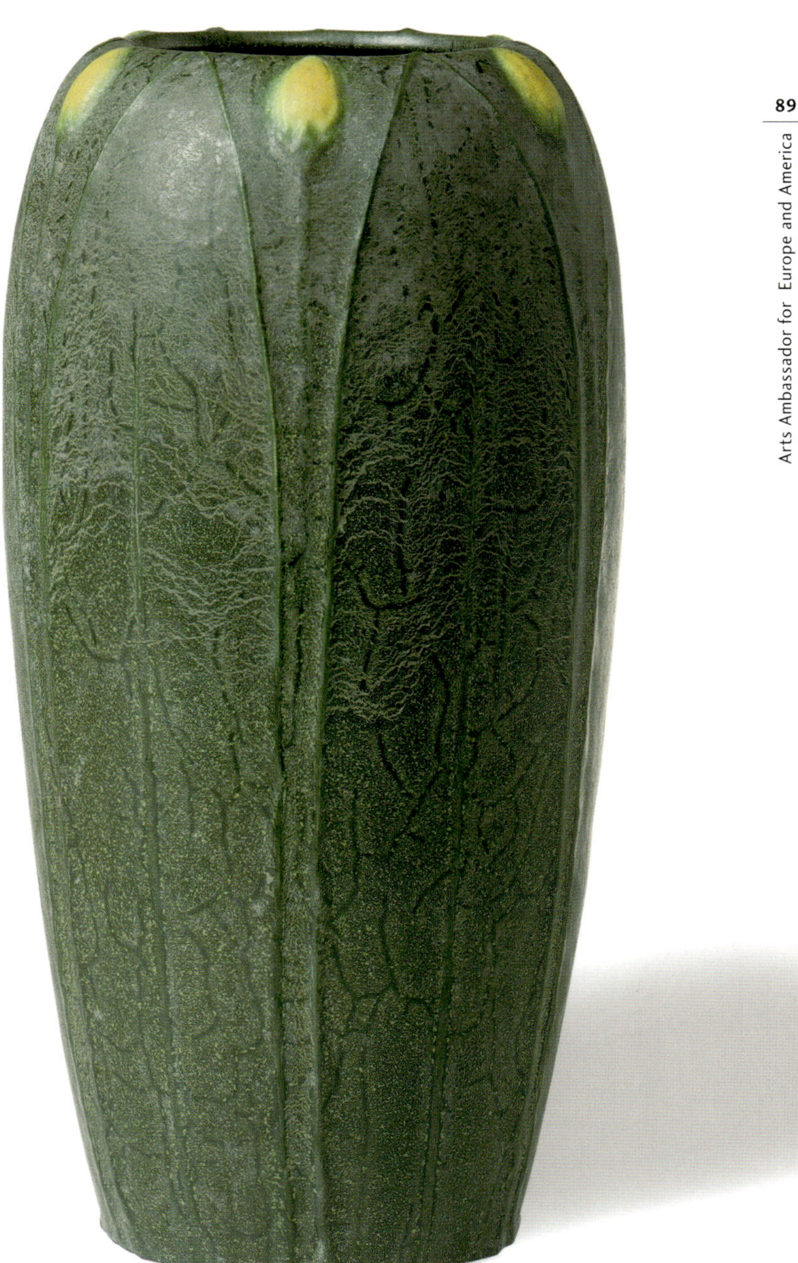

86
Grueby Pottery, Vase, c. 1900
Det Danske Kunstindustrimuseum, Copenhagen

MARKETING TIFFANY'S GLASS IN EUROPE

Following Bing's trip to the United States in 1894 and the subsequent opening of his first Salon de l'Art Nouveau in Paris, Bing maintained close ties with Louis Comfort Tiffany. In his dealings with the leading European museums, Bing emphasised the importance of Tiffany's unique contribution to the field of decorative arts, urging them to purchase Tiffany's works from him or, at the very least, hold exhibitions of the American designer's works in their galleries.[46] Bing's strategy of mentioning prior sales to other prominent collections to encourage prospective buyers to make their own purchases is clear from a letter he wrote in August 1897 to Arthur von Scala, the Director of the Österreischisches Museum für angewandte Kunst (Austrian Museum for Applied Arts) in Vienna: 'I suppose that you have heard of the artistic glass works produced by Tiffany in New York, which have surprised all those who have seen them in America or in my gallery (after the artist got into the habit of sending me specimens once in a while). I have sold examples to several French museums such as the Luxembourg, Sèvres, the Musée des Arts décoratifs in Paris, and Limoges, Arts et Métiers, Galliera, as well as to

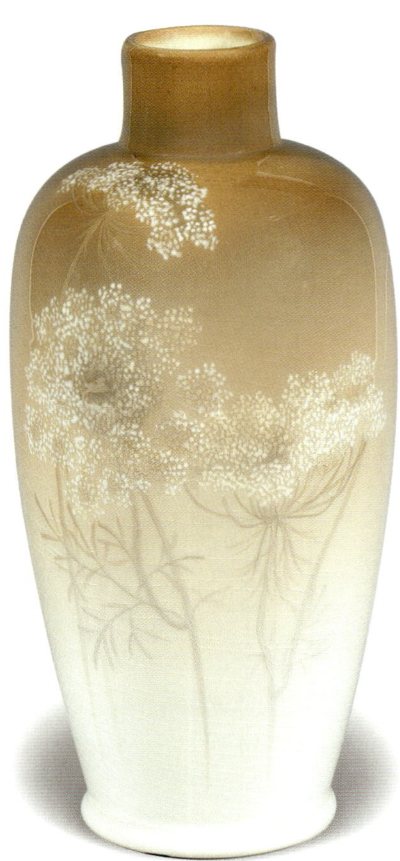

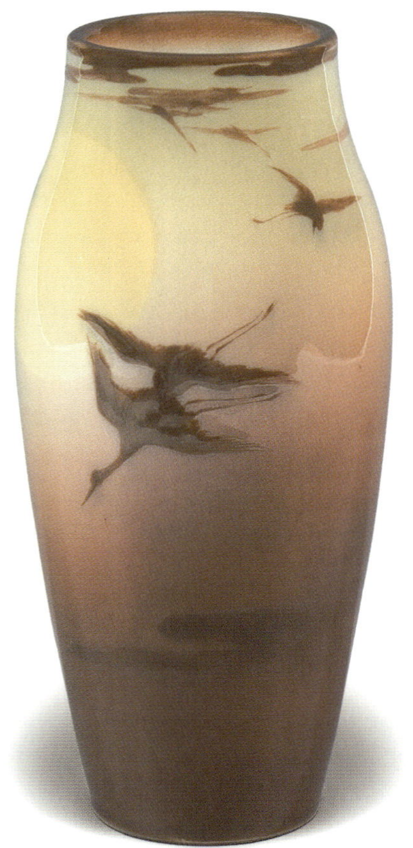

87
Rookwood, Vase, decorated by Amalia B. Sprague, 1899
Kunstgewerbemuseum, Berlin

88
Rookwood, Vase, decorated by Harriet E. Wilcox, 1899
Kunstgewerbemuseum, Berlin

> 89
Albert-Louis Dammouse, Vase, c. 1900
Kunstgewerbemuseum, Berlin

museums in Brussels, St Petersburg, among others. Professor Lessing, from Berlin, has purchased some Tiffany pieces for his museum directly in America (during his trip to Chicago); others were sold to the South Kensington Museum.'[47]

Bing's activity on behalf of Louis Comfort Tiffany between the years 1895 and 1897 resulted in his becoming the exclusive distributor of the American designer's works in Europe; it was through Bing, for example, that Tiffany's Favrile glass vases (figs. 78–84, 90, 278, 286) were added studied by artisans and designers as models for their own work. In short, Bing and Tiffany developed a close working relationship motivated by both men's desire to see Tiffany's pieces widely known throughout Europe.

In the summer of 1897, Bing organised an exhibition of Tiffany's latest glass pieces at his gallery on 22, rue de Provence.[48] Tiffany came to Paris along with his objects to attend the opening. Having Tiffany in Paris to discuss various pieces with potential collectors was a major coup for Bing; the show was well received, and Bing sold a number of pieces to collectors and museums. The success of the exhibition prompted Bing to promote the designer's work further by organising subsequent exhibitions in major European cities. In a letter to Scala, Bing outlined this expanded strategy: 'This summer, M. Tiffany came to Paris with a most magnificent collection. I exhibited it in my gallery where it had an enormous success because of the extraordinary technical achievements, never seen before, and also because of the purity of taste visible in the pieces. Since the exhibition has ended, and since I have received a supplementary shipment to replace the pieces that were sold, I think that, with the blessing of Tiffany, it would be good to show the exhibition in the principal European cities: Vienna, London, Berlin, St Petersburg. However, since the [summer] season is not favourable for touring an exhibition I have accepted the invitation of the Nordböhmischen Museum in Reichenberg to show the exhibition in their galleries.'[49]

With this goal of disseminating Tiffany's pieces more widely, Bing sent the exhibition to Reichenberg (now Liberec in the Czech Republic), where some examples were secured for the local museum.[50] His letters to Scala seem to have been effective, since in the autumn of 1897, the show arrived in Vienna at the Applied Arts Museum. In order to encourage museums to take the show, Bing offered to prepay the cost of shipping the objects, with the individual museum paying only transportation to the next venue. Always the astute businessman, Bing also proposed that the host museum receive a commission on each sale made while the show was at its location, while careful to recognise that some directors might be opposed to using their galleries as salesrooms.

The Favrile glass exhibition in Vienna coincided with an increased interest in Tiffany throughout Austria,

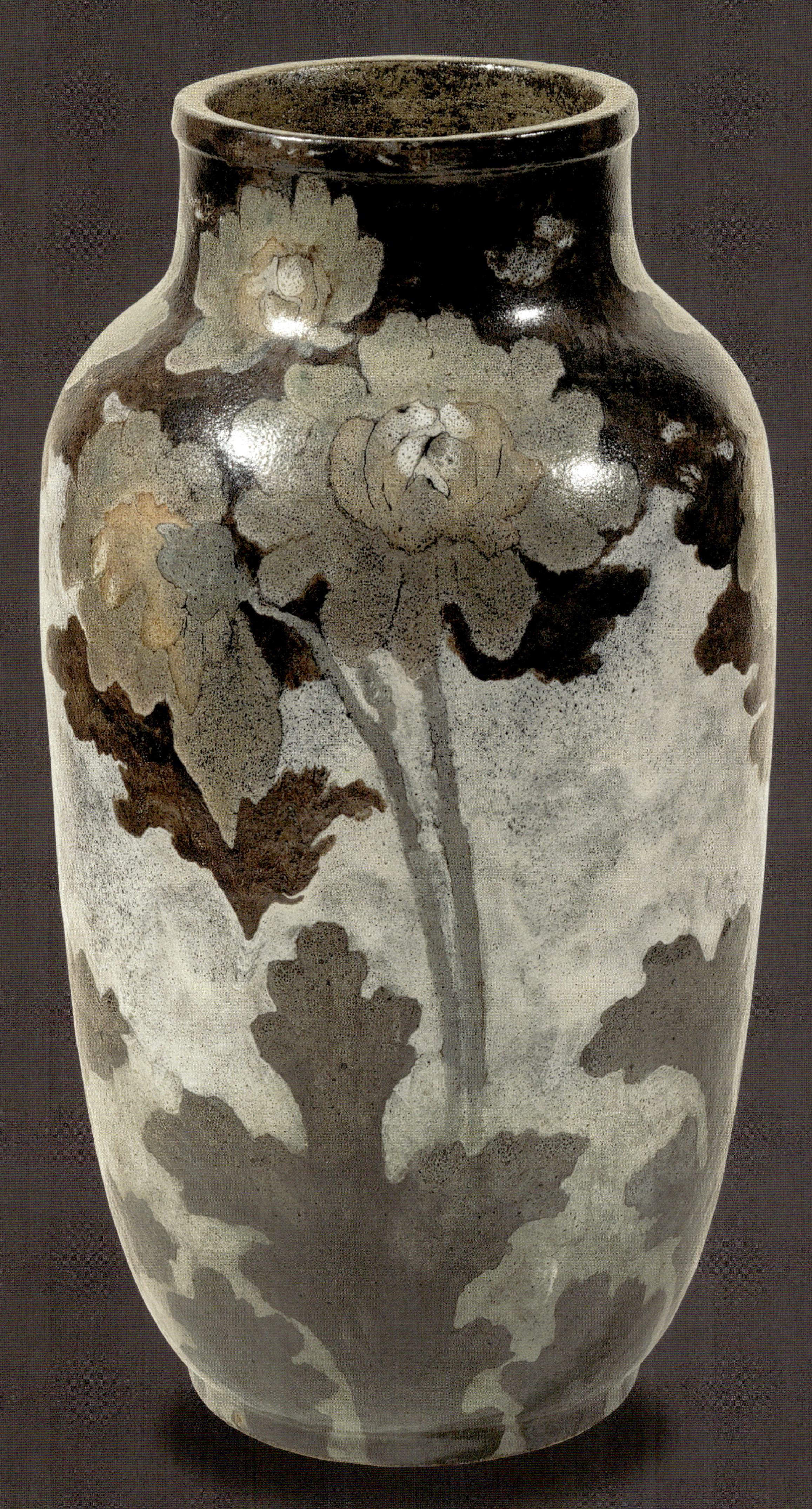

ensuring its success with the public. While the objects were still installed in the galleries of the Vienna museum, Bing continued his promotional campaign with messianic zeal, writing to the Director of the Országos Magyar Iparmüvészeti Muzeum (Hungarian Applied Arts Museum) in Budapest in October 1897: 'I had thought that before continuing the tour to Berlin, St Petersburg, etc. [...] you would be glad to profit from the presence of these pieces in Austria, and show them to the Hungarian public. If this is so, please advise me as soon as possible, so that I can organise a shipment to your museum. The collection is composed of about seventy pieces.'[51] The Hungarian director, Jenö Radisics, agreed to take the show at the end of 1897, but not before the Viennese director, Scala, had secured numerous pieces for the permanent collection of his museum (figs. 78, 81, 82, 90, 286). Bing, with the authorisation of Tiffany, offered him a 15% discount for the purchase of a substantial number of objects.[52]

In preparation for the show in Budapest and elsewhere, Bing, with the assistance of the young art critic Julius Meier-Graefe, placed articles and advertisements in widely read art periodicals. These emphasised Tiffany's originality and the American designer's links with Bing, who also published his own article on Tiffany in *Kunst und Kunsthandwerk*, illustrated with pieces from the touring show.[53] In 1898 and later in 1899, Meier-Graefe wrote two more articles on Tiffany, for *L'Art Décoratif* and *Dekorative Kunst*, further promoting Tiffany's reputation in Europe. The author wrote that Tiffany's vases were 'above reproach and beyond compare', exceedingly high praise for an American's work.[54]

The Tiffany show was scheduled to arrive in Budapest in May 1898. Following the example of his Viennese colleague, the Hungarian director had asked Bing for a special price on pieces he wished to buy for the permanent collection.[55] There was a glitch, however, regarding some of the best examples that had been in the Vienna show. Tiffany had requested that his favourite Favrile glass pieces be returned to Paris so that they could be included in the annual Salon of the Société Nationale des Beaux-Arts in April.[56] To assuage Radisics, Bing promised that the missing objects would be substituted with the best new works from his own Paris stock (supplied recently by Tiffany).[57] Throughout the early spring, Bing negotiated with Tiffany in New York and the Viennese director to ensure that high-quality pieces went to Hungary.[58] When the show opened in Budapest in May and Radisics balked at the prices of the vases, Bing explained that these pieces were original creations that had been

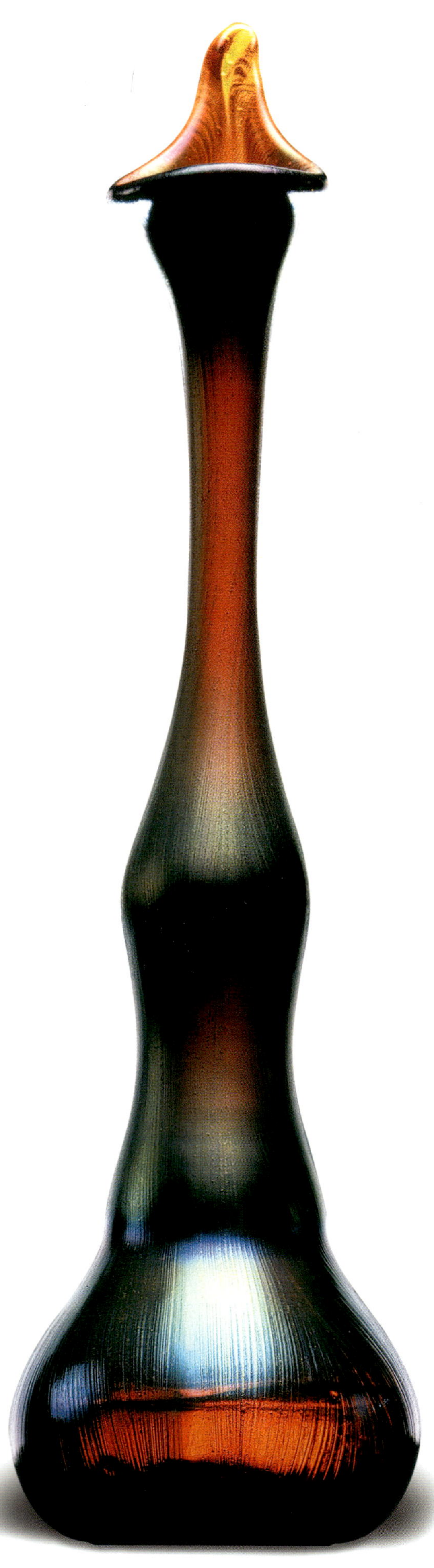

90
Louis Comfort Tiffany, Vase , c. 1896
Österreichisches Museum für angewandte Kunst, Vienna

achieved after considerable research and could not be easily duplicated, if at all.[59] His argument appeared to satisfy the director, for Bing sold twelve Tiffany pieces to Budapest from this travelling show, and for a substantial sum.[60]

In 1899, not content with spreading the word about Tiffany's glass across the European continent, Bing sent examples of the firm's creations across the Channel to Great Britain, to join other works in a group show at the Grafton Galleries in London. London was then perceived as somewhat antagonistic toward 'new art' ideas, whether from the continent or the United States.

For all of his efforts, Tiffany rewarded Bing with the title of 'exclusive representative' of his firm. The arrangement benefited both parties: Tiffany became well known in Europe and Bing became his primary dealer. This relationship was articulated in advertisements that Bing placed in magazines such as *Dekorative Kunst* in 1898. Leading up to the Paris World's Fair of 1900, Bing's promotional campaign made both their names synonymous with originality. At his pavilion at the Fair and afterward at his shop at 22, rue de Provence, Bing continued marketing Tiffany pieces throughout Europe. Buyers could be as far away as Trondheim, Norway, where Bing sold a beautiful white lamp (fig. 298).[61] Other examples were purchased in 1900 by the Museum für Kunst und Gewerbe in Hamburg, including three Tiffany vases; these were added to the already impressive collection of applied arts that had been built by the director and Bing's old friend and colleague, Justus Brinckmann.

ART POTTERY: ROOKWOOD AND GRUEBY

While Bing considered Louis Comfort Tiffany's glasswork the primary example of the 'new art' within the applied arts movement in America, he also kept up with other developments in other media. Well before his trip to the United States in 1894, he had been interested in ceramics, having been a ceramic manufacturer early in his career, and he was therefore very receptive to the American art pottery movement. Two firms especially caught his attention: the Rookwood Pottery Company in Cincinnati and the Grueby Faience Company in Boston.[62] By the time of the 1900 World's Fair, in which both firms were well represented, Bing had become their principal agent on the European continent. After the fair, Bing's promotion of these ceramics was aided by the fact that Rookwood had earned the grand prize for ceramic production and Grueby a gold medal, thus increasing their international stature.[63] Moreover, designers who worked for these companies also received individual recognition at the fair that year. Albert R. Valentien of Rookwood and William H. Grueby of Grueby were designated gold medal winners,[64] while Kataro Shirayamadani, the primary designer at Rookwood, was given space to exhibit his drawings for ceramic vases. The preparatory drawings showed potential buyers specific designs that could be manufactured upon request.[65]

Sometime prior to the opening of the 1900 World's Fair, the Rookwood Pottery Company made an arrangement with Bing to act as its 'general European agent' for a period of three years.[66] The terms were similar to those between Bing and Tiffany; Bing was to receive a commission of 10% on pieces that were sold during the Fair, and 25% on other sales, including those sold at his shop on 22, rue de Provence at the time of the Fair and afterwards. Even though Rookwood expenses were high, as they had to cover the installation at the Fair and compensation for salesmen, these were more than offset by profits made from the retail sales, less Bing's commission.[67] The gold medal Rookwood received in 1900 increased the firm's reputation in the United States and in Europe. Through its contract with Bing, the company was assured of major sales to the new European applied arts museums that were then building their collections. As pieces entered museums, Rookwood made the most of this: every pamphlet advertising the firm after 1900 listed the foreign museums that owned examples of its wares. It was also no small accomplishment for Bing to have negotiated these acquisitions.

Among the German museums that purchased Rookwood pieces from Bing during the course of the 1900 Fair was the Kunstgewerbemuseum in Berlin. In July, five Rookwood vases entered that collection (figs. 87, 88), including one by Harriet E. Wilcox, purchased for the considerable price of 276 marks. Bing also sold examples to the Museum für Kunst und Gewerbe in Hamburg, including an extremely large vase designed by Kataro Shirayamadani and a vase by Albert R. Valentien.[68] These joined the Tiffany glasswork as well as the many other decorative objects bought by Justus Brinckmann from Bing when the dealer handled Asian art exclusively. Another group of Rookwood pieces were acquired by the Gewerbemuseum in Nuremberg, including, again, vases decorated by Shirayamadani and Valentien. The Shirayamadani piece, chrysanthemums against a dark green background, is particularly impressive (fig. 91).

Eager to promote Rookwood pottery throughout Europe, Bing saw to it that two pieces were added to the

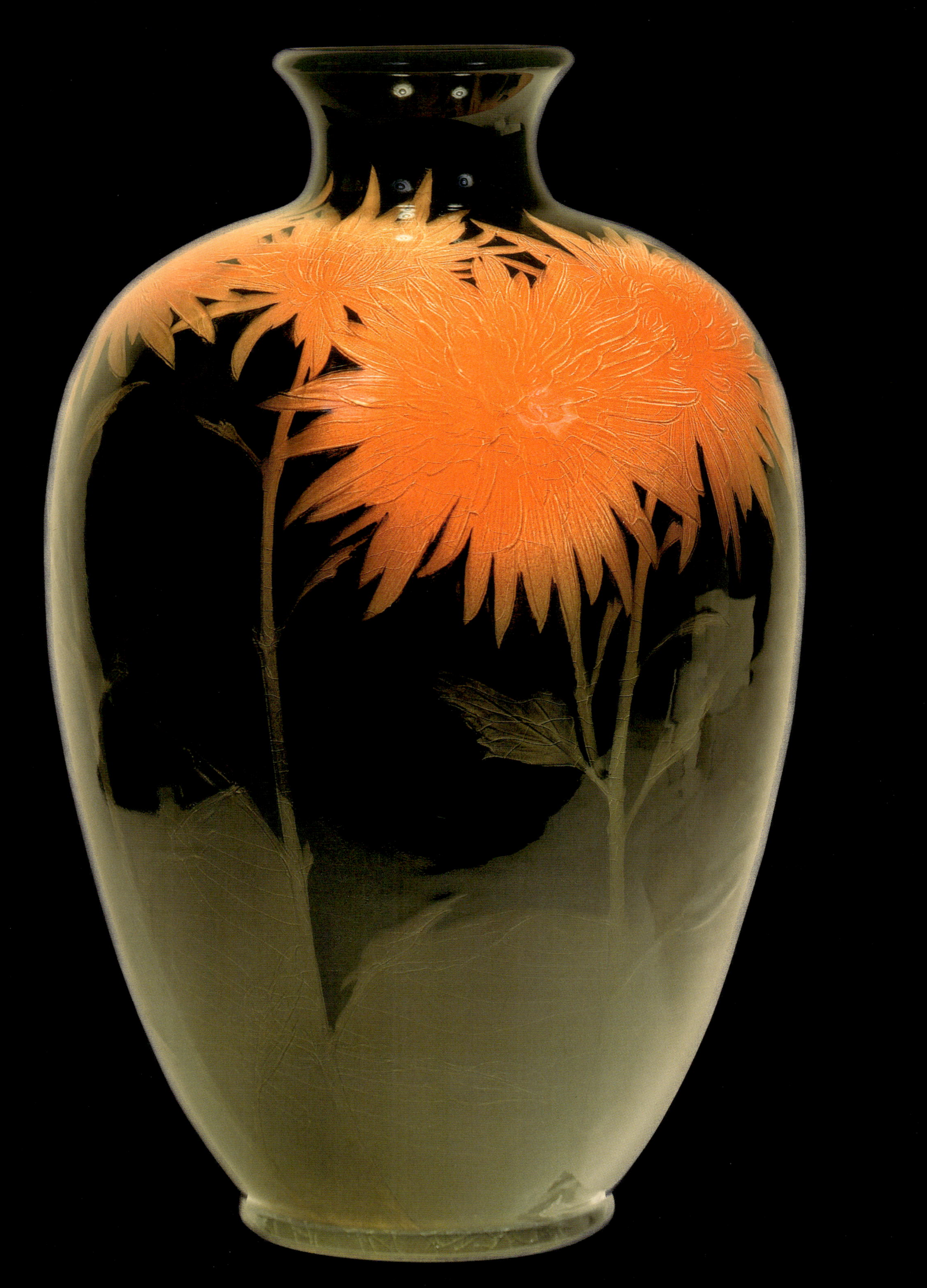

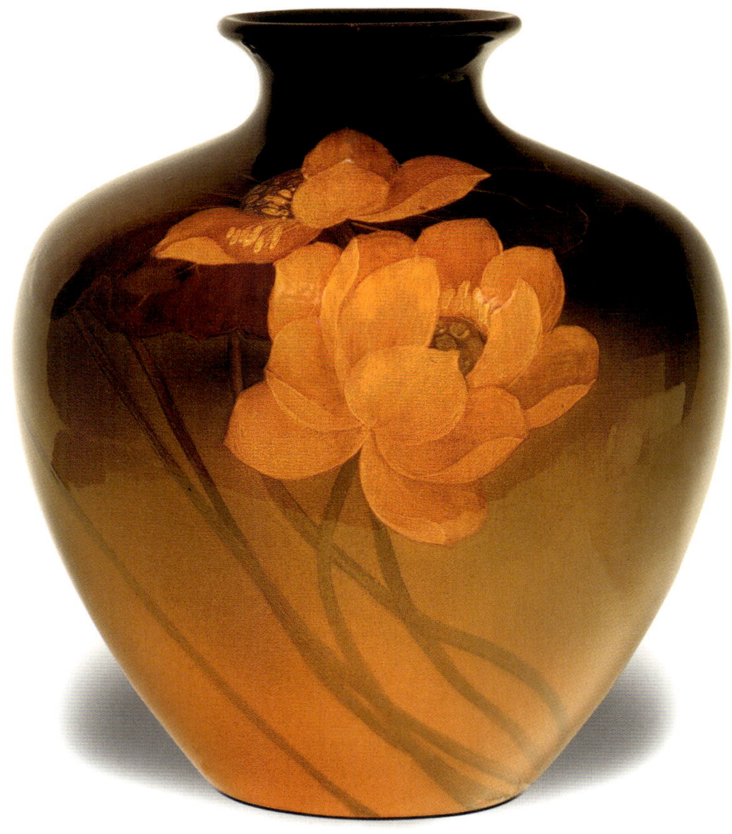

< 91
Rookwood, Vase, decorated by Kataro Shirayamadani, 1897
Germanisches Nationalmuseum, Nürnberg

92
Rookwood, Vase, decorated by Anna Maria Valentien, 1899
Germanisches Nationalmuseum, Nürnberg

Uměleckoprůmyslové Museum (Museum of Decorative Arts) in Prague.[69] To the Museum for Applied Arts in Vienna Bing sold a series of ceramic vases, two of which had been exhibited at the World's Fair, as is confirmed by exhibition stickers that are still on their bases. Further documentation reveals that, probably to stimulate sales, Bing granted the same 15% reduction that he had given to purchasers of Tiffany pieces. The substantial prices for the Rookwood objects ranged from 100 to 250 francs.[70] As he had done so often before in his search for the best in the applied arts, Bing zeroed in on an American firm at the apex of the design revolution in a particular medium, in order to enhance America's role in the international *art nouveau* movement. Rookwood's subtle colours, similar to those used in interiors in France, combined with an inherent love of nature, demonstrated just how these pieces were attracting European supporters of new art.

The 1900 World's Fair also demonstrated the vigorous reform of French decorative arts under the stimulus of Japanese art as promoted by Bing. This was especially evident in pottery, as exemplified by the highly creative works of Auguste Delaherche and Albert Dammouse (fig. 89). The taste for contemporary French ceramics in America had already been stimulated by the Chicago Exposition of 1893, and French pottery had a particularly strong influence on the Grueby Faience Company,[71] which was deeply involved in the Arts and Crafts movement in Boston.[72] Bing's activities in Paris – including the opening of his first Salon de l'Art Nouveau – would have been known to producers and collectors of decorative arts in the area, since Bing advertised in the Boston journal *Modern Art* as early as January 1897. The publication of his announcement calling for examples of 'new art' was greeted with considerable enthusiasm and most likely encouraged the designers at Grueby to contact the Parisian entrepreneur.[73]

Bing began promoting Grueby about three months before the opening of his pavilion at the 1900 World's Fair.[74] Exactly when Bing learned of Grueby pottery is unknown, but, like Tiffany and Rookwood, the company was well respected in the field of American design. The pottery firm had exhibited works in Boston in 1897 in a major show, pieces had been reproduced in the journal *International Studio* in 1899, and it is even possible that Bing had seen Grueby pottery during his 1894 trip to Boston.[75] Bing's friend Pietro Krohn, Director of the Danske Kunstindustrimuseum (Danish Decorative Arts Museum) in Copenhagen, selected a large Grueby vase from Bing's shop on 21 April 1900 (fig. 86).[76] Because Bing sold Grueby vases both in his gallery and in his 1900 pavilion, he was recognised as the principal dealer for Grueby in Europe. In December 1900, the South Kensington Museum acquired two Grueby vases with a matte glaze from Bing's pavilion. One of these, described as 'melon-shaped', elicited a comparison with the vases

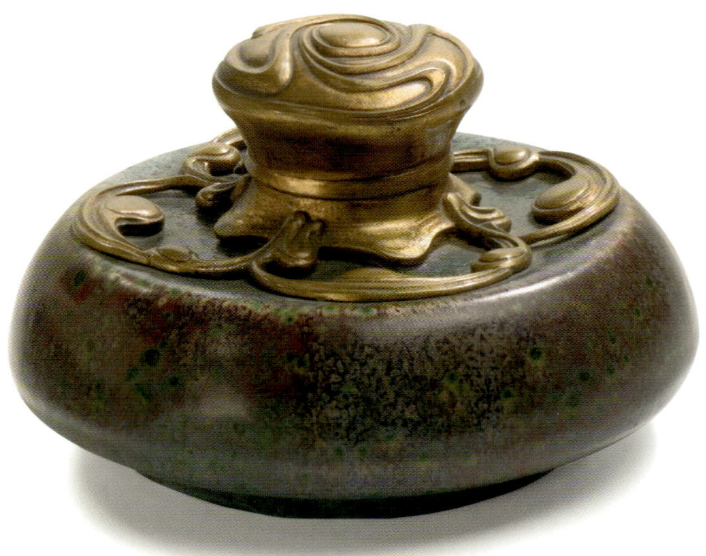

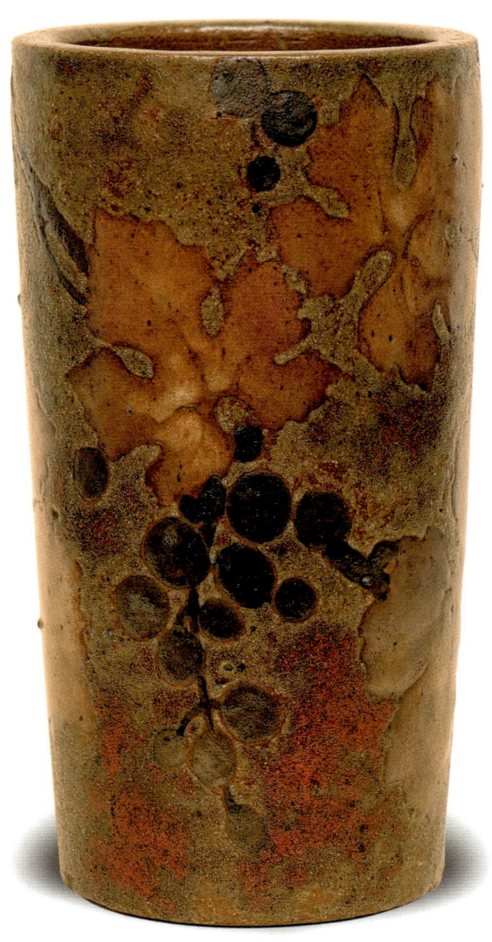

of Auguste Delaherche, thus articulating the truly international nature of design reform in the decorative arts at the turn of the century.

Bing's sponsorship led to Grueby pieces being acquired by the collections of European museums such as Prague, Berlin, Leipzig and Vienna.[77] When in the same year Bing was appointed president of the 'foreign committee' for a ceramics and glass exhibition in St Petersburg, several Grueby pieces were included, and the firm was awarded a gold medal.[78] Critics then regarded Grueby as a firm that produced simple designs, with glazes of subdued, rich colours, unique in the evolution of American art pottery. A series of original pieces reproduced in 1902 in the American journal *Brush and Pencil* show that Grueby designs had become somewhat more elaborate, incorporating a combination of flower and leaf motifs.

93
Adrien Dalpayrat, Inkwell, with mount by Edward Colonna, 1898–1903
Design Museum, Ghent

94
Albert-Louis Dammouse, Vase with vine decoration, 1897
Kaiser Wilhelm Museum, Krefeld

> 95
Edward Colonna, Canton Service in green, c. 1900
Musée national Adrien Dubouché, Limoges

GUSTAV STICKLEY AND THE ARTS AND CRAFTS MOVEMENT

Bing's prominence as a supporter of advanced American design brought him to the attention of other American craftsmen. Around this time, Gustav Stickley, a champion of American Arts and Crafts design in New York City, became the editor of the influential *Craftsman* magazine, and he visited France and England in 1898.[79] While contact with Bing can only be assumed from circumstantial evidence, it is certain that Stickley developed a more than casual interest in *art nouveau*.

In the end, Stickley was more attuned to English Arts and Crafts and the work of Charles Rennie Mackintosh in his designs for furniture, but he was much taken by certain examples of French *art nouveau*. When he decided to open his Craftsman restaurants in Syracuse, New York, and New York City, starting in 1899, he knew the Canton porcelain service designed for Bing by Edward Colonna in 1899–1900 (fig. 95). The Canton service became a model of advanced, abstract design in porcelain. Examples of the service still remain in the Stickley family. The two men may well have corresponded when Bing published his article 'L'Art Nouveau' in the October 1903 issue of *The Craftsman*. Among the numerous illustrations included in this survey article was a plate for the, by then, extremely famous table service, used both in the United States and in France.[80]

Stickley and Bing may also have engaged in a dialogue around the nature of 'new design' at the time of the Arts and Crafts exhibition held in Syracuse and Rochester, New York, in March and April 1903. This wide-ranging

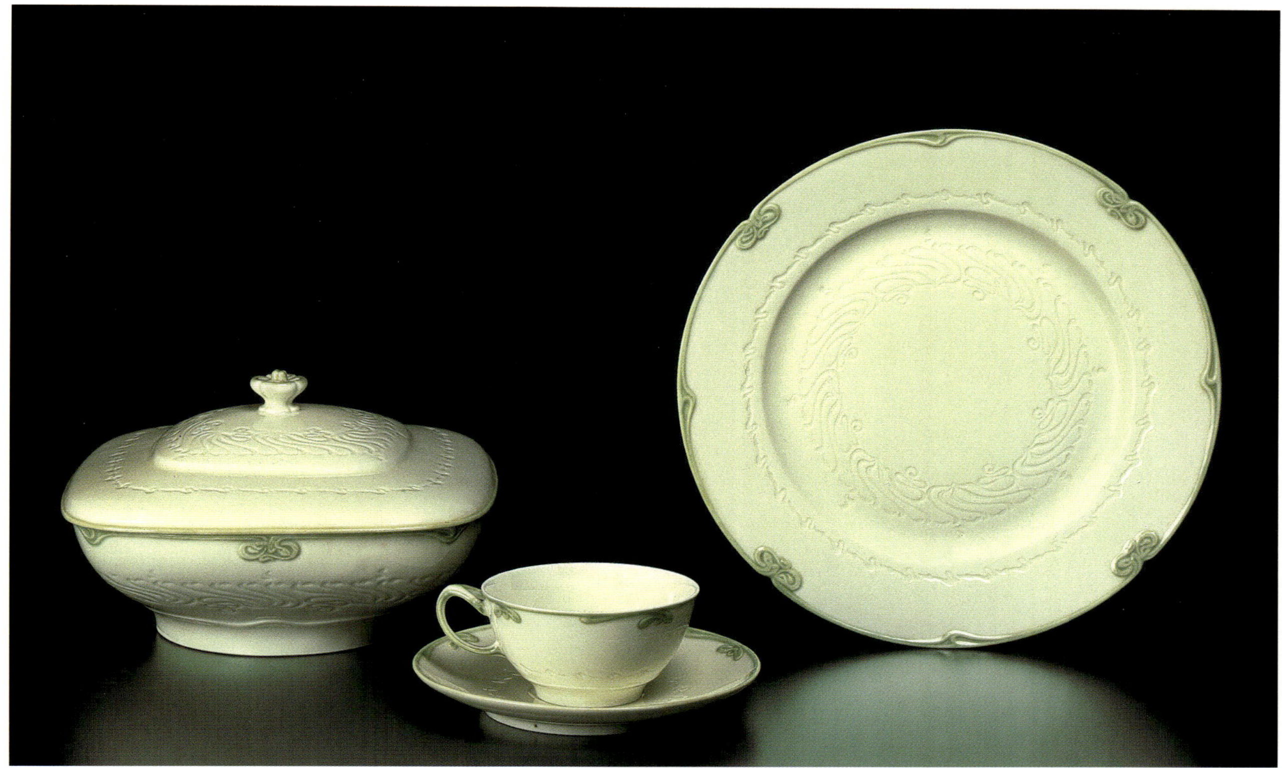

exhibition emphasised various aspects of American Arts and Crafts design. American examples were compared with pieces produced in England (by C.F.A. Voysey) and, significantly, with a group of porcelains, metalwork pieces, and electric lamps that came from Siegfried Bing in Paris.[81] This touring exhibition allowed American designers to see for themselves what tastemakers such as Stickley and Bing considered the most avant-garde examples in the applied arts, whether produced in America or Europe.

Acting as a self-appointed ambassador between the decorative art worlds on either side of the Atlantic, Bing not only drew the countries closer together through his business activities, but he also laid the groundwork for the acceptance of American design in Europe. In a reciprocal gesture, some American designers were willing to promote Bing's vision of design in the United States, as a way of increasing the international basis of design reform.

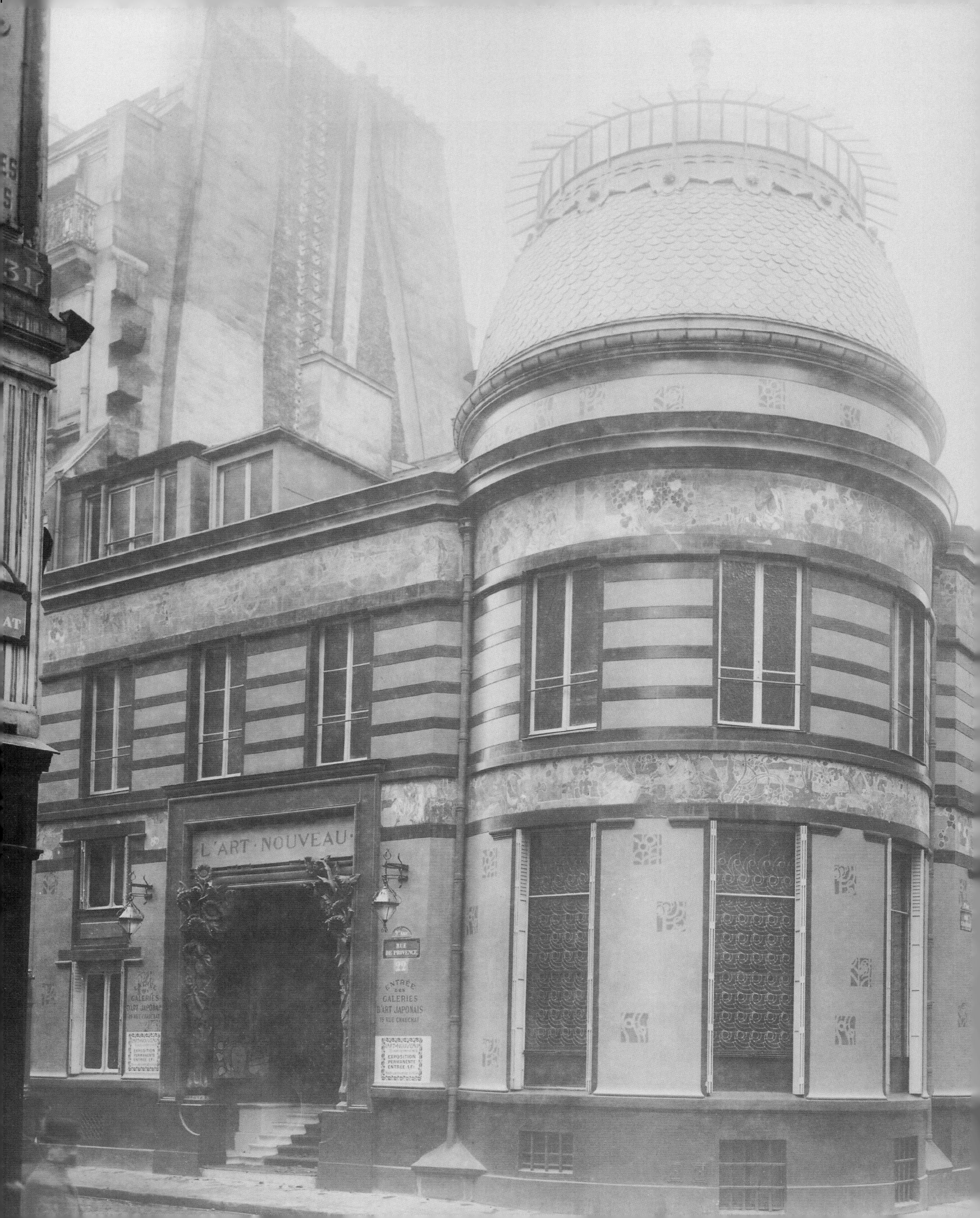
L'ART · NOUVEAU ·
RUE
DE PROVENCE
ENTRÉE
DES
GALERIES
D'ART JAPONAIS
19 RUE CHAUCHAT
EXPOSITION
PERMANENTE

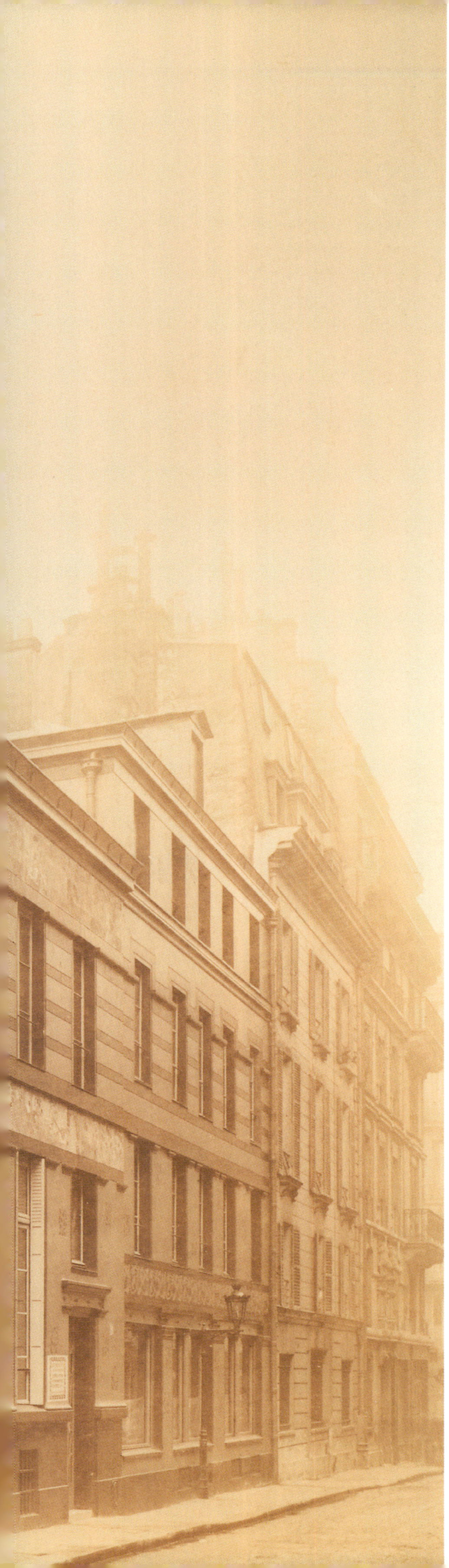

THE OPENING OF LA MAISON DE L'ART NOUVEAU

BING AND BELGIUM

PHILIPPE THIÉBAUT

'M. S. Bing, who was impressed, during a recent trip to Brussels, by the organisation of the Maison d'Art de la Toison d'Or, has recently decided to set up a similar gallery in Paris.' Such was the information conveyed in the spring of 1895 by *L'Art Moderne*,[1] the dynamic mouthpiece, since it was founded in March 1881, of the Belgian artistic and literary avant-garde. A few months later, following the inauguration of Bing's Paris gallery, L'Art Nouveau, in late December 1895, the original Brussels institution was twice mentioned in that same journal: 'An excellent programme, inspired by that of the Maison d'Art. We trust that the efforts of M. Bing and his artistic circle will reach an entirely satisfactory conclusion.' That was from the brief report of 5 January 1896;[2] a later and fuller article (19 January), still regarding L'Art Nouveau as a 'pale imitation' of the Maison d'Art, insists on the differences between the two

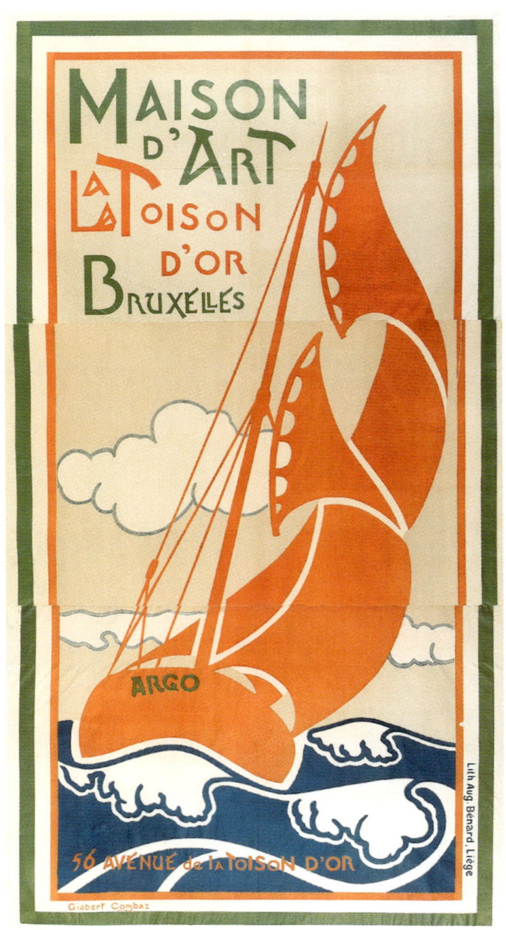

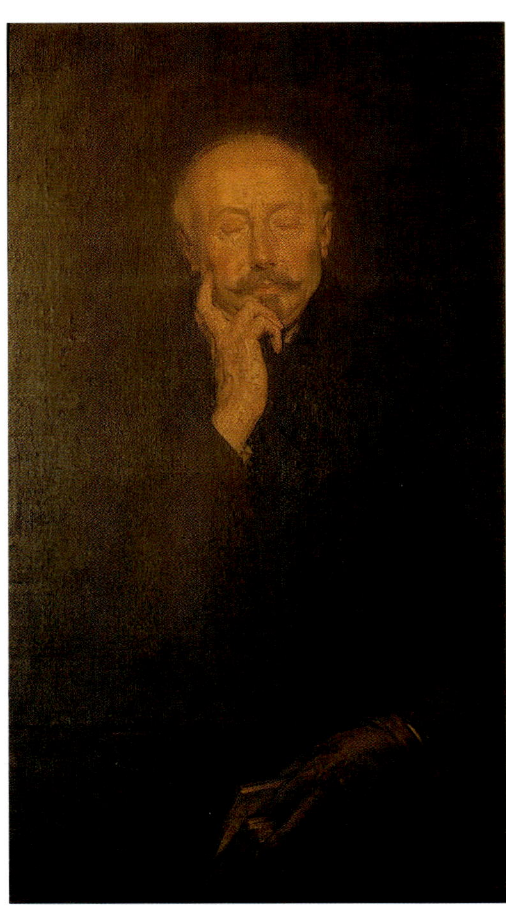

establishments: a certain commercial emphasis in Paris, totally absent in Brussels, and a regrettable lack of lectures, literature and theatrical programming in the former city.[3] The writer implies, though without bitterness, that the inspiration Bing derived from certain features of the Maison d'Art was applied both hastily and superficially and failed to recapture the spirit of the original. In fact, while Bing's efforts had the goodwill of Belgian art circles, it is by no means certain whether the enlightened minds who had presided over the creation of the original Maison d'Art in Brussels perceived L'Art Nouveau as a decisive step towards the realisation of their dream of seeing all the art galleries of Europe eventually 'united in a single federation, or, at least linked by a programme of information and exchanges'.[4] The reaction of Hippolyte Fierens-Gevaert, a literary figure particularly attuned to the work of the Belgian avant-garde – he was, for instance, a member and patron establishment was not the Maison d'Art but the exhibitions staged by La Libre Esthétique: 'The artists upon whom M. Bing relies have long been known in Brussels, and his gallery, so unjustly decried by some and vaunted so incontinently by others, is just a copy, somewhat larger and perhaps more complete, of the Libre Esthétique exhibitions, the first, to our knowledge, to permit an overall evaluation of the tendencies and productions of contemporary art.'[5]

<< 96
Exterior view of Bing's L'Art Nouveau, 1895
Fonds Louis Bonnier, Institut français d'architecture, Paris

97
Gisbert Combaz, Poster for the Maison d'Art, 1895
Bibliothèque royale de Belgique, Brussels

98
Auguste Levêque, *Portrait of Edmond Picard*, 1900
Koninklijk Museum voor Schone Kunsten, Antwerp

> 99
Façade at 19, rue Chauchat, 1895
Fonds Louis Bonnier, Institut français d'architecture, Paris

THE MAISON D'ART IN BRUSSELS

To appreciate the proper significance of these judgements – which it would certainly be wrong to ascribe to mere nationalism or sentiments of superiority[6] – we need to look further at the Brussels gallery, which has been the subject of an excellent study by Jane Block.[7] Although its origins were in the same avant-garde circle that had employed *L'Art Moderne* as a vehicle for their creed, the Maison d'Art was a recent creation. It was a subsidiary of a limited company (L'Art) formed on 7 March 1894 by the lawyer Edmond Picard (fig. 98), an ardent propagandist of 'social' art, with the support of his colleague Octave Maus – one of the founders of *L'Art Moderne* – and by personalities as eminent as the writer Emile Verhaeren and the Burgomaster of Brussels Charles Buls.

Their objective was twofold: to set up a permanent display for works that would normally be accessible only during temporary Salons and exhibitions, and to promote the development of art-related enterprises.

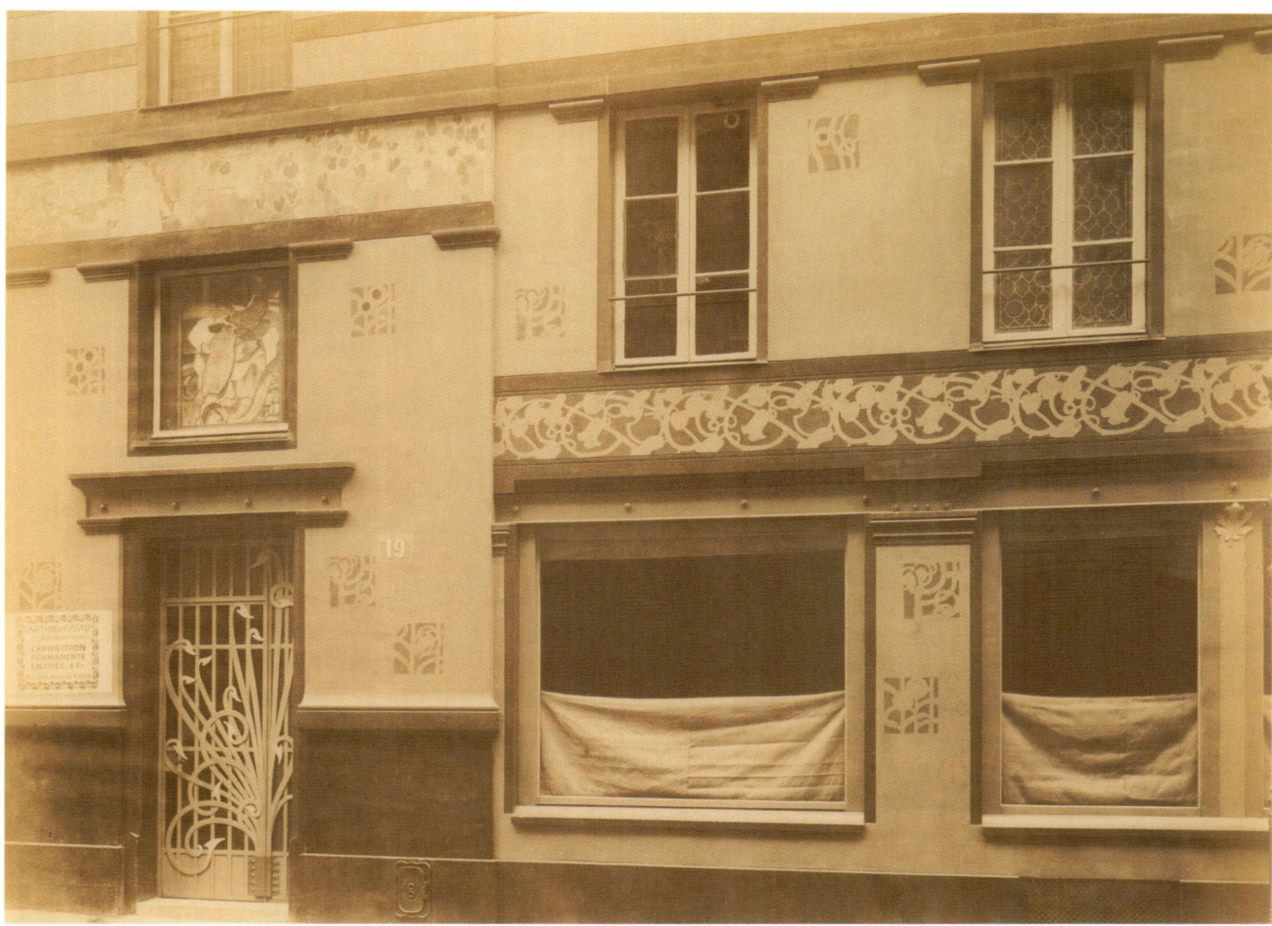

Inaugurated in June 1894 at 6, rue Montagne aux Herbes potagères, the Maison d'Art transferred in December of the same year to 56, avenue de la Toison d'Or, a large private house owned by Picard, which he had had modified at his own expense by the architect Ernest Van Humbeeck to accommodate the gallery.[8] In actual fact – and this was the novelty – the gallery, management of which was entrusted to Georges Picard, elder son of the founder, was far more than a gallery.

Fine and decorative art objects were arranged in actual settings appropriate to a deliberately 'modern' interior. 'Everything in the proper environment, clearly designed for everyday use, set out in the subdued light typical of an apartment and in its familiar place, no longer confined to the wretched jumble of a shop in unfortunate proximity to other merchandise, where its effect would be ruined – but still just as attractive to the customers, arousing their aesthetic inclinations, awakening an urge to reproduce these arrangements with all their connotations of gracious living, of emotions as varied as the unpredictabilities of social activity, both relaxing and stimulating, like the smoke of a cigarette. [...] The ludicrous notion of an *objet d'art*, always isolated from the environment it is designed to enhance, heaped up with other articles in those storehouses we call public museums, which resemble nothing so much as markets displaying their wares, will gradually disappear from our culture, and we will return to the good, healthy attitude of past centuries when everything in artists' work was ornamental and designed to beautify places frequented by Man.'[9] The last thing a gallery was to be was a *shop*. The word 'salon' would be more appropriate, since it was understood that this was a salon with a mission to educate taste and steer it towards decidedly 'modern' products.

In order to make the Maison d'Art the living symbol of the fusion of all the arts, the establishment organised lectures (Camille Lemonnier, Emile Verhaeren, Sâr Péladan...), concerts (César Franck, Gabriel Fauré, Ernest Chausson...) and theatrical performances (Maurice Maeterlinck, Henrik Ibsen, Charles van Lerberghe...). The sincerity and convictions of its promoter instilled in the Maison d'Art a real desire to reform both art and life;[10] it campaigned for a kind of art that would be intimately concerned with life, so that life could become art in its turn.

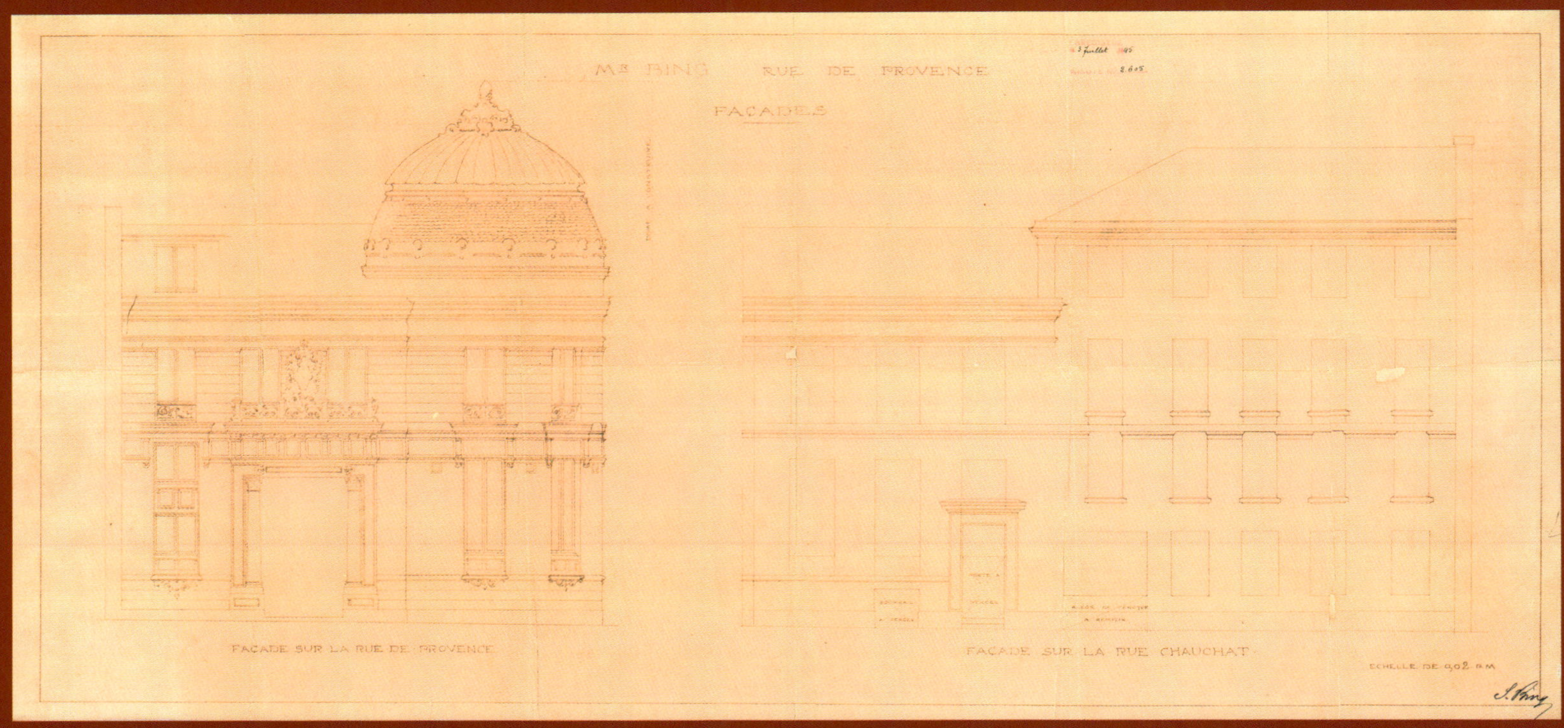
Mr BING RUE DE PROVENCE
FAÇADES
3 Juillet 95
2.605
FAÇADE SUR LA RUE DE PROVENCE
FAÇADE SUR LA RUE CHAUCHAT
ECHELLE DE 0,02 P.M.
S. Bing
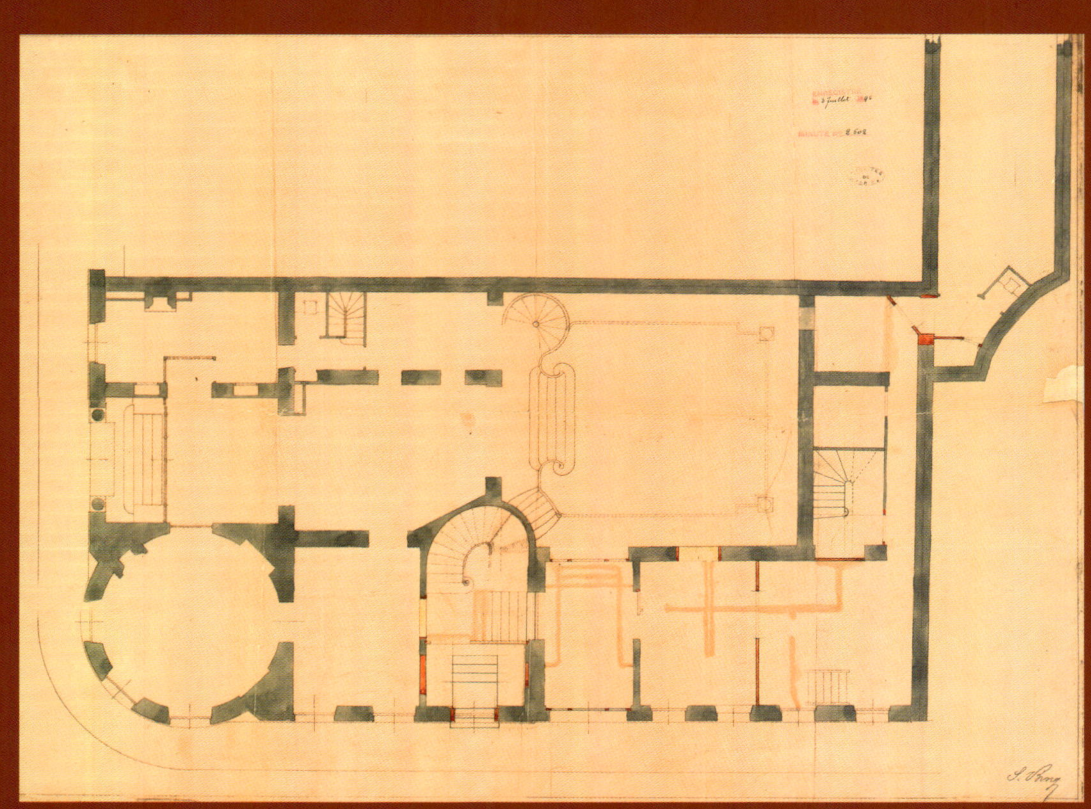
S. Bing

THE CREATION OF A 'MODERN ART' GALLERY

In his memoirs, Van de Velde claims that in May 1895 Bing called on him while on a visit to Brussels in the company of the art critic Julius Meier-Graefe, a distinguished collaborator on the avant-garde review *Pan*, first published that same year in Berlin. Meier-Graefe 'acted as his guide on a journey of discovery that was to open their eyes to the renaissance of artistic activities in England and various countries on the continent. [...] I learned in the course of conversation that, in the morning, he and Bing had spent a long time at the Maison d'Art. [...] Bing became very animated when he heard me describing the place, but took care not to reveal that his enquiries could lead him to create a "Maison d'Art" in Paris.'[11] Van de Velde's insistence that Bing and Meier-Graefe travelled together and visited him in each other's company has been contested convincingly by Catherine Krahmer.[12] What is not in doubt is that Bing made the acquaintance of Van de Velde during his visit to Belgium and visited the Maison d'Art. In all probability, he also met Picard – author of the article recording this visit in *L'Art Moderne* of 2 June 1895. Though the opportunity presented itself several times, notably on the publication in 1902 and 1903 of his articles on L'Art Nouveau,[13] Bing never gave any recognition to the innovative nature of the Maison d'Art. This attitude must have been shocking to those who were aware of the situation. One should place in this context the special issue that the *Revue Encyclopédique* devoted to Belgium in July 1897, in which the art critic Camille Mauclair, a protagonist of symbolism and a combative social reformer, warmly thanked Edmond Picard for his initiative and clearly demonstrated how the Maison d'Art was the precursor of L'Art Nouveau.

However, if Bing failed to mention the Maison d'Art, the reason may be quite simple: in his eyes, the two galleries were different in kind. Picard had acted like an enlightened *grand bourgeois* eager to take advantage of the mood of the times, while Bing acted as a businessman, equally enlightened but dependent on economic realities and wary of losing money. In addition, it is quite possible that his decision to direct the gallery's activities towards the 'modern' decorative arts derived from his realisation that the trade in Far Eastern artefacts was drying up, as the vogue for *japonaiserie* was evidently losing ground towards the end of the century after thirty years of success. Even though Bing clearly chose to break down the barriers between the arts in his proposed new

< 100
Louis Bonnier, Plan of 22, rue de Provence and 19, rue Chauchat, façades, 3 July 1895
Les Archives de Paris

< 101
Louis Bonnier, Plan of 22, rue de Provence and 19, rue Chauchat, central floor, 3 July 1895
Les Archives de Paris

102
Georges Lemmen, Invitation card for the opening of the gallery L'Art Nouveau, 1895
Museum für Kunst und Gewerbe, Hamburg

Mr S. Bing vous prie d'assister à l'inauguration des galeries de l'Art Nouveau qui aura lieu le jeudi 26 décembre 1895 à 8 heures du soir.

Entrée rue de Provence, 22, la porte de la rue Chauchat, 19, étant réservée aux galeries d'Art Japonais.

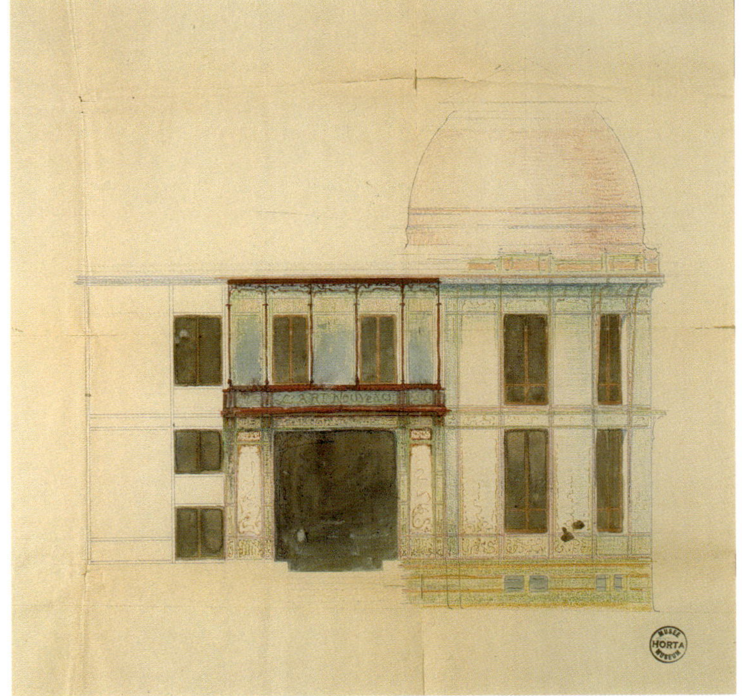

103
Victor Horta, Drawing for the façade of Bing's L'Art Nouveau, 1895
Musée Horta, Brussels

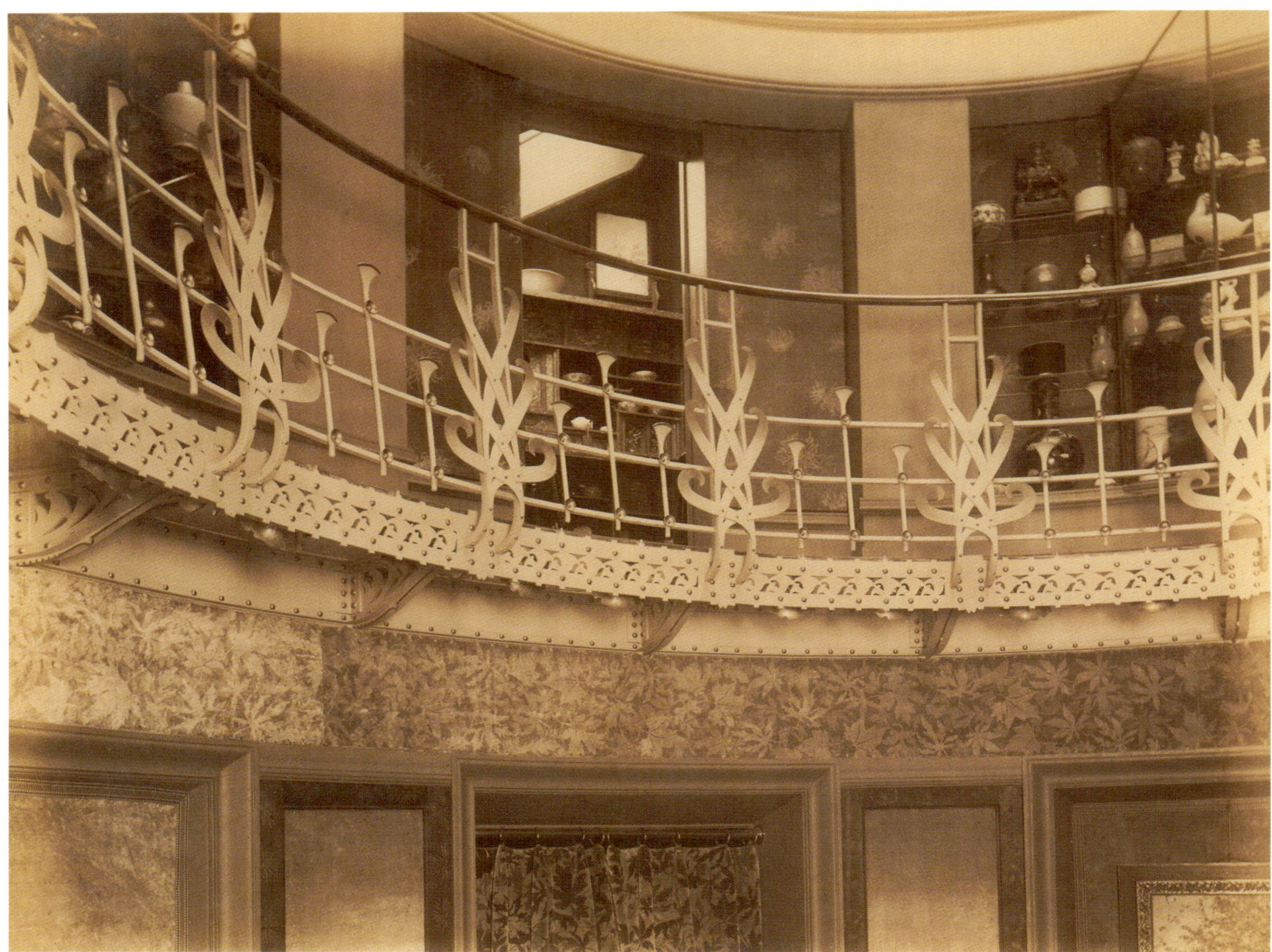

104
Louis Bonnier, Balustrade for the rotunda at L'Art Nouveau
Fonds Louis Bonnier, Institut français d'architecture, Paris

105
Louis Bonnier, Project for the balustrade in Bing's L'Art Nouveau, c. 1895
Fonds Louis Bonnier, Institut français d'architecture, Paris

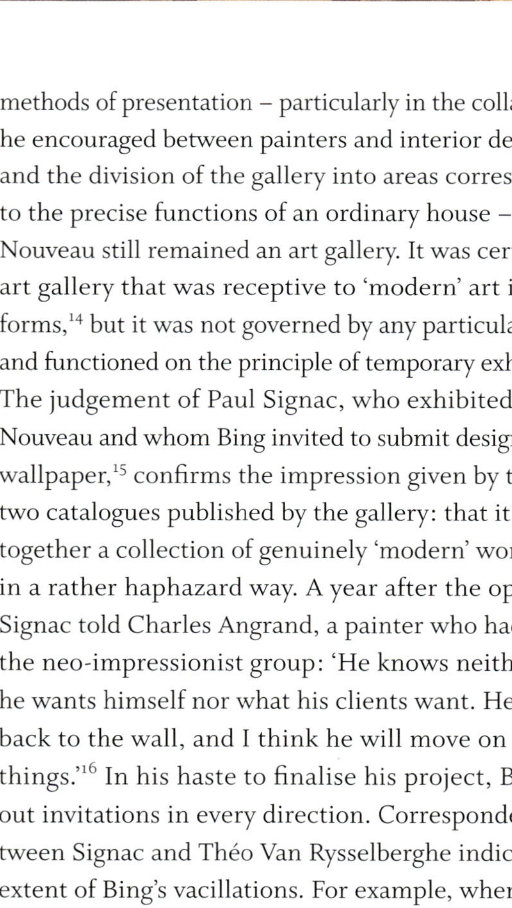

methods of presentation – particularly in the collaboration he encouraged between painters and interior decorators, and the division of the gallery into areas corresponding to the precise functions of an ordinary house – L'Art Nouveau still remained an art gallery. It was certainly an art gallery that was receptive to 'modern' art in all its forms,[14] but it was not governed by any particular agenda and functioned on the principle of temporary exhibitions. The judgement of Paul Signac, who exhibited at L'Art Nouveau and whom Bing invited to submit designs for the wallpaper,[15] confirms the impression given by the first two catalogues published by the gallery: that it brought together a collection of genuinely 'modern' works, but in a rather haphazard way. A year after the opening, Signac told Charles Angrand, a painter who had joined the neo-impressionist group: 'He knows neither what he wants himself nor what his clients want. He has his back to the wall, and I think he will move on to other things.'[16] In his haste to finalise his project, Bing sent out invitations in every direction. Correspondence between Signac and Théo Van Rysselberghe indicates the extent of Bing's vacillations. For example, when Signac expressed scepticism regarding the seriousness of the project, Van Rysselberghe replied: 'Why will he not involve us? He was the one who asked me to exhibit with him. He does talk, admittedly, about *us* and *'the younger generation'* rather vaguely, but I do think his intentions are good.'[17] In October, the participation of the neo-impressionists had still not been settled: 'As for Bing, the only news I have had is the invitation – but I know nothing is ready, and he won't be able to open his place for two months at least.'[18]

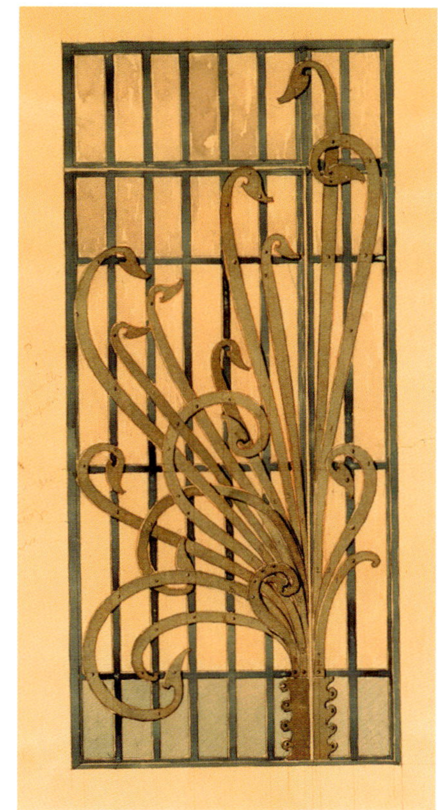

BING AND HORTA

However much Bing's eventual success was due to trial and error, it is certain that it was to Belgian artistic circles that he looked for support. The extent to which he relied on them is evident from the overtures he made to Victor Horta, the pioneer of *art nouveau* architecture, which were revealed in 1977 by Martin Eidelberg and Suzanne Henrion-Giele.[19] When Bing met him in July 1895 in Brussels, Horta had already designed the Maison Autrique and the Tassel, Frison and Winssinger town houses, and he was busy overseeing the construction of the Hôtel Solvay and the Hôtel Van Eetvelde. But Bing was somewhat naïve to think that the master would be happy with the role of consultant that was suggested and would be willing to work on a project that had already been broadly outlined by the French architect Louis Bonnier and the artist and interior designer Frank Brangwyn.[20] In their analysis of Horta's designs, Eidelberg and Henrion-Giele demonstrate clearly that Horta paid little attention to Bing's demands, especially as to the inclusion of Brangwyn's painted friezes (fig. 103). His proposals essentially reflected his own personal ideas and were very similar to the solutions already tried out in the Tassel, Winssinger and Van Eetvelde houses. In addition, the choice of freestone would have entailed a significant increase in the duration and cost of the work. It is a great pity that Horta's various designs failed to satisfy Bing, with the result that the French capital has no work by the celebrated Belgian architect. But was any other outcome possible, given Bing's impatience? Even had they joined forces, collaboration between Horta, who was a brilliant exponent of interior design, and Van de Velde might well have been tricky, not to say impossible, when one considers Van de Velde's fierce jealousy of Horta[21] and the scorn Horta entertained for Van de Velde, whom he regarded as nothing but a designer posing as an architect.[22]

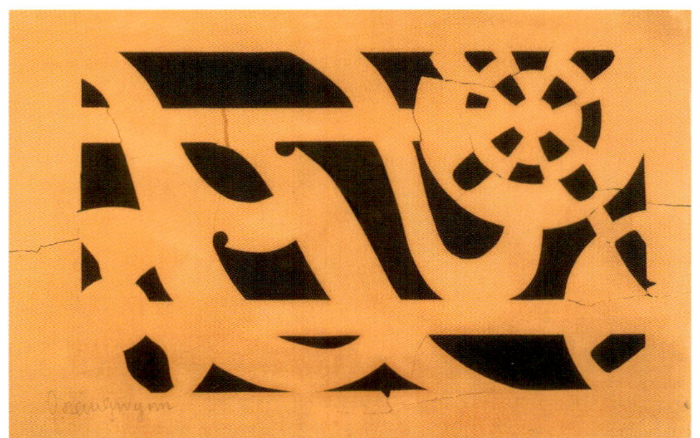

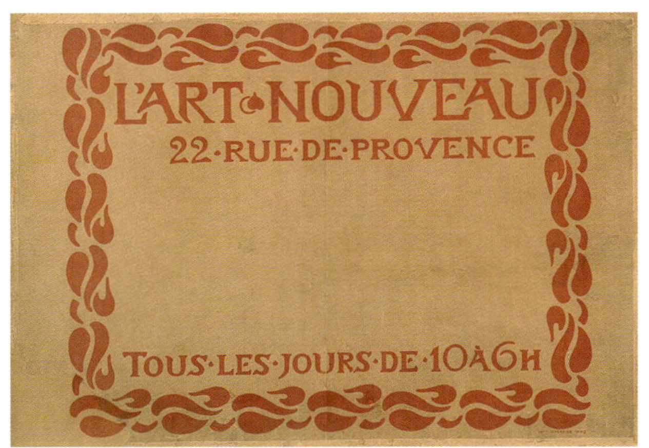

106
Louis Bonnier, Project for the doorway at 19, rue Chauchat, c. 1895
Fonds Louis Bonnier, Institut français d'architecture, Paris

107
Frank Brangwyn, Stencil design for the exterior of Bing's gallery, c. 1895
Fonds Louis Bonnier, Institut français d'architecture, Paris

108
Georges Lemmen, Placard for L'Art Nouveau, 1895
Museum für Kunst und Gewerbe, Hamburg

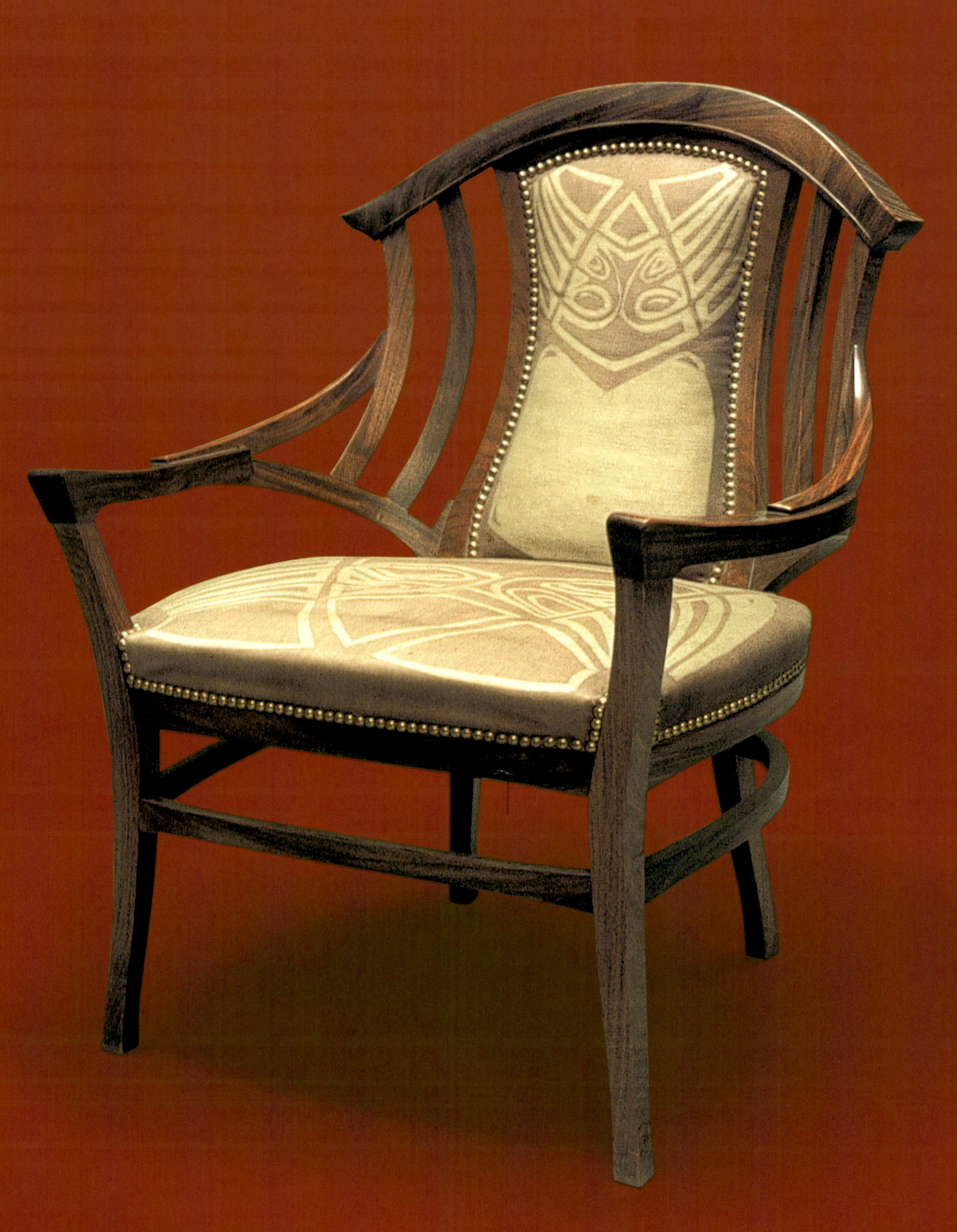

On the other hand, the commission awarded to the painter Georges Lemmen for the design of a 'graphic style' for L'Art Nouveau had a successful outcome. It was a wise choice, as the young artist had already proved his talent in this difficult field in his work for Les XX, *L'Art Moderne* and La Libre Esthétique. The experience he had gained with these groups bore fruit in his designs for a whole new range of publicity material for L'Art Nouveau: a placard, the invitation for the opening on 26 December 1895, two letterheads and a card (figs. 102, 108, 120).

HENRY VAN DE VELDE

There was one further Belgian involvement. Van Rysselberghe, whose special remit was to liaise with the French neo-impressionists, wrote to Signac in the summer of 1895: 'I must also tell you about something that is being prepared for next autumn. [...] Bing is giving up importing from China and Japan – turning his premises into an exhibition hall. Besides the large ground-floor room and the galleries, which will be given over to exhibitions of sculpture and painting, there are some twenty smaller rooms, many of them very well appointed, and these will be used for experiments in furnishing and interior design.'[23] What is more, it was Van Rysselberghe who provided Bing with the man who would successfully oversee alterations to the building[24] and provide lodgings for Van de Velde in Paris[25] – but about whom, alas, we know very little: Henri Jaeger.[26]

By turning to Van de Velde, Bing gave proof of real vision. Van de Velde was regarded as the living symbol of the multidisciplinary artist, with a passion for total art; under the twin influences of the theories of John Ruskin and the work of William Morris, he had, in 1892, taken the decision to abandon painting and devote his attentions to the modernisation of interior decoration. At the time when Bing asked him to help with the décor of L'Art Nouveau, Van de Velde's house in Uccle, the Bloemenwerf, soon to become the archetypal *beau foyer* and a rendezvous for European intelligentsia, was nearing completion. Bing must also have sensed that Van de Velde would throw himself wholeheartedly into the task, driven by his ambition to pose as the apostle of new aesthetic theories that were capable of changing the world. The letters Van de Velde sent to his wife in Belgium throughout December 1895 – he had left her behind to oversee the final touches to the interior of the Bloemenwerf – provide an intensely fascinating account of the man's artistic passion, at once arrogant and naïve.[27]

< 109
Henry Van de Velde, Chair, 1895–1902
Nordenfjeldske Kunstindustrimuseum, Trondheim

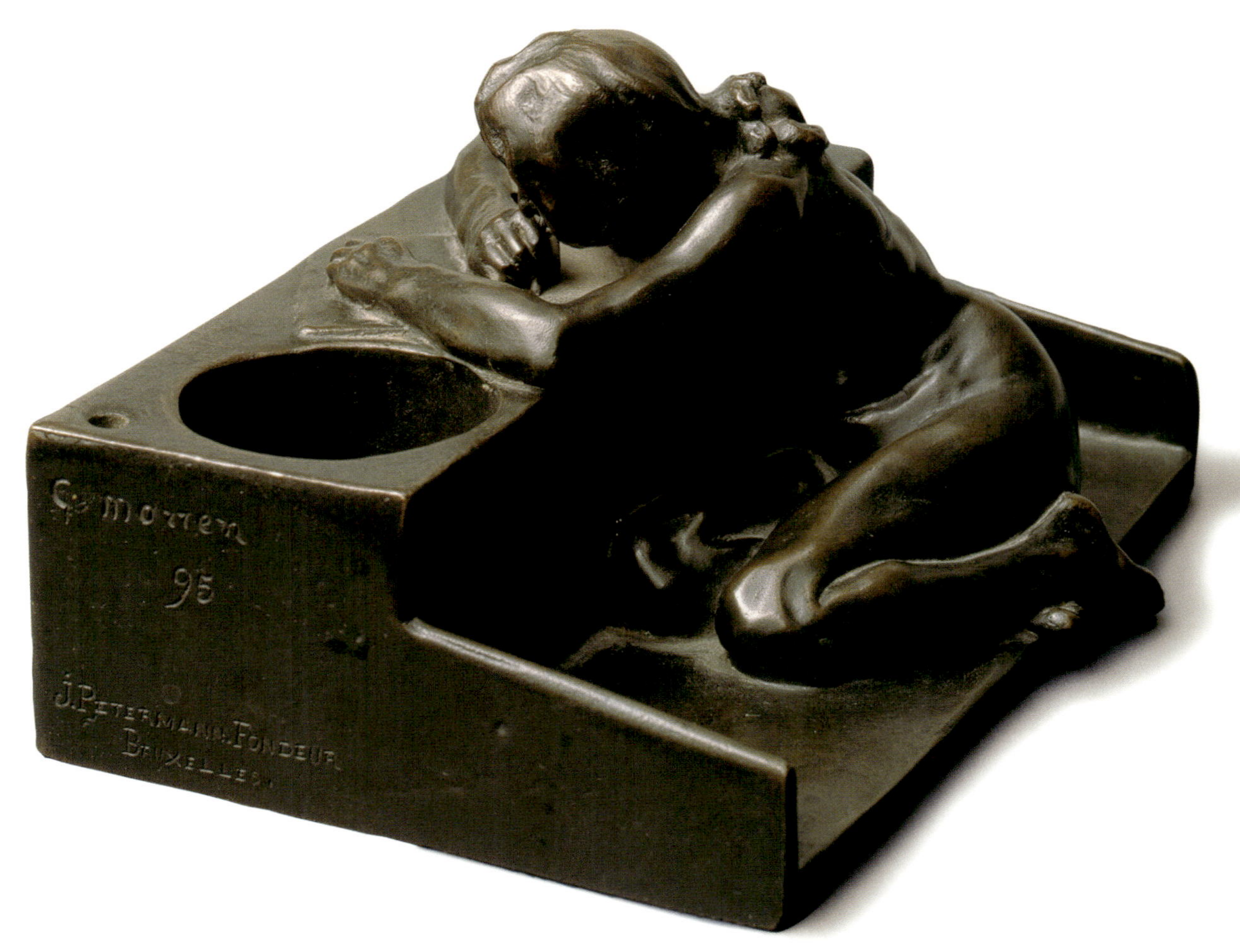

110
Georges Morren, Inkwell, 1895
Private collection

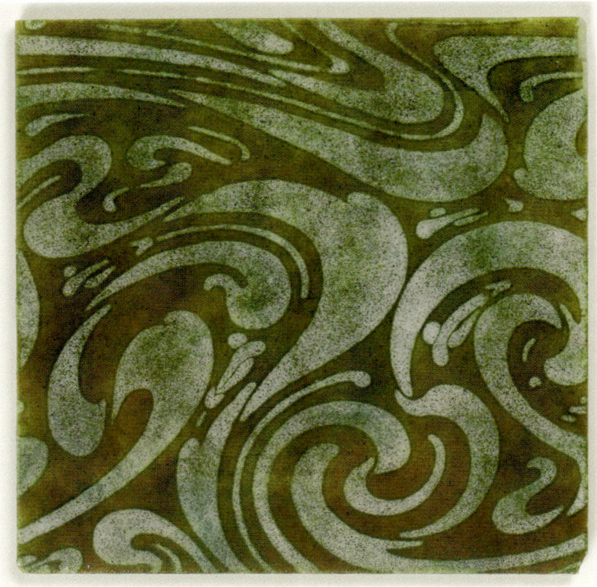

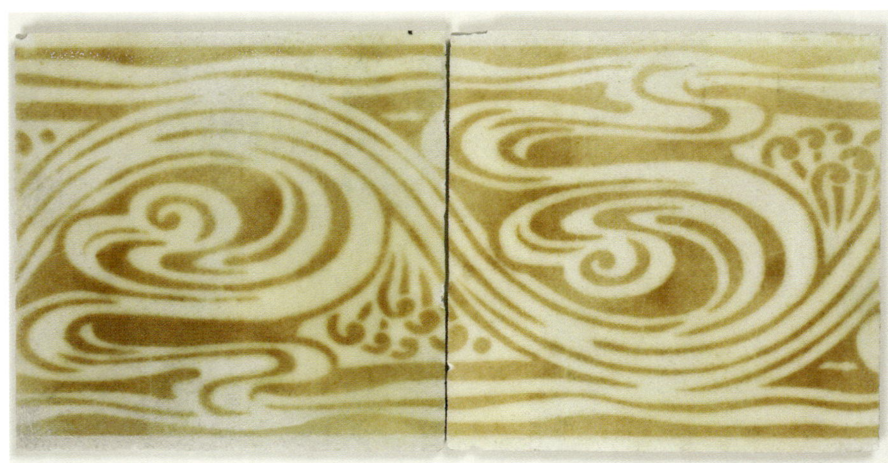

111
Henry Van de Velde, Tiles, c. 1900
Bernische Stiftung für angewandte Kunst und Gestaltung, Bern

First of all, we get a glimpse of his role as co-ordinator. Then we learn of difficulties and disappointments encountered as the various parts of the decoration were installed: 'Ranson's frieze (figs. 113, 114) is *worse than inferior!* I said so in front of Bing, and I am working with some of the others to try to avoid using it! [...] I have support, but Bing opposes me on grounds of sentiment. Will he let himself be persuaded? He knows how inferior Ranson's work is, but will he have the strength of character to break with him? Why couldn't I have worked with Théo or Lemmen!'[28] The bedroom, entrusted to Maurice Denis, appears to have aroused general consternation among the painter's friends, including Signac: 'It's so ugly that we had to disguise the furniture with bright silk stuffs. [...] Because I love the colours [...] I'm still enchanted by this failure, but I feel sorry for Denis, who can certainly do better than this miserable showing.'[29] Van de Velde too, at a later date, delivered an unqualified condemnation of Denis's work, referring to the furniture as a collection of 'mastodons', and claiming that it was as incongruous as the work of Rupert Carabin.[30] Given that Bing had undoubtedly given him the lion's share, Van de Velde's ingratitude at the end of the chapter of his memoirs devoted to L'Art Nouveau is astounding: 'Lacking aims, a programme or discipline, this first public event was completely useless as far as my purposes were concerned.'[31]

The opening of L'Art Nouveau may have been somewhat chaotic, and the fitting out of the building improvised, but Bing's commitment cannot be questioned. The fact that, following the limited success of his gallery, he was anxious to adapt his quest for a 'modern'

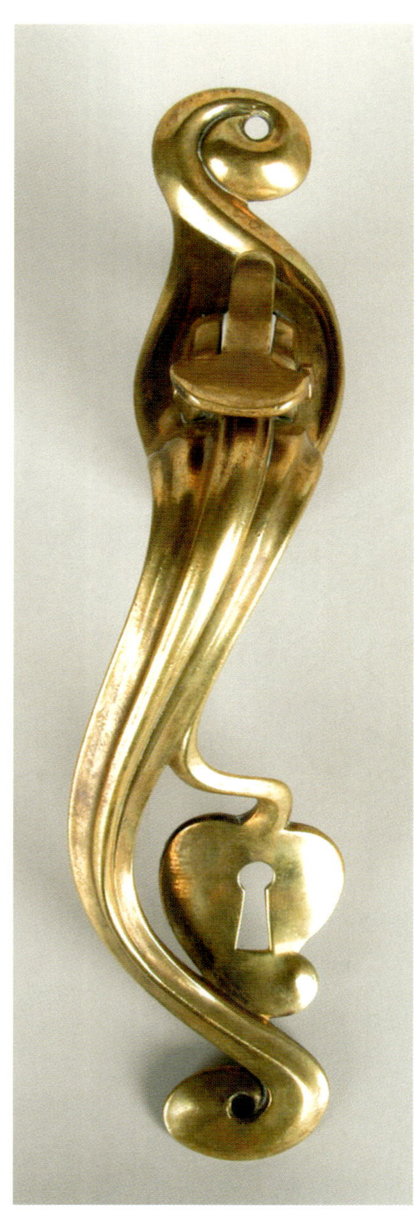

112
Henry Van de Velde, Door handle with key hole
Nordenfjeldske Kunstindustrimuseum, Trondheim

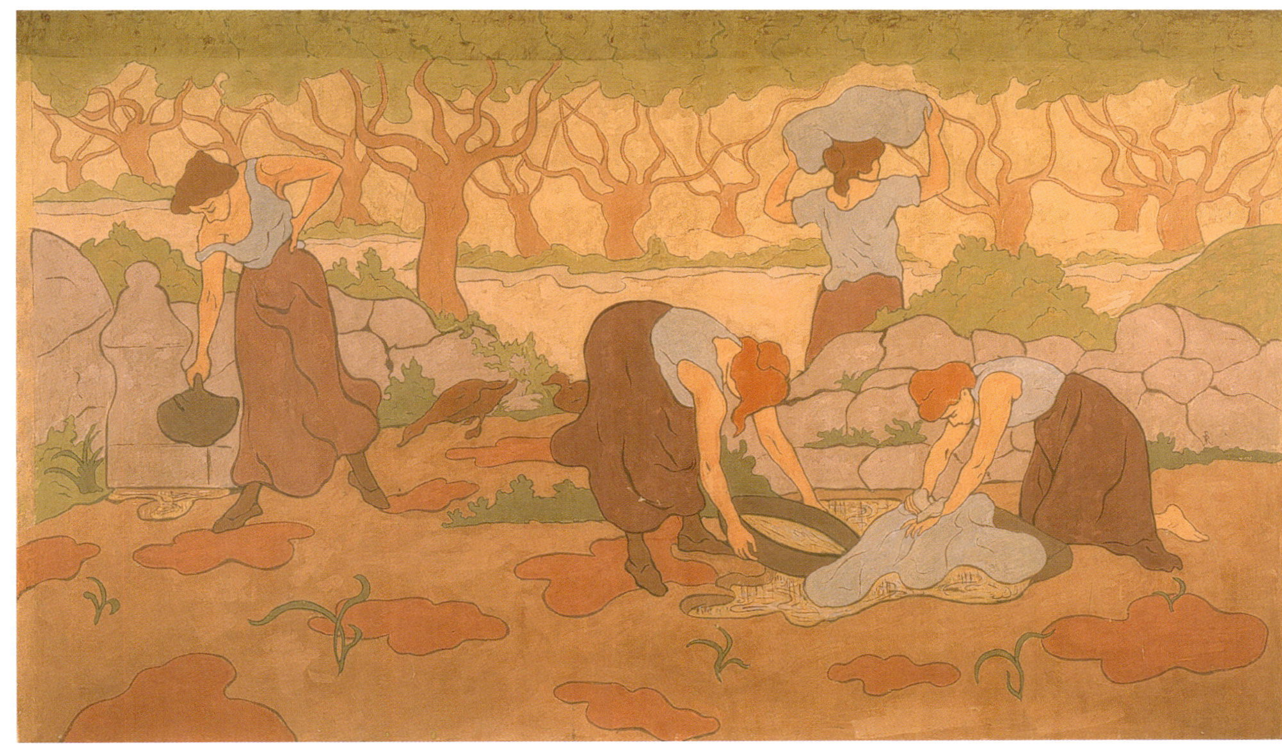

113
Paul-Elie Ranson, *Four Women at the Fountain*, 1895
Musée départemental Maurice Denis 'Le Prieuré', Saint-Germain-en-Laye

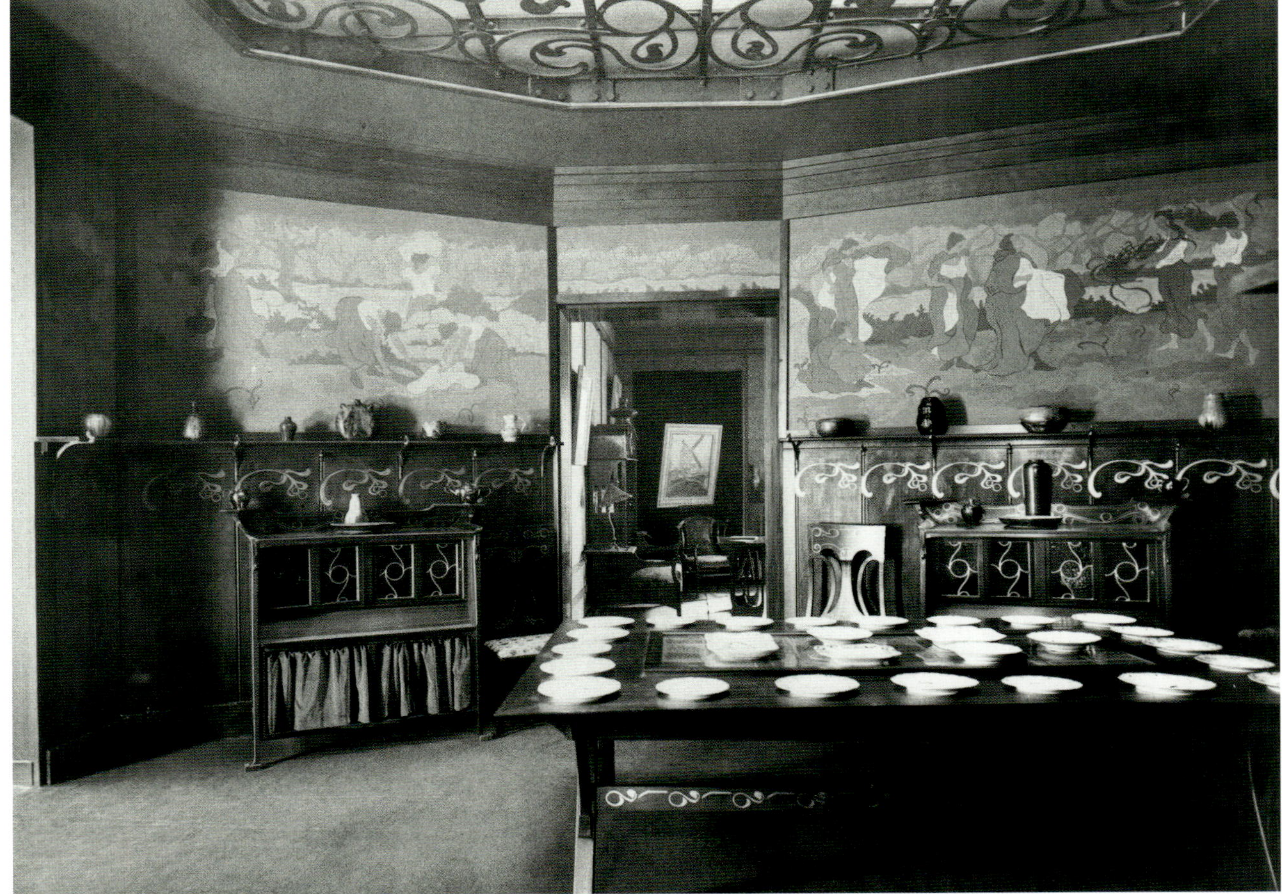

114
Dining room by Henry Van de Velde and decorative panels by Paul-Elie Ranson in Bing's gallery, 1895
Fonds Louis Bonnier, Institut français d'architecture, Paris

>> 115
Théo Van Rysselberghe, *The Canal in Flanders*, 1894
Private collection

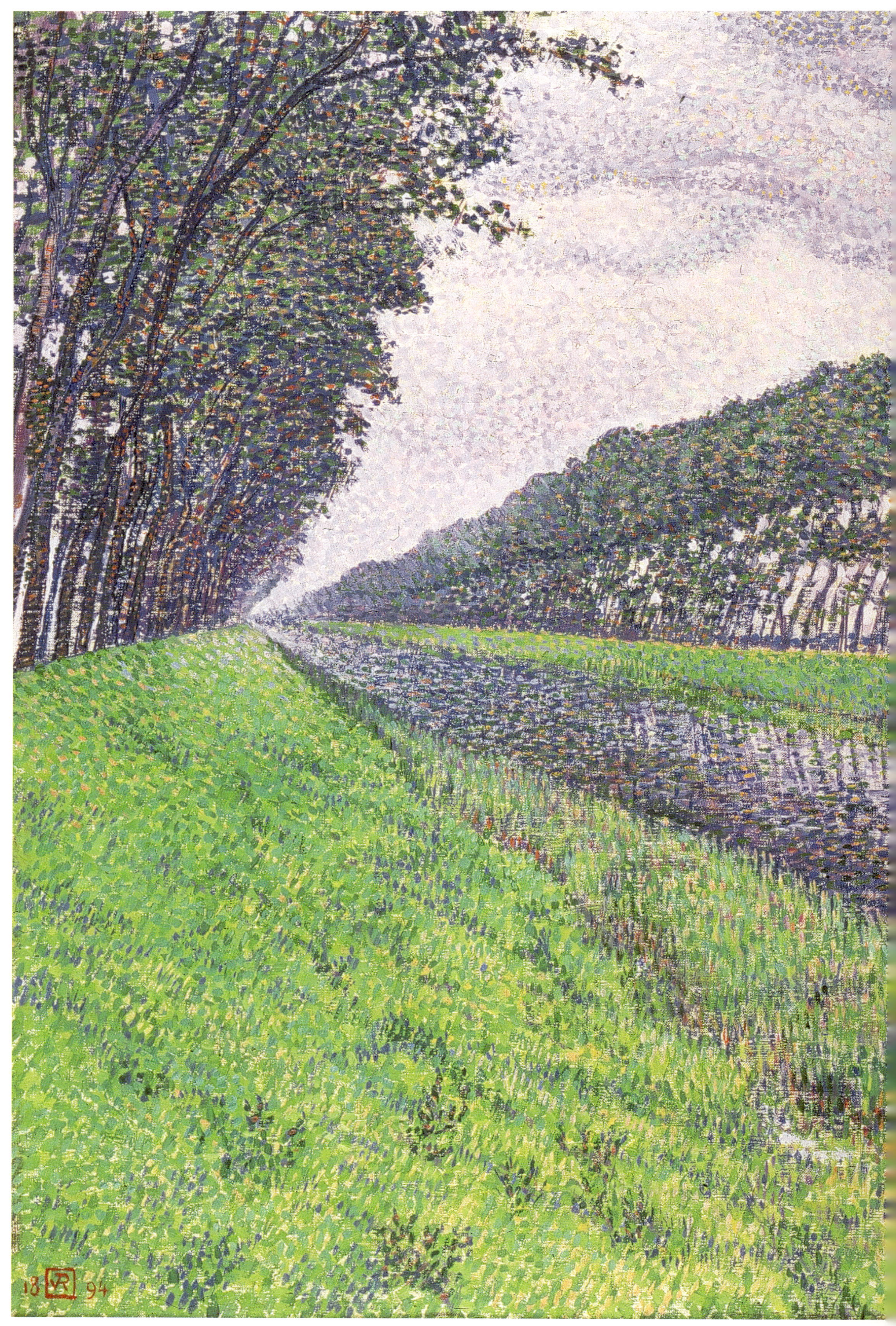

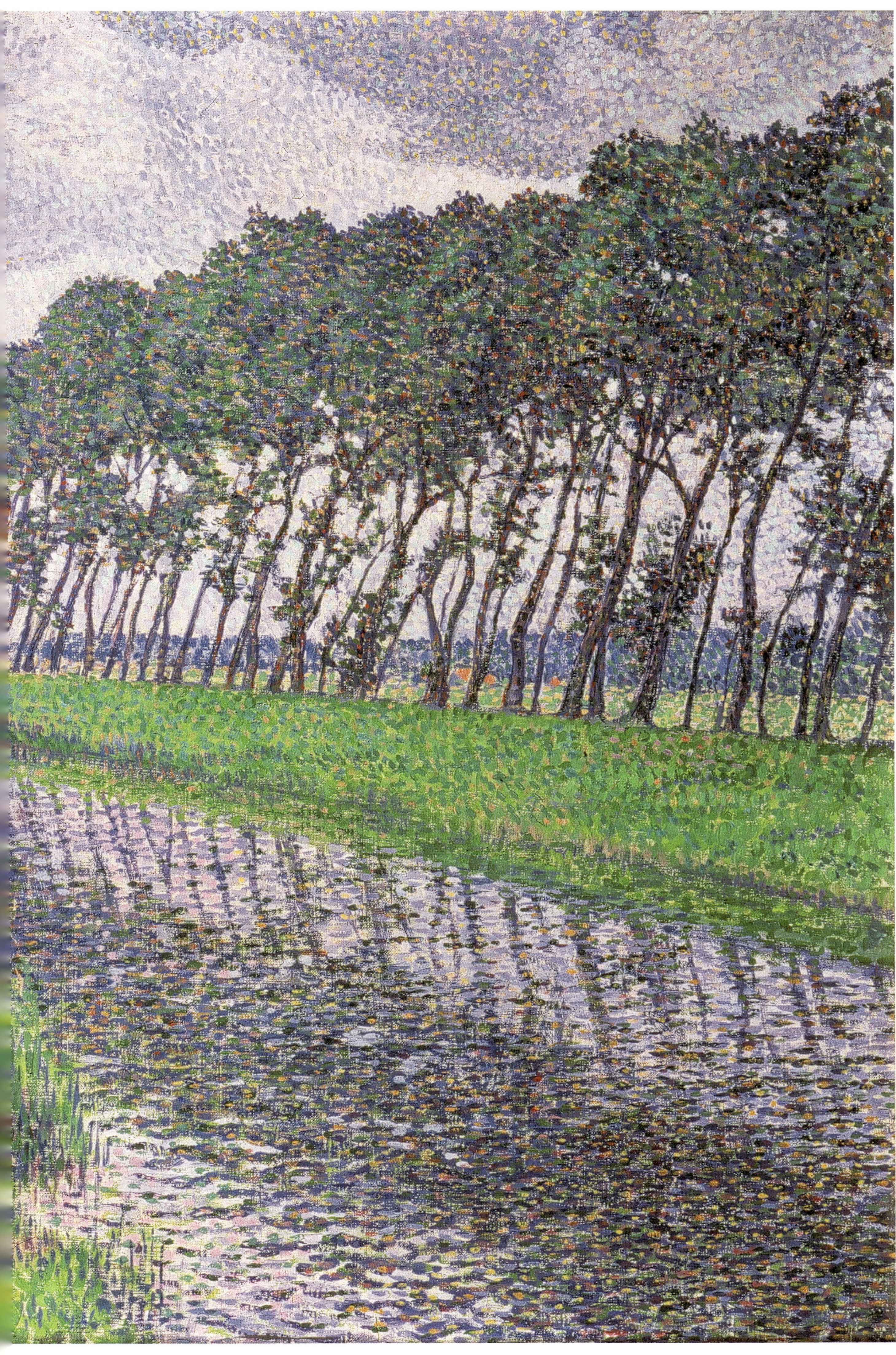

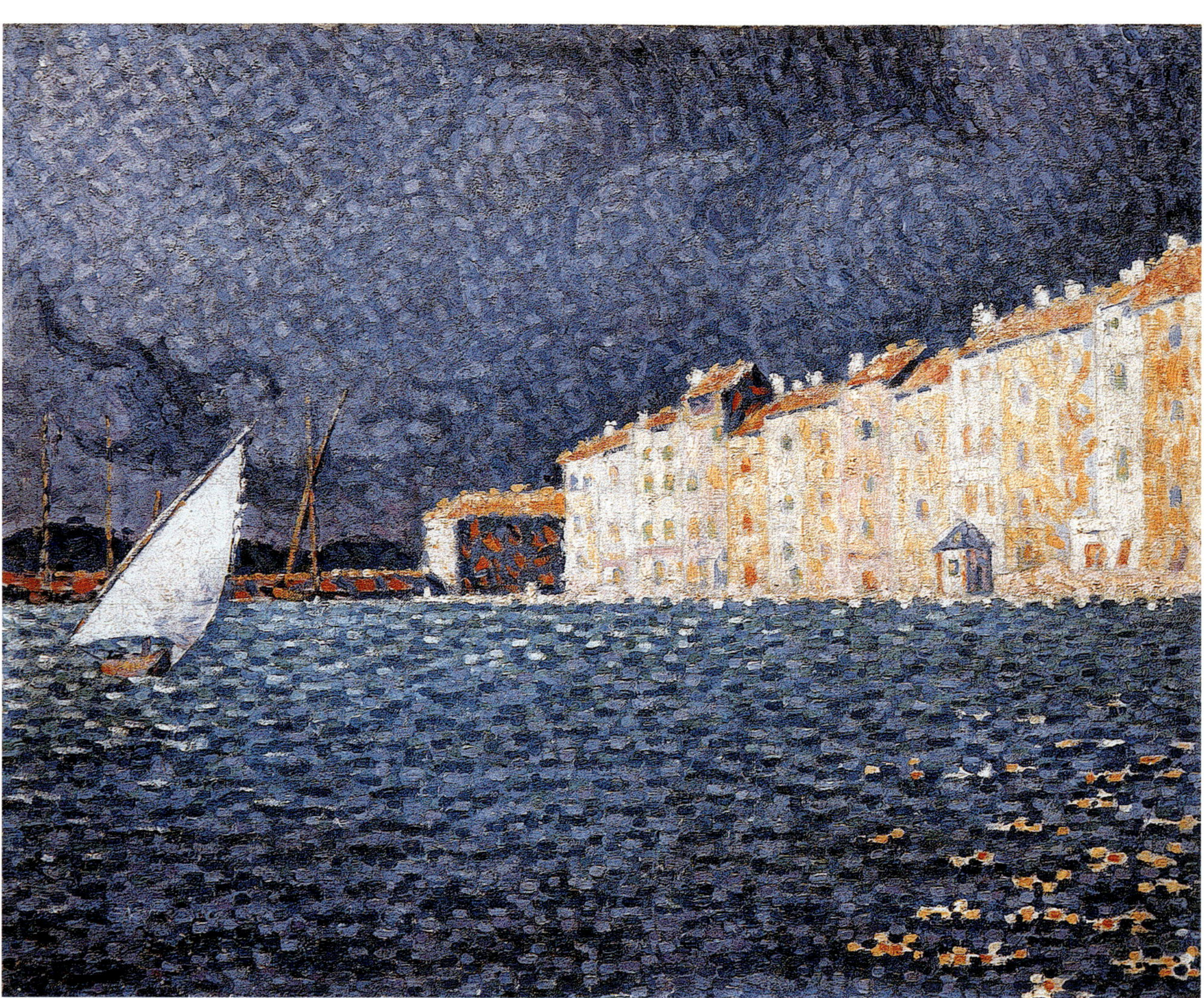

116
Paul Signac, *Saint-Tropez, The Storm,* 1895
Musée de l'Annonciade, Saint-Tropez

> 117
Félix Vallotton, Poster for L'Art Nouveau, 1895
Musée de la Publicité, Paris

lifestyle-oriented art to French and Parisian taste cannot – despite Van de Velde's scornful remarks – be ascribed to lack of conviction. His change of direction, working with a new team, was, on the contrary, the shrewdest possible move. It was to lead him to a triumph that was not only spectacular but representative in the highest degree of Parisian *art nouveau*: his pavilion at the 1900 World's Fair with all the ensuing acclaim. Here, the graceful, supple and elegant creations of Edward Colonna and Georges de Feure, in particular, were seen as 'modern' heirs to eighteenth-century elegance. The fact that the 'Belgian line' made little headway there was surely no reason to see the exhibition as a victory for 'titillation' and 'bewildering virtuosity'.[32] Did not Bing's ensembles rather demonstrate that they could really take their place in the true classical tradition, while at the same time avoiding any semblance of pastiche?

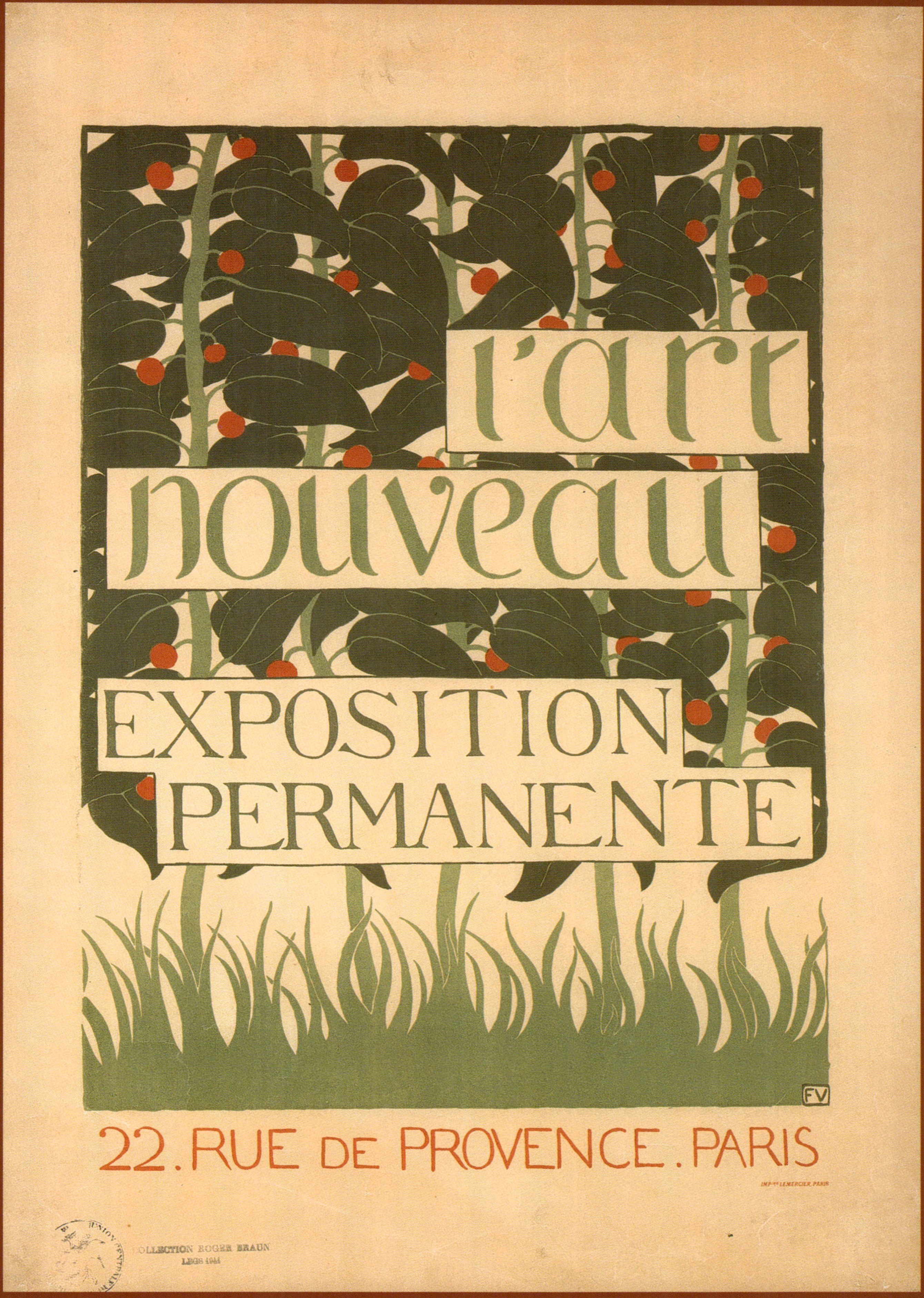

l'art nouveau

EXPOSITION PERMANENTE

FV

22. RUE DE PROVENCE. PARIS

IMP. LEMERCIER, PARIS

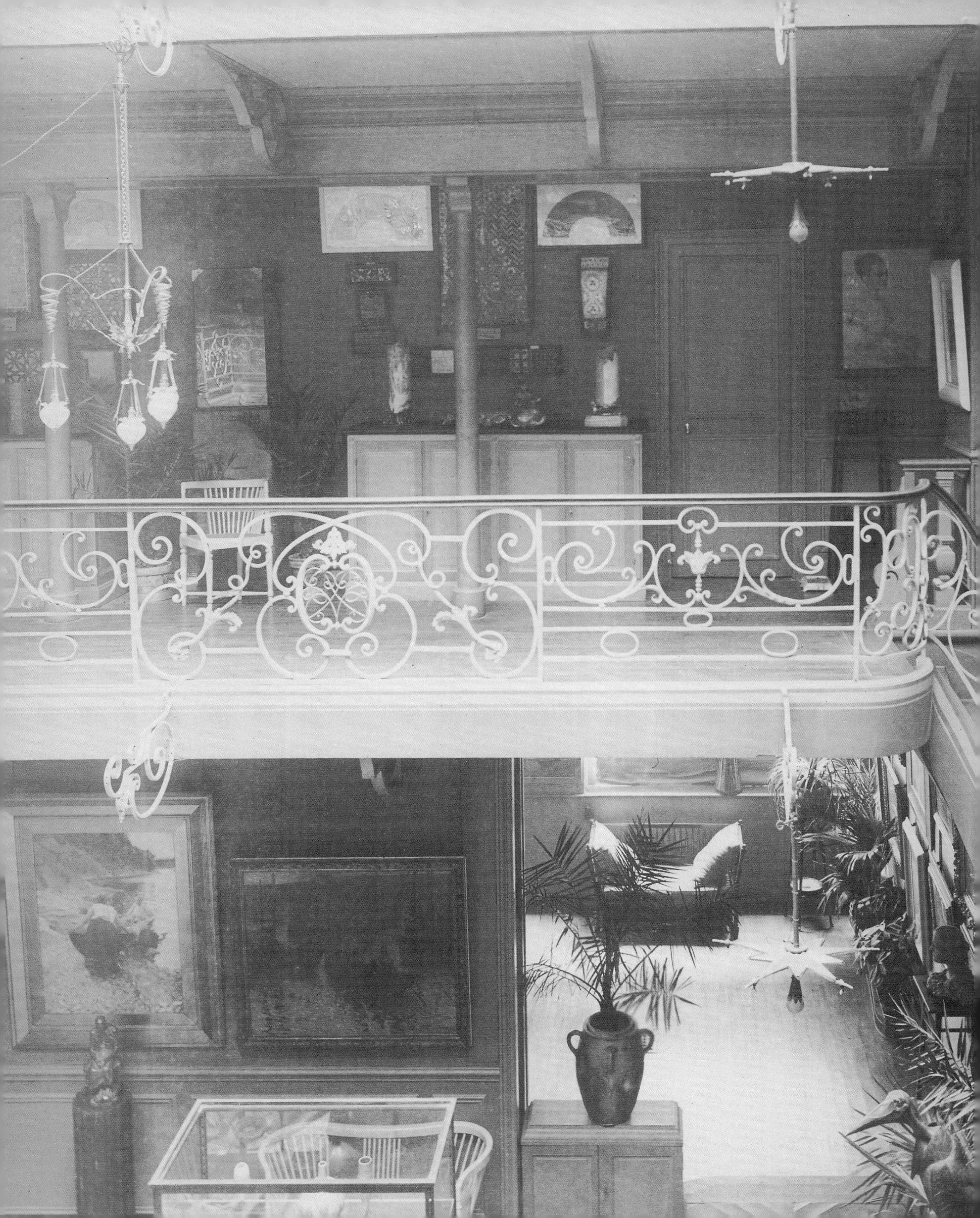

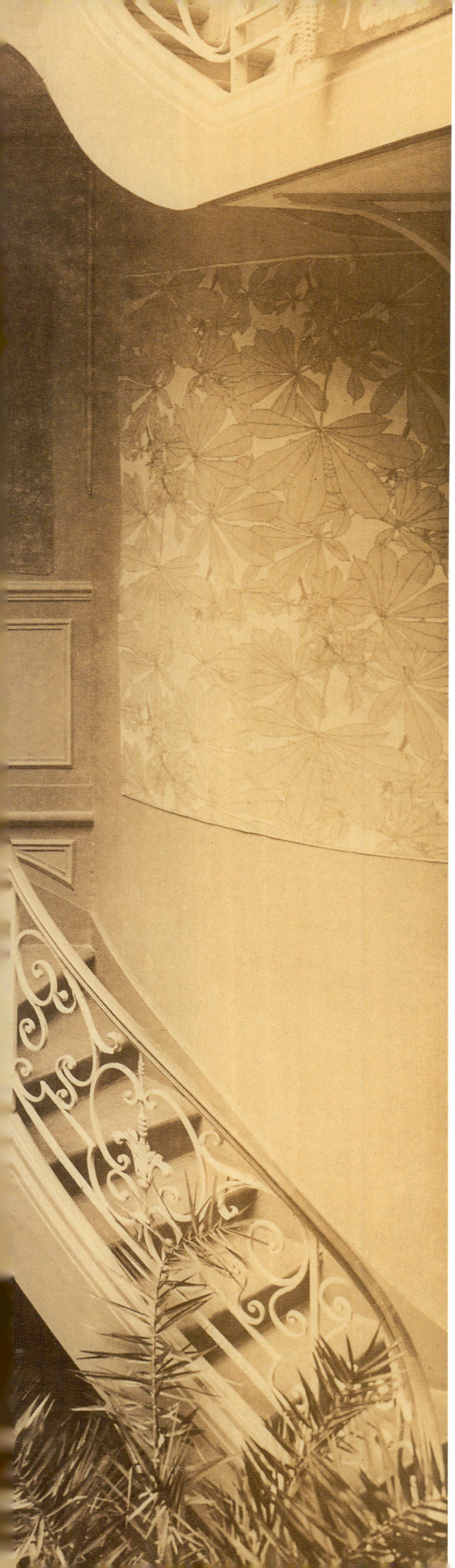

LES SALONS DE L'ART NOUVEAU

PERFECT HARMONY AND UNPRETENTIOUS BEAUTY

EDWIN BECKER

The inauguration of Siegfried Bing's gallery, named L'Art Nouveau, was a major event on the Parisian calendar. It opened its doors on Thursday 26 December 1895 at 22, rue de Provence, on the corner of rue Chauchat. That July Bing had already announced that he intended to present artistic furnishings – and the results were eagerly awaited.[1] There was great interest in this approach, and people hoped it would usher in a new period of harmony and elegance in the home, even for those with limited financial means. By opening this permanent exhibition of new art Bing intended to bring together works of art based not on the past but characterised by clearly personal approaches. 'L'Art Nouveau will strive to eliminate what is ugly and pretentious in all things that presently surround us in order to bring perfect taste, charm and natural beauty to the least important utilitarian objects.'[2] For the next ten years Bing was to organise countless

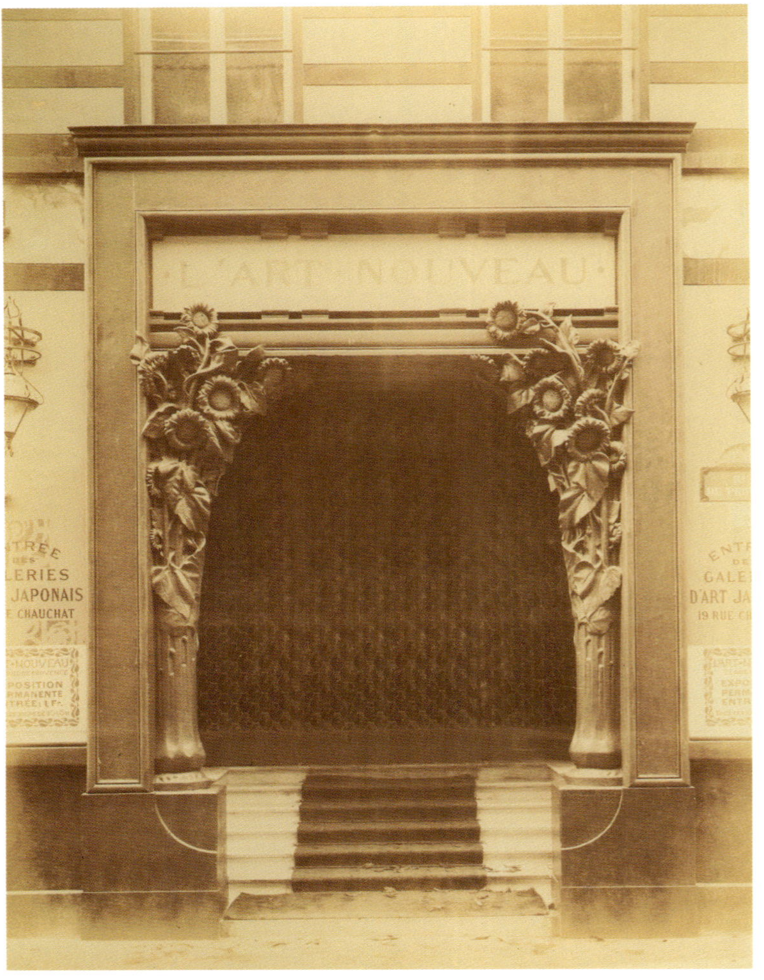

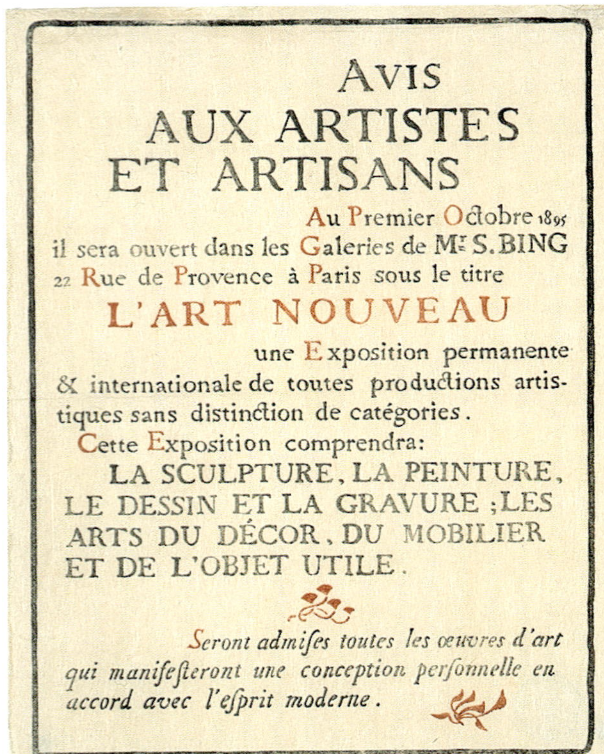

AVIS
AUX ARTISTES
ET ARTISANS

Au Premier Octobre 1895
il sera ouvert dans les Galeries de Mr S. BING
22 Rue de Provence à Paris sous le titre

L'ART NOUVEAU

une Exposition permanente
& internationale de toutes productions artistiques sans distinction de catégories.
Cette Exposition comprendra:
LA SCULPTURE, LA PEINTURE, LE DESSIN ET LA GRAVURE ; LES ARTS DU DÉCOR, DU MOBILIER ET DE L'OBJET UTILE.

Seront admises toutes les œuvres d'art qui manifesteront une conception personnelle en accord avec l'esprit moderne.

sales and exhibitions based on this mission statement, all of them testifying to his constant struggle for harmony. Such refined art would certainly not have been seen at its best in the cramped, somewhat outmoded premises where Siegfried Bing had shown his Japanese art. It was for this reason that he took care to ensure that the gallery was remodelled both inside and out to suit the taste and demands of the 'modern' age.

A PARIS GALLERY WITH INTERNATIONAL ALLURE

Working on a tight budget, Bing was able to afford only slight changes to the existing building; he was also restricted by the short amount of time he had to carry out the building campaign. Nevertheless, architectural connoisseurs showed their appreciation for the work of the architect Louis Bonnier, which they pronounced a success. The greatest change was made to the front façade. The ochre-coloured front, with brown and olive-green stripes, was adorned with decorative patterns by the Belgian-British artist Frank Brangwyn (fig. 96), which emphasised the two-dimensionality of the walls. Apart from these abstract, stylised motifs, which appeared to have been placed on the façade almost at random, there were two friezes showing Oriental figures making ceramics, as well as figures interspersed with scrolls and plant motifs. This pattern was especially appropriate because Eastern and Western ceramics were Bing's favourite forms of applied art. Moreover, the plant motifs bore a strong resemblance to work by Bing's much-loved hero William Morris.[3] As there was little time to waste, the blue outlines of the painting were drawn straight onto the wall and were afterwards brightened up with a few touches of colour. These friezes can be dimly seen in black-and-white photographs of Bing's gallery (fig. 1).

The renovated dome was also a real improvement, as it let in far more light. The ceiling, like the entrance doors, was made of hexagonal glass plates, a great novelty at the time. The wavy iris-leaf decoration on the doors had been fitted in most ingeniously,[4] while the stylised advertisement placards (fig. 108) from the hand of the Belgian Georges Lemmen, with their simple repeated

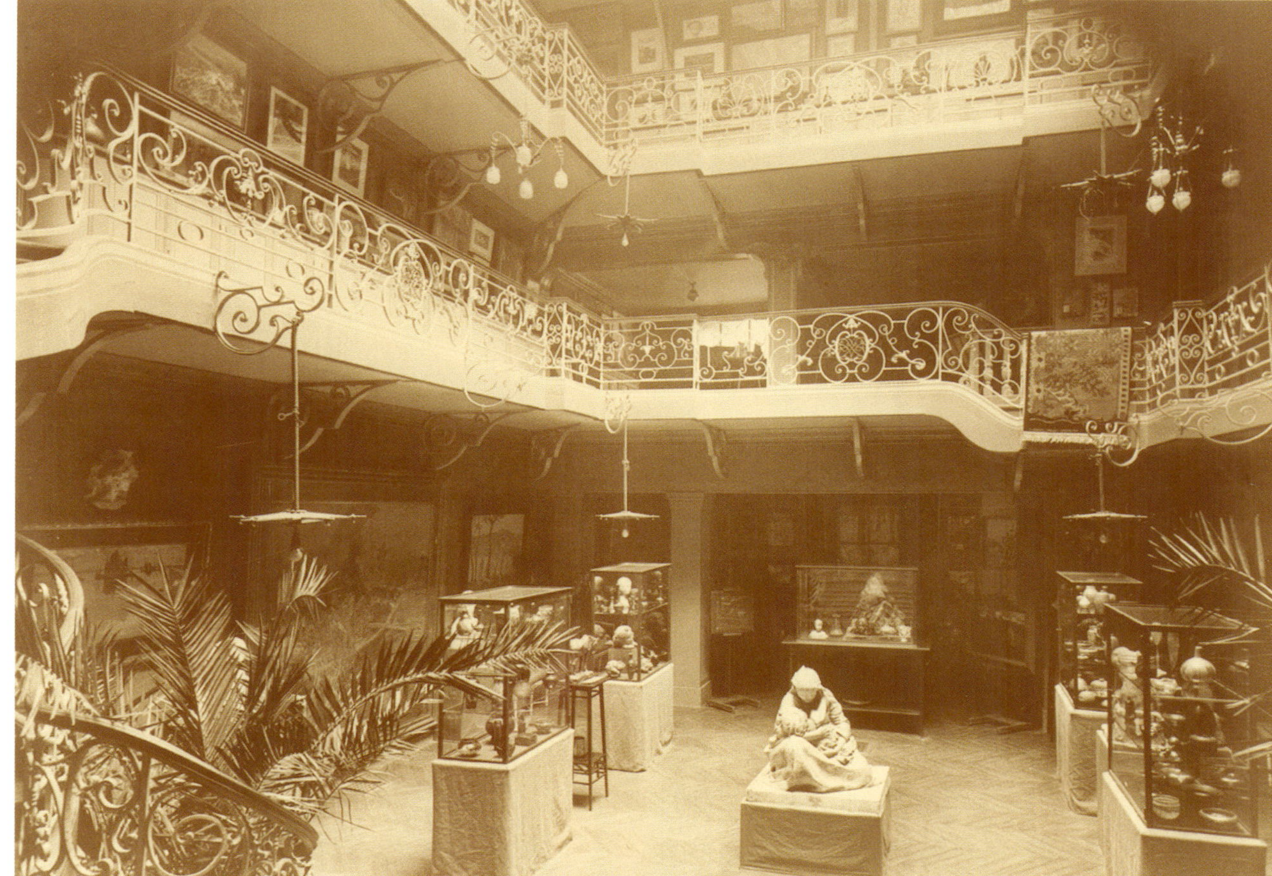

<< 118
View of the main exhibition hall and upper galleries at L'Art Nouveau (detail)
Fonds Louis Bonnier, Institut français d'architecture, Paris

< 119
Main entranceway of L'Art Nouveau, 1895
Fonds Louis Bonnier, Institut français d'architecture, Paris

< 120
Georges Lemmen, Notice to artists, 1895
Museum für Kunst und Gewerbe, Hamburg

121
The central exhibition hall of L'Art Nouveau, 1895
Fonds Louis Bonnier, Institut français d'architecture, Paris

122
Doorway, 19, rue Chauchat, 1895
Fonds Louis Bonnier, Institut français d'architecture, Paris

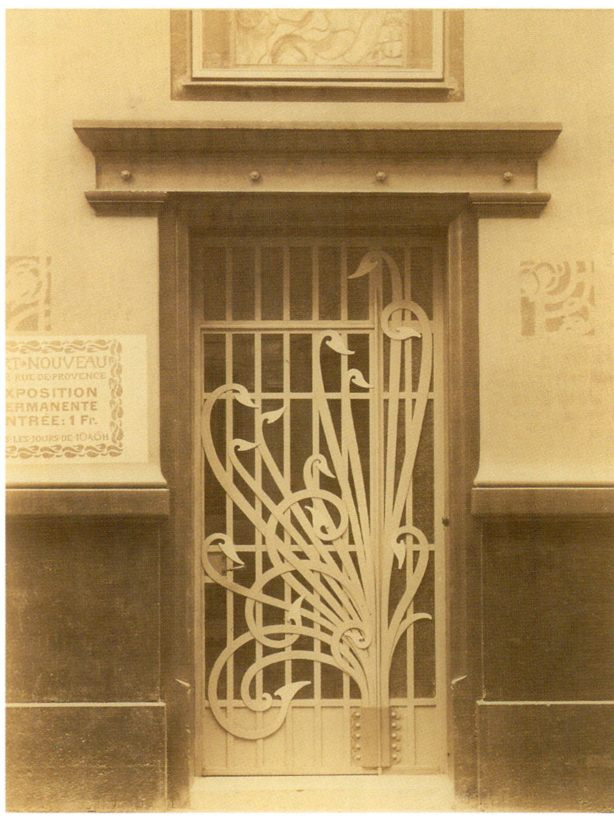

motifs, underlined the new concept. The entrance (fig. 119), flanked by naturalistically painted plaster of Paris sunflowers, was considered by most visitors to be a mistake, as these heavy, gigantic three-dimensional sculptures, made by Camille Lefèvre, bore no relation whatsoever to the smooth wall-decorations. The strongest criticism came from the pen of the critic Arsène Alexandre, who wrote a vitriolic piece in *Le Figaro* two days after the opening. He thought the new gallery was too contrived and drew too much attention to itself, and he pronounced the sunflowers next to the front entrance utterly repulsive, because there was no link between the architecture and the decoration, or, to be more precise, there was no connection except perhaps an ironic reference to the expression: 'there is nothing new under the sun'.[5]

A TOUR THROUGH BING'S L'ART NOUVEAU

The moment they entered the building, visitors caught sight of two large canvases by Frank Brangwyn based on the themes of 'Dance' and 'Music' (figs. 124, 125).[6] Brangwyn had successfully exhibited in the early 1890s in the Paris Salons, and his work was watched with some

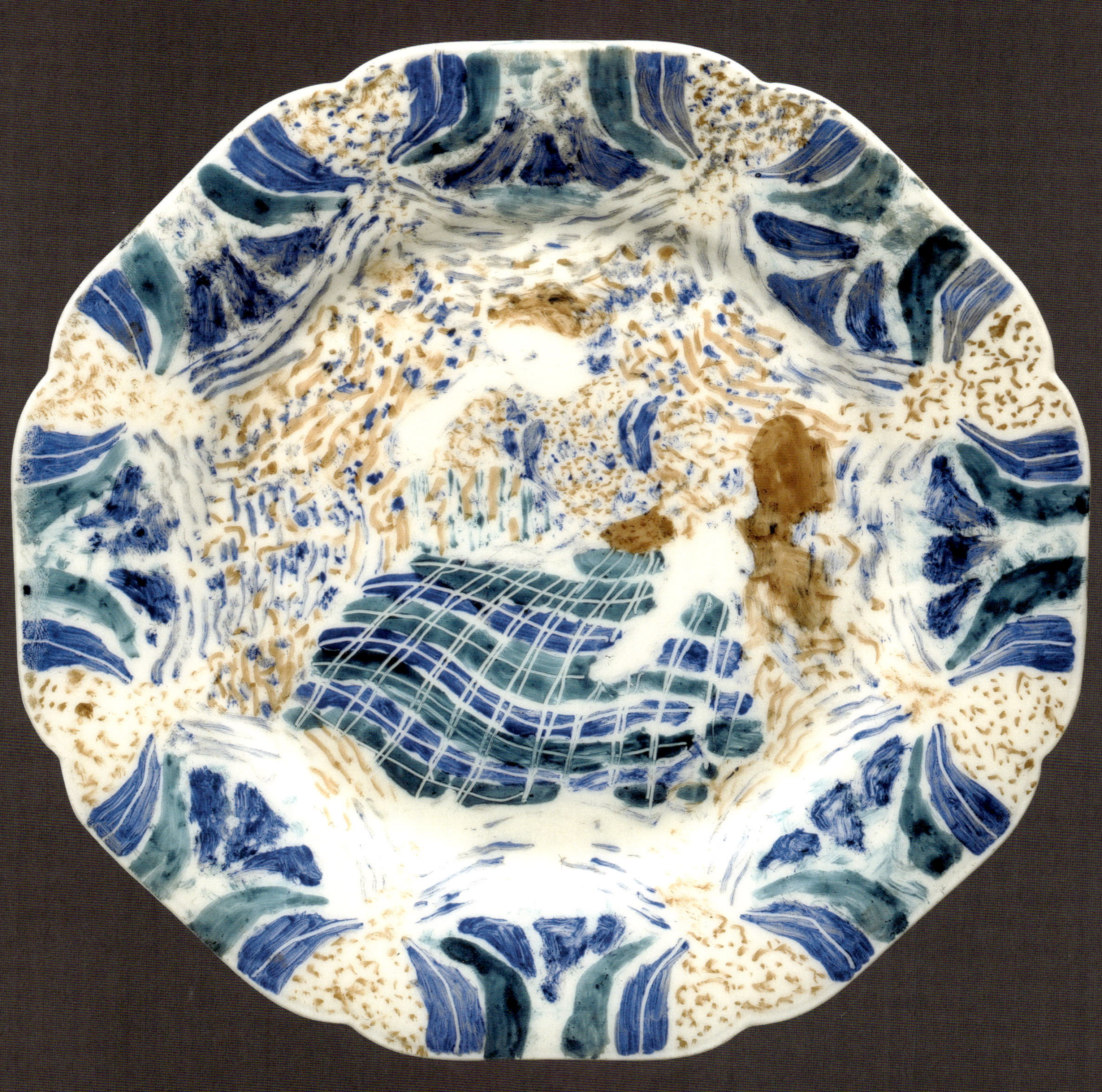

interest. Bing thought that the commission for the monumental wall-decorations for both the hall and the outside could best go to Brangwyn, who subsequently put all his energies into the task.[7] The painted canvases from the hall have been preserved. Referred to as 'stained cloths',[8] they appeared to be painted carpets; they show a two-dimensional world, with a Japanese feel for line and colour contrasts, and have an entirely idiosyncratic way of combining patterns and people. In iconographic terms, the two canvases underline the concept of the *Gesamtkunstwerk*, in which all the arts joined together to pursue a joint aim: lifting the banality of everyday life to a higher plane. Music, coupled with dance (ecstasy), was considered to be the highest expression of art, or at least the most universal.

Several years later, Brangwyn's large carpet 'Japanese Vine' was on show at Bing's L'Art Nouveau (fig. 160), with its fresh colours and an abstract design reminiscent of the patterns for the front façade (fig. 96). The ornamentation was inspired by William Morris's wallpapers, such as 'Vine' of 1874, and was a forerunner of the tautly designed ornamental carpets by artists like Gustave Serrurier-Bovy or Georges Lemmen.[9]

After the visitors had walked past the two Brangwyn paintings, and had paid their one franc entrance-fee at the ticket-booth, they could see the whole of the downstairs area at a glance (fig. 121). Not everyone was pleased with the numerous flights of stairs, galleries and split levels, but it was an ideal way of dividing the space into a number of open and closed areas, each with its own particular character.[10] At first sight, the large open space on the ground floor did indeed seem to contain a random mixture of applied and fine arts, but in fact there was a strict division between the paintings, watercolours and drawings on the walls and the ceramics and glass objects in the vitrines. A truly unified interior was only achieved in the various period rooms on the first floor and in the circular salon on the ground floor. Since Bing did not want the unified look of the period rooms to be disturbed by too many small trinkets, he used just a few objects as finishing touches, placing them here and there in a discreet way.

In the centre of the first floor was the dining room (fig. 114) with beautiful functional furniture by Henry Van de Velde, which sadly can no longer be traced. Apart from the dining-room table, inlaid with Bigot tiles, and the chairs, this innovative Belgian designer was responsible for the occasional sideboards and the wooden panelling made of light-coloured cedar inlaid with decorative brass plant motifs worked in an abstract repeating

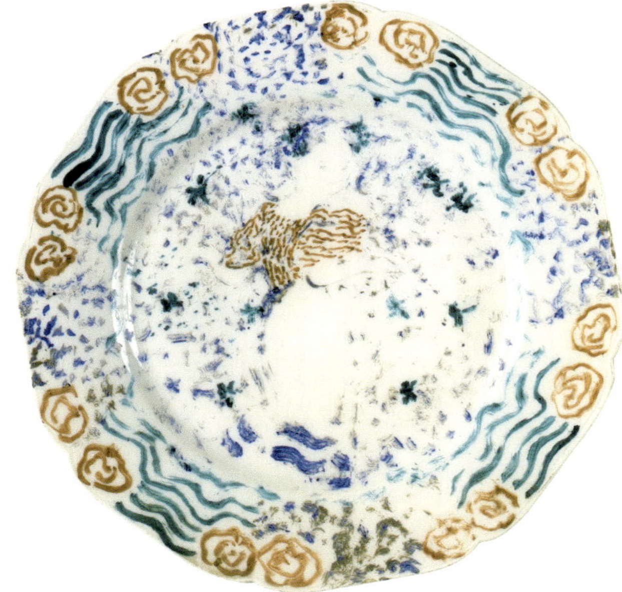

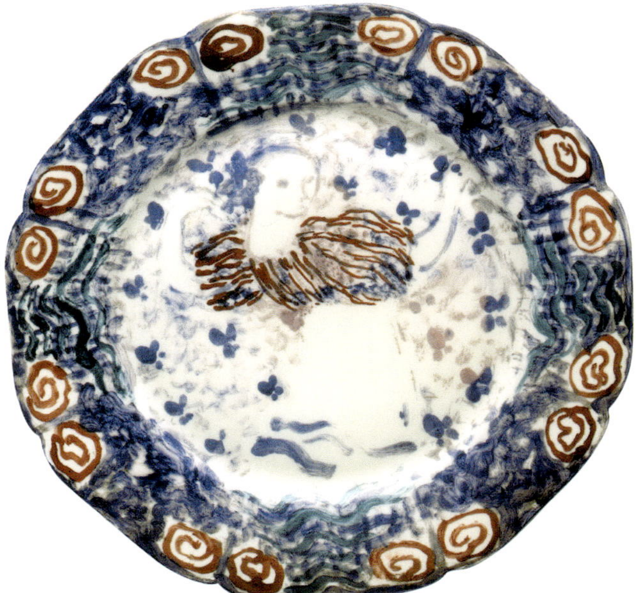

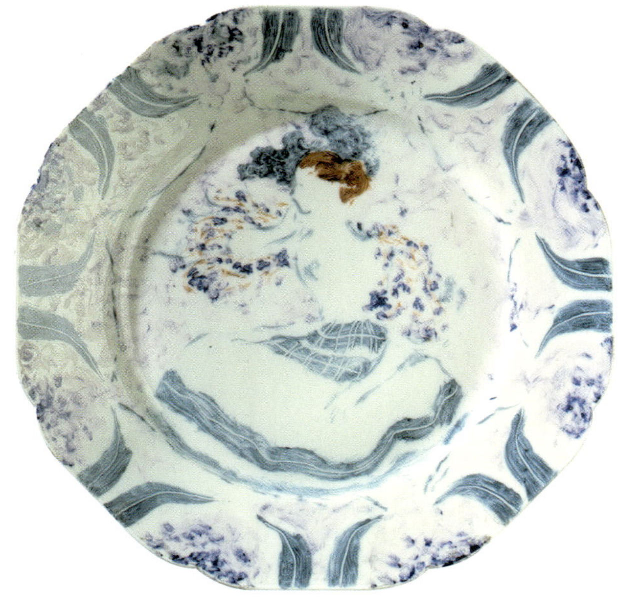

123
Edouard Vuillard, Four plates, c. 1895
Private collection

>> **124**
Frank Brangwyn, *Dance*, 1895
Collection Sir Angus and Lady Grossart

>> **125**
Frank Brangwyn, *Music*, 1895
William Morris Gallery, Walthamstow

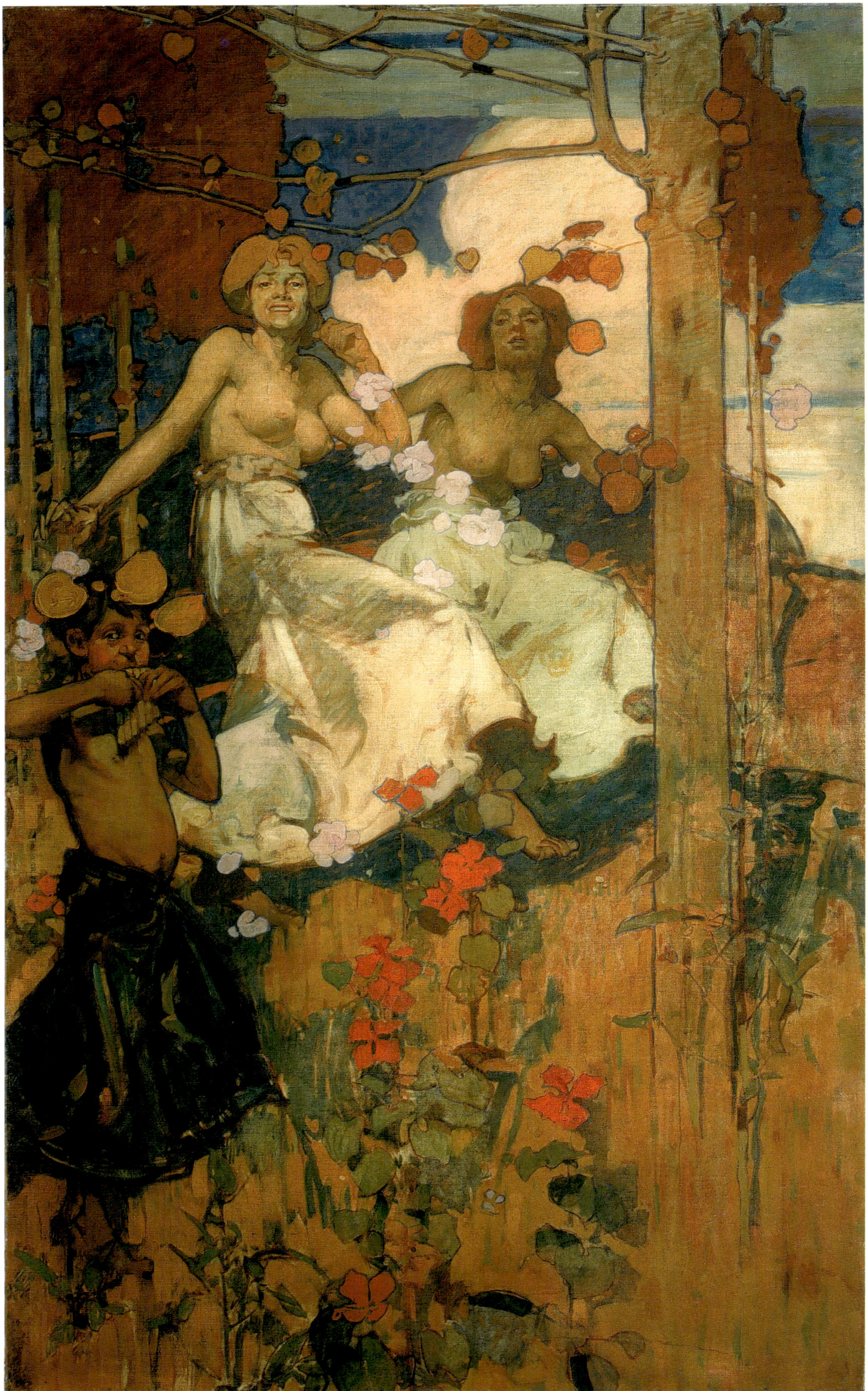

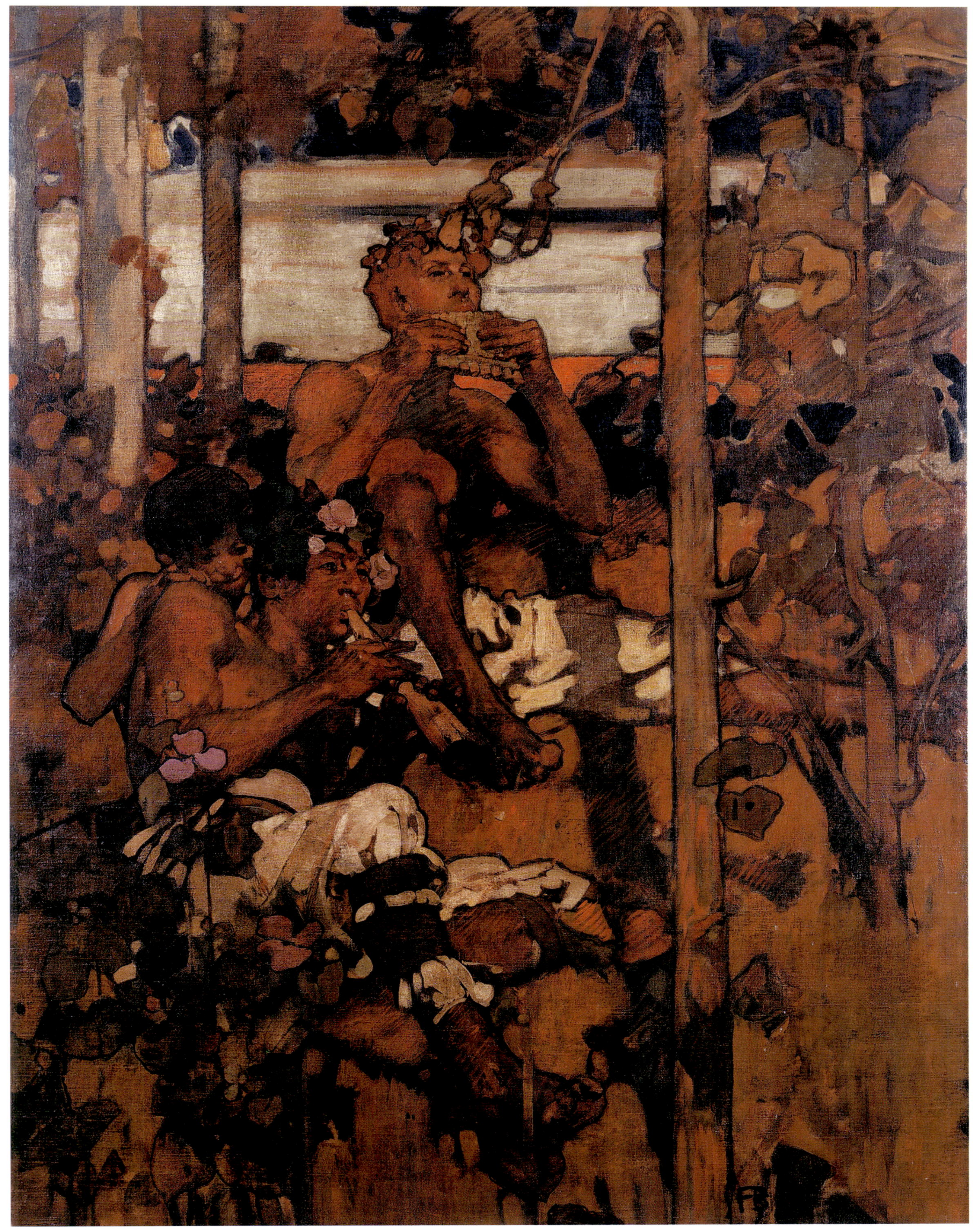

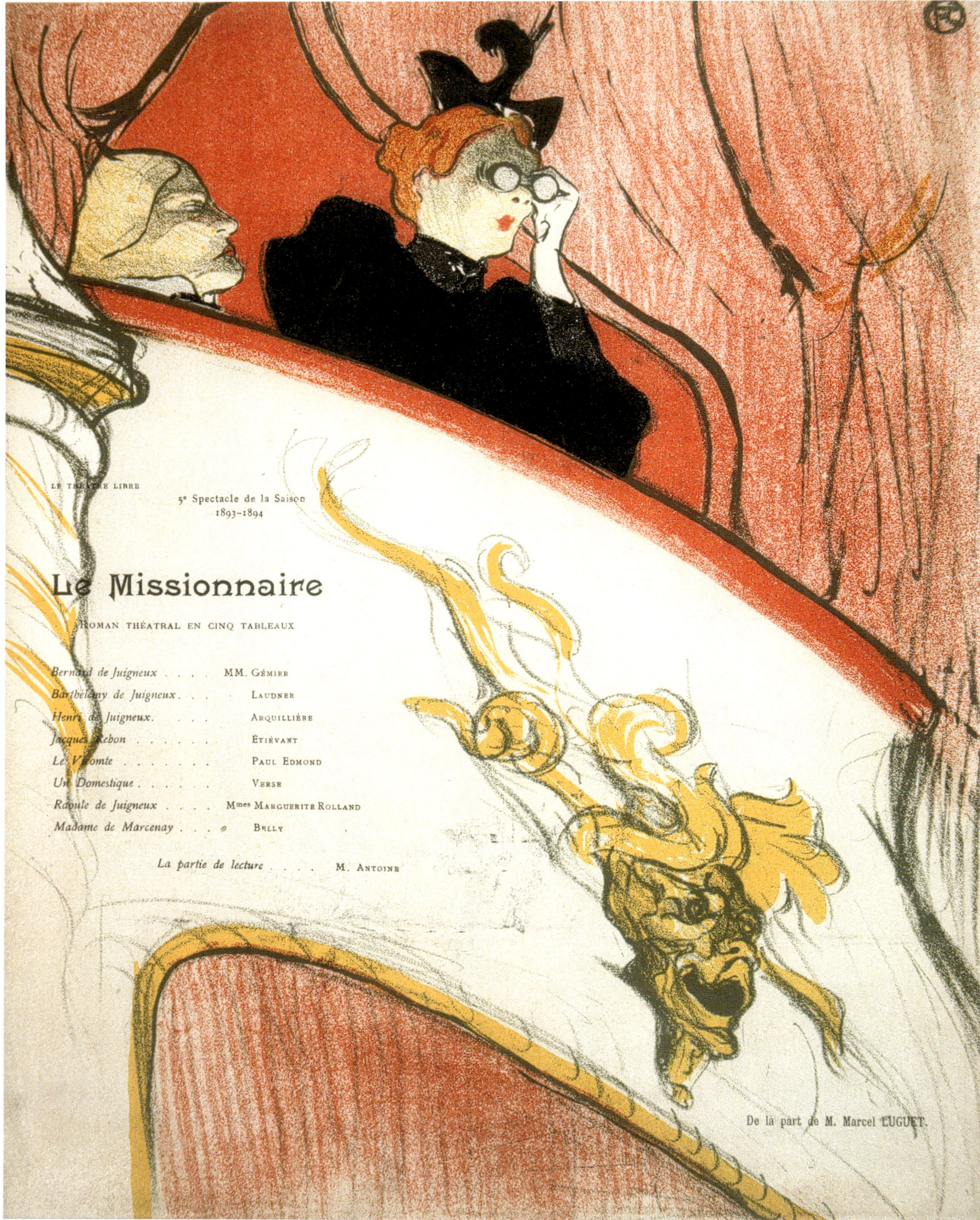
Le Théâtre Libre
5e Spectacle de la Saison
1893–1894
Le Missionnaire
Roman théatral en cinq tableaux
Bernard de Juigneux . . . . MM. Gémier
Barthélemy de Juigneux . . . . Laudner
Henri de Juigneux. . . . Arquillière
Jacques Rebon . . . . . . Étiévant
Le Vicomte . . . . Paul Edmond
Un Domestique . . . . . . Verse
Raoule de Juigneux . . . . Mmes Marguerite Rolland
Madame de Marcenay . . . . Belly
La partie de lecture . . . . M. Antoine
De la part de M. Marcel LUGUET.

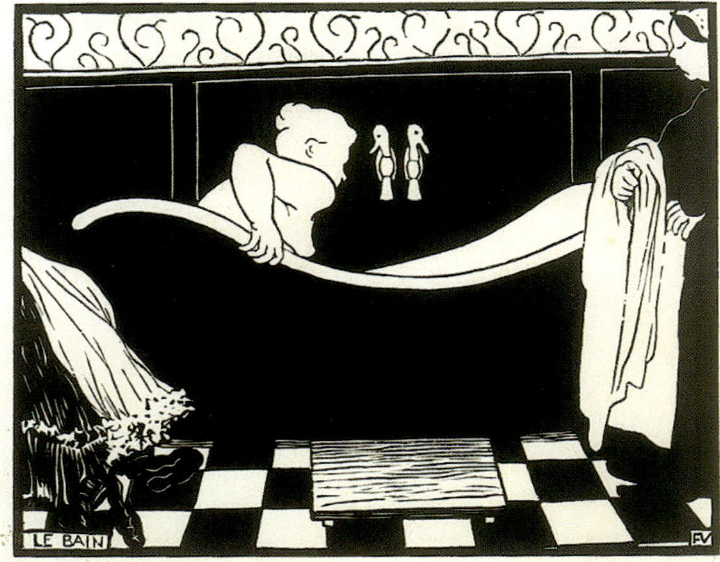

< 126
Henri de Toulouse-Lautrec, *Theatre Box with Gold Mascaron (mask)*, 1894
Van Gogh Museum, Amsterdam

127
Félix Vallotton, *The Bath*, 1894
Van Gogh Museum, Amsterdam

pattern. At that time, Van de Velde was still at the beginning of his career, and his work made an important contribution to this harmonious and functional interior. Above the wood panelling, in shades of brown and lilac, Paul-Elie Ranson's wall-decorations (fig. 113) combined with their surroundings, and the ceramic vases by Adrien Dalpayrat, Auguste Delaherche and Alexandre Bigot made the design complete. Even more striking than these ceramics was the display of porcelain plates by Edouard Vuillard (fig. 123) on the dining room table. The theme of the service was completely new, totally different from the typical flower and animal motifs prevalent during the period. Instead, each plate displayed different motifs of elegant women painted with flowing brushstrokes and in three colours: warm reddish-brown, green and blue.

The dining room led into both the smoking room and the study *(cabinet d'amateur)*. People thought the smoking room was the most daring, because here Van de Velde's furniture with its large undulating lines was in total harmony with the strongly linear frieze and Georges Lemmen's coloured-glass mosaic. The graphic artist-designer Lemmen had also designed the placards placed on both sides of the entrances and was responsible for other printed material used by Bing in advertising his gallery. Using a simple pattern with a strong linear emphasis, he had developed a gracious but sober style. Despite this restraint, everything exuded an air of refined luxury, although Bing's faithful devotee, the famous art critic Julius Meier-Graefe, had to admit that it made a colossal impression.[11]

The room known as the *cabinet d'amateur*, designed with the cultivated collector in mind, had a fresher, lighter tone, with pale yellow wallpaper and stained pine furniture by Van de Velde. The furnishings were very simple but elegantly shaped, and the sofa was covered with a William Morris fabric. This room created a successful ambiance for the post-impressionist paintings by Paul Signac and Théo Van Rysselberghe. In a photograph taken of the interior (fig. 114), the painting on the back wall, *The Windmill* by Van Rysselberghe (1894, private collection), takes pride of place, hung directly above a Van de Velde armchair (fig. 109).

As far as the remaining rooms on the first floor are concerned, two others are worth a mention. One was a boudoir, with a hint of French rococo, by P. A. Isaac, worked in soft, stylish fabrics. He used an unusual technique to achieve the special effect of the plant motifs: they were etched into the fabric. The other was the bedroom with murals by Maurice Denis based on the theme of Robert Schumann's song-cycle *Frauenliebe und Leben*.[12] It was essential that these wall-decorations in delicate pastel shades should harmonise with the furniture. From a letter written by Bing to Denis, it becomes clear how keen Bing was for Denis to reveal what shades he was thinking of using, so that plans could be made for the rest of objects in the room to be adjusted to the colour scheme.[13] Bing's first idea was to show furniture by Emile Gallé, hopefully less ornate and simpler than his well-known furniture with its fussy inlaid motifs; however, he realised that Denis thought this furniture would not fit in well with his wall-decorations, and Bing himself was not entirely convinced that the combination would work. Faced with this dilemma, Denis decided to design the furniture himself, to be made by Eugène Pinte. Both Bing and almost all the visitors to the Salon believed that the

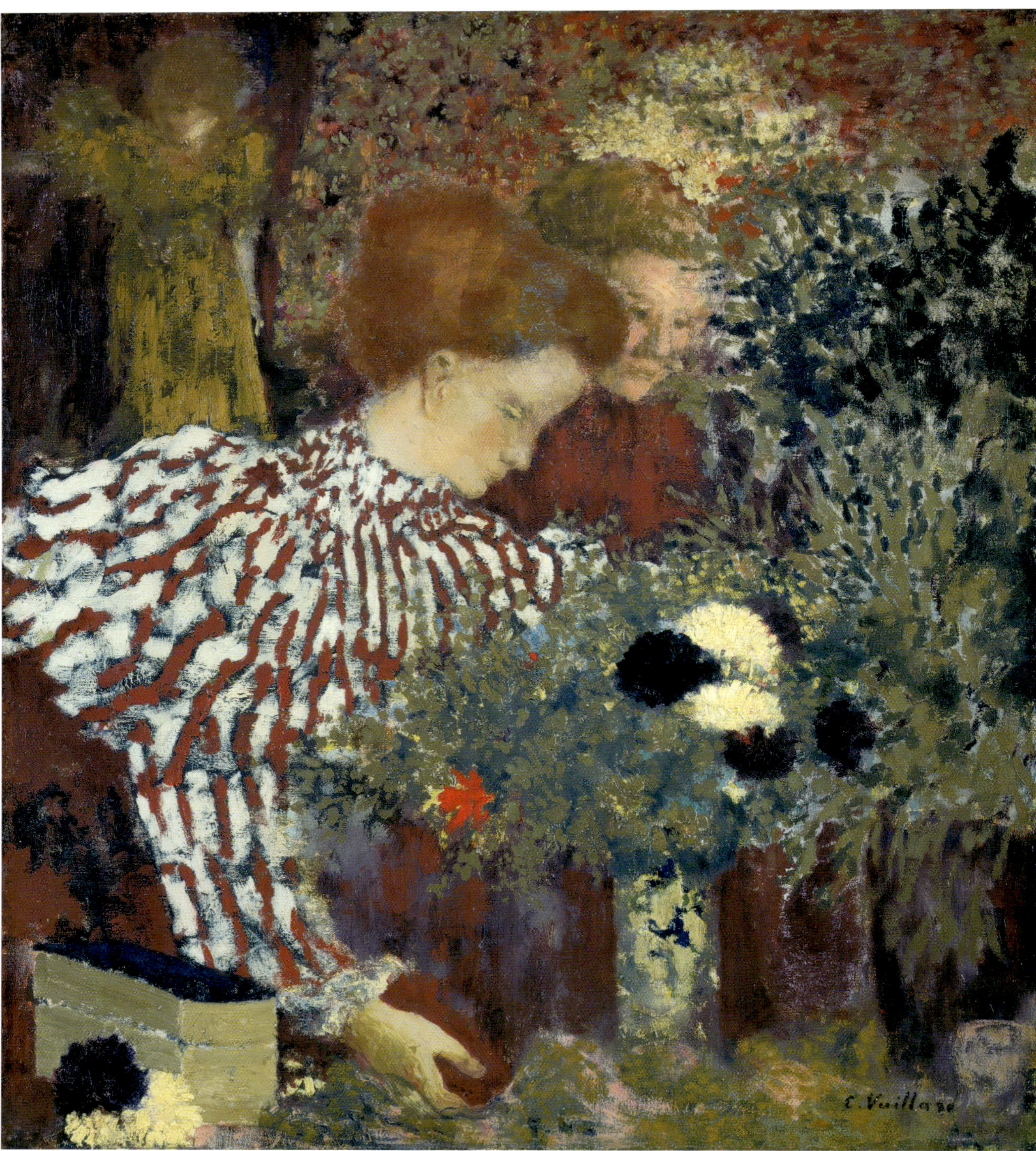

128
Edouard Vuillard,
***Woman in a Striped Dress*, 1895**
National Gallery of Art, Washington

> 129
Paul-Albert Besnard, Three decorative panels, c. 1895
Telfair Academy, Savannah

resulting pieces were too cumbersome and unattractive to remain on exhibition. One critic went so far as to call Denis's bedroom a mortuary decorated by a mind troubled by sinister fantasies, nourished by melancholy fairy-stories by Maurice Maeterlinck.[14]

While the bedroom was not a great success, the circular salon on the ground floor with painted decorations by Paul-Albert Besnard (fig. 129) was considered a far greater accomplishment. There was nothing but praise for the refined paintings, which consisted of eleven panels and a round painted ceiling showing dancing women. The theme of the panels was mountain scenery, painted in fluent brushstrokes, the dominant colour being lilac. Besnard was famous for his versatility and daring, and Camille Mauclair among others devoted enthusiastic articles to his technique and poetic taste.[15] Today it is rather difficult to imagine the success of such a traditional painter as Besnard, but perhaps he was so well loved because he was able to bridge the gap between the rather smooth and polished skill of academic art and the sketchy brushstrokes of impressionism.

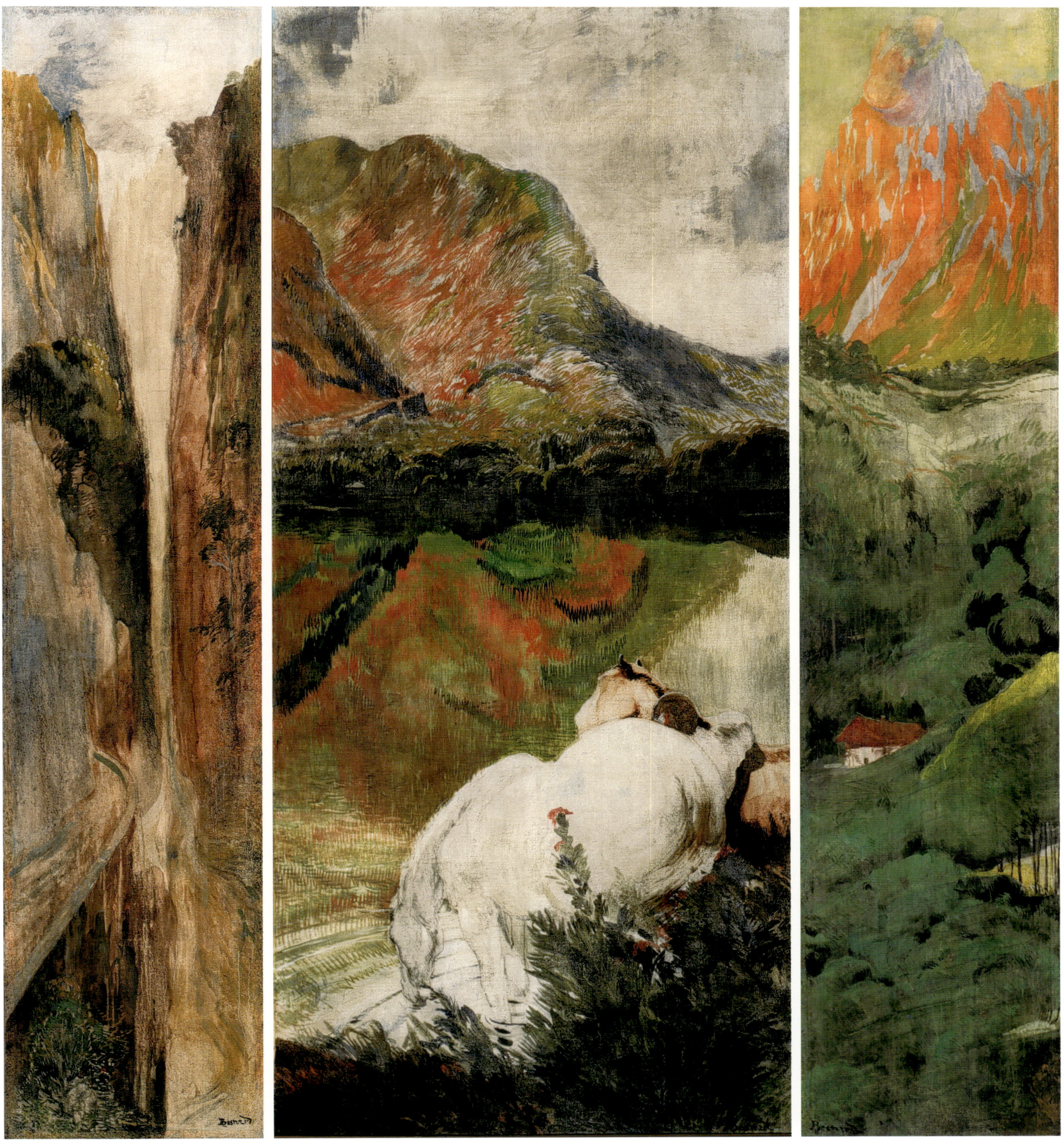

However, Besnard was sharply criticised by one of the impressionists: Camille Pissarro was unhappy with the resounding success of the celebrated artist. He pronounced the work awful, writing: 'It smacks of café-concert [décor] and Julian' (a reference to the traditional art of the Académie Julian).[16] But Pissarro was almost alone in his views. Even the most critical reviewer of Bing's efforts thought Besnard's salon a triumph of workmanship. Especially by daylight, the fine colour distinctions and the poetic atmosphere were seen at their best.

Curiously, the series of five panels by Vuillard, known as the 'Album', hanging to the right of the Besnard salon, failed to attract much attention (fig. 128).[17] The title is a reference to the second panel, in which three women on a sofa are looking at an album. Vuillard had finished the series of paintings a few weeks before the opening of Bing's first Salon. Camille Mauclair, a fervent advocate of the Nabis, was nevertheless sceptical about Vuillard's series. He thought the panels failed to harmonise with the dim light of their surroundings and found the repetition of what he considered a banal motif of women emerging from masses of flowers, painted in unpleasant impasto brushstrokes, ineffective. Others did not agree: Edmond Cousturier appreciated the intimate, mysterious atmosphere and the subtle range of colours, while Octave Mirbeau thought Vuillard was at his best if his 'musical' imagination could be given a free run over the surface of a wall.[18] The 'Album' series can truly be considered a superb combination of an almost symbolist mood with decorative, carpet-style patterns. The large undulating movement, the design in the characteristic arabesque of *art nouveau*, created a similar effect to that of Maurice Denis's frieze or Paul-Elie Ranson's paintings in the gallery. Félix Fénéon called them in essence abstract.[19] The panels had to be made in different sizes to fit the walls of Bing's gallery: where the wall was wider, Vuillard had extended the panel horizontally, and in the narrow section of wall between the two windows the panels had been elongated vertically. After the paintings had been on view for a few months in Bing's L'Art Nouveau gallery, they were installed in the house of Thadée Natanson, who had commissioned them. Natanson was supportive of Bing's accomplishments; like him he was greatly enamoured of Vuillard and symbolist painting.

In addition to the purely decorative objects and wall-decorations, the colourful stained-glass windows made by Louis Comfort Tiffany and designed by Paul-Elie Ranson, Ker-Xavier Roussel, Pierre Bonnard, Henri-Gabriel Ibels, Edouard Vuillard, Henri de Toulouse-Lautrec, Félix Vallotton, Eugène Grasset and Paul Sérusier, attracted a great deal of attention (figs. 69–71, 74, 76–77). Toulouse-Lautrec's window (fig. 74) was placed above the door of the entrance on the rue Chauchat (fig. 99). It must have been quite striking from the inside during the day, or from the outside when lights were on in the gallery. The other windows were located around the interior. It is true that they had already been exhibited a year earlier at the Salon du Champ-de-Mars, but here, in Bing's gallery, they appeared to greater advantage. They bore witness to a successful symbiosis between a two-dimensional scene – which ignores any illusion of depth – and an elegant use of line. It was Siegfried Bing who coupled the subtle technique of the American glass craftsman with the daring designs of French artists, who were inspired by everyday themes like elegant Parisian ladies out walking (fig. 77), a theatre seen from the gallery (fig. 74), children playing in a park (figs. 69, 70), or the bustling 'fleeting' life of the street (fig. 71). In doing so, Bing broke down the barriers between the arts and mixed a creative cocktail of fine and applied arts.

Each room had its own special atmosphere. The emphasis in Besnard's salon was on nature rendered in poetic and beautifully harmonised colours; the theme of Denis's bedroom decorations was the tender relationship between mother and child or, in a more general sense, family happiness; and in Ranson's dining room paintings the focus was on life in the countryside. The stained-glass windows were also a reflection of contemporary life, just like the wall-decorations, but the sparkling character of stained glass with its bright colours meant that the effect was more direct, more confrontational and less spiritual and diffuse. All in all, the rooms were so different in outlook and style that they must have had a stunning impact on the visitor, and the presence of many foreign designers gave Bing's first Salon tremendous international allure.

> 130
William Degouve de Nuncques, *Child with Owl*, 1892
Private collection, courtesy Van Herck, Antwerp

ART IN THE HOME

Apart from the stained-glass windows and the painted decorations that had been integrated into the various model rooms, it was mainly the ground floor of the gallery that provided a fine selection of independent paintings on canvas; this 'autonomous' art in turn accentuated the decorative features of the gallery. Paintings by the symbolists Fernand Khnopff, William Degouve de Nuncques or Félix Vallotton, and the pointillists Théo Van Rysselberghe or Henri-Edmond Cross, used the flat surface and the manipulation of space as their point of

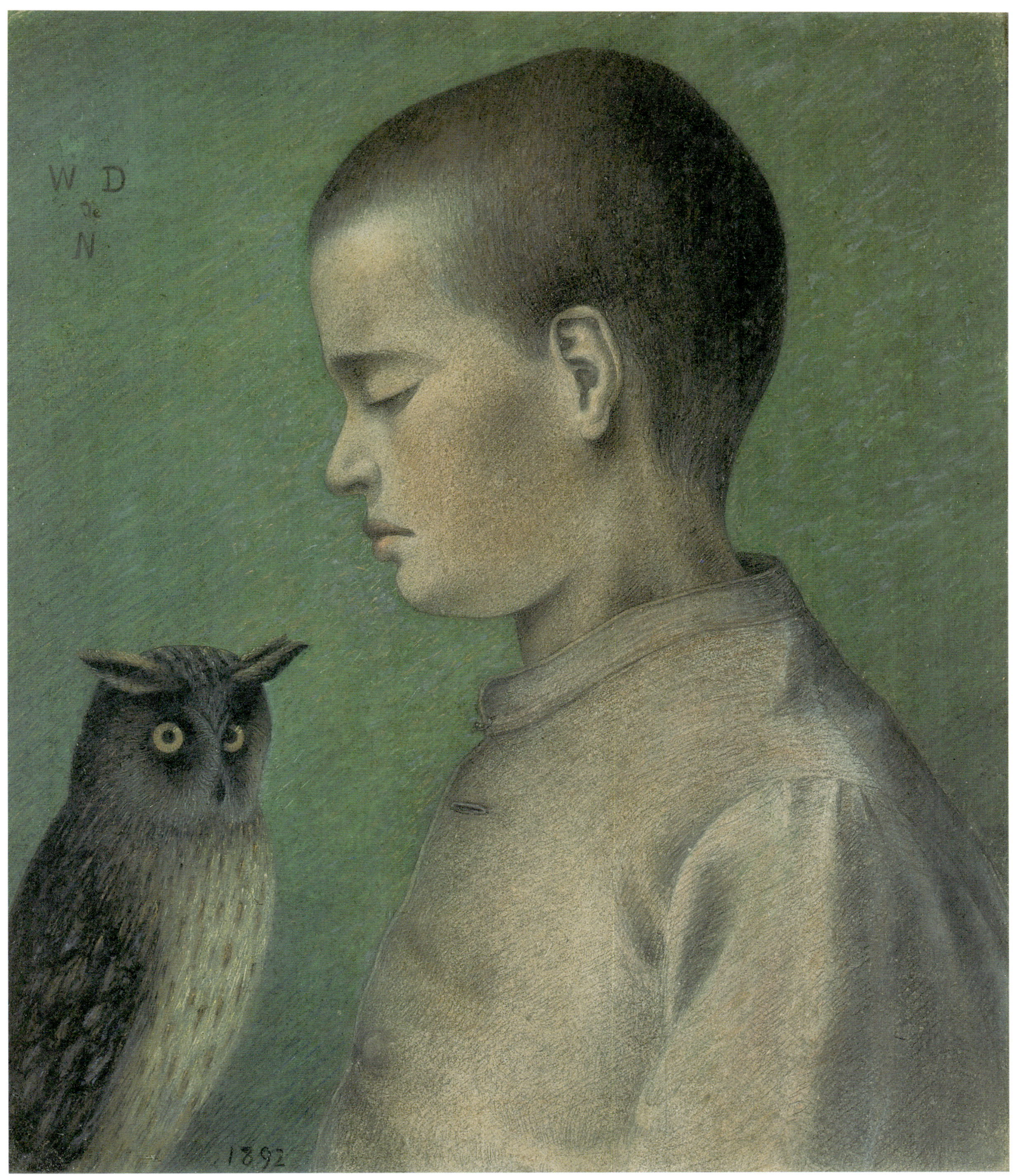
W D
de
N
1892

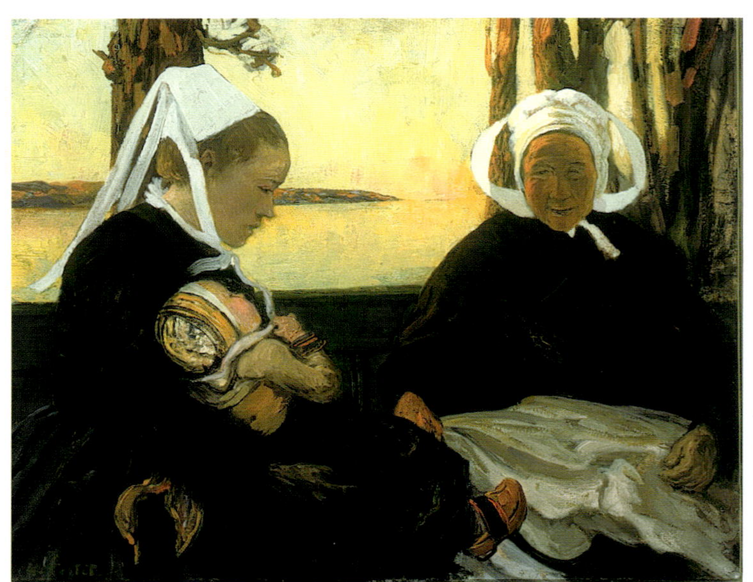

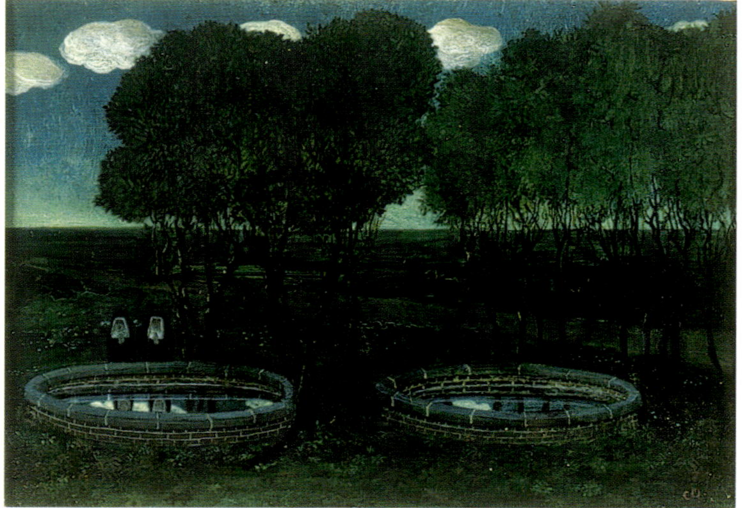

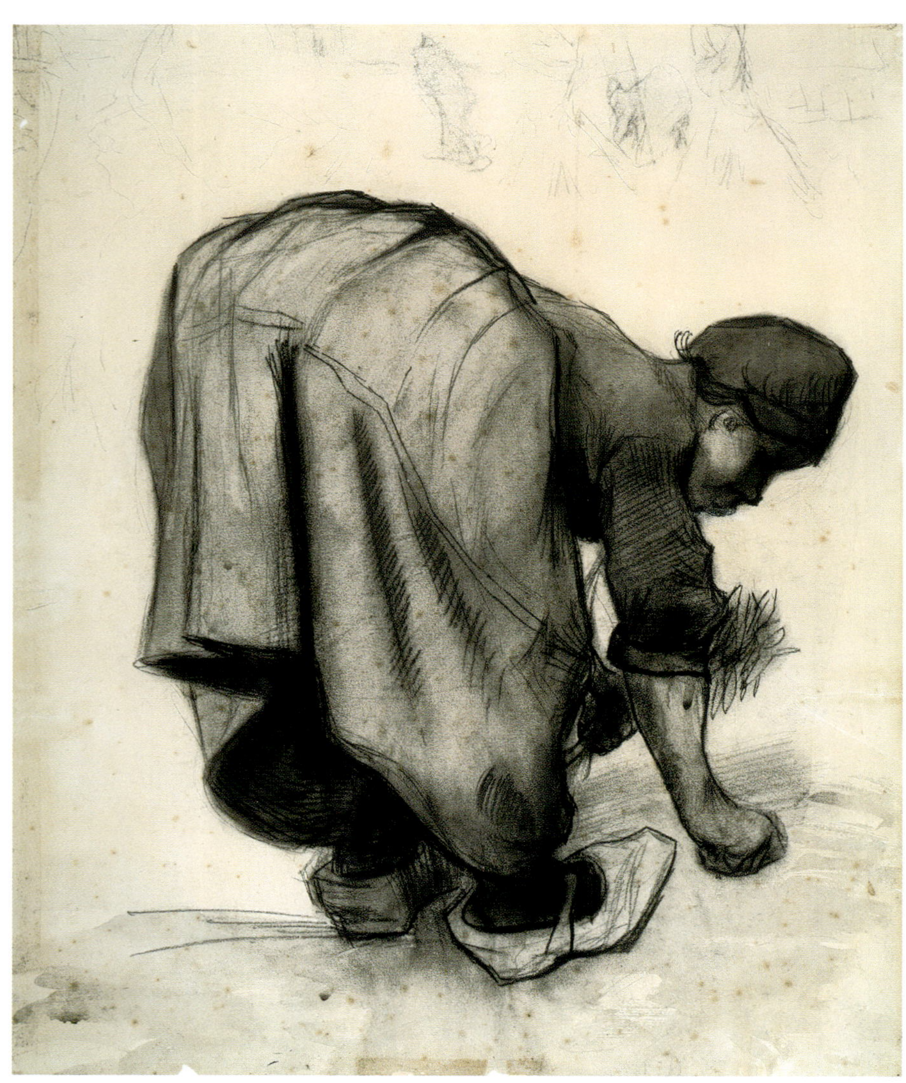

departure. With a decorative interplay of lines and forms, the often off-centre compositional arrangements – combined with the emphasis on surface designs – became the most prominent features of these advanced works. Thematically speaking, the painters, even the impressionists and neo-impressionists, were often trying to capture the expression of emotions such as melancholy, loneliness, tranquillity and contemplation. In fact, it was only the colourful windows that offered a happy and lively note in a predominantly solemn artistic décor. This fin-de-siècle mood expressed in somewhat sombre art suited Bing, who was known for being very erudite, thorough, serious, professional and fanatical, as well as insisting on the importance of minute detail. The choice of artists and works for the gallery was also reflected in his own collection of fine art, pieces that were auctioned at the Hôtel Drouot in 1900 to help Bing finance his *art nouveau* business. This collection mixed different styles: traditional Brittany landscapes and genre scenes by Charles Cottet (fig. 131), depictions of Normandy by the Norwegian painter Fritz Thaulow, elegant decadent watercolours by Georges de Feure (fig. 192), intimate, tiny paintings by Charles Doudelet (fig. 133), Xavier Mellery and Alphonse Osbert, but also two drawings by Vincent van Gogh, including a women bending down, from the painter's Brabant period (fig. 132).[20]

This latter drawing by Van Gogh may have been acquired in exchange for *ukiyo-e* prints, for during his Paris period (1886–8) Van Gogh regularly visited Siegfried Bing to browse through his Japanese prints. Van Gogh acted as an agent for Bing; he had his own 'depot' at Bing's and brought him new clients. It was not that he earned a great deal of money, according to his own account; his main motive was to surround himself with Japanese artefacts, and he advised other people to do the same. In a letter dated 15 July 1888 Vincent asked his brother Theo to keep the depot going: 'We get them so cheap, and can give pleasure to so many artists with them altogether we must keep what favour we have with old Bing [...] There is an attic at Bing's with millions of prints piled up, landscape and figures, and old prints too. He will let you choose for yourself some Sunday, so take plenty of old prints as well.'[21] Bing's Japanese art was a major influence on Van Gogh's oeuvre, leading to an unusual series of interpretations of Japanese prints, like the paintings *The Blossoming Plum Tree* or *Bridge in the Rain*, both after prints by Hiroshige and made in Paris in the autumn of 1887.

The influence of Far Eastern art also played a prominent role in the work of other artists who exhibited at Bing's later on, as can be seen in the silhouette-like women by de Feure (fig. 193) and Toulouse-Lautrec (figs. 74, 75, 126) or the willowy dancers by Frank Brangwyn (fig. 124), who all bear a resemblance to the graceful geishas in Japanese prints. The two-dimensional quality of colour, line and surface permeated contemporary art at the end of the nineteenth century. Bing's passion for modern art was therefore a logical progression stemming from his predilection for Eastern art. At the same time, it should be noted that the source of Japanese art was gradually running dry, and that all the important museums and collectors had already been supplied with outstanding examples of Eastern arts and crafts and prints.[22] This meant that Bing, always a shrewd businessman, was forced to try new approaches. But, as Meier-Graefe so rightly remarked in 1896, Japanese art had generated a wealth of ideas and had been a great stimulus in the development of modern aesthetics. Japanese art had always been recognised and appreciated for its ability to create art out of the simple events of everyday life. It focused its attention on the smallest and seemingly the least significant objects used in the home in order to evoke a thoroughly artistic environment. Europe, on the other hand, had always held to the principle of 'art for art's sake', and decorative art objects were created for their own intrinsic value. In Meier-Graefe's view the ideal of a house like that of the Goncourts, in an eighteenth-century setting, was passé. 'A modern person cannot live in the bric-à-brac surrounding of the Second Empire. Wrenching something from another period and putting it in a new setting can be just as much of a disaster as barbarian imitations of old models in the applied arts.'[23]

< 131
Charles Cottet, *Fine Evening in Brittany*, c. 1896
Rogalin Gallery, Poznán

< 132
Vincent van Gogh, *Woman Bending Down*, 1885
Kröller-Müller Museum, Otterlo

< 133
Charles Doudelet, *Devotion*, c. 1894
Rogalin Gallery, Poznán

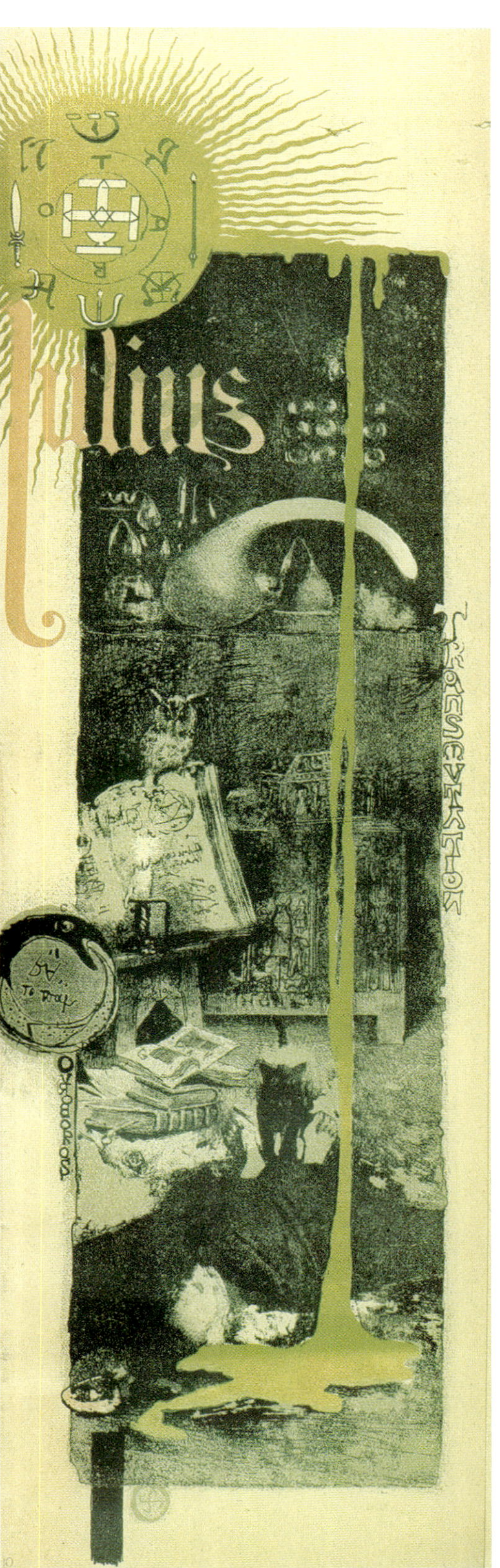

134
Manuel Orazi, Illustration for Austin de Croze, *The Magic Calendar*, 1895
Collection Jacques et Rolande van der Heyde

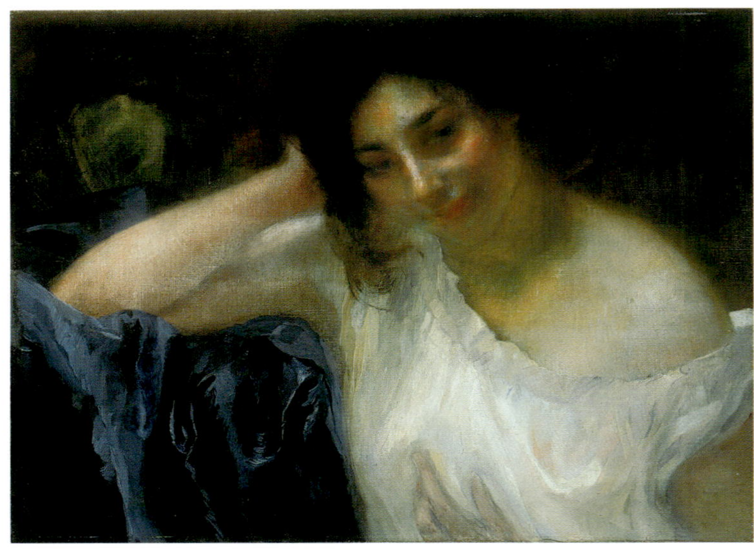

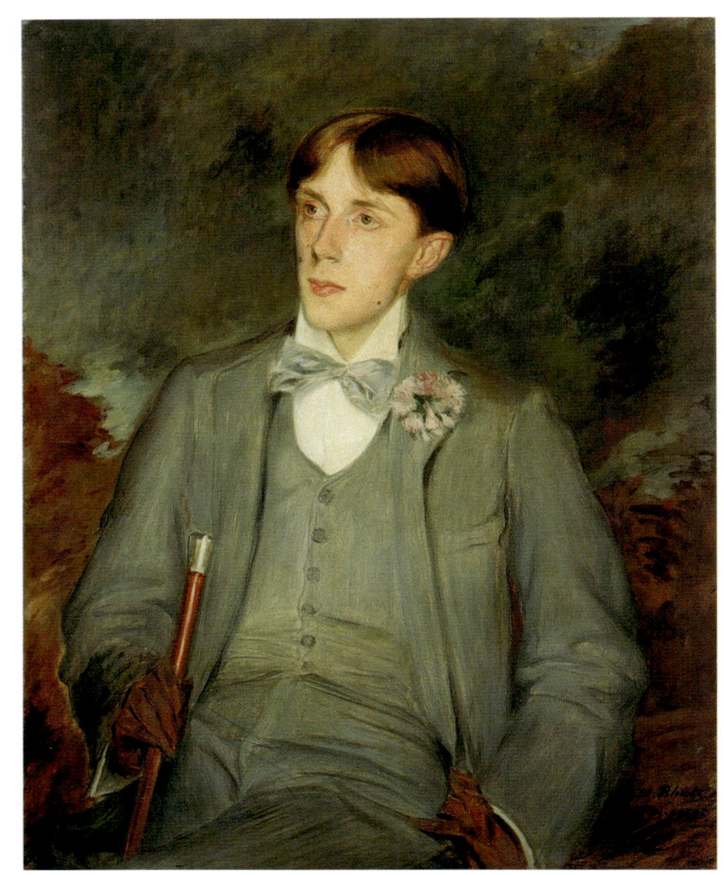

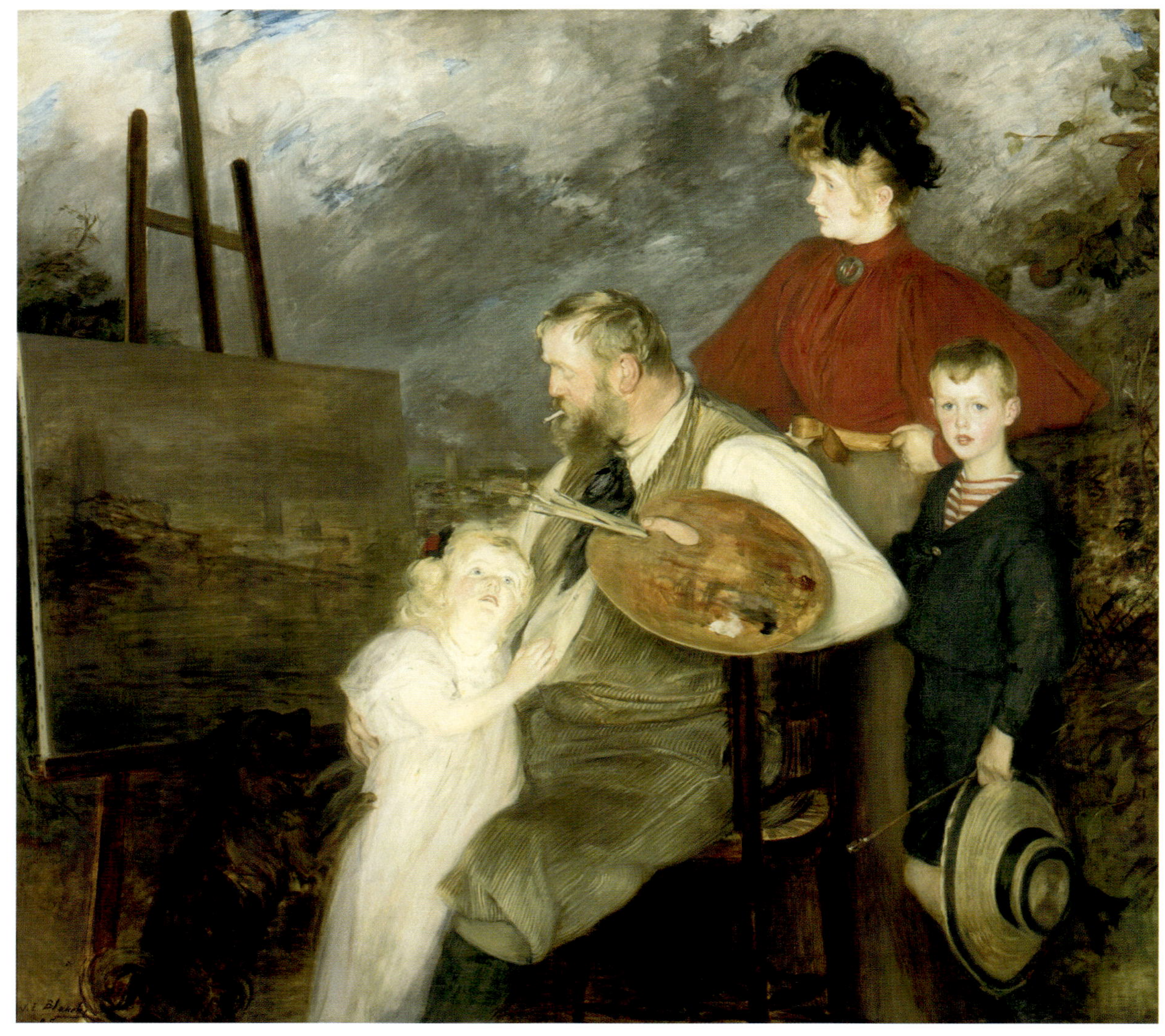

Imposing academic works, exhibited at countless Salon exhibitions, which were beginning to resemble market halls, were not to be found at Bing's, who, in addition to paintings, exhibited many intimate drawings, sketches and graphic works. The exhibition catalogues are very brief and usually only mention the artist and the title of the piece,[24] which makes a reconstruction of the works Bing exhibited no easy task. Nevertheless, apart from the elements from the various style rooms described above, we have been able to trace a few outstanding examples of both fine and applied art shown in Bing's gallery.

< 135
Paul-Albert Besnard, *Woman with Blue Drapery*, c. 1900
Rogalin Gallery, Poznán

< 136
Jacques-Emile Blanche, *Portrait of Aubrey Beardsley*, 1895
National Portrait Gallery, London

< 137
Jacques-Emile Blanche, *The Painter Thaulow and his Children*, 1895
Musée d'Orsay, Paris

SALONS 1 AND 2: DREAMY POETRY AND GEOMETRIC DOTS

When considering the more moderate modern artists, a figure like Albert Besnard automatically springs to mind; it was he who he had been commissioned for the paintings for the circular salon, and there were also a number of his works in Bing's personal collection. One of them, *Woman with Blue Drapery* (fig. 135), sold at Drouot, passed into the hands of the Polish Count Raczynski, who was an avid collector of late nineteenth-century French art.[25] Stylistically speaking, works by Besnard leaned towards the type of society portraits typical of Jacques-Emile Blanche, a very talented portrait painter, whose attractive painting of the Thaulow family (fig. 137) and unusual portrait of the twenty-three-year-old English draughtsman Aubrey Beardsley (fig. 136) were also on show. The lean face of the sickly, dandified Beardsley and the ostracism he suffered were beautifully rendered by Blanche. The man in the portrait and his work were much to Bing's taste. A few months after Blanche completed the painting, Bing presented a number of Beardsley's works at his 1896 international book fair, including a good selection of decadent illustrations executed in harsh, poignant brushstrokes.[26] The bibliophile Bing exhibited more than a thousand books, including his own publications, such as *The Magic Calendar*, a mystical, astrological publication (fig. 134), and two illustrated works by the Belgian decadent writer Georges Rodenbach.[27]

An important number of paintings at Bing's first Salon de L'Art Nouveau were symbolist in style. Whilst the pastel *Child with Owl* by William Degouve de Nuncques (fig. 130) reminds us of the meditative atmosphere of the Flemish primitive painters, Charles Doudelet's *Devotion* (fig. 133), with its theme of introspection and reflection, has an even more monastic aspect; likewise Fernand Khnopff's *Under the Fir Trees* (fig. 142), a melancholic introspective piece in which the rarefied natural shapes of autumn

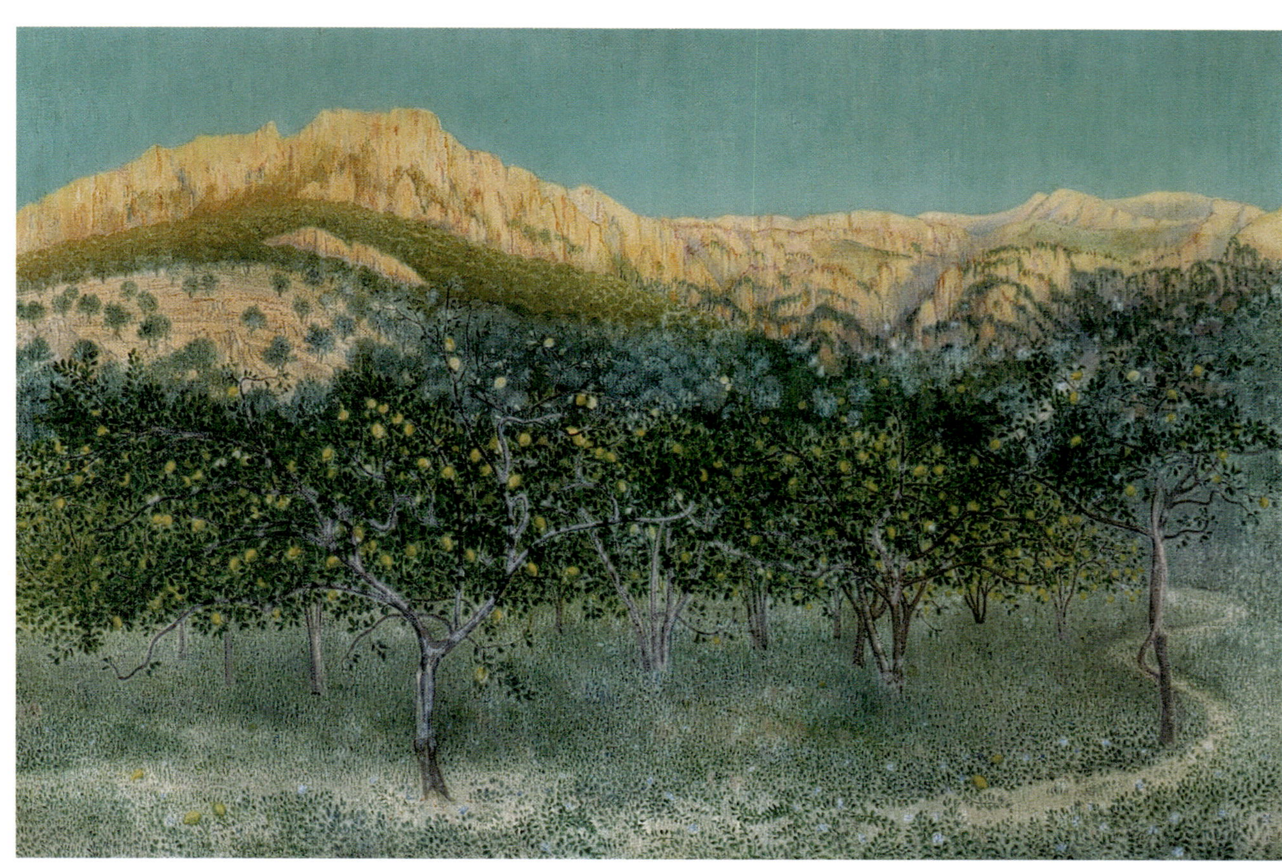

138
William Degouve de Nuncques, *Lemon Trees in Majorca*, c. 1901
Private collection

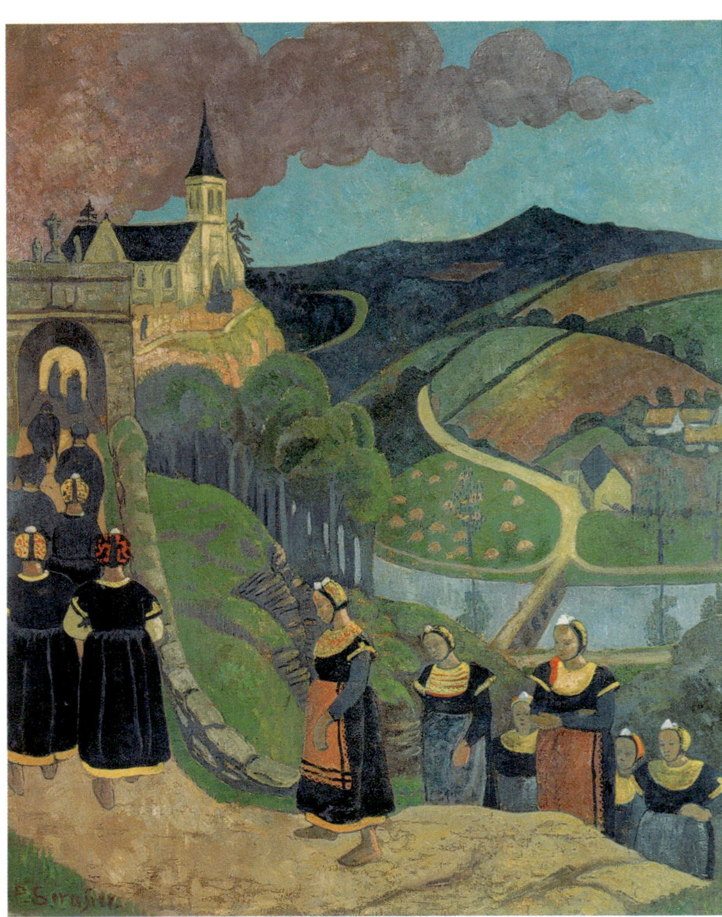

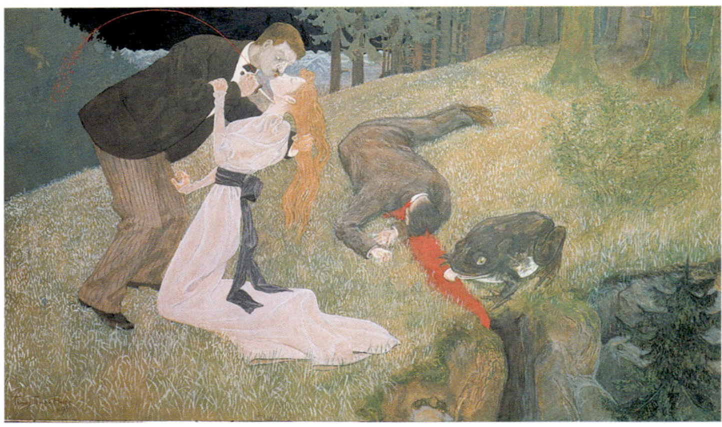

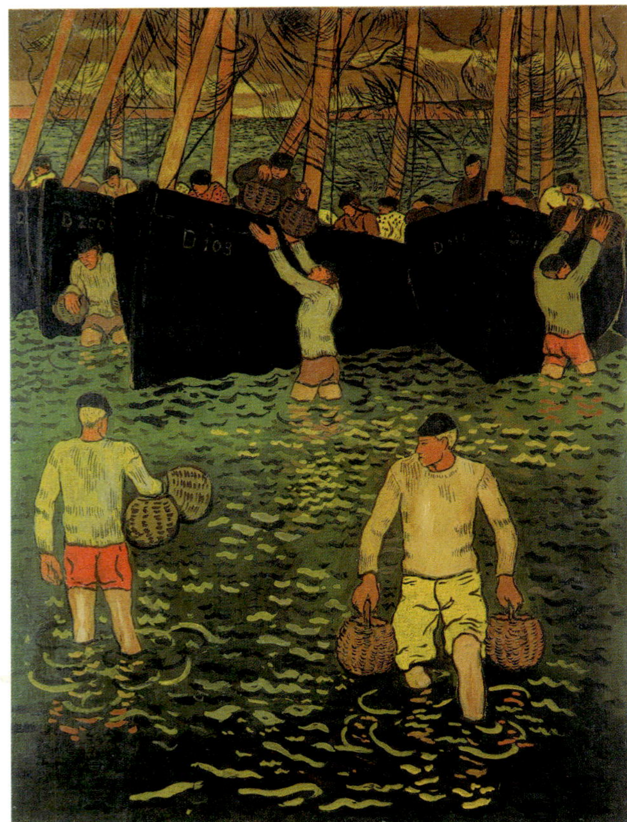

139
Paul Sérusier,
The Pilgrimage to Notre-Dame des Portes,
1894–95
Musée des Beaux-Arts, Quimper

140
Georges Lacombe,
***Return of the Sardine Fishers,* 1895**
Private collection

141
Thomas Theodor Heine, *Jealousy,* 1894
Private collection

> 142
Fernand Khnopff,
***At Fosset/Under the Fir Trees,* 1894**
Musées royaux des Beaux-Arts de Belgique, Brussels

are a reflection of the soul. It is not surprising that these Belgian artists were on show at Bing's, since they had all previously exhibited in Brussels at La Libre Esthétique or Picard's Maison d'Art, both of which served as models for Bing's own Salon de L'Art Nouveau. Furthermore, symbolism was gaining far more coverage in the press, and this style was attracting an increasing following.

Bing wanted to introduce the charm of simple beauty into everyday life, and it was this simplification of the language of shape and image that was characteristic of the Nabis (from the Hebrew word for 'prophets'), a group of artists under the leadership of Paul Sérusier, who leaned heavily on symbolism. Sérusier exhibited at Bing's his *Pilgrimage to Notre-Dame des Portes* (fig. 139), a procession held at the consecration of a new church in Brittany. It does not depic the real event but is, rather, a symbolic evocation of the location, where the winding roads in the landscape and the abstract figures combine with the marked contrast of the colour surfaces, emphasising a primitive, religious experience of nature, stripped of all distracting and superfluous details.

Another striking category of works at the first Salon were the neo-impressionist paintings by Henri-Edmond Cross, Théo Van Rysselberghe, Maximilien Luce and Paul Signac (figs. 115, 116, 143). According to Meier-Graefe, these artists were a new generation who used painting

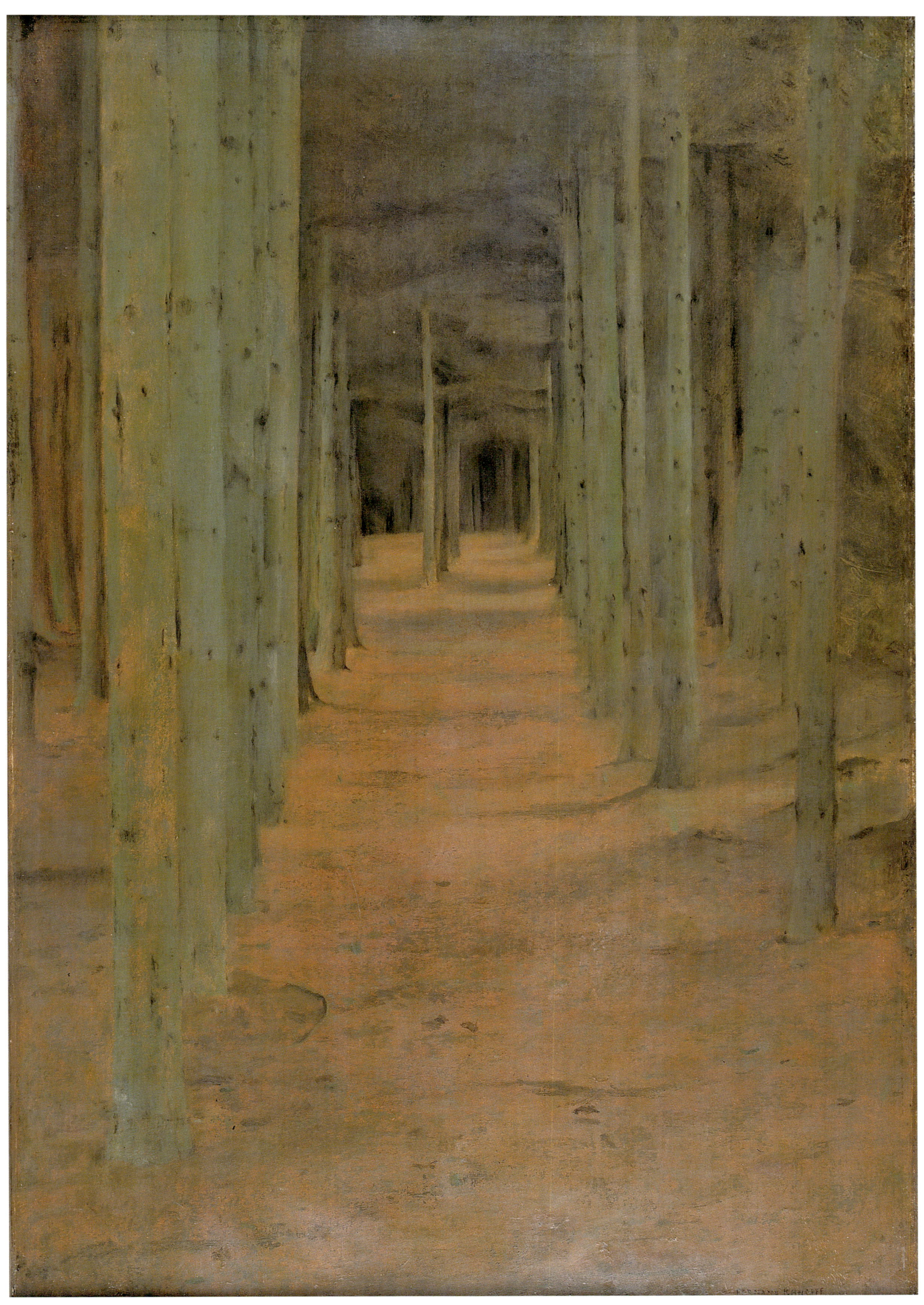

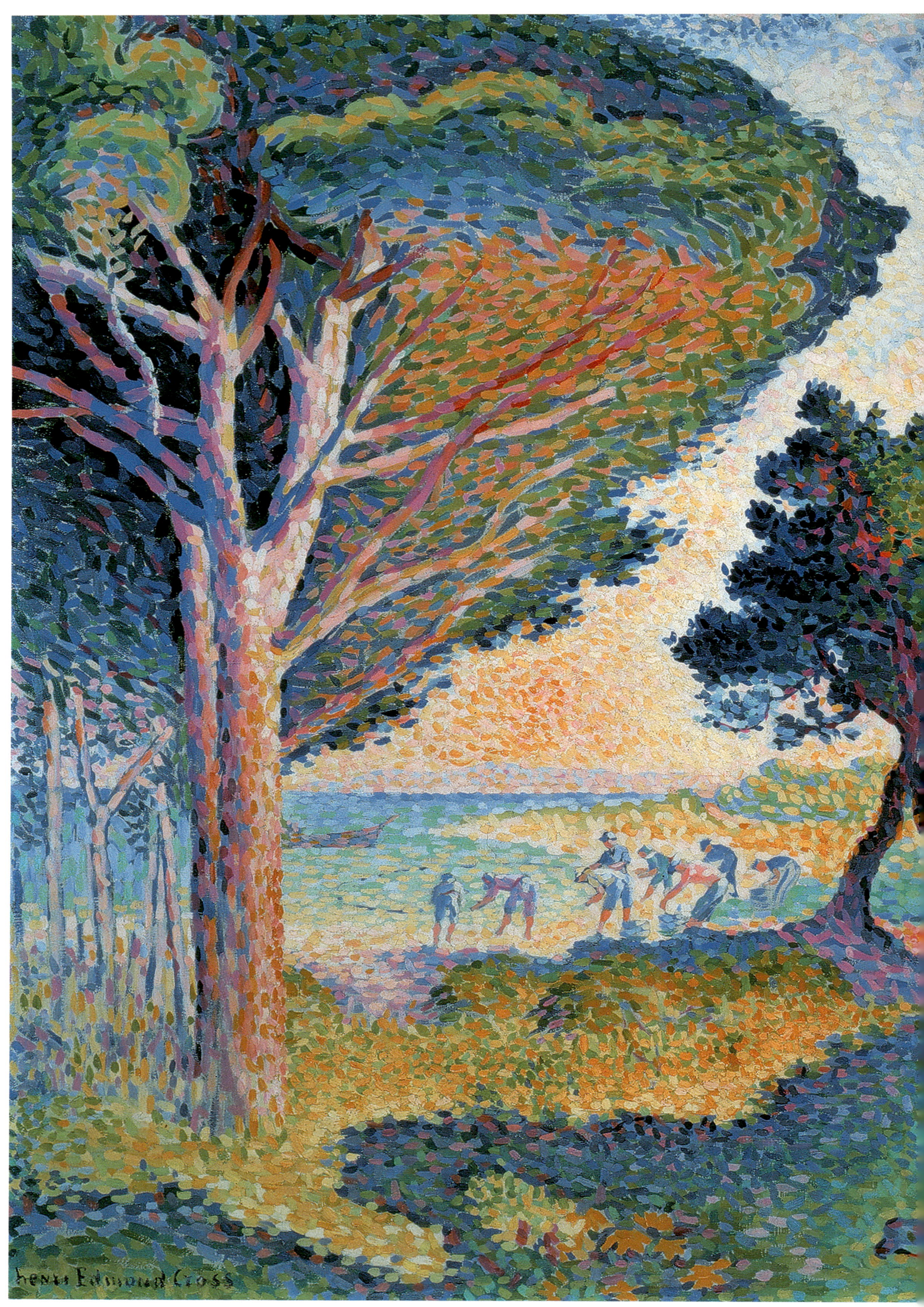
henri Edmond Cross

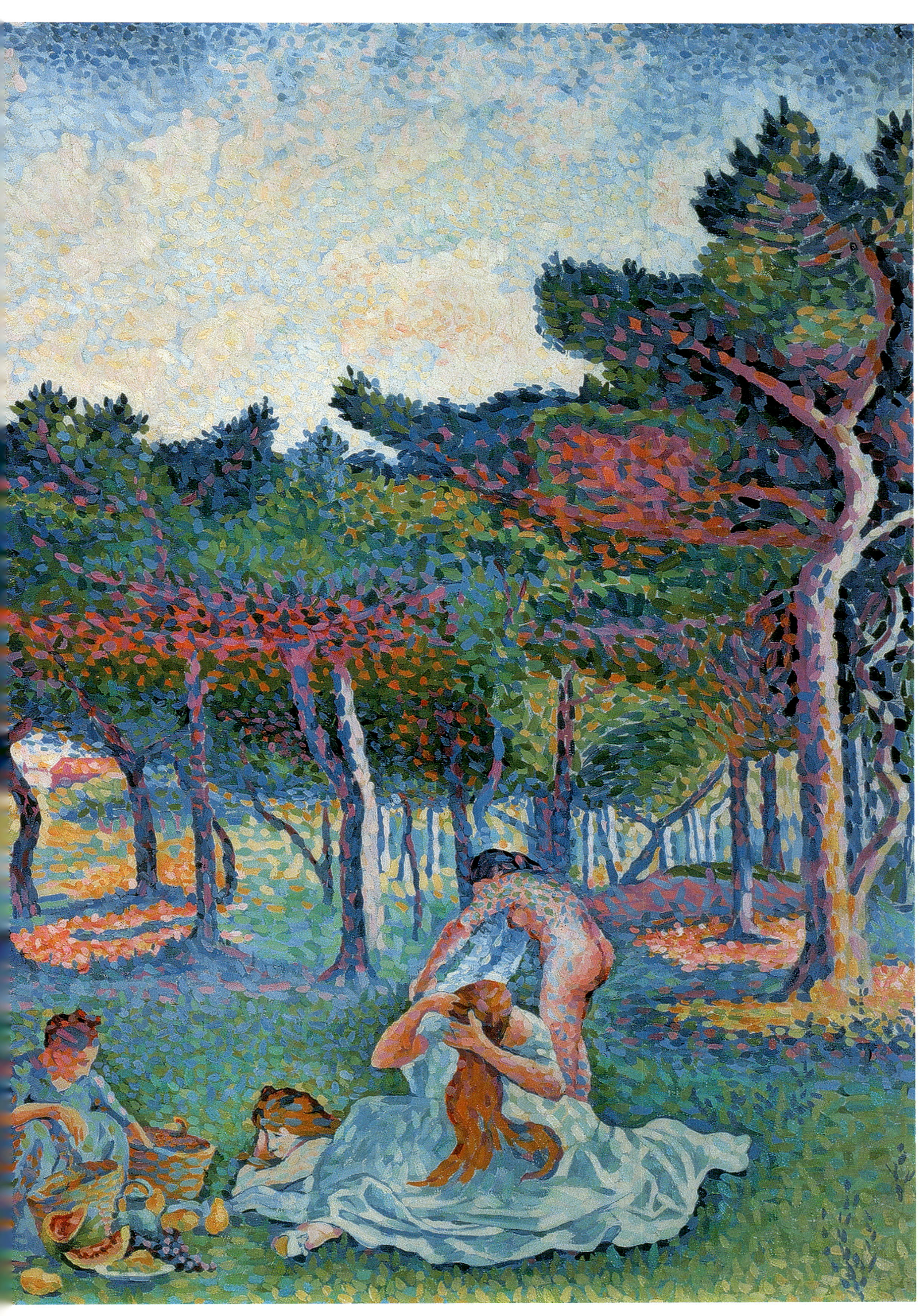

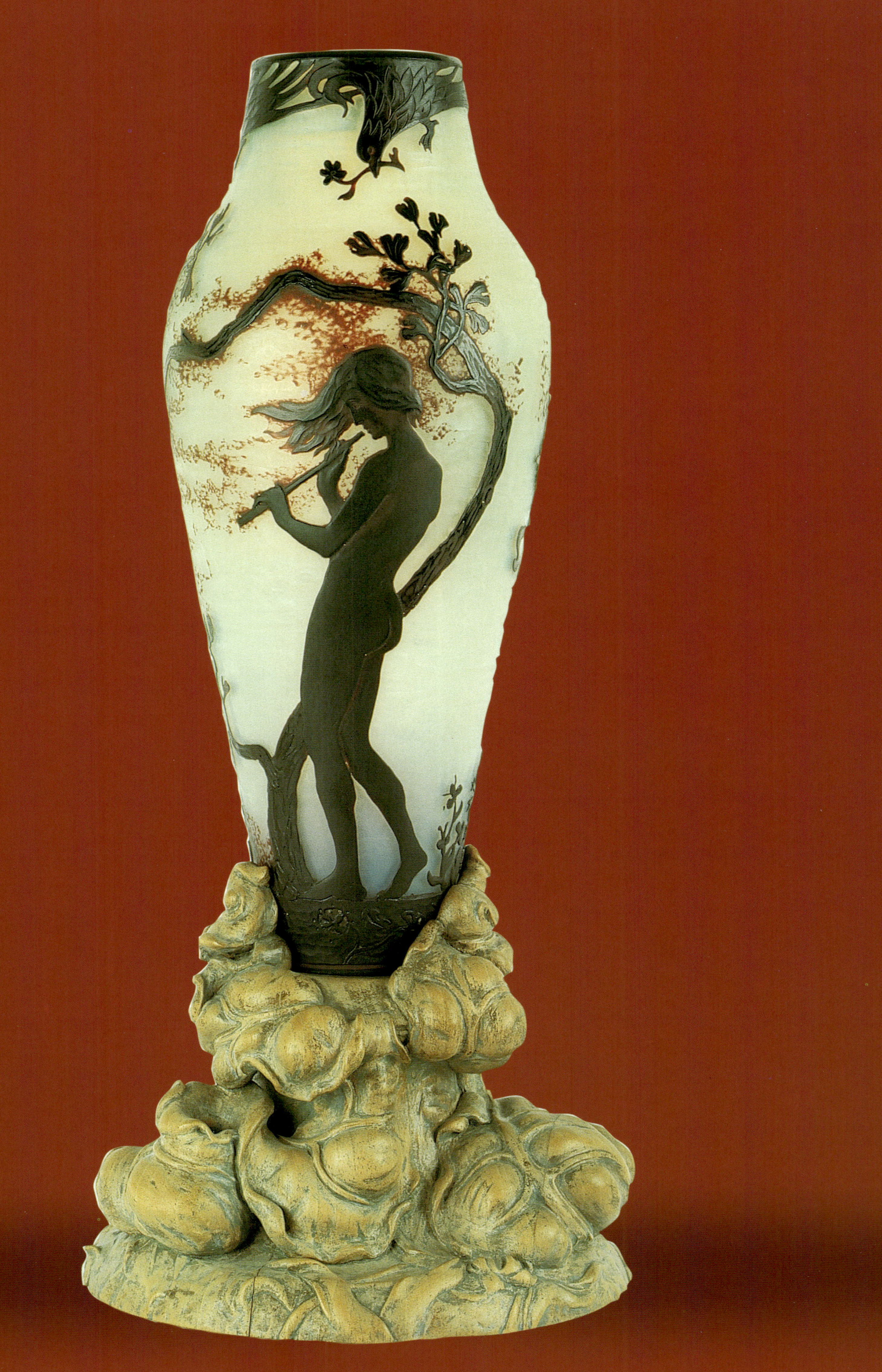

techniques and colour as a means of expression. As an influential critic, Meier-Graefe also noted that Michel-Eugène Chevreul's publication on colour theory was invaluable to the development of modern painting and, by extension, for enterprises like Bing's that sponsored new art. He saw Chevreul's work on colour contrasts as a handbook for modern interior design, based on the harmony of colours, where each object (and stroke of colour) are in accordance with the nature of the object or the objects and their context.[28] This idea is supported by the importance the neo-impressionists (supported by Chevreul) attached to matching frames and to the place in which the work of art would be hung. Once again, Belgium was a guiding light in this matter. From its very beginning in 1883 the artists' group Les XX, who were based in Brussels, had shown their works in peaceful, harmonious surroundings, thus attempting to present them at their best, while taking into consideration the total effect they created.[29] The artist Gisbert Combaz put the decorative effect of the neo-impressionist painters even more succinctly when he called Van Rysselberghe a 'décorateur belge', thereby referring to the pure colours in rhythmic lines often used in mosaics and carpets.[30]

The paintings of the pointillists were very much in vogue. When the architect Louis-Charles Boileau asked one of the assistants at Bing's gallery, the so-called 'inspecteur des galeries',[31] the price of some of the works, he remarked that the luminists and pointillists were shockingly expensive.[32] However, inventory books for Bing's gallery are not available to confirm this, so one can merely guess at the prices. It is only through the bills of purchase from the various museums, which were always bills for works of applied art, that we gain some idea of the prices of objects bought from Bing's. The prices are known for all the items auctioned from Bing's collection in 1900, thanks to an annotated version of the auction catalogue.[33] These confirm the reputation of some of the artists discussed above. The highest prices were paid for works by Albert Besnard (for instance, 4,200 francs for fig. 135). Paintings by Fritz Thaulow and Charles Cottet, neither considered nowadays to be top artists, also fetched high prices. Unfortunately the neo-impressionists were not part of this sale, so we do not know anything about what they fetched, but in the gallery they were priced at a few thousand francs, comparable in cost to art by famous impressionists like Monet.[34]

Just as two-dimensional art shown at Bing's gallery can often be referred to as 'decorative', Bing's applied art often had 'painterly' or 'sculptural' qualities. One craftsman who fell into this category was René Lalique,

<< 143
Henri-Edmond Cross, *Mediterranean Shores*, 1895
Walter F. Brown Collection

< 144
Daum Frères, *Calm Hour/Twilight Incantation*, 1895
Musées royaux d'Art et d'Histoire, Brussels

145
Daum Frères, *The Violet Mourning of the Colchicum*, 1893
Musée d'Orsay, Paris

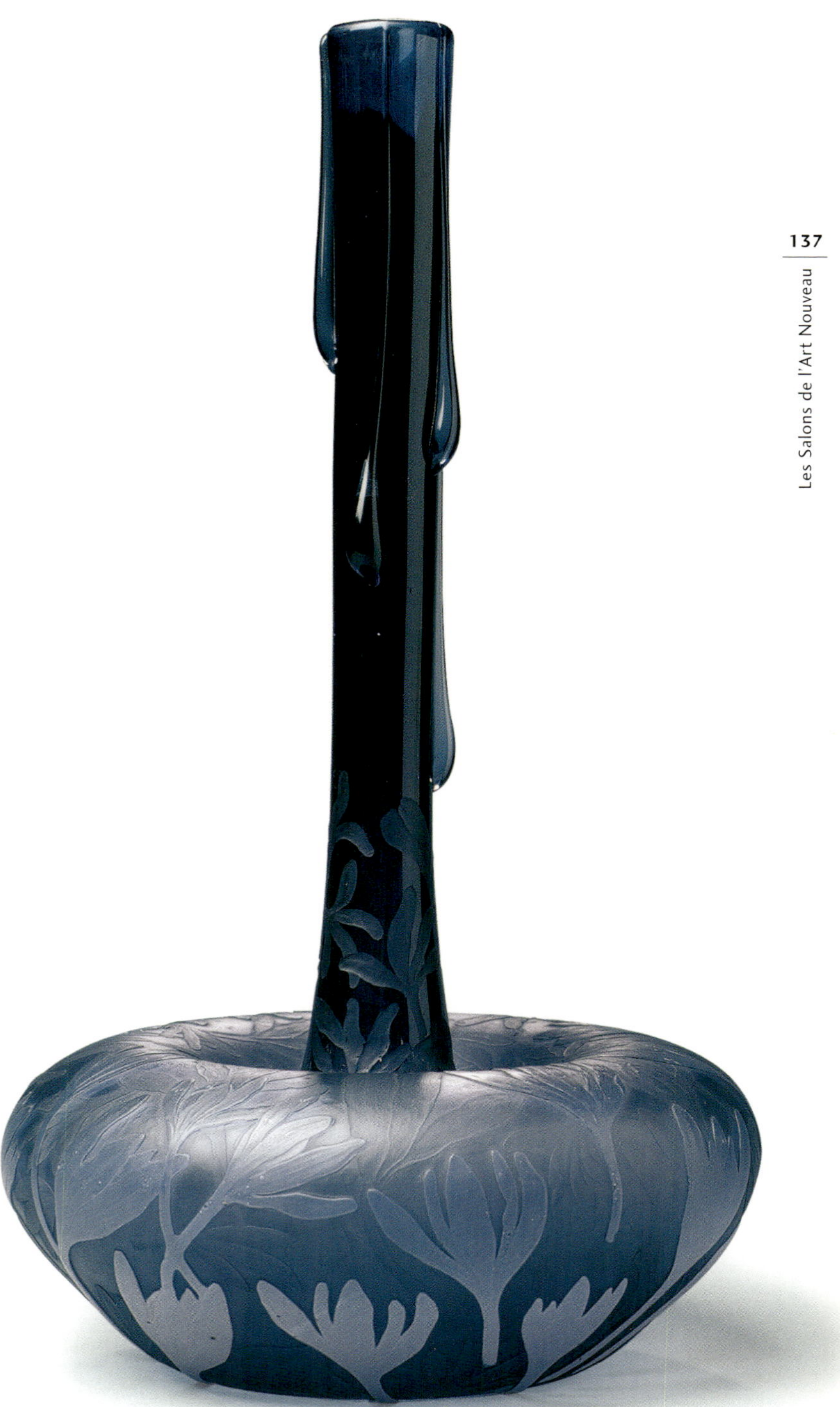

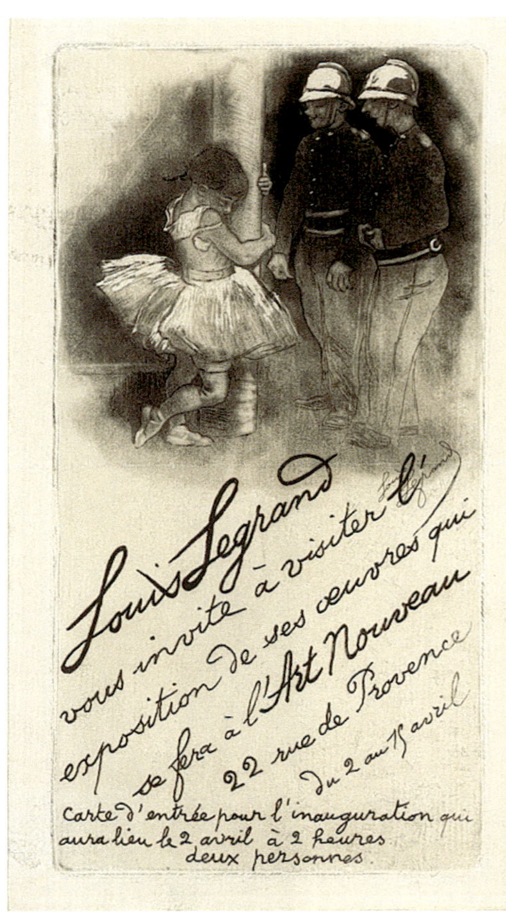

then at the beginning of his career, who showed a number of pieces of jewellery with masks and chimeras (mythological creatures), which are no longer traceable. There was also Georges Morren, who, in addition to jewellery, produced small decorative utilitarian objects, including an inkwell with a seated female nude (fig. 110). Another artist who, like Morren, combined art and functionality was Alexandre Charpentier, who designed small bronze door plates.

In the field of artistic glassware, the vases by the Daum brothers were striking in appearance. They were given symbolic titles like *Calm Hour* (fig. 144), *The Violet Mourning of the Colchicum* (fig. 145), or *Elsa's Dream*.[35] They were unique pieces, and due to their range of colour tones and rich jewel-like quality they rose above the level of an ordinary utilitarian object. As well as *Elsa's Dream*, named after the first act of Wagner's opera *Lohengrin*, *Calm Hour* (or *Twilight Incantation*) was also based on a Wagnerian theme. On this vase, designed by Jacques Gruber but made by Daum, there is a depiction of an elegant male figure playing the flute, hair flying in the breeze, and encircled by three eagles. It is a free interpretation of Siegfried, the Germanic hero, who is trying to make contact with the birds by playing his musical

146
Louis Legrand, Invitation for Legrand's exhibition at Bing's, April 1897
Museum für Kunst und Gewerbe, Hamburg

147
Auguste Rodin, *Head of St John the Baptist*, 1892–93
Private collection

> 148
Victor Rousseau, *Happiness*, 1894
Musée des Beaux-Arts, Tournai

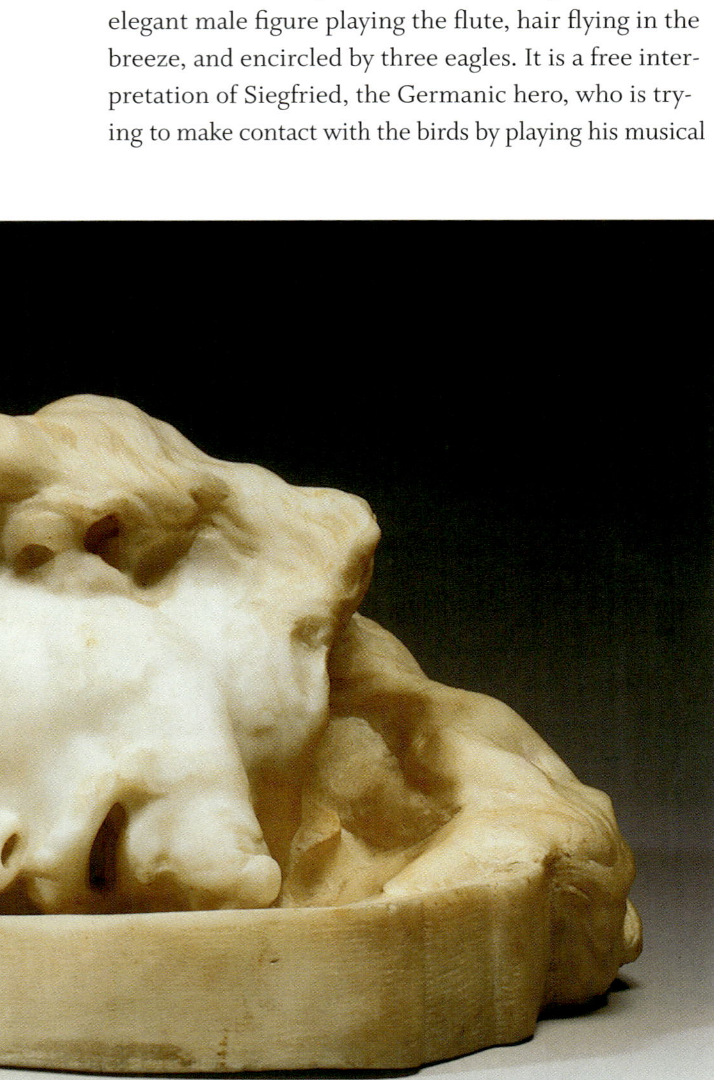

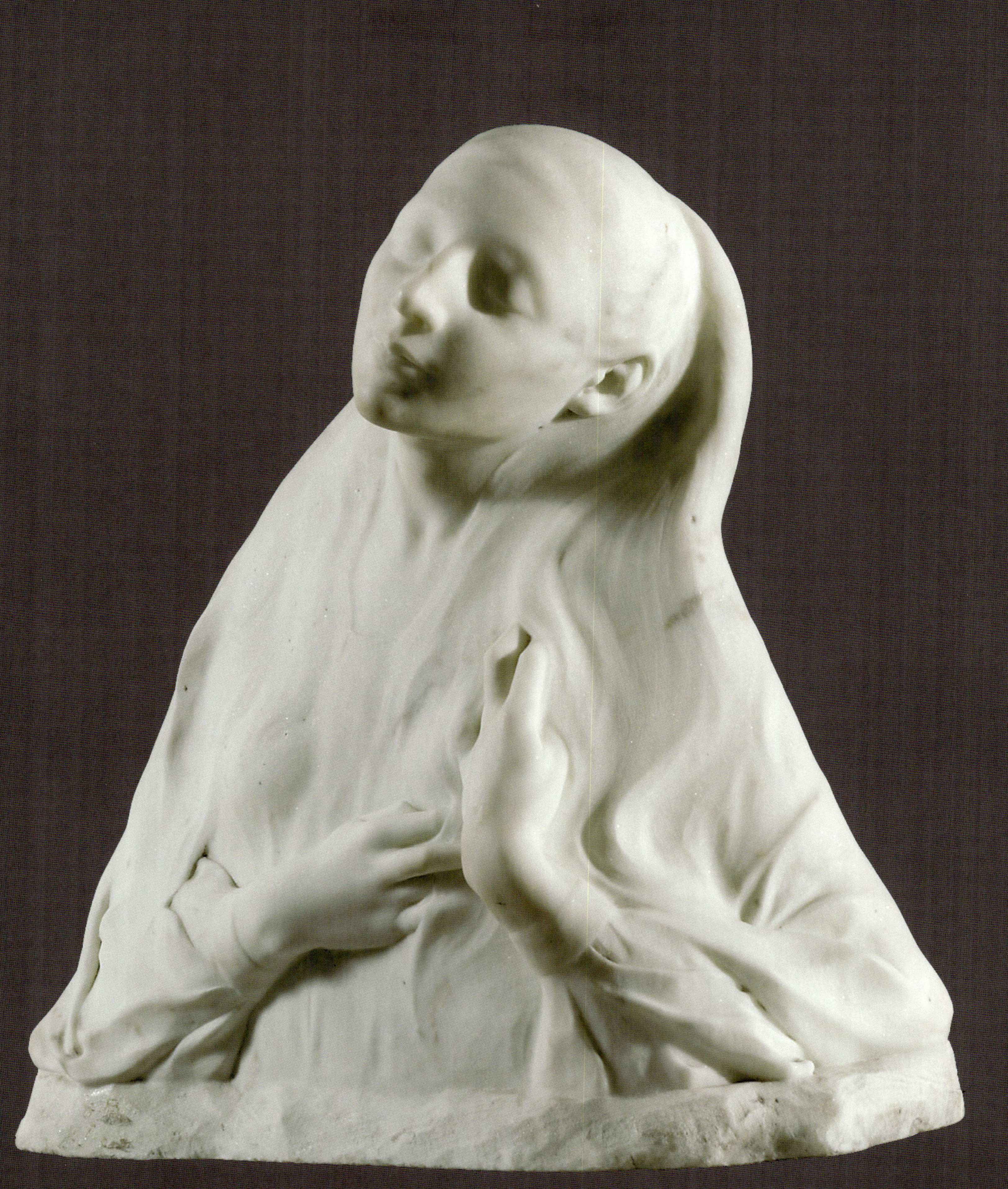

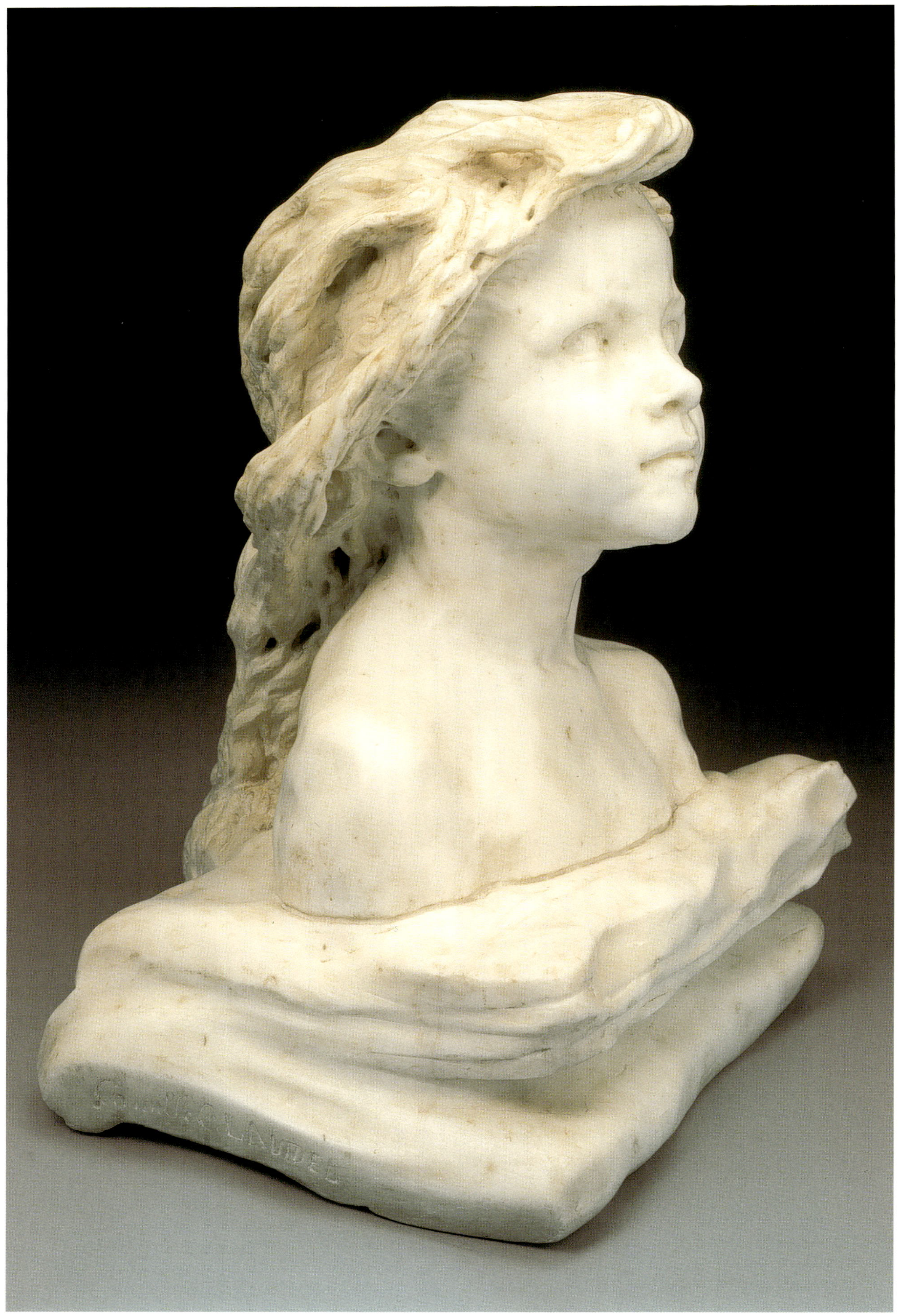

149
Camille Claudel,
***The Little Châtelaine*, 1896**
Musée d'Art et d'Industrie, Roubaix

> 150
Camille Claudel,
***The Waltz*, 1896**
Private collection

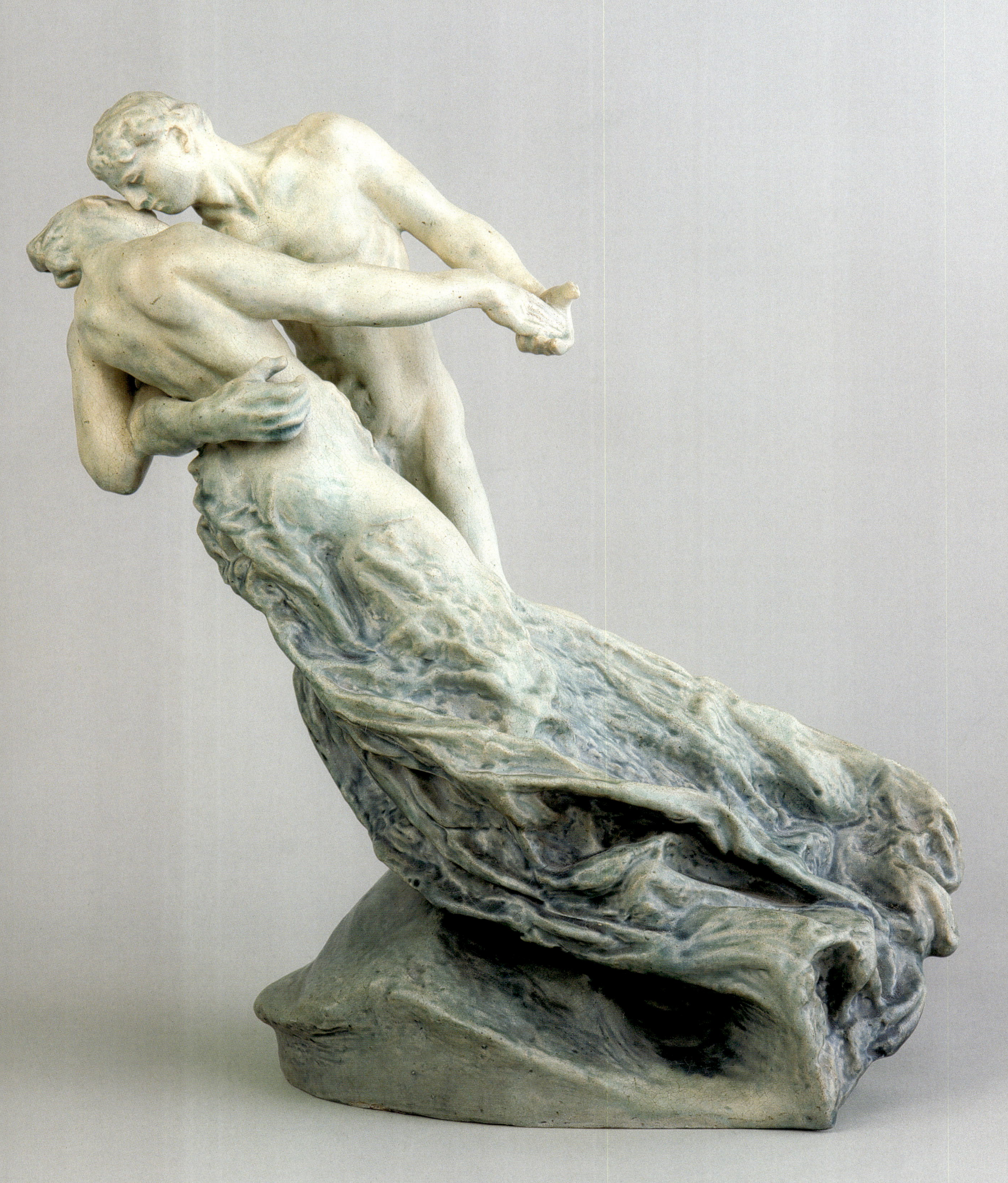

instrument. The decoration owes its inspiration to Greek vase-painting and Roman cameos as well as Japanese aesthetics, while the plinth has an entirely separate organic sculptural shape. In almost every respect – in function and form – the boundaries have become blurred: the titles give the vase, originally a practical object, a meaning and a symbolic significance; the combination of the knotty wooden plinth with the various complicated glass techniques elevate it to a true work of art; and there is a synthesis of references to antiquity, medieval sagas, Wagnerian music and Japanese art. Bing's aim to achieve a *Gesamtkunstwerk* is supremely embodied in this vase.

MONOGRAPHIC EXHIBITIONS: FROM REALISM TO EXPRESSIONISM

After the first two Salons, at which a wide selection of different works was to be seen, Bing started to focus on smaller-scale, usually monographic, exhibitions. From February to March 1896 the painter-sculptor Constantin Meunier (figs. 151–3, 285) showed his sculptures and drawings at Bing's. It was the first time that an independent exhibition had been devoted to this major artist. Georges Lecomte, who wrote the introduction to the catalogue, summed up the following characteristics of Meunier's work: monumental, distinctive and – perhaps not what would first spring to mind – exceptionally 'decorative'.[36] In Lecomte's view, Meunier was capable of expressing an idea or emotion in an exceedingly harmonious way, in which all the proportions of the human body were well balanced, and in which the form was simplified, thus placing the pictures on a higher plane than the merely picturesque. His moving portraits showing dock-workers, miners and labourers are given 'soul' and expression; above all the protagonists become heroic figures of tragic beauty. The critics unanimously praised the show, and a week after the opening the French State bought an important drawing, while eight sculptures were sold to private buyers.[37] A month later, Bing organised an exhibition with about two hundred pieces of mostly graphic work by Louis Legrand, who also designed the invitation card (fig. 146).[38] His favourite theme was mondaine ballet girls, comparable to Degas's, but with a more natural and less abstract quality about them. Many of Legrand's prints also had slightly erotic or symbolic overtones, which was not surprising as he had studied with the 'satanic' master-engraver Félicien Rops. Once again, it was a successful exhibition that attracted

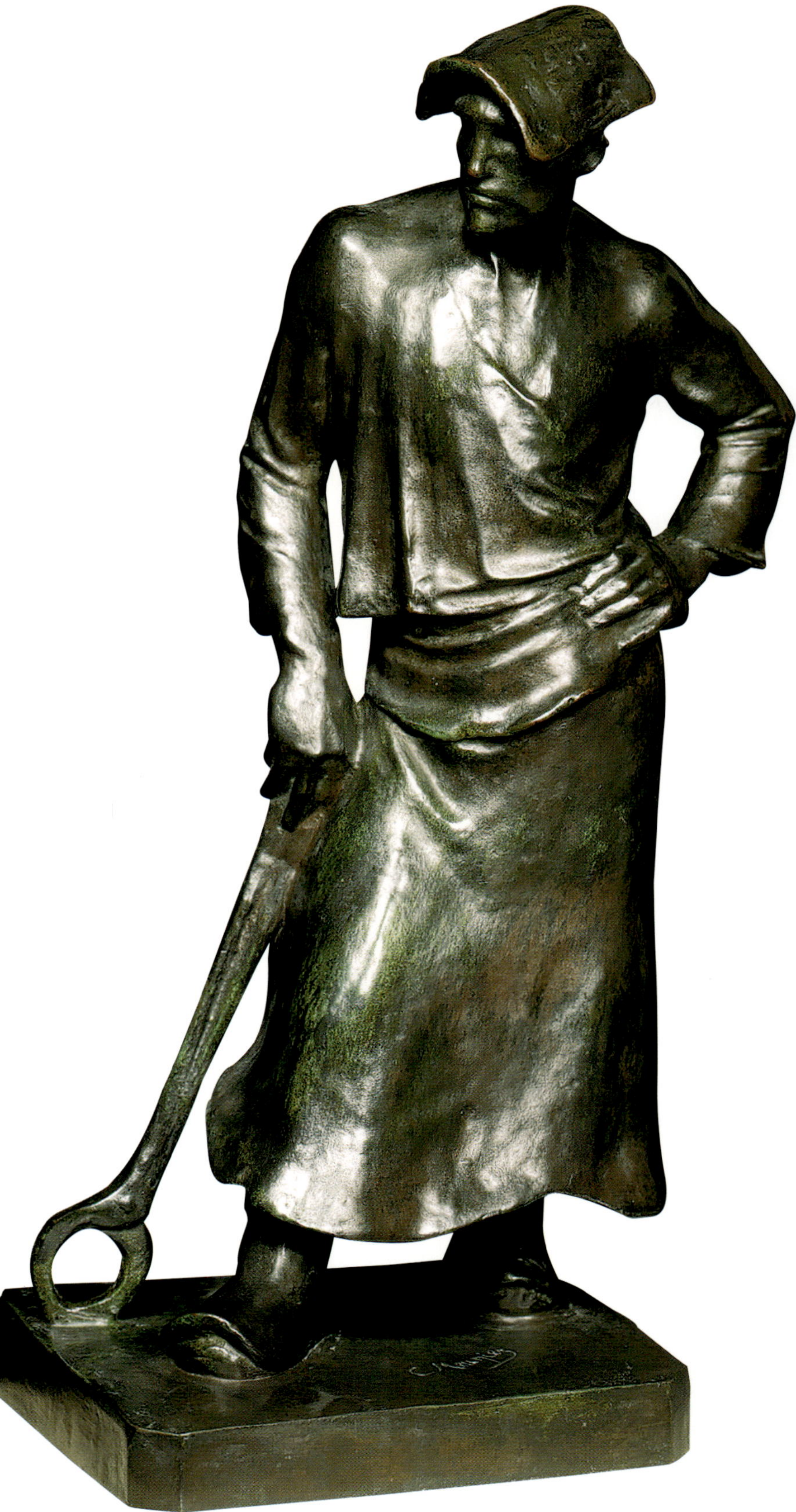

< 151
Constantin Meunier,
***The Metalworker*, 1886**
Musée Constantin
Meunier, Brussels

152
Constantin Meunier,
***Woman Coalminer with Shovel*, 1888**
Museum für Kunst und
Gewerbe, Hamburg

153
Constantin Meunier,
***The Dockworker*, 1893**
Musée Constantin
Meunier, Brussels

>> 154
József Rippl-Rónai,
***Pale woman*, 1896**
Magyar Nemzeti Galéria,
Budapest

>> 155
József Rippl-Rónai,
***Woman with Birdcage*, 1892**
Magyar Nemzeti Galéria,
Budapest

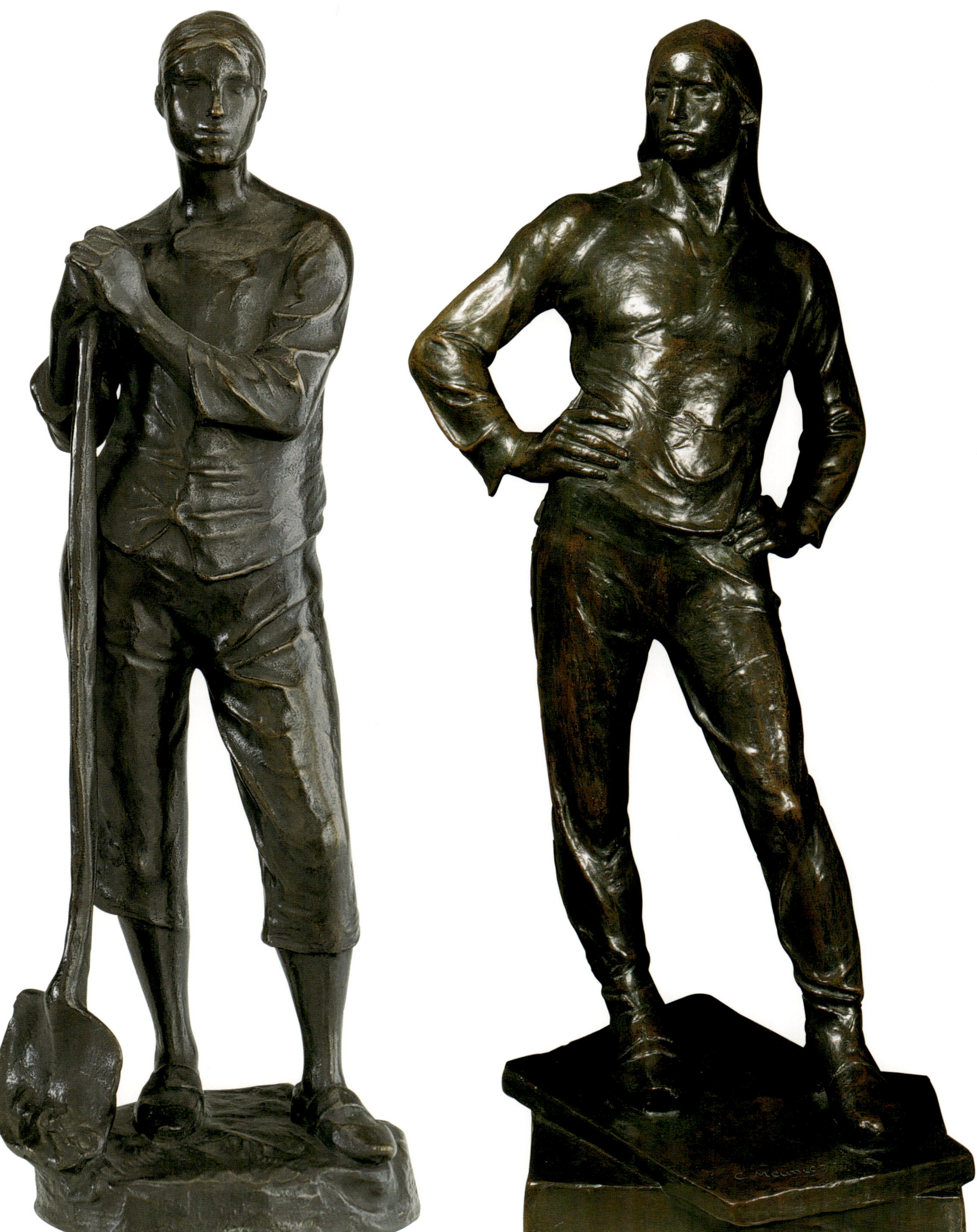

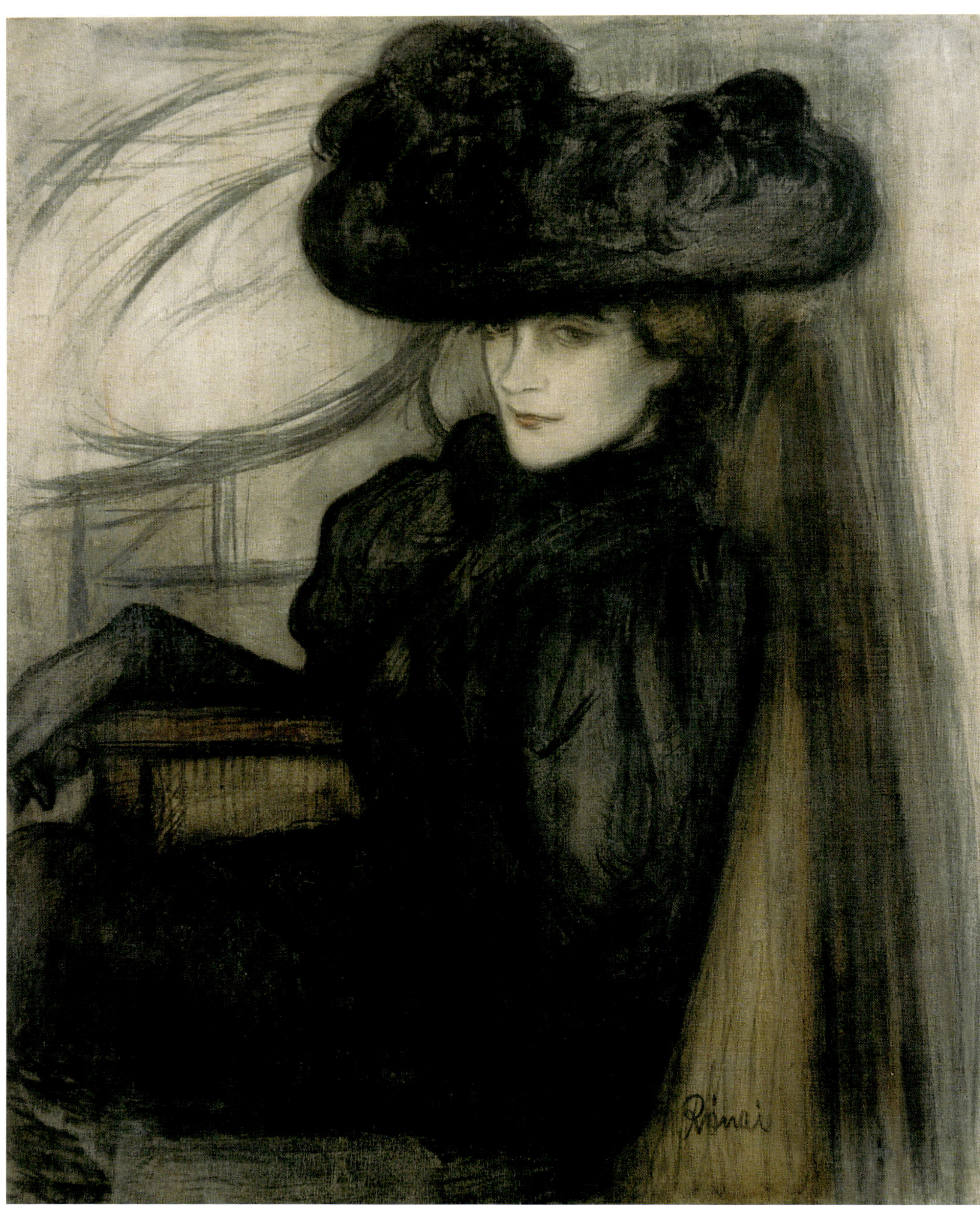
Rónai

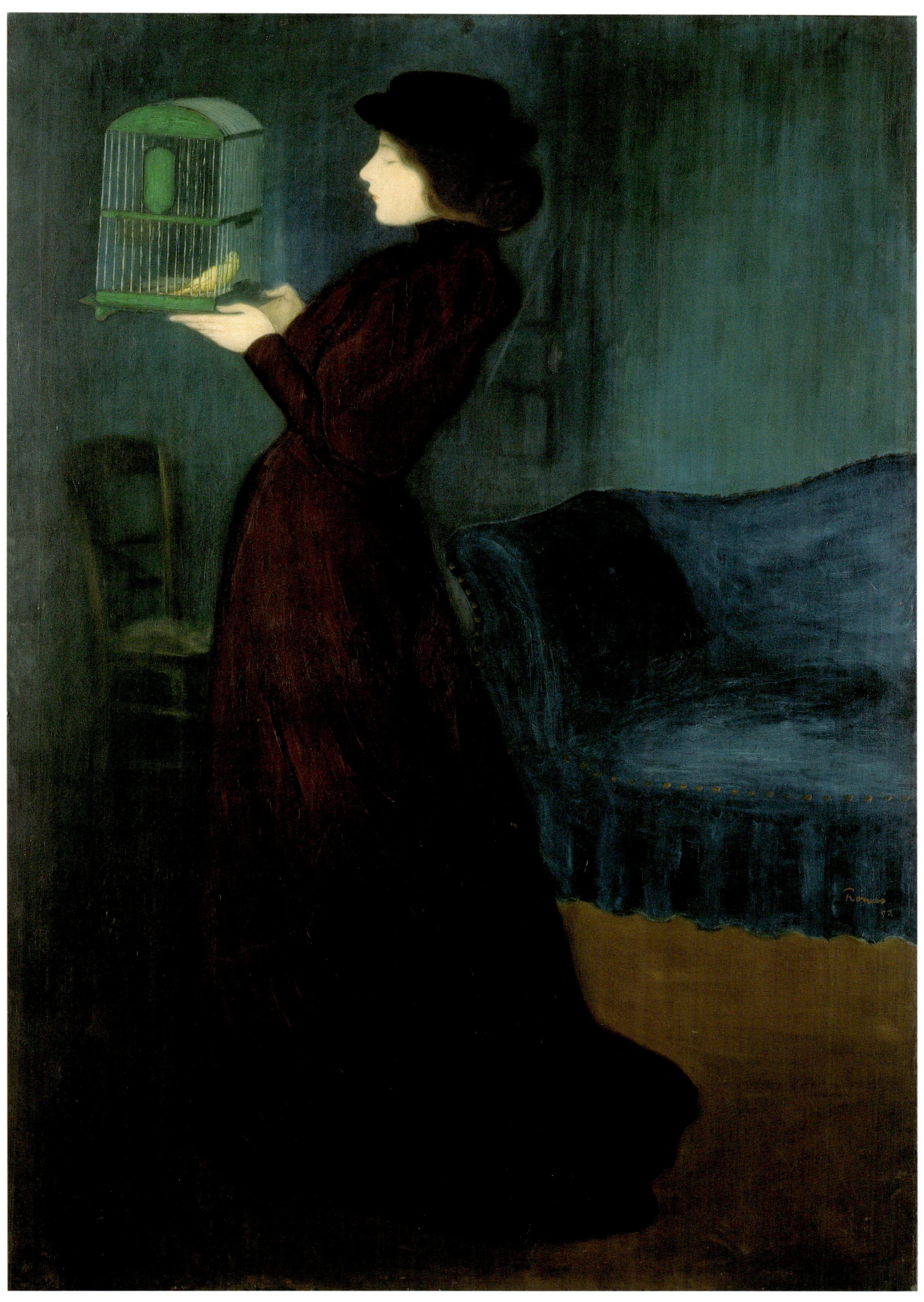

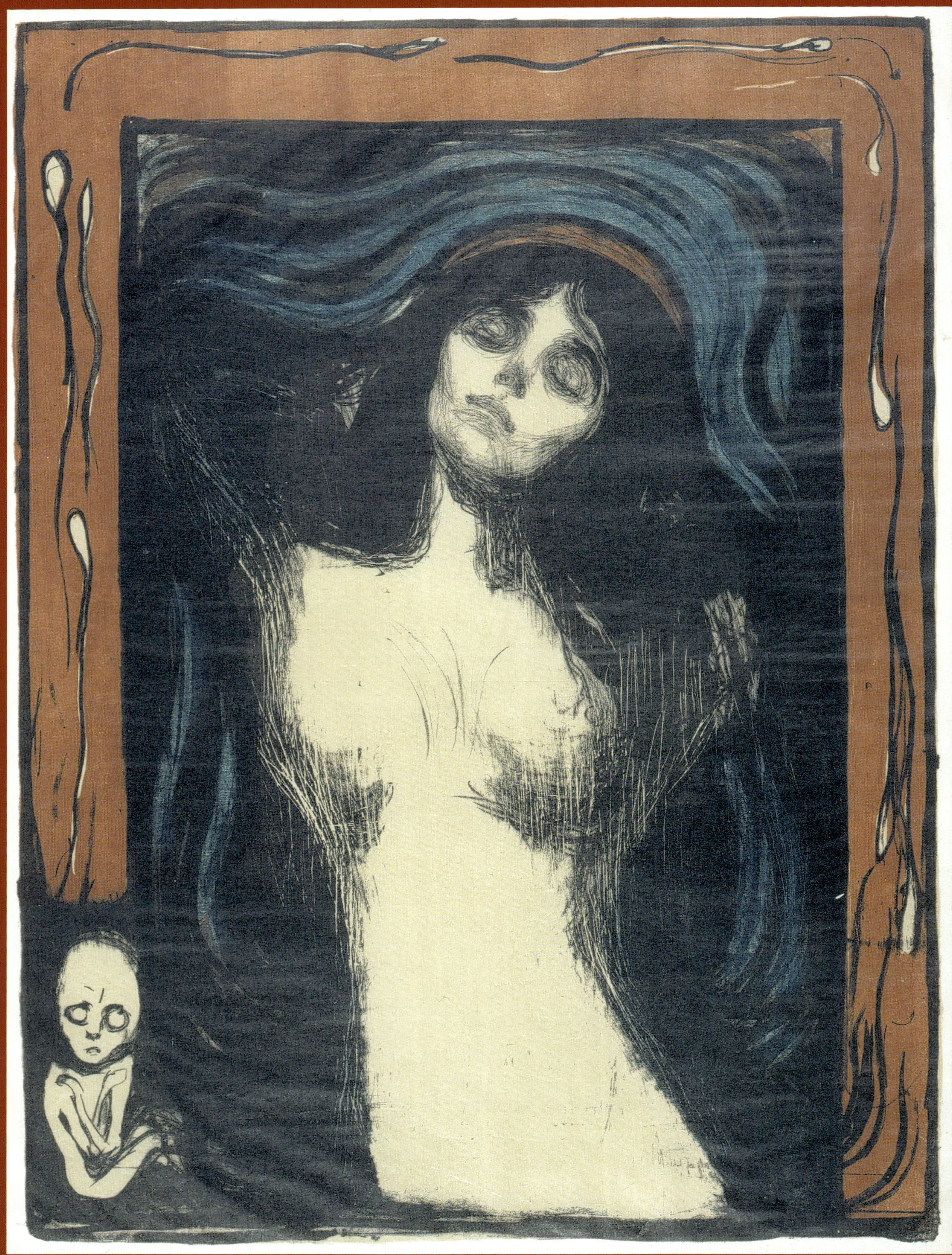

a great deal of attention. One of the art critics wrote about Legrand as follows: 'a form of art that is close to life, and which with minimal means achieves a maximum of expression.'[39]

During the Legrand exhibition people were already eagerly looking forward to the next exhibition with fifty-seven paintings and drawings by Eugène Carrière. The artist himself wrote the foreword to the exhibition catalogue, which contained the crucial words: 'The love of the external forms of nature is the instrument of comprehension that nature imposes upon me. [...] The forms which, not of themselves, but by the multiplicity of their relationships, all, in a distant perspective, come before us through subtle transitions.'[40] A mysterious, mystical atmosphere hangs over all Carrière's works, and it is as if all his characters were floating on clouds, far removed from reality. His aim was to penetrate deeper until he reached their essence, while at the same time reducing the colour to almost monochrome shades. It is this dreamy quality that brings Carrière close to the symbolists, but his personal approach was unique. The critic Gustave Geffroy, who also had his portrait painted by the artist (fig. 158), once said: 'The hands which he describes and models in a few strokes of the pencil, can bear comparison with the most celebrated hands in the most impeccable of drawings.'[41] Hands painted by Carrière often seem to lead a life of their own and appear to reveal the character of the person being portrayed.

< 156
Edvard Munch,
***Madonna*, 1895**
Albertina, Vienna

It would take us too far afield if we were to discuss all the subsequent monographic exhibitions at Bing's in detail, even though many of them were first showings or unique presentations of hitherto unknown artists. Included in their number was Charles Cottet (1896), the Nabi József Rippl-Rónai (1897), who had already shown his monumental *Woman with Birdcage* (fig. 155) at the first Salon, Alphonse Legros (1898), Jean-François Raffaelli (1898), Santiago Rusiñol (1899) and, importantly, Paul Signac, who was given his first monographic exhibition at Bing's in 1902. Pierre-Paul Jouve, who, once outside Bing's sphere of influence, moved toward art deco motifs, was the beneficiary of the last exhibition (March 1905), after S. Bing's gallery had closed and just prior to Bing's death in September 1905. One exhibition also deserves a special mention, that devoted to Edvard Munch. It was a unique event, and the choice of artist would prove to be a very risky undertaking.

As can be seen from the correspondence between Meier-Graefe and Munch,[42] Meier-Graefe had to do his best to convince Bing to show a few controversial paintings like *The Scream* and to get him to exhibit representative pieces of Munch's graphic work like the *Madonna* (fig. 156) or the *Vampire*. The criticism levelled at Bing for the international art he had presented at the first two Salons de L'Art Nouveau was still ringing in his ears, and it probably made him somewhat more cautious. Nevertheless, in May 1896, in a room dedicated to Munch, Bing presented twelve paintings, six studies and forty-two sheets of graphic work.[43] Camille Mauclair, a critic of modern art (but also highly sceptical), had nothing but condemnation for Munch's expressive language of form: he spoke of 'paintings with no feeling for line and painted in barbaric colours, with their repugnant subject matter which is heavy and unharmonious, decked out with symbolic titles, [which] shock the life out of the onlookers.'[44] He absolutely could not understand the art of the 'esoteric painter of love', as the painter was called by the writer and artist August Strindberg.[45] However, not everyone was so outspoken. Frantz Jourdain, the architect of the department store La Samaritaine, thought that Munch's creations, born from a dislike of the banal, were closely related to the literature of Edgar Allan Poe or Maurice Maeterlinck and the art of Odilon Redon, Félix Vallotton or Henri de Toulouse-Lautrec. True innovators were in his view always impulsive.[46] The fierce reactions showed that Bing's Salon had once more caused quite a stir, and it was thanks to Bing's foresight and pioneering spirit that there was again a striking exhibition to be seen in Paris, one that stood head and shoulders above the rest.[47]

THE CRITICAL VOICE: A WHIM OF FASHION OR A VISION OF THE FUTURE

Not everyone was convinced of the importance of Bing's exhibition concept. Soon after the opening of Bing's L'Art Nouveau certain critics launched a furious attack against the concept of the gallery, the selection of the artists and against Bing himself. Arsène Alexandre was particularly scathing. He touched a sensitive nerve when he immediately questioned the validity of the gallery's name. In his view there was no such thing as 'Art Nouveau', or new art, only art at its present state of development. He wrote that any artist who says of himself that he is making new art is claiming all the glory.[48] Art Nouveau was in his eyes unjustifiable as a title for a gallery and far too pretentious. Alexandre complained that all the artists Bing put on show had already made their debuts at other exhibitions, like the Salons du Champ-de-Mars, Le Barc de Boutteville or Père Tanguy's small shop, where many impressionists and neo-impressionists were exhibiting. The critic found that Bing lacked original innovative artists like Degas, Renoir, Monet, Cézanne, Gauguin, whereas the artists he did show like Besnard, Blanche or Anquetin had already been seen at the Salons du Champ-de-Mars. Finally he summed up his remarks with, 'Applied art: what do you mean new? We already knew that the English were good cabinetmakers, and that the Belgians have no feeling for line. Everything reeks of the depraved English, the morphine-addicted Jew, or the cunning Belgian, or a cocktail of all three.'[49] He also sneered at foreign artists who, in his view, were leading the French artists astray; nor did he spare the public, whom he accused of being in hot pursuit of the latest trend and terrified lest they should miss out on a new craze.

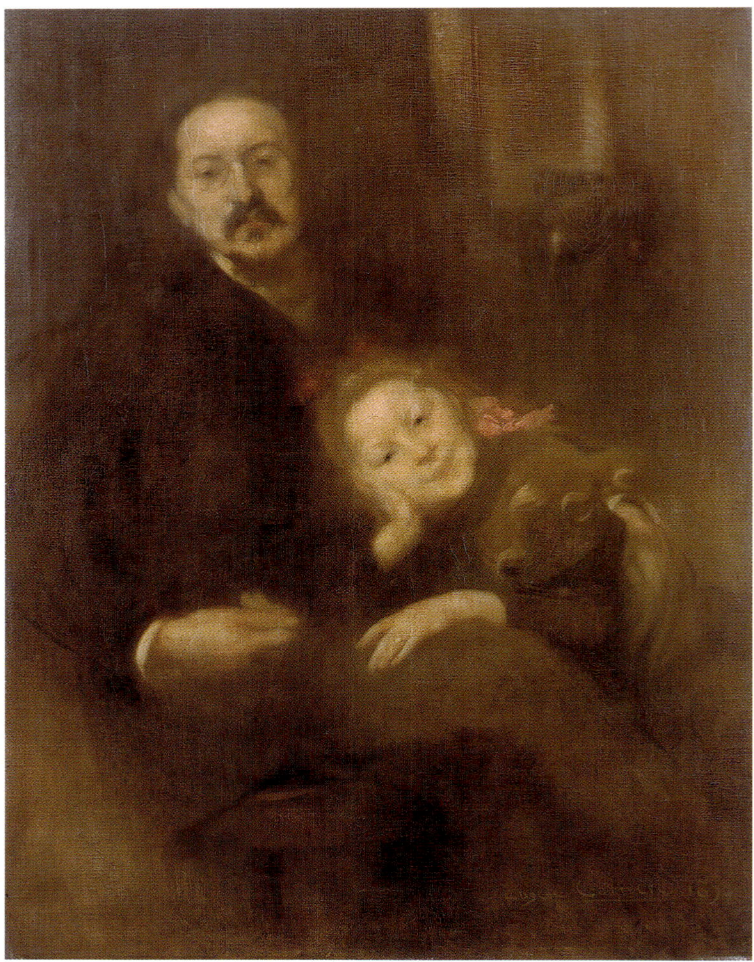

The Belgian press, on the other hand, dismissed Alexandre's fiery nationalistic, xenophobic criticism. After all, they had already got to know the Maison d'Art in Brussels with its successful combination of foreign and national art, ranging from decorative objects to the fine arts, and furthermore they were really proud that many Belgian artists, like Van de Velde, Lemmen, Van Rysselberghe and Khnopff, were represented at Bing's Salons. It was thanks to Bing's good contacts in Brussels with Van de Velde and Edmond Picard that many renowned Belgian artists and designers had been encouraged to exhibit at the Salons.

Thadée Natanson, a French collector and journalist, also supported Bing when the enterprise was under fire, writing: 'Do we have to wait until the "old" forms have slowly evolved, or encourage the initiative of artists who supply new models, so that craftsmen are furnished with new inspiration?'[50]

Of course, it had been a race against the clock to get everything finished on time for the presentation at the first Salon. And, in retrospect, Bing himself had to admit that it was partly due to his own inexperience that he had not been entirely successful when he brought together such a variety of artists under one joint name. But the term 'Art Nouveau', he said, was merely a title, a logo, two words which could of course not encompass all the ideas they embraced. He thought that there was a lack of stimulus for artists to explore new avenues, and no suitable place for artists to show their art to the public; that was one of the most important motives for his setting up the gallery.[51] Bing had realised, idealistically, partly due to the reactions his enterprise aroused, that by stimulating craftsmen and artists to work together the danger could be averted that Art Nouveau would disintegrate into incoherent chaos due to an overemphasis on individuality.

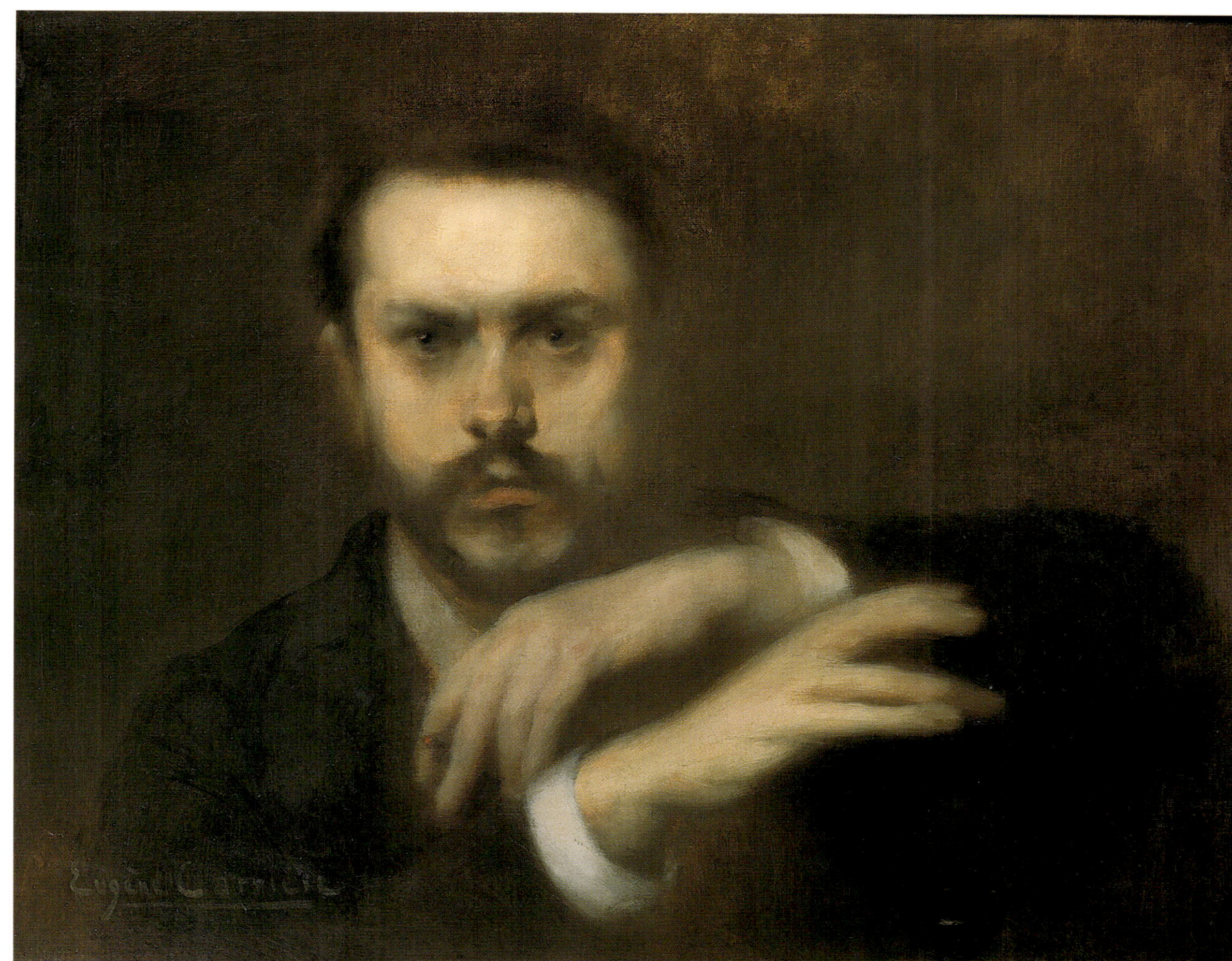

< 157
Eugène Carrière,
***Gabriel Séailles and his Daughter*, 1893**
Musée d'Art moderne et contemporain, Strasbourg

158
Eugène Carrière,
***Portrait of Gustave Geffroy*, 1890**
Musée d'Orsay, Paris

Fortunately, there were also critics who, despite the variety of styles, praised the general harmony and the combination of the practical with the aesthetic beauty of the line. Bing had, after all, dared to show the public these ongoing experiments, which had certainly not crystallised into their final shape. He had craftspeople and artists join forces as had been done earlier in England in the Arts and Crafts movement, or as would happen later in Vienna in the Wiener Werkstätte, which would evolve in 1903. It was not just this diversity and freedom of style and technique, but more the crossing of national borders that led to so much criticism in France.

In any case, Bing's ambition to achieve perfect harmony was not hampered by all the adverse criticism: it only made him all the more determined. He finally achieved his aim and came into his own after setting up his ateliers in 1899, and he was to reach his aesthetic climax in his pavilion at the 1900 Paris World's Fair.

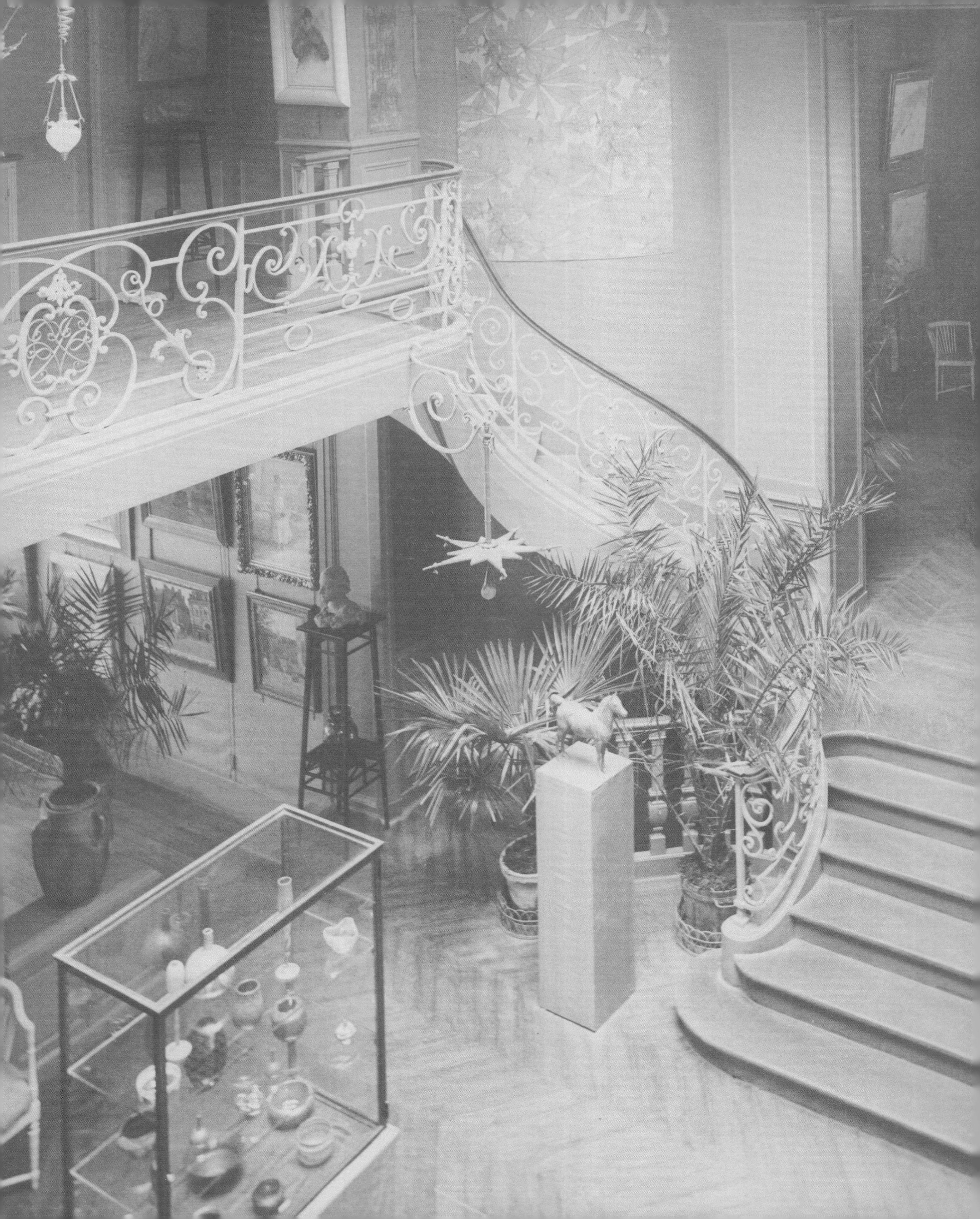

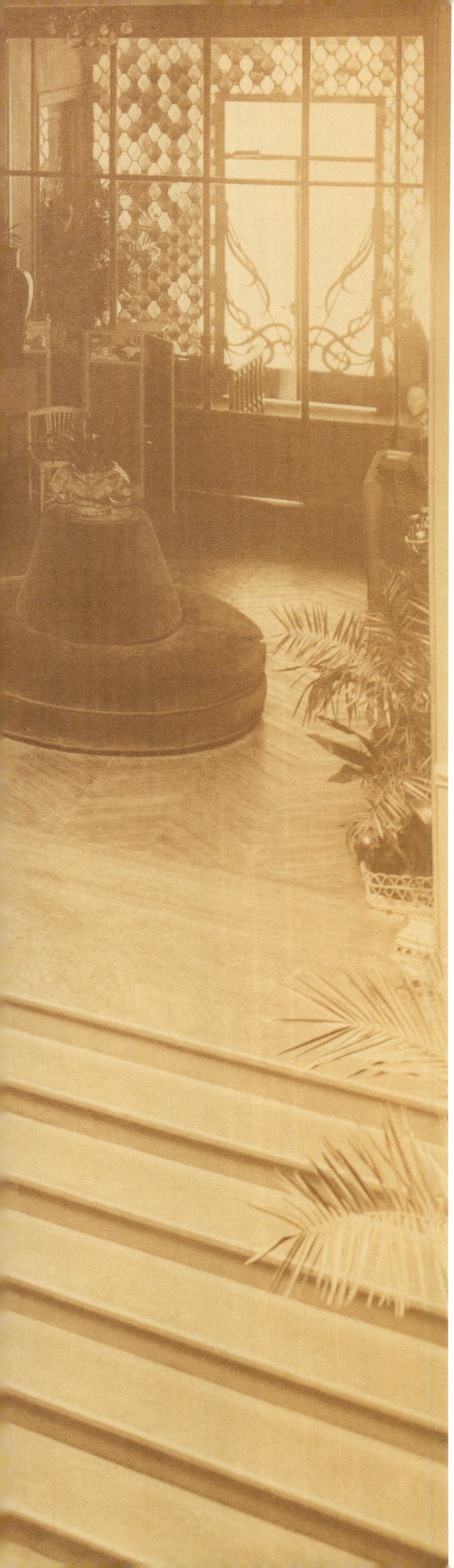

BING AND ENGLAND

ÉVELYNE POSSÉMÉ

The numerous studies devoted to Siegfried Bing and his artistic and commercial activities have all been prepared on the basis of fragmentary sources and in the absence of his personal archives. Whether the latter have been destroyed or merely misplaced is uncertain; the only archival material known today consists of a large bound album preserved in the Bibliothèque des Arts décoratifs in Paris. This book contains 524 photos of individual items or sets of furniture produced by his gallery, L'Art Nouveau. Until now, only those showing interior views of the Art Nouveau pavilion at the 1900 World's Fair have been studied and reproduced. If this *Album de références* constitutes a unique source for the study of furniture created by Bing's gallery, it is equally precious for identifying the items sold and distributed by that establishment, particularly the English furniture that appears in large quantities in the first fifteen pages and at various points thereafter.[1]

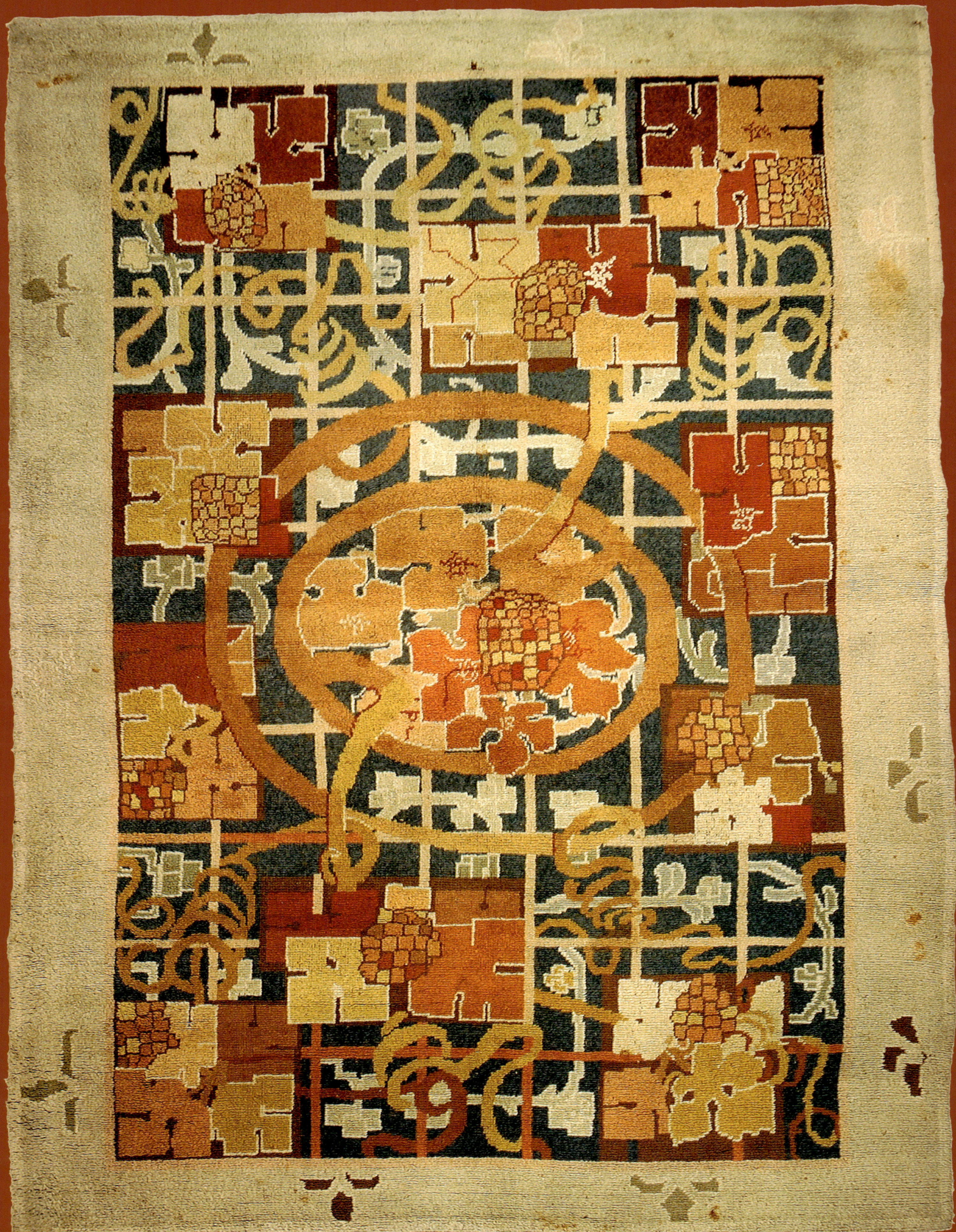

When Bing's gallery was opened, the critics made great play of the varied origins of the furniture on sale. Beside Belgian groups by Henry Van de Velde, Georges Lemmen and Théo Van Rysselberghe, 'a few interesting rustic items from Holland' were also noted.[2] Jens Thiis, during his visit in 1896, emphasised the stark contrasts between the work of French, British, American, Belgian, German, Dutch and Scandinavian artists.[3] The photos of the gallery's interior at its inauguration provide a few clues about the arrangement of the English furniture: along the walls of the central hall, under the glass roof, we see a *banquette* (bench or settee) with white-painted wooden slats, as well as an armchair of similar design in the mezzanine of the first floor (fig. 118).[4] Possibly they were located in the circular salon that P.A. Isaac decorated with plush panels; an article in the *Revue Blanche* mentions in this connection 'white benches, their seats consisting of *lanières* (thin strips), out of keeping with the elegant appearance of the walls';[5] or perhaps in the boudoir, with its silk paintings by the Australian artist Charles Conder.

The participation of the Galerie de l'Art Nouveau in the 1897 Dresden International Art Exhibition included several of the ensembles from 1895. This entailed some redesign at 22, rue de Provence as the art press reported in 1898:[6] Van de Velde's dining room, in the glass-roofed area on the first floor, was replaced by an English-style dining room (fig. 163);[7] Isaac's circular salon was furnished with pieces of various origins, among them a rectangular Colonna table, a 'Thebes' stool by Liberty (fig. 182) and some English chairs (fig. 164). In the room visible in the background, in front of the 'Boulogne' wardrobe attributed to Gaillard, are an armchair by the London maker J.S. Henry and a stool also of English manufacture. In a publication of 1899 (fig. 165) English furniture can also be seen in the large, central glass-roofed hall used in 1895 for the display of sculptures and objects in showcases.[8] The middle of this area is occupied by Brangwyn's 'Japanese Vine' carpet (fig. 160) – already in the English dining room in 1898 – on which stand a table with an openwork base, one of Bing's designs, and English 'Lily' chairs (fig. 179), whilst visitors would recognise a small table by Benson and Bigot (fig. 161), padded Chesterfield-type armchairs, the piano stool previously displayed in the Isaac salon and an English music cabinet.

These various items are to be found in the opening pages of Bing's *Album de références*, but none bears any indication of its origin except, for some ten pieces, the

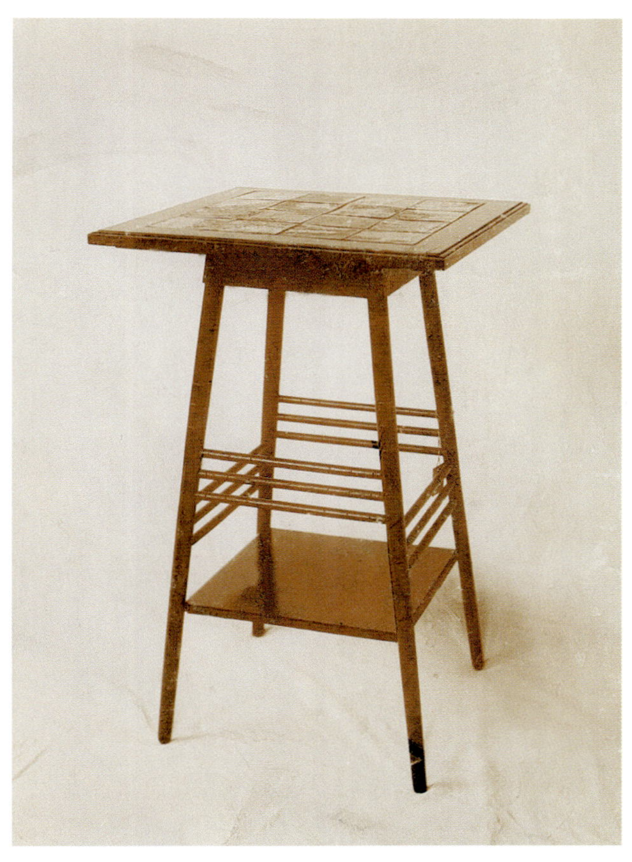

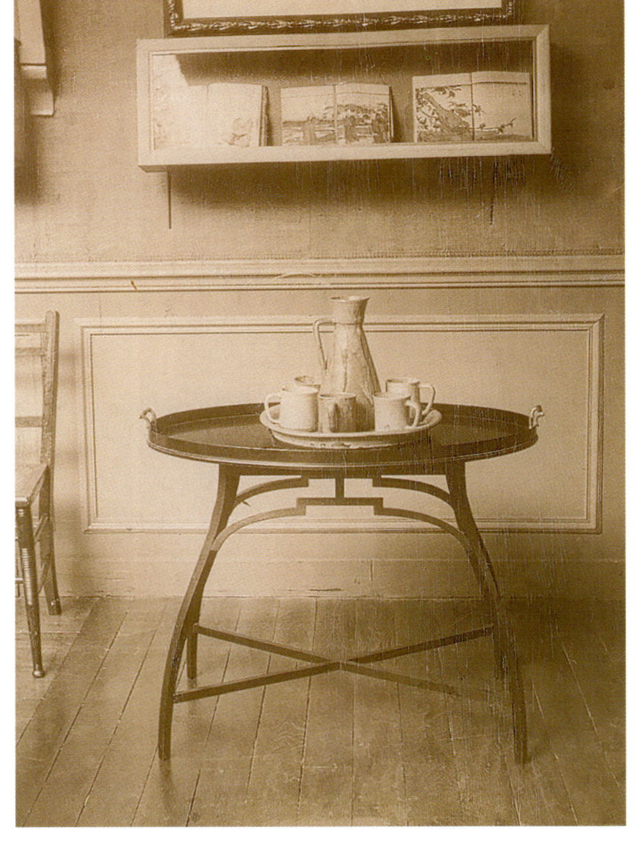

<< 159
Interior of the hall of Bing's L'Art Nouveau, view towards the main entrance, 1895
Fonds Louis Bonnier, Institut français d'architecture, Paris

< 160
Frank Brangwyn, 'Japanese Vine' carpet, 1896–97
Stedelijke Musea, Brugge

161
William Benson and Alexandre Bigot, Table, *Album de références*, 13/192
Bibliothèque des Arts décoratifs, Paris

162
Oval tea-table, signed CM, *Album de références*, 8/105
Bibliothèque des Arts décoratifs, Paris

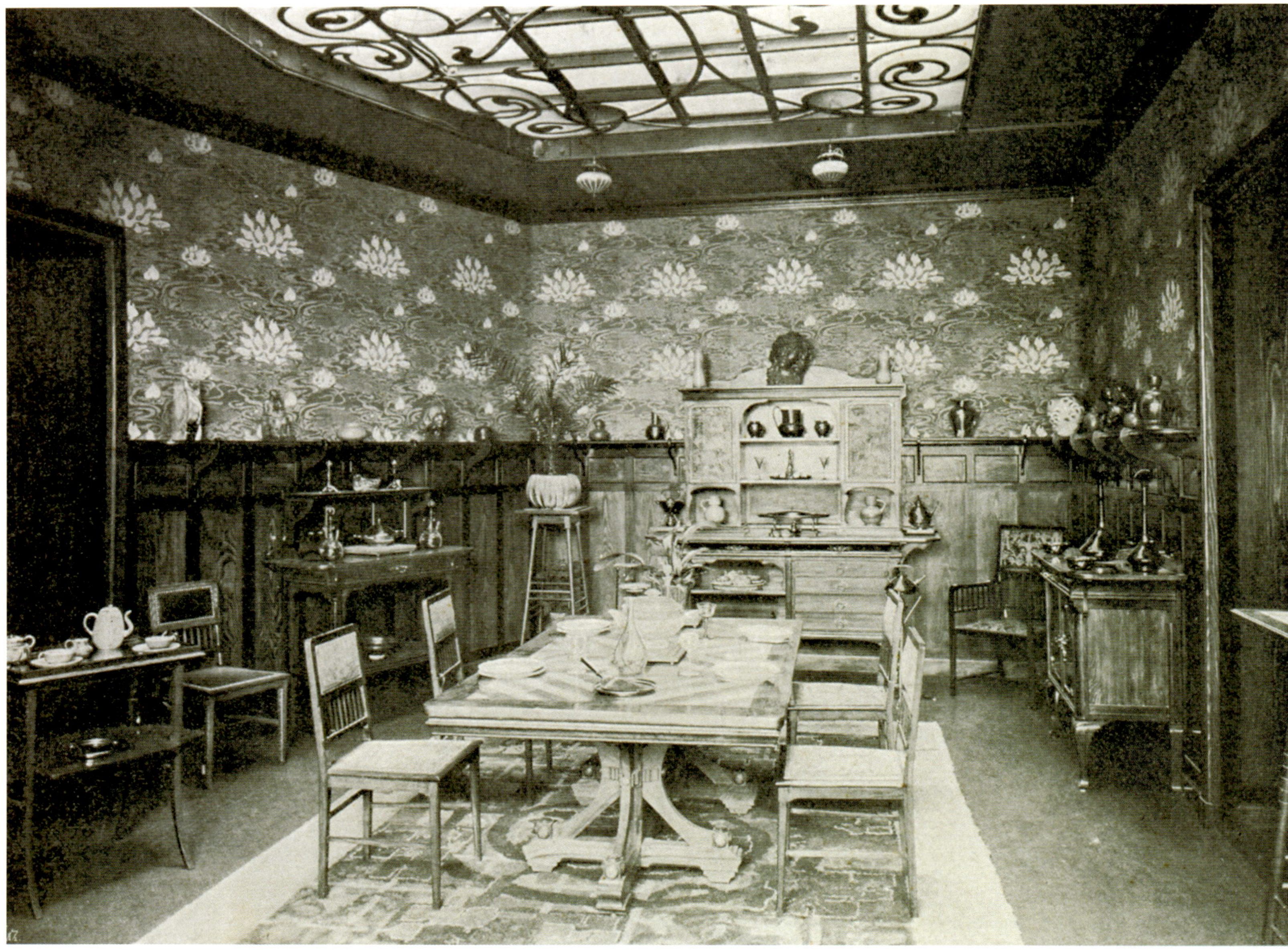

initials CM or MC (fig. 162). It will be a difficult and time-consuming task to identify these English designs. For Bing, only the English, Dutch and Belgians had discovered how to create a new form of decorative art, as he explained in two articles published in German and English.[9] In mid-nineteenth century England, Ruskin adopted a pioneering approach, claiming that the only way to explore the future was to understand the past. But his disciples William Morris and Walter Crane were too absorbed in imitating their predecessors and forgot that times had changed; this, according to Bing, was their mistake: 'The archaism of their creations prevents their own age from recognising them as their own.' Britain underwent a moment of creative stagnation until, around 1900, pupils of Morris such as C.F.A. Voysey introduced a new impulse that would sweep away Japonisme and the last traces of historicism. Bing, despite these few criticisms of a type of furniture he regarded as an 'extension of the Queen Anne style', recognised that British designers of Voysey's generation had taken a step forward. Among their work he discovered items that were simple, functional in their lines, and produced industrially by important English firms, the prototype of which was Morris and Co.

INDUSTRIAL DESIGN COMPANIES IN ENGLAND: MORRIS, LIBERTY AND HENRY

These items, then, were not one-off pieces but belonged to industrial series turned out by the big manufacturers. England was, at that time, in a leading position not only

< 163
Dining room at Bing's L'Art Nouveau, from *Dekorative Kunst*, 1898, no. 9

164
Isaac's circular salon at L'Art Nouveau, from *Art et Décoration*, August 1898, supplement

165
General view of L'Art Nouveau, *Revue internationale des expositions. Moniteur général de l'Exposition 1900*, 16–31 January 1899

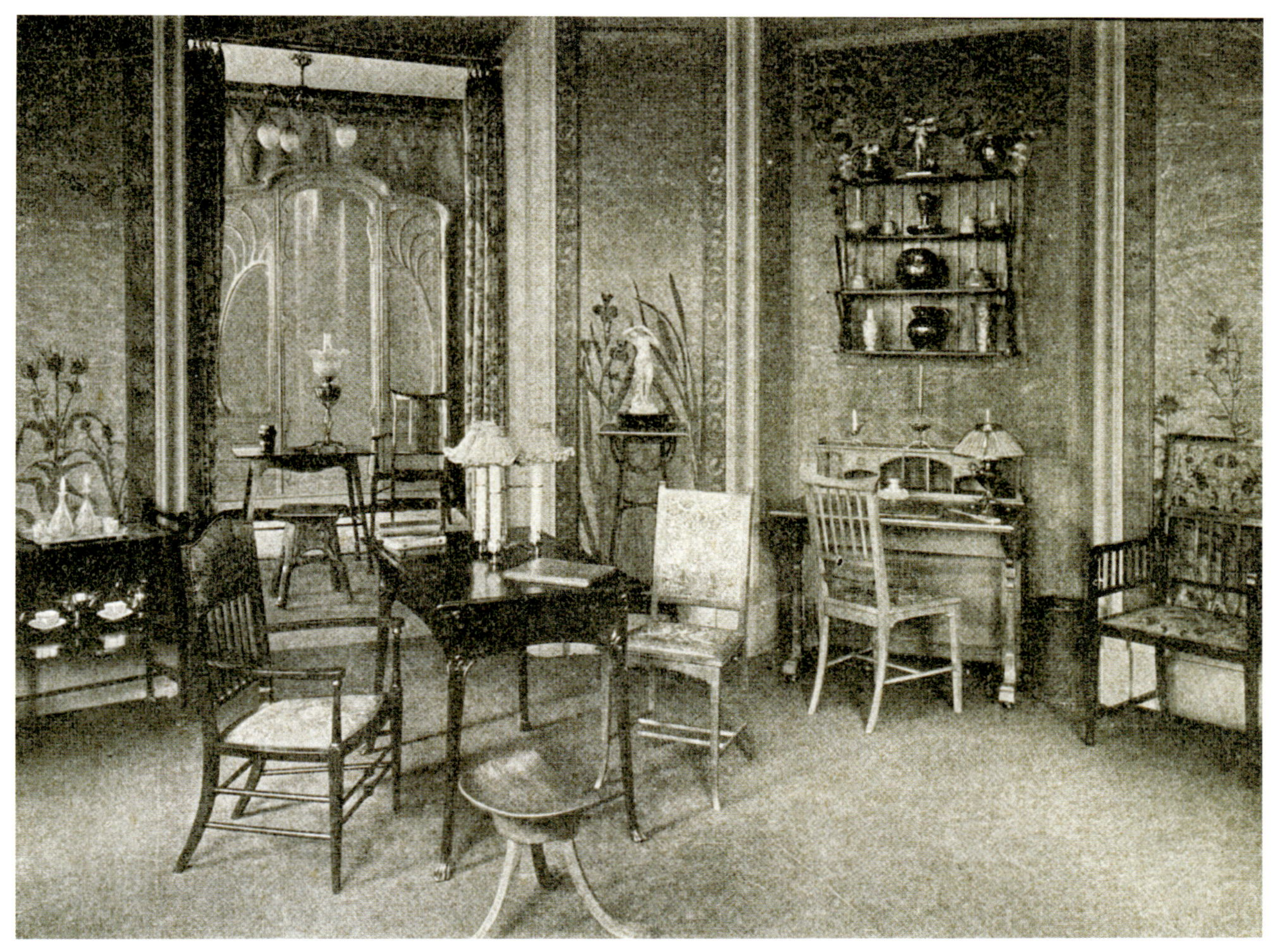

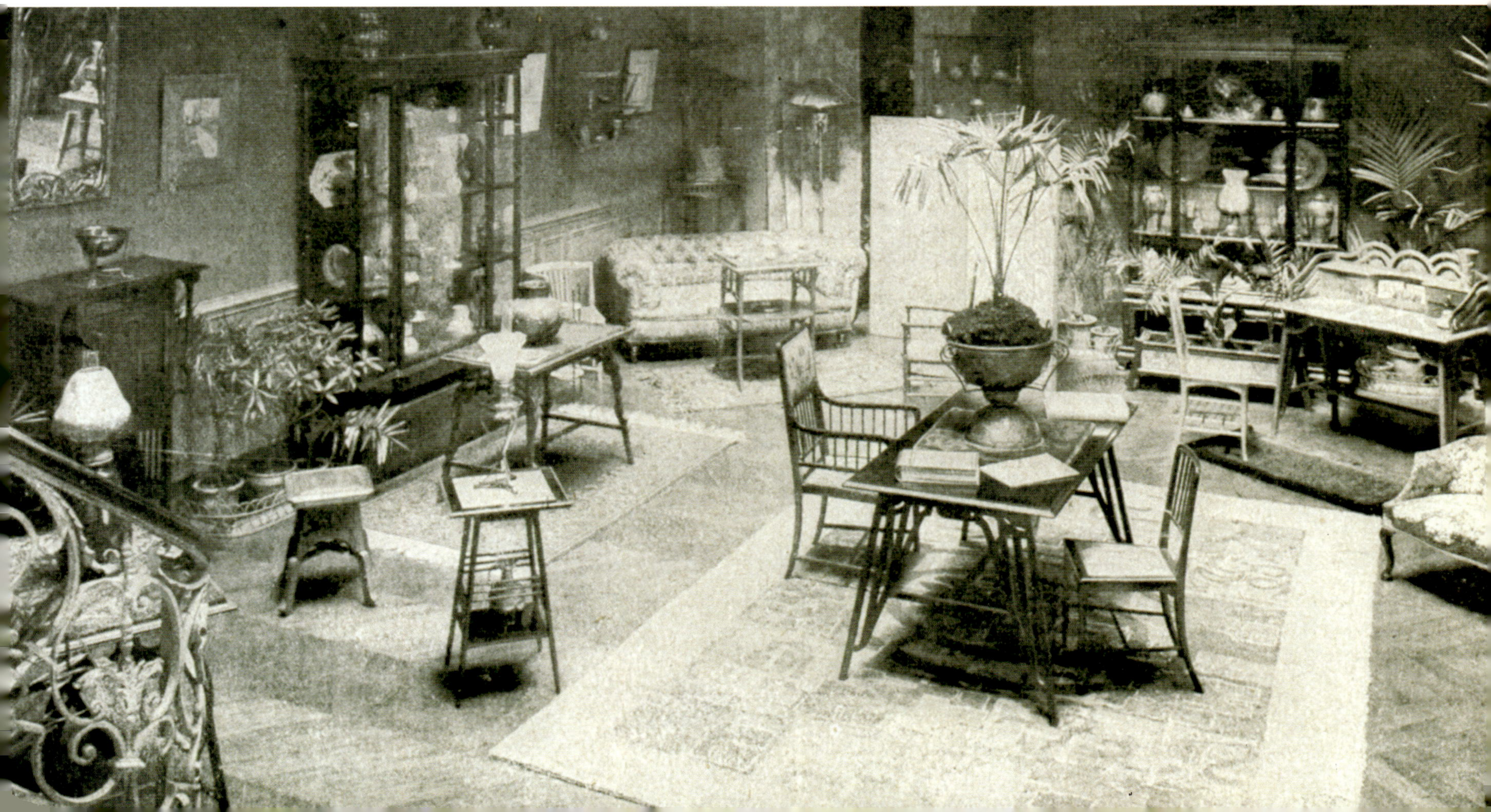

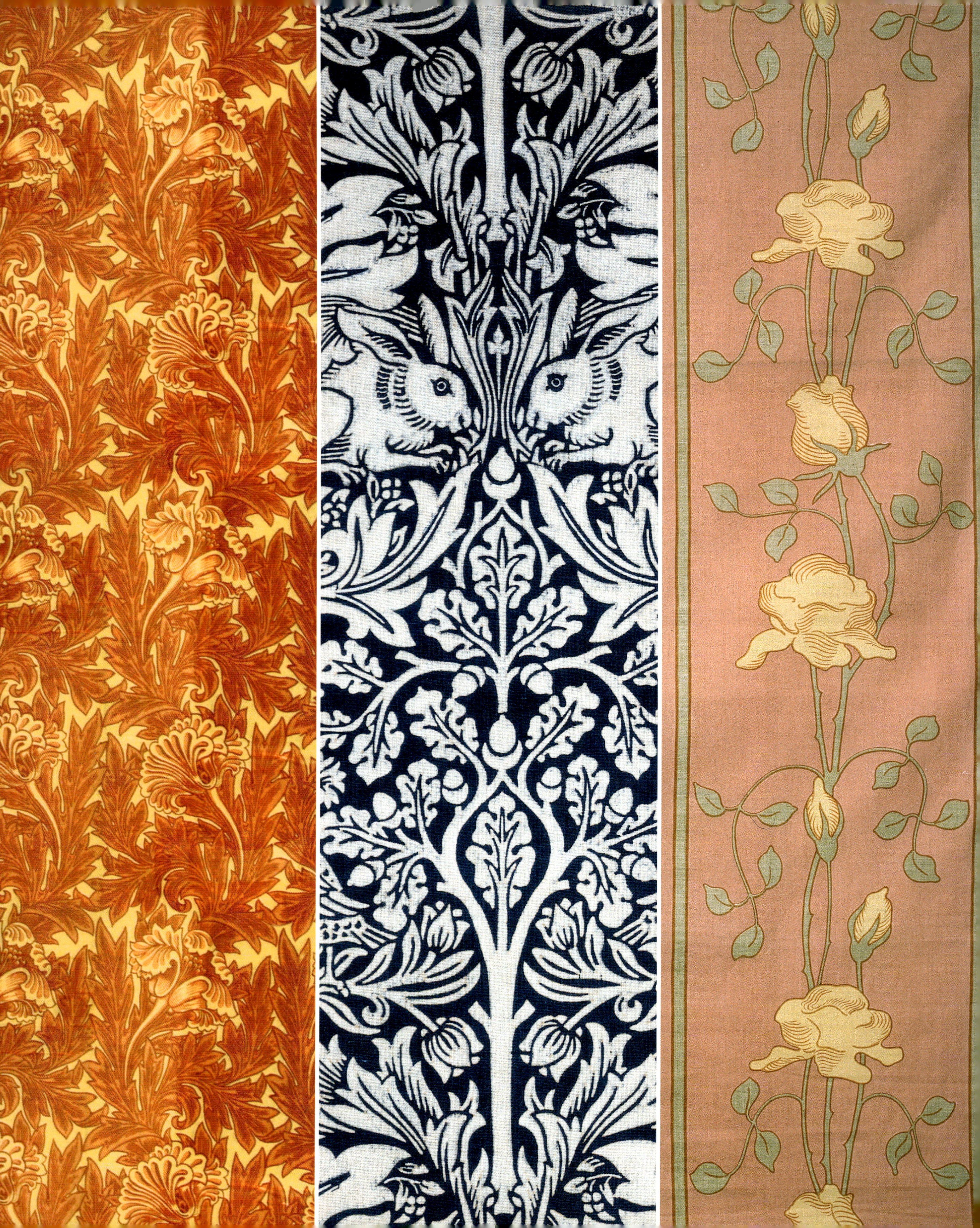

in the matter of design but in her ability to implement large-scale production, with the designers supplying a wide range of patterns to sizeable factories. Companies like Morris and Co. or Liberty had a field day, and their output was extremely varied – from Moorish-style and ornate turned pieces to the most avant-garde creations – to satisfy the broad spectrum of their clientele. Some of the foremost English firms even set up in Paris in the second half of the nineteenth century: William Morris, Maple, Liberty, and Waring and Gillow among them. Their output is particularly difficult to identify because the majority of these companies have not yet been studied by British researchers, and the most famous, like Morris and Liberty, have gaps in their archives, especially for the years 1895–1905.[10]

< 166
William Morris, Fabric 'Tulip', 1875
Nordenfjeldske Kunstindustrimuseum, Trondheim

< 167
William Morris, Fabric 'Brer Rabbit', 1883
Nordenfjeldske Kunstindustrimuseum, Trondheim

< 168
William Morris, Fabric 'Roses and Trellis', 1885
Nordenfjeldske Kunstindustrimuseum, Trondheim

The most famous of Bing's suppliers was the firm established by the Londoner William Morris. While textiles clearly made up the bulk of orders – for instance the large-scale purchases for the Nordenfjeldske Kunstindustrimuseum in Trondheim from 1897 onwards (figs. 166–8) – many items of furniture sold by Bing's gallery undoubtedly originated from the London store, although none has so far been identified. After William Morris's death in 1896, the artistic direction of the company passed to William Arthur Smith Benson, who, through his own business, furnished Bing with lamps and objects in copper and brass (figs. 169, 170, 181).[11] Benson had already collaborated with Morris on an occasional basis, supplying the firm with furniture designs. Other items reproduced in the *Album de références* can definitely be attributed to Benson. This is the case with the little table with tiles by Alexandre Bigot on the top, bought by the Trondheim Museum (no. 13/192). Another table, in ebony and copper and offered at 500 francs (no. 25/300, fig. 174), has been identified recently, since a similar design appeared in print in 1906.[12] Apart from these firm attributions, it is very possible that the furniture for the English dining room, displayed in 1898 in the galleries of L'Art Nouveau, was designed by Benson with the work carried out by Morris and Company.[13]

The other major supplier of Bing's gallery was Liberty and Company, with its famous three-legged 'Thebes' stool produced in 1884 (no. 4/50, fig. 182). The various Liberty registers reveal no trace of orders from Bing, nor any record of the Liberty fabrics sold by him, principally to the Trondheim Museum in 1897 (figs. 171, 279).[14] Does this mean that the quantities were infinitesimal and for that reason do not feature in the books alongside orders from Doucet, Bernhardt, Damon and Colin? This appears most unlikely, given that certain small

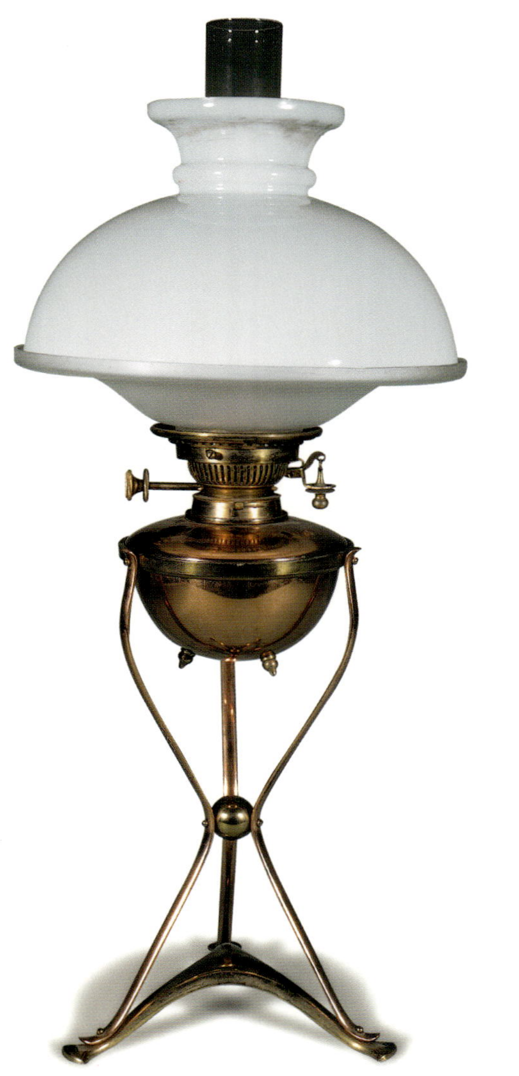

169
William Benson, Paraffin lamp, c. 1895
Nordenfjeldske Kunstindustrimuseum, Trondheim

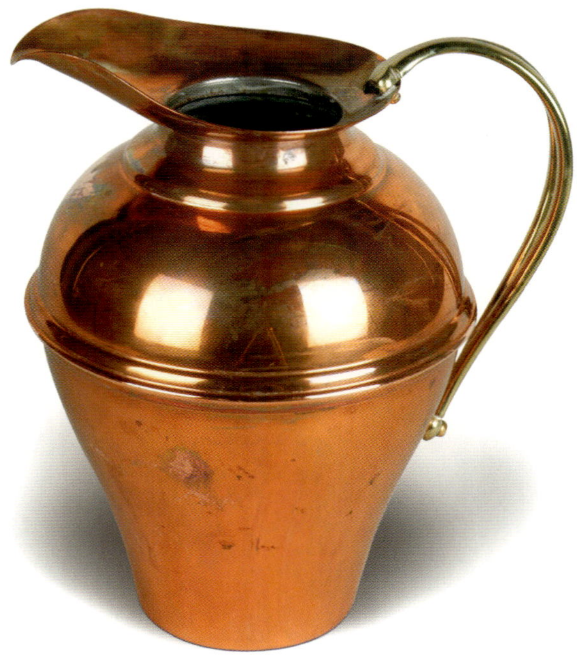

170
William Benson, Pitcher, c. 1895
Nordenfjeldske Kunstindustrimuseum, Trondheim

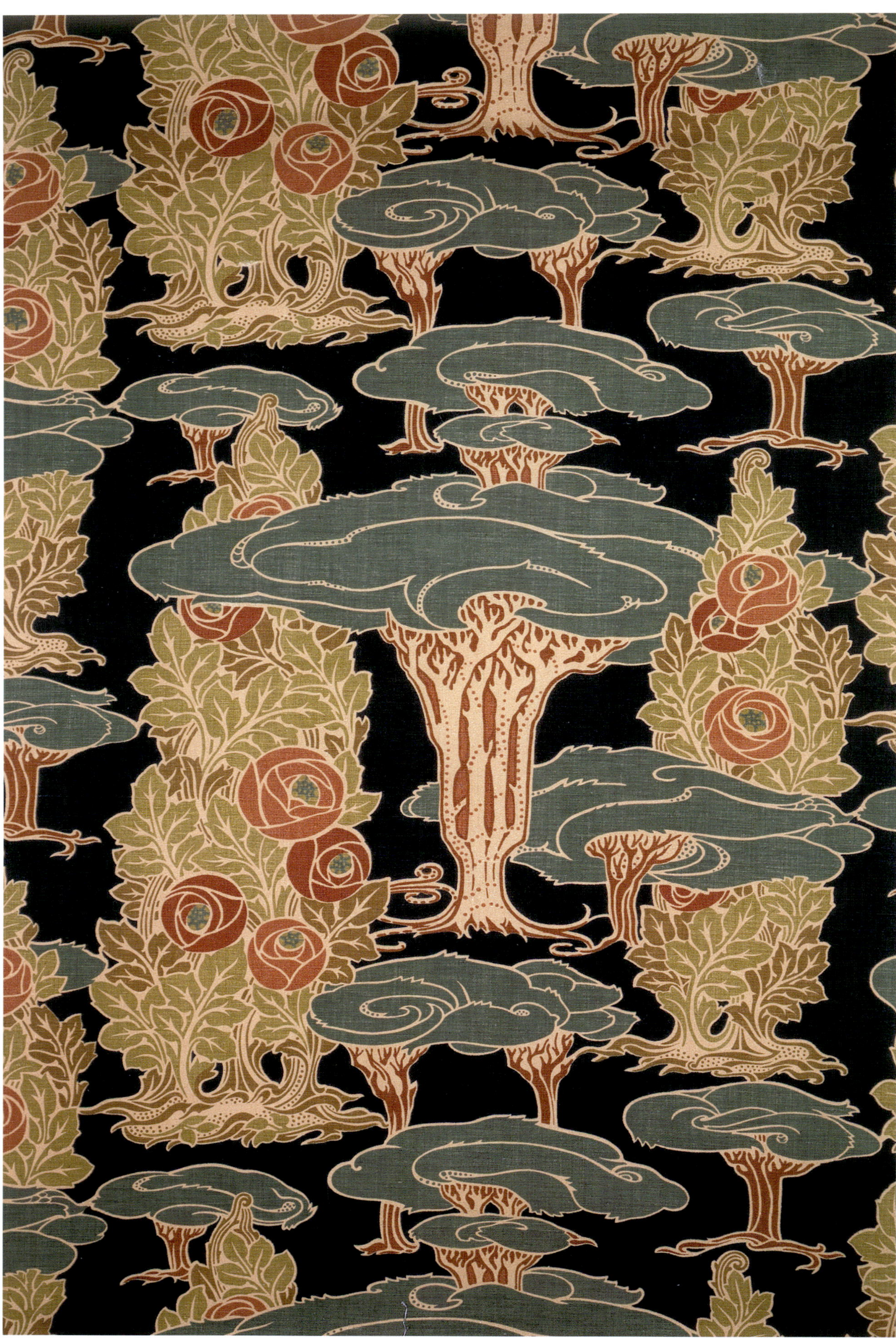

171
Liberty & Co., Fabric, abstract plant design, by Arthur Silver, c. 1896
Nordenfjeldske Kunstindustrimuseum, Trondheim

> 172
Clément Heaton, Large round dish, 1898
Musée des Arts décoratifs, Paris

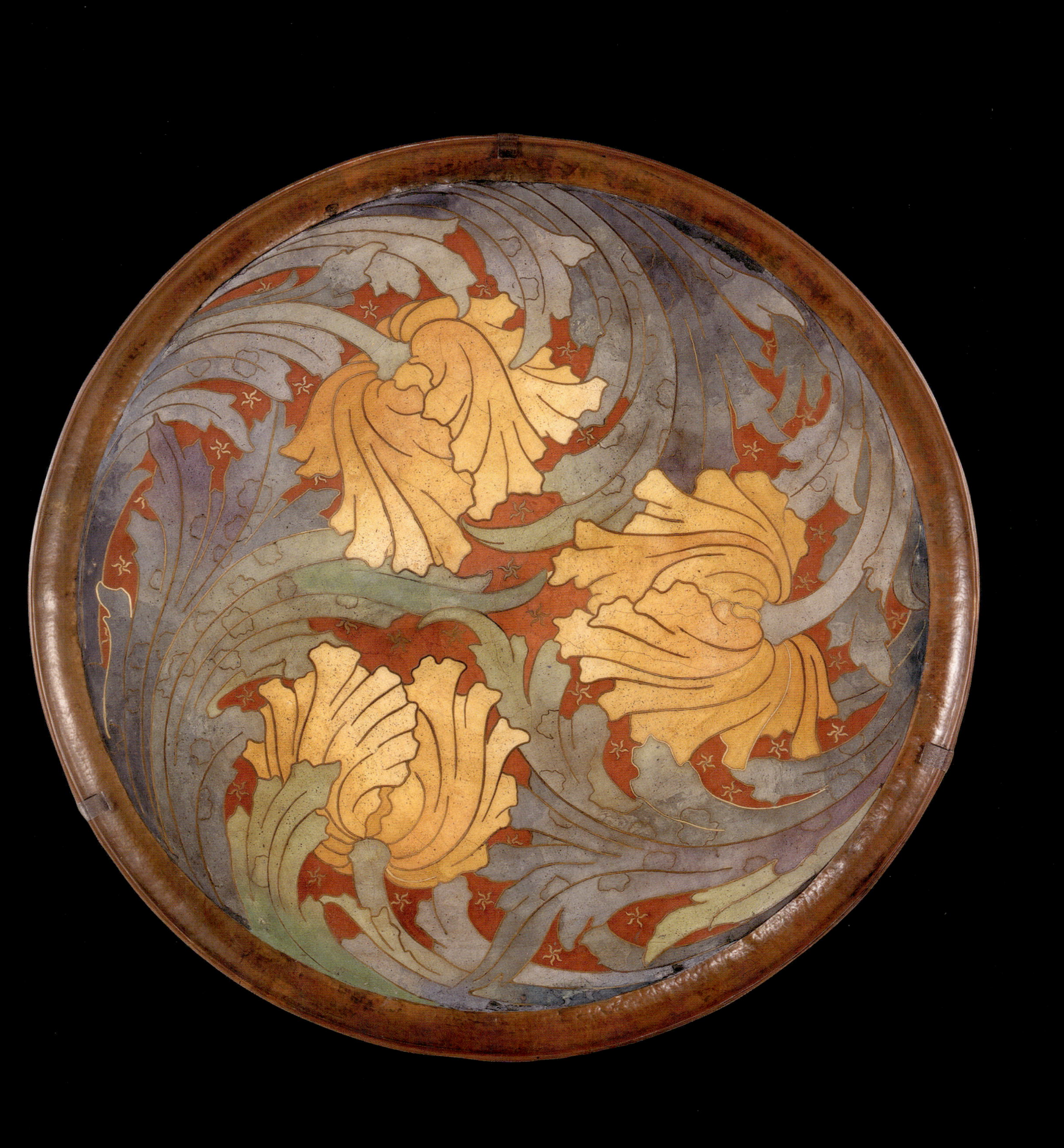

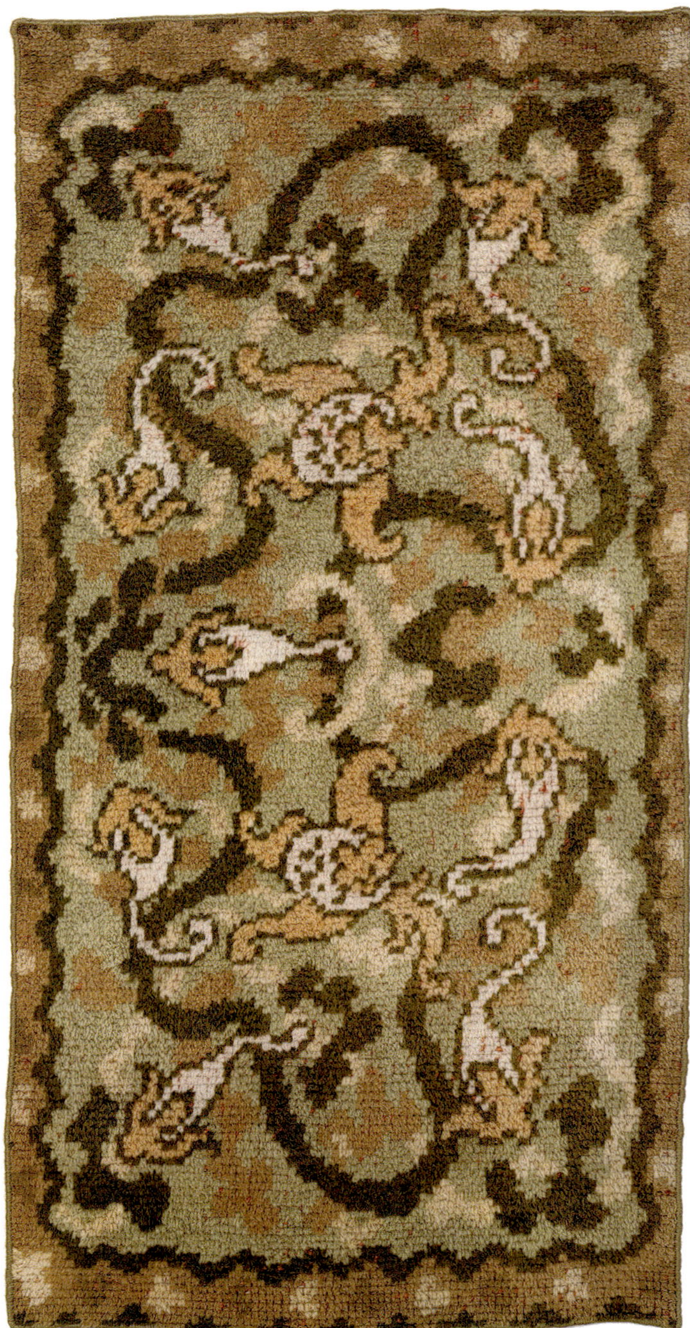

tables and sideboards reproduced in the *Album de références* bear a close resemblance to Liberty designs.[15]

Finally, the firm of J.S. Henry, of 287–9 Old Street, London – manufacturers of quality furniture for the middle classes, including ranges by Voysey and George Montague Ellwood – also appear among Bing's British suppliers. The *Album* entries 'Banquette et chaise Macarons' (no. 1/9, fig. 176) have been identified thanks to a publicity insert from the *Cabinet Maker* magazine of June 1896. 'Chaise et fauteuil Pépinière' (nos. 13/190 and 191, fig. 177) are recognisable in a catalogue of the Henry firm preserved in the files of the furniture department of the Victoria and Albert Museum. A third group, 'Chaise et fauteuil Marqueterie' (nos. 9/115 and 117, fig. 175) have been tracked down with the most appreciated aid of English specialists.[16] Other attributions of furniture to Godwin, William Birch or Norman and Stacey remain unsubstantiated.

BRITISH ARTISTS: HEATON, BRANGWYN

British artists who distinguished themselves in fields of the decorative arts other than furniture were also exhibited at Bing's gallery. A case in point was the Anglo-Swiss Clement John Heaton, who sold cloisonné ware at Liberty's and at the Galerie de L'Art Nouveau.[17] A large Heaton dish was purchased from Bing by the Musée des Arts décoratifs, Paris, in 1898, for the price of 250 francs (fig. 172), and other artefacts were sold to museums in Vienna and Berlin. The *Album de références* reproduces a 'socle Heaton' in metal (no. 7/86). In the same book are four 'Iris' glass vases (no. 28/350, fig. 180) by the London manufacturer James Powell and Sons, whose sole surviving client register includes a mention of 'Bing, Paris'. Finally, among British artists, it was undoubtedly Frank Brangwyn who enjoyed the closest co-operation with Siegfried Bing. His share in the decoration of the façade of 22, rue de Provence and the preparation of two painted panels for the gallery's entrance are well known as a result of various published researches,[18] but his commissions in the decorative arts are more obscure, with studies at present in progress.[19] It appears that Brangwyn produced no furniture at all for Bing and would only become interested in this field much later, in 1900. In a sketchbook dating from the period 1895–8, Brangwyn notes that he is working on five carpet designs for Bing. The best known is the 'Japanese Vine', designed from 1896 to 1897 and probably executed by J. Ginskey in Bohemia.[20] The

173
Frank Brangwyn, Bedside carpet, c. 1898
Musée des Arts décoratifs, Paris

> 174
William Benson, Table, *Album de références*, 25/300
Bibliothèque des Arts décoratifs, Paris

> 175
'Marqueterie' settle, *Album de références*, 9/115
Bibliothèque des Arts décoratifs, Paris

> 176
Wooden settle 'Macarons', *Album de références*, 1/9
Bibliothèque des Arts décoratifs, Paris

> 177
'Pépinière' chair and armchair, *Album de références*, 13/190 and 191
Bibliothèque des Arts décoratifs, Paris

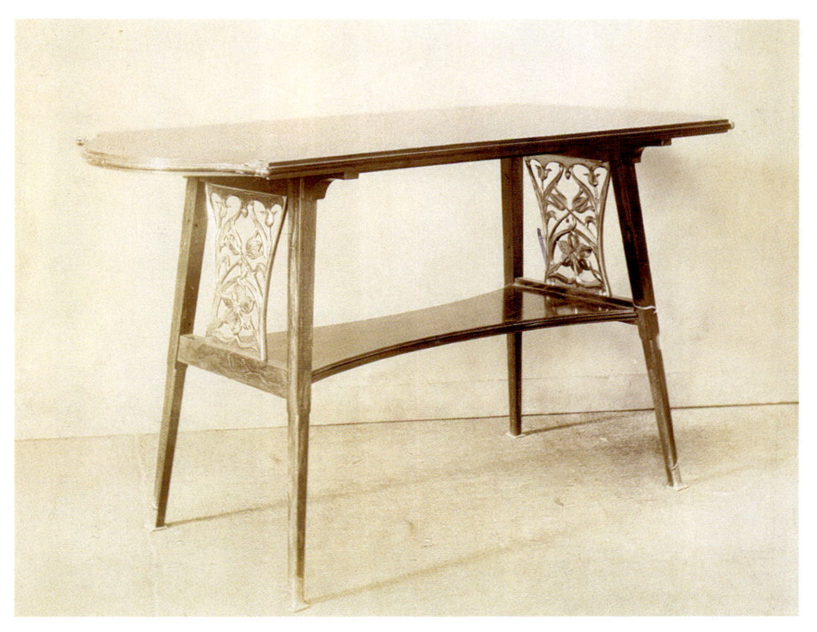

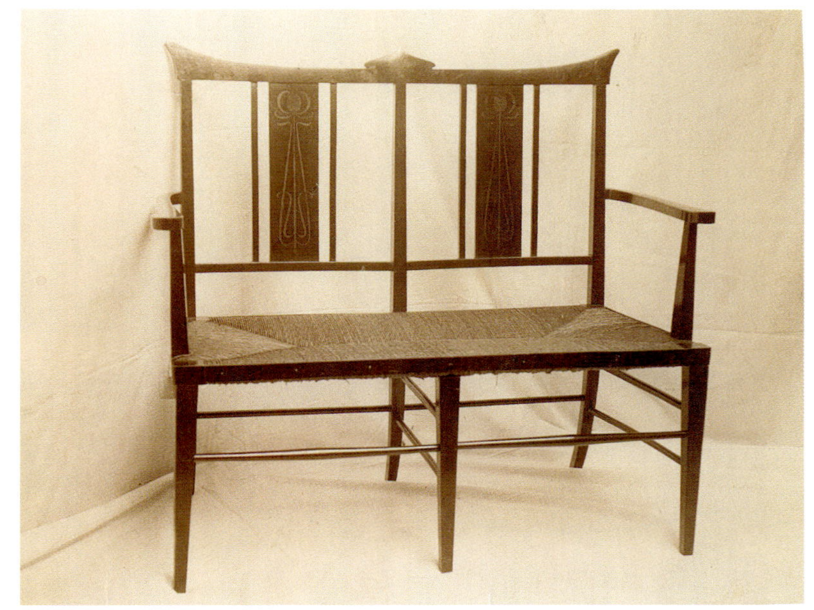

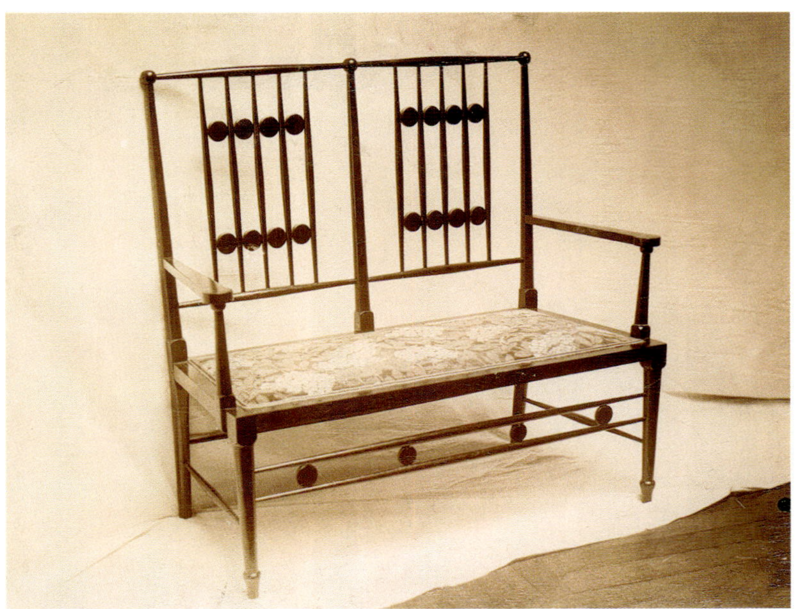

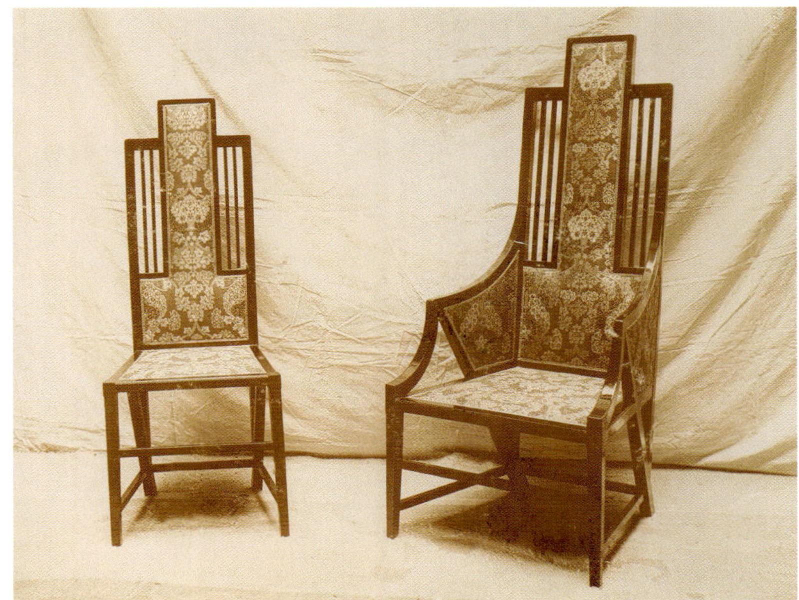

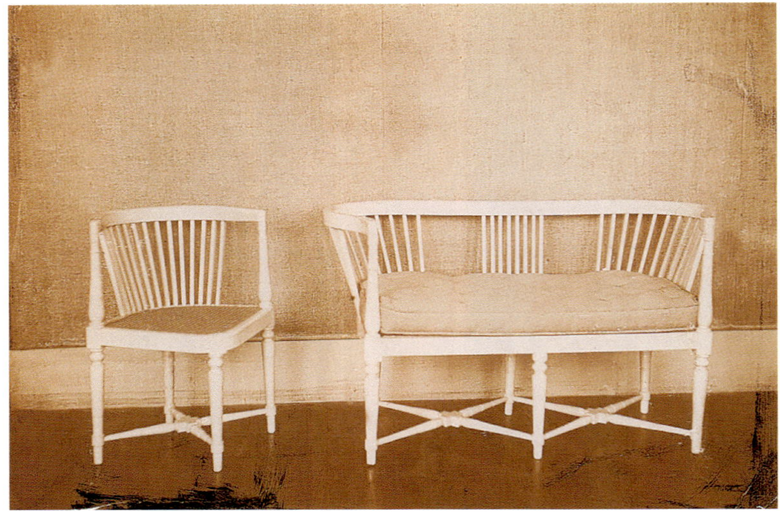

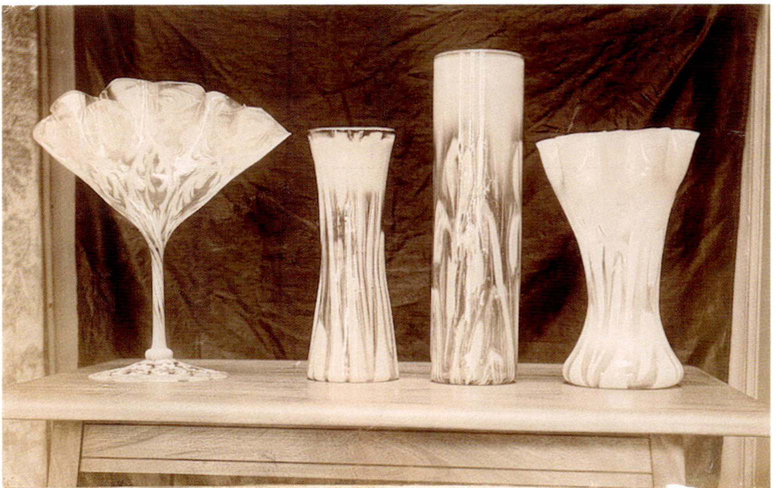

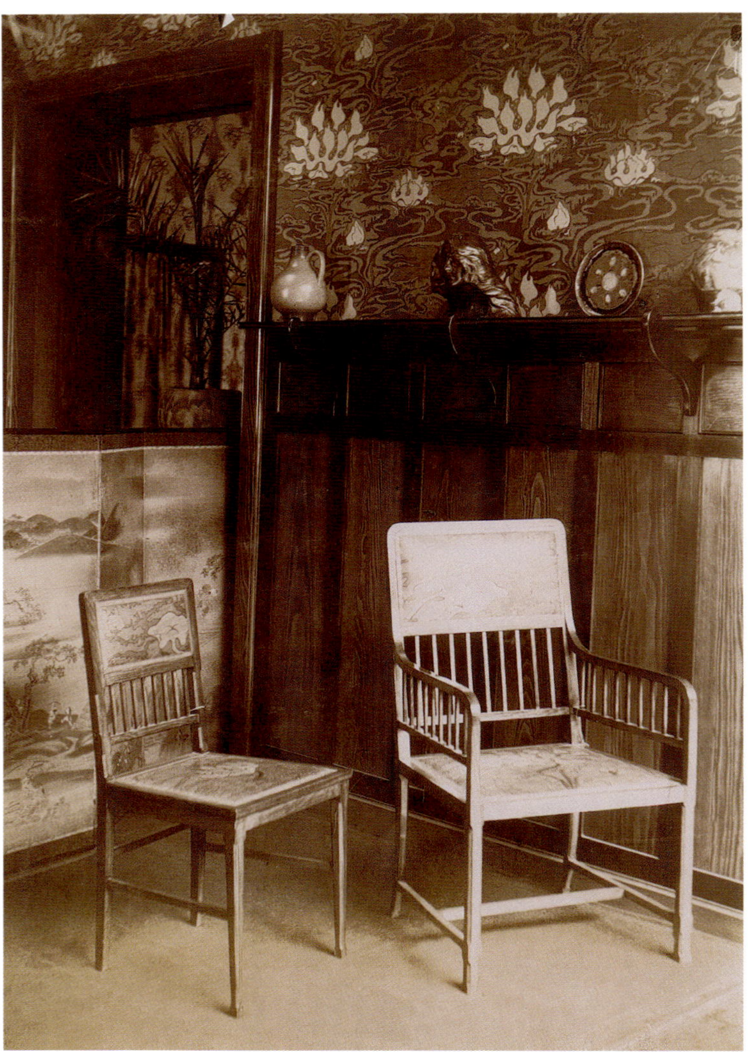

paintings (figs. 124, 125), carpet designs (figs. 160, 173) and the stained glass appear to have been among the many areas of collaboration between Bing and Brangwyn for which there is clear evidence.

SIMPLE DESIGNS FOR MASS PRODUCTION

If some of the British artists who worked for Bing produced work that was unique, or at least of a high artistic quality, the same was not true of items by industrial companies. We learn from the *Album de références* that the price of chairs varied from 50 francs ('Deauville' model, no. 6/77) to 80 francs (J.S. Henry chair, 'Pépinière' type, no. 13/190). British-made *banquettes* fetched from 75 to 200 francs, while sale prices for pieces made in 1900 by artists from L'Art Nouveau reached considerable sums. Eugène Gaillard's leather chair was sold for 350 francs to the Copenhagen Museum; Georges de Feure's giltwood sofa made 2,500 francs. Discussing this apparent contradiction, Marcel Morot explained: 'He was well aware that he was not in business to supply merely the rich and famous. He never lost sight of the objective he had established from the very first moment, that the most modest interior had a right to beauty. [...] The three years following the Fair were spent on large-scale commissions, and Bing began to consider doing something new for the majority of ordinary clients: he wanted simple designs that could be mass-produced to suit the pockets of those with more limited or even very modest means.'[21]

These remarks by his close collaborator echo Bing's own thoughts expressed in his article on artistic culture in America and the important role played by the machine in the improvement of public taste. Bing's preoccupation, which haunted him until after the success of 1900, appears substantiated by the critic Camille Mauclair: 'The excellent Bing lovingly prepared designs for complete dining rooms for the man in the street. These were simple but agreeable, and everything was signed, from Baffier's soup tureen to Charpentier's spoons. But there

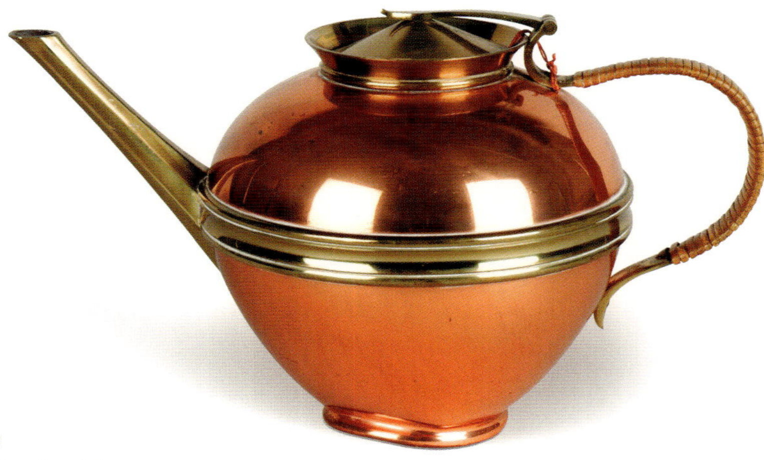

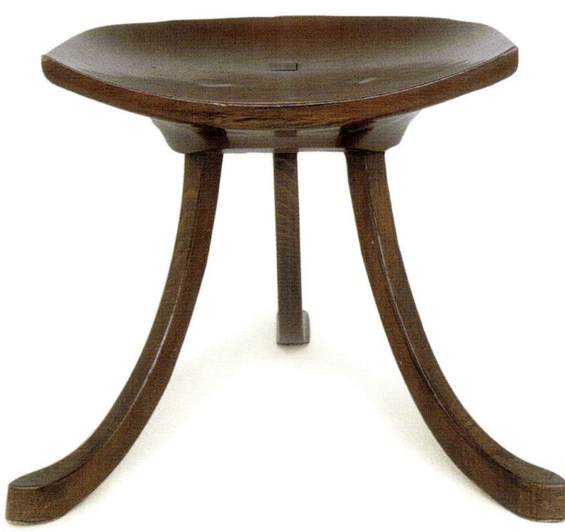

< 178
Furniture for a hall, *Album de références*, 7/82 and 83
Bibliothèque des Arts décoratifs, Paris

< 179
'Lily' chair and armchair, *Album de références*, 6/77 and 78
Bibliothèque des Arts décoratifs, Paris

< 180
James Powell and Sons, 'Iris' glasses, *Album de références*, 28/350
Bibliothèque des Arts décoratifs, Paris

181
William Benson, Tea pot, c. 1895
Nordenfjeldske Kunstindustrimuseum, Trondheim

182
Liberty & Co., 'Thebes' stool, designed by Laget, 1884
Nordenfjeldske Kunstindustrimuseum, Trondheim

were no buyers.'[22] It is possible to see here the origin of certain small pieces in non-precious materials now in museums in Berne, Vienna and Berlin.[23]

Siegfried Bing, with his background as a porcelain manufacturer and his innate business sense, was not working merely for the elite; he knew all about industrial production. For most of his life, he ran a commercial trade in expensive Japanese *objets d'art* while circulating items mass-produced in Japan and designed for export.[24] His delayed success and his illness seemingly prevented him from redeveloping this commercial policy within the framework of his gallery – with the exception of furniture, for which he had reason to thank British companies for their assistance.[25]

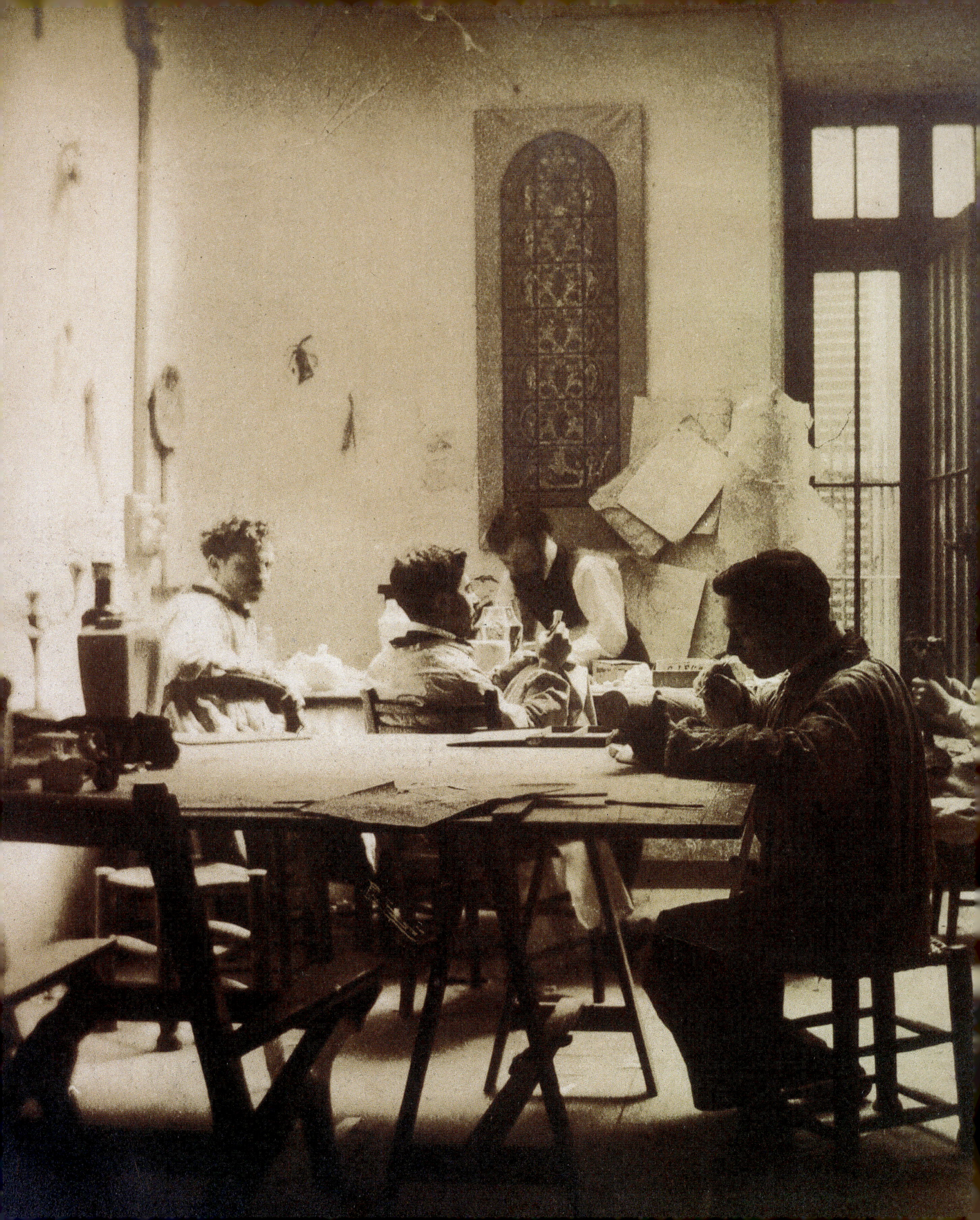

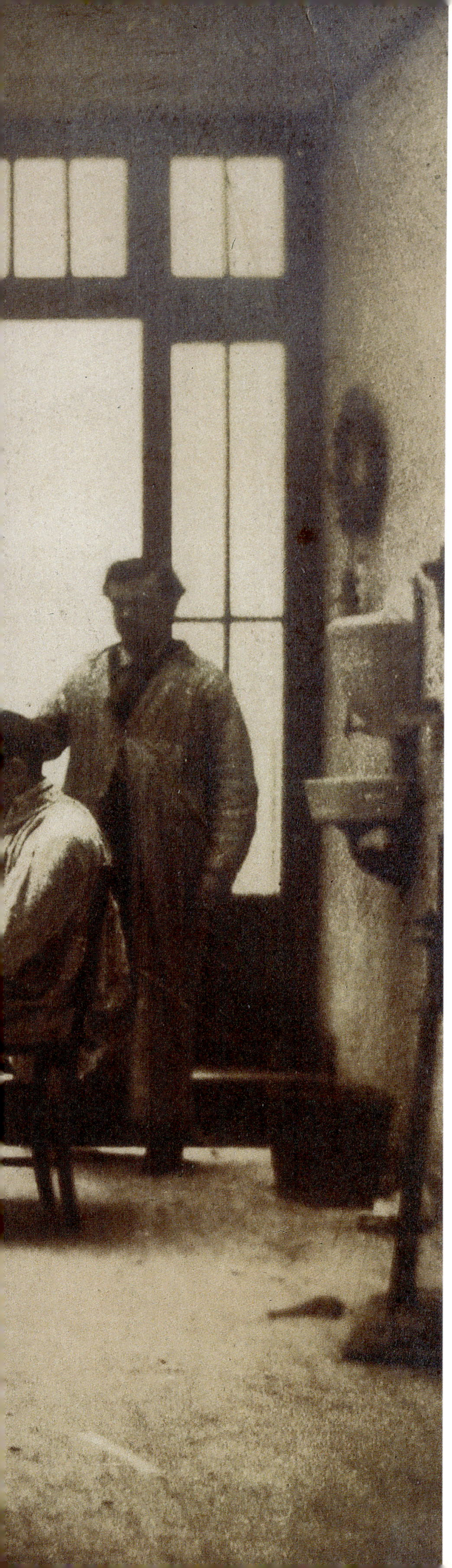

REDESIGNING THE HOME

BING'S ART NOUVEAU WORKSHOPS

GABRIEL P. WEISBERG

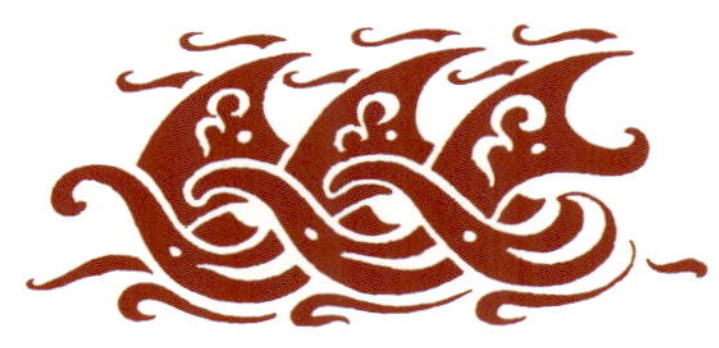

In preparation for the first exhibition at his Salon de l'Art Nouveau in 1895, Bing began to think about how home interiors might be transformed to correspond to new ideas about daily living: how to allow more light and air into living quarters, as well as how to move away from outdated decorative traditions. He asked a number of prominent European designers to create furniture ensembles that would fit a more modern concept of interior décor. Bing commissioned a bedroom from Maurice Denis; a waiting room from Edouard Vuillard (fig. 128); a salon with wall-decoration from Paul-Albert Besnard (fig. 129); a boudoir from the Australian Charles Conder; a smoking room from the Belgians Henry Van de Velde and Georges Lemmen; and a sitting room and a dining room, also from Van de Velde (fig. 114). These furnishings – combined with paintings by such Nabi artists as Paul-Elie Ranson and Maurice Denis – conveyed the sense of newness that Bing was

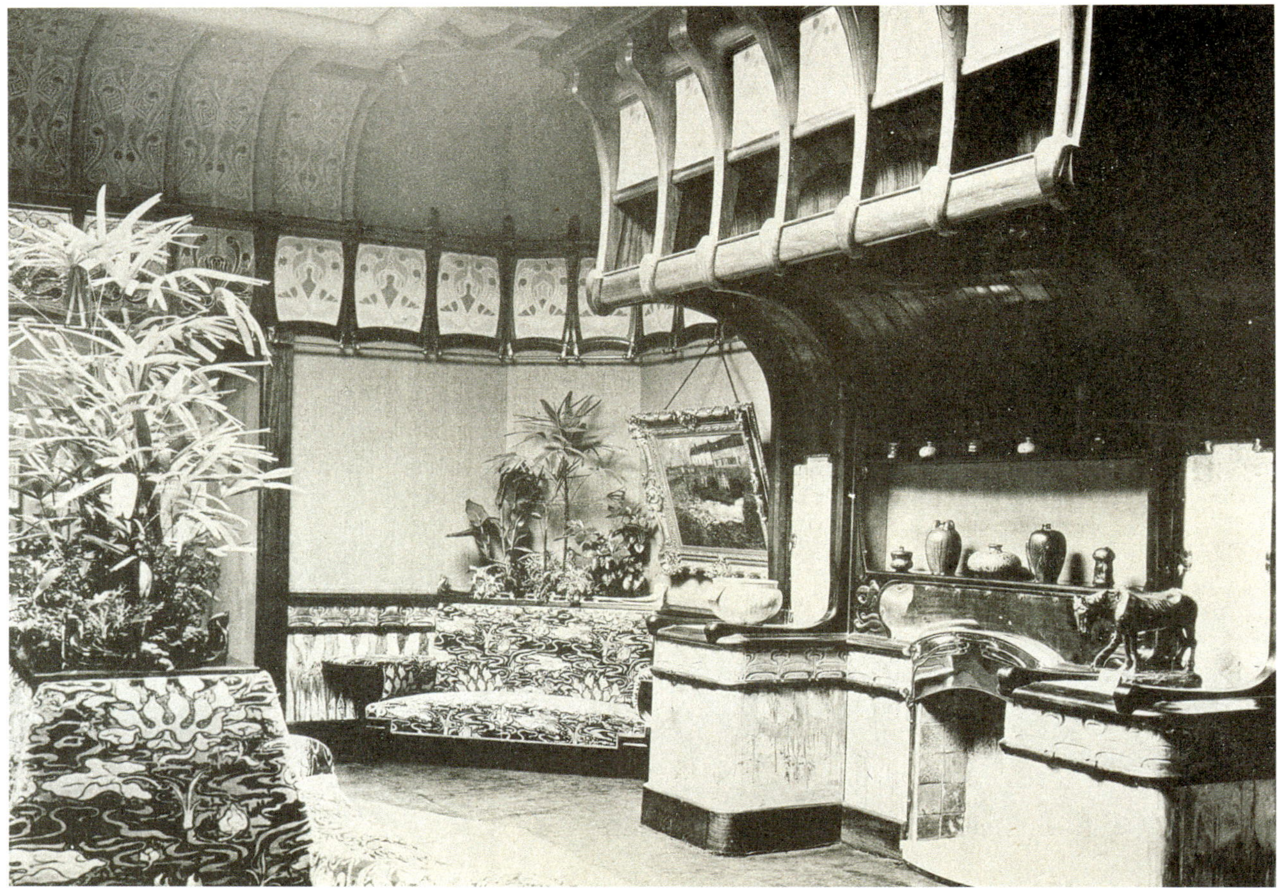

<< 183
Interior of the modelling workshop, c. 1899–1900

184
Sitting room by Henry Van de Velde at the International Art Exhibition, Dresden, 1897
Kunstbibliothek, Dresden

> 185
Léon Jallot

after. Five of these rooms were exhibited in his remodelled galleries at 22, rue de Provence and 19, rue Chauchat, where they were part of the first Salon de l'Art Nouveau that opened in December 1895.

The rooms received mixed reviews in Paris. But whether they were regarded as successful is almost beside the point; what is significant is that Bing used the model room concept to demonstrate that domestic spaces needed fundamental reshaping. In contrast to the prevailing style, with heavy, ornate furniture, Bing's interiors now incorporated subtler colours and less ornate furniture that emphasised the integrity of the materials, and a simple, uncluttered design. Smaller practical objects – ceramics, dishes, lamps – as well as curtains and rugs, incorporated the same design principles as the furniture, which added up to a unified environment. Bing was at the vanguard of a whole new concept in interior design, familiar to homeowners today but unknown in the late nineteenth century: the idea that complete rooms could be transported and installed in the home of a potential client. Historicism, a reliance on styles of the past, had come to an end.[1]

1897 INTERNATIONAL ART EXHIBITION IN DRESDEN

Bing's interiors continued to provoke debate through early 1897. He decided to promote his rooms beyond France, to tap into a wider market and perhaps to neutralise the somewhat negative reception they had received in Paris. In May 1897, Bing sent the five rooms to an international art show in Dresden.[2] This wide-ranging exhibition, which included other model rooms produced elsewhere in Europe, offered Bing the opportunity to promote his artists and wares and to compete with other design firms.

Each of Bing's rooms was carefully installed in the exhibition hall. Photographs of three of Van de Velde's rooms – the salon with wall fabric designed by Paul-Elie Ranson, the chimney from the sitting room (fig. 184), and the dining room with wainscoting – were reproduced in *Dekorative Kunst* and *L'Art Décoratif*.[3] A large number of smaller objects, including ceramics by Adrien Dalpayrat of the firm Dalpayrat et Lesbros and glasswork by Louis Comfort Tiffany, were added to the newly installed rooms.[4] This exhibition established Bing's shop as the primary outlet for *art nouveau* and his designers as being at the forefront of a totally new interior decorating style.

The German press responded mostly favourably to the innovative model rooms, and the reviews were abstracted for a publication that serves as a useful discourse on Bing's new direction in interior design.[5] One critic wrote that while ' "l'art nouveau" has often been ridiculed [...] one has to admit that indeed new beginnings for a 'new art in the house' are present. [...] The furniture and entire décor of [Bing's] rooms are certainly stripped of excessive decoration and traditional forms and created entirely in pure materials that show delicately balanced, utilitarian forms. [...] Every piece shows that it was created for a practical purpose, but at the same time that artistically trained hands were involved in its creation.' The impact of the interiors on prospective buyers was consistently discussed by reviewers, for example: 'The customer [...] does not have to live in the midst of modern banalities, but among the best taste in furnishing.'[6] While acknowledging Bing as the driving force behind the promotion of *art nouveau*, the critics credited the Belgian designer Henry Van de Velde as the visionary behind the new look. It is not known what happened to the rooms after the close of the Dresden exhibition or whether Bing even attended the show. Nevertheless, it is safe to say that he was thinking about how to increase his role in the design reform movement that was evolving simultaneously in several countries.

LIAISONS WITH EXISTING MANUFACTORIES AND THE ORIGINS OF THE BING WORKSHOPS

Bing concluded that to compete successfully in the burgeoning design reform movement he had to do two things: increase his ties with industrial firms so that designs produced by artists working for him could be widely produced; and organise his own crafts workshops. He knew that the English designers William Morris, Frank Brangwyn and W.A.S. Benson had had their objects produced by various firms,[7] and he was probably also aware of designers in other countries, such as Clément Heaton in Neuchâtel, Switzerland, who had organised workshops to make objects for the international market.[8] To promote his brand of *art nouveau*, Bing decided to set up his own workshops for the production of jewellery and furniture. At the same time, he provided designs made by his artists to outside factories that could produce a wider range of decorative objects.

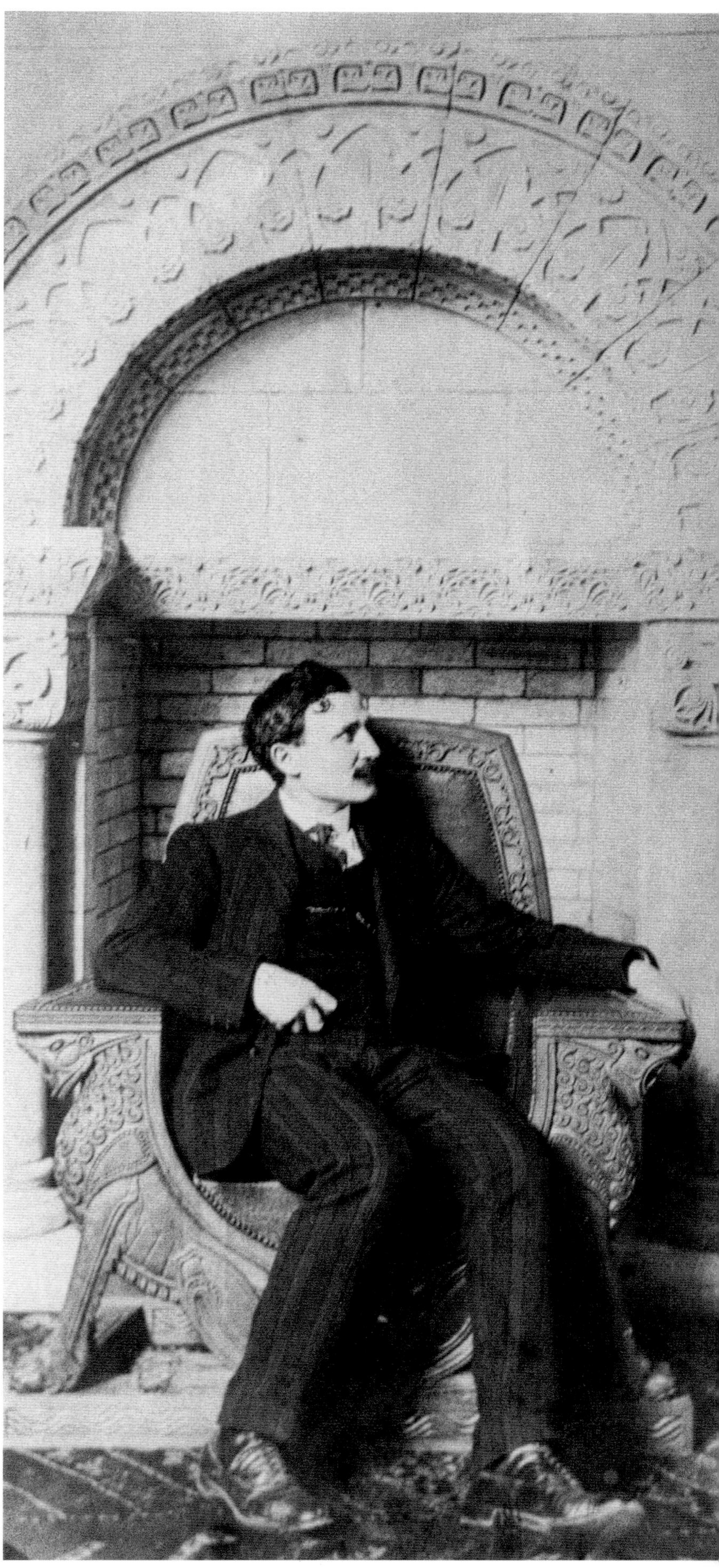

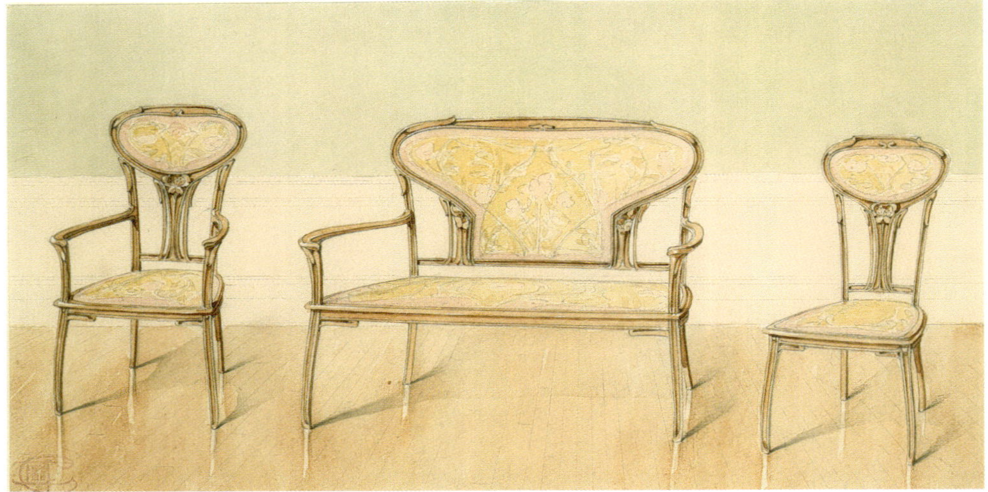

186
Georges de Feure, Drawing for chairs in a drawing room, 1895–1903
Musée des Arts décoratifs, Paris

187
Louis Bonnier, Plan of the jewellery and cabinetmakers' workshops, 3 June 1899 (detail)
Les Archives de Paris

> 188
Interior of the jewellery workshop at L'Art Nouveau, c. 1899–1900

> 189
Interior of the design studio, c. 1899–1900

> 190
Interior of the carpenters' workshop, c. 1899–1900

> 191
Interior of the cabinetmakers' workshop, c. 1899–1900

The starting date of the Art Nouveau workshops is difficult to establish because of the lack of company records, but by early 1897 Bing was commissioning designs for picture frames, mirrors and various other utilitarian objects, noting that the 'drawings were being completed in his own ateliers'. If these preliminary drawings were approved, the works shown in the designs were assigned to craftsmen or to firms able to manufacture them. By late 1897 and early 1898, Bing was asking artists to draw designs for dyed fabrics to be used for his 'Japanese installations' at his gallery. One of these artists was P. A. Isaac, whose fabric designs were so successful that he abandoned painting for a career in the applied arts.[9] Bing commissioned designs for impressions on velvet, silk, cretonne and woollen fabrics; these drawings could have been executed on his own premises as well, since he did not mention the name of a firm in connection with them. At the same time, Bing invited 'painters who are my friends' to create cartoons for rugs to be woven at the well-known tapestry manufactories at Aubusson.[10]

The names of the dealer's painter-friends remain unrecorded, although it is possible that one was Frank Brangwyn, who was then expanding into the applied arts; judging from their style, several rugs that Bing commissioned may have been designed by Brangwyn (figs. 160, 173).[11] The number of rugs produced, the names of the designers who made patterns for them, and the current location of most of the carpets from this early period are unknown, but the business link with Aubusson alone is significant. As Bing could not possibly open ateliers for every branch of the applied arts, he relied on outside firms that could produce the many types of objects he wished to market. In fact, as will be discussed below, he jobbed out most of the works that he commissioned, with the exception of jewellery, furniture and perhaps embroidery. Thus, fabrics for wall coverings and furniture, rugs and especially porcelains were executed by outside firms.

EARLY WORKSHOP ACTIVITY

Exactly where Bing's workshops were located prior to 1899 remains a mystery, but if they were already located at 19, rue Chauchat space must have been at a premium. This may have been why in that year Bing added a third

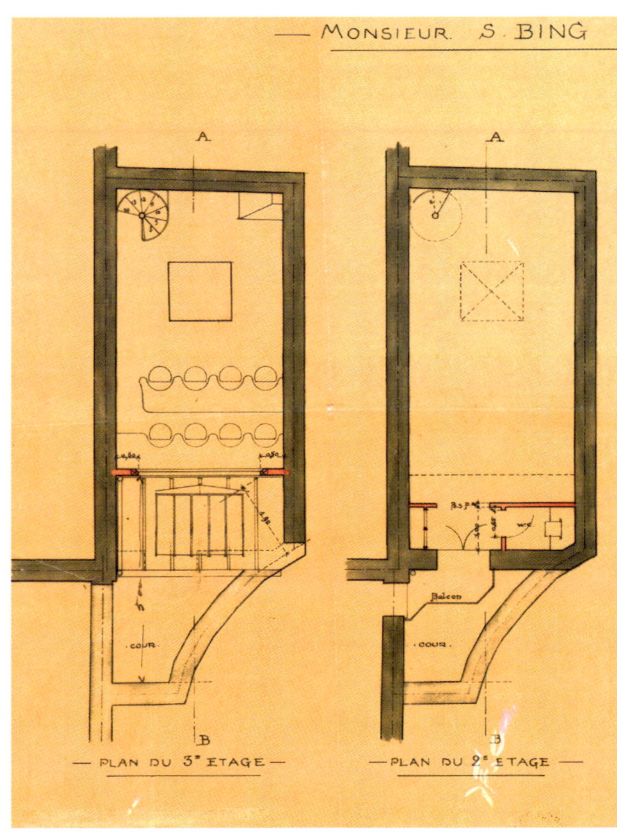

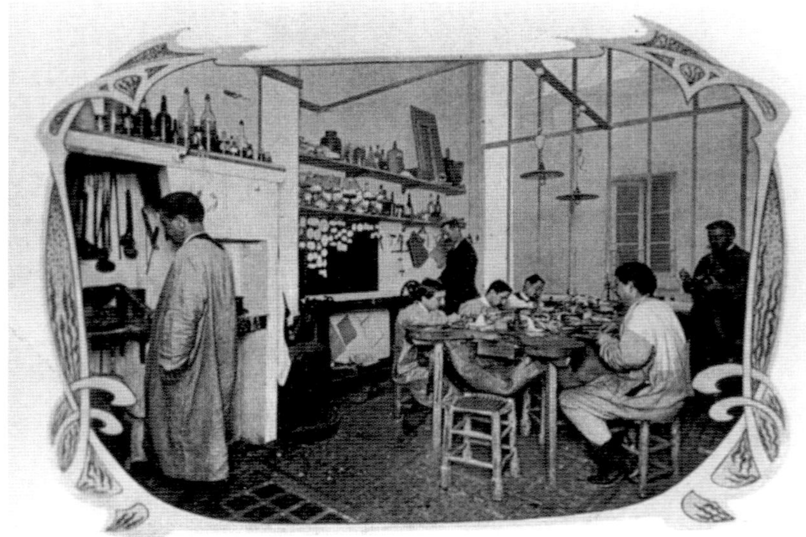
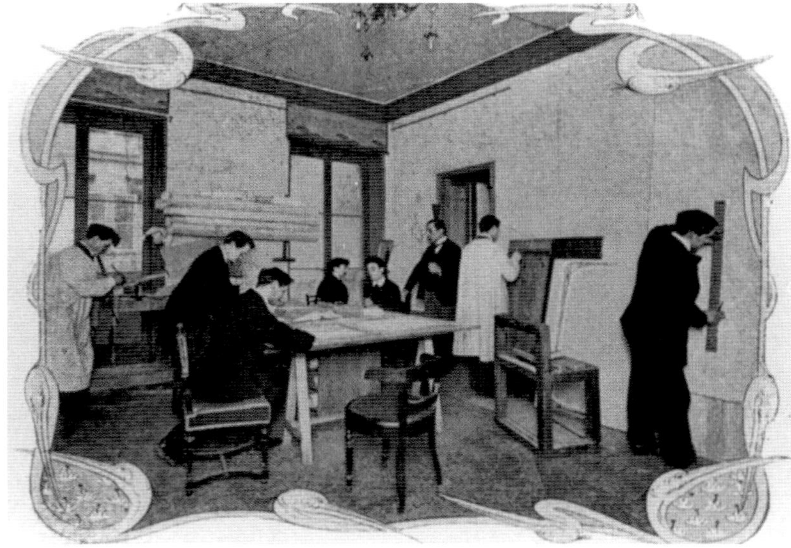
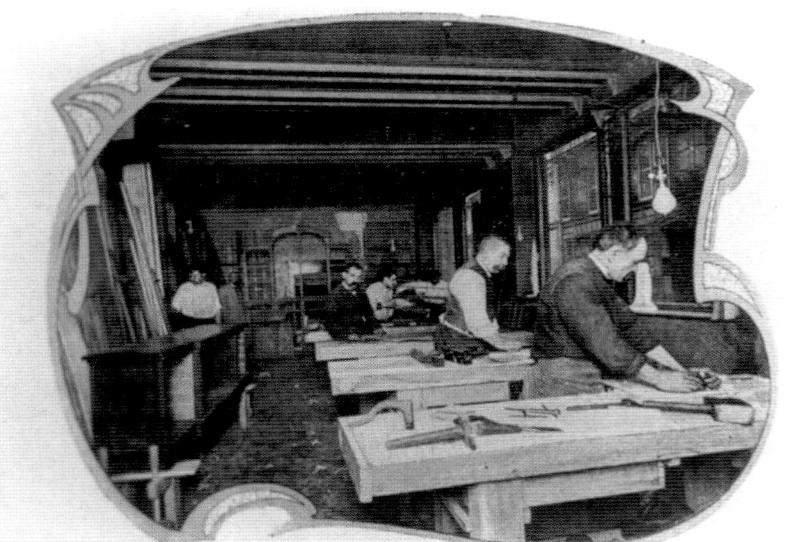
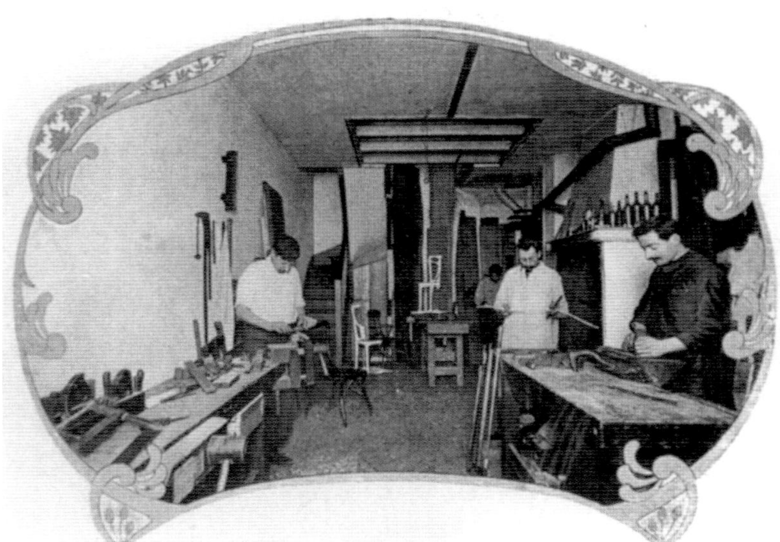

floor to the building. It was here that he set up two ateliers: one for woodworkers and one for jewellers.[12]

Through newly examined letters between Bing and Friedrich Deneken, Director of the Kaiser Wilhelm Museum in the industrial city of Krefeld, some details of the early phase of these workshops can be reconstructed. In early February 1898, Deneken wrote to the dealer regarding a home furnishings exhibition he wished to mount in his applied arts museum that would include artists from several countries, including Germany and France.[13] He asked Bing to provide carpets, wallpaper and furniture, including a set of furniture by Henry Van de Velde. In April, Bing responded that he had no current pieces by Van de Velde, noting that he was 'involved in the design and manufacture of his own, which was now directed toward a more current taste than the Belgian concept is at the moment,' but regretting that examples of his furniture were not ready to be shown, as they were still being produced by his craftsmen. Bing promised that he would send copper decorations, writing desk sets, and other small decorative objects instead.[14] However, in May Bing wrote Deneken that, 'in consequence of lively demand, none of the items I had in mind for you are available at the moment. Besides, these are items which are not made by special artists I commissioned but they are manufactured by the personnel of my own firm.'[15] Based on previous information about the expansion of Bing's gallery in 1899, it was thought that it was only then that Bing began to produce his own line of home furnishings in his own workshops. However, the correspondence between Bing and Deneken shows that Bing was already producing a wide range of works as early as April 1898. Moreover, it reveals that Bing was attempting to produce a unique style of French furniture under his own name, independent of outside influences.

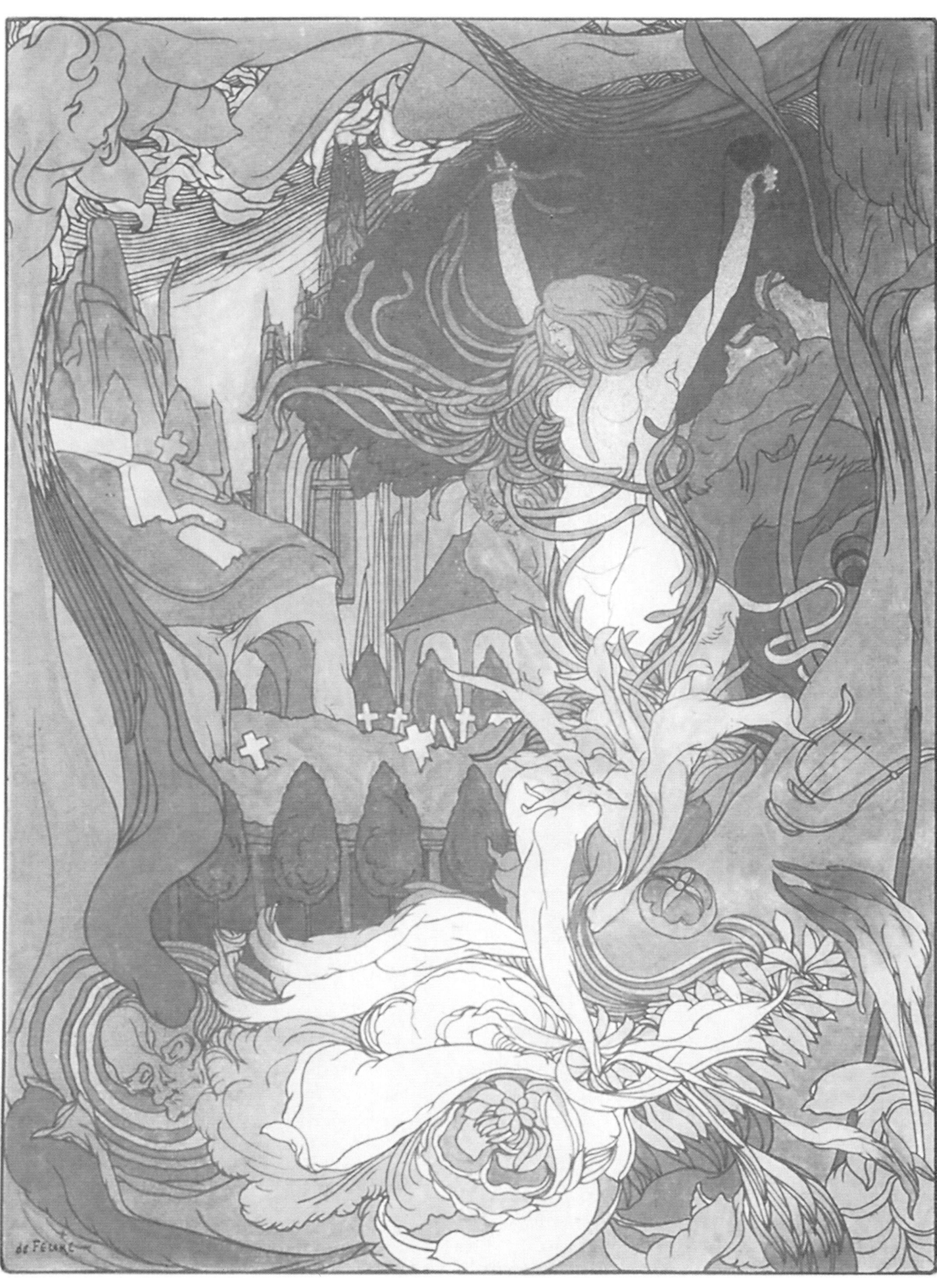

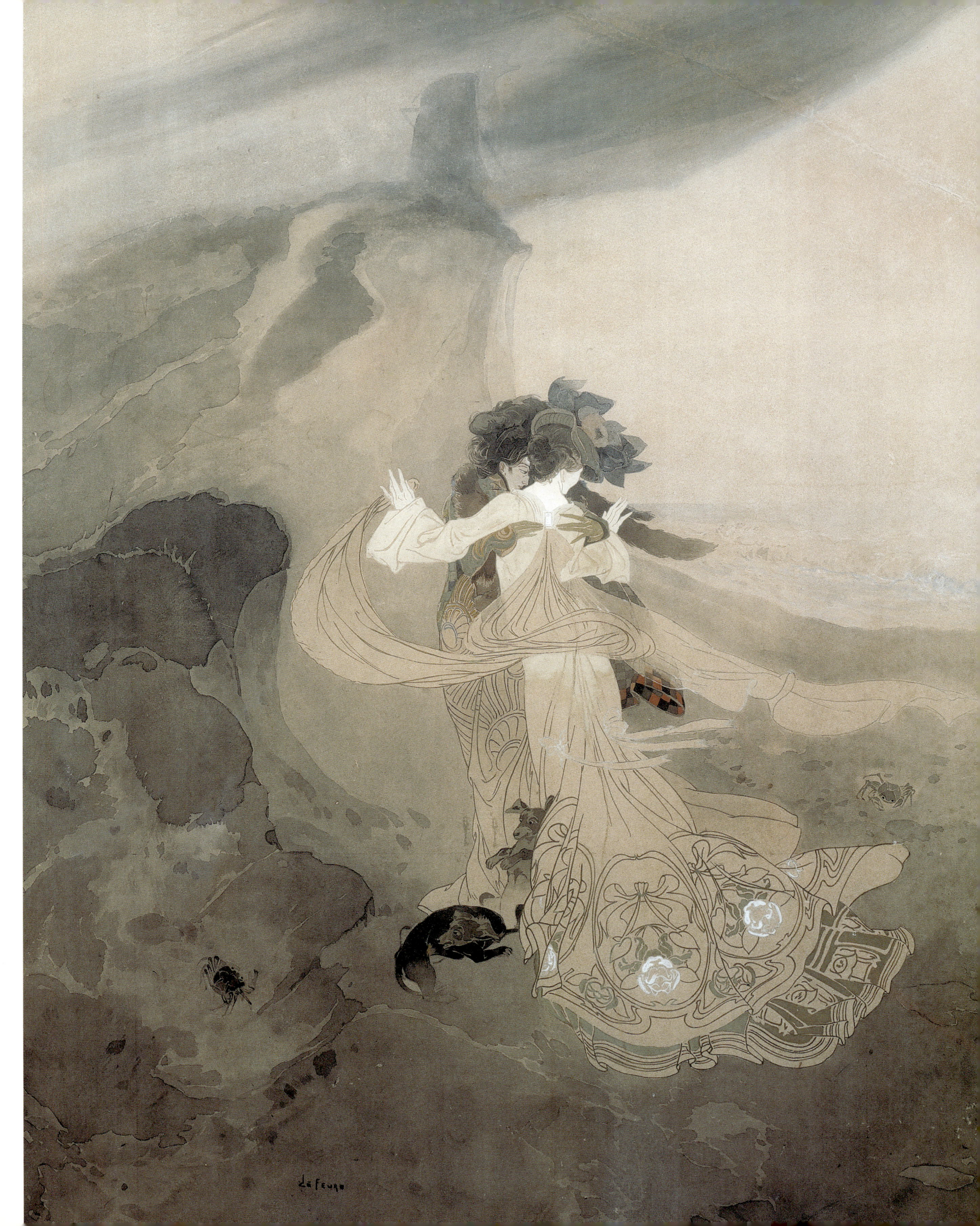
de Feure

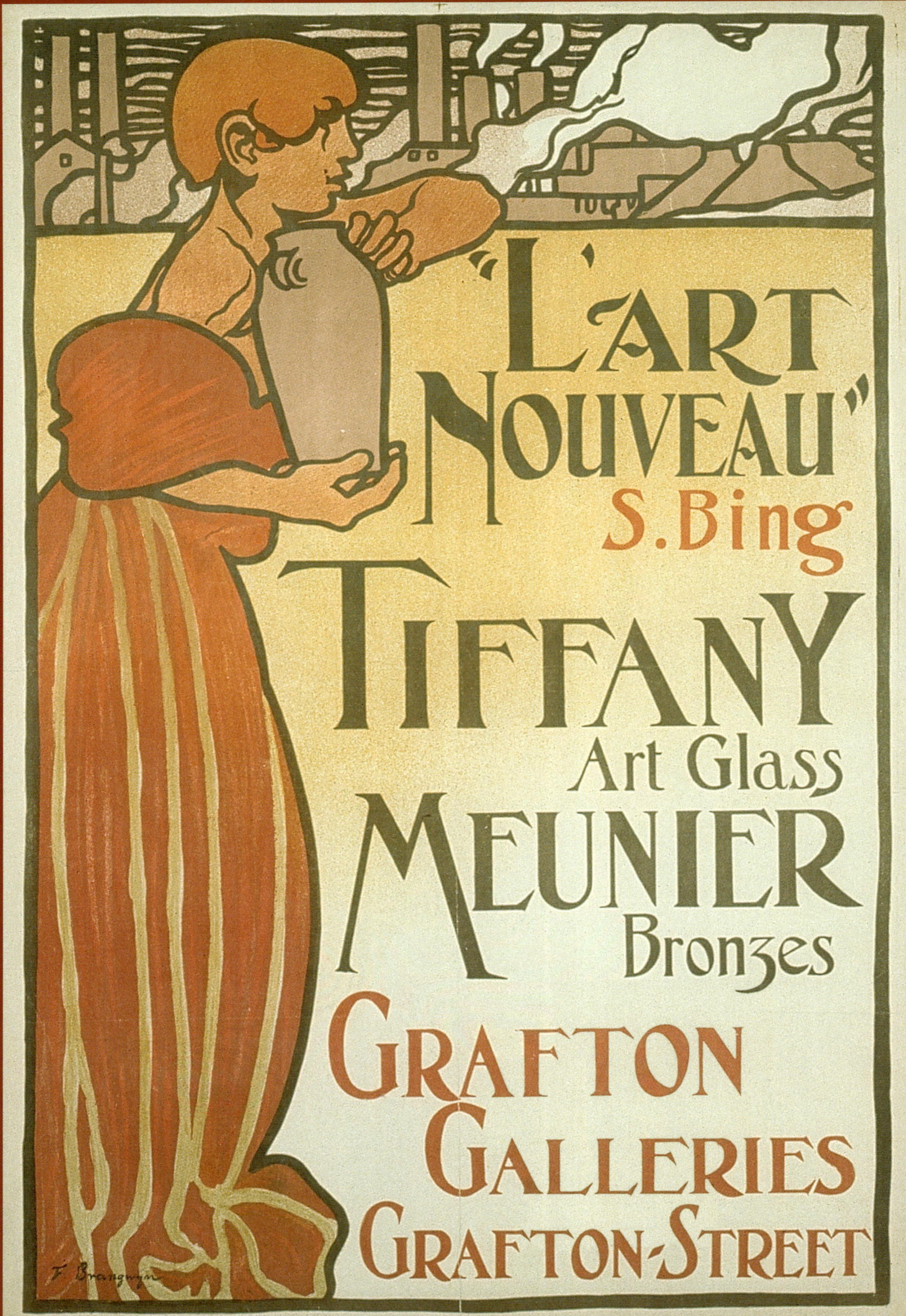
"L'ART
NOUVEAU"
S. Bing
TIFFANY
Art Glass
MEUNIER
Bronzes
GRAFTON
GALLERIES
GRAFTON-STREET
F. Brangwyn
Printed By CHARLE VERNEAU. Oberkampf Street . PARIS

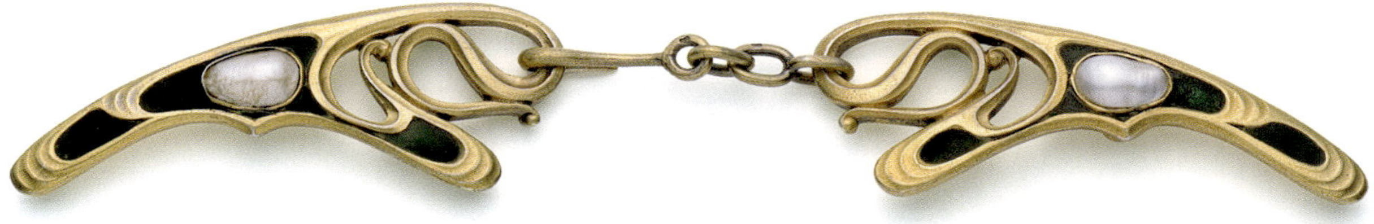

<< 192
Georges de Feure, *Damned Women*, 1897–98
Victor and Gretha Arwas Collection, London

<< 193
Georges de Feure, *Elegant Women on the Beach*, 1900–02
Collection Jane Abdy, London

< 194
Frank Brangwyn, Poster for L'Art Nouveau's exhibition at the Grafton Galleries, London, 1899
Musée de la Publicité, Paris

195
Edward Colonna, Fastener or clasp, c. 1900
Musée des Arts décoratifs, Paris

Again the lack of company records frustrates any attempt to determine what designers were employed by Bing in this early phase of the workshop activity. It is possible that Bing had already hired Léon Jallot (fig. 185), who became the head of his furniture workshop and, likely, his general overseer by 1900. In any event, Bing was undoubtedly on the lookout for young, creative artisans who could make designs that conformed to his own vision. Some of these early models for furniture are documented in a photographic album Marcel Bing gave to the Musée des Arts décoratifs, Paris, in 1908. Unfortunately, few of the pieces bear a precise date or the name of the designer.[16]

CONSTRUCTION OF THE WORKSHOPS

At the same time that Bing was negotiating with artisans to produce objects, and sending the resulting pieces to museums and galleries in various countries to promote his vision of an *art nouveau*, he was reviewing architectural plans for new ateliers at the rear of 19, rue Chauchat.[17] By renovating a space that had provided storage for Japanese objects and by constructing a third floor, Bing created new spaces for his cabinetmakers and jewellers (figs. 188–91). The jewellery workshop, with its large windows facing the interior courtyard, received the daylight required for working on small objects (fig. 188). By this time, the jewellers were supervised by Bing's son, Marcel, a jewellery designer in his own right. The construction of the addition was authorised by the city of Paris in May and June 1899; the new workshops were most likely fully operational by the autumn.[18] Since a number of pieces produced in the Bing ateliers were shown as early as May 1899 at the Grafton Galleries in London, it can be presumed that the workshops already existed off-site or in another part of the building at 19, rue Chauchat at the time of this London show.

Concurrently with the expansion of his workshops, Bing mounted a publicity campaign in the Parisian art magazines. Through his friend Julius Meier-Graefe, editor of *L'Art Décoratif*, Bing promoted *art nouveau* in the pages of that journal. In October 1899, an article appeared with many illustrations of pieces of jewellery by Edward Colonna. Another article appeared in December 1899, featuring jewellery pieces by Colonna, small vases by Tiffany with Colonna mounts and perfume bottles made of agate with mounts also by Colonna. An article in *La Revue Illustrée* predicted that Bing's jewellery would become treasures in contemporary museums, describing the delicate, shimmering pieces as 'artistic jewels'.[19] With these notices all published by the end of 1899, Bing could rest assured that the name of his shop, the artists he commissioned and the objects he sold were becoming known to the French public.

THE GRAFTON GALLERIES EXHIBITION, LONDON, 1899

Bing's boundless energy is evident not only in the creative output of his new workshops but also in his efforts to promote his brand of *art nouveau* in the leading European capitals. London had been slow to support continental *art nouveau* in any of its manifestations, but Bing, who would have been well aware of the dominance of the British Arts and Crafts group in the art schools of England, was not dissuaded from establishing a foothold in the English capital. He may have gained some confidence that his line of decorative arts might be accepted in London from his slightly younger colleague Arthur Lasenby Liberty, who had helped Bing promote Japanese art relatively early on, and whose own firm, Liberty and Company, produced a diversity of decorative objects.[20]

Bing found the Grafton Gallerie of London amenable to hosting an exhibition of his own choosing from May

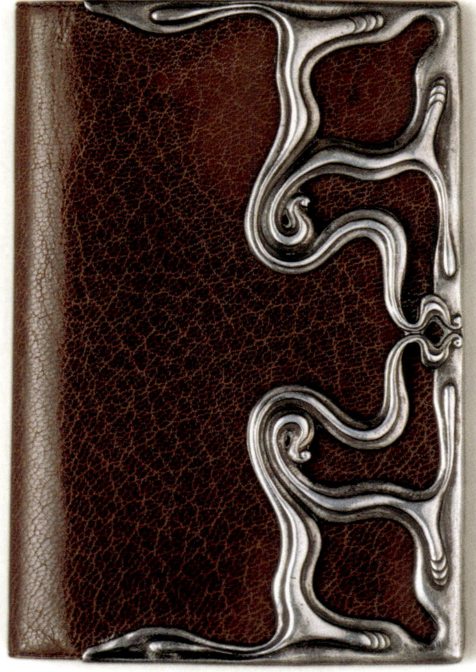

to July 1899. This extensive display presented works from all of the areas that the dealer had championed over his long career, with the result that it offered several overlapping and simultaneous viewpoints, not unlike a cubist painting. The exhibition included: Japanese prints; Indo-Persian miniatures; oil paintings by such French artists as Albert Besnard, Ary Renan and Camille Pissarro; sculpture by Constantin Meunier; silk designs for a sitting room by Charles Conder; jewellery and other small objects, many of which had been designed by Edward Colonna in Bing's new workshops; and finally, glasswork by Louis Comfort Tiffany.[21] Regarding the latter, Bing could call attention to American artists working in the *art nouveau* style, while also demonstrating how members of his own ateliers were designing mounts for Tiffany's Favrile glass vases (fig. 199). Some pieces from the show were bought by the South Kensington Museum for their permanent collection. The exhibition closed that summer but reopened after a few months, in October.[22]

Bing's exhibition generated a lively discourse in the press. A reviewer for the London *Times* paid particular attention to the glasswork of Tiffany, which explored 'with great success, the possibilities of a beautiful but intractable material'.[23] The *Westminster Gazette* called the exhibition 'heterogeneous' and also singled out Tiffany and the 'ingenuity' of colouristic effects achieved in his stained-glass windows.[24] However, not all the critics were supportive. One took aim at Bing's essays in the accompanying catalogue for heaping too much praise on Tiffany, as well as Meunier. The anonymous reviewer wrote: 'I might have appraised Mr. Tiffany's efforts more highly had not M. Bing assessed their artistic value at so ridiculous a figure.'[25] He noted that 'one is always inclined to resent having an author, or an actor [...] or even an artist in glass, forced down one's throat.' In England, as in France in 1895, Bing experienced the chauvinist reaction of the art establishment toward foreign elements.

When the London exhibition reopened in October, there were some forty additional small objects on display. Designed by Edward Colonna and produced in Bing's ateliers, these included belt buckles, tie-pins, brooches, coat fasteners, rings (figs. 7, 195, 202, 203) and leather card cases (fig. 196), all demonstrating the high level of sophistication that the workshops had achieved in a short period of time.[26] A number of these pieces were reproduced in *The Studio*, and the author of the article, Horace Townsend, declared: 'Colonna is proceeding on absolutely correct lines. [...] He relies on his jewels simply to accentuate the line of the designs. [...] The interest lies chiefly in the beauty of line and form, and the truly decorative quality of the gold work of the settings, rather than in the pecuniary value [...] of the jewels themselves.' Townsend grasped early on the achievements of these objects produced in Bing's workshops – the skilful use of various materials and the elegant, abstract designs – leading him to state unequivocally that 'artistically they are all beautiful'.[27]

These press notices of the Grafton Galleries show would have attracted many visitors, among them craftsmen, designers and potential collectors. No doubt buoyed by the excitement and controversy over this recent venture, Bing forged ahead with preparations for his pavilion, L'Art Nouveau Bing, at the 1900 World's Fair in Paris.

196
Edward Colonna, Card case, c. 1898–99
Musée des Arts décoratifs, Paris

> **197**
Edward Colonna, Fabric, c. 1899–1901
Manufactured by Lamy et Bornet, now Maison Prelle, Lyon

>> **198**
Vase, with crystalline glazes by Millet and silver mount by Léon Jallot, c. 1900
Victoria and Albert Museum, London

>> **199**
Louis Comfort Tiffany, Vase, with silver mount by Edward Colonna, c. 1900
Det Danske Kunstindustrimuseum, Copenhagen

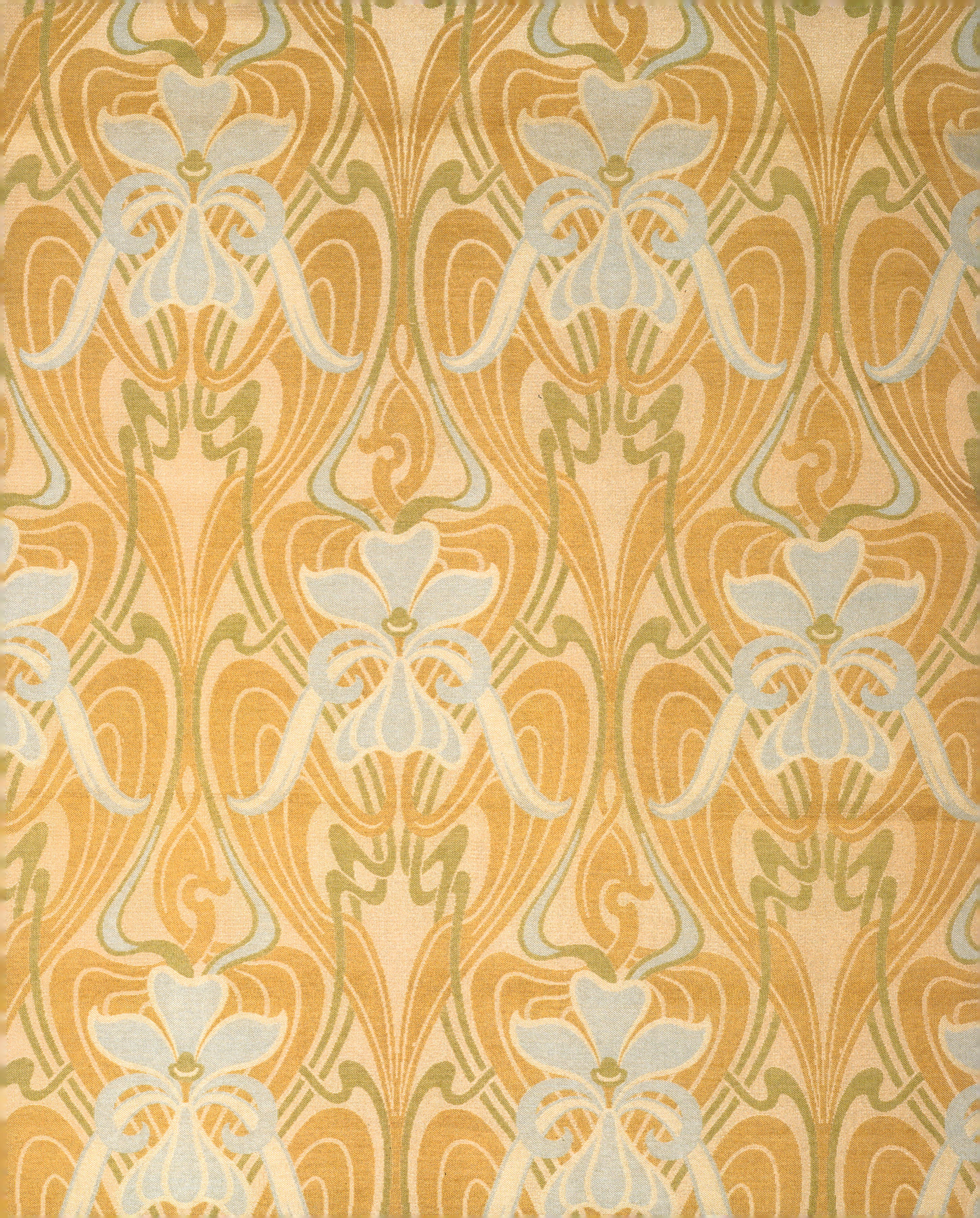

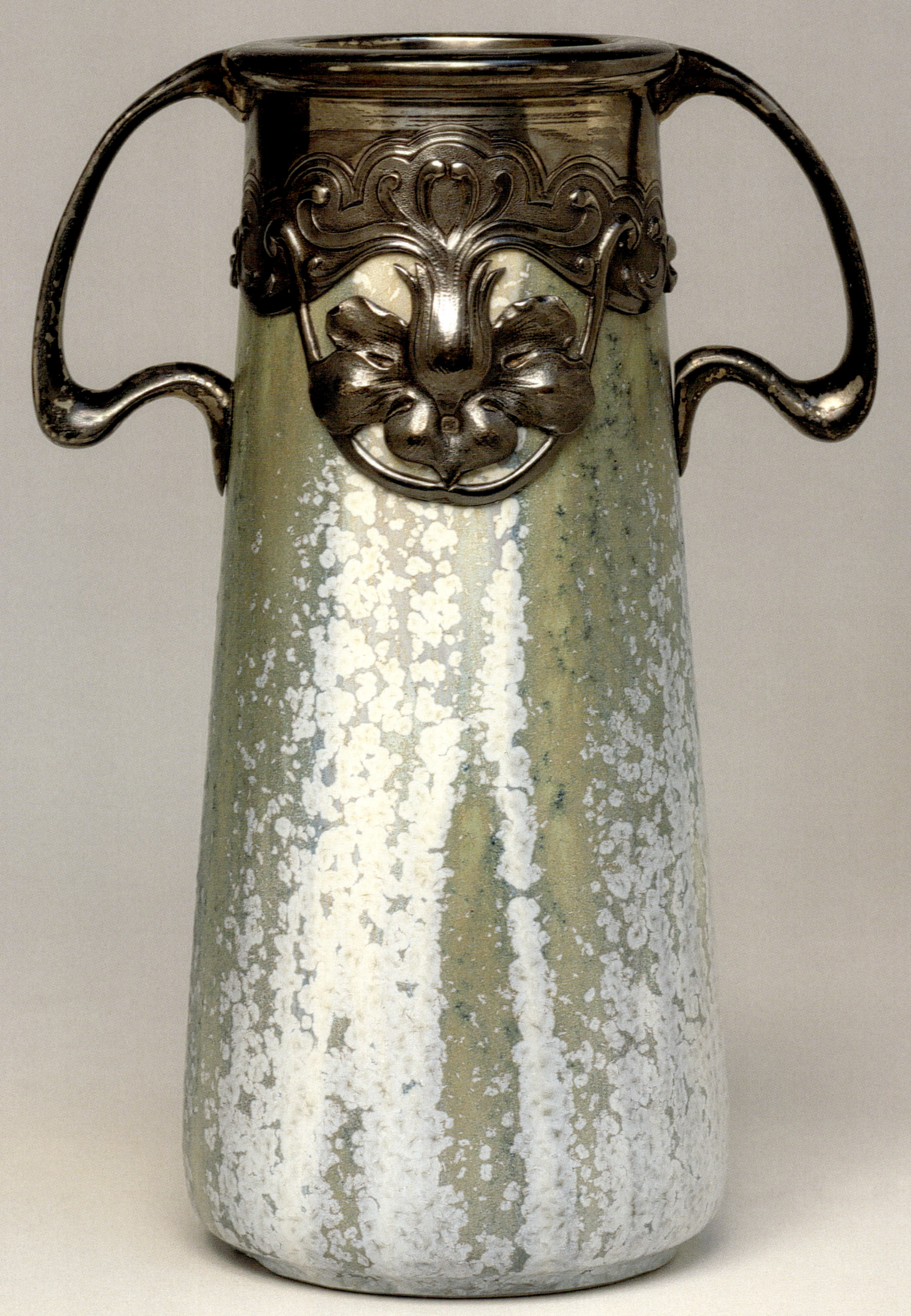

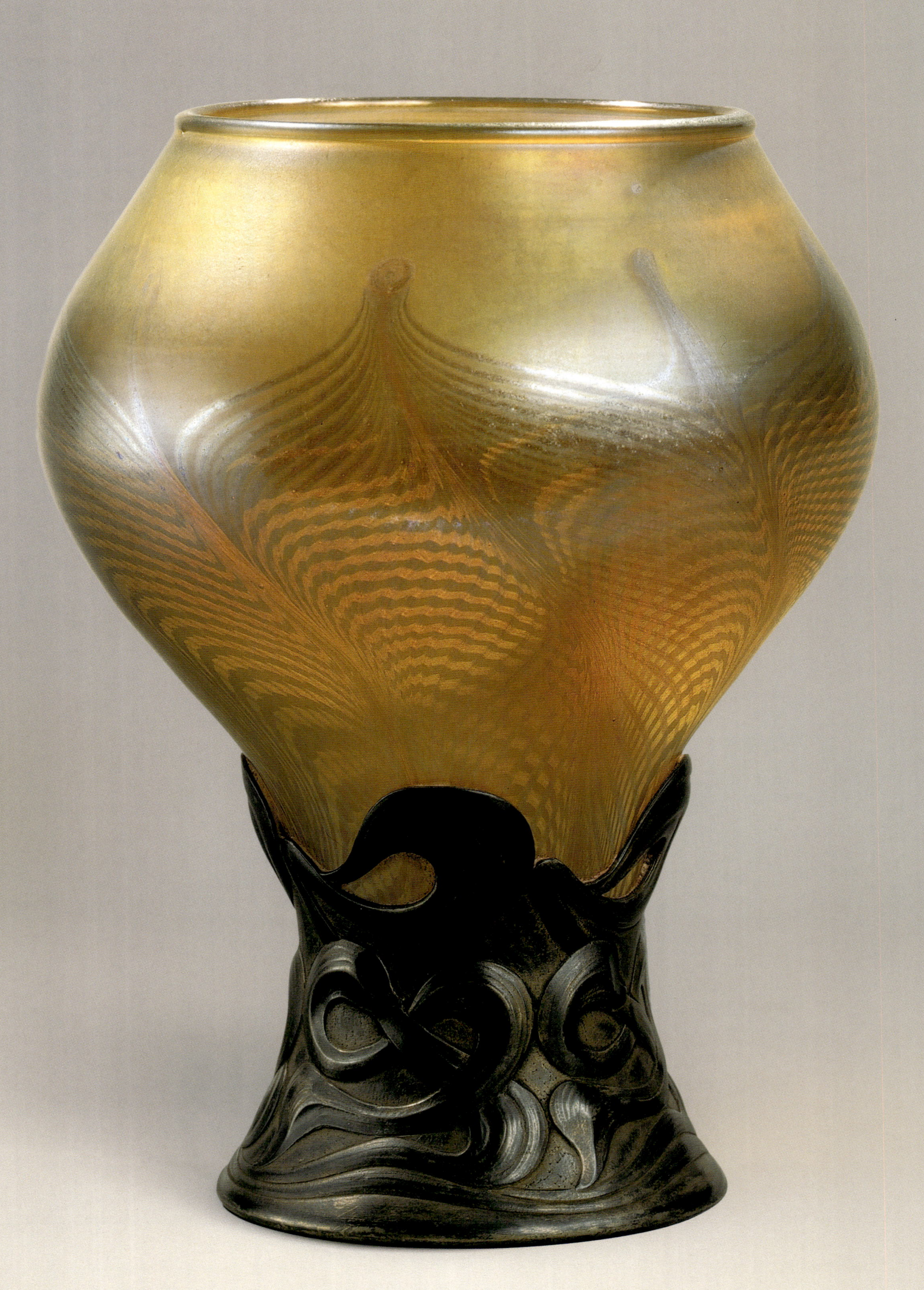

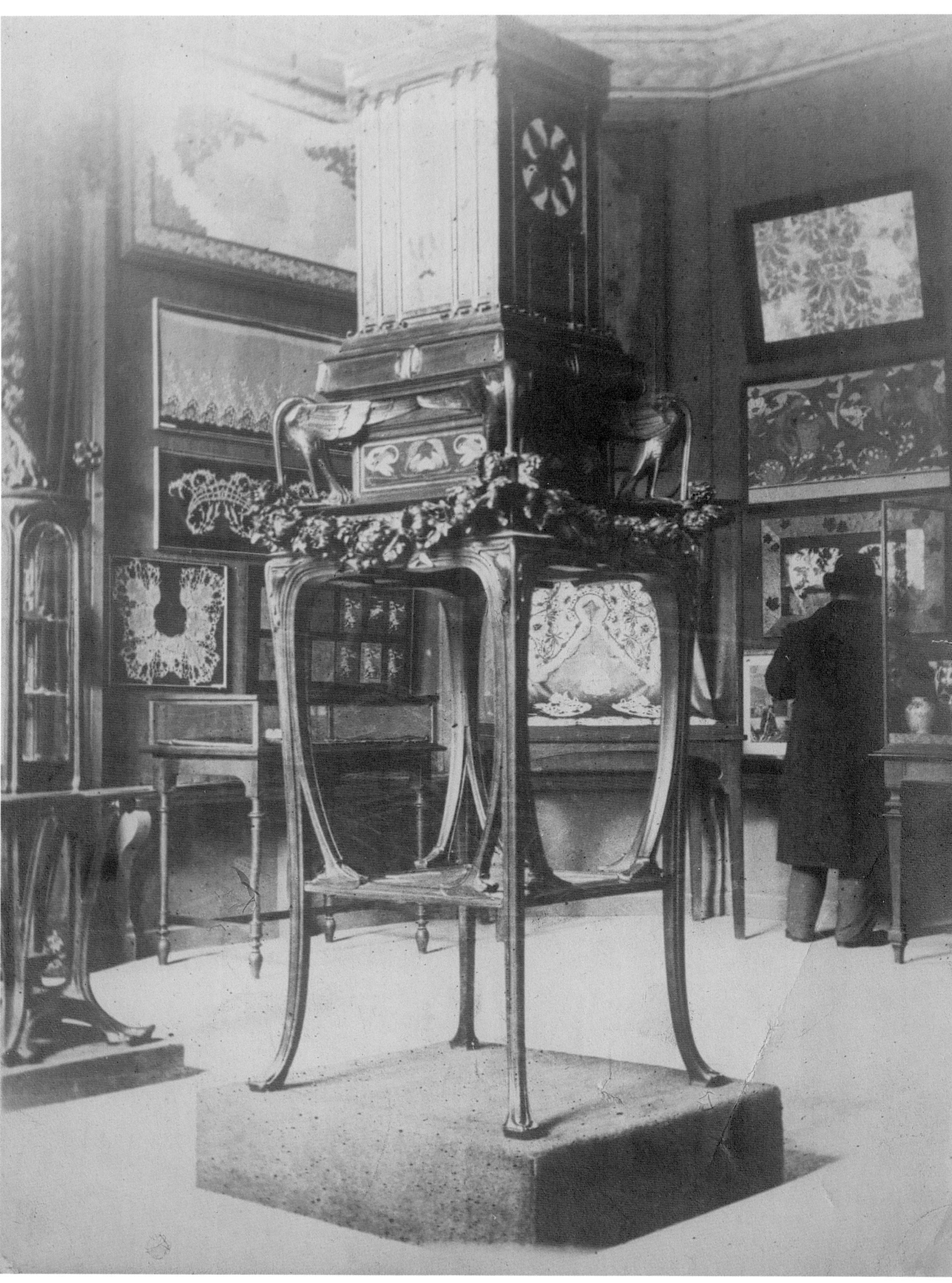

< 200
Interior of Bing's L'Art Nouveau with a piece of furniture by Léon Jallot

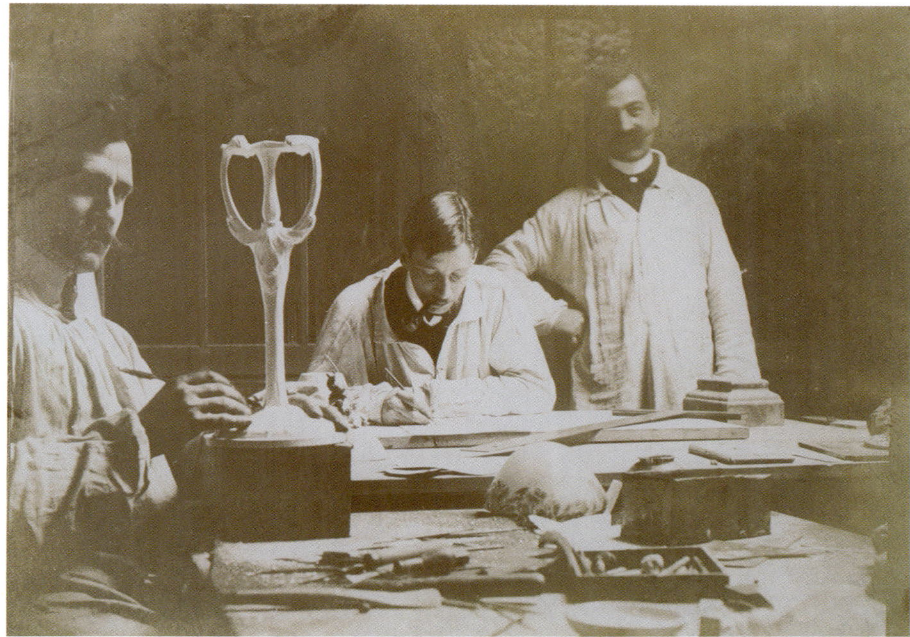

201
Modelling workshop with Marcel Bing (centre) and Léon Jallot (standing), c. 1899–1900

>> 202
Edward Colonna, Pendant brooch, c. 1900
Musée des Arts décoratifs, Paris

>> 203
Edward Colonna, Ring, 1899–1900
Musée des Arts décoratifs, Paris

>> 204
Marcel Bing, Pendant, 1900
Musée des Arts décoratifs, Paris

>> 205
Marcel Bing, Pendant, 1900
Musée des Arts décoratifs, Paris

THE CRAFTSMEN AT WORK

Once the new workshops were open, Bing lost no time in publicising them in *La Revue Illustrée*. Several photographs in the article show different groups of artisans – furniture designers, cabinetmakers, and jewellers – working at their tasks. The angle of these shots conveys the impression that the workshop spaces were larger than they actually were (figs. 188–91).[28] Moreover, while the workshops were certainly better organised than they had been earlier on, it is likely that only the jewellery items were fully made in-house. Certainly drawings of all types were produced on site. Many more designs on paper were made than pieces were executed, either because they failed to meet the necessary prerequisites of beauty and usefulness or because there was not enough time or money to develop all the ideas generated by the designers. Furniture designs and prototype models were created in the workshops, but the pieces to be sold were fabricated offsite under the watchful eye of Bing's foreman, the young cabinetmaker Léon Jallot (fig. 185).[29]

Jallot and Bing enjoyed a close relationship, as Jallot himself recalled during an interview conducted in 1968.[30] The young craftsman valued what the dealer was trying to do, especially as the venture was a tremendous financial risk. The cost of producing furniture designed in the workshop was high; before a piece was deemed ready for manufacture, models were often produced in wax, then in plaster, then in wood, with a prototype being made in the final materials.[31] During this process, Jallot supervised the other men and assured overall quality. Among the different designers who joined Bing's workshops was Eugène Gaillard, who designed furniture for a dining room and a bedroom for the World's Fair of 1900. Jallot recalled that Gaillard received 1,000 francs a month, even though the designer espoused the view that one 'could not produce pieces of furniture quickly'. In fact, according to Jallot, Bing paid all his men 'too well', but in return, they produced outstanding work. What impressed Jallot most was that the dealer worked like a *mécène* (a patron of the arts) and spared no expense to accomplish his goal of developing new products in the *art nouveau* style.

Jallot's own work involved designing mounts for decorative objects. Heavier than those created by Edward Colonna for Favrile glass pieces by Tiffany, Jallot's Asian-influenced settings were used for ceramics by Adrien Dalpayrat. An example is his mount employing the motif of a dragon for the handles, which complements Dalpayrat's large vase with curvilinear patterns.

One of Bing's principal designers of furniture as well as other decorative objects was Georges de Feure, whose reputation as a poster artist and symbolist painter was already well established.[32] Unless the archives of his gallery and workshops are located someday, we will never learn the names of all the lesser-known members of Bing's workshops. Yet several can be identified, thanks to the 1968 interview with Jallot.[33] In the furniture workshop, there was J.P. Niederkorn, a cabinetmaker *(ébéniste)*, and a Monsieur Colinot, a carpenter *(menuisier)*.[34] In the jewellery area was Tony Laforêt, a metal chaser *(ciseleur sur métaux)*, whose special skill made him a valued

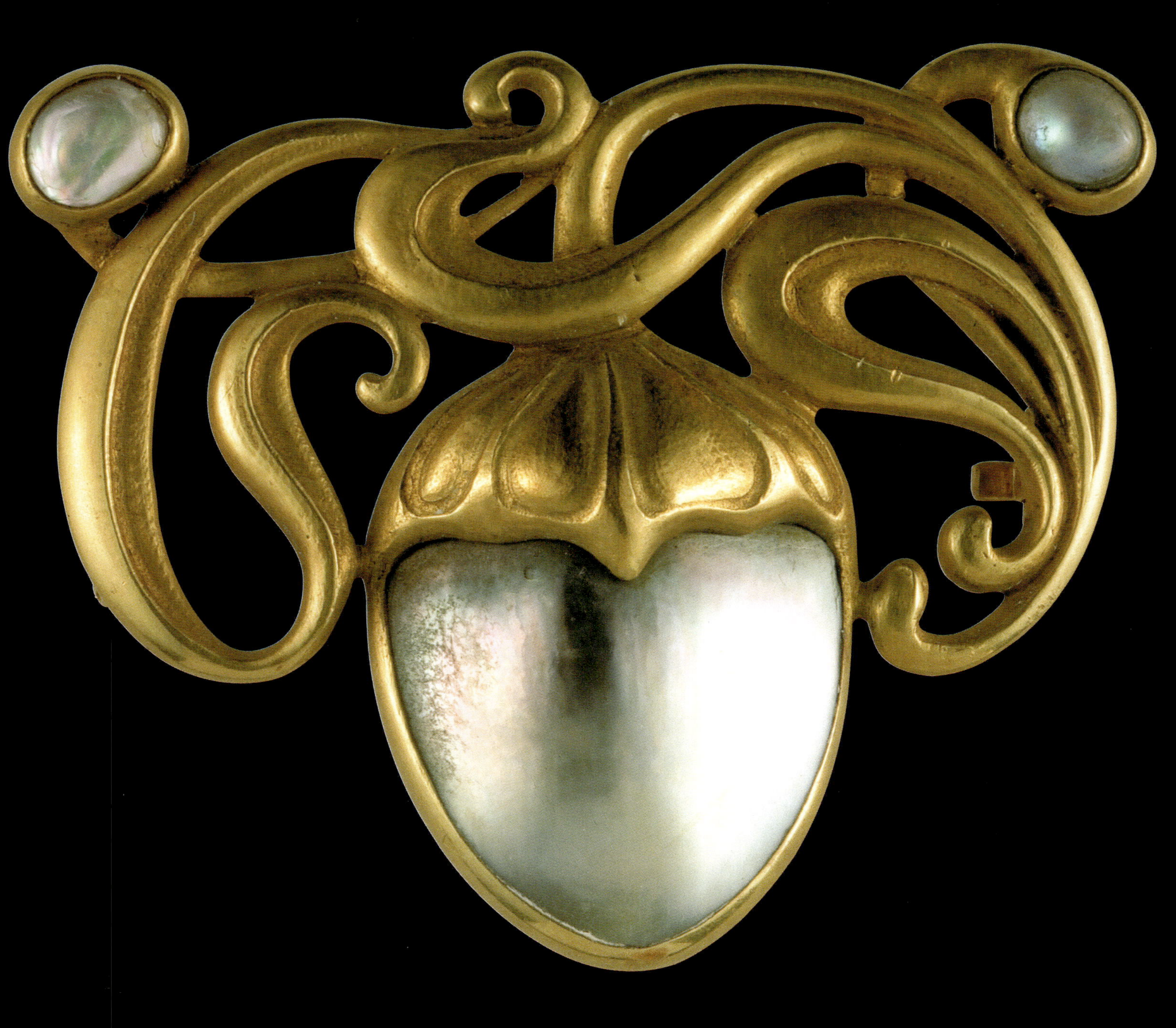

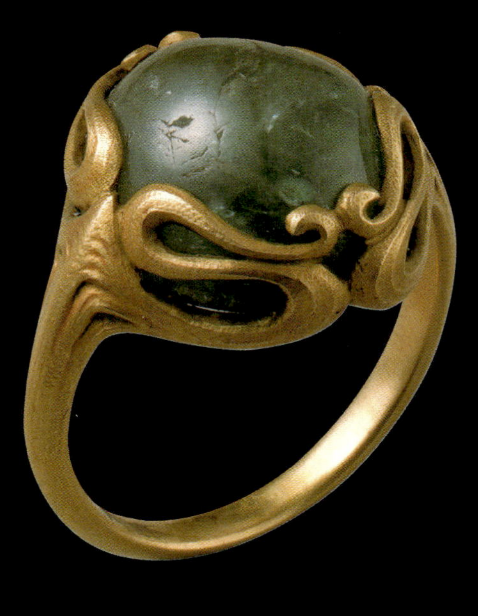

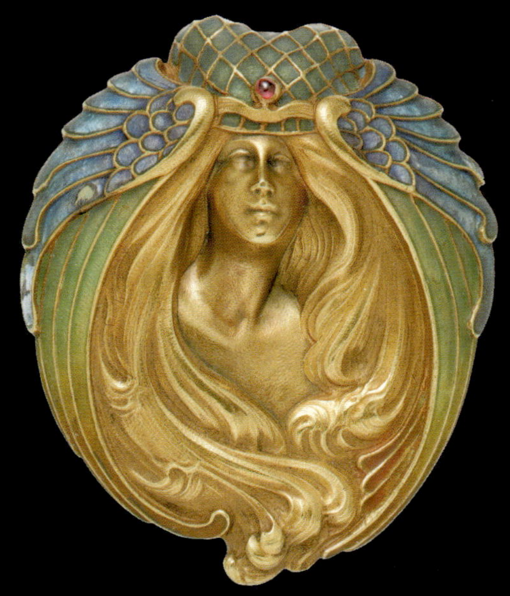

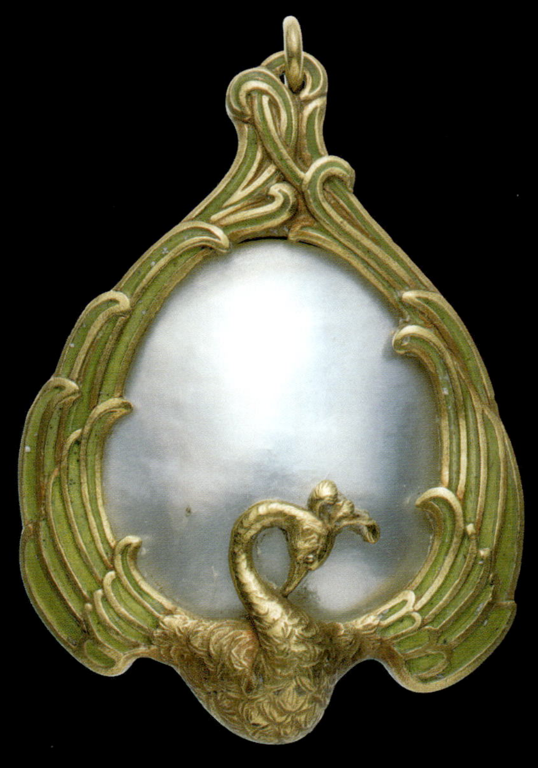

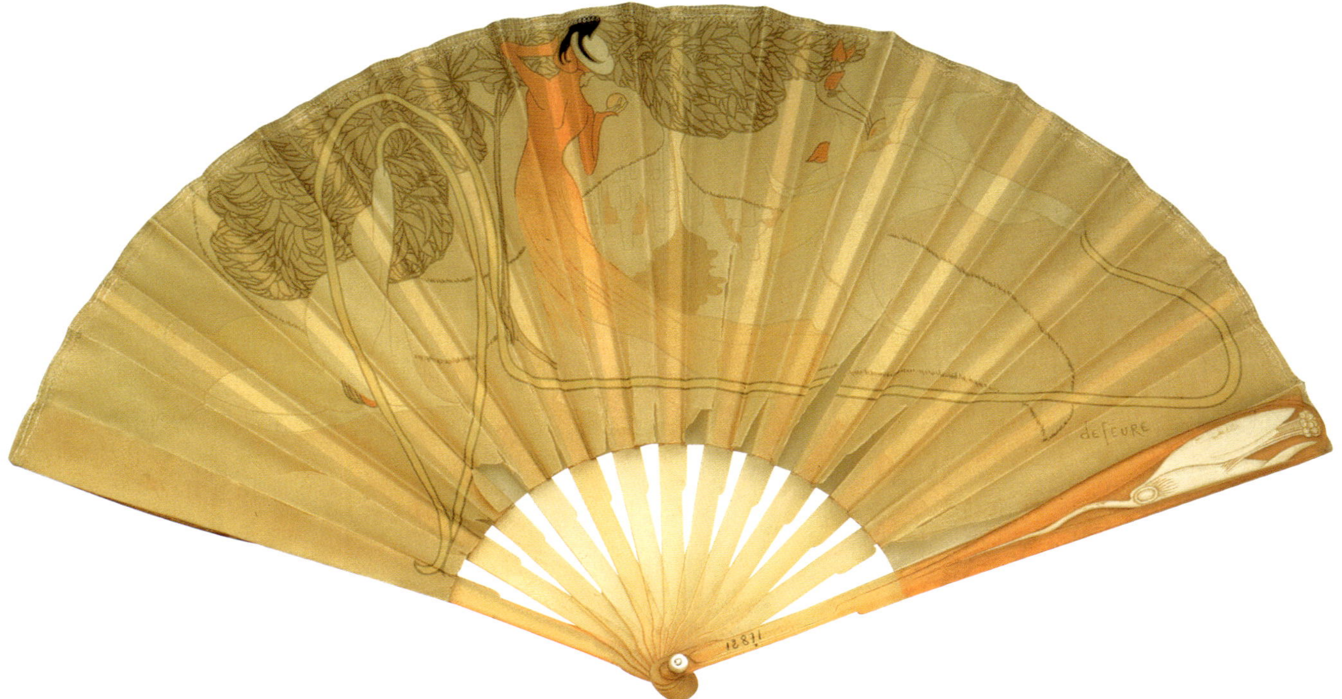

member of the jewellery atelier, and who had his own workshop elsewhere in Paris. This indicates that some craftsmen worked part time in Bing's workshops as they were needed. Other jewellers included Eugène Pigeon, who gilded pieces of jewellery, and Alfred Daguet, who worked on repoussé designs in metal, producing jewel cases for precious objects; some of these were identified with the name of Bing's ateliers on the side.[35]

Bing and the two workshop foremen, Jallot and Marcel Bing, stressed a professional atmosphere, while encouraging a strong sense of congeniality. Photographs taken by Jallot show members of the group along the Boulevard near Montmartre, posing on the steps of the Paris Opéra with Siegfried Bing standing in the background (fig. 210), or moving briskly along the sidewalk near the doorway of 22, rue de Provence.[36] The demeanour of the men suggests that they enjoyed being together.

Jallot's recollections correspond with what was already known about the way in which the Bing ateliers functioned. Craftsmen worked side by side with the head foremen and designers. One photograph shows Jallot and Marcel Bing examining plans before a plaster cast (fig. 201), while others show Marcel and his jewellers working in the remodelled interior space (fig. 183) or the men sitting on the floor during a moment of respite. As indicated by the plans of the third-floor addition and renovation, the workshops were not large and could not have accommodated too many craftsmen working on site. Yet the small, cohesive workshops allowed for the careful oversight of production and thus quality control.

OUTSIDE MANUFACTURING FIRMS

During this period, around 1899–1900, due to the wealth of ideas generated by his designers, Bing began to rely more and more on outside firms to fabricate objects. He needed the skills of workers in various industries whose technical expertise in the production of fabrics or ceramics, for example, exceeded the capabilities of Bing's own workshops. These outside industries were able to manufacture, on demand, individual pieces, separate elements of pieces, or, as in the case of ceramics, a complete line of wares. Bing remained closely involved with these firms, so that every object marketed under his name would conform to the unified look he desired.[37]

This was the hidden aspect of Bing's business practice – one that enabled the dealer to extend his production of *art nouveau* objects in a manner unprecedented in the field of decorative arts. Such a marketing approach was possible thanks to the dealer's contacts with well-established industrial firms and his intuition about how modern design and industry could work together. While some in the international applied arts movement opposed the use of machines in the production of objects, Bing was more open to new technology. However, from his advertisements and the publicity photographs of his workshops, Bing conveyed the impression that everything sold under his name was produced in his own ateliers. To be sure, furniture prototypes were assembled at 19, rue Chauchat, but the final pieces for sale were made elsewhere. Likewise, fabric used to upholster the furniture was manufactured outside Paris.

206
Georges de Feure, Fan, c. 1900
Musée des Arts décoratifs, Paris

> **207**
Georges de Feure, Clock with figure of a woman, c. 1900–1901
Porcelaines GDA, Limoges

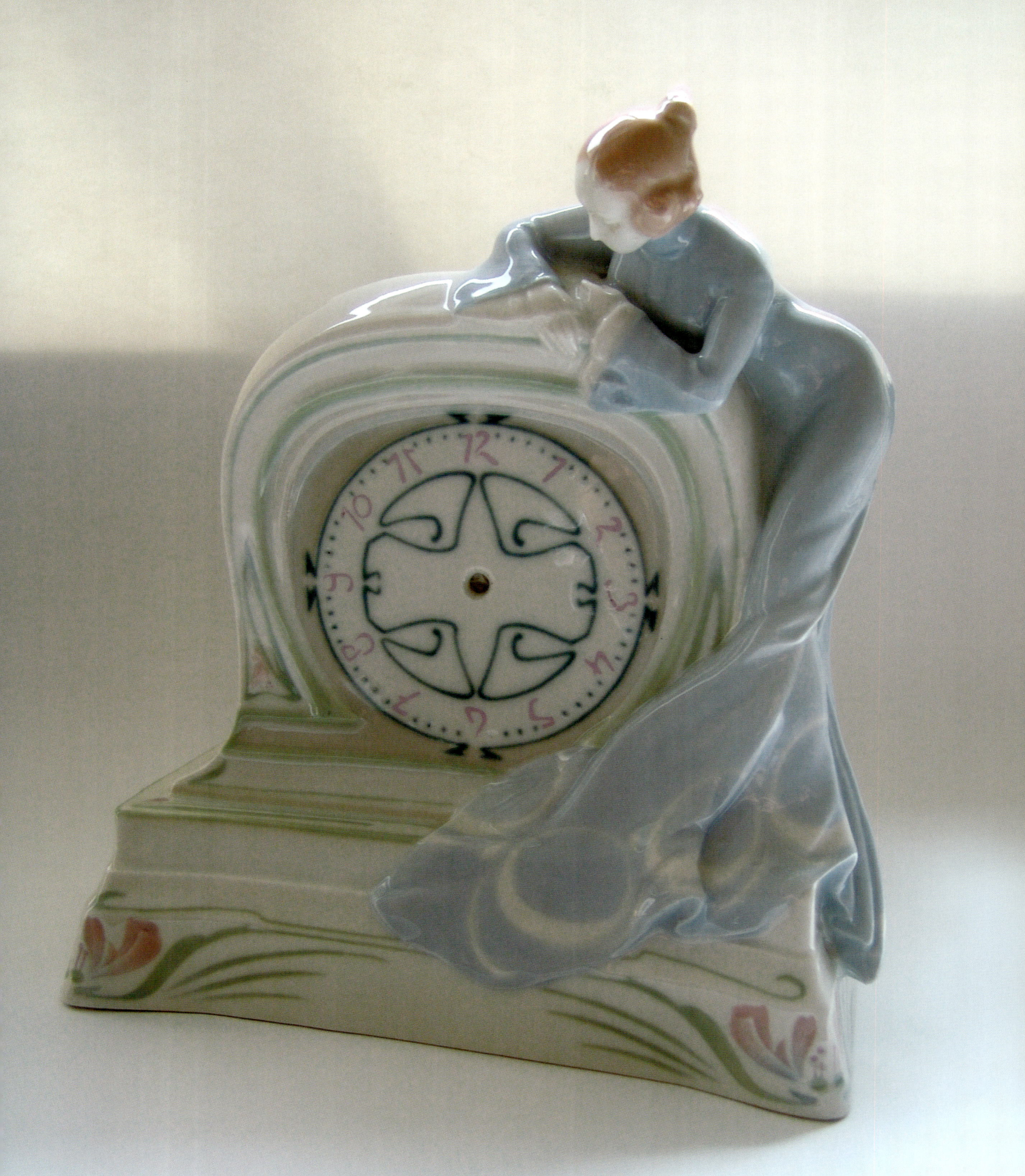

FABRIC FROM LYON

This scenario is certainly borne out by the furniture for several of Bing's rooms exhibited at the 1900 World's Fair in Paris.[38] First, the designs of Georges de Feure, Edward Colonna and Eugène Gaillard were used to make the prototypes in Bing's shop. Bing then acted as a middleman between his designers and the manufacturers, taking care that the outside firms respected the original drawings and that the final products met his and his foreman Jallot's high standards of quality. Thus far, the factory that produced and assembled the furniture has not been identified.

On the other hand, the identity of the textile manufacturer of the fabric used in two rooms exhibited at the fair has been established with certainty. This is the firm of Lamy et Bornet (now the Maison Prelle) in Lyon, which collaborated closely with Bing from 1899 to 1901. In particular, the firm produced the luxurious fabric on the chairs in Edward Colonna's celebrated drawing room ensemble (fig. 235). Following Colonna's original designs, the manufactory produced over 130 metres of silk damask with a lily motif in blue, yellow and rose. For Georges de Feure's boudoir (fig. 251), Lamy et Bornet developed a silk wall-hanging based on the designer's drawing of peonies. In this work, grey leaves combine with orange-tinted flowers against a maroon ground, which created a rich setting for de Feure's gilded furniture (fig. 16). These two splendid rooms, which were featured in Bing's pavilion at the 1900 World's Fair, demonstrate the dealer's interest in combining rich textures, floral motifs and subtle combinations of colours to convey elegance and harmony in his line of interior furnishings.

Bing likely selected the Lyon firm based on its reputation for producing luxurious material in pure silk or cut velvet, which conveyed an aura of elegance and discrimination (figs. 16, 197, 220, 239, 256). At a time when many textile factories were moving toward mechanisation, using power looms to increase productivity, Lamy et Bornet continued to employ skilled weavers, thereby ensuring the highest quality.

Since the archives of Lamy et Bornet are relatively complete, the fact that no orders for additional fabric were placed after that manufactured for the 1900 model rooms is revealing.[39] It appears that during the two years of collaboration with Bing, the firm worked exclusively on fabrics for these suites of rooms. Bing may have been waiting to see what the response was to the showroom prototypes before committing to further production.

208
Georges de Feure,
Statuette of a woman,
c. 1900
Musée des Arts décoratifs, Paris

> **209**
Georges de Feure,
Statuette of a woman,
c. 1903
Victor and Gretha Arwas Collection, London

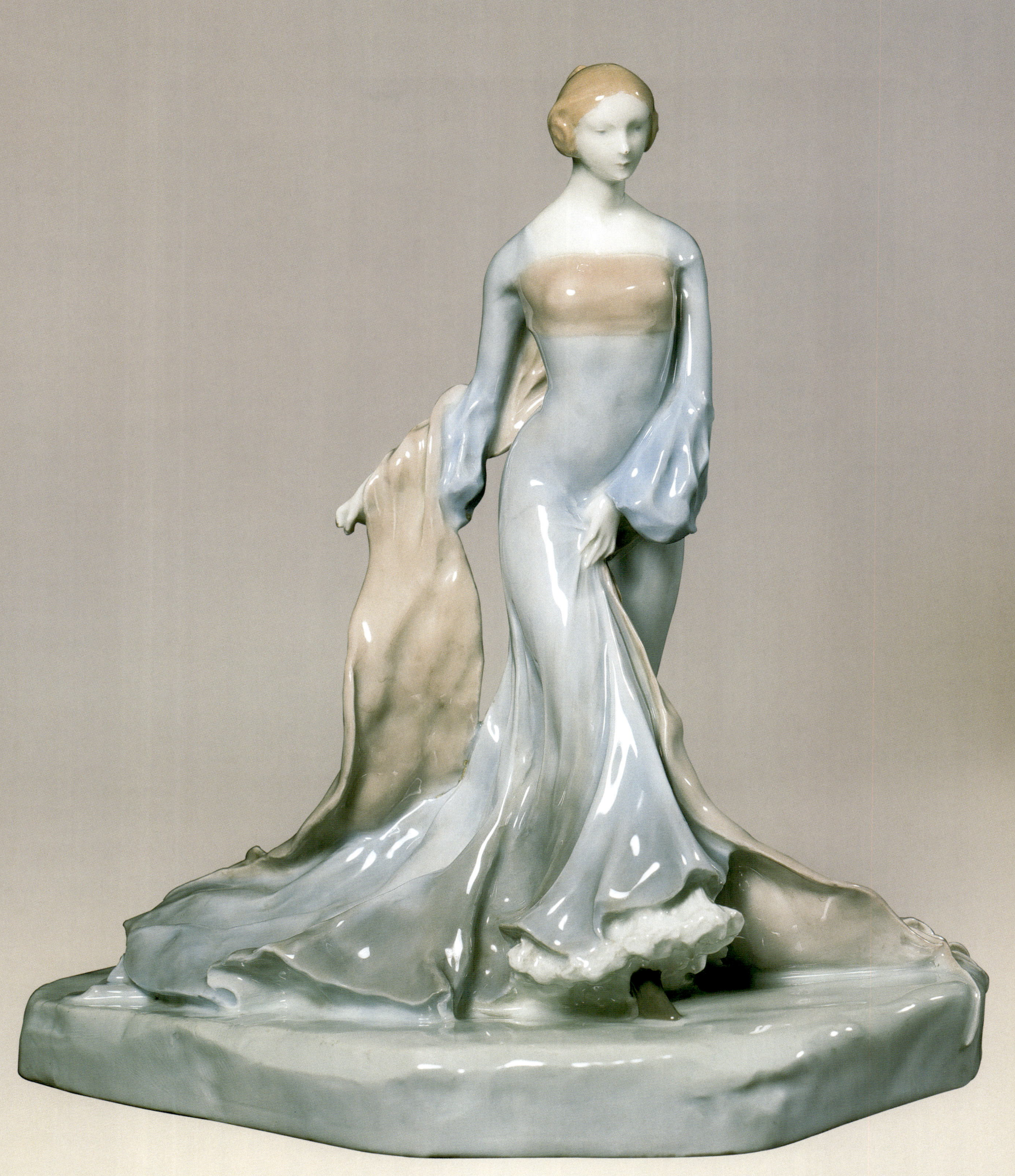

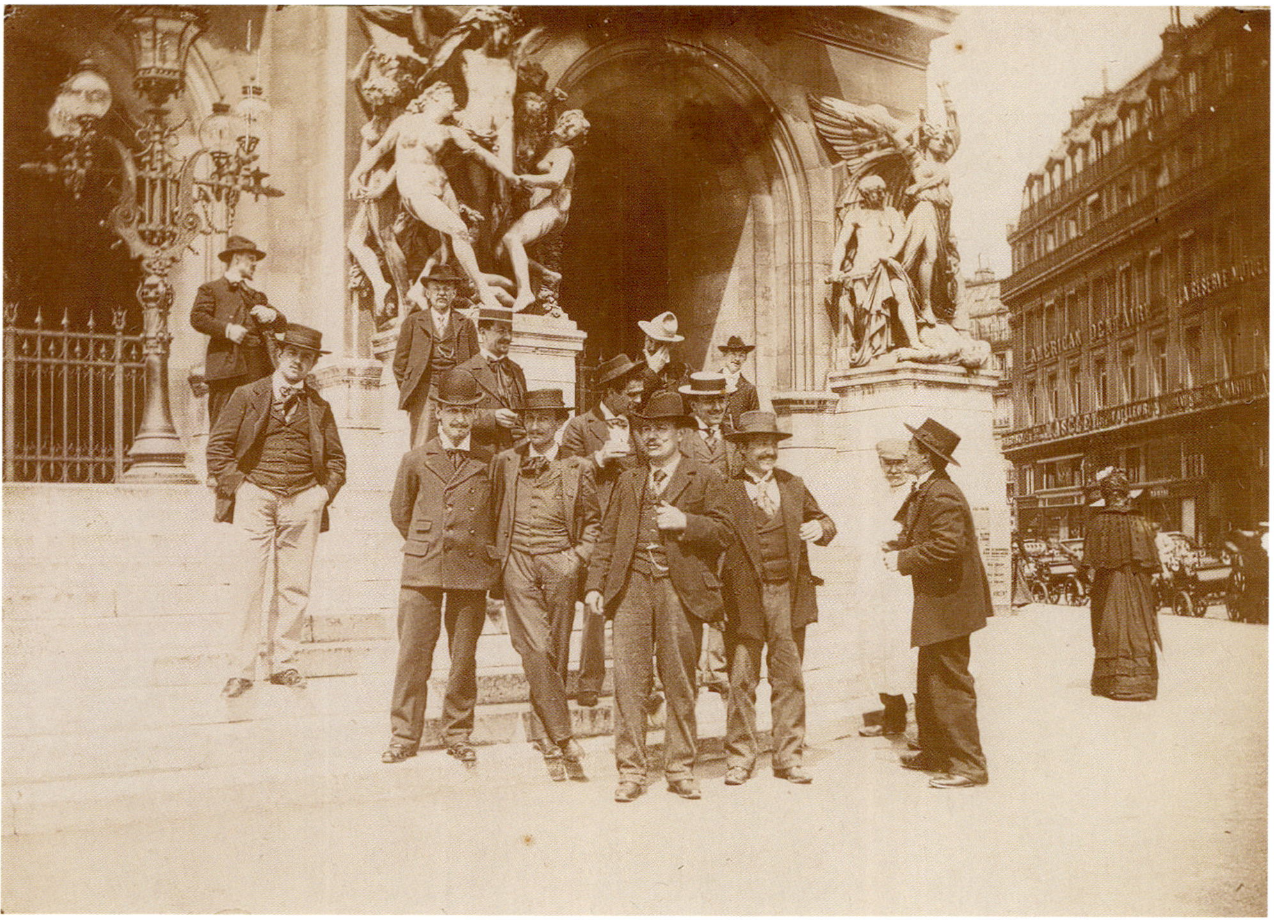

210
Members of the Bing workshops posing on the steps of the Paris Opéra (with Siegfried Bing standing at the back, in front of the sculptural group *Danse* by J.B. Carpeaux), 1900

On the other hand, he may have intended these rooms to be one-of-a-kind examples, recognising that they would be too expensive or idiosyncratic for the modern home. If this is the case, the sample rooms created for the 1900 World's Fair that have entered museum collections in Hamburg, Krefeld and Copenhagen are exceedingly important, since they would be the only evidence of Bing's vision for a unified home interior. In addition, since the museums preserving these rooms were often connected to schools for the applied arts, they served as teaching examples for young craftsmen in the early twentieth century.

PORCELAINS FROM LIMOGES

Another well-documented case of Bing working with an outside manufactory at the moment when his workshops were in high gear involves the production of porcelains, Bing's personal passion. Working with Georges de Feure and Edward Colonna, Bing hoped to produce a line of elegant porcelains that would combine the best design qualities of symbolism and abstraction. For this project, he chose Gérard, Dufraisseix et Abbott in Limoges, a firm that respected the tradition of craftsmanship, yet experimented with new technologies.[40]

Bing's relationship with the Limoges firm began in 1899, with the production of the Colonna Canton Table Service (fig. 95). This joint venture coincided with the porcelain manufacturer's interest in exploring new ways to expand sales and involve new partners in order to attract more capital.[41] Bing sent a series of drawings so that the factory could begin producing trial pieces, which he would either approve or reject. Some of these porcelains bear the marks of both 'Gérard, Dufraisseix et Abbott' and 'L'Art Nouveau Bing', while others carry the mark of only one firm. What this suggests is that Bing and the Limoges manufactory had arrived at some type of formula for sale and distribution that allowed both parties to sell pieces on their own. The selected works (figs. 207, 209, 233, 234, 245–50) were produced from plaster moulds (fig. 208) – including statuettes and a clock – and could be reproduced in quantity according to market demand.

These two cases of Bing working with outside firms reveal his careful management of an expanding decorative arts business. By choosing the best companies, he could maintain the highest standards of quality, whether the final product was silk damask or a complete buffet service. While Bing appreciated the possibilities of new technology, he nevertheless was not a proponent of mass production; he remained firmly committed to the artist's original concept and the important role of the craftsman.

REGISTRATION OF SAMPLES IN 1900

Bing's belief in the value of good design and fine craftsmanship in the field of applied arts is reflected in his practice of registering all the prototypes created in his Art Nouveau ateliers. To establish his claim to works of art he commissioned and to assure that no one else could use the designs for five years after the date of their creation, Bing filed his models with the patent office of the French government. The first patent, for furniture, is dated 7 March 1900. Bing filed photographs of chairs, tables, a sofa for a salon and a buffet, among others.[42] A second document, filed 16 July 1900, was also signed by Marcel Morot, an associate who was given power-of-attorney regarding Bing's business affairs. This patent was for sixteen additional models, including a showcase, four chairs, a bed and a dining room table.[43] On 7 September 1900, a third patent, accompanied by photographs of additional furniture, also reveals that Bing's workshops were designing metal keyholes and bronze fittings for the drawers of furniture.[44] These patents establish Bing's determination to establish intellectual property rights for objects produced in his workshops.

Interestingly, in all these instances, Bing filed photographs rather than actual models or drawings, probably to demonstrate that the pieces had already been created. This would have warded off attempts at copying his objects. The documents also stipulate that he retained the right to approve other examples to be manufactured after the five-year period. Shrewdly availing himself of the laws governing artistic property, Bing hoped to prevent artists, manufacturers and even his own designers from pirating designs or replicating pieces that he had commissioned.

While the registration of certain works provides dates for the completion of major furniture pieces shown at the 1900 World's Fair, we still do not know, and may never know, how many pieces were made of each model recorded between 1898 and 1902. No official patents seem to have survived for other types of L'Art Nouveau objects. While they may be lost, it is also possible that none was ever filed. This may be explained by the fact that Bing would have had to wait a longer time between the design phase and the placement of orders for furniture, whereas jewellery and ceramics, which could be produced more quickly, did not present such constraints. In the end, it is quite possible that the patents exist, but that they have not been found or looked at.

The workshops closed in 1904, at least five, and possibly seven, years after they had opened, and a year before Siegfried Bing's death. These ateliers were indeed the culmination of Bing's dream of revitalising French design according to the highest standards of quality and innovation. He had gambled a considerable amount of his private fortune to finance the venture, paying his workmen extremely well and producing many prototypes that were never replicated for the market. The 1904 auction included large numbers of *art nouveau* objects still left in stock in his galleries, attesting not only to the diversity of works that had been made in the ateliers, but also to the sad fact that many of these items never found buyers.[45] Some Art Nouveau objects remained with Marcel Bing until 1909.[46] The fact that these objects also remained unsold must have disappointed Bing, but, in matters of taste, he was ahead of his own time and of his own adopted country. He might have taken solace, however, in the tremendous success of his Art Nouveau Bing Pavilion at the World's Fair of 1900, where the products of his workshops drew praise from a broad international audience, if not from the French.

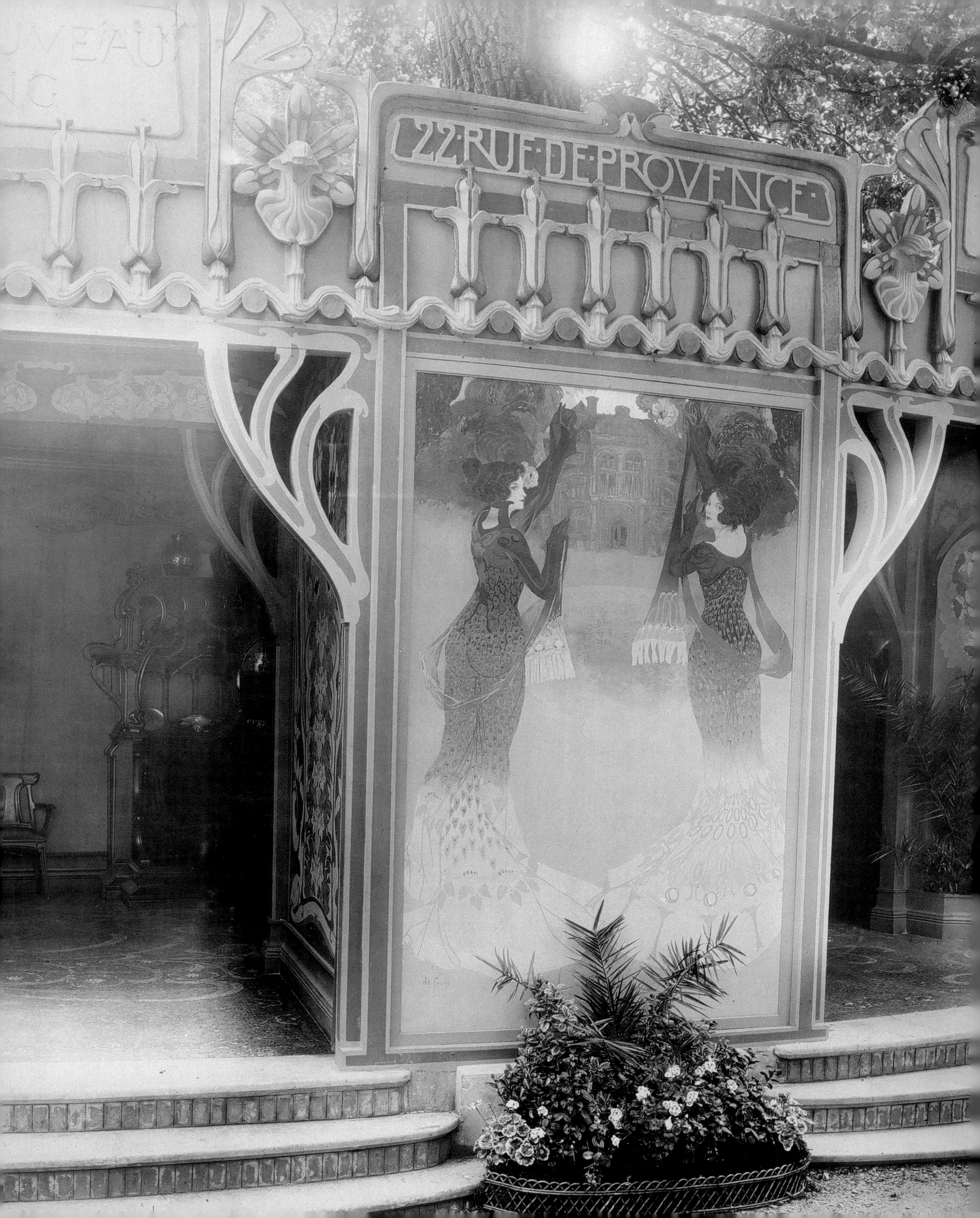
22·RUE·DE·PROVENCE·

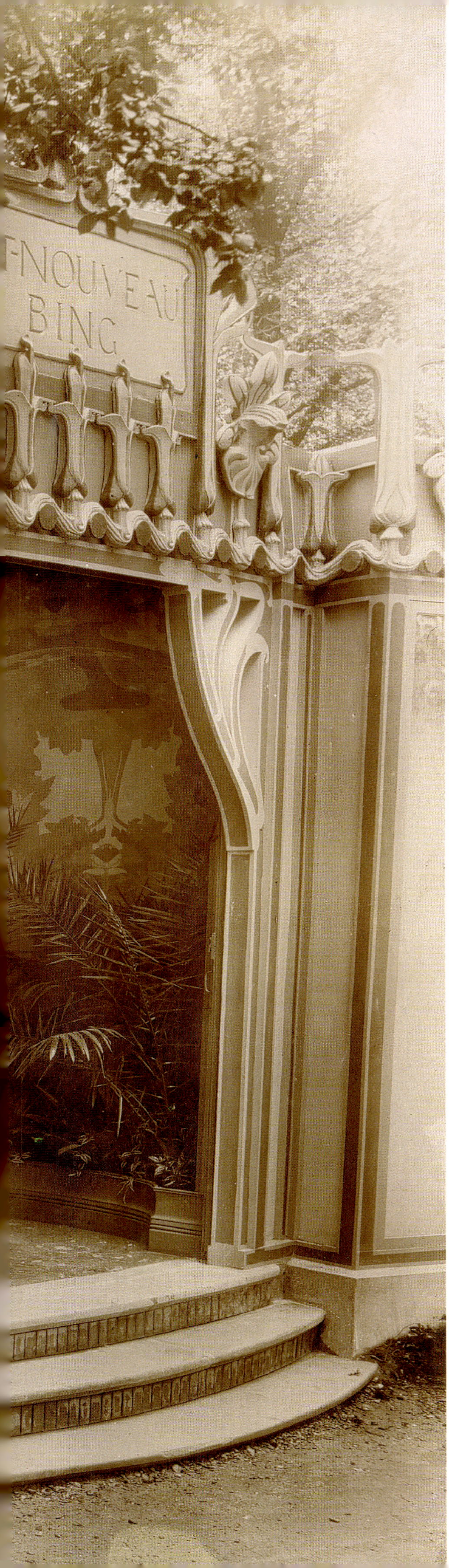

THE BING ART NOUVEAU PAVILION AT THE WORLD'S FAIR OF 1900

'NEW' ART FROM OLD

KARINE LACQUEMANT

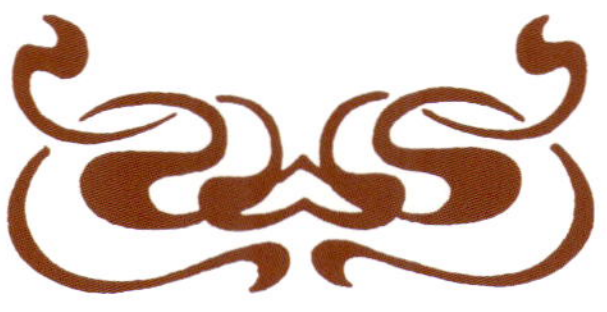

'The 1900 World's Fair represented a distinct backward step in relation to that of 1889. The latter had been bold enough to show iron constructions in all their nakedness, whereas the former concealed it beneath a covering of plaster.'[1] Louis Hautecœur's comment is directed at the extreme conservatism of the event and the profound ambiguity between a return to the values of ornamentation and the rational austerity dictated by the advances in building techniques. In fact, there are plenty of examples of buildings that were conceived as out-and-out historicist pastiches constructed on an avant-garde metal framework. For instance, the glass and iron cupola of Louis-Albert Louvet's Grand Palais is hidden beneath a monumental colonnade, while the steel arch of the Pont Alexandre III – a marvel of technical skill – is camouflaged by baroque ornamentation. This hybrid vision was reinforced by hastily built 'exhibition architecture', consisting of

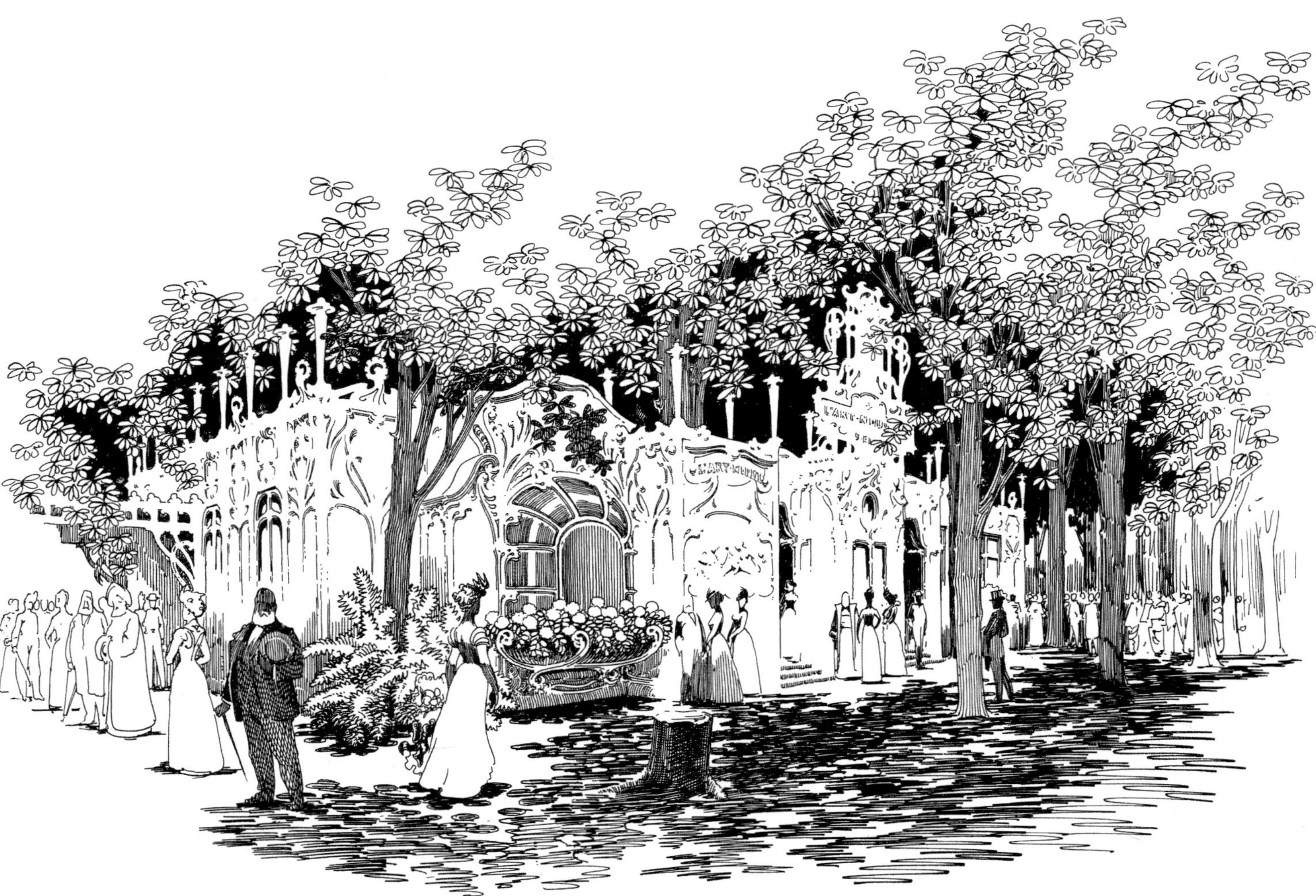

<< 211
Exterior view of the L'Art Nouveau Bing pavilion, 1900, *Album de références*
Bibliothèque des Arts décoratifs, Paris

212
Louis Bonnier, Preliminary sketch for L'Art Nouveau Bing pavilion at the Paris World's Fair, 1900
Fonds Louis Bonnier, Institut français d'architecture, Paris

ephemeral foreign or regional pavilions, which frequently borrowed from the vernacular architecture of famous local monuments. Standing at the junction between the nineteenth and twentieth centuries, the Fair appeared more like a kind of catalogue of the previous century, with its many exhibitions celebrating progress in the arts and sciences. This nostalgic return to the past was particularly evident in the retrospective exhibition of French art housed in the Petit Palais, which was built specially for the occasion by Charles-Louis Giraud in a style full of Louis xv references.

IN SEARCH OF THE MODERN STYLE

Despite being swamped by this pasteboard architecture, a few isolated buildings, mostly the result of private initiatives, still managed to provide evidence of a positive effort to be innovative. These pavilions, all too few to satisfy the critics, were chiefly grouped along the Esplanade des Invalides.[2] They included the Loïe Fuller Theatre by the young architect Henri Sauvage and the sculptor Pierre Roche, and the restaurant 'Le Pavillon Bleu', the work of René Dulong and the Liège artist Gustave Serrurier-Bovy. Surprisingly, the great foreign designers Van de Velde, Horta and Mackintosh – the real precursors of *art nouveau* – were not represented at the Fair. The experiments heralding the new style were to be seen instead in projects for interior decoration or in the creation of individual pieces. Although the exterior of the pavilion of the Union centrale des Arts décoratifs returned to the elegant, historicist formulae of an eighteenth-century folly, an original, innovative repertoire of floral designs was developed for the interior, with its famous Salon du Bois designed by Georges Hoentschel.

The Pavillon de l'Art Nouveau itself did not appear in the official fair catalogue. It should be stressed that, as a member of the jury for the ceramics section, Bing was not eligible to participate in the competition.[3] In any event, the pavilion opened late, well after the World's Fair itself, which was inaugurated on 14 April 1900.[4] It might well be that the practical reasons for this delay were that the gallery had probably received rather a late invitation to take part in the event, and that permissions for private pavilions were apparently hard to obtain.[5] Bing had originally intended entrusting plans for the pavilion to the architect Louis Bonnier. The two men were used to working together, as Bonnier had collaborated closely with Bing on the extension to the Galerie l'Art Nouveau in the rue de Provence. However, the project got no further than the preliminary sketches (fig. 212), as Bonnier was appointed architect-in-chief of the Fair. As a result, the design of the pavilion was handed over to André Arfvidson, a young architect undoubtedly recommended by Bonnier.[6] The building was erected away from others, in a part of the Esplanade des Invalides close to the Breton Village. They opted for a classic rectangular plan comprising six rooms. Alfred Picard described it in his general report on the 1900 World's Fair: 'This wood and plaster pavilion occupied around 260 m² on the rue de Constantine. Its façade was decorated with paintings after sketches by M. de Feure, as well as a large amount of plasterwork' (figs. 211, 242, 243).[7] The main body of the exterior of the pavilion was surmounted by a heavy frieze of orchids in pierced relief, designed by La Forest. For the occasion, Bing had a plan of the Fair, showing the site of the pavilion, printed on the back of his visiting cards, using modern lettering designed by Georges de Feure (figs. 213, 215).

A RETURN TO TRADITION

In more ways than one, the interior of the pavillon de l'Art Nouveau was to provide a laboratory for all the experiments in modern decorative design. This new attitude was neatly encapsulated by Marcel Morot, a close collaborator of Bing's: 'After much consideration, Bing had evolved a "theory" which was, on the whole, tenable. He declared that the new decorative art should not, and could not, emerge fully armed from the brain of a modern Jupiter, but should adhere, though not slavishly, of course, to the French tradition.'[8]

Bing obviously wanted this new approach to be enshrined in the very heart of the pavilion, after experiencing the failure of his gallery to achieve critical success during the first few years of its existence. It should be said that at the start of his commercial venture, with his well-known flair for talent-spotting, Siegfried Bing had sought out and selected the best international designers of the age. He had been severely criticised for this desire to promote foreign artists, which had also helped to rekindle a bitter debate on the supremacy of French taste, fuelled by the deep-rooted nationalism inherent in the French character. The moderate change of direction he envisaged in the context of the pavilion

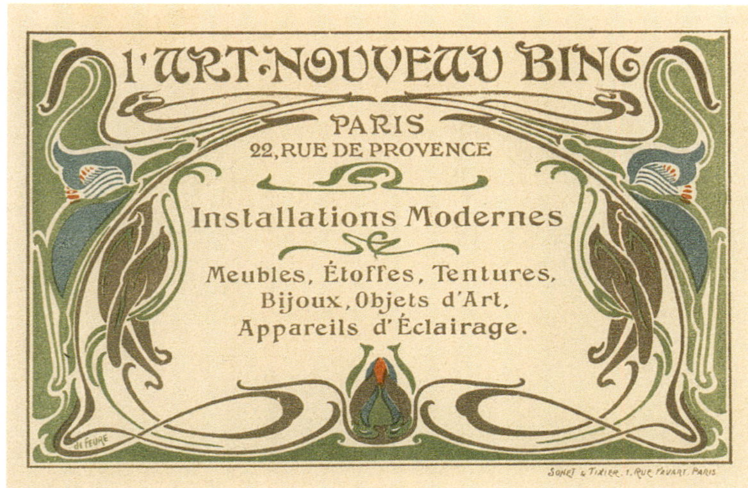

213
Georges de Feure, Advertising card for the L'Art Nouveau pavilion, 1900
Museum für Kunst und Gewerbe, Hamburg

Monsieur S. BING
vous prie de lui faire
l'honneur de venir visiter
le Pavillon de L'ART NOUVEAU
situé à l'Exposition Universelle sous
les quinconces des Invalides côté
de la Rue de Constantine.

214
Georges de Feure, Invitation to L'Art Nouveau, 1900
Museum für Kunst und Gewerbe, Hamburg

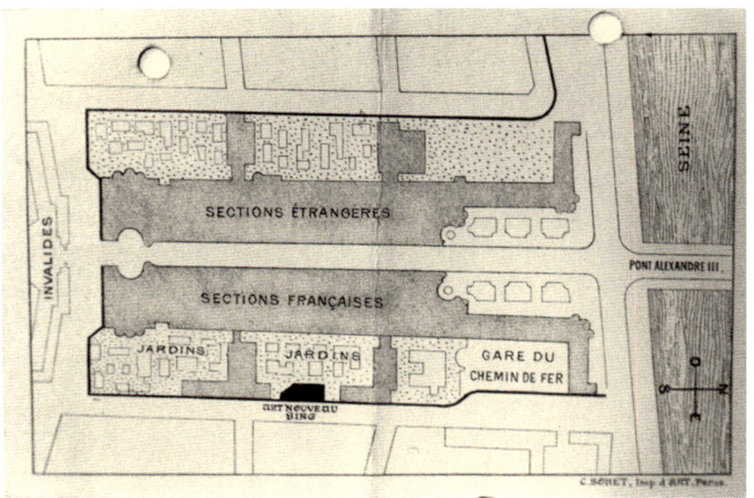

215
Georges de Feure, Verso of the Advertising card for the L'Art Nouveau pavilion, with the location of Bing's pavilion at the Paris World's Fair pinpointed, 1900
Museum für Kunst und Gewerbe, Hamburg

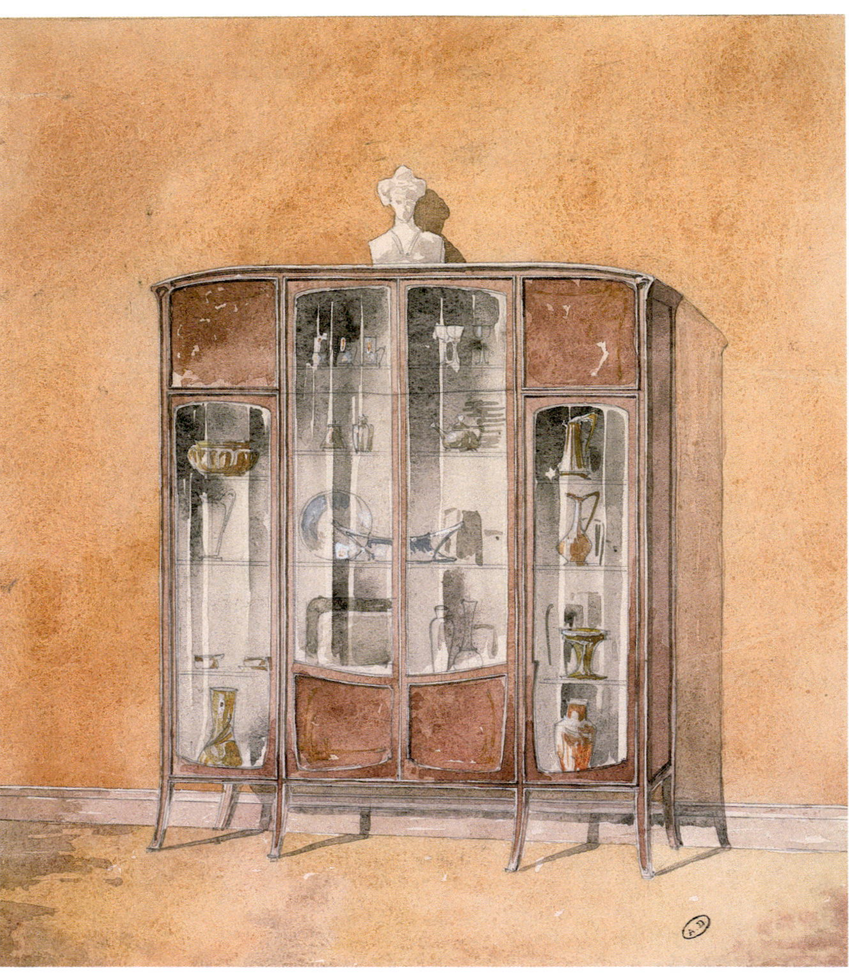

216
Georges de Feure, Drawing for a vitrine, c. 1900
Musée des Arts décoratifs, Paris

reveals all his acumen as an astute businessman, mindful of the response of both the critics and the public.

The art critic and dealer Meier-Graefe, a close friend of Bing's, succeeded in capturing all the qual-ities of this man of art doubling as a man of action: 'It is hard to imagine that one single man can possess so many skills, not to mention the prodigious energy needed to arrive where he is today from where he started a few years ago. The intuitive ability to choose the right path from among the many false trails along which others stray; exquisite taste; the sound yet sensitive understanding of every art form; the knack of discovering, one might almost say creating, the right person for every job – artists, craftsmen, industrial workers; the charisma to impose his views on them by persuasion, without their being aware; the ability to organise all these people and things into a single homogeneous unit: these gifts, exercised in the service of a cause, with a youthful ardour combined with all the experience gained from a long career, must contribute greatly to his success.'[9]

A TEAM STRATEGY

As an experienced project manager, Bing came up with the idea of bringing together three young and promising artists, still relatively unknown to the public, and personally co-ordinating and supervising their collaboration, aided by his foreman, Léon Jallot.[10] He approached Eugène Gaillard during the course of 1897,[11] Edward Colonna – whose jewellery had been exhibited in the early summer of 1898[12] – and Georges de Feure, who was already well known as an illustrator and whom Bing recruited shortly before the exhibition, at the end of 1899.[13] The unstinting efforts of all three men chosen to carry out the complete decoration of the six rooms in the pavilion were greeted with much critical acclaim: 'The Pavillon de l'Art Nouveau, set among the rows of trees in the Invalides, conceals the results of considerable labour. Complete decorations and sets of furniture, allowing each artist to create a co-ordinated ensemble, show evidence of very interesting characters.'[14] The main entrance hall, designed by Gaillard as a kind of furnished antechamber, gave access on the left to a dining room by the same artist.

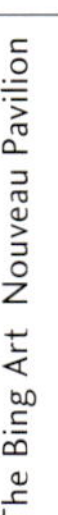

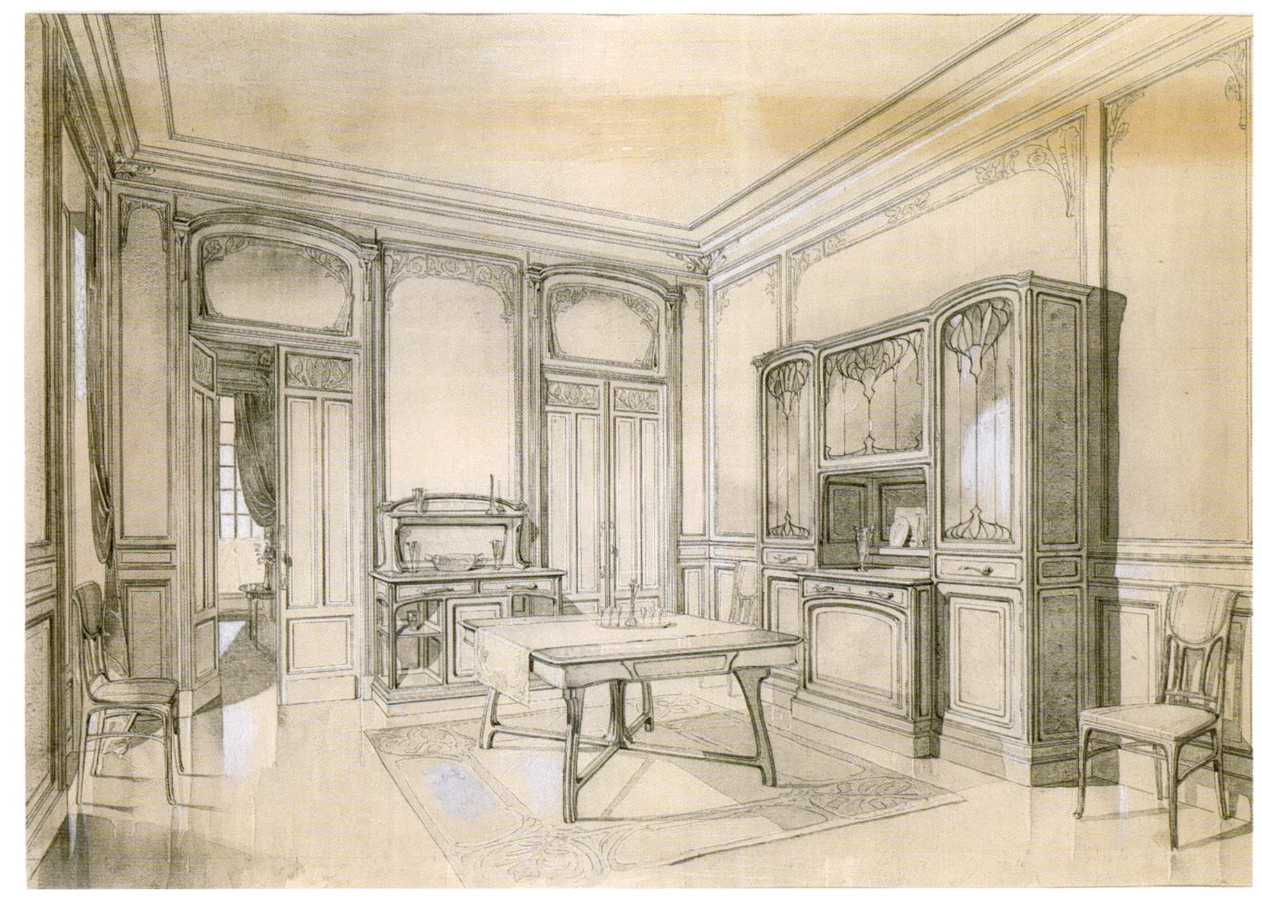

217
Georges de Feure, Drawing for a dining room, 1895–1905
Musée des Arts décoratifs, Paris

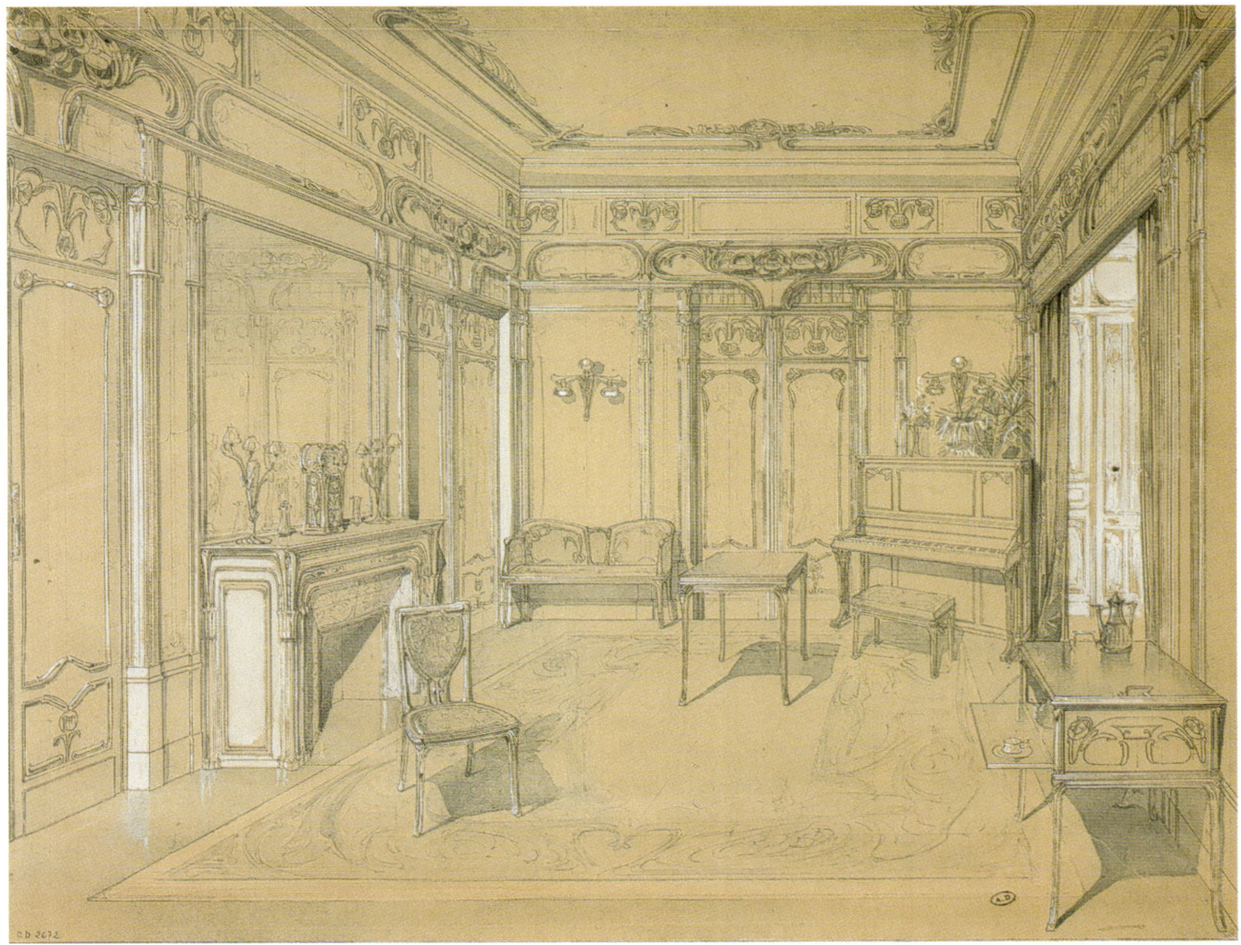

218
Georges de Feure, Drawing for a boudoir, 1895–1903
Musée des Arts décoratifs, Paris

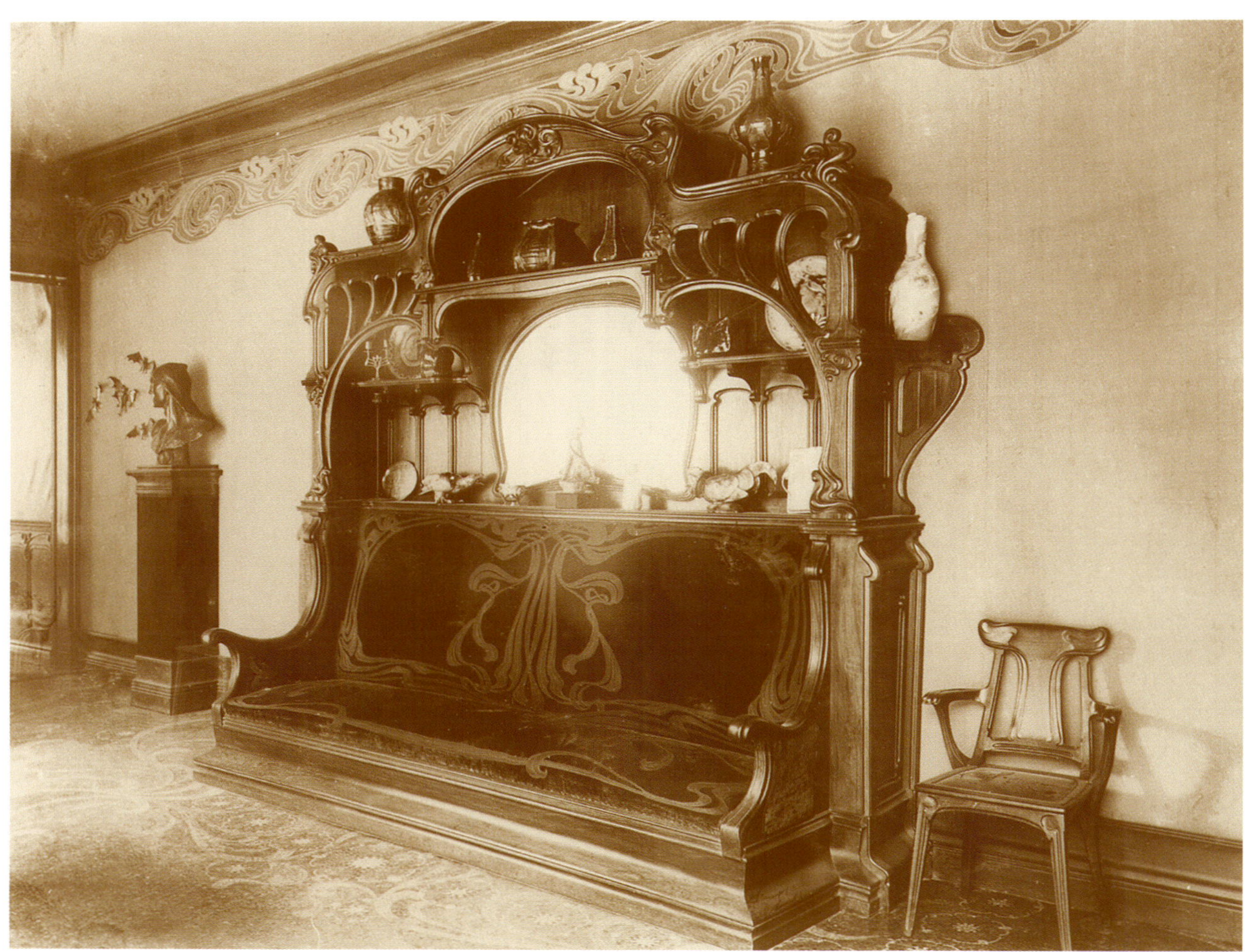

The drawing room was divided into two, forming a reception area and a music room with decorations by Colonna. One bedroom was the work of Gaillard, and after that came a dressing room and boudoir, both by de Feure. These were linked to the bedroom by a short vaulted passage decorated with stained-glass panels symbolising the four seasons, also designed by de Feure. 'Here we recognise the de Feure we know from his prints, with his mysterious-looking women, their eyes full of the unknown, tall, slender, both sacred and beguiling under their enormous hats, intended (I presume) by the artist as *fleurs du mal*. [...] They are awash with colour in sumptuously contrasting masses; the composition remains elemental, phantasmagorical [...] that is the main thing.'[15]

219
Eugène Gaillard, Antechamber, 1900, ***Album de références***
Bibliothèque des Arts décoratifs, Paris

220
Eugène Gaillard, Fabric with floral design, c. 1899
Museum für Kunst und Gewerbe, Hamburg

> 221
Eugène Gaillard, Chair, c. 1899
Musée des Arts décoratifs, Paris

>> 222
Eugène Gaillard, Sideboard, c. 1899
Museum für Kunst und Gewerbe, Hamburg

ENTER THE SUPPLIERS

All Bing's workshops were involved and they worked together in perfect harmony. 'In order to make constant supervision of such a project possible, workshops were set up for gold and silver, jewellery, cabinetmaking, wallpaper and stained glass; the production of the fabrics,

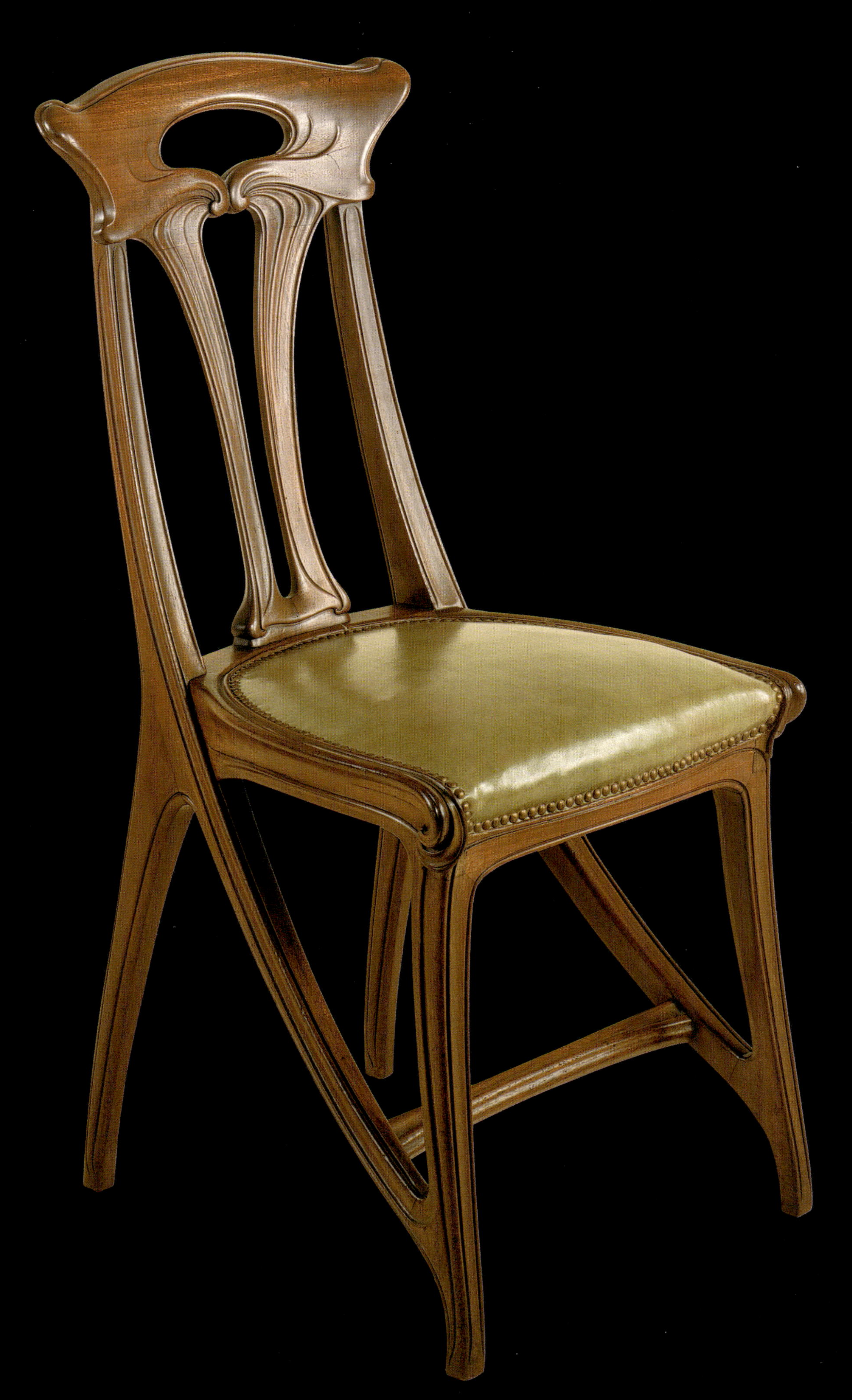

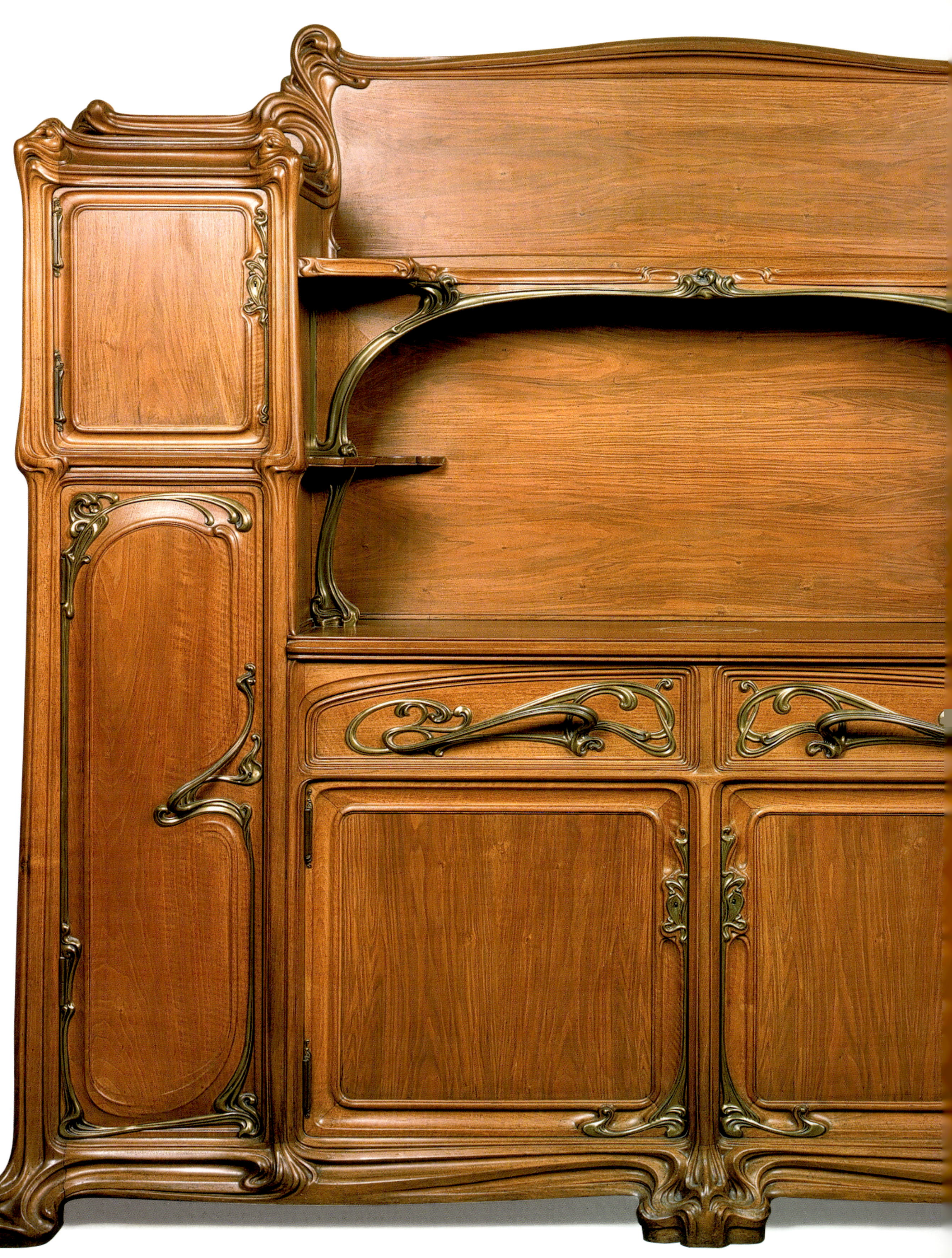

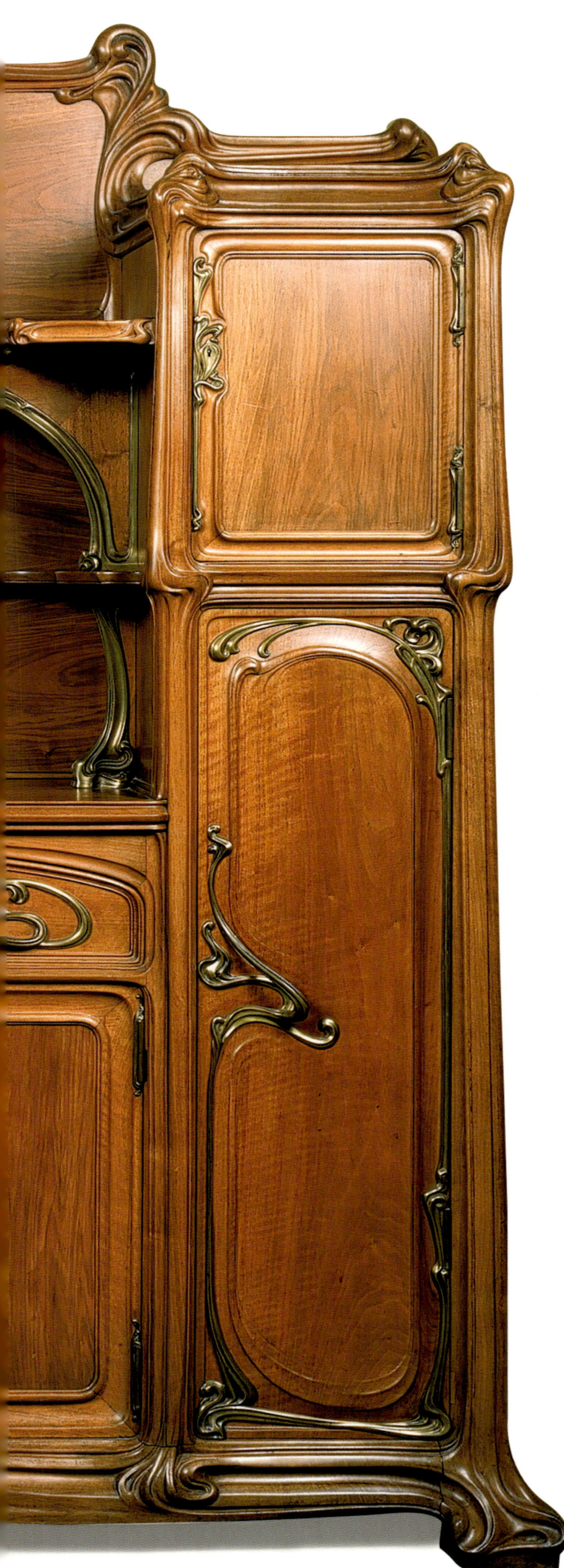

carpets and embroideries was entrusted to the leading French manufacturers.'[16] The furniture was the framework around which the project was built, but various techniques were delegated to external subcontractors. When it came to the silks for the drapes and chair seats, Bing had no hesitation in calling on the best companies and craftsmen of the time, the guardians of generations of traditional expertise. In Lyon, the silk capital, he placed an order with Lamy et Bornet, which later became the firm of Prelle, and he approached Cornille Frères with regard to their printed fabrics. He also ordered velvets from Scheurer, Lauth et Cie., who had premises in Thann, near Mulhouse, a centre of textile manufacturing. The wallpapers were printed by Forrer.[17] Bearing in mind his origins, Bing also bought from German companies, ordering a number of silks from Deuss und Oetker in Krefeld.

The majority of the interior furnishings were produced by the workshops in Bing's premises in the rue Chauchat, working in collaboration. De Feure, Gaillard and Colonna drew preliminary sketches, which were approved by Bing, with production supervised by Jallot. Everything was meticulously planned to ensure that every detail, every nuance, would be in harmony with the composition as a whole. This stylistic unity could only have resulted from a complete symbiosis between the various teams involved, even if the collaborating artists, with their very diverse temperaments, appear to have been permitted a certain creative freedom. Its success was, of course, due to the stubborn determination of the team captain, Bing.

A DIFFERENT AMBIENCE FROM EACH DECORATOR: EUGÈNE GAILLARD – STRENGTH AND RATIONALISM

Once inside either of the pavilion's two entrances, the visitor found himself face to face with an imposing hall seat (fig. 219). This piece by Gaillard was skilfully set off by a floor mosaic with large, flowing arabesques and a brick-red wall-covering with a stencilled frieze decorating the top. For the upper part of the bench seat, Gaillard used a sinuous, openwork line, a motif that can be found in a whole range of furniture named 'Boulogne' in Bing's pattern book. A young Catalan painter, José Maria Sert, was chosen for the art work in the dining room (fig. 231).[18] This consisted of decorative panels of charcoal drawings with coloured highlights on the theme of abundance (Bacchus, Pan, Pomona).[19] Octave Maus, the founder of the review *L'Art Moderne*, explained its profoundly

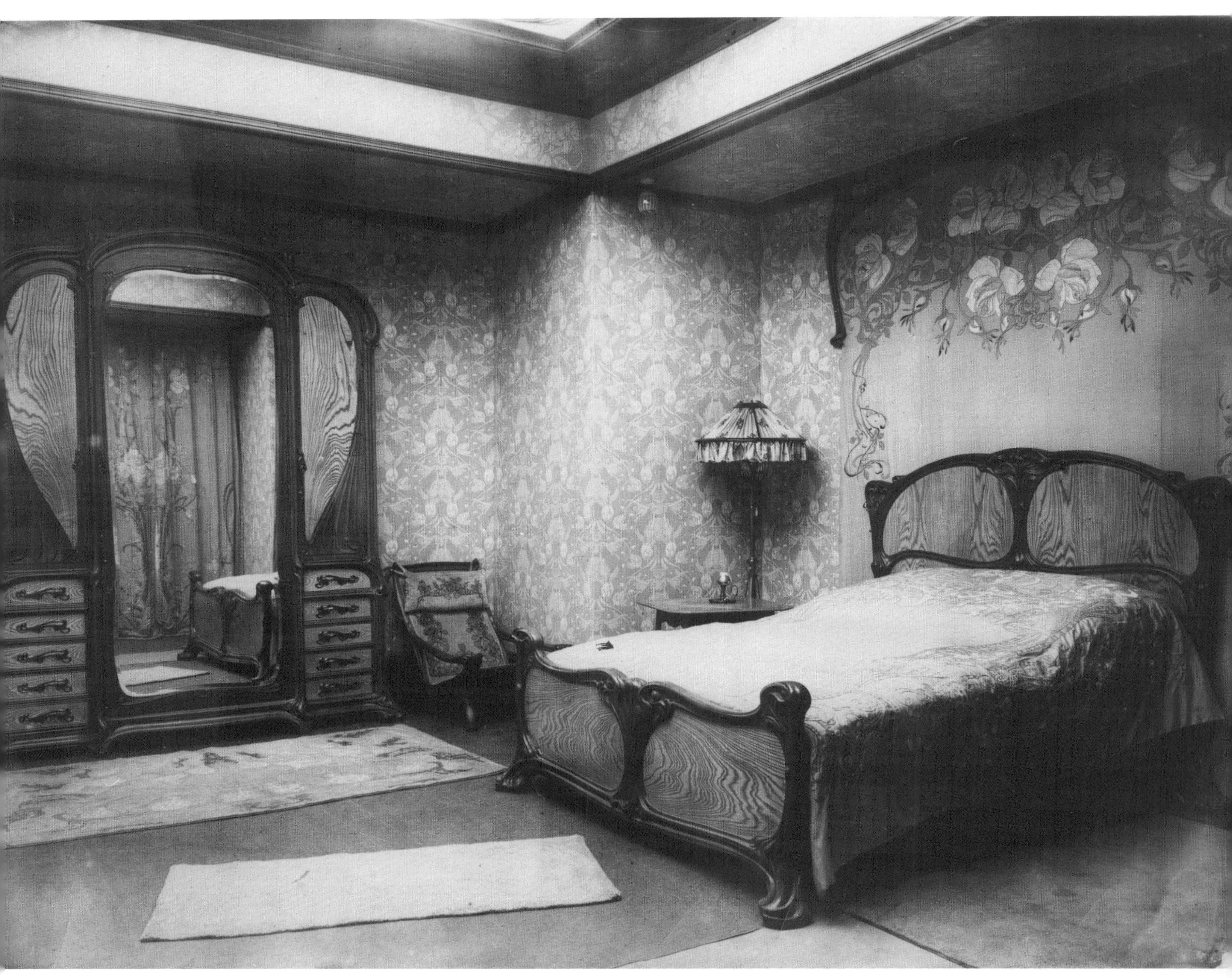

pantheistic content: 'The subject, which could be called *The Triumph of Abundance*, is unfolded in a series of panels containing figures treated broadly and appearing remarkably three-dimensional. Animals, elephants, buffalo laden with amphorae, groups whose only link with academicism is the absence of clothes, form a procession in honour of Abundance, who is portrayed as a well-built female, whose enormous loins appear capable of giving birth to a whole world. Here fruits are piled up in the manner of a Jordaens still life; there a child shamelessly sucks on the swollen udders of a sow. Everywhere there is exuberance, joy unconfined.'[20] The panels were set on a breast-high wainscoting, with applied 'whiplash' motifs in bronze.

The dining room furniture, in polished walnut, consisted of a table, sideboard, dresser, chairs and armchairs. Solid, but not heavy, it was perfectly suited to its purpose. The structures were emphasised by a scrolling leaf motif, in relief or sunk relief, in a perfect blend of form and decoration: 'M. Gaillard has clearly drawn his inspiration for the contours of the large items of furniture in the dining room and bedroom from the Louis xv style, in that, wherever it was possible to do so without offending reason, he has taken pains to replace straight lines and angles with the kind of curves that delight the French eye.'[21] This use of lines to make the decoration part of the body of the piece proved not to be to everyone's taste: 'The artist should, however, be warned against the desire to exaggerate the impression of the wood's plasticity in the details of the carving.'[22] Of all the pieces in this collection, the chair (fig. 230) was particularly noteworthy, as it was a commercial success for the artist. Produced in various woods, it would be acquired by all the European museums of the decorative arts.[23] Its originality is clearly displayed in the way wood is combined with studded and finely crafted leather. Its arched and curving legs are connected by two uprights forming an ogive at the front; the structuring diagonal is reminiscent of one of 'the latest incarnations of the cantilever advocated by Viollet-le-Duc and already used by Grasset in 1880 and Guimard around 1889'.[24]

The bedroom by Eugène Gaillard (fig. 223), a more intimate room, plays on contrasts of colour, using the light tones of pear-wood for the panels and the darker colours of ash for the uprights of the furniture. The green silk bedspread is embroidered 'with large, white silk flowers arranged to form a delightful rosette',[25] a motif that recurs on the curtain at the head of the bed. This floral luxuriance is repeated in a vertical arrangement

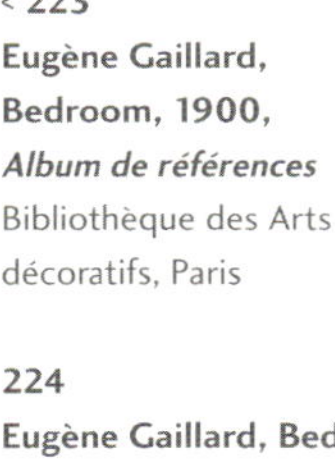

< 223
Eugène Gaillard, Bedroom, 1900, ***Album de références***
Bibliothèque des Arts décoratifs, Paris

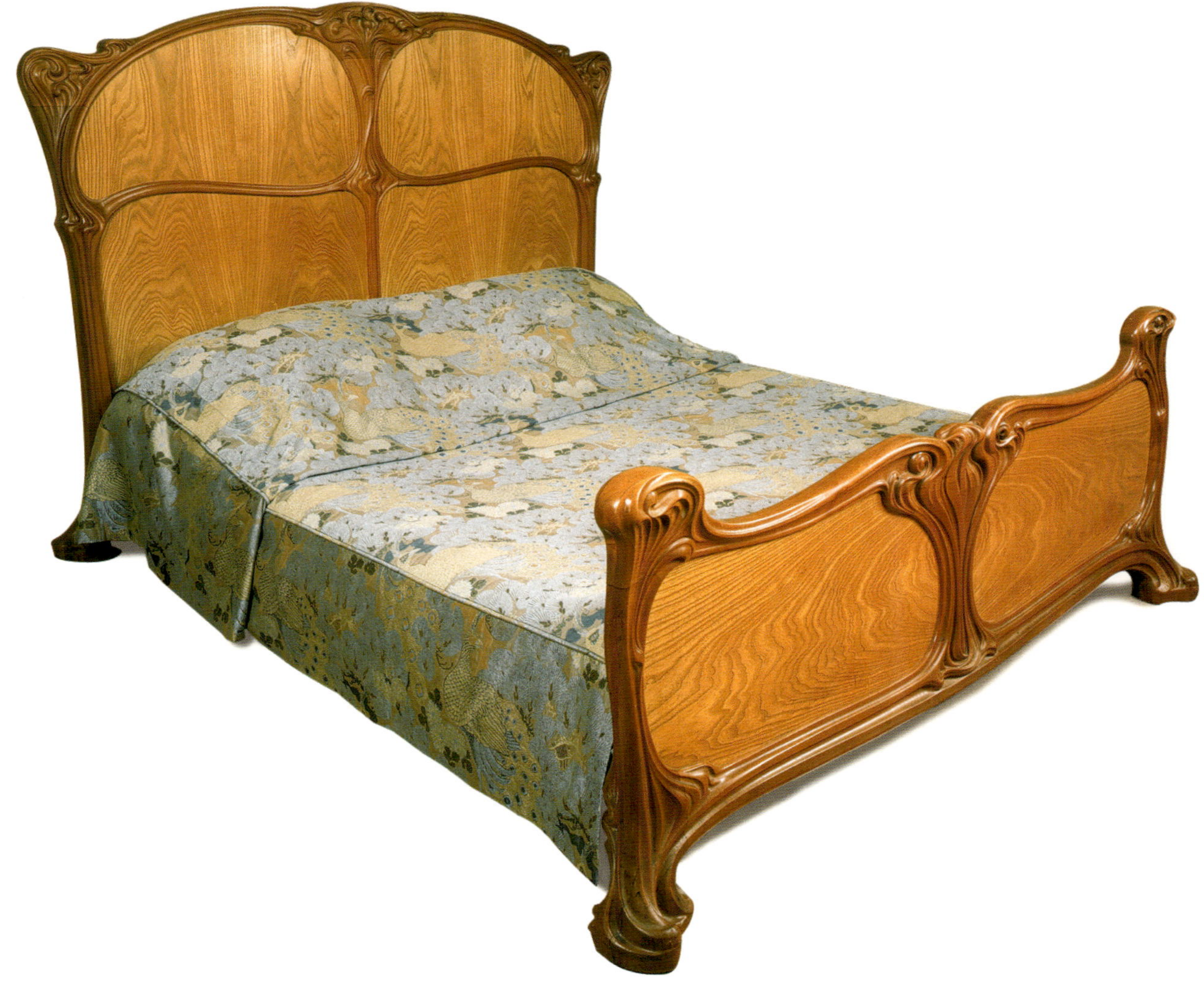

224
Eugène Gaillard, Bed from the bedroom suite, c. 1899–1900
Private collection

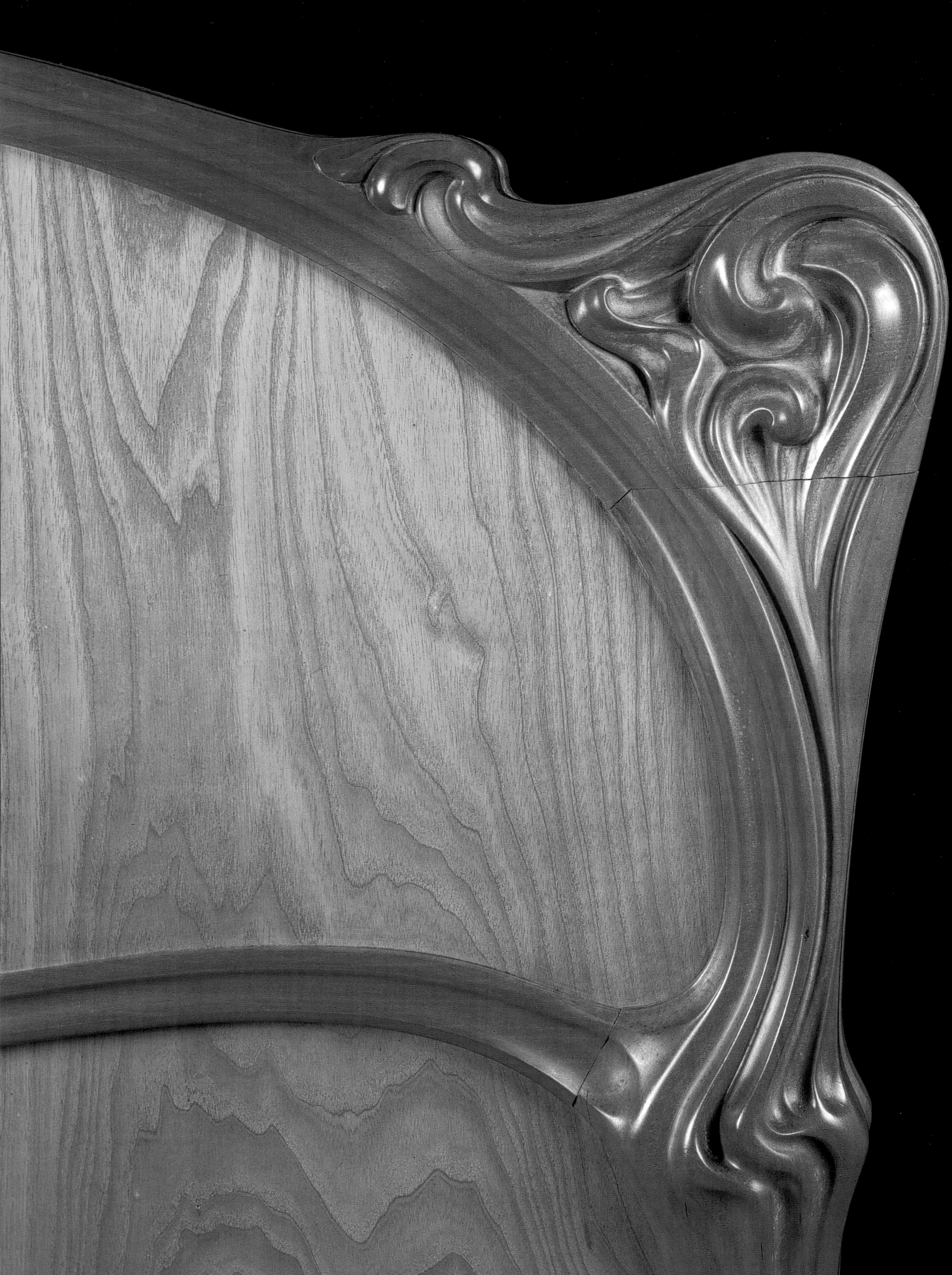

< 225
Eugène Gaillard, Detail of the bed from the bedroom suite

226
Eugène Gaillard, Wardrobe from the bedroom suite, c. 1899–1900
Private collection

227
Eugène Gaillard, Detail of the wardrobe from the bedroom suite

228
Eugène Gaillard, Detail of the bed from the bedroom suite

229
Eugène Gaillard, Detail of the wardrobe from the bedroom suite

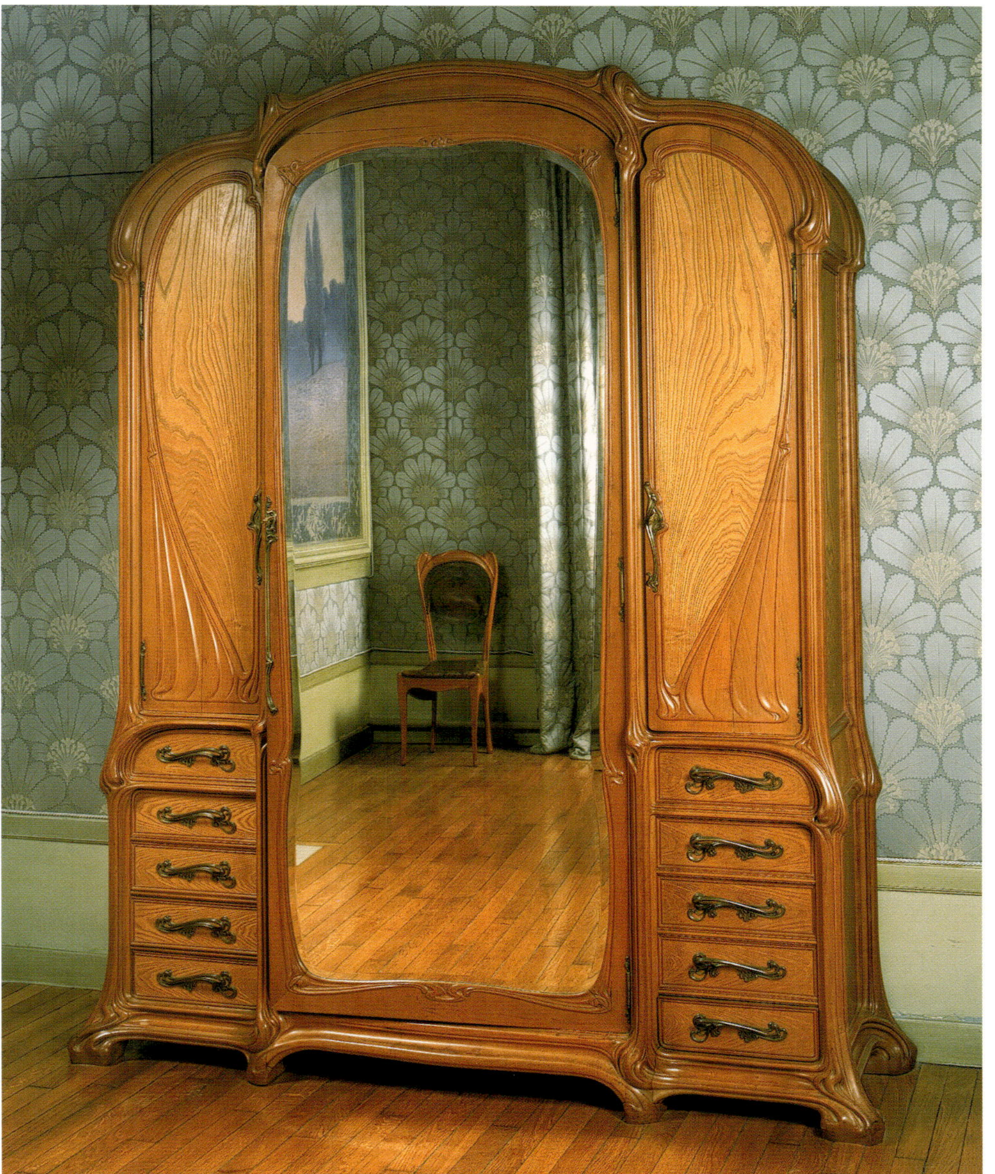

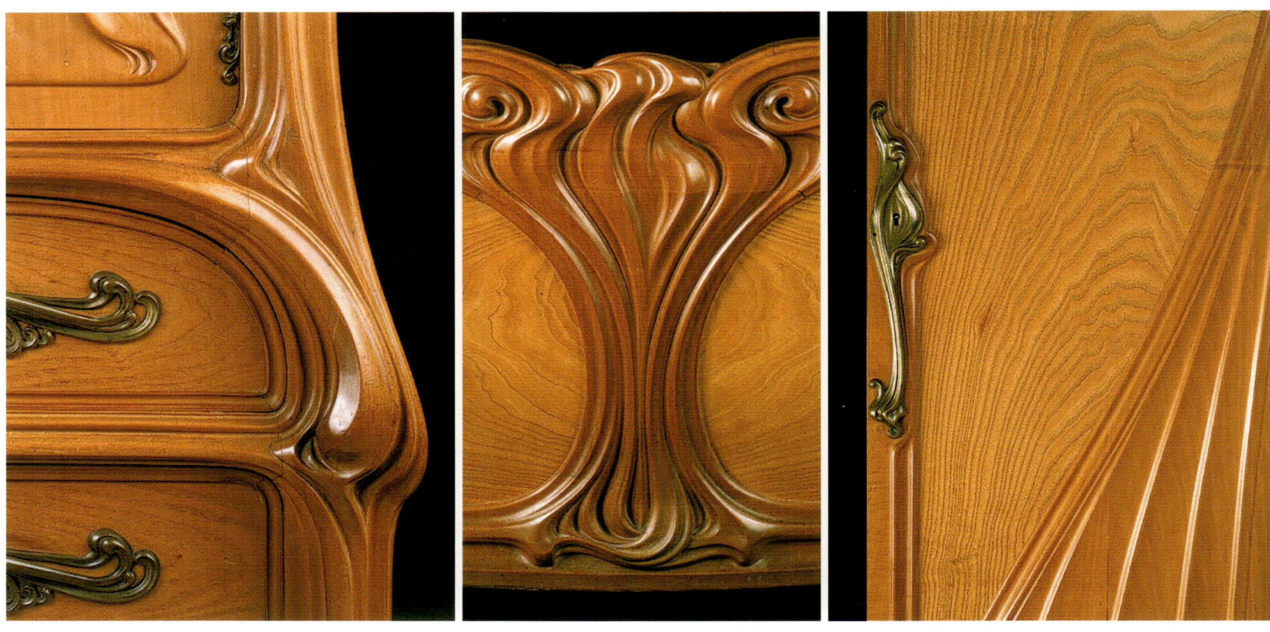

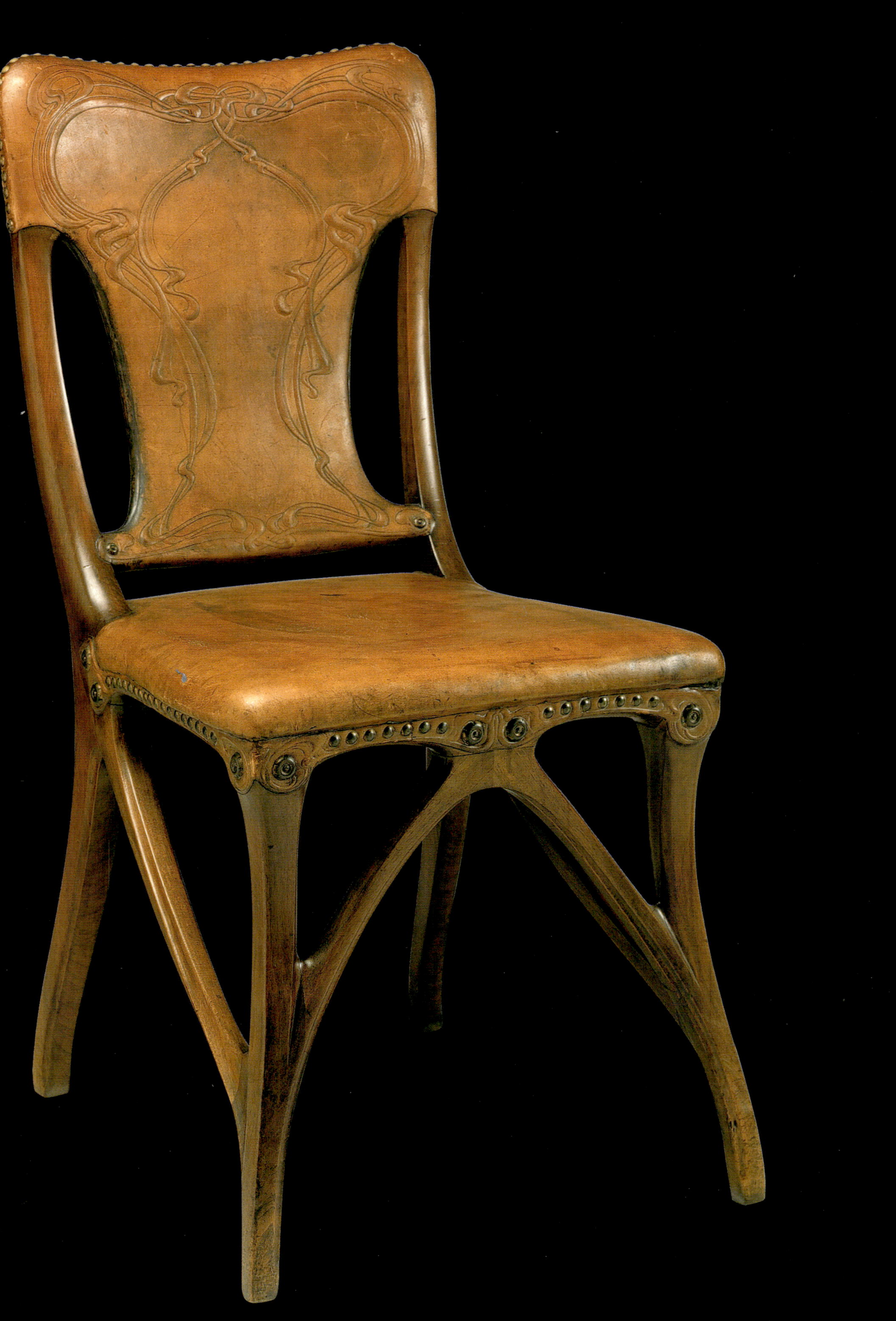

< 230
Eugène Gaillard, Chair, c. 1899
Museum für Kunst und Gewerbe, Hamburg

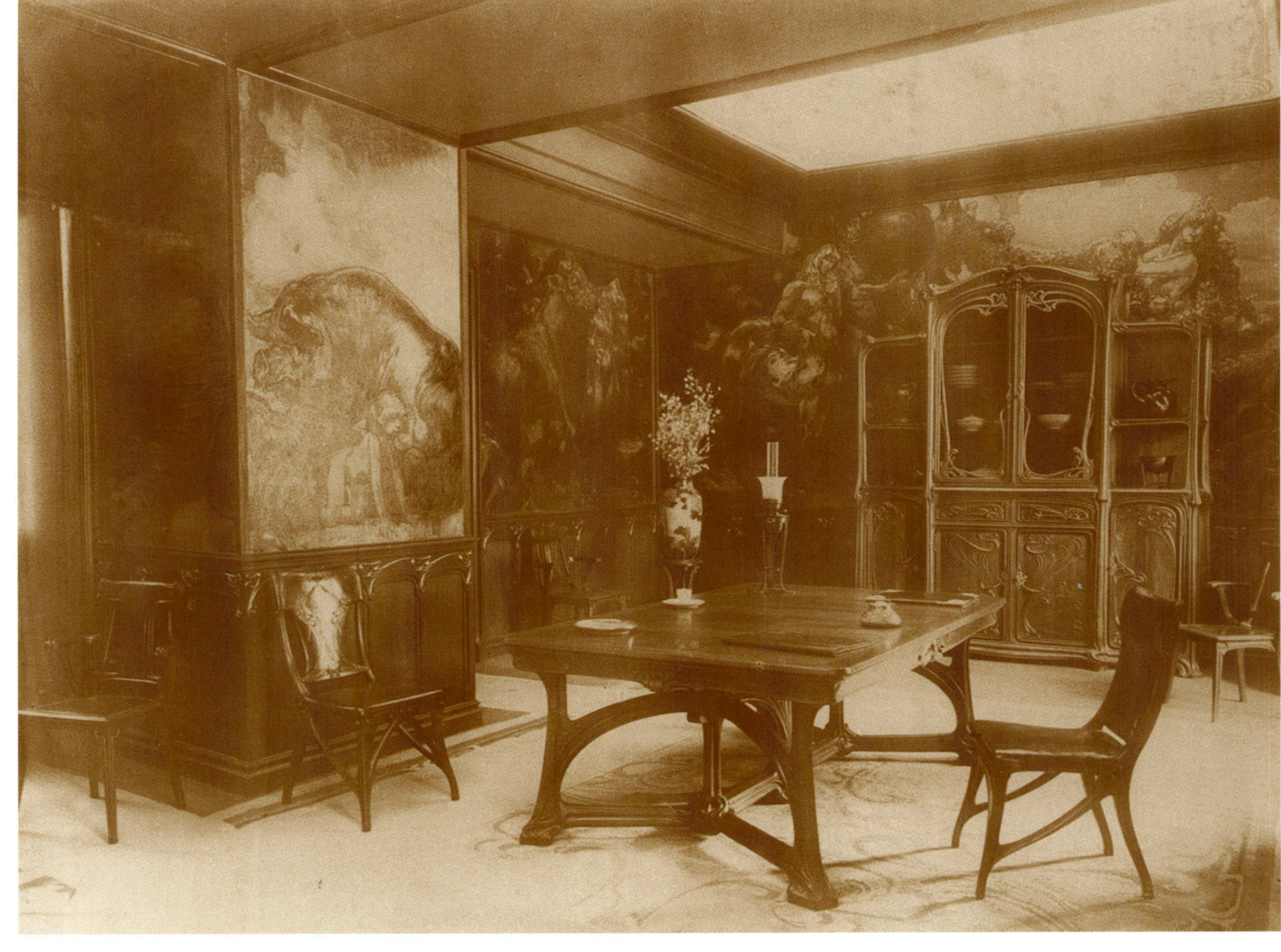

231
Eugène Gaillard, Dining room at Bing's L'Art Nouveau, 1900, *Album de références*
Bibliothèque des Arts décoratifs, Paris

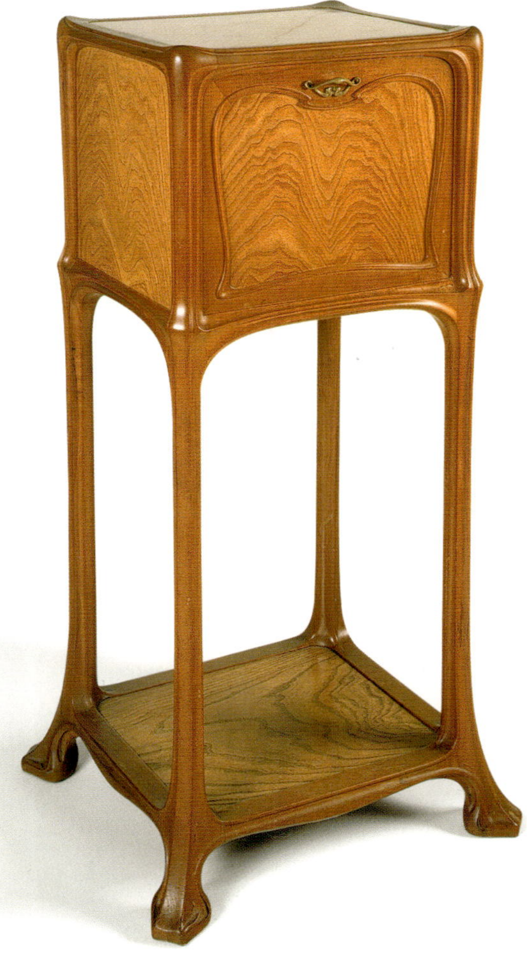

232
Eugène Gaillard, Bedside table from the bedroom suite, c. 1899–1900
Private collection

to form the motif on the door-curtain (which can be seen reflected in the wardrobe mirror).[26]

EDWARD COLONNA: DISCREET ELEGANCE

By contrast with the work of Eugène Gaillard, 'M. Colonna has a very different artistic temperament. The lines are more fluid, more graceful and slender; the colours soften into subtler harmonies.'[27] Adjoining Gaillard's dining room, the drawing room in pale satinwood designed by Edward Colonna was divided into two areas – a reception room and a music room – with an assortment of furniture: tables, armchairs, sofa, upright chairs, display cabinet, writing desk, piano and music cabinet (fig. 235). It is a refined collection: the legs, uprights and stretchers are all perfectly proportioned and remarkably well executed. The overall impression is one of homogeneity in the way the ornamentation – a stylised, scrolling plant motif – is integrated with the structure of the furniture, though there are differences in the detail. The structural line in the small drawing room (sofa, armchair, chair) is undulating and emphasised by

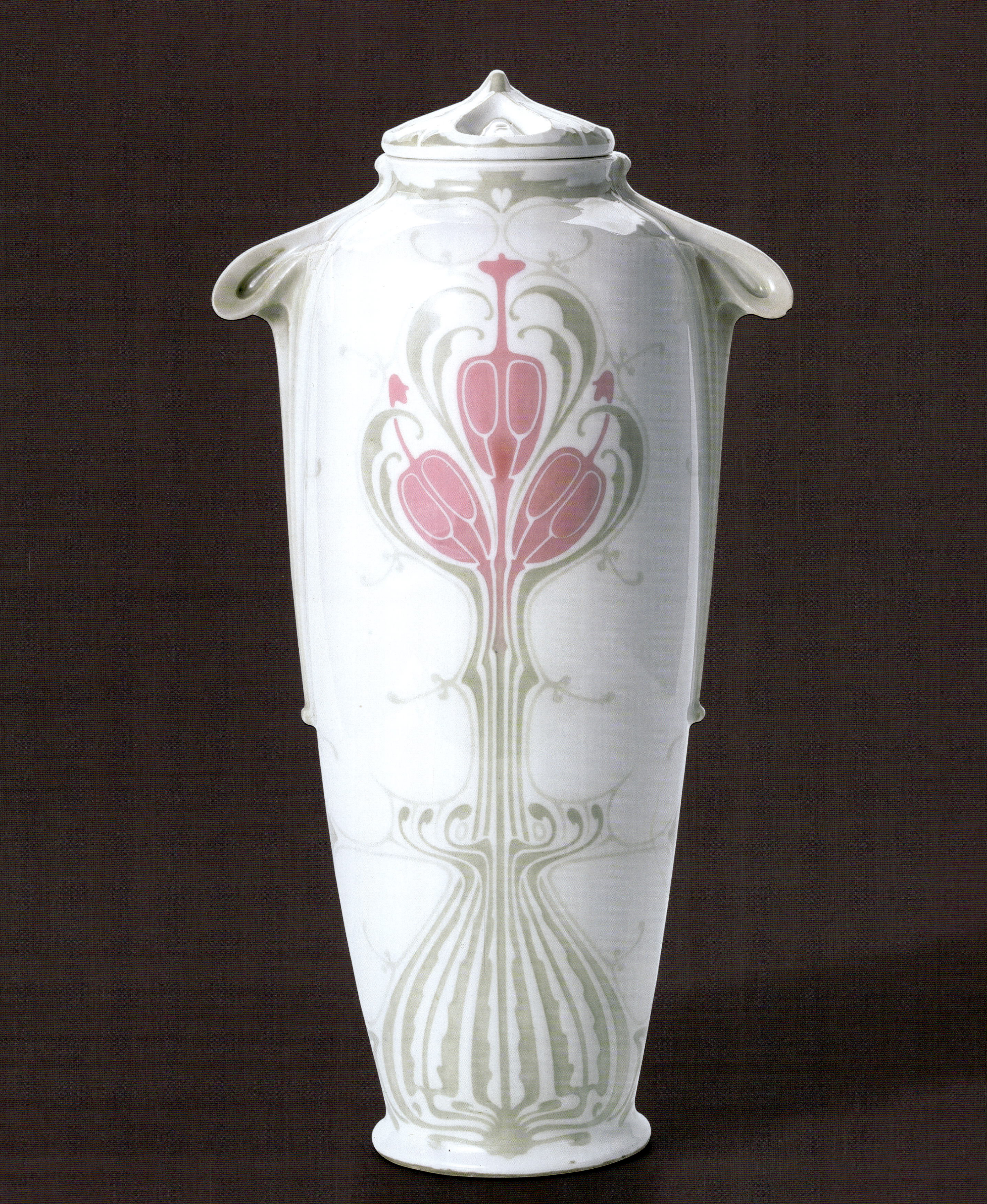

mouldings and a motif sculpted in relief. The bases flare out slightly towards the bottom. The recurring orchid motif is developed in the silk fabric covering all the seats, including the 'palmette' chair with its pierced back. Colonna also used an ornamental stem motif in serial fashion, carved in high relief on the upper third of the wooden uprights of the display cabinet and the desk, as well as on the table legs and the piano stool. Other items of furniture are notable for the decorative inlay work using a technique inherited from the Louis xv style, particularly the round table (fig. 237), the desk, the music cabinet and the piano. Skilful juxtapositions of different woods – rosewood, grained woods and satinwood – enabled Colonna to maximise the effect of the line and ally fluidity with lightness, realism with stylisation. 'This deliberate simplification of the decorative theme is not, however, carried so far as to become lifeless. [...] The motifs of his marquetry retain their associations with the plant kingdom through the simplicity of their design.'[28]

< 233
Edward Colonna, Covered vase, 1902
Musée des Arts décoratifs, Paris

234
Edward Colonna, Vase, c. 1900
Musée national Adrien Dubouché, Limoges

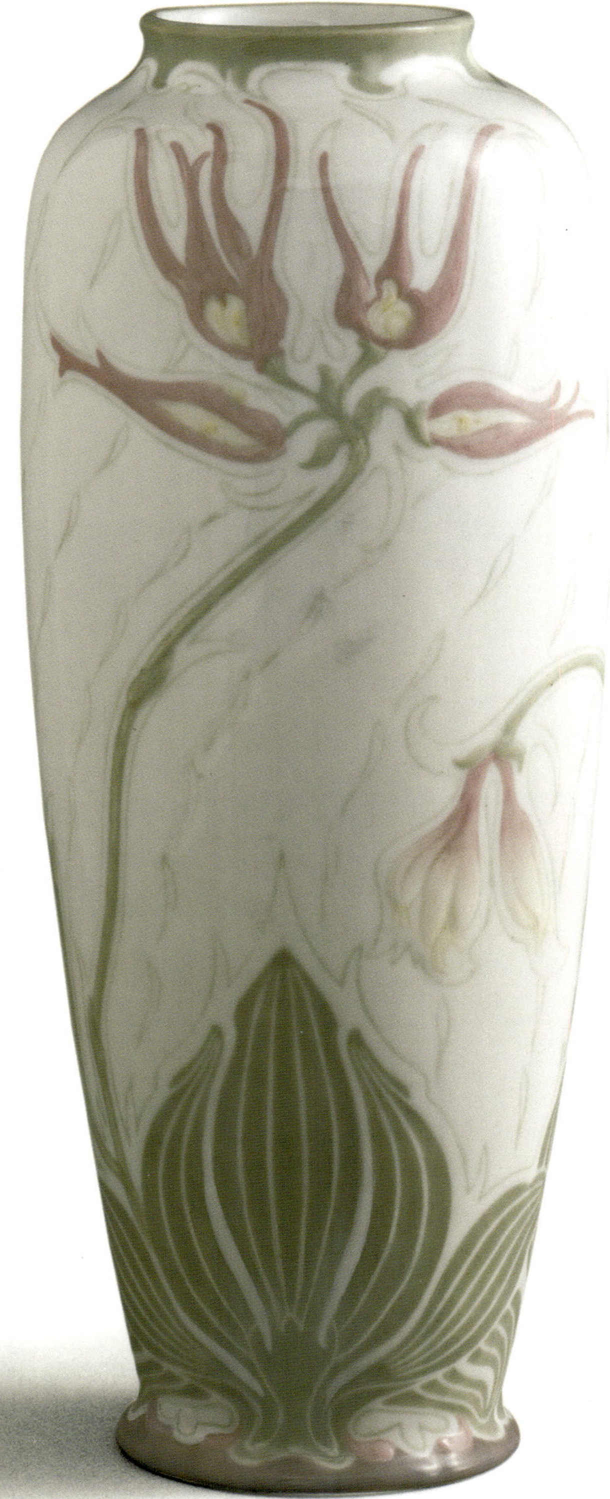

GEORGES DE FEURE: THE HAUTE COUTURE OF DECORATIVE ART

Under the brush of Georges de Feure, the façades of the pavilion were peopled with 'elegant and svelte' female figures.[29] The theme of woman, which recurs throughout this artist's paintings and drawings, was here symbolised in the form of allegorical figures. Set between the two main entrances, the figures of Ironwork, Jewellery, Glass, Pottery, Leatherwork, Sculpture and Architecture, 'sovereigns of all the arts',[30] invited the passer-by to enter (fig. 243). The panel representing *Glass* (fig. 242) is the only visual evidence of the group to survive. The elegant silhouettes and supple lines of this work, enhanced by a subtle gradation of greys and pinks, are typical of de Feure. The stylised motif and the pastel shades of the gown inevitably recall some of the ceramic decorations designed by de Feure at the same period (fig. 247). Here, he won critical acclaim for his painted compositions, bursting brilliantly into the domain of mural decoration.

The same very feminine grace was displayed in the furnishing of the boudoir, in gilded wood, and the dressing room. De Feure not only designed the furniture but also the fabrics and accessories. In the boudoir (fig. 251), which is outstandingly well finished and executed, all the items of furniture harmonise with one another, thanks to the pastel tones of the chairs and seats upholstered in silk, embroidered in petit point with stylised

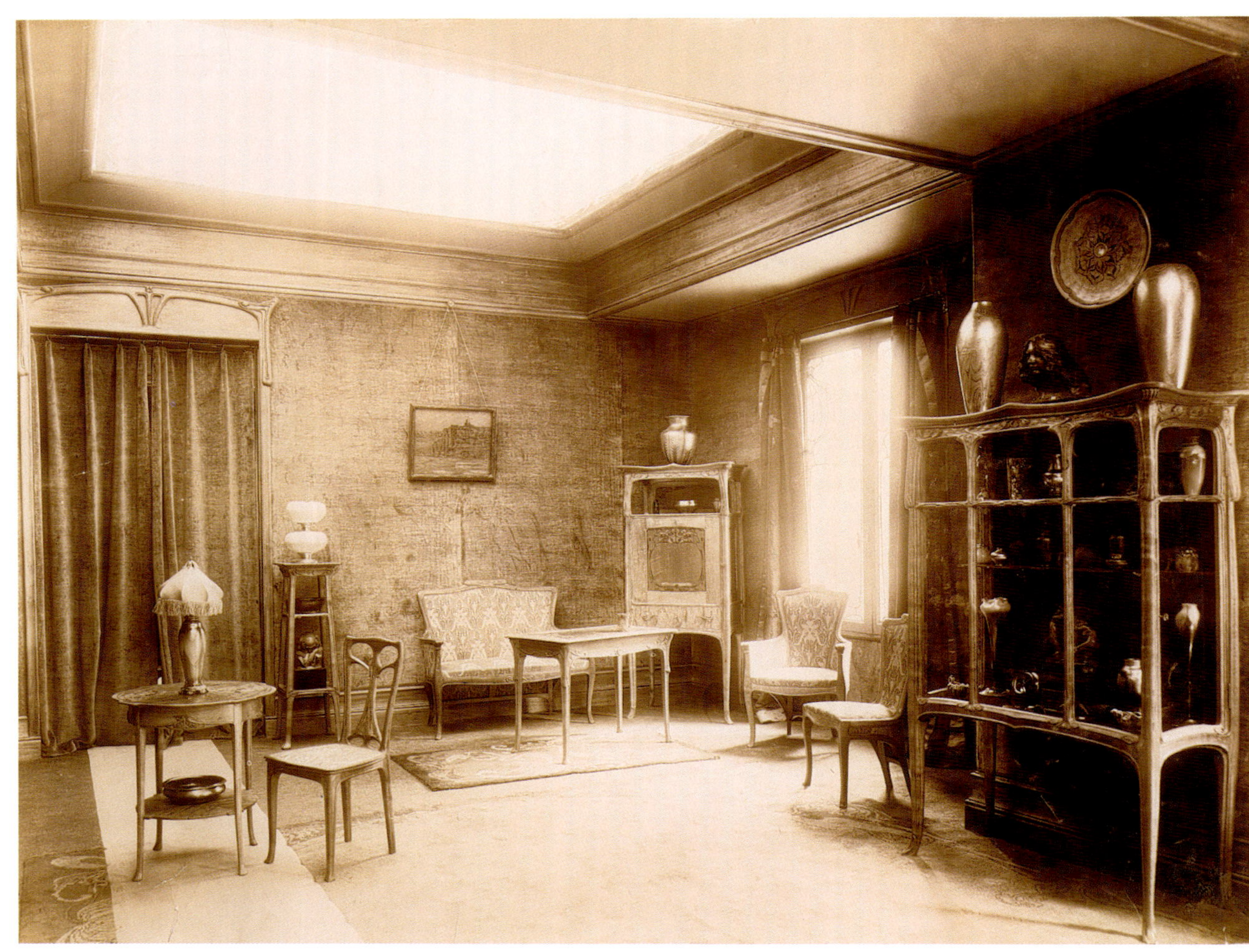

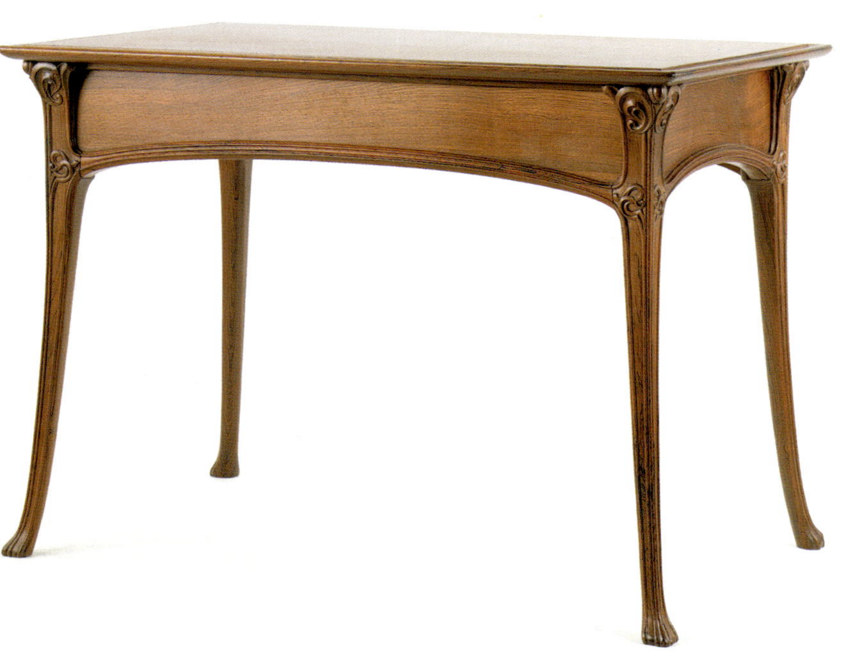

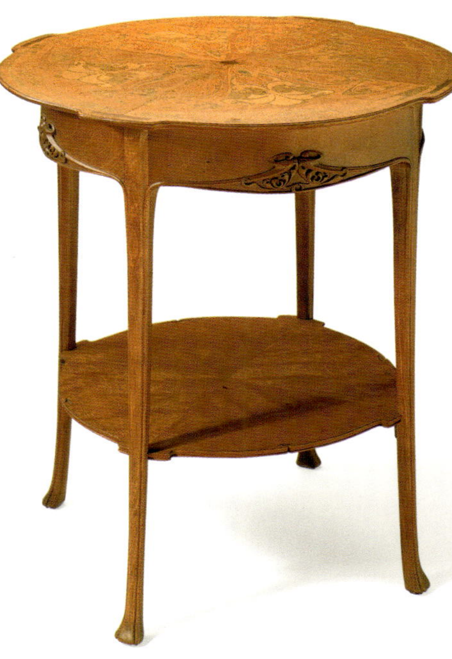

235
Edward Colonna, Drawing room, 1900, *Album de références*
Bibliothèque des Arts décoratifs, Paris

236
Edward Colonna, Table, c. 1900
Musée des Arts décoratifs, Paris

237
Edward Colonna, Round table, c. 1899–1900
Museum für Kunst und Gewerbe, Hamburg

> 238
Edward Colonna, Display cabinet, c. 1899–1900
Museum für Kunst und Gewerbe, Hamburg

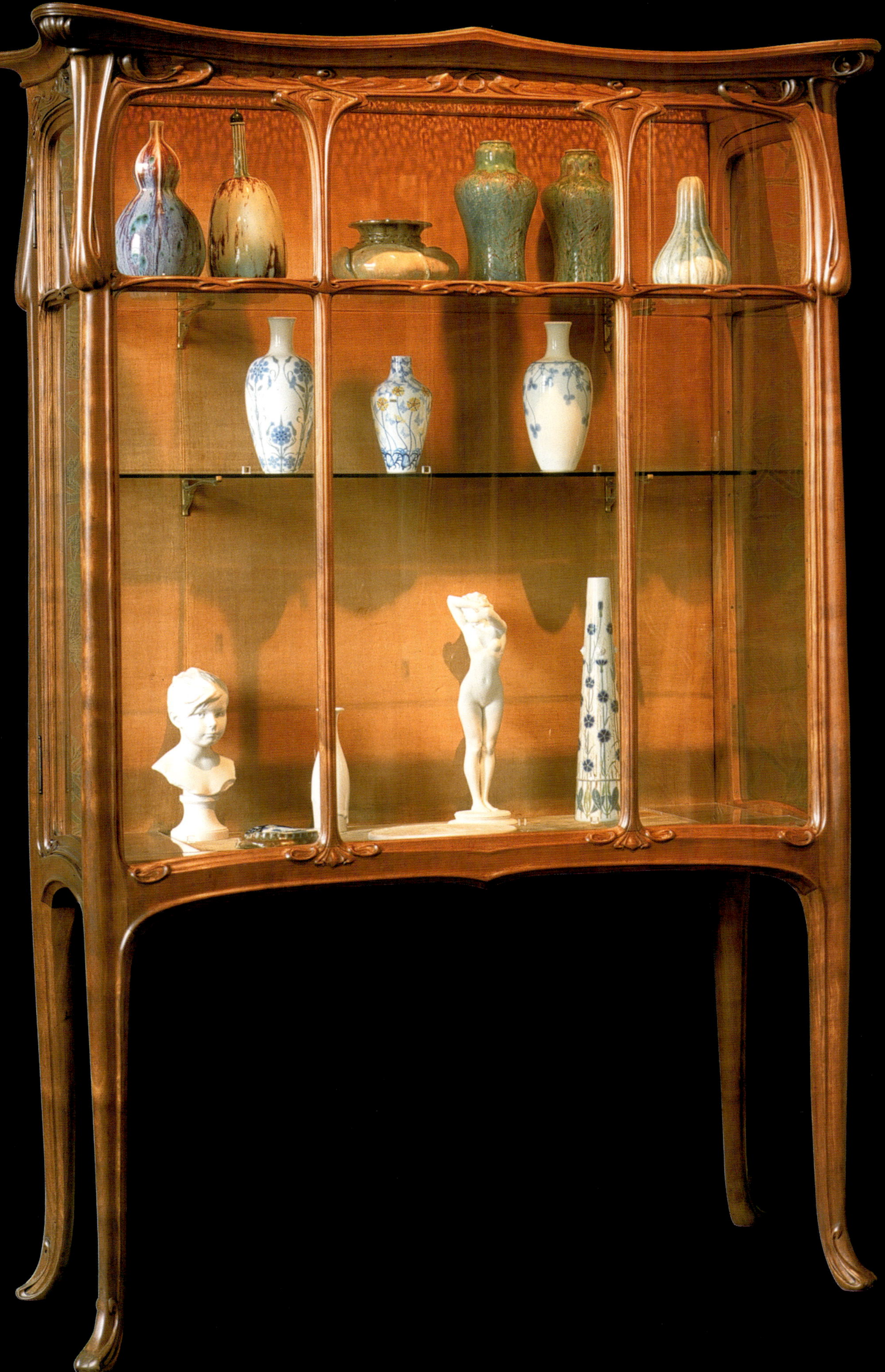

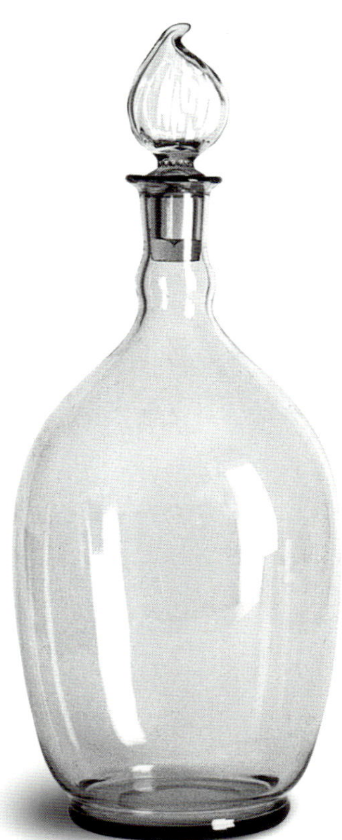

239
Edward Colonna, Fabric 'Orchids', c. 1899
Museum für Kunst und Gewerbe, Hamburg

240
Edward Colonna, Wine carafe, c. 1900
Nordenfjeldske Kunstindustrimuseum, Trondheim

> 241
Edward Colonna, Knotted rug, c. 1899
Österreichisches Museum für angewandte Kunst, Vienna

>> 242
Georges de Feure, *Glass*, c. 1900
Galerie Tonon, Genève

>> 243
Corner view of Bing's L'Art Nouveau pavilion, 1900, *Album de références*
Bibliothèque des Arts décoratifs, Paris

plant motifs. The artist did not hesitate to allude to late seventeenth-century styles, even if his furniture appeared 'modern and new in its architecture, and in the lines, design and contouring of its structure'.[31] The armchair mimics the shape of a transitional-style bergère chair, with straight legs that are very slightly curved. The same type of base is used for the occasional table, the chairs and the sofa, giving the whole collection a feeling of lightness and unity. These sober lines contrast with the decorative complexity of the floral motifs on the back of the 'medallion' sofa (fig. 255), while the console table is decorated with a stem of poppies opening into two flowers (fig. 252), a motif repeated on the screen and the display cabinet.

For the dressing room furniture (fig. 258), de Feure made use of the grain of Hungarian ash to produce a moiré pattern that harmonised well with the panels of brocaded silk in monochrome grey-blue, grey-mauve or grey-green, reminiscent of the iridescent glassware of Tiffany. The atmosphere was muted and confined, an effect reinforced by the luxury of the materials – opaline and onyx for the washbasin, furniture fittings of silvered bronze – and the rich fabric of the wall-hangings. The clarity of the whole was maintained by the straight lines of the furniture bases and frames and the sobriety of the Empire-style day-bed upholstered in sea-green wool embroidered with roses.

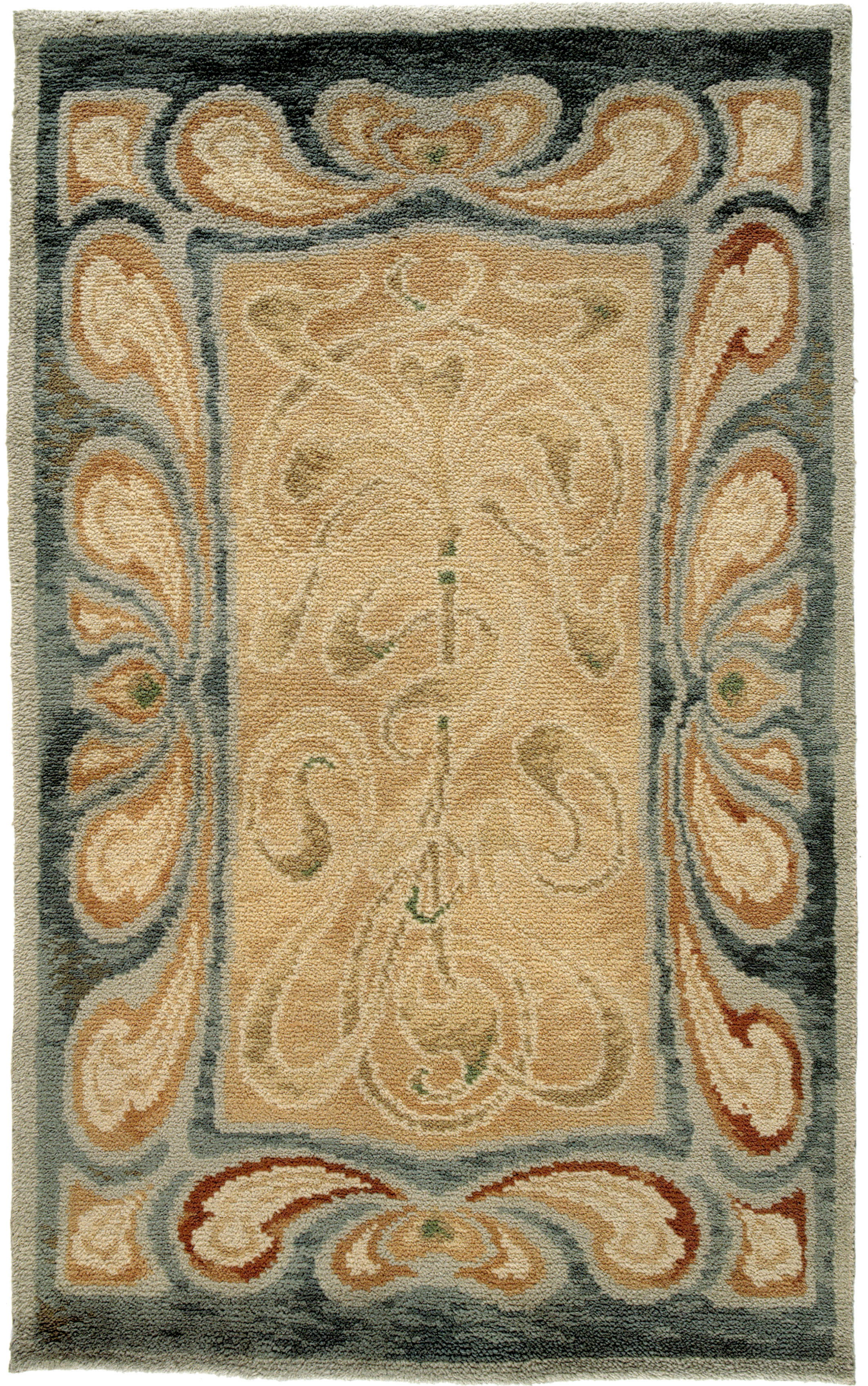

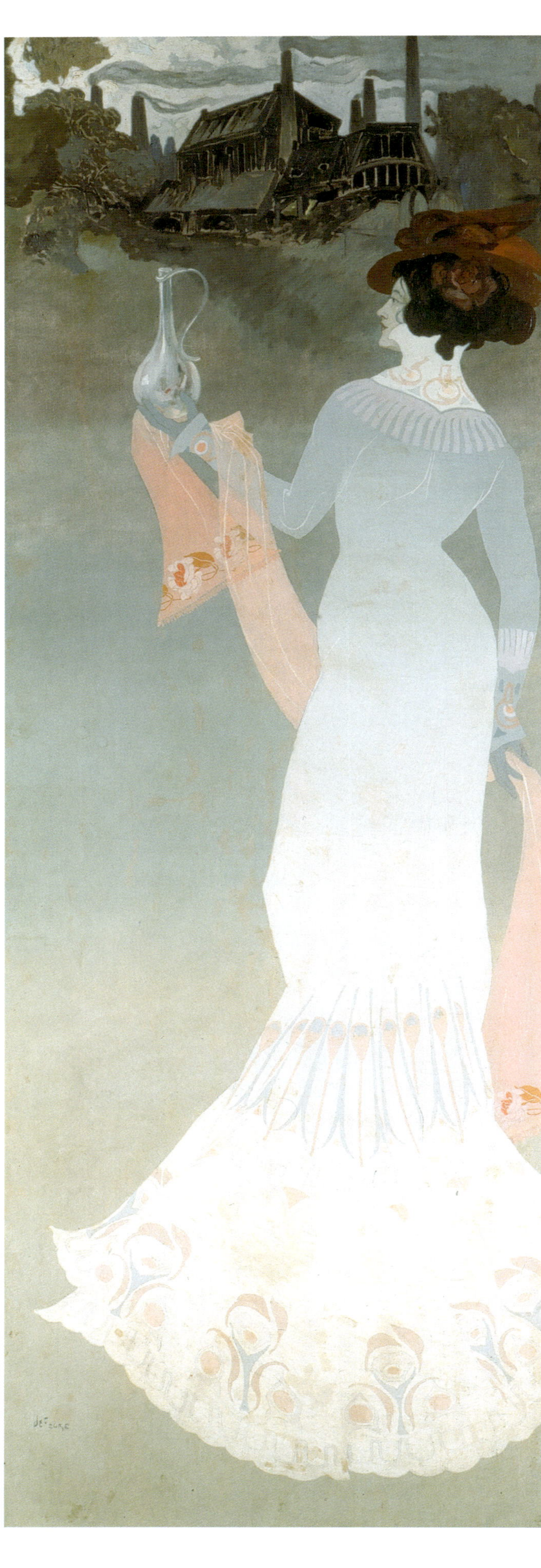

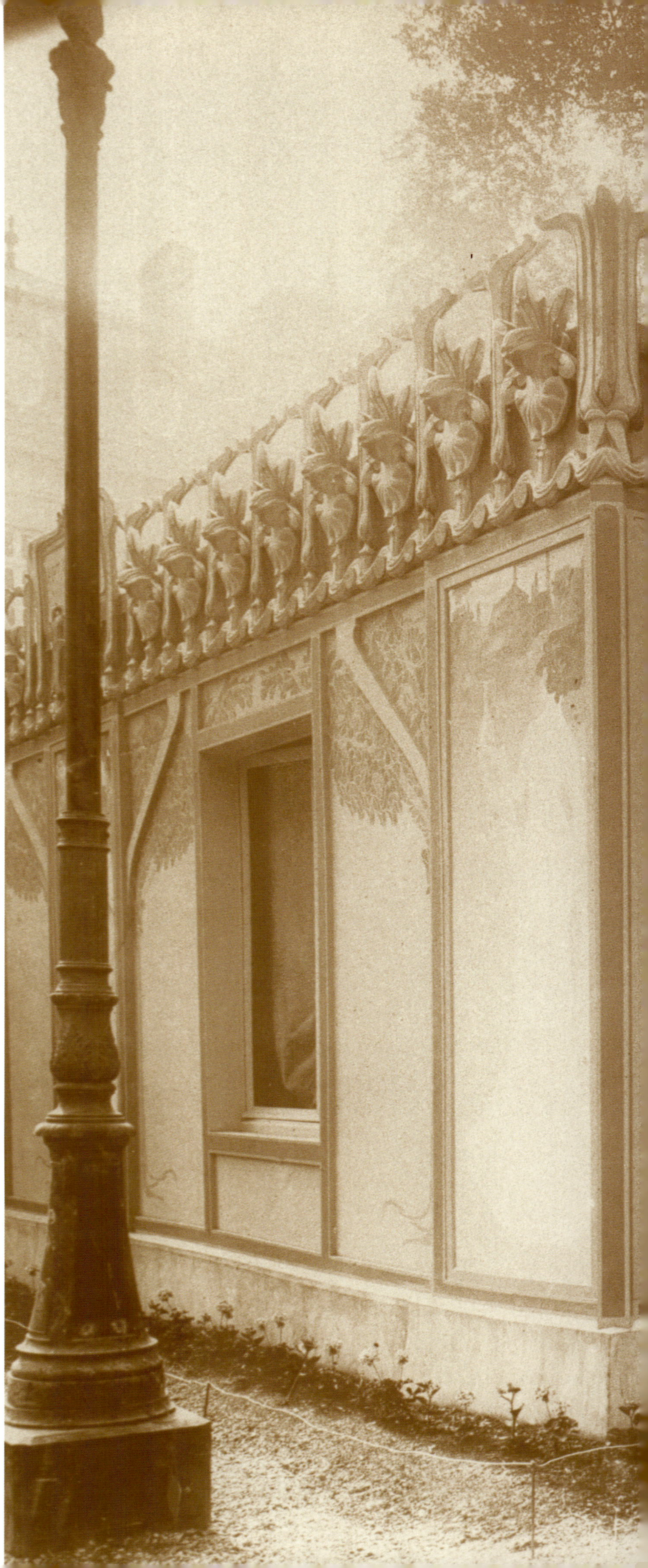

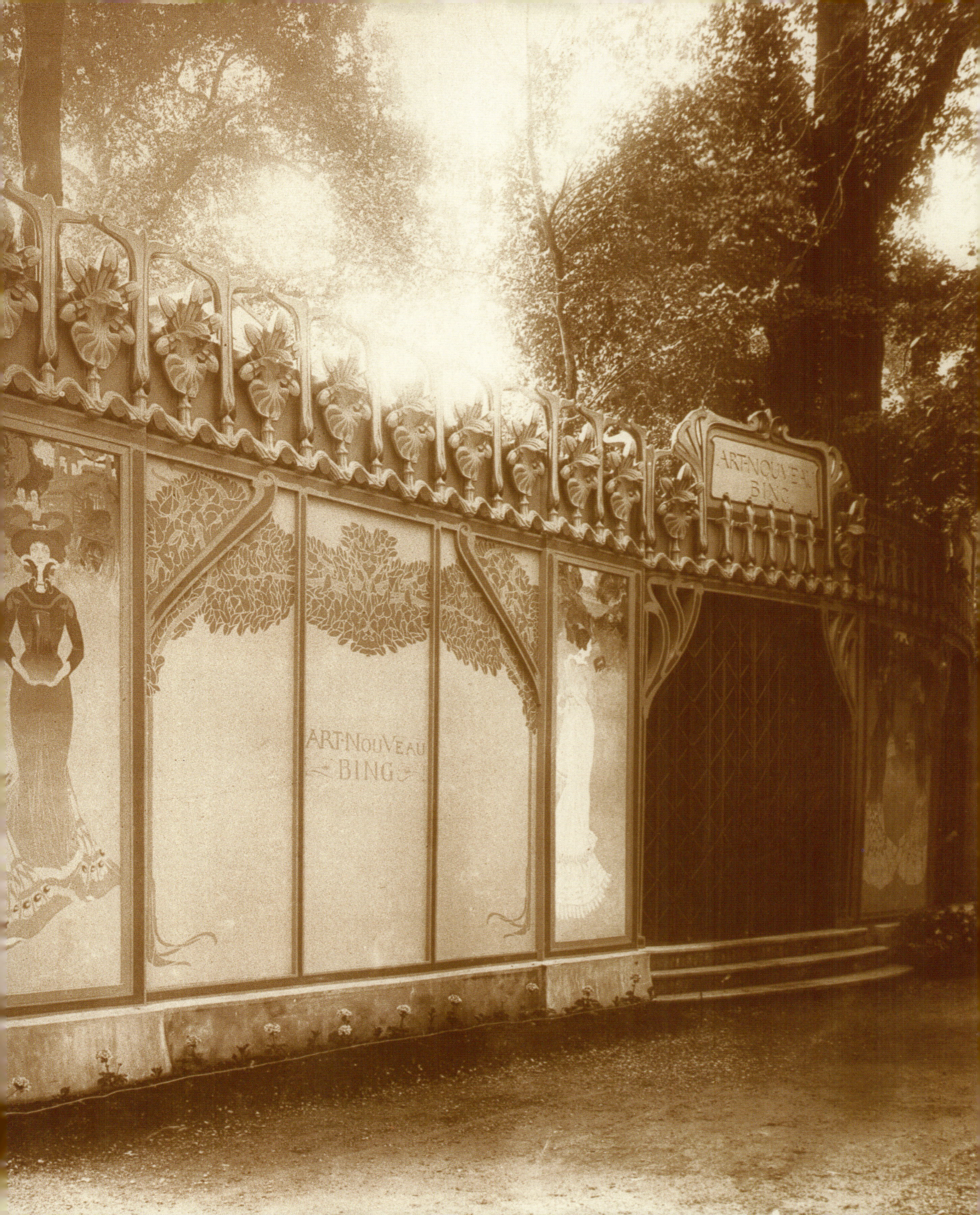
ART-NOUVEAU
BING
ART-NOUVEAU
BING

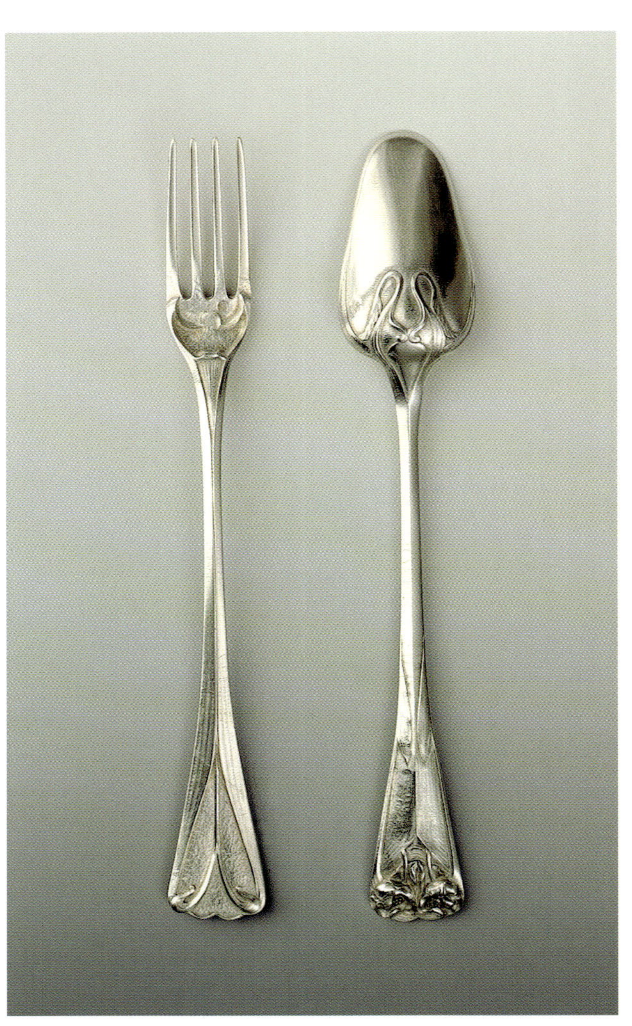

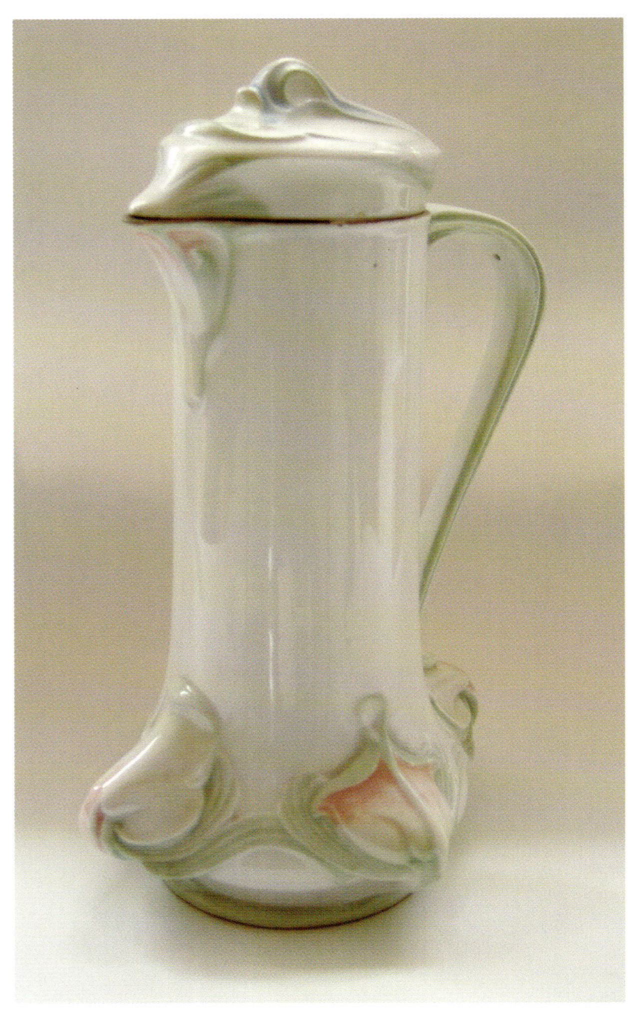

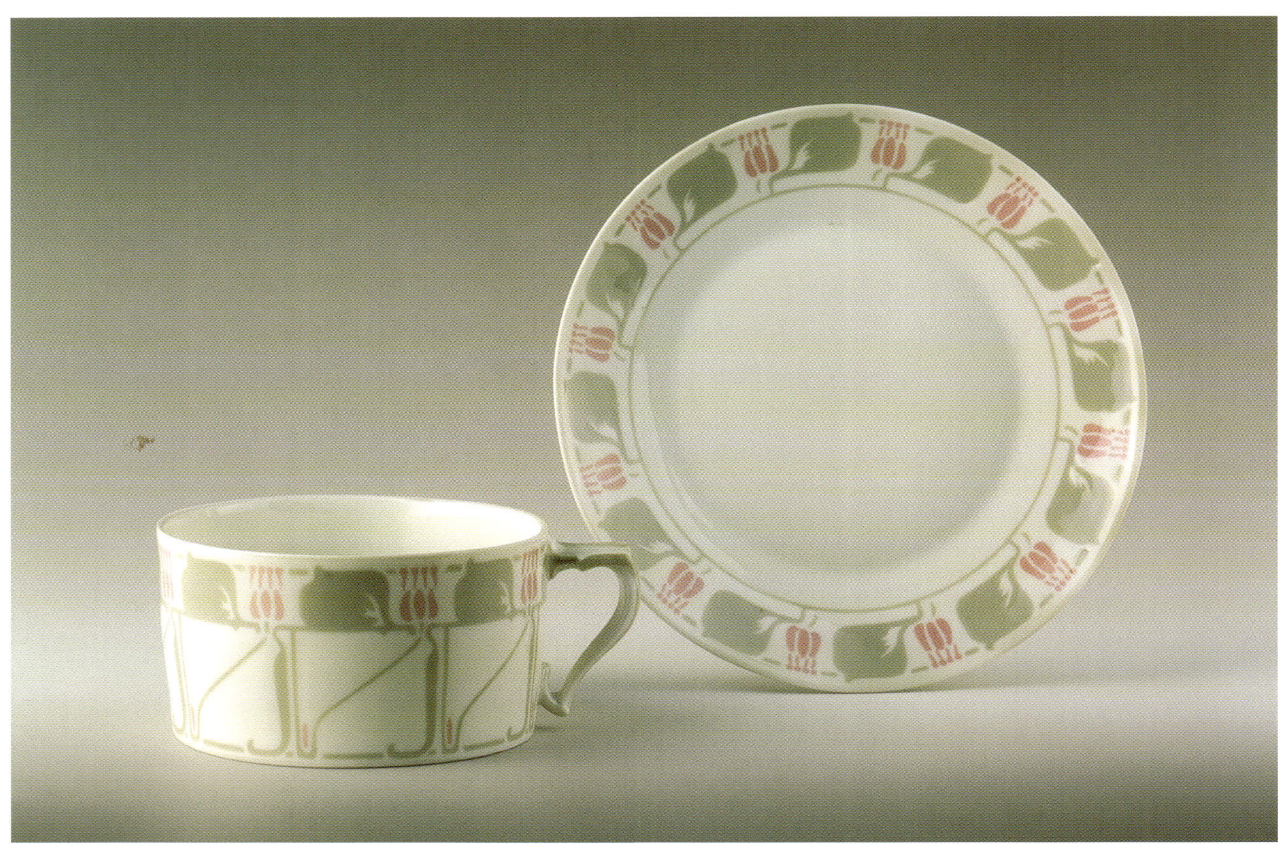

244
Georges de Feure, Cutlery, dessert spoon and fork, 1900
Germanisches Nationalmuseum, Nürnberg

245
Georges de Feure, Chocolate pot, c. 1902
Porcelaines GDA, Limoges

246
Georges de Feure, Cup and saucer, abstract flower design, c. 1900
Musée des Arts décoratifs, Paris

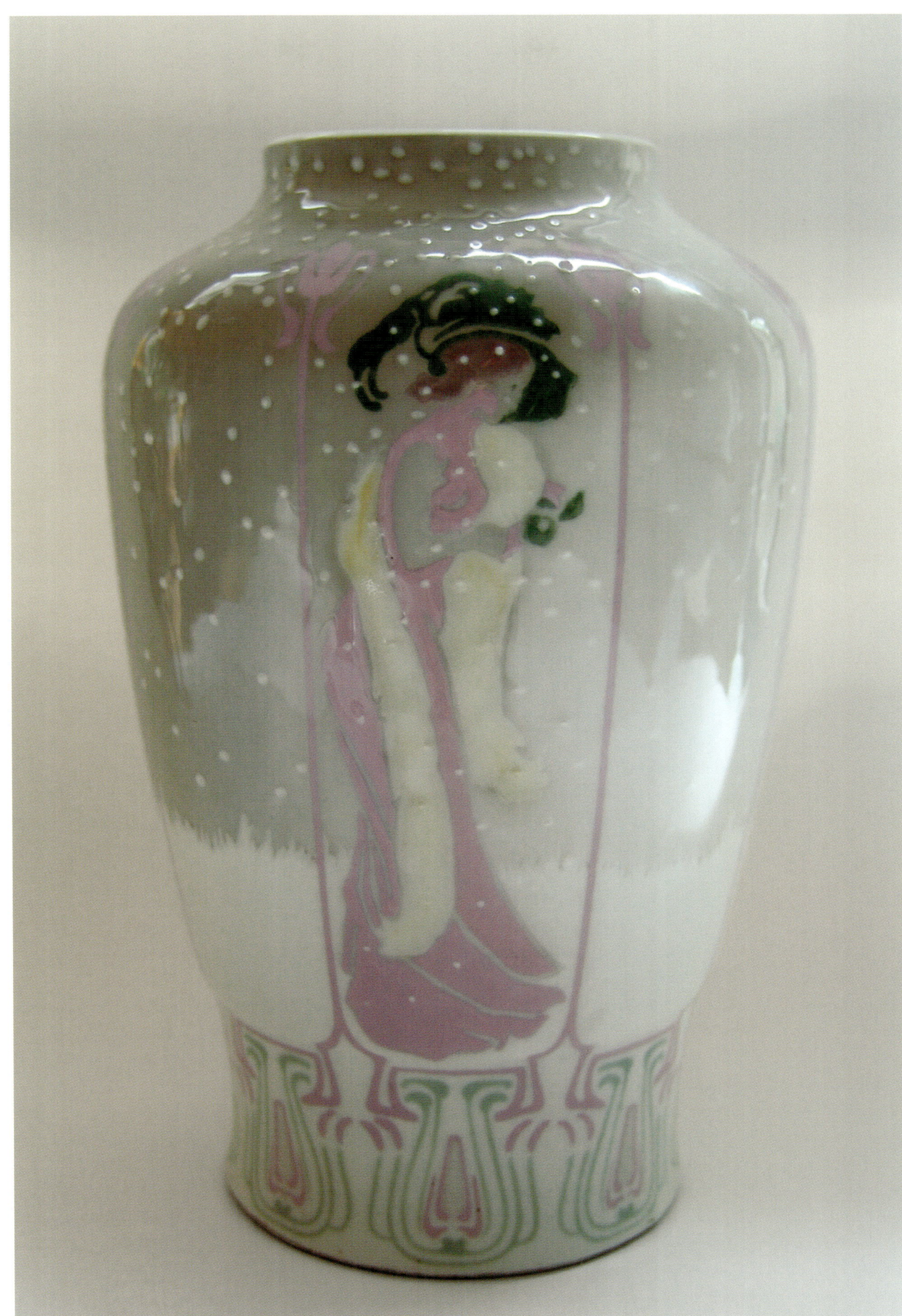

247
Georges de Feure, Vase 'Woman in Snow Scene', c. 1901–02
Porcelaines GDA, Limoges

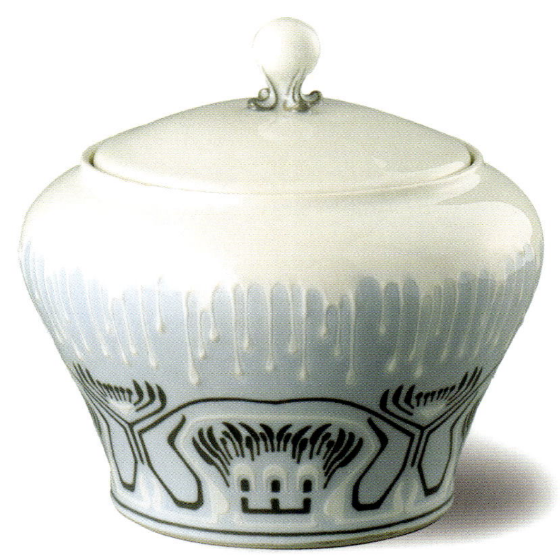

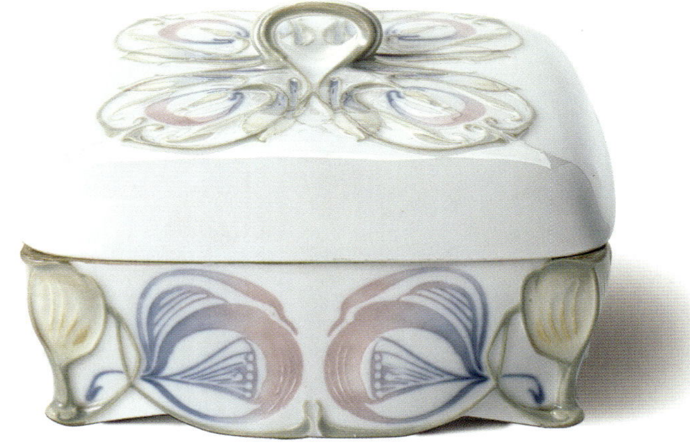

248
Georges de Feure, Sugar bowl, c. 1900–01
Musée des Arts décoratifs, Paris

249
Georges de Feure, Bonbonnière, c. 1900
Musée des Arts décoratifs, Paris

> **250**
Georges de Feure, Vase, c. 1900
Porcelaines GDA, Limoges

The final piece was a tutelary figure of Woman in the stained-glass windows of a little hall connecting the boudoir to the bedroom designed by Gaillard.

A FAVOURABLE RECEPTION: THREE REPUTATIONS ESTABLISHED

The best proof of the resounding success of the 1900 World's Fair was the number of visitors attending it: no less than 48 million in the space of six months. Foreign critics particularly praised the Art Nouveau pavilion.[32] Bing's policy of presenting new, elegant designs in styles to suit French taste appears, on this occasion, to have been best represented by Georges de Feure. Some even saw him as the outstanding success of the Fair. 'I like to think that M. de Feure's boudoir is one of the most perfect and exquisite examples of decorative art our times have produced. [...] It really is the best piece in the Bing pavilion, and perhaps even the entire 1900 World's Fair.'[33] Meier-Graefe's review, *L'Art Décoratif*, waxed enthusiastic over de Feure's eclectic originality, which it discerned particularly in his fabric designs: 'Taking the beautiful arabesques discovered by Belgian artists and already transformed by the Germans, he has very cleverly eliminated the gloomy violence of the former and the latter's tendency towards heaviness. The lines have become more supple, lighter, kinder to the eye. And finally, our French instincts are satisfied by the discreet introduction of highly stylised floral elements, so ingeniously married to the arabesques that one can scarcely distinguish what belongs to which.'[34] *Art et Décoration* also emphasised how far de Feure had succeeded in fitting into the French tradition of elegance constantly demanded by all the critics: 'We can see that, in his boudoir and dressing room, M. de Feure has made every effort to create the most elegant and feminine interior possible, and one which clearly conforms to our native traditions.'[35]

Eugène Gaillard did not generate the same enthusiasm from the critics, but they still commented very favourably on the originality of his forms and his choice of wall decoration: 'The eye is captured, conquered, by this splendour, before it is possible to analyse it.'[36] A compliment from the pen of Gabriel Mourey still seems the best definition of this decorator's style: 'His furniture is vigorous, without being pompous or heavy, simply because of its sound and logical structure; there is muscle beneath these forms.'[37] It is true that Gaillard's contribution was almost the complete antithesis of the slenderness of de Feure's or Colonna's, and perhaps that is where one must look for the real innovation in the Art Nouveau Pavilion. As Octave Maus very pertinently remarked: 'Work of this kind reveals a designer of quality, who has cast aside conventions and the usual insignificant nonsense. It is in marked contrast to the rather precious overall effect of the Bing pavilion, giving it an unexpected note of virility.'[38]

'M. Colonna seeks to give his furniture simple and elegant lines, whose essential qualities are effortless fluidity and perfect proportions.'[39] Of the three artists whose work was on show in the pavilion, Colonna attracted the least comment from the critics. Some, no doubt, saw a greater lack of consistency in his mode of

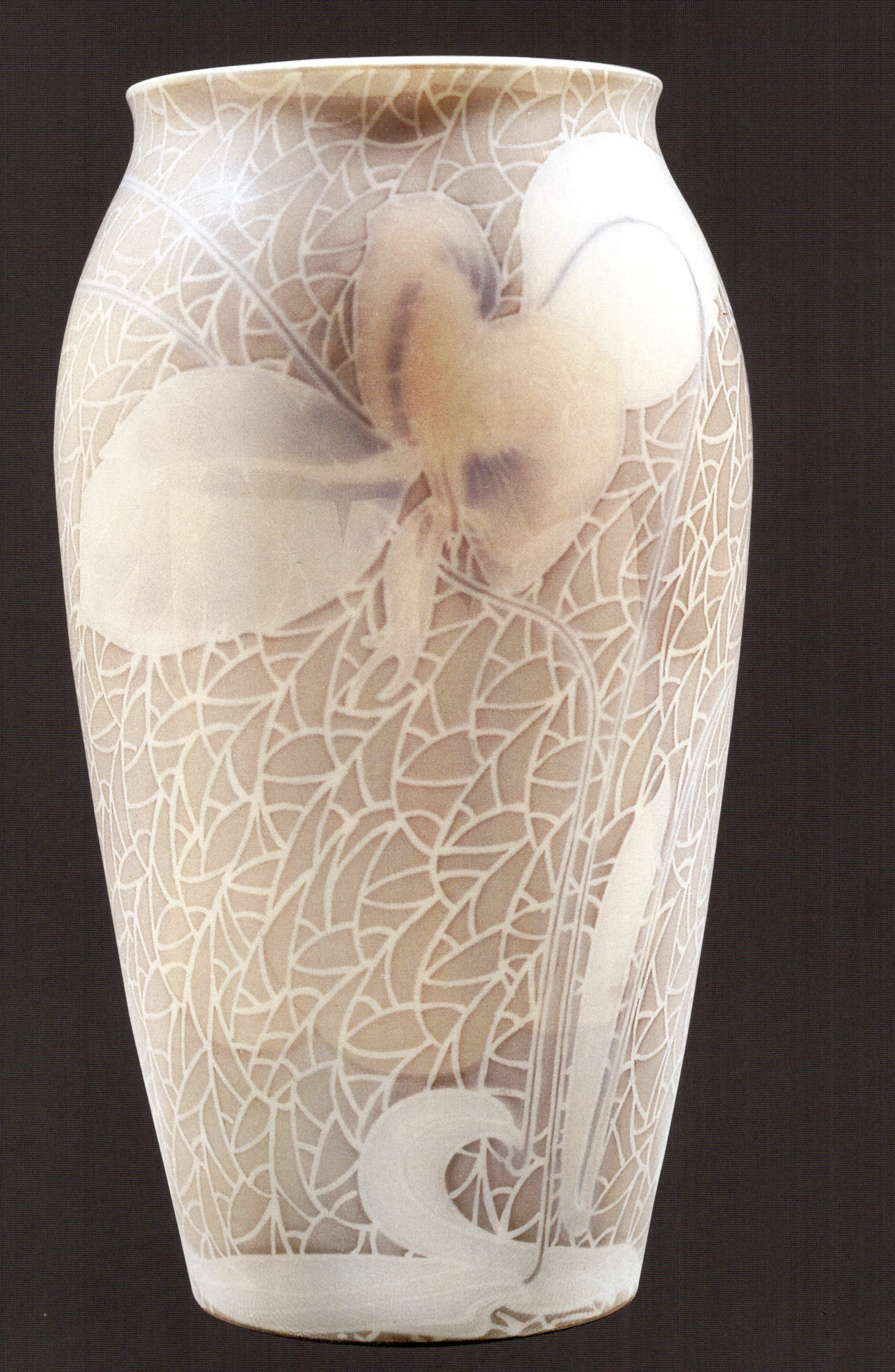

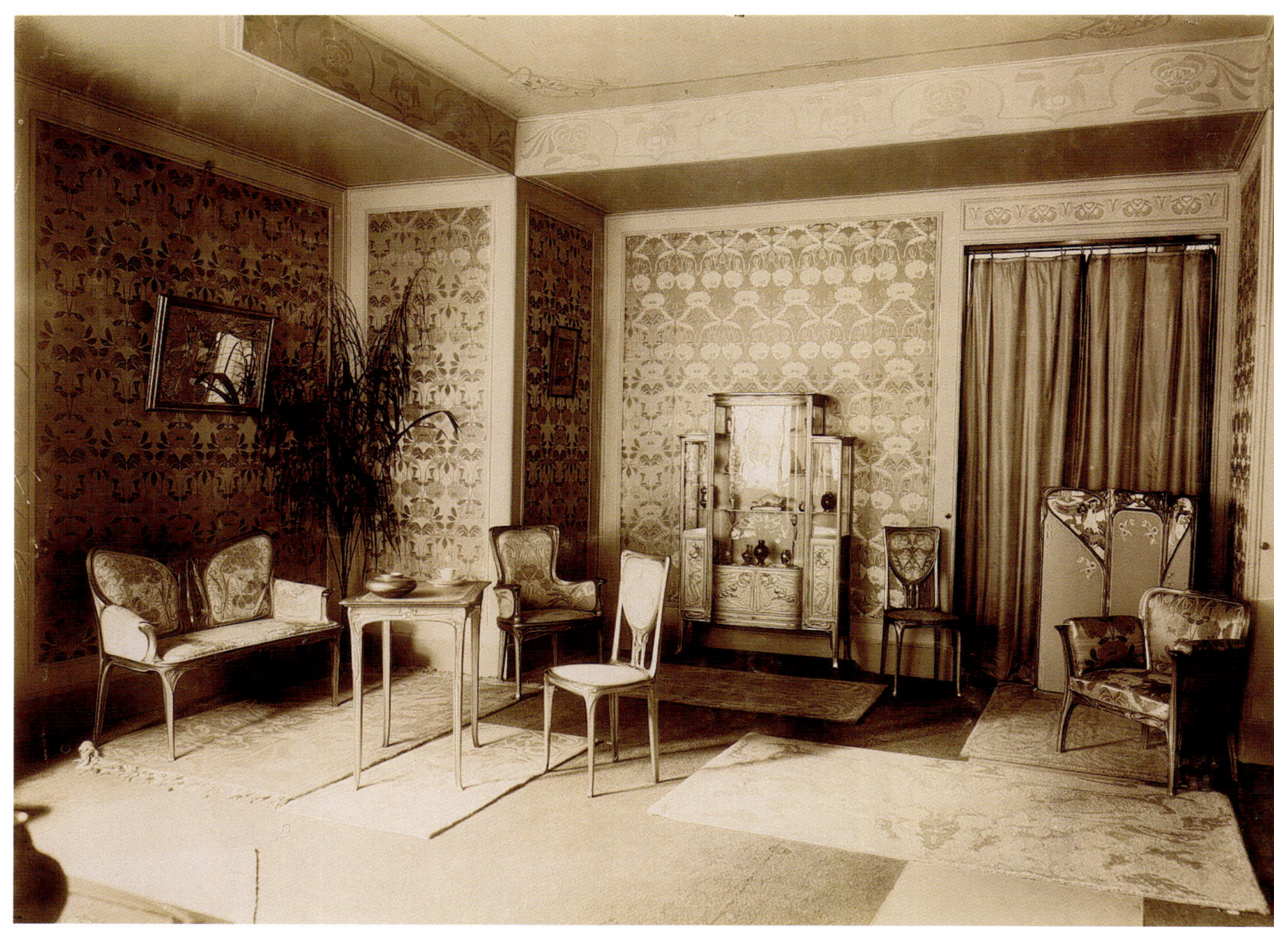

251
Georges de Feure,
Boudoir, 1900,
Album de références
Bibliothèque des Arts décoratifs, Paris

252
Georges de Feure,
Console table, 1900
Musée des Arts décoratifs, Paris

> 253
Georges de Feure,
Display cabinet, c. 1900
Musée des Arts décoratifs, Paris

>> 254
Georges de Feure,
Screen, 1900
Musée des Arts décoratifs, Paris

>> 255
Georges de Feure,
Sofa, chair, table and wall hanging from the boudoir, c. 1900
Det Danske Kunstindustrimuseum, Copenhagen

expression. Meier-Graefe was the critic who best summed up Colonna's talent, by preferring to emphasise his brilliance in the fields of jewellery and gold and silver work rather than in the design of soft furnishings. 'Despite all his skill, the Belgian origins of the design remain too apparent. And although certain details of this design (in particular the hook shape with a bulge at the bottom of the curves) serve M. Colonna extremely well in relief, they do not appear so much to his advantage when applied to flat surfaces. M. Colonna's superiority is rather more evident in jewellery and gold and silverwork.'[40]

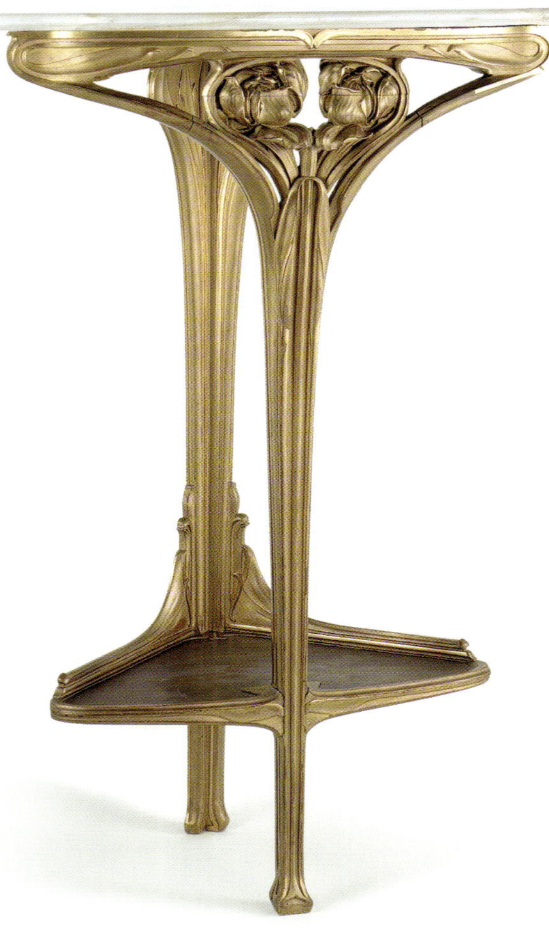

A LIMITED INFLUENCE

It was mainly foreign museums that bought from Siegfried Bing at the time, but there were also a few private individuals. 'We see from a notice that de Feure's dressing room has been acquired by the Princess of T.'[41] 'In addition to a few famous people, it is the museums of Hamburg, Berlin, Copenhagen, Budapest, Graz, Krefeld, Trondheim, Tokyo, etc., which bought the principal items exhibited by the firm of Bing'.[42] Of course, by building his own pavilion, Bing had taken on a colossal financial burden,

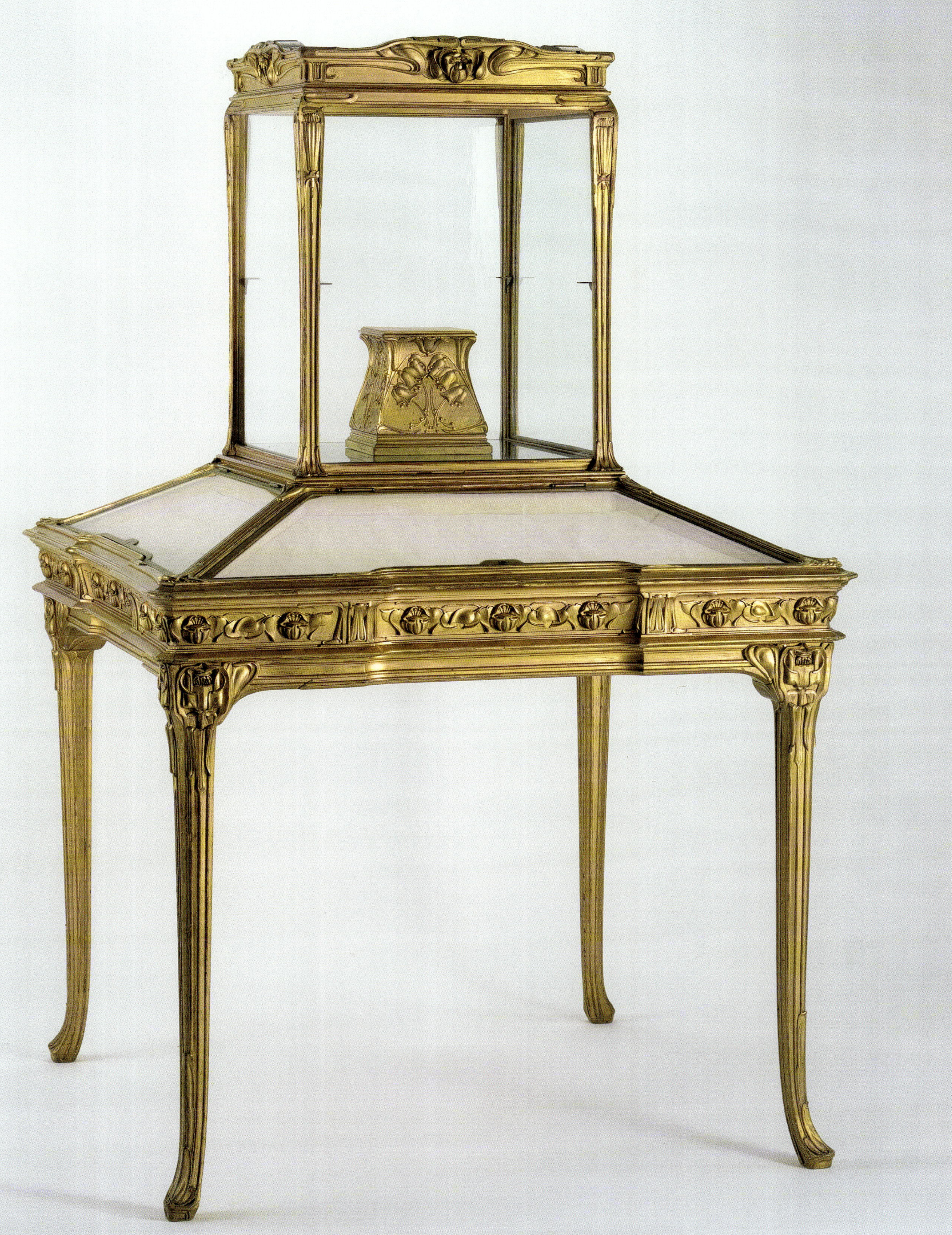

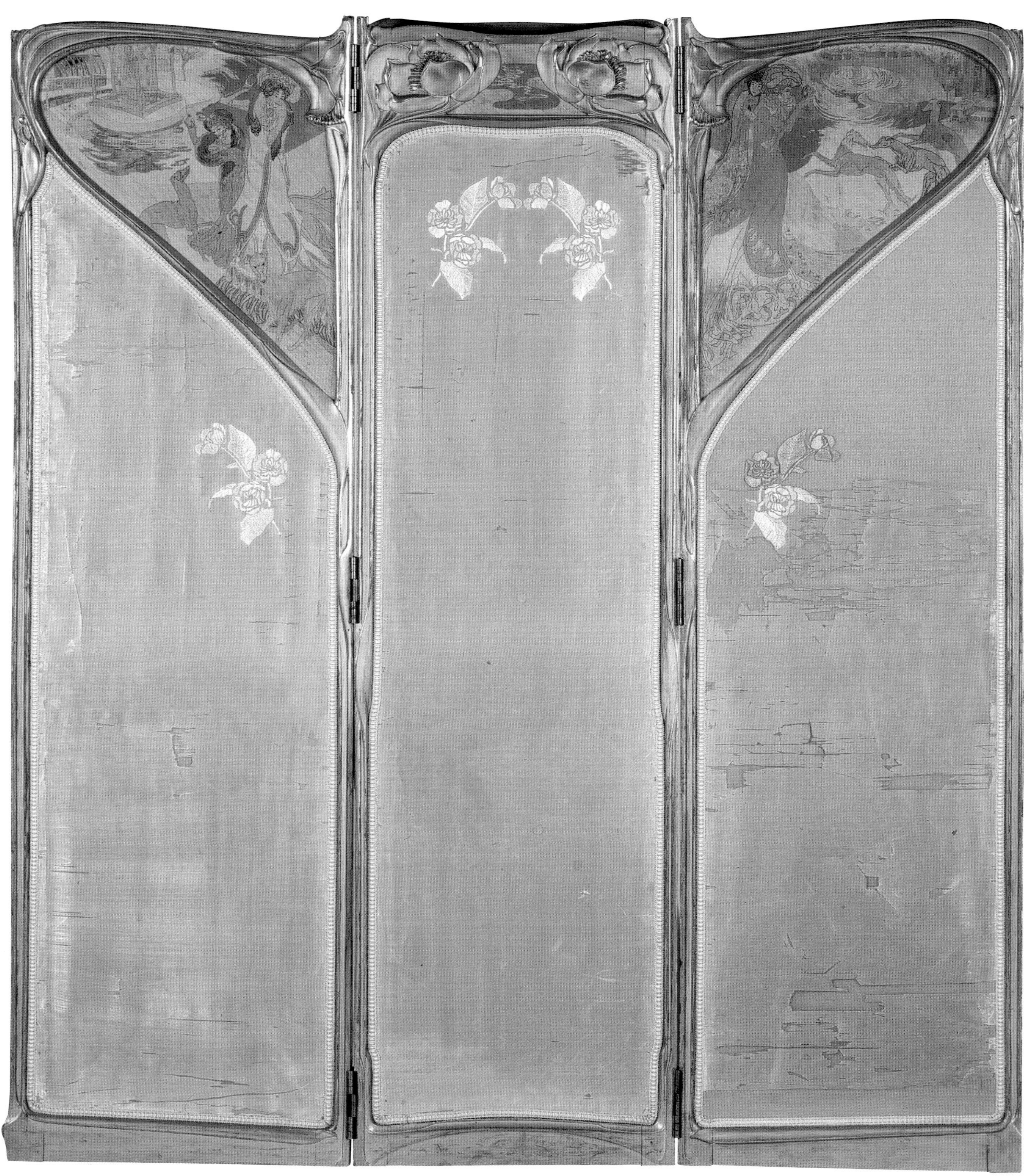

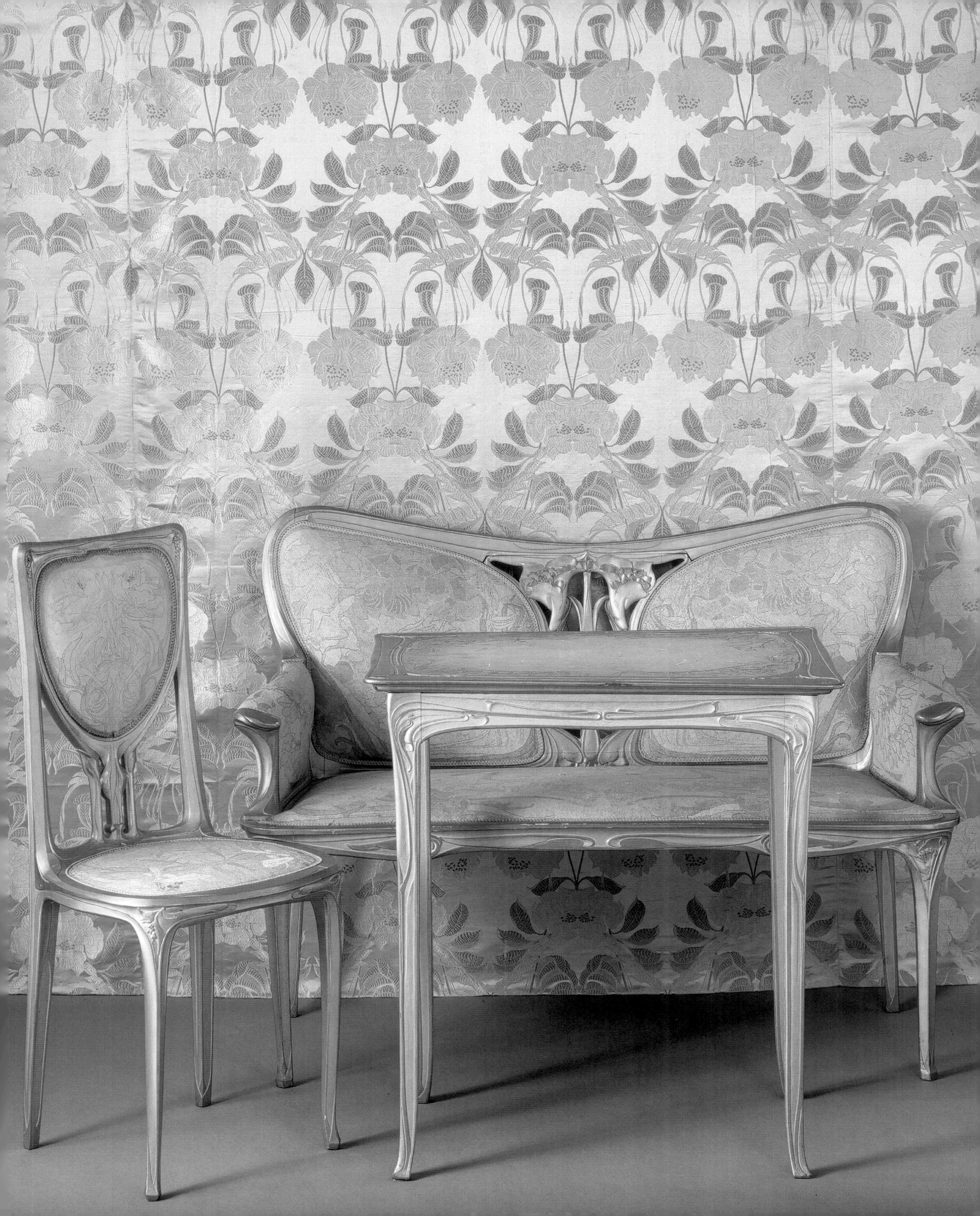

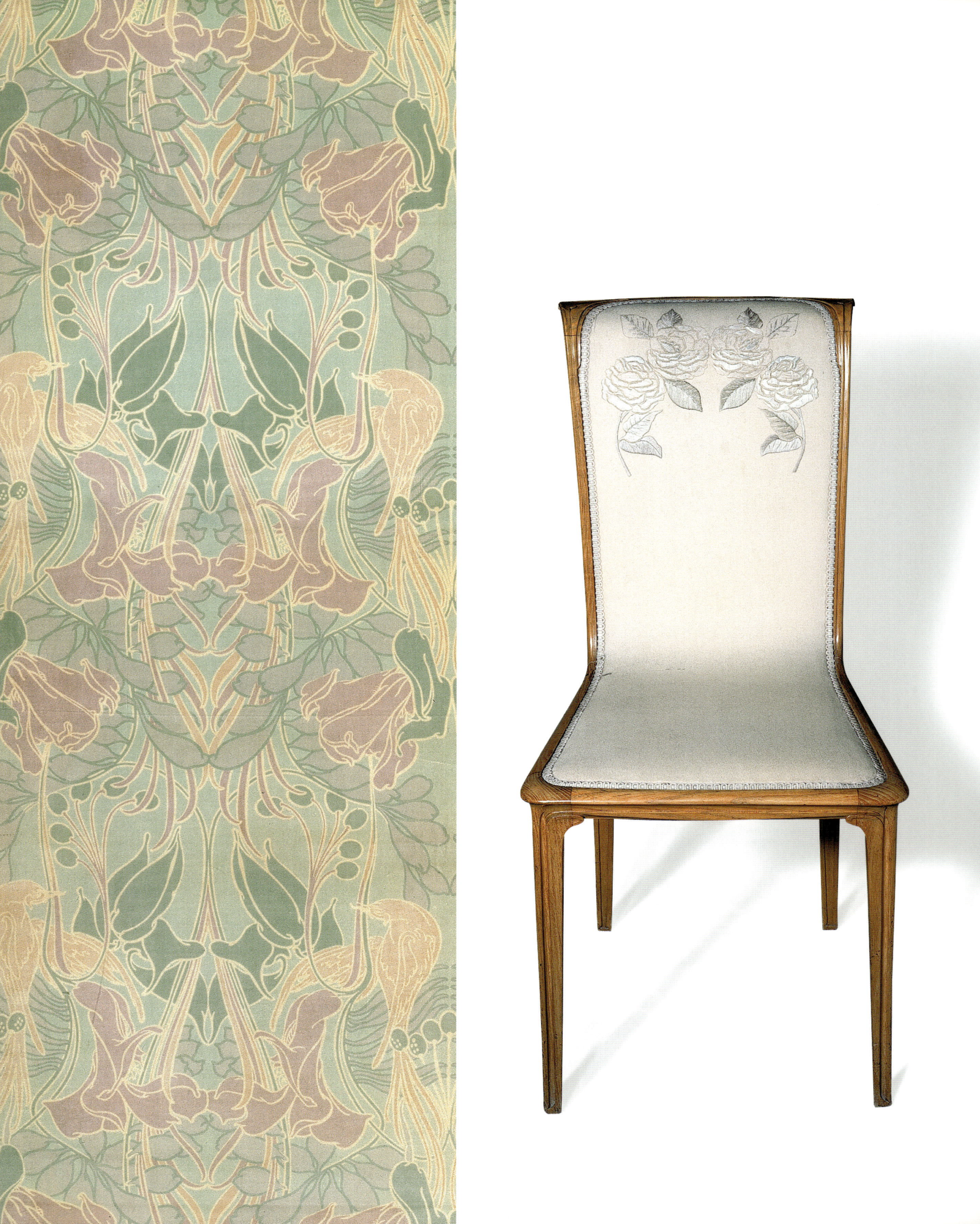

< 256
Georges de Feure, Fabric with birds among vines, c. 1899–1900
Museum für Kunst und Gewerbe, Hamburg

< 257
Georges de Feure, Dressing room chair, 1900
Nordenfjeldske Kunstindustrimuseum, Trondheim

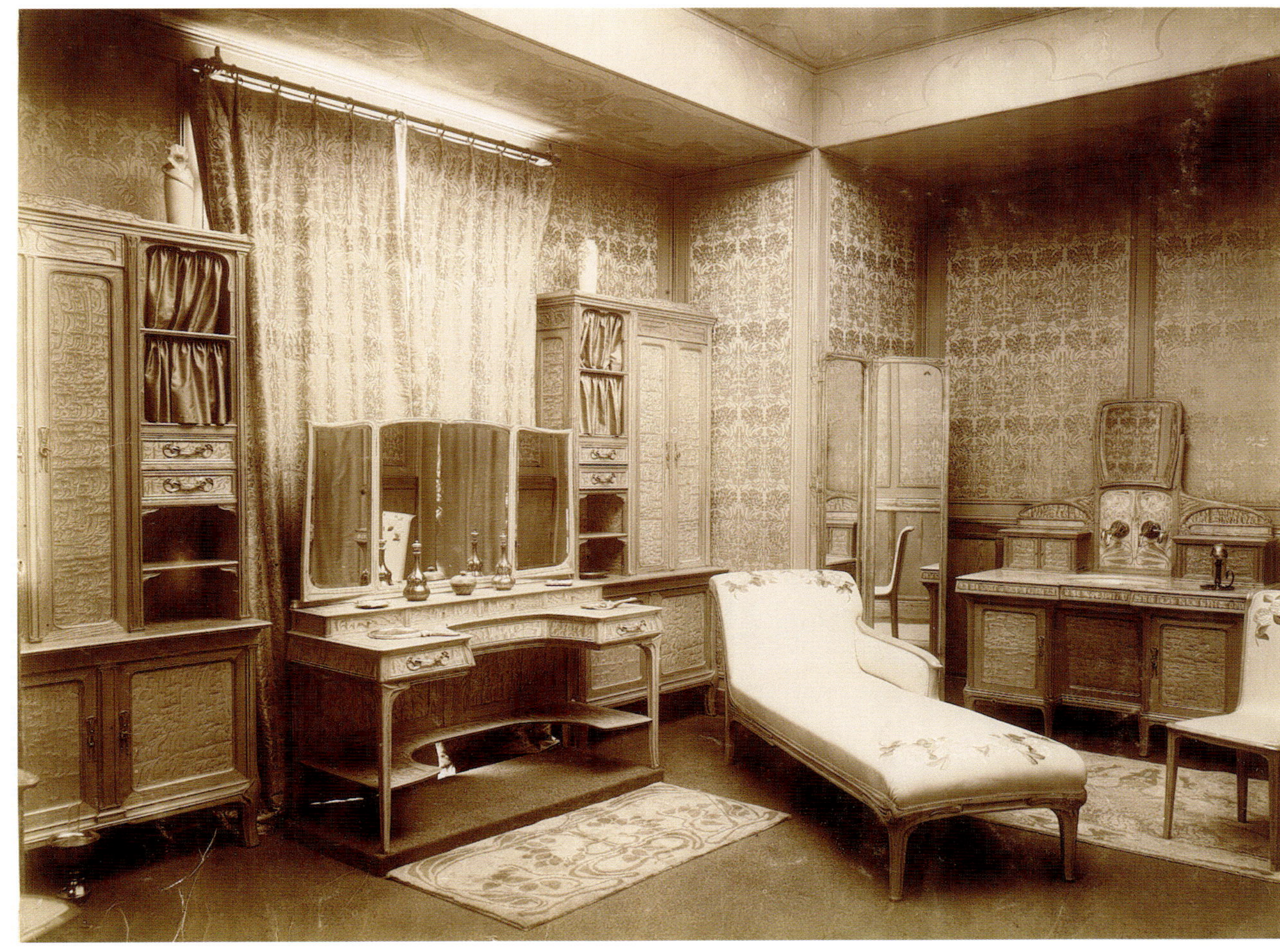

258
Georges de Feure, Dressing room, 1900, *Album de références*
Bibliothèque des Arts décoratifs, Paris

which he hoped he would quickly be able to turn into profit. Although it is difficult now to evaluate the consequences of his participation in terms of figures, it seems to have had a beneficial effect on the reputation of his company, certainly with the French public, but even more with foreign visitors. Business seems to have prospered in the period following the Fair. Some of the furniture displayed in the pavilion 'has been reproduced. M. Bing commissioned their designer, M. Georges de Feure, to decorate a drawing room in his private house in the rue de Provence.'[43] Bing's collaborator, Marcel Morot, reinforces this belief: 'For the three years following the Fair, the firm was kept busy fulfilling large orders.'[44] This evidence would lead us to believe it was a commercial success, but if we look through the catalogue of the Bing sale of 1904,[45] we are now forced to conclude that this refined type of decoration remained the prerogative of an elite clientele.

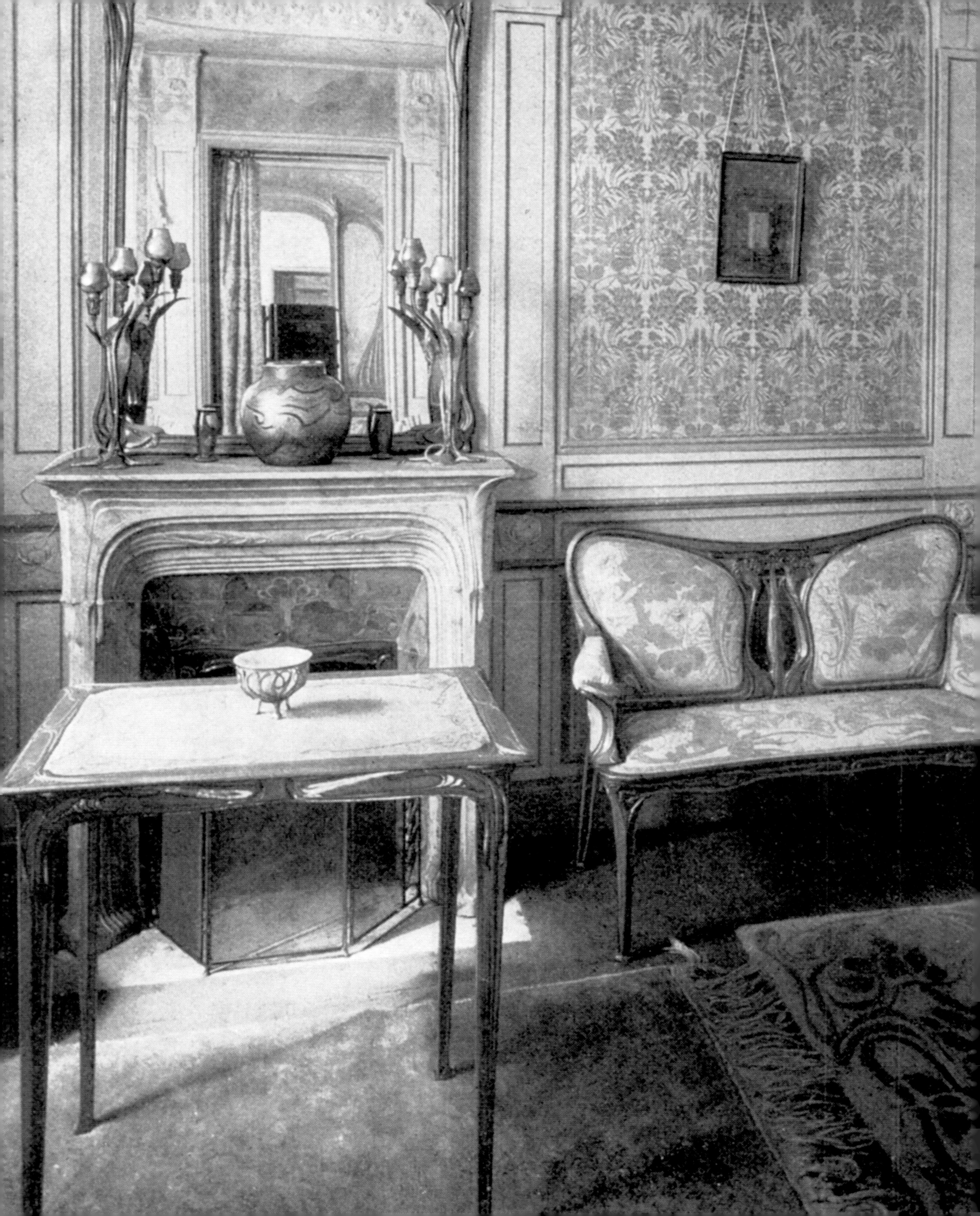

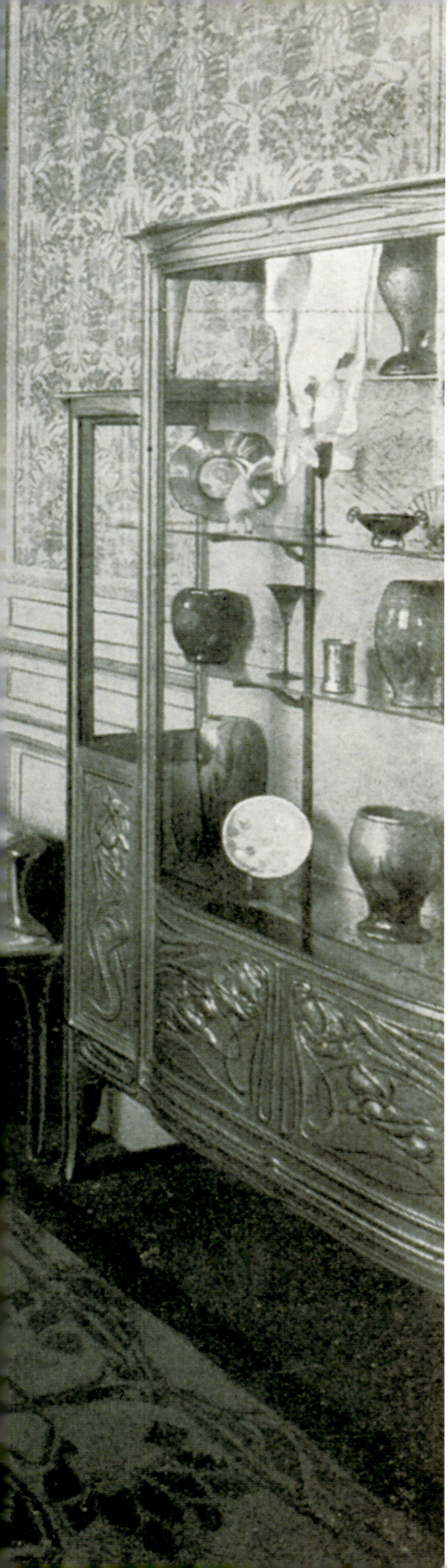

BING AND INTERIOR DECORATION

THE EXAMPLE OF THE CHÂTEAU DE TRÉVAREZ

ÉVELYNE POSSÉMÉ

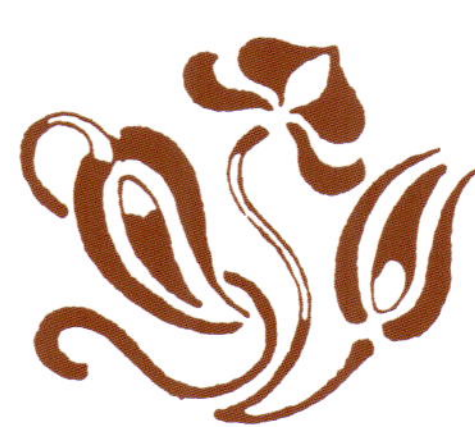

At the time he set up the Galerie de L'Art Nouveau, Siegfried Bing's intention was not only to encourage the emergence of a modern movement in the decorative arts, but also to present interior design to the public as coherent ensembles – entire rooms, in which all the furniture, decoration and art objects would be in harmony – that could be transposed straight to the buyers' homes. While expressing admiration for the achievements of the Bing pavilion at the 1900 World's Fair, Julius Meier-Graefe (writing as G.M. Jacques) was nevertheless surprised that, 'despite wonderful furniture and a collection of art objects representing the greatest and one of the best attempts of our time to modernise interior design, the final result does not match up to the effort. Why? Because the second aspect of the question, concerning interior architecture and wall decoration, has remained almost unnoticed.'[1] The subsequent development of Bing and

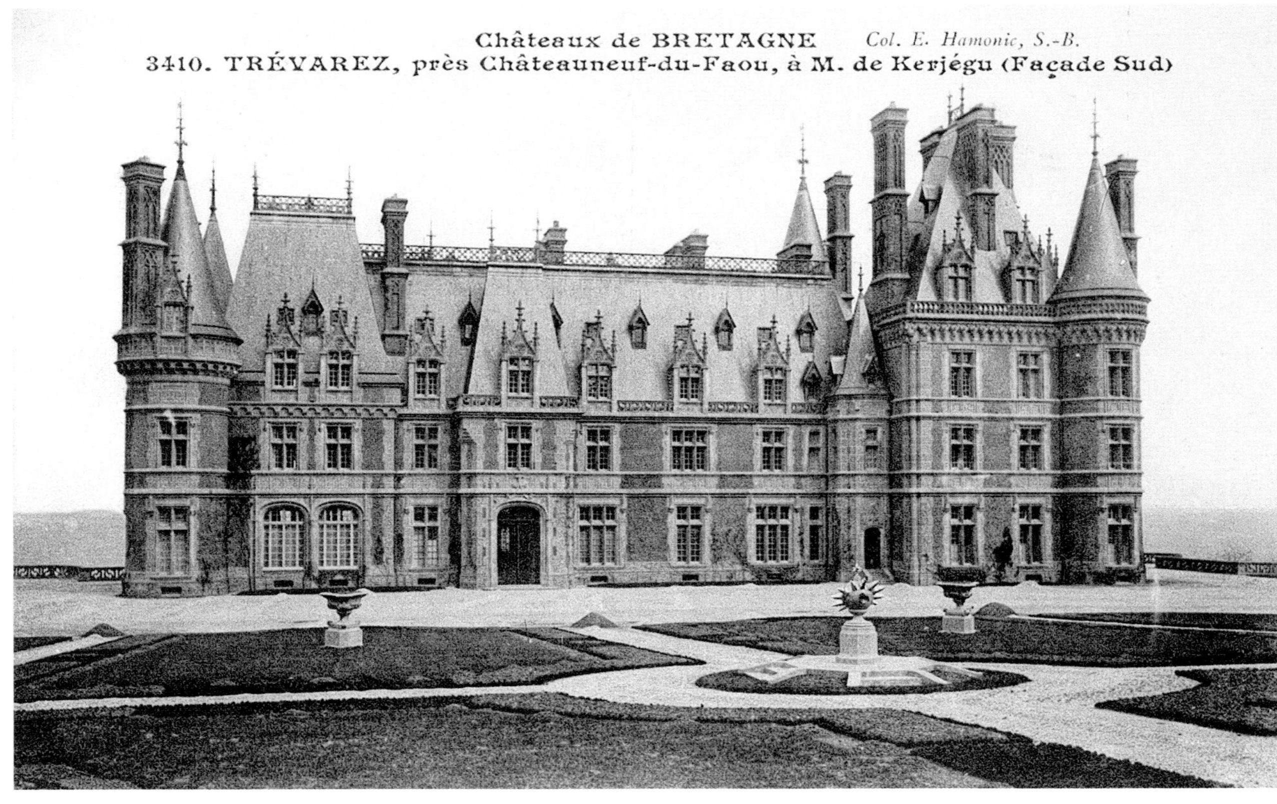

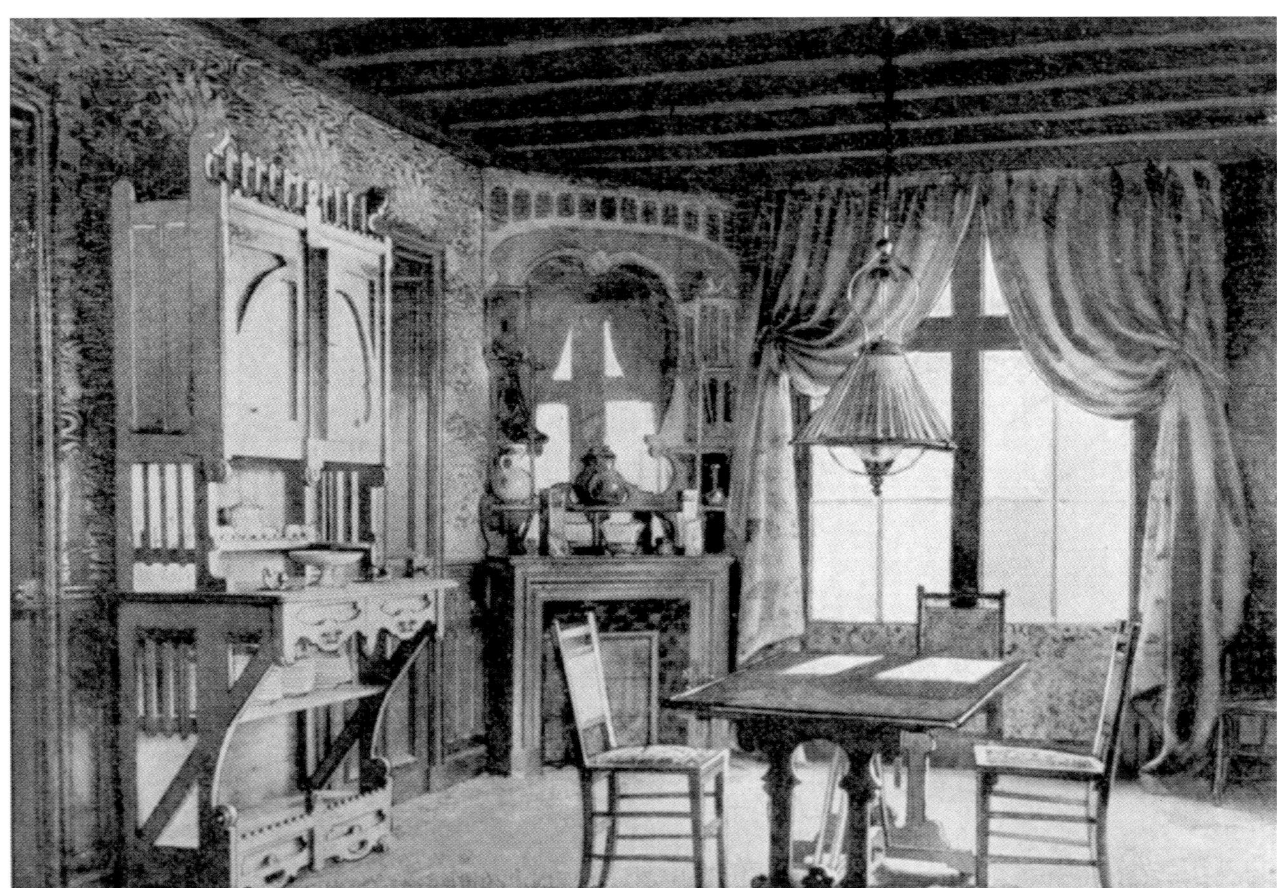

<< 259
Georges de Feure, Drawing room in gilded wood, in Bing's gallery L'Art Nouveau, 1901, from Octave Gerdeil, 'An artist's studio', *L'Art Décoratif*, January 1902

260
The Château de Trévarez, *Album Maciet* 44/8
Bibliothèque des Arts décoratifs, Paris

261
Dining room for a villa in Deauville, from *Le Gaulois du dimanche*, 16-17 April 1898

his designers, in particular Georges de Feure, would provide an appropriate response to the problem of total decoration. Though he was known mainly for the furniture and art objects he sold, Bing also carried out the decoration of complete rooms or houses, albeit in smaller numbers. A few traces of these have survived in the designs preserved in the *Album de références* or in contemporary articles.

HOME DECORATION

On the day the Galerie L'Art Nouveau opened, 26 December 1895, Bing's desire for 'total art' could be seen in the three rooms he commissioned from Henry Van de Velde. As early as April 1898, Bing informed his customers that 'L'Art Nouveau has taken on the task of revivifying our interiors by giving all the diverse elements that go to make up furnishings or decoration a modern character.' He explained that 'L'Art Nouveau has just been specially reorganised with the decoration of country and seaside homes in mind [fig. 261].'[2] A collection reproduced in 1898 appears in the *Album de références*.[3] This is the dining room with half panelling and ash furniture made for a villa in Deauville. It is not easy to attribute the general forms of the Henri II-style table and sideboard to one of the designers known to have worked for Bing, but the sideboard doors are decorated with circular arc motifs very similar to the ornamentation on the bedroom furniture designed at the same period by the architect Louis Bonnier for the Flé house, which was situated by the sea.[4] This intention to sell complete interiors was brilliantly displayed in the Art Nouveau pavilion at the 1900 World's Fair.[5] The rooms presented by Bing's three designers showed a concern for unity and harmony that goes a long way towards explaining the enthusiasm of both public and critics. However, Gaillard was the only one to use wood panelling in the dining room; the other rooms were decorated with textile wall-coverings. For the small drawing room created in 1901 in the rue de Provence (fig. 259) to house the giltwood furniture from the 1900 Fair, de Feure designed wainscoting with panels in addition to pilasters and capitals, as well as a ceiling with a central recess, which had painted decorations on the tympana, the top of the recess and parts of the cornice in soft colours that accentuated the refinement of the décor. G.M. Jacques recognised in de Feure 'an astonishing talent for relief and combinations of volume',[6] qualities that are confirmed by the many designs for panelling published on the occasion of the

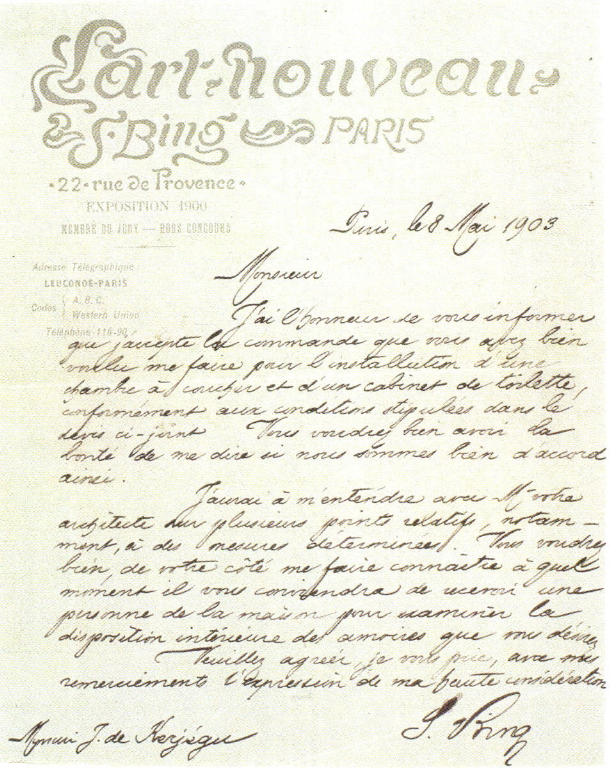

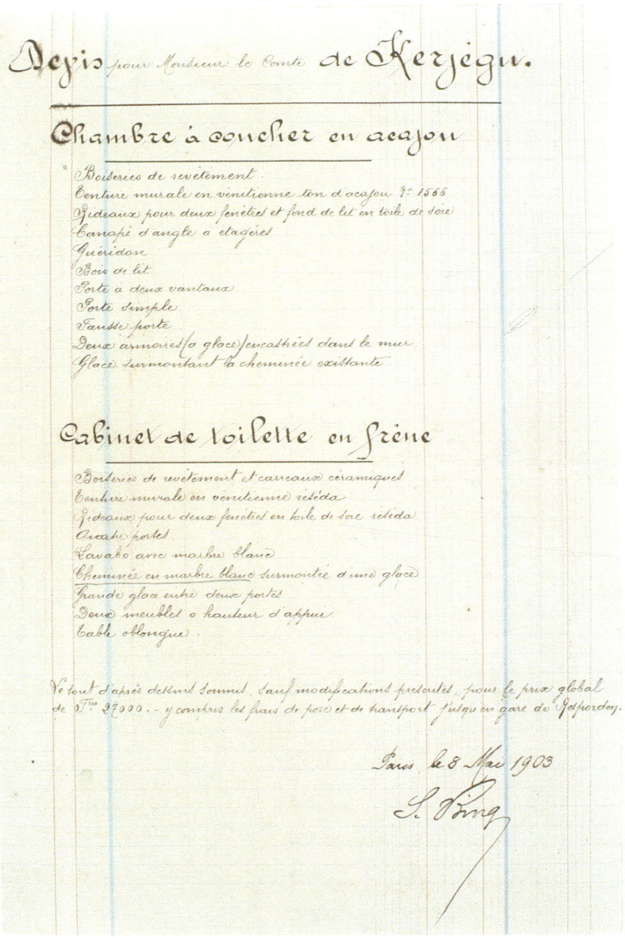

262
Letter from Siegfried Bing to James de Kerjégu, 1903
Archives départementales du Finistère

263
Estimate from Siegfried Bing to James de Kerjégu, 1903
Archives départementales du Finistère

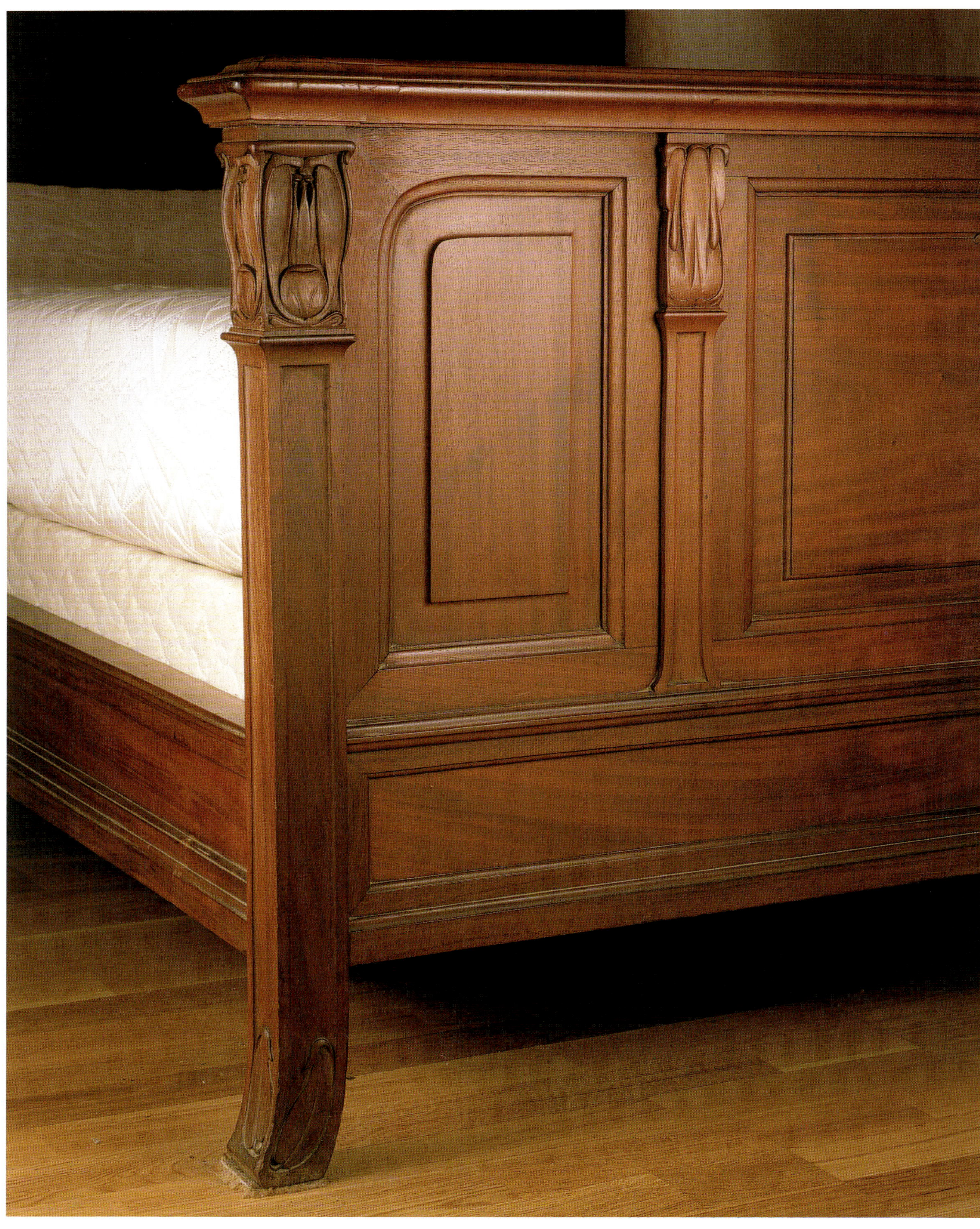

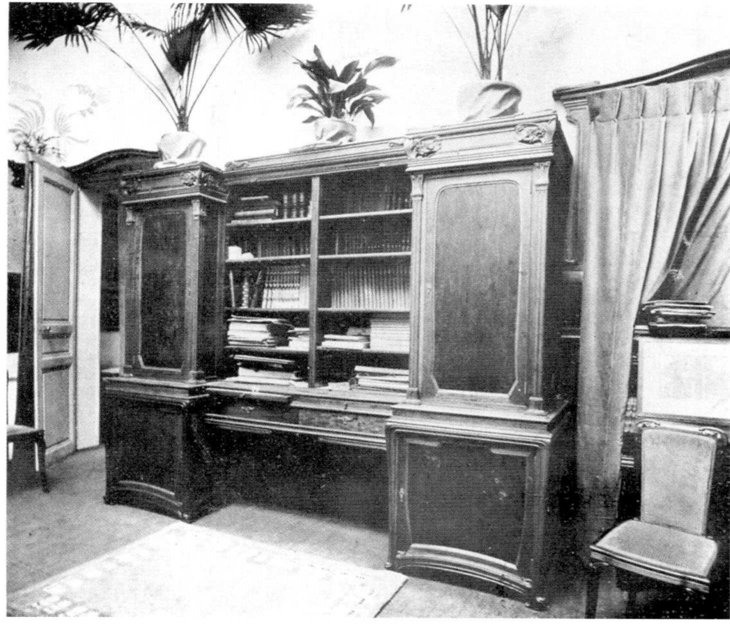

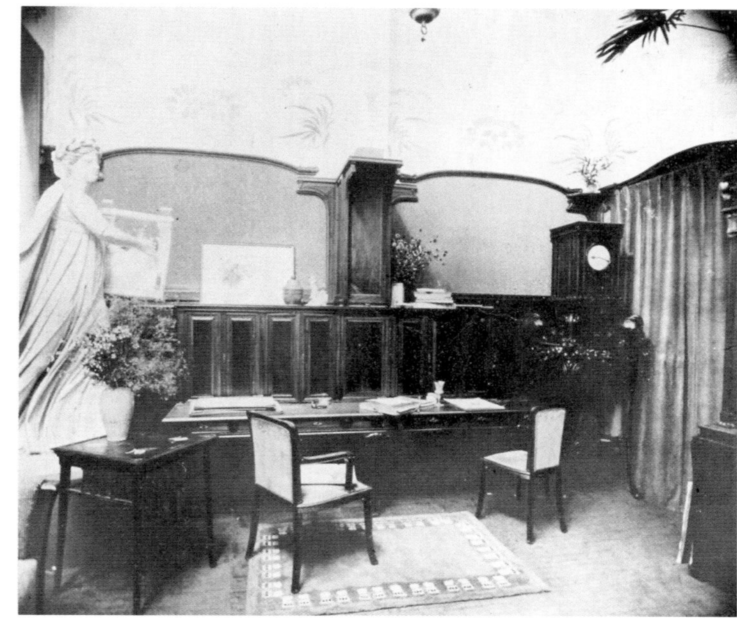

< 264
Georges de Feure for L'Art Nouveau, Bedframe in James de Kerjégu's bedroom at the Château de Trévarez, 1903

265
Georges de Feure's studio, from O. Gerdeil, 'An artist's studio', *L'Art Décoratif*, January 1902

266
Georges de Feure's studio, from O. Gerdeil, 'An artist's studio', *L'Art Décoratif*, January 1902

retrospective exhibition of his work, which Bing mounted in his gallery in 1903. De Feure then became Siegfried Bing's principal collaborator, and his creations are the final expression of the ideas of his patron.[7]

A CHÂTEAU WITH ART NOUVEAU ROOMS

As a result of the media preoccupation with the World's Fair, and thanks to the creations of Georges de Feure, it seemed that fortune was at last smiling on Bing. Marcel Morot, a close collaborator, noted that 'for the three years following the Fair the firm was kept busy fulfilling large orders.'[8] These almost certainly included the decoration of three rooms carried out for James de Kerjégu[9] in 1903 at the Château de Trévarez, near Quimper (fig. 260).[10] First a diplomat, then a politician, James de Kerjégu decided around 1892 to restore the old manor house and build a prestigious residence nearby. He entrusted the construction work – eventually finished in 1906, two years before the owner's death – to the architects Hippolyte and Walter-André Destailleurs.

The château, a pastiche of Renaissance architecture, is built of brick faced with Kersanton stone. Standing on top of an isolated hill, it dominates the Aulne valley. The main body of the building was divided into three parts. The south-west wing was reserved for private apartments, with the owner's apartments and the two rooms decorated by L'Art Nouveau occupying the ground floor. The central building was used for receiving and lodging the many guests, while the west wing was intended for official receptions. In addition to the richness of its decoration, the château had every modern convenience available at the time, including two lifts, a goods lift, a power plant and an extensive network of pipes enabling water to be fed to the many bathrooms as well as the park.[11]

In May 1903, the year of the de Feure exhibition, James de Kerjégu, who owned a large private house in the rue de Chaillot in Paris, commissioned Bing to install a bedroom and a small dressing room. The estimate (figs. 262, 263),[12] in the name of 'Monsieur le Comte de Kerjégu', describes a mahogany bedroom with wood panelling, a double door, a single door, a false door, wall-coverings of mahogany-coloured silk, curtains for two windows and a bed head panel on the wall in silk. The bedroom furniture comprised a corner sofa with shelves, a round table, a bed, two mirror-fronted wardrobes built into the wall and a mirror above the existing fireplace. In July, additional furniture was added, in the form of a table, a visible wood armchair, an upholstered armchair and two upright chairs. The panelling and part of the furniture have recently been rediscovered. The panelling and the corner sofa had been stored in the cellars of the château, after being dismantled to protect them from an attack of dry rot.[13] The bed and the bedside table were in the house of a private individual, who had acquired them at a public sale organised at the château in 1970. The only surviving photographs of the panelling *in situ* show it in an already damaged state, but they still give us a good understanding of how the different elements were arranged.[14]

James de Kerjégu's bedroom, situated on the ground floor in the east wing of the château, adjoining his study and dressing room, has a very high ceiling. The panelling

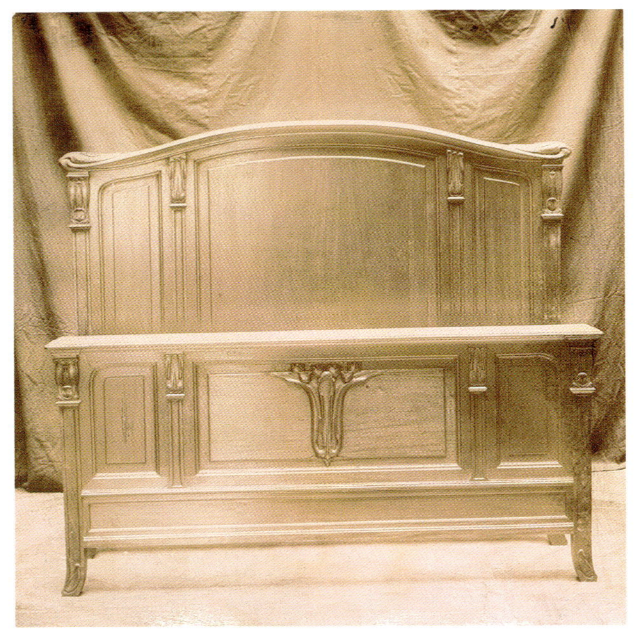

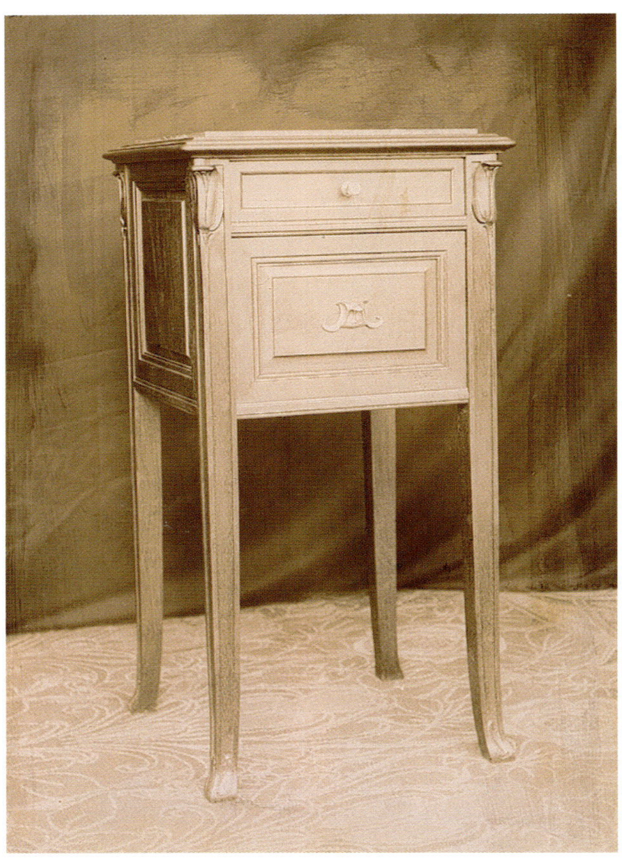

produced by L'Art Nouveau reaches half way up the wall; the upper part of the walls is covered in mahogany-coloured Venetian silk, and the ceiling arch is painted in the same colour. The panelling is in three tiers, with square panels at the bottom, followed by upright rectangles, and rectangles set widthways at the top (fig. 272). The panels surrounding the bed and the two semi-fitted, mirror-fronted wardrobes are surmounted by a rounded pediment decorated with ornamental carving. This pedimented wainscoting is flanked by pilasters, which have capitals carved with flowers with very simplified stamens. The central sections of the pediments of the wardrobes and the bed head (figs. 264, 267) are ornamented with bunches of tulips, composed of six flowers surrounded by broad leaves. Other leaf motifs can be found on the pediment of the bed panel, which has scrolls of foliage at the corners.

The quality of the carving and the structure of the panelling in Trévarez are undeniably very similar to those de Feure created for his own studio. Gerdeil described the panelling of the studio in an article published in 1902: 'Here, the simple shapes of the furniture are complemented by the harmonious way the walls are divided up to combine with them. In short, the wainscoting, doorframes, fireplace [...] complement the furniture, forming a co-ordinated ensemble. The room has a very lofty ceiling, like all artists' studios. It was decided that the line of the upper edge of the fixed panelling should be at the same height as the tops of the large items of furniture, and the monotony resulting from the elimination of the usual irregularities caused by furniture jutting up above the wainscoting was avoided by making this line curve in a series of very elongated arches [figs. 265, 266].'[15] At Trévarez, the features corresponding to the arcading on the panels are the pediments of the wardrobes and the bed head, which add interest to the line of the top of the panelling. The fitted wardrobes and the corner sofa with shelves represent very innovative ideas in the field of interior design.

A study of the carved elements on the bedside table and the bed, photographs of which are to be found in the *Album de références* (nos. 36/513 and 514, figs. 267, 268), confirms the attribution of the ensemble to de Feure, as does the identification of the metalwork on the bedside table, which is the same as that found on models by Georges de Feure housed in the Victoria and Albert Museum in London.

The ash-wood dressing room has panelling and ceramic tiles (fig. 269); the wall space was once covered in Venetian silk fabric in reseda, the same colour as the

267
Georges de Feure,
'Bed costing 750 francs',
Album de références,
36/513
Bibliothèque des Arts décoratifs, Paris

268
Georges de Feure,
'Bedside table',
Album de références,
36/514
Bibliothèque des Arts décoratifs, Paris

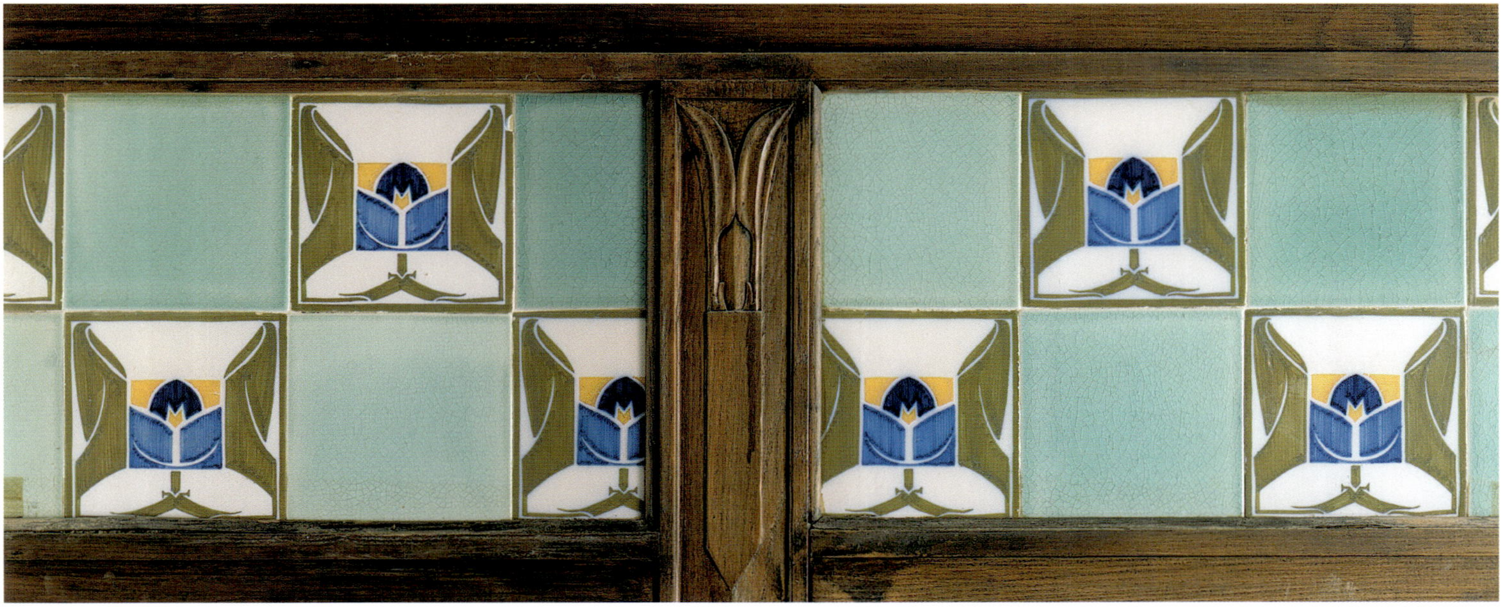

269
Anonymous for L'Art Nouveau, Ceramic tiles from the dressing room, Château de Trévarez, 1903

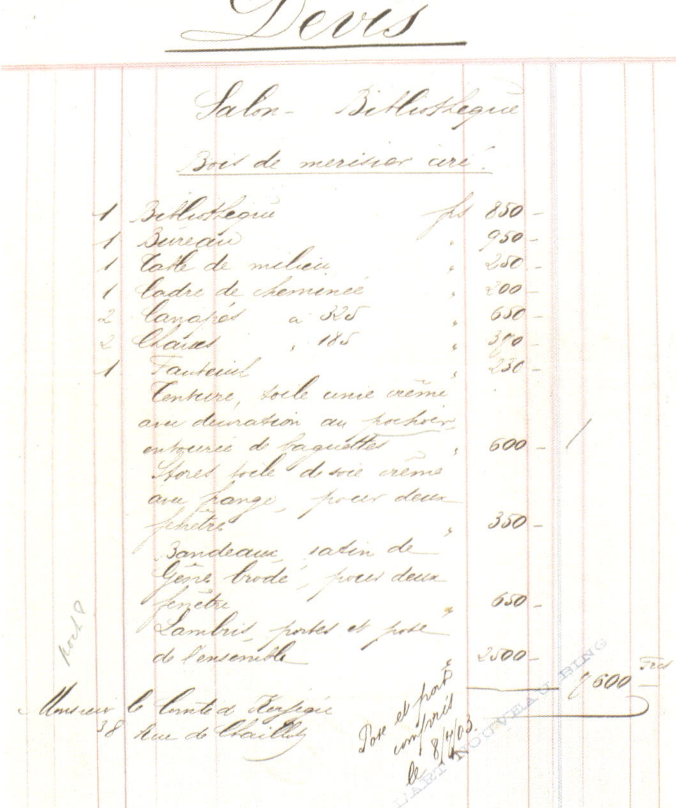

Devis

Salon – Bibliothèque

Bois de merisier ciré

1	Bibliothèque	frs	850 –
1	Bureau	"	950 –
1	Table de milieu	"	250 –
1	Cadre de cheminée	"	200 –
2	Canapés à 325	"	650 –
2	Chaises " 185	"	370 –
1	Fauteuil	"	230 –
	Tenture, toile unie crème avec décoration au pochoir entourée de baguettes	"	600 –
	Stores toile de soie crème avec frange, pour deux fenêtres	"	350 –
	Bandeaux satin de Gênes brodé, pour deux fenêtres	"	650 –
	Lambris, portes et pose de l'ensemble	"	2500 –
			7600 Frs

Monsieur le Comte de Kerjégu
38 Rue de Chaillot

Pose et port compris le 8/4/03

L'ART NOUVEAU BING

270
Quotation from Siegfried Bing for James de Kerjégu's sitting room/library, 1903
Archives départementales du Finistère

>> **271**
Study at the Château de Trévarez, from Luc, 'Le château de Trévarez', *Le Figaro*, 15 October 1903

>> **272**
Bedroom at the Château de Trévarez, from Luc, 'Le château de Trévarez', *Le Figaro*, 15 October 1903

>> **273**
Attributed to Georges de Feure, Drawing of interior décor, *Album de références*, 35/495
Bibliothèque des Arts décoratifs, Paris

>> **274**
Drawing room at the Château de Trévarez, from Luc, 'Le Château de Trévarez', *Le Figaro*, 15 October 1903

silk curtains intended for the two windows. The four ash doors supplied by Bing were complemented by a white marble washbasin, a white marble fireplace – still in place – surmounted by a mirror, with another large mirror between two of the doors. The furniture included two cupboards of medium height and an oblong table. The panelling preserved *in situ* can also be attributed to de Feure, whereas it has not been possible to identify the source of the tiles and the style of the cupboards.

The supplementary order for the bedroom in July 1903 was accompanied by the estimate for a new order for a drawing room cum library in polished cherry-wood (fig. 270).[16] The estimate describes the elements included in the ensemble, with wainscoting and doors supplied and fitted, furniture comprising a bookcase, a desk, a centre table, two sofas, two chairs, an armchair and a mantelpiece. The textiles section describes a plain cream rounded by wooden beading, fringed cream silk blinds and heavy embroidered satin pelmets for two windows. No trace of this small drawing room remains at the Château de Trévarez. However, we know how it looked from a photograph published in *Le Figaro* in 1903 (fig. 274):[17] a small room with cut-off corners with at least two windows and a door – two doors, in fact – and very elegantly furnished. In his private apartments on the ground floor, James de Kerjégu already had a study, decorated by the English firm of Waring and Gillow, a photograph of which was published in *Le Figaro* in 1903 (fig. 271). In the margin of the invoice summarising the order,[18] next to the small cherry-wood drawing room, is the handwritten note 'mademoiselle'. This must therefore have been a room created for James's daughter,

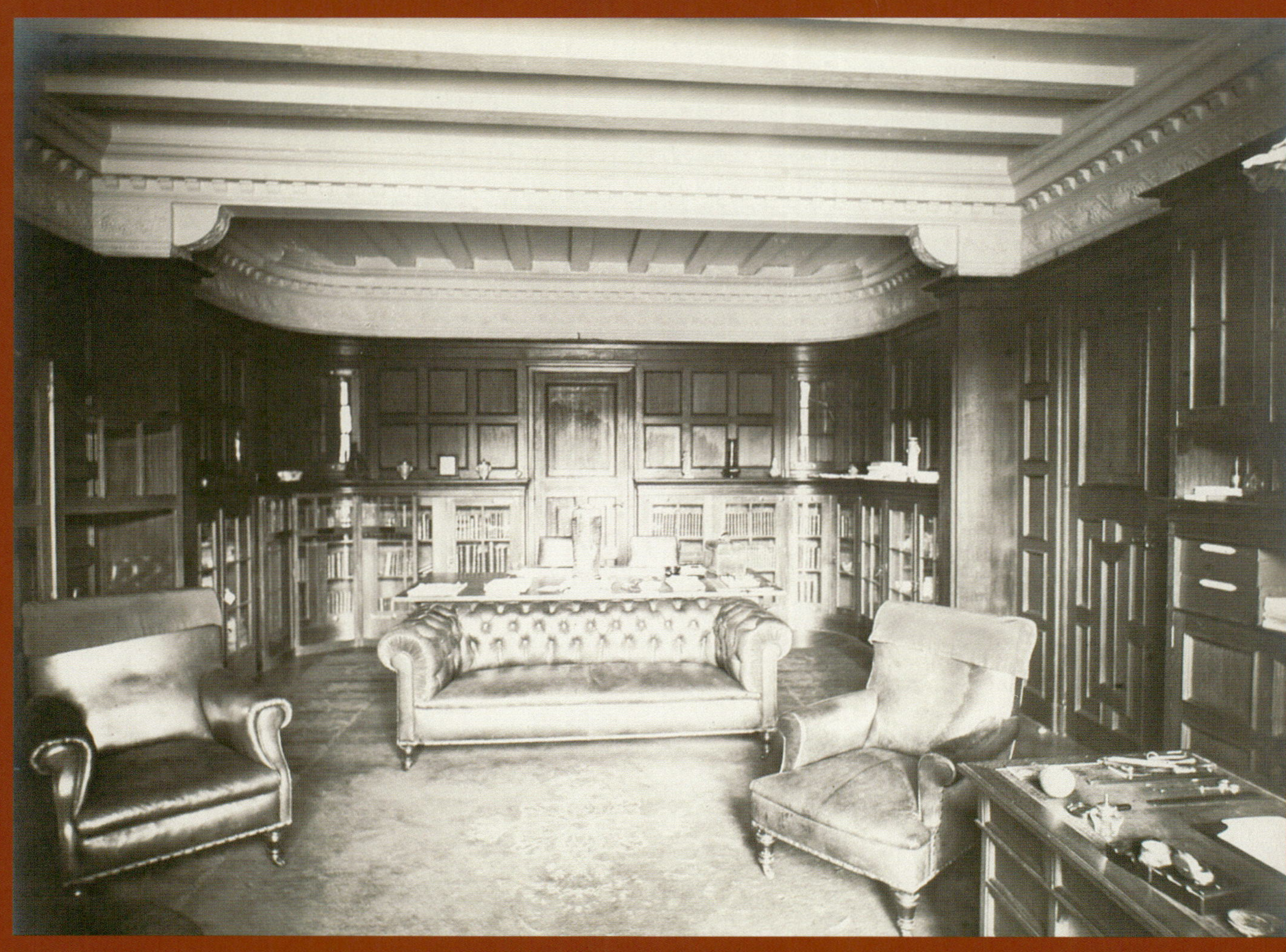

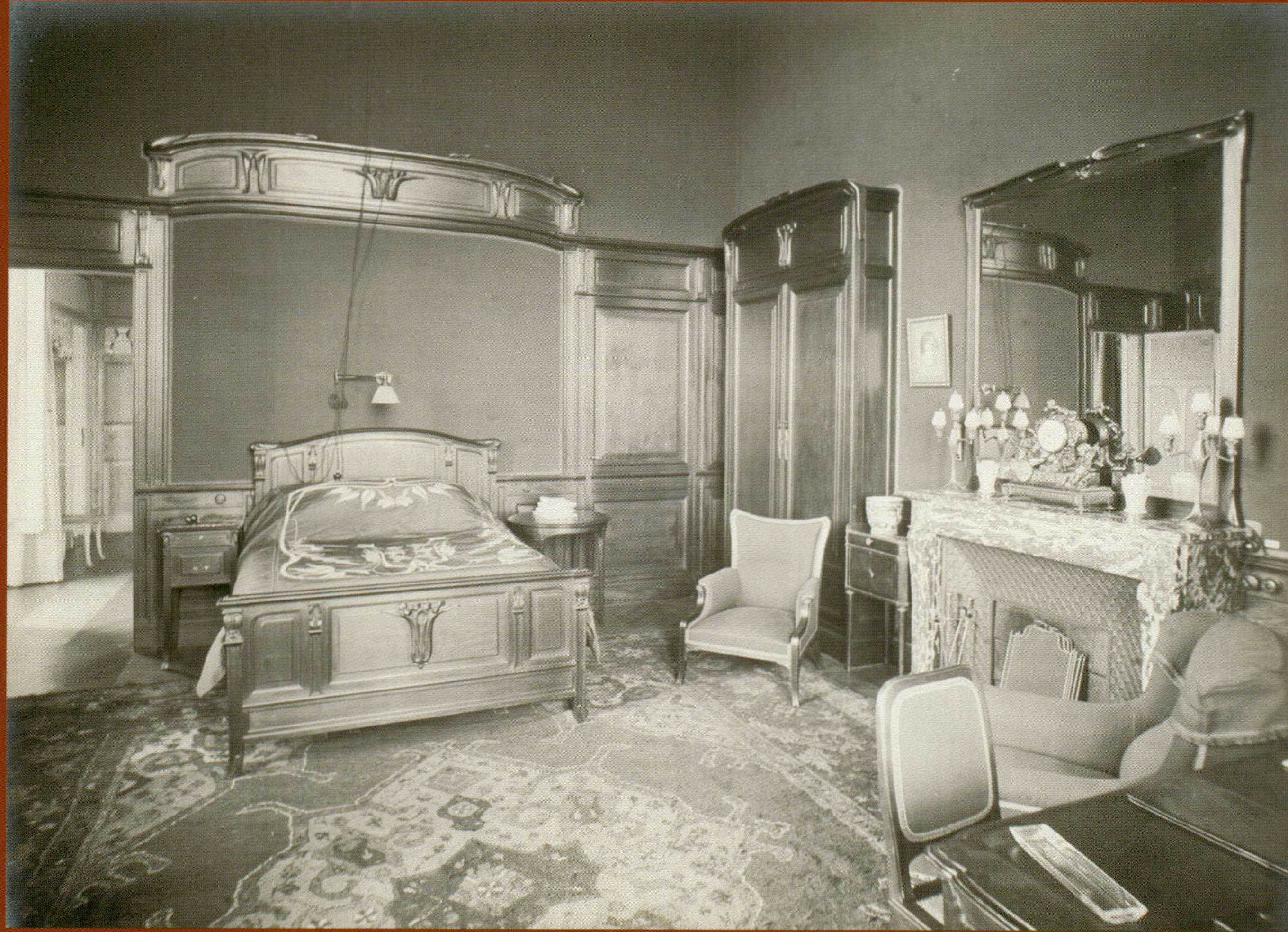

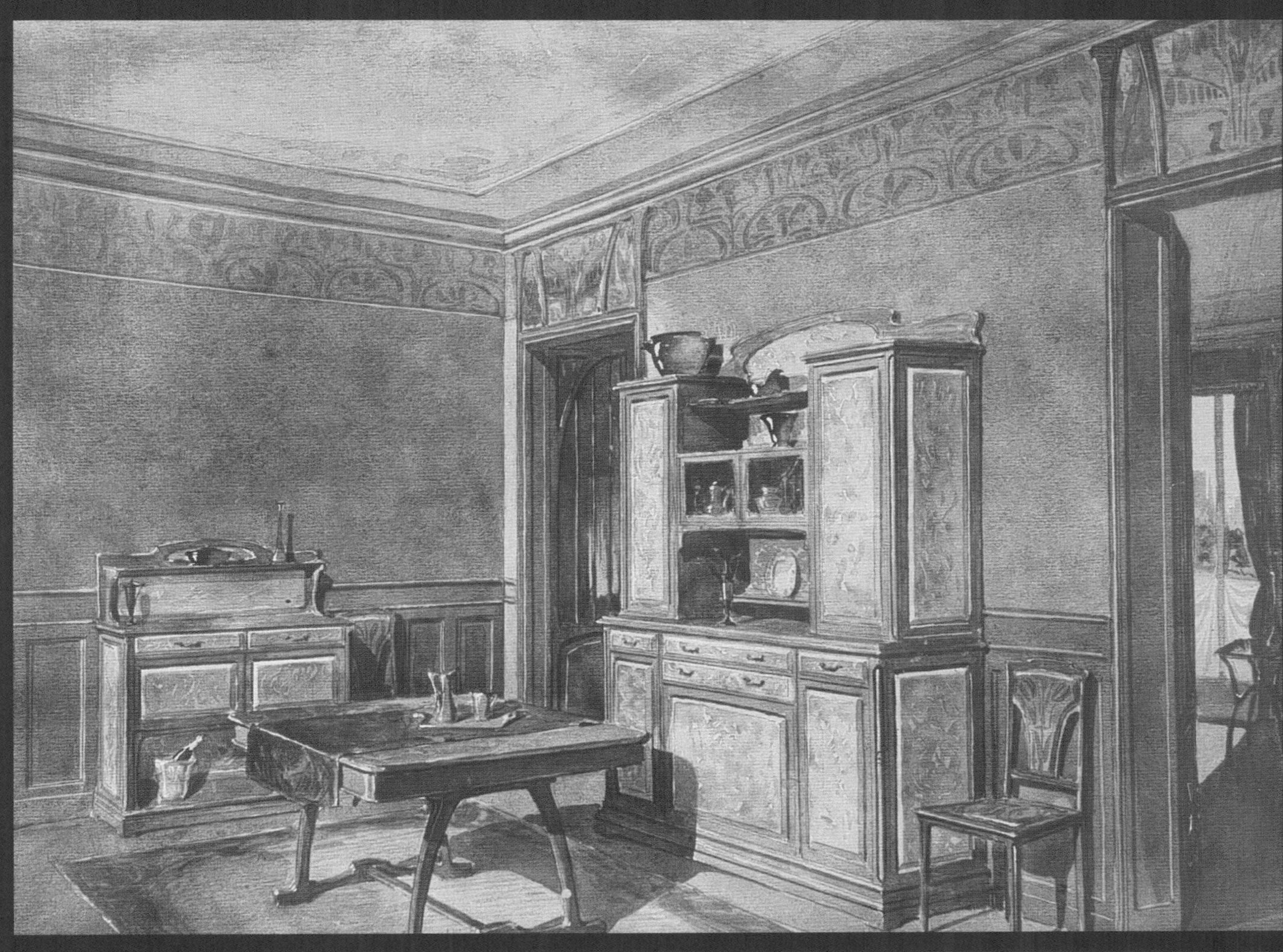

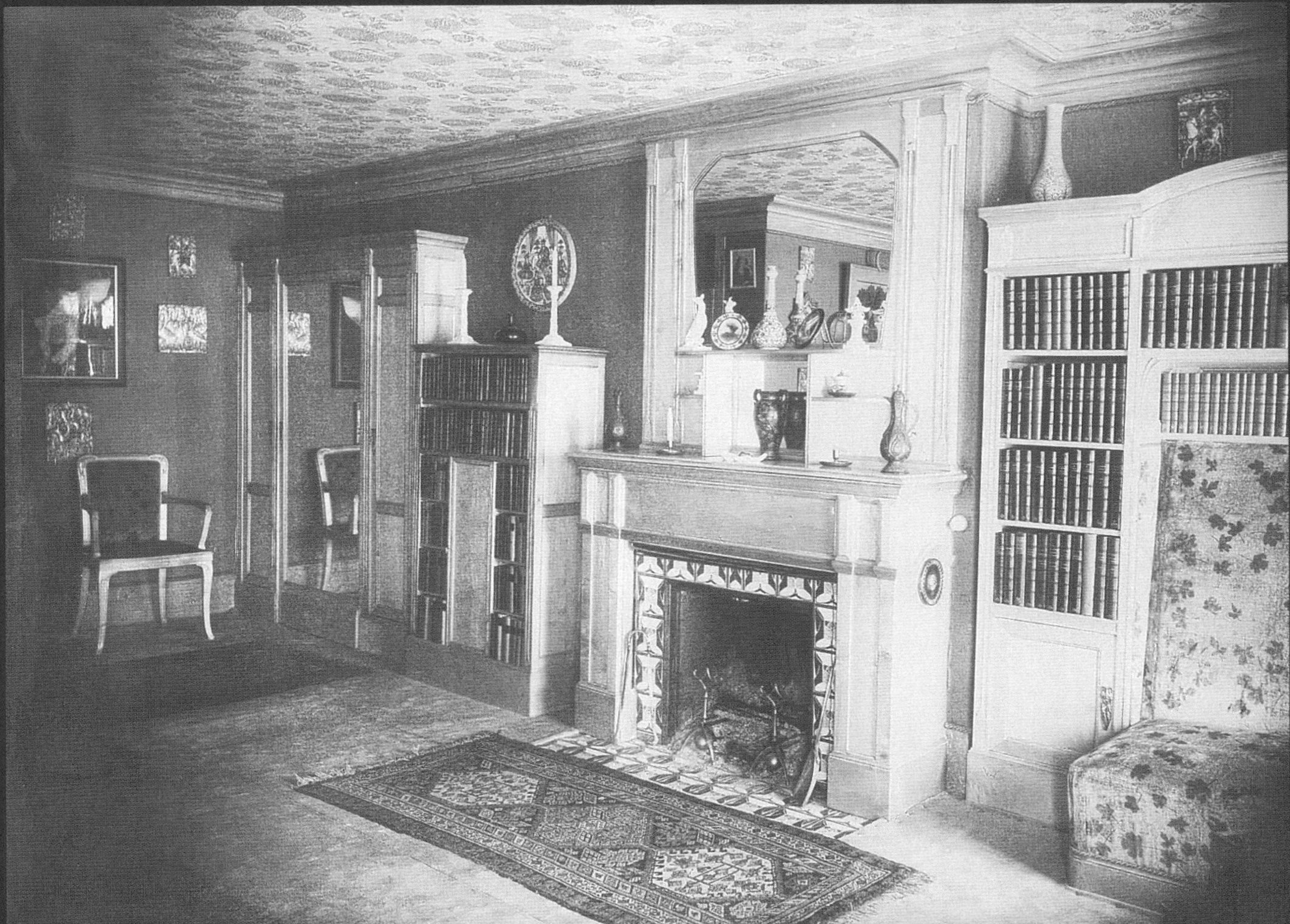

Françoise de Kerjégu, who was eighteen at the time and whose apartments, situated on the first floor above those of her father, included a very small drawing room in the south-east tower. It has been possible to identify several pieces of furniture from this drawing room in shades of cream, yellow and nasturtium, notably the armchair and the upright chair, in the *Album de références* (fig. 276), while the bookcase and the desk are reminiscent of some of the furniture designs preserved in the Musée des Arts décoratifs (fig. 275).[19]

Although two of these significant orders have been partly preserved, it appears that other, smaller, collections may also have been ordered from L'Art Nouveau. In fact, a number of pieces of furniture discovered in the cellars can be related to another of Bing's designers, Eugène Gaillard, in particular a suite of bedroom furniture, of which the bed frame, part of a wardrobe – very badly damaged – and a bedside table in very good condition have survived.[20] Two other items in the L'Art Nouveau style – one consisting of the top section of a wardrobe and a bed head, the other a rounded bookcase and a frame – may have been made for guest rooms, possibly by the Bing gallery. The Trévarez ensembles were chosen from designs that do not appear in the *Album de références*. Only one or two individually reproduced pieces are identifiable. Few photographs of complete ensembles appear in this book,[21] which seems to have been no more than a catalogue of models of furniture, which customers, or Bing himself, would choose from when putting collections together. The panelling and interior decorations are known from the drawings that are scattered among several museums – when they have not been lost.

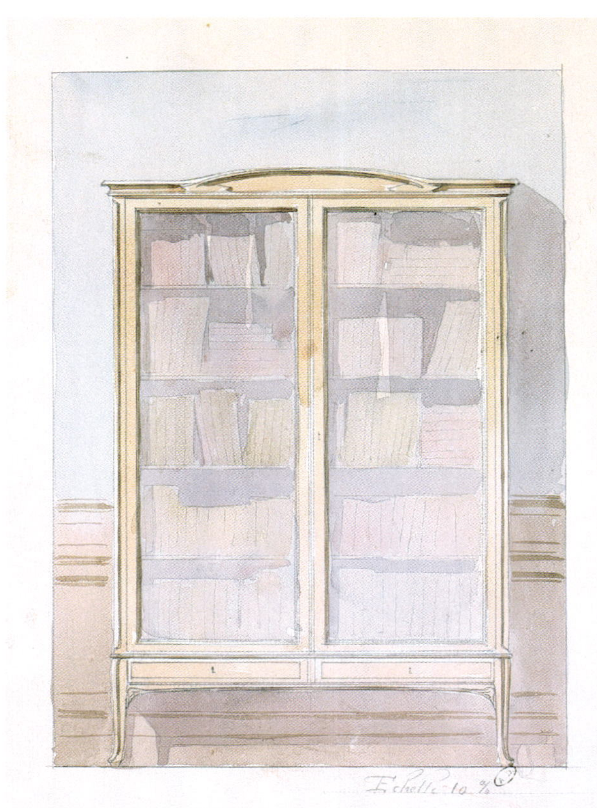

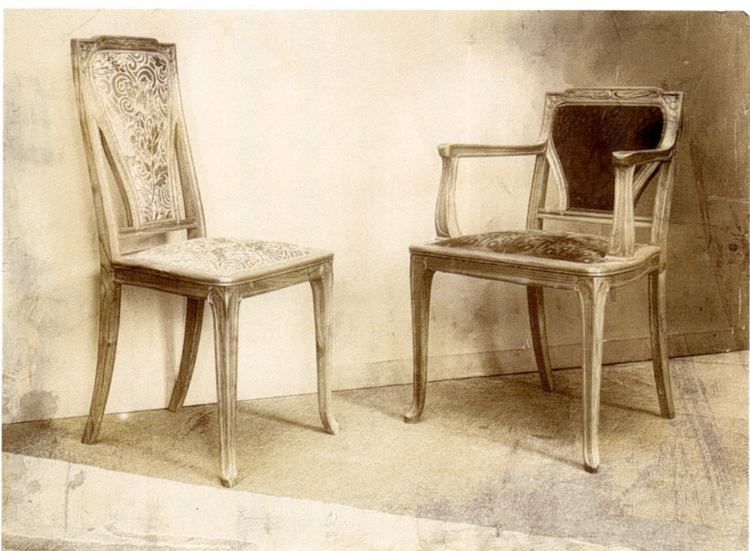

275
Georges de Feure, Drawing of a bookcase
Musée des Arts décoratifs, Paris

276
Models of chair and armchair for the sitting room/library, *Album de références*, 37/521 and 522
Bibliothèque des Arts décoratifs, Paris

STRIVING TOWARDS THE FUTURE WITHOUT NEGLECTING THE PAST

The verdict of the *Figaro* journalist on the Trévarez collection provides a good illustration of Bing's return to favour with the public and French art lovers after the success of the 1900 World's Fair: 'The three rooms [...] are not only miracles of decorative art, they also provide striking examples proving that Bing is not the revolutionary he has often been accused of being and that Art Nouveau does not claim to be a revolution, but rather a very fertile development. Far from repudiating the past, it is related to it and flows naturally from it, as it has its starting point in the great eighteenth-century French tradition, particularly the Louis xv style.'[22] After the 1900 Fair, and with the aid of De Feure, Bing succeeded in giving his gallery's creations a real unity, in the tradition of French taste, having come a long way from the accusations of confusion and internationalism of the early years. The complete room decorations carried out for Trévarez show Bing beginning to attract a new clientele from a rich, refined milieu, members of the country's political and cultural elite. The importance of the Trévarez order and the writings of Marcel Morot make us inclined to question Bing's supposed financial difficulties, particularly as the same M. Morot explains Bing's cessation of business activities in 1904 as being due to illness and to Marcel Bing's lack of interest in continuing his father's work in this area.[23] It appears that with the Art Nouveau pavilion at the 1900 World's Fair Bing finally achieved the commercial success he had been waiting for since December 1895.

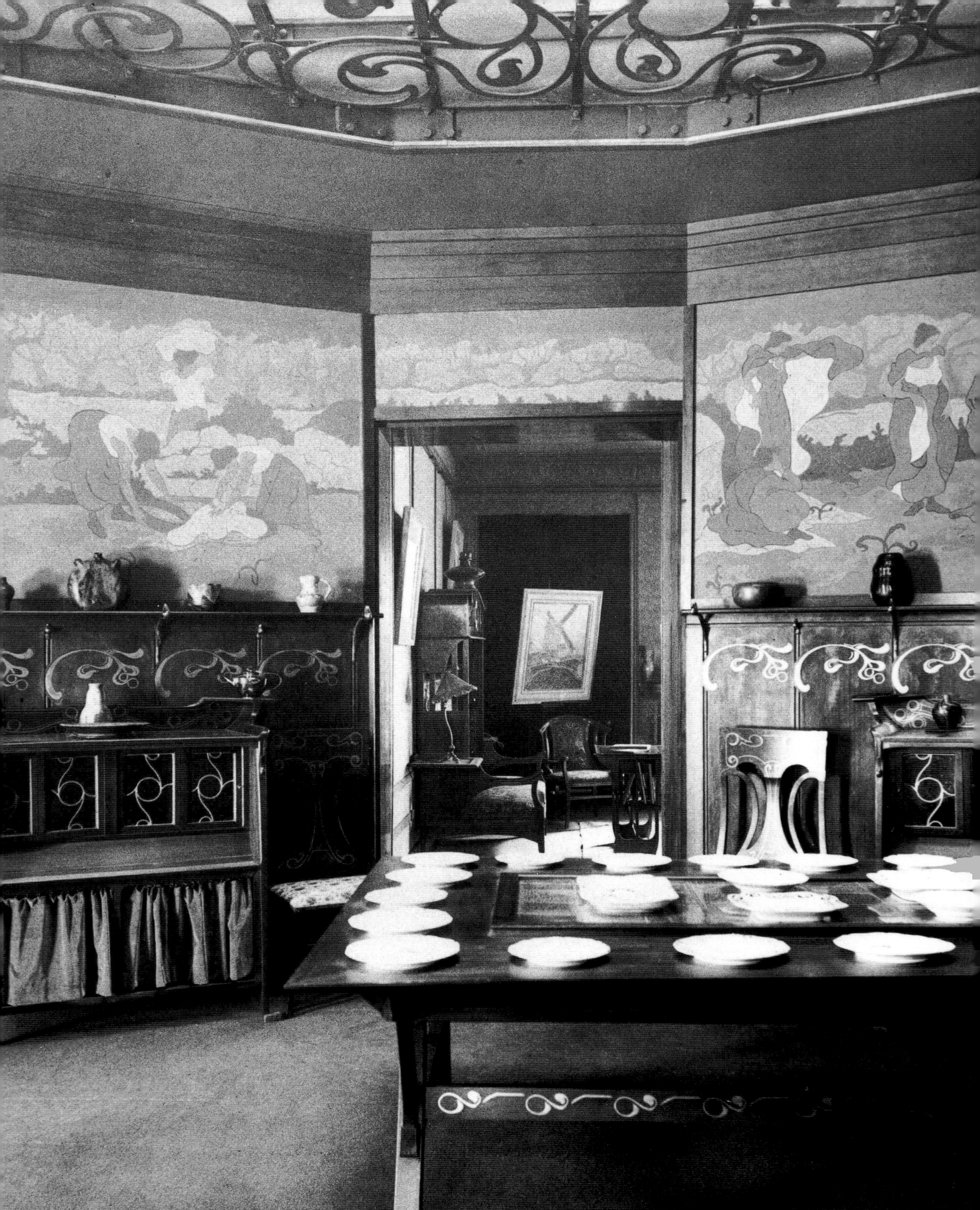

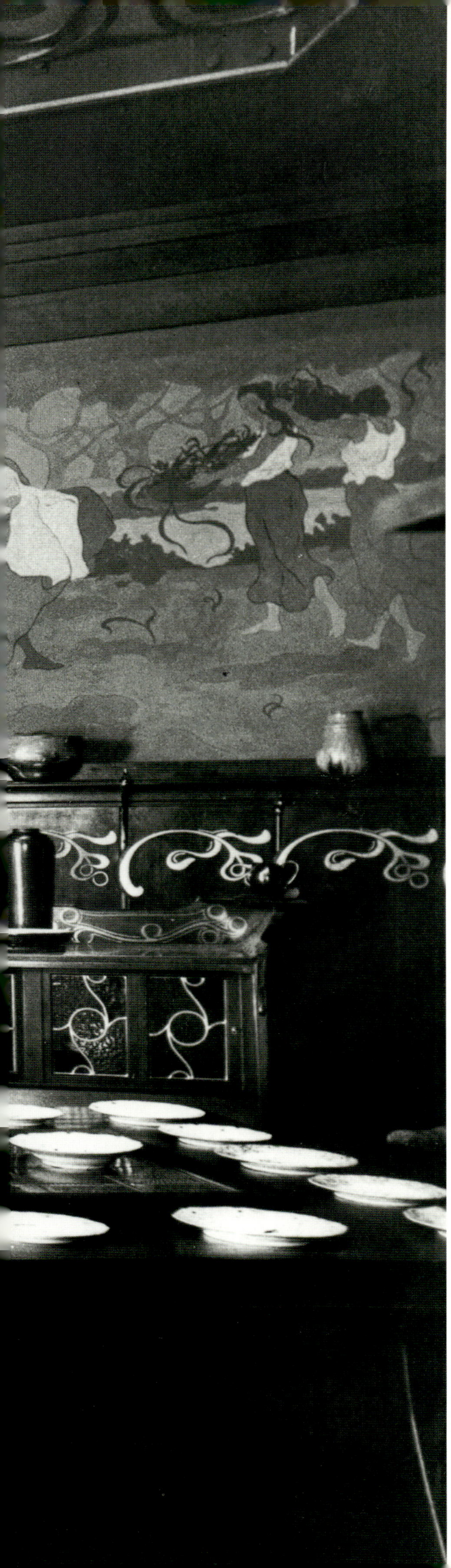

BING'S INFLUENCE AND PLACE IN THE ART OF HIS TIME

RÜDIGER JOPPIEN

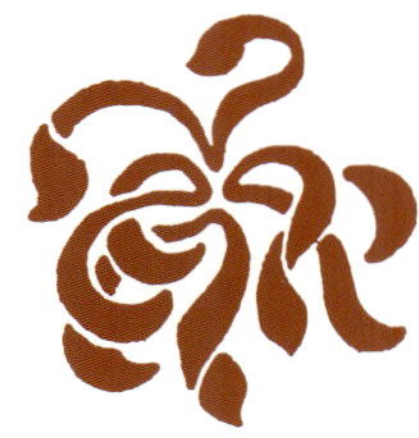

The words Max Osborn used to describe Julius Meier-Graefe's Paris gallery 'La Maison Moderne' could have been applied equally well to Siegfried Bing's 'L'Art Nouveau' art gallery, founded four years earlier. Osborn wrote: 'One of the more recent phenomena typical of the present age, in which art and craft have become reunited after all too long a separation, is the modern bazaar of arts and crafts, an unusual combination resulting in a hybrid establishment, somewhere between an art dealer's and an emporium stocking luxury items as well as consumer goods of a practical nature, owned and run by people who usually represent a peculiar blend of connoisseur, artist, art critic, patron and businessman in the most refined sense of the word.'[1]

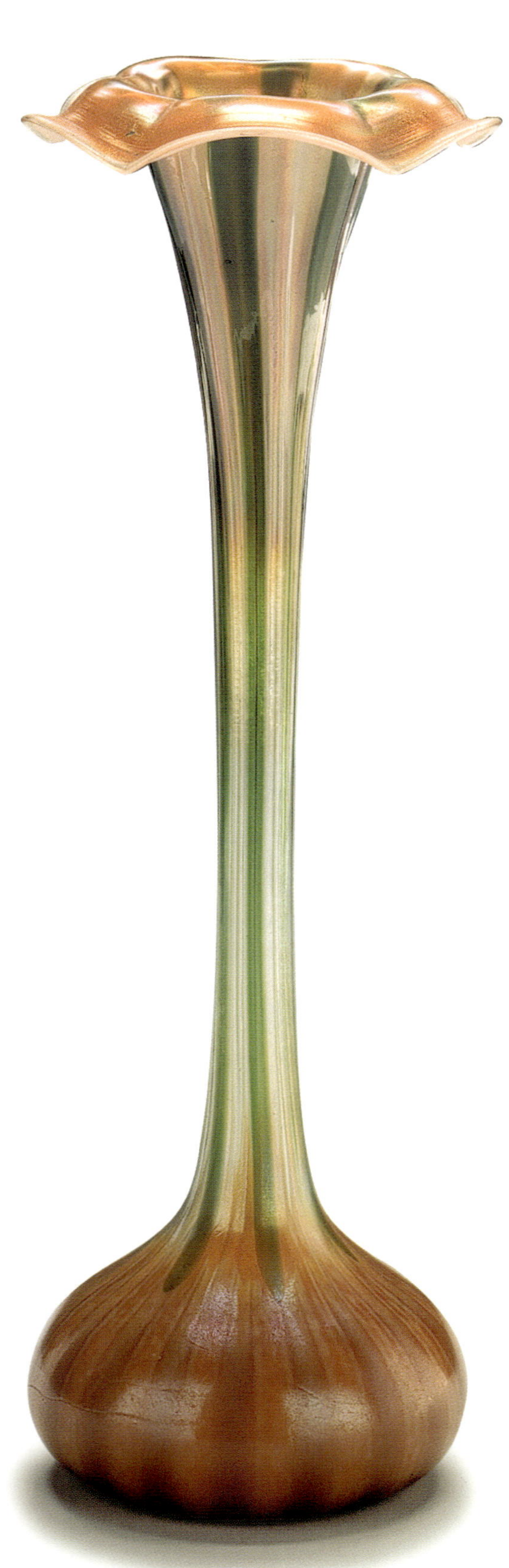

BETWEEN GALLERY AND WAREHOUSE

Osborn's words describe the kind of gallery that had begun to spring up towards the end of the nineteenth century, reaching its zenith with Bing's establishment.[2] He might also have added that this kind of gallery was an appropriate and logical product of the emergent new genre of art. The fact that he was actually describing Meier-Graefe rather than Bing in no way alters the relevance of the view expressed by Osborn; Bing and Meier-Graefe were colleagues, pursuing the same ideals at the same time. In November 1895, after burying all hope for an art gallery of his own, Meier-Graefe joined Bing's establishment, where he spent six months as an art consultant. Many of the displays and exhibitions held there were at his instigation.[3] Even after leaving the gallery, he continued to be warmly enthusiastic, in words both erudite and enlightening, on the subject of Bing and his gallery, until 1899, when he was finally able to open a gallery of his own at 82, rue des Petits-Champs.[4]

Bing enjoyed the challenge of fresh projects. A visit to the U.S.A. in the spring of 1894 was to signal a turning-point in his life: it was there, while on a collecting trip, that he made the acquaintance of Louis Comfort Tiffany and his work. He visited the latter's workshops, where all consumer and luxury items for household use were centrally produced, regarding them as a perfect example of progressive production methods. Bing was so taken with Tiffany's glass manufacture that, on his return to Paris, he invited several young artists of the 'Nabis' group to produce designs for stained-glass windows, which he then sent to New York to be manufactured; the finished stained-glass windows were eventually exhibited at the Salon de la Societé Nationale des Beaux-Arts at Paris in 1895. Bing could rightly claim to have pioneered the trans-Atlantic partnership between designers and manufacturers. Bing commissioned this same group of artists, which included Pierre Bonnard, Maurice Denis, Paul-Elie Ranson, Edouard Vuillard and others, to design items of furniture, textiles, dinner services, book bindings etc. for his planned L'Art Nouveau gallery. This was significant, since it was a complete departure from the norm for an art dealer himself to commission work in this way, and it gained Bing the reputation of being a 'promoter'.

During the 1890s, the notion of workshops and the idea of channelling new kinds of design in a specific stylistic direction were still in the air; they had, to some degree, been tried by William Morris, A.H. Mackmurdo (Century Guild, 1882), C.R. Ashbee (Guild of Handicraft, 1888) and, of course, Louis C. Tiffany. All these,

<< 277
Dining room by Henry Van de Velde and decorative panels by Paul-Elie Ranson in Bing's gallery, 1895 (detail of fig. 114)

278
Louis Comfort Tiffany, Onion flower vase, c. 1899–1900
Museum für Kunst und Gewerbe, Hamburg

> 279
Liberty & Co., Fabric, abstract plant design, by Silver Studio, c. 1896
Nordenfjeldske Kunstindustrimuseum, Trondheim

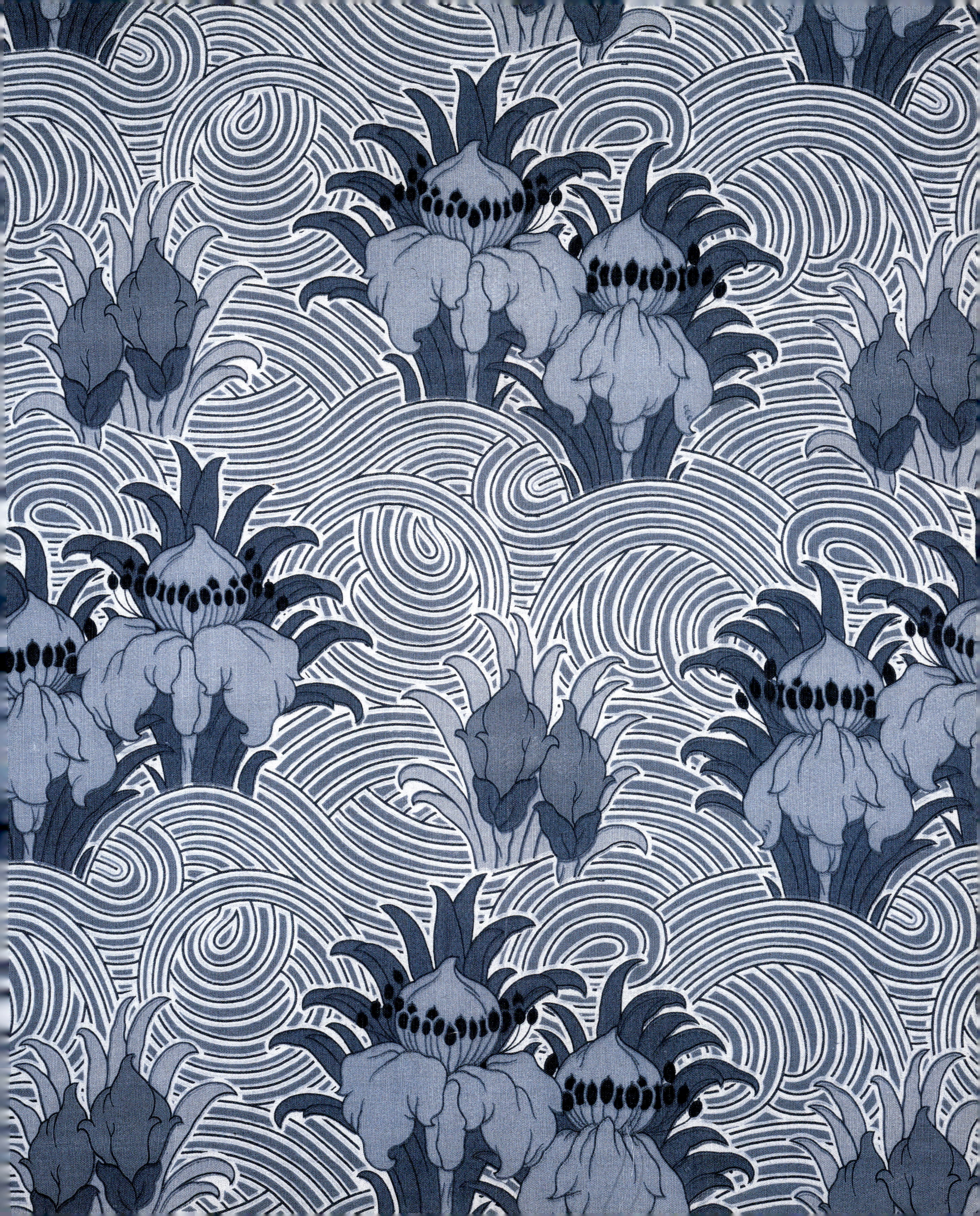

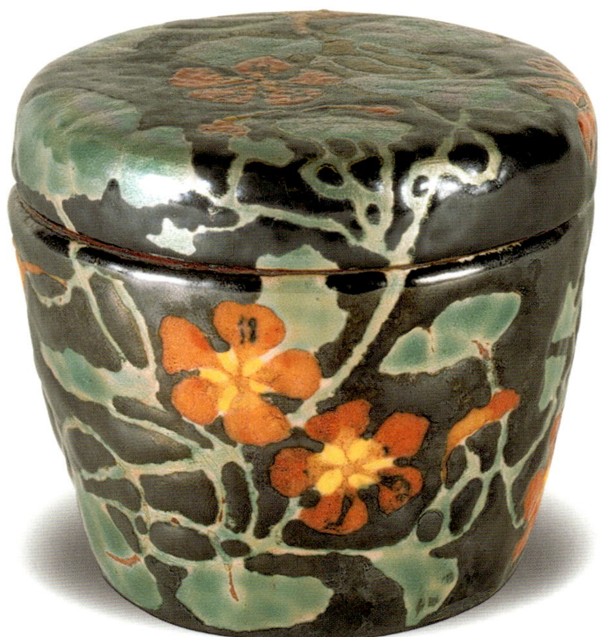

however, were creative artists in their own right, who were intent on reforming the existing world of interior design by their own efforts and using their own resources. Bing was the first 'outsider' to embrace the same goals and take the initiative of approaching individual artists with proposals for different projects. He was an entrepreneur whose priority was selling.

Bing opened his new gallery on 26 December 1895, a postponement from the original proposed opening date of 1 October. It was advertised as a permanent exhibition of international art, embracing the various categories of sculpture, painting, drawings and prints, decorative arts, furniture and items of practical use *(objets utiles)*,[5] covering the same categories as the official Salon exhibitions, but on a more permanent basis. Furthermore, the objects were not separated into categories of works, but grouped together in settings of almost domestic intimacy. Bing gathered together all the avant-garde strands of European reformist art, concentrating them in one place, like rays of light in a burning-glass; the overriding emphasis was on the concept of newness.

The opening exhibition was greeted with a mixed reaction on the part of the public and art critics alike. People were irritated by the conglomeration and eclectic mix of items on display and felt that the style of the furniture did not reflect French taste. The art critic Otto Feld believed that the fault lay in the fact that too many artists were copying Japanese works of art without understanding them. He ascribed Bing's involvement with the *art nouveau* movement to a shortage of high-quality Japanese artefacts.[6] This view was shared by others and could not be entirely dismissed. Nevertheless, Bing's determination, after decades of dealing in Japanese antiquities, to turn his attention for the first time to contemporary art and find collectors and patrons to promote it, was unquestionably an admirable one.

FROM ART SUPPLY TO ART PRODUCTION

Bing drew the necessary conclusions from the French public's rejection of his exhibits and subsequently narrowed the range and improved the quality of goods on offer. In 1896, he enjoyed the energetic support in this respect of Meier-Graefe. As a businessman and dealer in Japanese decorative arts, Bing had not had much contact with contemporary art, and even in the field of applied art his knowledge must have been rather limited up until that time. Had it not been for Meier-Graefe's input, exhibitions such as those featuring international book art or Munch's paintings would probably not have come about.[7] Similarly, the range of the international fine and applied art on show in Bing's gallery was probably also achieved with outside advice. It seems likely that works by Berlin artists such as Walter Leistikow, Max Liebermann and Adolph von Menzel were exhibited at Bing's gallery at the suggestion of Meier-Graefe; as editor (since 1894) of the art magazine *Pan*, Meier-Graefe had up-to-date contacts with the world of contemporary art. Meier-Graefe was already making plans with Hermann Pächter, the Berlin gallery owner who exhibited Menzel's work, to open an art gallery of his own, so it is perfectly feasible that he gave his backing to Menzel in Paris.[8] Similarly, Justus Brinckmann, the Director of Hamburg's Museum

280
Louis Comfort Tiffany, Covered box, c. 1900
Kunstgewerbemuseum, Berlin

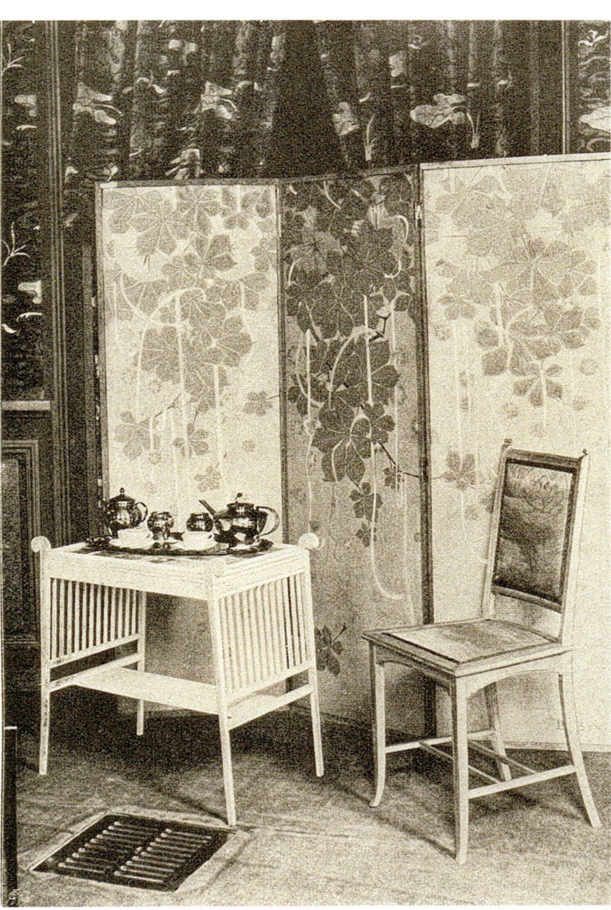

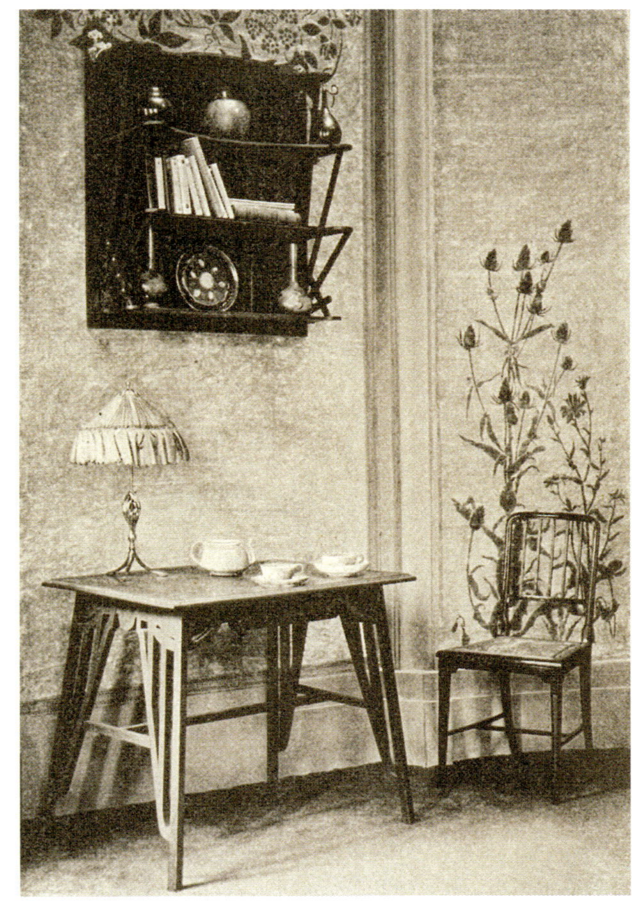

281–282
Furniture at L'Art Nouveau, from *Dekorative Kunst*, 1898, no. 9

283
Advertisement for lamps from L'Art Nouveau, from *Art et Décoration*, February 1898, supplement

für Kunst und Gewerbe, with whom Bing had been in contact for fifteen years, was also an important source of ideas. In its early days, therefore, Bing's gallery followed a loosely structured programme of art with no rigid conceptual framework; it was only during the course of the next five years that Bing was able to refine his programme and develop an individual direction of his own.

From 1895, Bing continued along his chosen path as a purveyor of furniture and consumer goods, engaging experienced designers for specific projects. These included Frank Brangwyn, Georges Lemmen, Paul-Elie Ranson, and the wife of the painter Fritz Thaulow.[9] Despite the criticism that greeted many of the objects in his interior designs, Bing continued to develop his furniture theme. Nor was he alone in this: towards the end of 1896, for example, the 'groupe des cinq' held its first exhibition in the Galerie des Artistes Modernes at 19, rue Caumartin, displaying a beautiful collection of furniture by Jean Dampt and Georges Plumet. A new style was emerging and, with it, a growing demand for professional design.[10]

In 1898, Meier-Graefe described the change of direction evident in Bing's establishment as being the natural progression from the original idea of supplying art to producing it, 'which alone enabled the gallery to survive'.[11] In its first issue, in October 1897, the journal

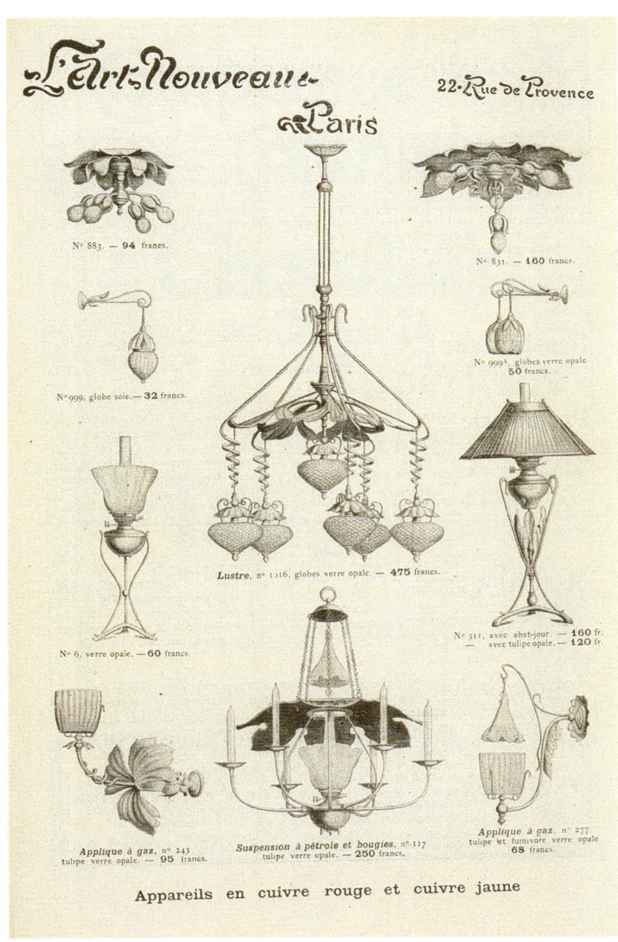

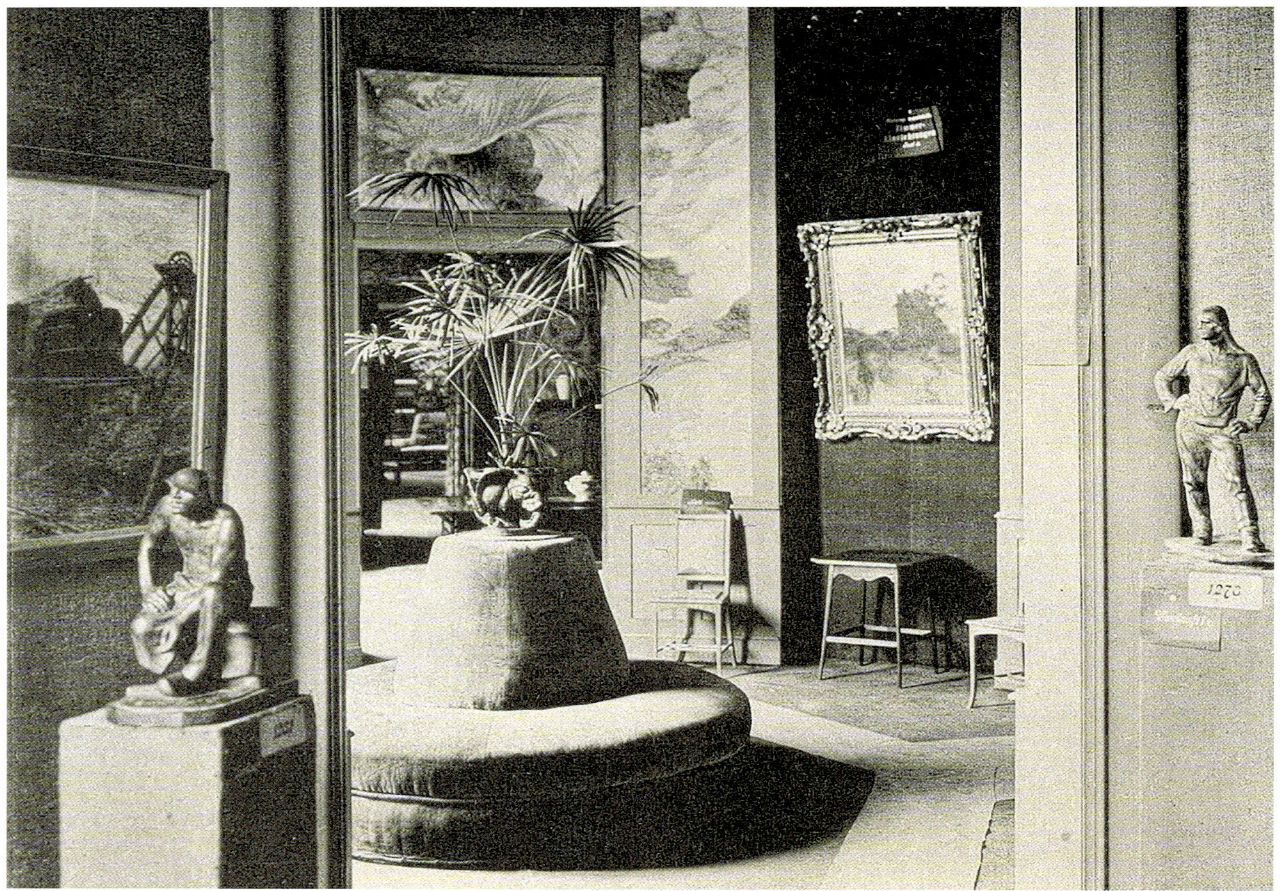

284
The International Art Exhibition, Dresden, 1897, with, left and right, works by Constantin Meunier
Kunstbibliothek, Dresden

> 285
Constantin Meunier, *Glassblower*, 1889
Musée Constantin Meunier, Brussels

Dekorative Kunst carried Bing's advertisement for 'Ameublement Moderne'; in its next issue, it reported: 'A number of rental villas around Trouville have been furnished in a simple and attractive style by L'Art Nouveau for the well-known industrialist Menier.'[12] Barely one year later, in 1898, *Art et Décoration* published a photo of a dining room which had been produced by Bing's workshops for a villa in Deauville (fig. 261).[13] The furniture is still somewhat historicist in style and was not as remarkable as the furniture by Henry Van de Velde that Bing had exhibited at his Paris gallery in 1895 and again in 1897 in Dresden. Bing, however, had now recognised the need to adapt to French taste. The names of the artists who created these designs are not on record, but they probably came from the ranks of people working in the workshops. In an advertisement featured in *Dekorative Kunst* in 1898, Bing advertised 'furniture made to individual design'.[14] It is likely that, for reasons of commercial viability, Bing's workshops could not restrict themselves to producing modern-style furniture, but also accepted commissions for ordinary everyday furnishings. In 1899, an advertisement in *Dekorative Kunst* offered 'rénovation générale des intérieurs',[15] thus bearing out Meier-Graefe's view that the workshops' production had to help underpin the gallery's work.

In 1898, Bing was joined by Edward Colonna, a professional designer. He was a master of all aspects of design, from furniture to jewellery, and quickly made a name for himself. A year later, Georges de Feure and Eugène Gaillard also joined the establishment. The high point of the three designers' work was Bing's pavilion at the 1900 World's Fair. Having this team of designers meant that Bing had again taken up the role he had had several years earlier with the Nabis, the sole difference being that this time his new designers were not 'outsiders', but were creating a *style art nouveau* as part and parcel of the business.

BING'S SUCCESS IN GERMANY

Bing pursued his work as an art dealer on several levels. The type of clientele he aimed to attract to his fine arts business, particularly with regard to his comprehensive selection of graphics, was an up-market class of collector. His exhibition at London's Grafton Galleries in 1899 included works by Paul-Albert Besnard, Eugène Carrière and Fritz Thaulow, as well as paintings by Henri Fantin-Latour and Edouard Manet, which he had taken on

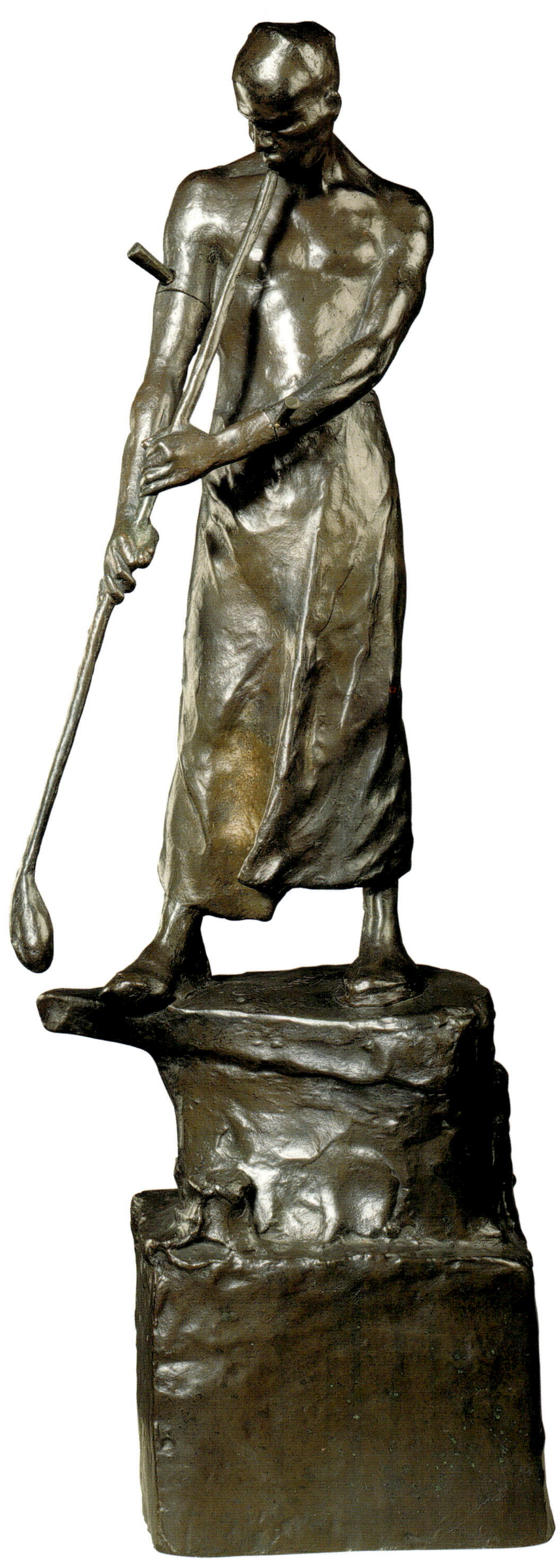

commission from Durand-Ruel. Other important exhibits included bronzes by Constantin Meunier, glassware by Tiffany and a choice collection of Japanese and Indo-Persian miniatures. Japanese artefacts were conspicuously absent from the exhibition, however, possibly because English collections already contained a rich variety of first-rate Japanese works. In other words, there was no need for him to court this particular market.

In continental Europe, however, the situation was quite different. Collections were still in the process of being built up in northern and central Europe. Bing had already enjoyed some success during the late 1880s and early 1890s mounting travelling exhibitions of his goods. He continued with this strategy during the second half of the 1890s, although he concentrated on works of modern applied art, with Japanese handicrafts still an attractive second string to his bow. In 1895, the Dresden art dealer Ludwig Gutbier, who ran the Ernst Arnold Hofkunsthandlung, mounted an exhibition of Japanese coloured woodcuts, acknowledging the 'backing given by a well-known Paris art collector', who is likely to have been none other than Bing.[16] The year 1897 was a particularly important one for Bing as far as promoting his image in Germany was concerned: he displayed five rooms at the Dresden International Art Exhibition, three by Van de Velde, which had already been exhibited at his 1895 Salon de L'Art Nouveau but had not sold; a fourth room, the 'salon de repos', was a new ensemble, specially designed by Van de Velde (figs. 184); while the fifth one, a salon, was the work of Paul-Albert Besnard. There was considerably more interest in Van de Velde in Germany than in France, so Bing could be sure of making a sale. The title in the official catalogue was 'Modern French room furniture produced by L'Art Nouveau (S. Bing)'.[17] It was probably Meier-Graefe who urged the inclusion of 'modern French room furniture' in the Dresden exhibition, since he had for many years been one of Van de Velde's staunchest admirers. Meier-Graefe compiled a detailed description of the rooms, which not only elucidates Van de Velde's room concept, but also describes the wall-coverings and frieze in stoneware tiles by Alexandre Bigot, as well as textiles and a stained-glass window by Georges Lemmen.[18] Particular attention is drawn to Bing's contribution, including the comment that, in the context of generosity, the rooms had come a long way since the early beginnings of William Morris and the 'Tearoom arrangements of the English'.[19] In *Deutsche Kunst und Dekoration*, Paul Schumann commented on the uniqueness of the rooms' colour schemes, and the Director-General of the Berlin Museums, Wilhelm Bode, was similarly moved to heap

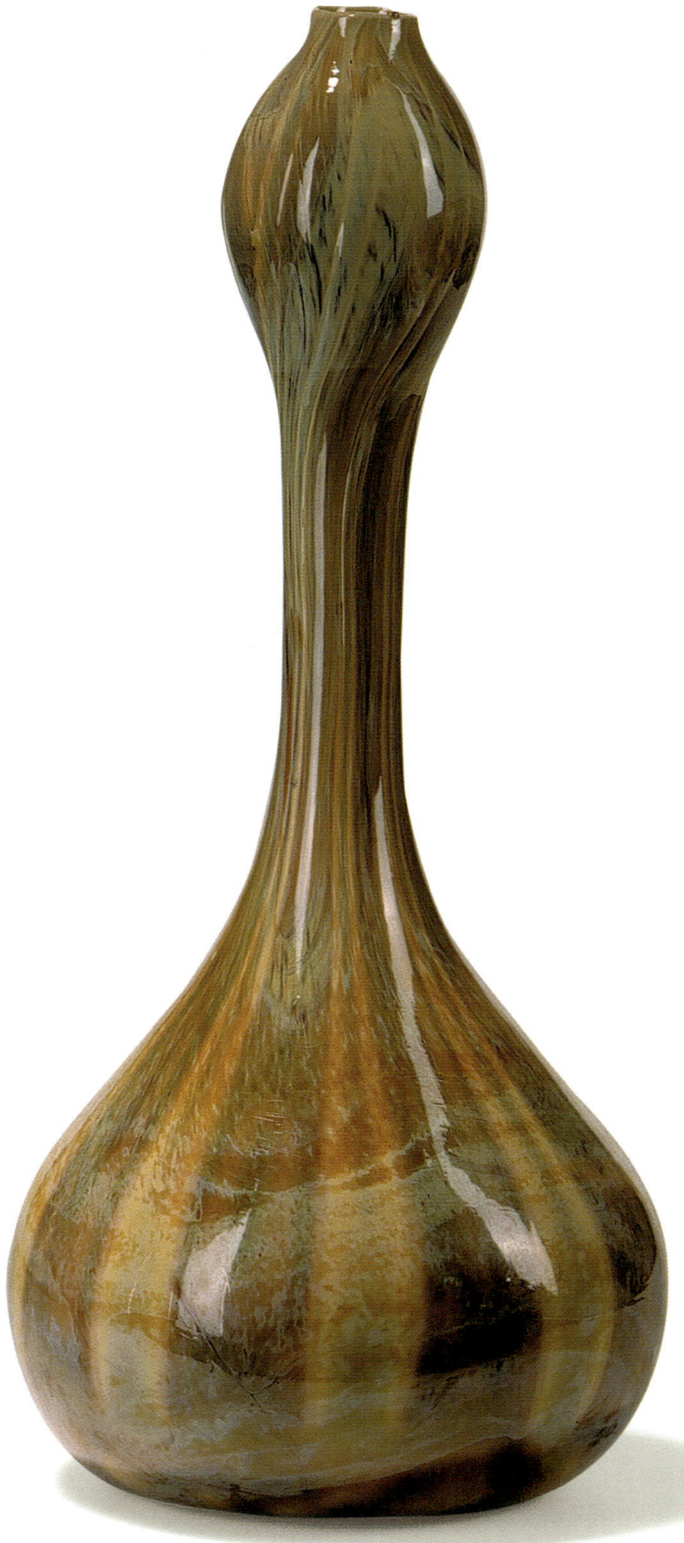

great praise on the room ensembles, saying that such work had 'almost never before been seen' in Germany.[20]

The walls of the rooms were hung with paintings by Charles Cottet, Besnard, Thaulow and others, while positioned between the pieces of furniture were freestanding sculptures by Meunier. Glass cases displayed ceramics by Bigot and Dalpayrat et Lesbros next to vases by Emile Gallé and Tiffany. The catalogue also lists a Tiffany window based on a design by Ranson. So, a mere eighteen months after the opening of his gallery in Paris, Bing found himself presenting a collection that focused on his chosen artistic direction. His name and reputation now extended to other art circles further afield, and the media response was phenomenal.

The Dresden exhibition displayed a number of objects that had already been exhibited at the Paris gallery, but it managed to impart an even stronger sense of authenticity, giving the impression of rooms actually in use. This helped present the new style in a much more convincing manner than individual objects could ever have done.[21] Furniture and textiles, as well as bronzes and paintings, had an extremely important role to play in this respect. Having said that, the transport and setting up of these room layouts must have been a very costly business, which could not be easily repeated; it is significant that Bing did not send any more furniture or paintings to Germany during the ensuing years.

286
Louis Comfort Tiffany, Gourd vase, c. 1895–96
Österreichisches Museum für angewandte Kunst, Vienna

For 1897/98, Bing organised a touring exhibition of Tiffany glassware, which visited museums in Hamburg, Reichenberg (Liberec), Vienna and Budapest.[22] There was enormous interest in Tiffany, and sales were going extremely well, thanks to Bing's acumen in business diplomacy. Bing's natural command of German meant that he was able to hold a constructive dialogue with all the museum directors and succeeded in coming across as a careful, accommodating business partner. It was part of his sales policy to present gifts and give price reductions, which were all the more gratefully received as Bing's stock, though very desirable, was regarded as rather expensive. The correspondence between Bing and Friedrich Deneken, Director of the Kaiser Wilhelm Museum in Krefeld, for example, suggests more than a mere business relationship. Bing was assisting the latter in building up a fine collection of applied contemporary art and he loaned him some old Japanese works of art for his display – never failing to hint, at the same time, that he would be willing to sell.[23] Deneken had been Justus Brinckmann's assistant in Hamburg until 1897 and shared the latter's passion for all things Japanese and for modern reformist art.

In the early 1880s, Bing had published a series of articles on Japanese art and established himself as the publisher of *Le Japon Artistique*; but he was also the author of a study of American Arts and Crafts and wrote enthusiastically in various articles, such as 'Where are we drifting', on the subject of contemporary reformist art.[24] Thanks to his enlightening contributions on the subject, he, more than any other art dealer of his time, played an influential part in the discussion surrounding contemporary applied art, thereby acquiring a reputation as an expert whose judgement was unquestionably highly respected.

His article entitled 'The glassware of Louis C. Tiffany', which appeared in 1898 in *Kunst und Kunsthandwerk*, endorsed this reputation.[25] Following his visit to America in 1894, his establishment had become Tiffany's European outlet. He acted as spokesman for Tiffany, explaining the latter's intentions and justifying his rather high prices.[26] The novelty of Tiffany glassware and the general interest in American Arts and Crafts in the wake of the Chicago World's Columbian Exposition in 1893 had made these items so sought after that virtually no European art museum of any calibre from Brno to Trondheim, from Budapest to Stockholm, wanted to be without an example of it. No other *art nouveau* glassware artist – apart from Gallé – was so fêted by the media as Tiffany, whose name became inextricably linked with that of Bing.

It has only been possible to unravel the intricate network of business contacts between Bing and German art dealers piece by piece. What we do know is that Tiffany's glassware found its way to the Arnold Gallery, Dresden, the Hirschwald Gallery, Berlin, the Keller & Reiner Gallery, Berlin, the Leykauf Gallery, Nuremberg, and the Littauer Gallery, Munich.[27] It goes without saying that some of Bing's other artists also gained entry to these galleries. In 1899, for example, the Berlin art dealers Keller & Reiner held an exhibition of bronzes by the

287
Karl Koepping, Glass, c. 1896
Musée des Arts décoratifs, Paris

288
Victor Vallgren, Vase with figure (Pain), 1894
Ateneum, Helsinki

>> **289**
Rörstrand, Vase with fish, c. 1899
Österreichisches Museum für angewandte Kunst, Vienna

>> **290**
Rörstrand, Vase, c. 1898
Musée des Arts décoratifs, Paris

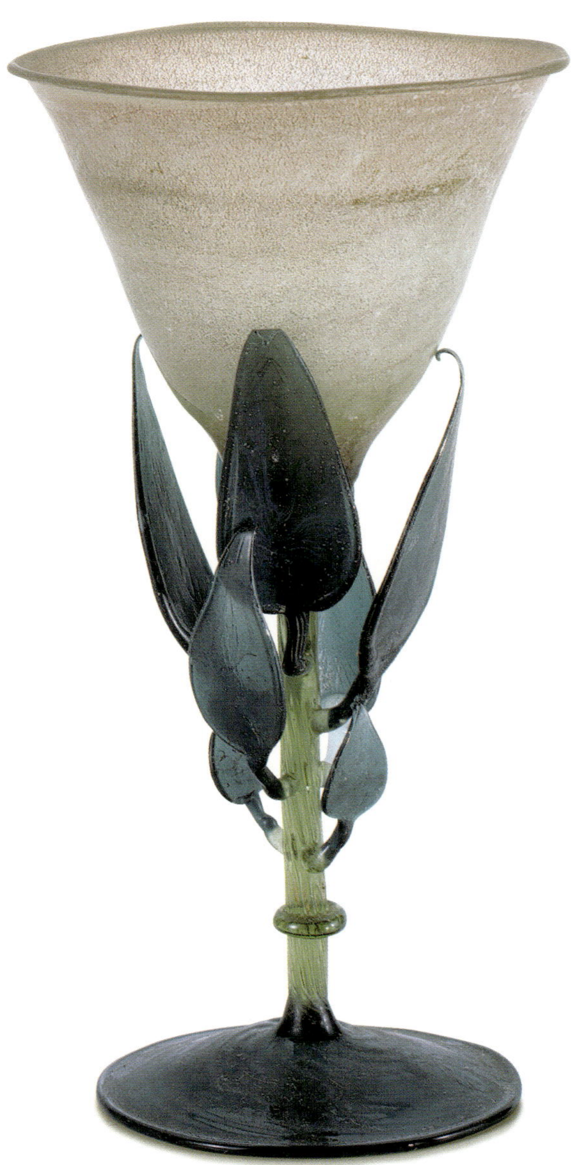

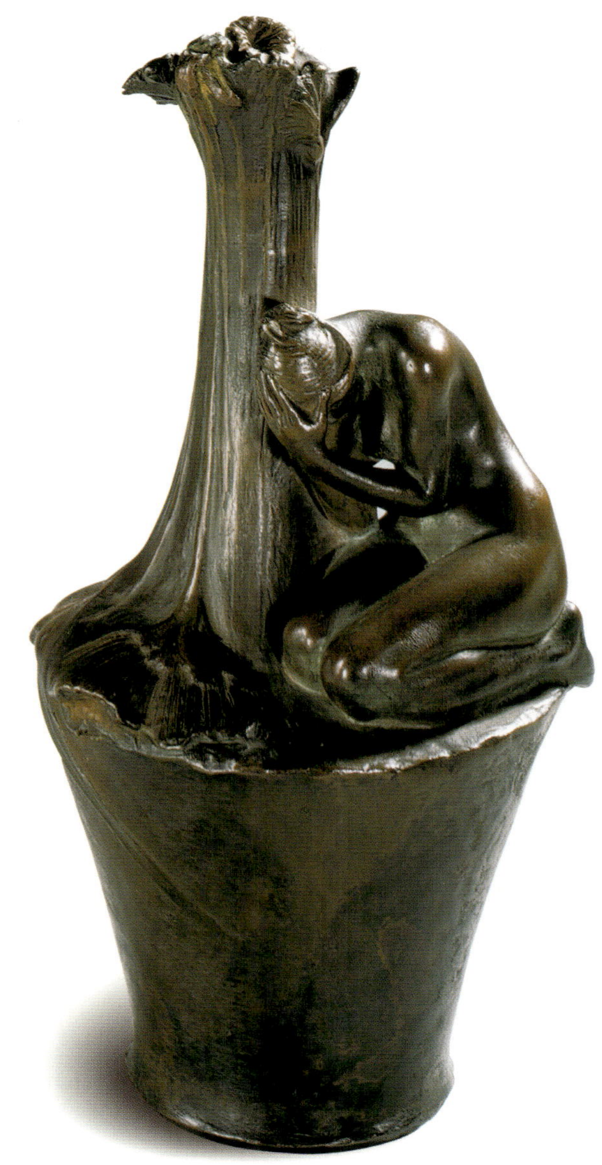

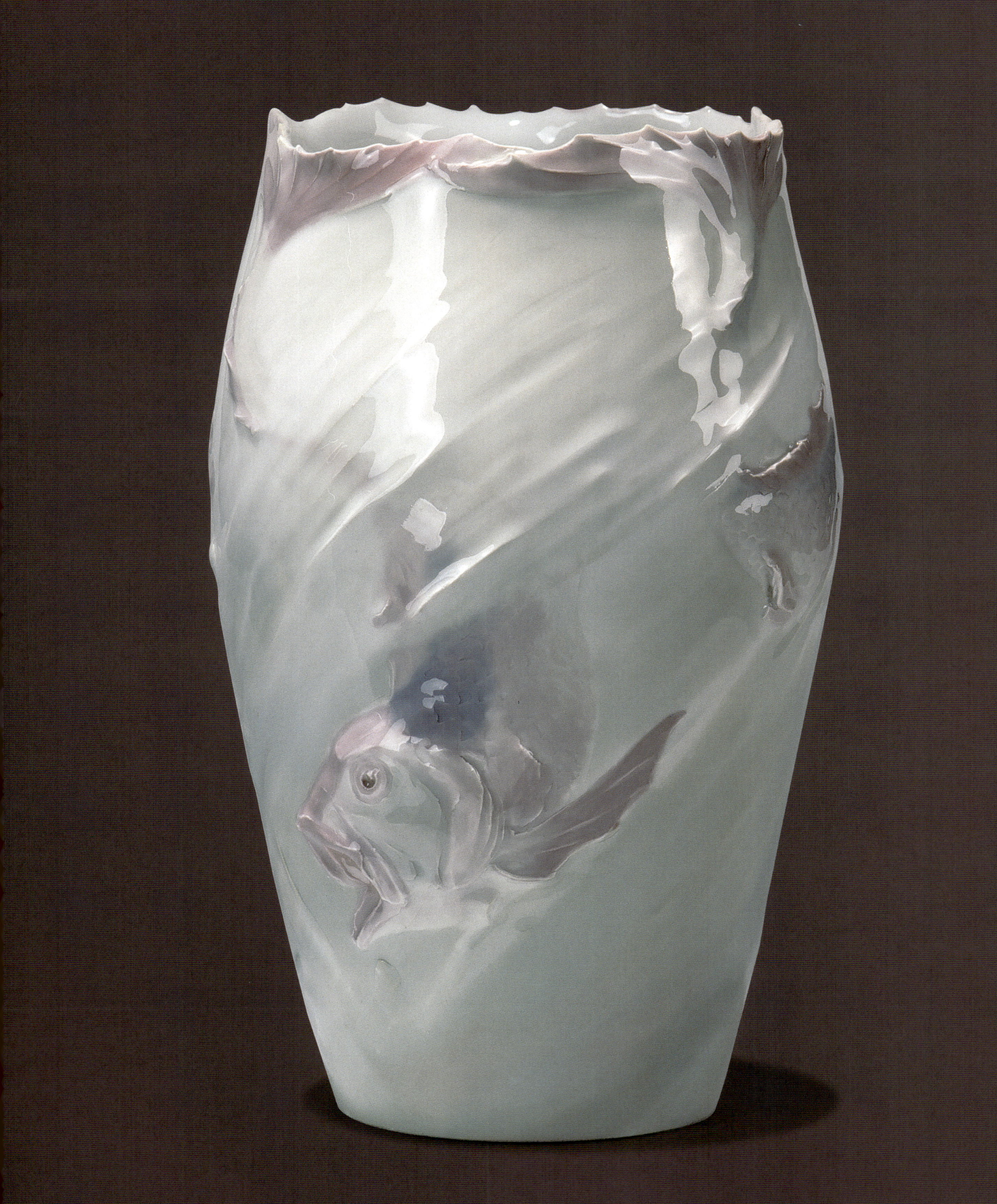

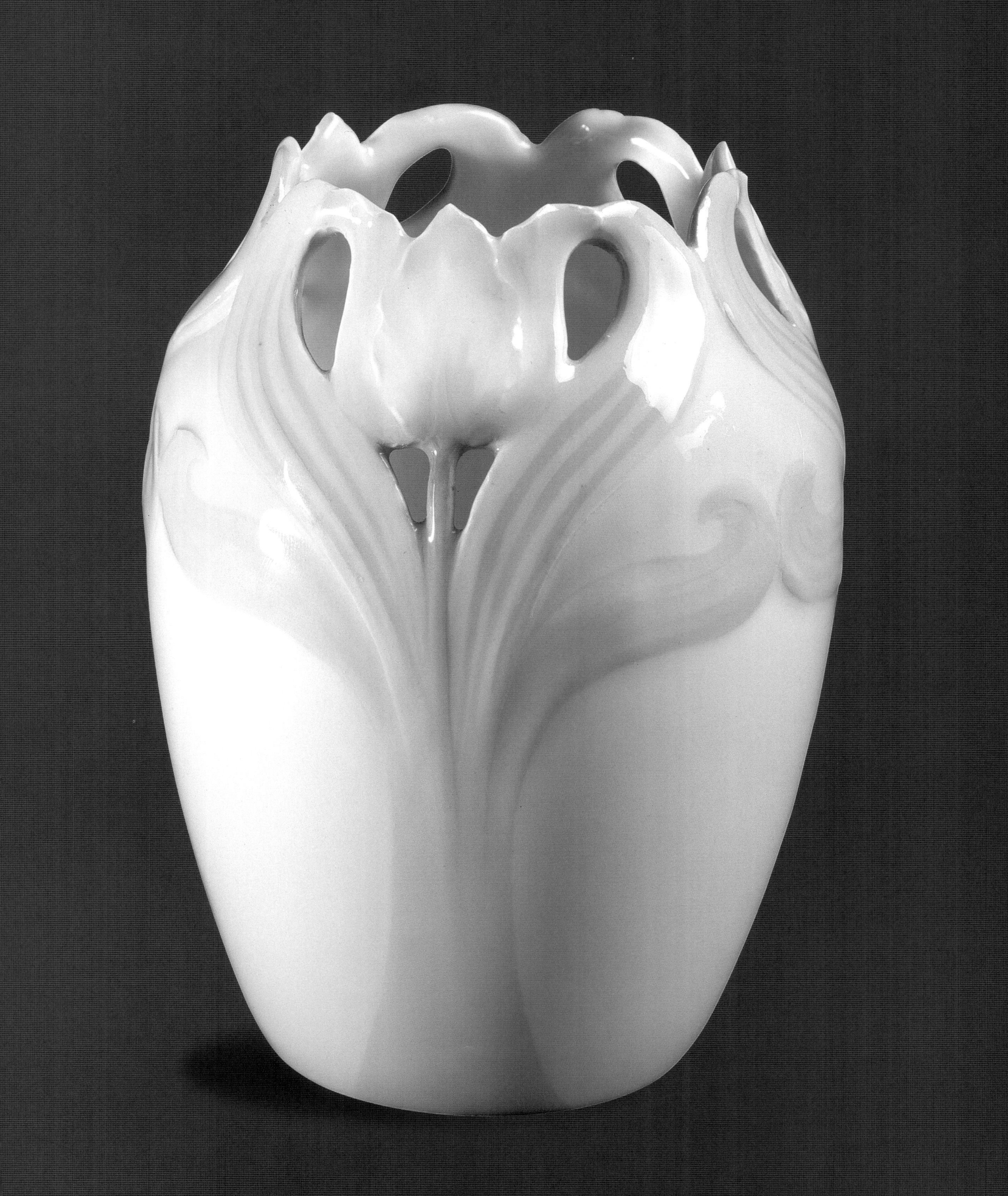

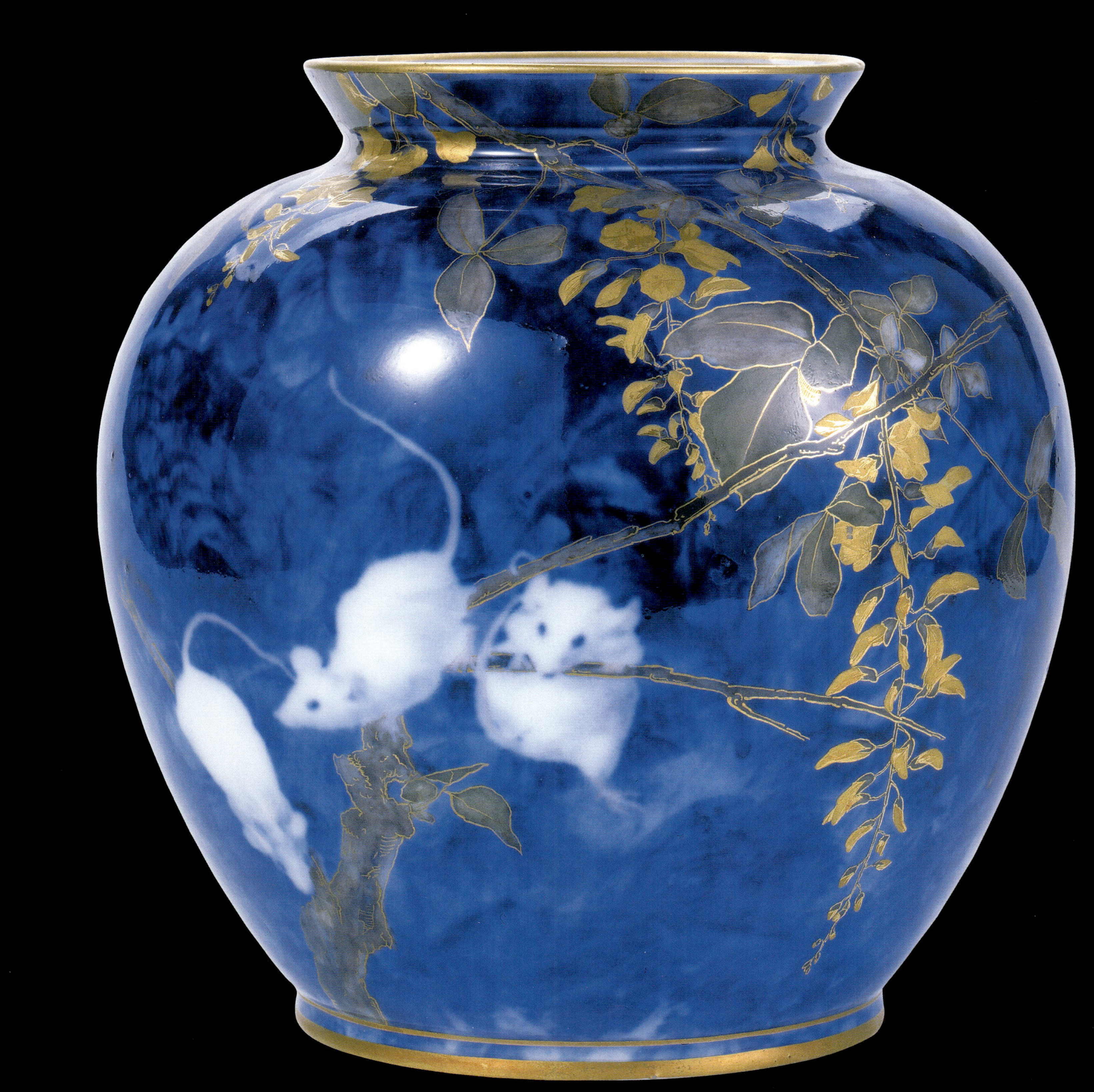

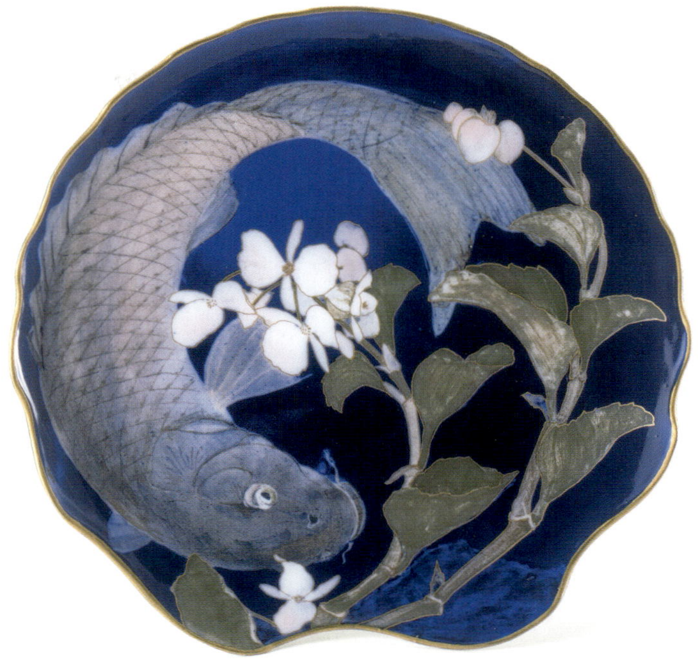

< 291
Royal Copenhagen, Vase, c. 1888
Musée des Arts décoratifs, Paris

292
Royal Copenhagen, Platter, c. 1888
Musée des Arts décoratifs, Paris

Finnish sculptor Victor Vallgren, who had already worked with Bing back in 1895 (fig. 288), and it is known that Keller & Reiner also had a keen interest in the jewellery produced by Colonna.[28]

BING AND BERLIN: HIRSCHWALD AND KELLER & REINER

Bing maintained close business relations with Berlin's largest art dealers, the Hohenzollern Kunstgewerbehaus run by Hermann Hirschwald. Of particular note is a carpet made for Bing in 1897 from a design by Frank Brangwyn and offered for sale in the autumn of 1898 at Hirschwald's.[29] Hirschwald reciprocated by occasionally supplying Bing: one of the artists whose work Hirschwald exhibited was Karl Koepping, whose delicate filigree glasses were regarded as among the most exciting glassware designs of the 1890s; Bing exhibited them in his first Salon de l'Art Nouveau in 1895.[30] He also maintained a mutual arrangement with the Rörstrand porcelain manufacturing firm; Bing had the sole distribution franchise for France, while Hirschwald was the manufacturer's representative in Berlin.

It made sense for Hirschwald and Bing to maintain a close business relationship, as both their companies conducted business on similar basic principles. Hirschwald had started business in 1879 with a store stocking small works of art and crafts, to appeal directly to Berlin's upper classes. The Director of Berlin's Kunstgewerbemuseum, Julius Lessing, was one of his customers, as was the Prussian Crown Prince and his wife. This patronage later led to the store being renamed the Hohenzollern Kaufhaus or Kunstgewerbehaus. The fact that the wife of Frederick, Crown Prince of Prussia, was a daughter of England's Queen Victoria also contributed to the fact that Hirschwald started to import English goods quite early on, rising to become the main German dealer in English Arts and Crafts.[31] Justus Brinckmann purchased William Morris textiles from him, but Hirschwald also stocked works by Ashbee, Benson and Voysey. Hirschwald is thought to have been the first German entrepreneur to import 'products of the American art industry, in particular, decorative glassware, lamps and furniture' in the wake of the Chicago Exposition.[32] 'It was at this time that he decided to completely redesign his store. From now on, it was to include arts and crafts items from abroad.' Lessing commented that, 'a tour of the rooms at the Hohenzollern store was one of the most enlightening experiences to be had in the field of arts and crafts; nowhere else in Germany, or indeed in continental Europe, was there a similar establishment, fitted out so perfectly with every kind of desirable material, to compare with this one, which resembled a "world's fair in miniature".'[33]

A further parallel between Hirschwald and Bing was the fact that it was not long before Hirschwald was adding interior design studios to his business, intended for the manufacture of furniture and leather goods, among other things. To begin with, these were very much bound by historical constraints of style, but eventually they began to move with the times. *Deutsche Kunst und Dekoration* reported in 1898 that Hirschwald had supplied leather-upholstered armchairs from designs by Otto Eckmann.[34] When Henry Van de Velde moved from Brussels to Berlin

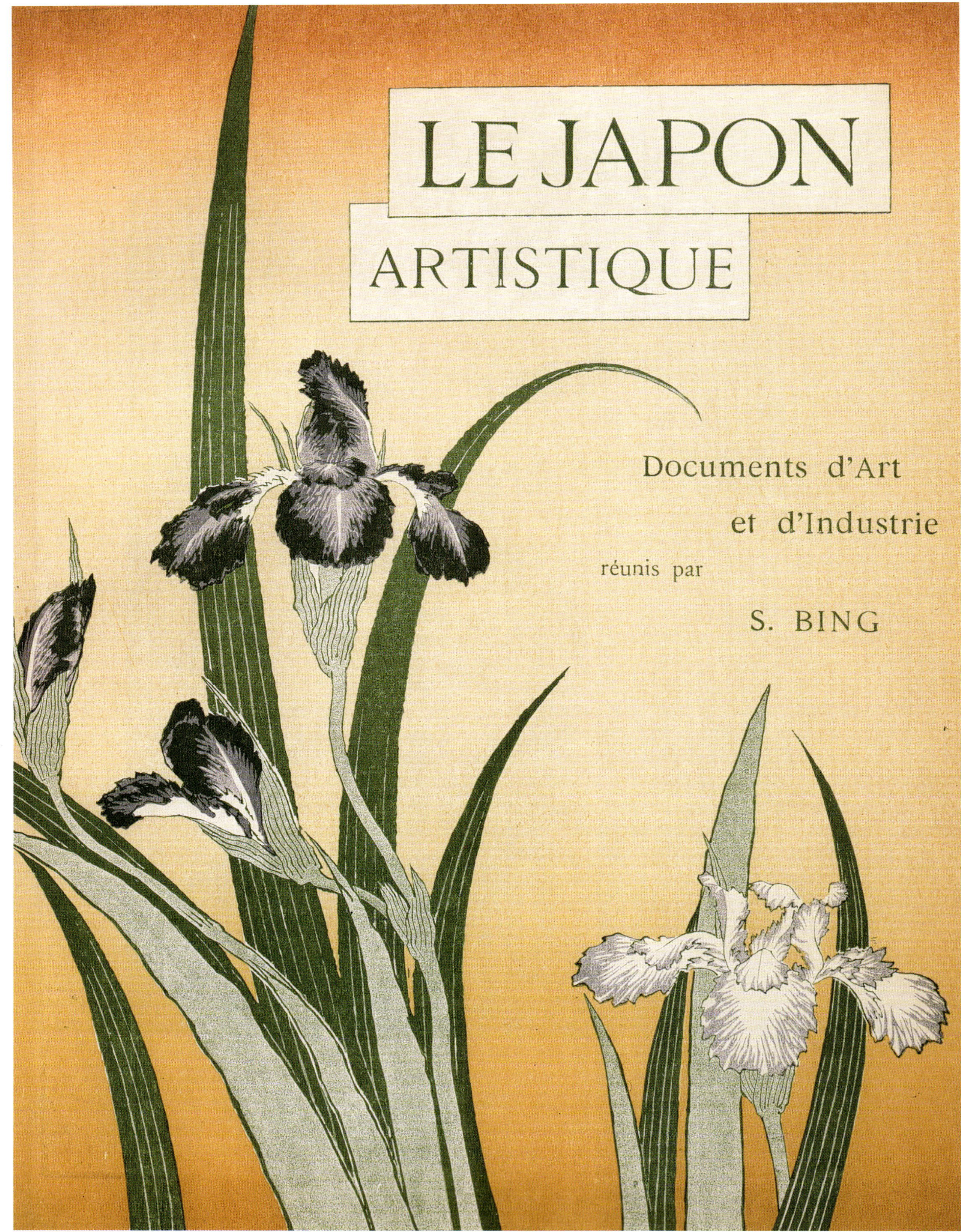
LE JAPON
ARTISTIQUE
Documents d'Art
et d'Industrie
réunis par
S. BING

in 1899, hoping to produce his furniture more lucratively, and set up the 'H. Van de Velde Werkstätte für Angewandte Kunst', it was on the understanding that the manufacture would be carried out in the Hirschwald workshops. Despite the fact that this cooperation was not destined for much success – it was legally terminated in 1901 – it is nevertheless clear how much importance Hirschwald attached to expanding his capacities and implementing his programme.

A firm with an even more modern approach was the Berlin firm of Keller & Reiner, which, in contrast to Hirschwald, focused to a greater extent on paintings, particularly those in the neo-impressionist style. Established in 1897, fitted out in part by Van de Velde, it quickly grew to become one of the leading art dealers in the city. The Director of Hamburg's Kunsthalle, Alfred Lichtwark, wrote: 'They [Keller & Reiner] are at pains to furnish your rooms in the style of an apartment befitting a rich man of modern taste.'[35] An advertisement, designed by Georges Lemmen, bearing a striking resemblance to his 1898 design for Bing's L'Art Nouveau, extols 'modern painting and sculpture' and also mentions 'furniture, textiles, wall-hangings, carpets, decorative metalware, stained glass etc. and native and foreign ceramics'.[36] Keller & Reiner also produced furniture, as is evident from the examples cited in the literature, but they lacked vision in finding an individual direction of their own. What distinguishes Bing from Hirschwald and Keller & Reiner is the fact that they ran their art galleries primarily as business enterprises, albeit with great taste and elegance, but without Bing's missionary zeal for exploring new avenues of distribution, discovering new artists and converting them to his own creative ideals.

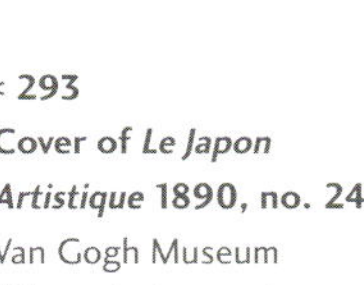

< 293
Cover of *Le Japon Artistique* 1890, no. 24
Van Gogh Museum (Library), Amsterdam

294
Max Laeuger, Pitcher, c. 1898
Musée des Arts décoratifs, Paris

>> 295
Alexandre Bigot, Creamer, with silver-gilt mount by Edward Colonna, c. 1899
Musée des Arts décoratifs, Paris

>> 296
Alexandre Bigot, Bowl, with silver-gilt mount by Edward Colonna, 1895
Victoria and Albert Museum, London

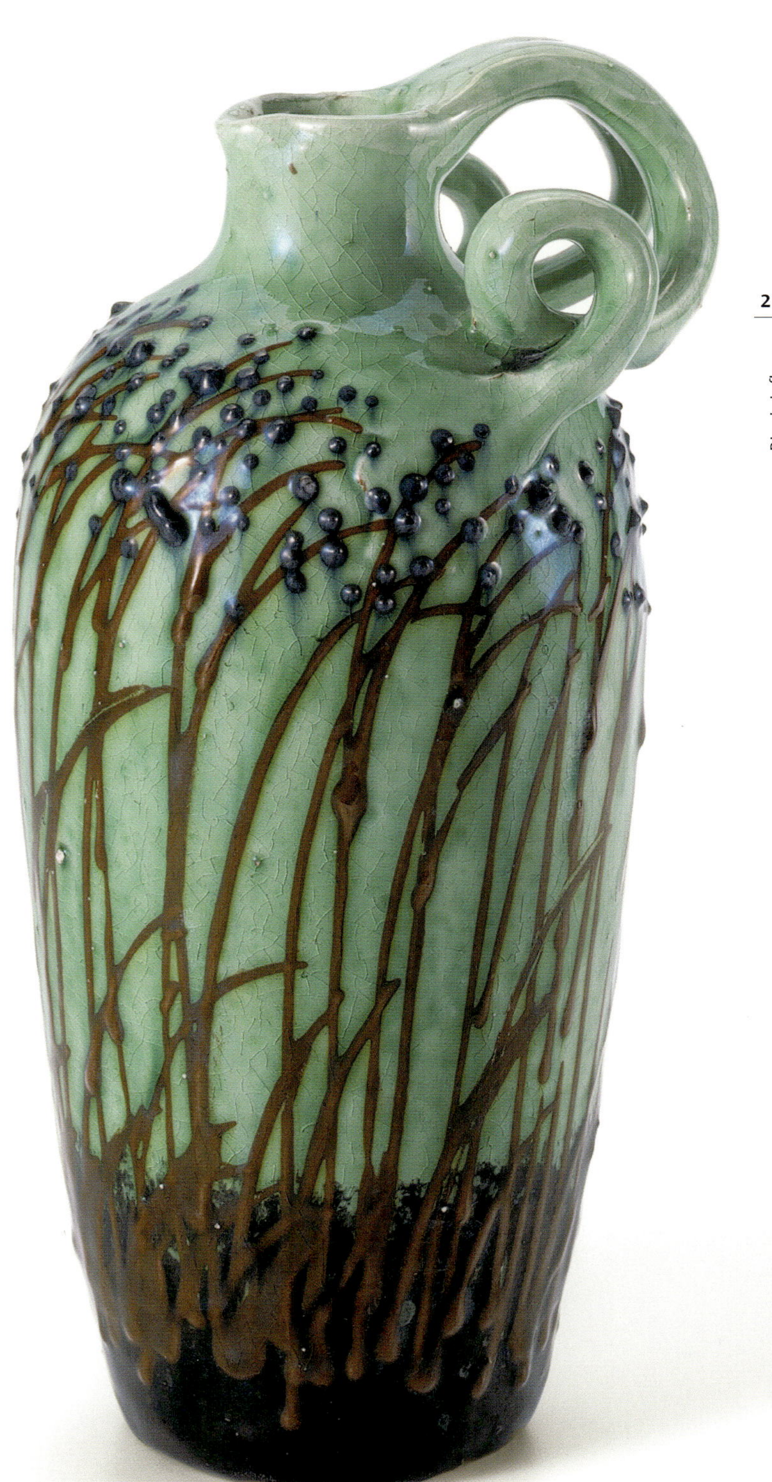

BING AND HAMBURG: JUSTUS BRINCKMANN

Around 1900, the European museums of applied art began to call for changes in their policy of collecting. In the past, the principal aim had been to collect exemplary objects from the past for the purpose of training craftsmen. Their *raison d'être* was now seen as being to seek out outstanding examples of contemporary art. Everywhere, the prevailing desire was for fresh beginnings; art should have a 'healing' effect, become strong, stand on its own two feet and echo the feelings of the time. The prototype of this new generation of museum directors, who felt committed to this burgeoning art, was Justus Brinckmann, Director of Hamburg's Museum für Kunst und Gewerbe. Not only was he director of the museum in Bing's home town

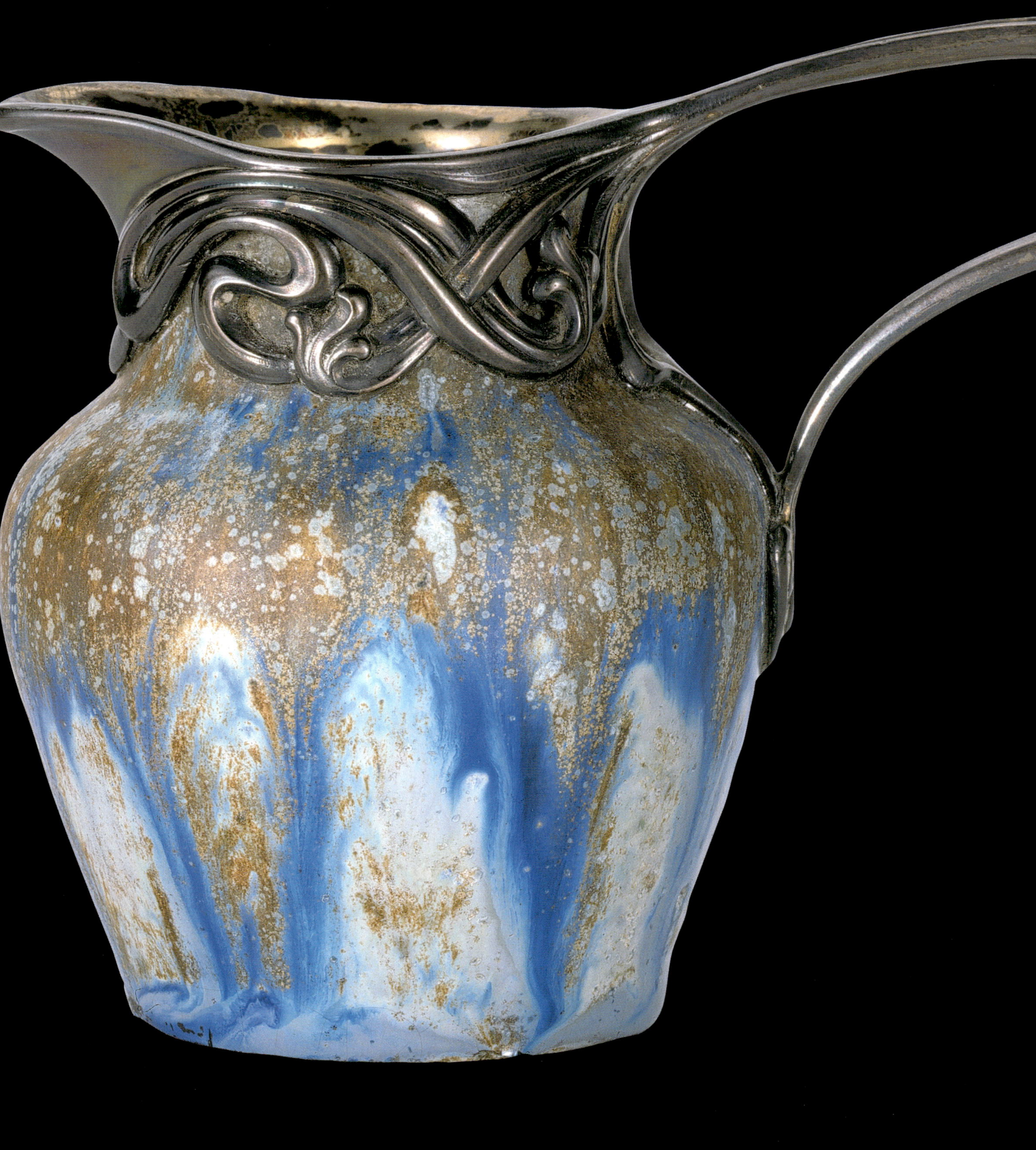

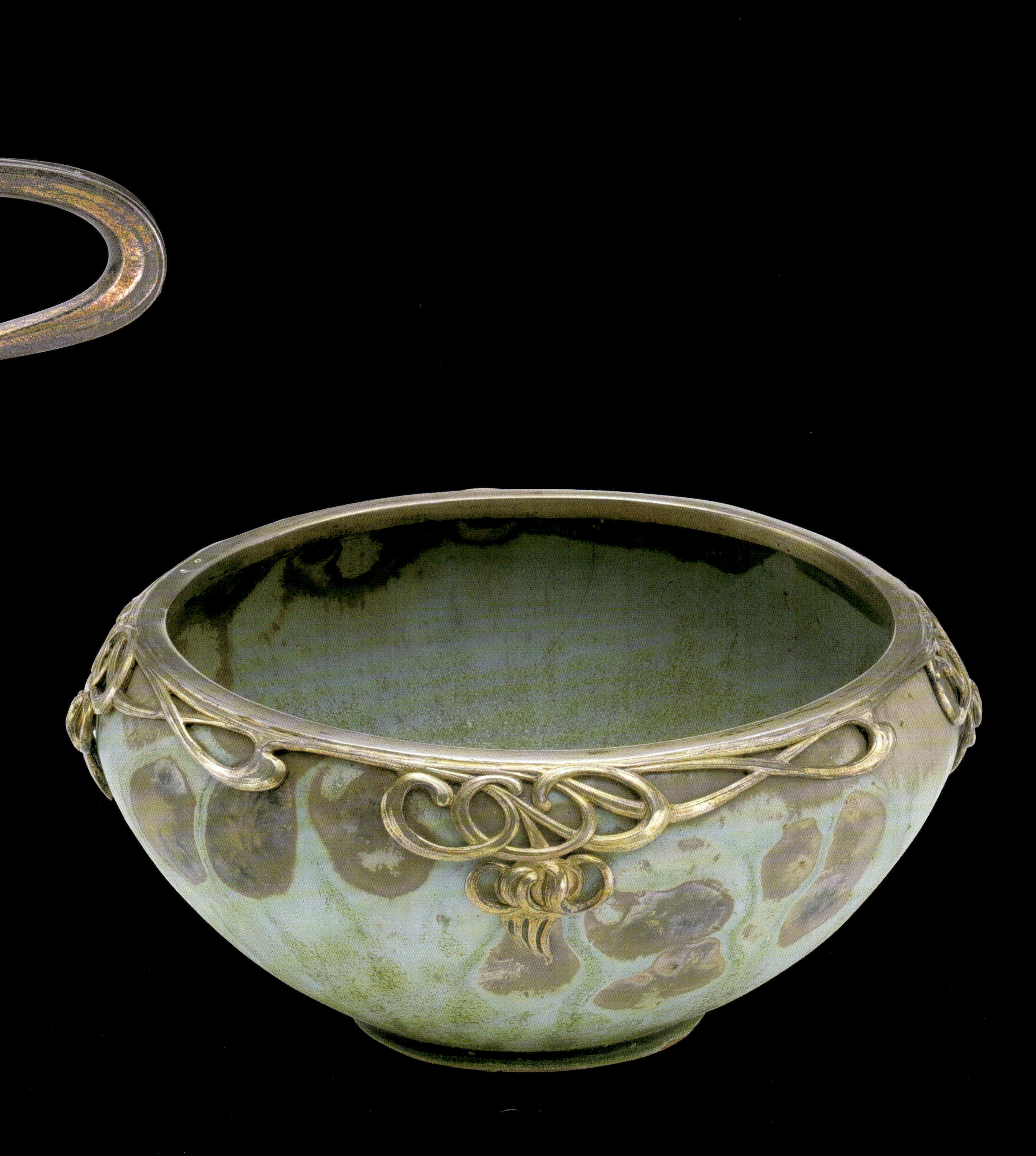

where he had gone to school, but he also had a special affinity for French art. As a member of the Franco-Japanese Society, he was renowned as one of the leading experts of his day on Japan. He was a member of the *Japon Artistique* team in German: *Japanischer Formenschatz*) and author of a book entitled *Kunst und Handwerk in Japan* (Art and Craft in Japan) (1889); his collection of Japanese arts and crafts was one of the most significant in Europe and had been acquired predominantly from Bing's gallery.[37]

Bing and Brinckmann were on a friendly footing. Their correspondence refers to numerous meetings as well as to breakfasts together at Bing's private apartment in the rue de Vézelay and at his country villa.[38] There is no doubt that Brinckmann profited from Bing's expertise, but, equally, he was in a position to make a valuable contribution in helping Bing assess developments in the world of contemporary applied art.[39] Annual visits to France kept him up-to-date with the French scene, and he had, since the early 1890s, been one of Germany's first collectors of French poster art and decorative ceramics. In 1893, he acquired four Japanese-style vases in *grès flammé* technique from the studio of Auguste Delaherche and an 1889 mask self-portrait from Jean Carriès together with three stoneware pots. Brinckmann's role as a pioneer of French applied art in Germany, which reached a climax in 1900 with the purchase of the L'Art Nouveau room, has until now been touched upon only peripherally in the literature on Bing. It is no coincidence that Brinckmann was apparently the only German museum director to buy three items – three vases by Tiffany, Bigot and Dalpayrat – at Bing's first Salon de L'Art Nouveau in 1895.[40]

Brinckmann's purchases were greatly admired, and his opinion carried a great deal of weight. He was in close, friendly contact with his colleagues Julius Lessing in Berlin and Pietro Krohn in Copenhagen, to whom he imparted valuable advice on matters related to the art trade. It is interesting to read a letter from Brinckmann to Lessing after his visit to Paris, as it also throws some light on Bing's business: 'If you are seriously interested in buying desirable Japanese *objets d'art*, ceramics in particular, now is a good time to do so. Our esteemed Herr Bing has made great sacrifices in the cause of *art nouveau* and will have to continue to do so. The fresh sense of enthusiasm with which he has thrown himself into this new trend is amazing. In order to give himself a bit of leeway, Herr Bing is apparently prepared to delve into the stocks he keeps in the attic and sell them at very moderate prices.'[41]

Brinckmann also served as a shining example to his younger colleagues in the field, such as Friedrich Deneken,

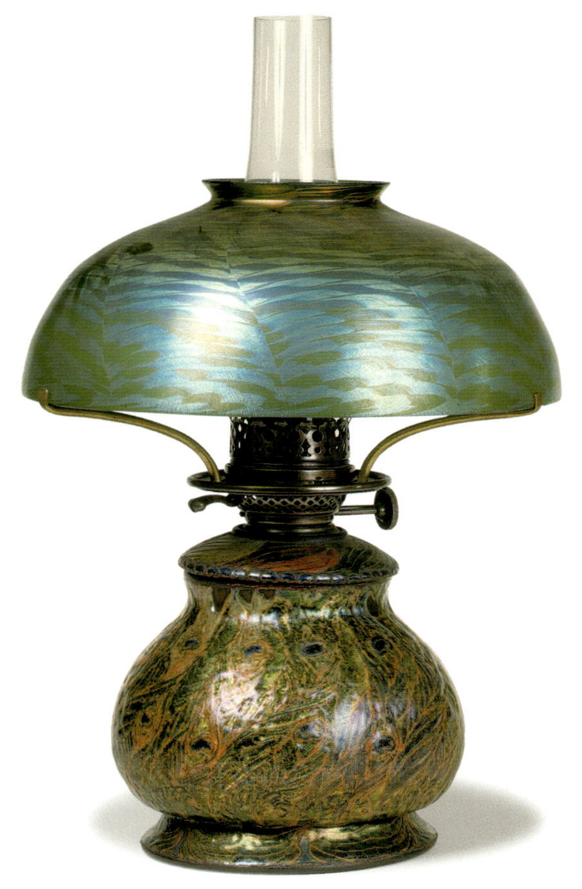

297
Louis Comfort Tiffany, Lamp, c. 1900
Det Danske Kunstindustrimuseum, Copenhagen

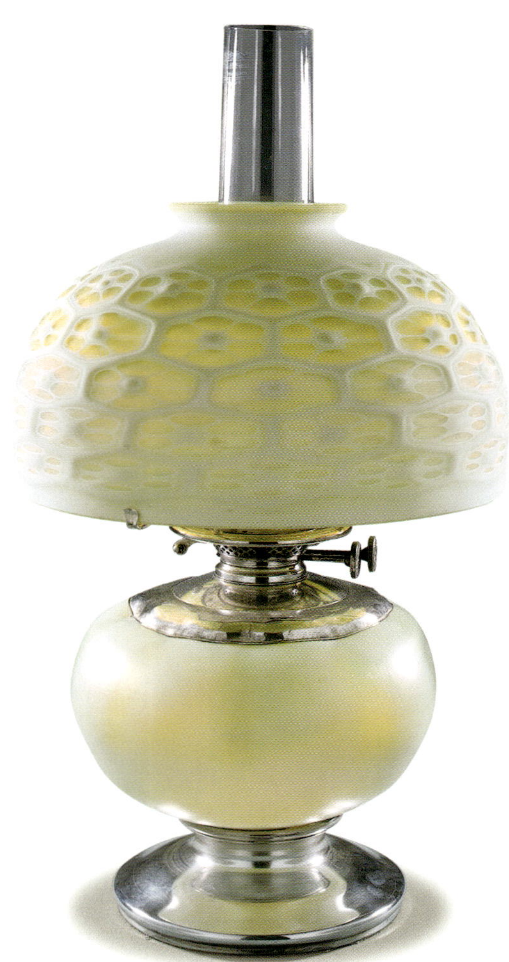

298
Louis Comfort Tiffany, Lamp, c. 1900
Nordenfjeldske Kunstindustrimuseum, Trondheim

who became museum director in Krefeld in 1897, and Jens Thiis of Trondheim. Brinckmann met up with with the twenty-five-year old Thiis towards the end of January 1896 in Bing's gallery. The latter, having recently been appointed museum director, had spent the previous few months on a study tour and during the autumn of 1895 had stayed as Brinckmann's house guest in Hamburg, where he also completed a course of training. Thiis had come to Paris with substantial funds provided by one of his patrons and during these few weeks was able to assemble the basic elements of what was to become an impressive *art nouveau* collection in Trondheim.

BING'S ART BUSINESS POLICY

The customary way of acquiring examples of contemporary art was, generally speaking, to visit the artists themselves in their studios; purchases could also be made at world's fairs. This, however, involved extensive travelling and carrying large sums of money, something that was not always easy to do. Establishments like those of Bing, Hirschwald and Meier-Graefe, which had an existing selection of *objets d'art* to choose from, offered a solution to this problem, although it was still necessary to make a personal visit to the premises. Bing must surely have been the only art dealer of his time to find an effective solution to this state of affairs by actually sending his artefacts on tour, either to museums or by passing them on to art dealers with whom he was associated to sell on commission. He offered museum directors the opportunity of seeing the goods on their home ground, so that patrons could be approached and the necessary funds raised to purchase them.

Bing's ideas took him into uncharted and unexplored areas of the art trade. They proved successful in a period that had the express aim of measuring every object, whether decorative or utilitarian, against a uniform yardstick of quality, eliminating any distinctions between fine and applied art and providing artistic examples for tasteful living. Bing, however, wanted more than simply to offer products from a broad range of contemporary designs. He wanted to help ensure originality and inspire artists to work. He also wanted to play an active part in presenting these items to collectors and, by so doing, help the new style gain acceptance and achieve success. It was this way of thinking that set the seal on his artistic and marketing genius.[42]

NOTES

A FAMILY AFFAIR

1 'Du 25 Mai, Vente de marchandises neuves "Art Nouveau" en vertu du jugement. Requête de M. Bing du 15 Juin. Décharge du produit de la dite vente' (Archives de Paris, D 42 E 3 111, 880, 1909). The objects were organised into appropriate groupings as Marcel Bing had to sell them either as lots for 20 francs or as lots for 150 francs. It was a very sizeable sale.

2 Ibid. Marcel Bing's interest in Near Eastern ancient art, in addition to objects from the Far East, emerged gradually. By 1904, and later, he was selling Persian objects to leading collectors and museums, including pieces to a major museum in Berlin. For further reference to this side of Marcel Bing's activities, see letters from Marcel Bing to Dr Wilhelm Bode, Director of the Kaiser Friedrich Museum (Zentralarchiv der Staatlichen Museen zu Berlin, Preussischer Kulturbesitz: Acta, vol. 1, Von 23. 1. 05 bis 30 Juni 1908).

3 'Don de Monsieur Marcel Bing', 26 October 1908 (Musée des Arts décoratifs, Paris). Appended to this document is a letter from Marcel Bing to Louis Metman, Director of the Museum, dated 6 June 1906, which suggests that at one time this might have been part of a larger correspondence.

4 See n. 1. This is the only written document from Marcel Bing that reveals information about the organisation, in 1895, of his father's shop, L'Art Nouveau, at 22, rue de Provence. Bing's two addresses at 19, rue Chauchat and 22, rue de Provence were contiguous spaces although on different streets.

5 10, rue Saint-Georges became Marcel Bing's place of business as well as his living quarters. It is also the address Siegfried Bing moved to after he ended his activities on rue de Provence. However, he died in Vaucresson, just outside Paris.

6 'Inventaire après le décès de M. Bing, 6 July 1921', p. 23.

7 Taken together, what was given to the Musée des Arts décoratifs in 1908, what was sold in 1909 and what was left in Marcel Bing's estate after his death in 1920 comprised a large stock to have held on to after the closure of the gallery on rue de Provence in 1904.

8 See Weisberg 1986a, which first established some of the family associations and ties that are enlarged upon here.

9 The author is indebted to the assistance of Walter O. and Carola Michael in helping to document the activities and interrelationships between various members of the Bing family. Walter Michael's help during the past twenty-five years in deciphering the documentation gleaned from the commercial archives in Hamburg has been invaluable. The first mention of Moses Michael Bing in the Hamburg business registry occurs in 1823 at Bohnenstrasse, no. 3; by 1824 and until 1828, he is listed in the same directory with the title of 'merchant' at Roedingsmarkt, no. 90, and also from 1826 at Altewallstrasse, no. 95 as 'merchant' and merchant of 'French porcelains' (Akten des Hamburger Handelsgerichts, B2 No. 61: Administrationssachen der Firma Bing Gebrueder & Co., 1857–60).

10 Bing Gebrüder & Co. were listed in the Hamburg commercial registry in 1829/30 at Altewallstrasse, no. 95, as merchants/importers of French porcelains (see n. 9). By 1831, and probably until 1836, the firm was listed at a second address, Muehlenbruecke, no. 15. Jacob Bing had settled in Hamburg in 1825 and became an 'Upper Middle Class' citizen of the city on 13 April 1849. In his application he noted that he had lived in the city for twenty-four years (Vorschrift fuer Diejenigen die das Buergerrecht nachsuchen No. 387 4. April 1849 [352–7] Staatsangehoerigkeitsaufsicht B 1 a 1849 No. 387).

11 For reference to this firm, see 'Hundert Jahre Bing', *Frankfurter Zeitung*, 13 June 1926. The article notes that Bing Jun. & Co. was in 1827 already selling 'French and English porcelains as well as English and French dry goods and fashions'. The firm had a Paris branch at 6, rue Portefoin. See also Hans Majer-Leonhard, *Altfrankfurter Firmenhandbuch*, Frankfurt 1925, and Alexander Dietz and Isobel Mordy, *The Jewish Community of Frankfurt: a genealogical study 1349–1849*, Camelford, Cornwall (UK) 1988, p. 570. Moses Salomon and Isaac Bing were brothers, first cousins of Siegfried Bing. Their two other brothers, Loeb Modo Leopold and Michael Salomon Bing, established a similar business at Zeil, no. 31 in Frankfurt in 1838. Loeb Modo Leopold moved to Paris in 1841.

12 Jacob Bing had married Friedericke Renner (1811–1893), sister of Joseph Samuel Renner, in Hamburg, on 12 January 1834. On the Bing/Renner partnership, see French liquidation proceedings for 1869 (Tribunal de Commerce du Département de la Seine: Remplacement de liquidateur: Ste. Bing Renner. Mardi, 9 Mars, 1869. Enregistrement 9 Juillet, 1869). The new partnership Bing/Renner was formed for the 'manufacture, sale, purchase, consignment, commission and exportation of porcelains'. It was to last ten years (Archives de Paris, D 31 U3 184: Actes de Société – Dissolutions de Société, 25 January 1854). The partnership had an outlet on 12, rue Martel, Paris. It purchased (c. 1855) a porcelain manufacture at Saint-Genou (Indre) from Charles Gendarme for 115,000 francs. On the Saint-Genou purchase, see information collected by Albert André Chapu (Saint-Genou). *Didot-Bottin* 1854, pp. 837, 1631, lists Bing Frères with the Saint-Genou porcelain manufactory (under Indre, Saint-Genou: 'Fabrique de Porcelaines, Gendarme et Cie., dépôt à Paris, Chez Bing Frères et Cie., rue Martel 12'). By 1855 the designation had changed to 'Bing et Renner, Commissionaires en porcelaines et cristaux, dépôt des manufactures de Saint-Genou (Martel 12), clearly suggesting that Bing and Renner were now owners of the firm. See also *Didot-Bottin* 1862, p. 129: 'Bing and Renner, porcelaines et art d'Allemagne'. It is difficult to know when Jacob Bing sold the Saint-Genou factory, but the Société Bing frères, 12, rue Martel is still noted up to *Didot-Bottin* 1863 as an outlet for Saint-Genou ('négociants', p. 971). On the link with the porcelain manufactory at Saint-Genou, see also Tardy, *Les Poteries et les Faiences Françaises*, Paris 1949, p. 1480, which lists a business office for the firm at 12, rue Martel. For further reference, see letter from Direction des Services d'Archives de la Nièvre to Peter Van Dam, 22 May 1980 (much of the information on Saint-Genou collected by Albert André Chapu was kindly provided by Mr Van Dam).

13 Akten des Hamburger Handelsgerichts, B2 No. 61: Administrationssachen der Firma Bing Gebrueder & Co. (1857–60). In his documentation on Saint-Genou, Albert André Chapu has questioned why the Bing group sold the factory and mentions the Hamburg receivership as a possible cause. In fact, the Bing/Renner group had entered into a business relationship with the local factory owner, who became insolvent.

14 Walter O. Michael has established the extensive list of creditors, noting the wide range of 'global' contacts that were maintained by the Bing Gebrüder firm. He is still examining the commercial archives and receivership materials to try to ascertain whether the specific nature of merchandise exchanged between various locations and Bing Gebrüder can be firmly established (letter from W.O. Michael to the author).

15 See Weisberg 1983, pp. 84–5.
16 Ibid.
17 Ibid.
18 Archives Nationales, Document no. 3819X9: Demande de naturalisation, 22.8.1876.
19 *Didot-Bottin* 1865 under 'manufacture de porcelaine'. This was maintained in *Didot-Bottin* 1866, p. 1063.
20 *Didot-Bottin* 1869, p. 1215.
21 For further reference, see Musée national Adrien Dubouché (former Musée de Limoges) inv. nos. 3509–11. Several of the pieces, which are exhibited in the cases of the museum, carry handwritten paper stamps on their bases that document the donation. Chantal Meslin, Chief Curator, has given kind assistance in trying to identify further documentation on these pieces, but any further correspondence relating to the donation has been lost.
22 See n. 18.
23 Ibid.
24 This marriage demonstrates how wealthy Jewish families consolidated not only family but business relationships. Johanna Baer's brother, Michael Martin Baer (1841–1904), became German Consul in Japan, and Siegfried Bing relied on him heavily for his contacts with that country when he developed in Japan import-export business. Between 1869 and 1875, four sons were born to Siegfried and Johanna: Jacques (1869–1891), Georges (September 1870-November 1870), Michel (May 1873-November 1873) and Marcel (1875–1920). Two of the boys died in infancy. See Weisberg 1986a, pp. 13–14.
25 Translation supplied by Walter O. Michael and based on documentation provided by the Hamburger Handelsgericht.
26 *See Catalogue des oeuvres et des produits modernes, Union centrale des Beaux-Arts appliqués à l'industrie, Exposition de 1869*, Paris 1869, p. 18. See also Weisberg 1986a, p. 14.
27 *Didot-Bottin* 1875, p. 831.
28 Weisberg 1986a, p. 14.
29 Hisao Miyajima, 'Martin M. Bair – A Foreign Merchant in the Early Meiji Period', *Bulletin of the Kyoto Institute of Technology 'Jinbun'* 35 (1986), pp. 3–14. Miyajima notes Bair (i.e. Baer, see n. 24) as a Consul/Agent in 1871.
30 Ibid. Miyajima, in notes provided to the author, carefully documented the mercantile activities of H. Ahrens for Heinrich Ahrens and Company from 1870 to 1886. See also Hisao Miyajima, 'S. Bing's Visit to Japan', *Bulletin of the Study of Japonisme* 2 (1982), pp. 29–33.
31 For further reference to the way Japan was regarded at this time in the West, see Weisberg 1975; and Weisberg 1990.
32 The partnership was known as 'S. Bing et Proost Besce'. See *Didot-Bottin* 1878, pp. 148, 928, listed under the rubric of 'curiosités'. In 1879 only S. Bing is listed under 'curiosités' at 19, rue Chauchat.
33 See Elizabeth K. Menon, 'Henry Somm's *Japonisme*, 1881, in context', *Gazette des Beaux-Arts* (February 1992), pp. 89–98.
34 *Didot-Bottin* 1880, p. 468.
35 Information on August Bing supplied by Walter O. Michael in consultation with Bing family descendants. A specific history of August Bing, in the context of Japonisme, awaits further documentation and clarification.
36 Bing's possible early trip to Japan is mentioned in at least two obituaries following his death. See 'Nécrologie, S. Bing', *L'Art Moderne*, 17 September 1905, p. 306; and *Bulletin de l'Art Ancien et Moderne* 272 (1905–6), p. 243. Geneviève Lacambre, in discussions with the author, has also suggested the strong possibility of an early Bing trip to Japan, based probably on these two sources. Information found among documents that belong to the descendants of August Bing, such as a map of a trip to the Far East in 1875, suggests that a trip took place in 1875. These documents were seen by Mr and Mrs Walter O. Michael in 1976 but were not seen by the author, who is still trying to gain access to them. Doubts about Siegfried having gone to Japan in 1875 are raised by the remarks made by the daughter of August to Mr and Mrs Michael referring to Siegfried's fragile health and dislike of long trips. His own words about his first trip, when he wrote, 'In 1880 I could stand it no longer, I left family and business and set course towards the adventurous shores of the Far East,' may have been chosen judiciously to indicate his original aversion to long trips (*Kunstbladet* 9–10 (1888), pp. 119–21). The question is: why would S. Bing conceal the 1875 trip? And why would he write in 1888 about the 1880 trip, 'I could stand it no longer?' Furthermore, no documents found in Japan, pertaining to westerners' trips to Japan, have come to light about S. Bing for 1875.
37 See *Kunstbladet* (n. 36) and *Japan Weekly Mail*, 16 July 1881, p. 830, noting S. Bing as a passenger to Japan on the *Genkai Maru*.
38 A. Bing is mentioned as a passenger on the *Tokio Maru* in *Japan Weekly Mail*, 1 October 1881, p. 1148.
39 These journeys to the Far East have been confirmed by Bing family documents, discussions with W. O. Michael, and the existence of maps and possibly journal entries that document aspects of the journeys. They involved trips to India, China and Japan.
40 Information supplied by Hisao Miyajima to the author. See n. 30.
41 Weisberg 1986a, p. 19.
42 *Didot-Bottin* 1882, p. 165: 'curiosités' – 19, rue Chauchat and 23, rue de Provence (the house number of his shop in rue de Provence changed to 22, probably between 1880 and 1883); and p. 1067: 'articles anciens' at the same two locations. 13, rue Bleue was also listed under 'articles nouveaux'.
43 In *Cadastre 1876*, D P 4 919: 23, rue de Provence, Bing is noted as renting a space on the ground floor and first floor. *Cadastre 1876*, D P 4 132, 133, 134: 13, rue Bleue, notes that Dubuffet, Siegfried Bing and August Bing rented space from 1881 onward.
44 See Tribunal de Commerce, Paris: Registres du commerce après 1881, Dépôts des statuts de la société en commandite par action S. Bing et Cie. avec déclaration de souscription et de versement, no. 1388, Paris, 14 June 1884.
45 Ibid.
46 Ibid. The loss of these accounting books severely hampers an ability to reconstruct the business transactions of this company.
47 In *Cadastre 1876*, D P 4 C 251: 19 rue Chauchat, the glass roof is listed as an 'addition de construction de 1883'. Bing paid rent for this site from 1883 for fifteen years, six months. The amount was 25,000 francs per year for the land.
48 See 'Un Musée Japonais Bing, 22 rue de Provence, et rue Chauchat,19' in *Catalogue Illustré du Salon*, Paris 1884, pp. 249-51.
49 Ibid., p. 251.
50 Letter from S. Bing to the Director of the South Kensington Museum, London, 1 May 1885.
51 Weisberg 1986a, p. 24 (original information on these offices supplied to the author by Hisao Miyajima).
52 See letter from S. Bing to M. Lockroy, Ministre du Commerce et de l'Industrie, on stationery of the 'Agence Générale Française, S. Bing et Co., Siège social, Paris, 13 rue Bleue', 24 January 1887 (Ministère des affaires étrangères, Direction des affaires commerciales et consulaires). Significantly, the letterhead notes three telegraph addresses in France, China and Japan as 'ESBing ... Paris, Shanghai or Yokohama', attesting to the far-reaching tentacles of the company. Other letters found in *Correspondance commerciale*, Tokyo, vol. 5 (1887–8), nos. 315, 318, 428, 429, between state officials, discuss the same issues and underscore the need to help Bing & Co. in their endeavours.
53 Ibid.
54 Weisberg 1986a, p. 24.
55 The significance of *Le Japon Artistique* is further discussed in Weisberg, 'The Creation of Japonisme' in this catalogue, pp. 52–7.
56 Weisberg 1986a, p. 29.
57 'Collection de pièces de porcelaines japonaises fournie au musée par Bing en 1888', inv. nos. 11353–400 (Archives, Conservatoire National des Arts et Métiers, Don Bing).
58 'Bing, Siegfroy (Siegfried)', 24 July 1890 (Archives Nationales, Dossier, Légion d'Honneur). He was given the award for three things: dissemination of Japanese art in France, artistic publications and for holding numerous exhibitions.

59 Hisao Miyajima noted that August Bing was connected with S. Bing et Cie. until 1894 (communication to author). Walter O. Michael in discussions with Bing family relatives noted that the family reported that August moved to Kassel by the mid-1890s.

60 Notes provided to the author by Walter O. Michael based on discussions with August Bing's family.

61 August had three children. His daughter Irene was still alive in 1981, and she is the Bing family member Walter O. Michael and his wife Carola met in 1976 (notes provided to the author by Walter O. Michael).

62 See Tribunal de Commerce, Paris: Registres du commerce après 1881, 'Dépôt des statuts, Société Dubuffet et Cie., Commandite simple, Exploitation de l'ancienne Maison S. Bing et Cie.', no. 2402, Registered 10 December 1892. Among the limited partners were Daniel Furcy Dubuffet, Nephtalie Lévy, Bernard Merzbach, Hector Wargny, and Siegfried Bing, among others. The new company was constituted for five years. Its purpose was to purchase and run the old S. Bing et Cie. There was some urgency in obtaining the documents from the authorities, as they had to be sent to Japan.

63 Ibid., 'Dépôt des statuts, Société Dubuffet et Cie., ancienne Maison S. Bing', no. 793, Registered 18 June 1901. This reorganisation of the company eliminated any reference to Siegfried Bing, except that the mention 'ancienne Maison S. Bing et Cie.' had to be kept.

64 Letter from Walter O. Michael to the author, 6 January 2003. Mr Michael has based his information on Paul Michael's *History of the Bing-Michael Family* prepared in 1967 and in his possession.

65 *Didot-Bottin* 1882, p. 468, under 'manufacture de porcelaine', lists Alfred Haase as the successor of Leullier fils et Bing at the same address as the earlier firm. *Cadastre 1876*, D P 4 no. C 412: 48, rue du faubourg Saint-Denis, notes the dissolution of Leullier fils et Bing.

66 The inventory of Marcel Bing's estate (see n. 6) lists René Haase as an heir who was to receive 35,000 francs. Haase helped disseminate porcelain objects from Bing in the United States, donating and selling works to the Metropolitan Museum of Art in New York. René Haase also purchased the client list from Marcel's shop and had the right to hold onto the gallery at 10, rue Saint-Georges. Both points are noted in the inventory.

67 Weisberg 1986a, p. 32.

68 See Weisberg 1987a, pp. 51–68.

69 *Didot-Bottin* 1896, pp. 1352, 1691.

70 Ibid., pp. 905, 1123, 1204.

71 *Didot-Bottin* 1903, pp. 19, 70, 1222, 1490.

72 Jacques Bing, Bing's eldest son, died in Blidah, Algeria, in 1891. See O. Serieux, 'Echos et Nouvelles', *Gazette de l'Hôtel Drouot*, 5 October 1891. Jacques Bing was in military service as a 'brigadier au 1er Chasseurs [sic] d'Afrique'.

73 'Marcel Bing', *American Art News*, 20 November 1920, p. 6.

74 Ibid. See also 'Ecole du Louvre, Registre des Cartes de Cours, années, 1893, 1894, 1895, 1896, 1897' (Archives du Louvre). Marcel studied Oriental archaeology and Classical sculpture (1893–4) with M. Pottier, the history of painting (1893–4) with M. Lafenestre (probably Louis Lafenestre), and the history of sculpture (1893–4) with M. Courajod. In 1895, at age twenty, Marcel should have been fulfilling his military service; however, because his brother Jacques had died on active duty, Marcel was exempted from military service.

75 For reference to the Vever shop being close to one of Bing's stores, see *Cadastre 1876*, D P 4 C 837: 19, rue de la Paix. Bing rented a ground-floor boutique from 1881 to 1886; Paul Vever also rented a ground-floor boutique on the right of the building from 1877. The name of his son, Henri Vever, appears in 1883. This would suggest an early tie between the two men.

76 Weisberg 1983.

77 See letter from S. Bing to Jules Adeline from Berck-sur-Mer, 17 August 1896 (Bibliothèque de la ville de Rouen, 4991 256).

78 Letter from A.G. Duizend to Madame Renée Genay, 4 May 1971 (in the possession of the author).

79 R.S., 'The Passing of Siegfried Bing', *Brush and Pencil* (November 1905), pp. 161–4.

80 See 'Du 7 Mai, Vente d'objets d'art et peintures du Japon et de la Chine composant la Collection S. Bing. Requête de M. Marcel Bing, F. Lair-Dubreuil, Commissaire-Priseur à Paris' (Archives de Paris, D 42 E 3 522: Extrait du registre des déclarations préalables aux ventes de meubles, 1906).

81 See letters from Marcel Bing to Dr Bode (Zentralarchiv der Staatlichen Museen zu Berlin, Preussischer Kulturbesitz: Acta, vol. 1, Von 23. 1. 05 bis 30 Juni 1908).

82 Letters from Louis Sarre to Dr Bode, 1905 to 1909 (ibid.).

83 Ibid., letter dated 10 July 1906. Sarre was especially concerned with tiles Bing sent, which he thought were fakes. He added that after consultation with Dr Mittwoch, his doubts had been confirmed.

84 The letter from Bing to Freer is dated 6 January 1916 and is sent from his post in the army. Freer's answer is dated 2 February 1916. In it Freer notes that the 'lot of bronzes which you entrusted to Mr. Loo has been divided between the collection of Mr. Eugene Meyer Jr. and my own.' (Archives, Freer Gallery of Art, Smithsonian Institution, Washington, D.C.: Letters between Marcel Bing and Charles Lang Freer). The list of Asian objects purchased by Freer from Bing is quite extensive.

85 See Archives Nationales, F 21 4447 (Ministère de l'Instruction Publique et des Beaux-Arts). These documents, dated between 1921 and 1936, are a record of all the objects Haase sold to the Louvre.

86 See Archives de Paris, D 42 E 3 no. 2628: Extrait du registre des déclarations du bureau d'enregistrement des Commissaires Priseurs, (Fernand Lair-Dubreuil), 7 February 1927.

87 Purchases of *art nouveau* pieces from René Haase were approved on 21 December 1925 out of the Edward C. Moore Jr. 'gift for the purchase of modern decorative art' (Archives, Metropolitan Museum of Art).

88 Gift of *art nouveau* pieces from René Haase. Gift received by letter to Mr Breck, Curator of Decorative Arts, on 7 September 1926. The gift was approved and accepted on 15 November 1926 (ibid.).

89 *Vente à la requête du Commissaire gérant. Biens Israélites. Ancienne Maison Maurice [sic] Bing – René Haase, Successeur, Art Antique [...], Art d'Extrême-Orient [...]*, Sale, Paris (Hôtel Drouot), 10–11 May 1943, Commissaire Priseur M. François Thullier (Bibliothèque de l'Union centrale des Arts décoratifs, G. V.o 41).

90 See letter from Isabel Fonseca to the author, 5 May 1983.

THE APPRECIATION AND STUDY OF JAPANESE ART

1 On Wakai Kenzaburô, see Brigitte Koyama-Richard *et al.*, *Correspondance adressée à Hayashi Tadamasa*, Tokyo 2001, p. 603; also Koyama-Richard 2001.

2 On the early shops and japonisants, see Lacambre 1980.

3 On William Michael Rossetti and Japonisme, see Julie L'Enfant, *William Rossetti's Art Criticism, The Search for Truth in Victorian Art*, New York 1999, especially chapter 4.

4 Sichel 1883.

5 See Weisberg, 'A Family Affair' in this catalogue, pp. 16–18, for confirmation of the early date for Bing selling Japanese art.

6 Chesneau 1878a, p. 387.

7 Throughout their history the Japanese worked mainly in wood. By comparison the use of bronze was limited; however, the gigantic statue of the Kamakura Buddha (thirteenth century), described by early travellers to the country, and nineteenth-century bronzes were seen by the French as typical.

8 The huge Buddha (around 1750) from the Banryôji Temple in Meguro (Tokyo) brought back by Cernuschi is on exhibition at the Musée Cernuschi, Paris.

9 For reference to these pieces, see the following inventory records at the Victoria and Albert Museum: inv. nos. 85–76; 187–76; 163–76.

The purchase prices of these pieces were respectively £7 (175 francs), £6 (160 francs) and £11 (275 francs).

10 See Victoria and Albert Museum inv. no. 1904–76.

11 Gonse 1883, vol. 2, p. 64 and plate 5.

12 Raymond Koechlin, *Les Collections d'Extrême-Orient du musée du Louvre et la donation Grandidier*, Paris 1914, p. 17.

13 Chesneau 1878a, p. 388.

14 This firm was founded in 1873, after the close of the World's Fair in Vienna, to produce and export ceramics, metalwork, cloisonné enamel and lacquer ware. Wakai Kenzaburô served as Vice-President, and Hayashi Tadamasa worked for the firm as an interpreter. For further information and references on this group, see Koyama-Richard 2001, pp. 39–40.

15 For a discussion of bronzes in the Meiji period, with reference to the activity of Suzuki Chôkichi, see Joe Earle, 'Japanese bronzes of the early Meiji Period', *Apollo* 154, no. 477 (November 2001), pp. 36–41.

16 See Victoria and Albert Museum inv. no. 188–1883. See also Gregory Irvine and Anna Jackson, 'The finest piece of bronze which an artist's hand has ever produced. The life and time of a Japanese incense burner', *Apollo* 152, no. 465 (November 2000), pp. 18–23.

17 Chesneau 1878b, p. 842.

18 P. Gasnault, 'La Ceramique de l'Extrême-Orient à l'Exposition Universelle', *Gazette des Beaux-Arts* 18 (December 1878), pp. 890–911.

19 Gonse 1886.

20 Many Japonistes had their own libraries, including Burty and, obviously, Bing. For reference to Burty's, see Weisberg 1993, Appendix I, The Japanese Library and Art Collection, pp. 271–5. For the donation to Arts et Métiers, see Inventory 11404–0001–002.

21 Beginning in 1875, Ernest Grandidier established a significant collection of Chinese porcelain, which had been largely secured from Langweil, Sichel and S. Bing. By 1894, this collection had been donated to the Louvre (now in the Musée Guimet, Paris).

22 S. Bing, 'La Céramique', in Gonse 1883, vol. 2, p. 241.

23 Leullier et Bing began as an outlet for the sale of contemporary French porcelains. They began selling some Japanese ceramics in the mid-1870s. See Weisberg, 'A Family Affair' in this catalogue, pp. 15–16. On the Sèvres pieces, see MNC 7045–55; MNC 7045 is reproduced in Shimizu 2001, p. 72.

24 While Hayashi's knowledge was often substantial, there were still many instances where places of production were misidentified or potters confused.

25 Noted as inv. no. MNC 7103 and reproduced in Shimizu 2001, p. 32.

26 The diptych by Zeshin was in the 1906 sale of Bing's collection, where it was catalogued as 'Paire de kakemono figurant un aigle...' Records of the sale indicate that it fetched 150 francs. For further reference, see 1906 Paris, no. 877. The work is listed in Hamburg as inv. 1906–743 a,b.

27 For a solid introduction to the issue of Japan learning the themes and technique of Western-style oil-painting, see Shuji Takashina, J.Thomas Rimer and Gerald D. Bolas, *Paris in Japan, The Japanese Encounter with European Painting*, Tokyo & St Louis (Washington University) 1987.

28 Cited by Kigi Yasuko, 'Hayashi Tadamasa: gloire et tourments', in Brigitte Koyama-Richard *et al.*, *Correspondance adressée à Hayashi Tadamasa*, Tokyo 2001, pp. 14–15.

29 Gonse 1883, vol. 2, p. 318.

30 Koechlin 1930, p. 17. Koechlin notes that Bing and Hayashi were the 'zealous propagators of a new cult'.

31 See Weisberg, 'The Creation of Japonisme' in this catalogue, pp. 52–7.

32 Koechlin 1930, p. 21. Koechlin provides a list of many Japonistes who came to Bing's house to see the works of art there, including Alexis Rouart, Charles Gillot, Manzi, Hugues Krafft, among many others.

33 See Préface [by Gaston Migeon], *Collection Ch. Gillot, Objets d'art et peintures d'Extrême Orient*, Sale, Paris (Galeries Durand-Ruel), 8–13 February 1904.

34 Van de Velde 1992, vol. 1, p. 271.

35 Camille Mauclair, 'Servitude et grandeur littéraire', *Mercure de France* (February 1896), pp. 265–9.

36 Koechlin 1930, p. 7.

37 Sichel 1883.

38 S. Bing, 'Les Origines de la peinture dans l'histoire', *Le Japon Artistique* 3, no. 13 (May 1889), pp. 13, 151–62.

39 Van de Velde 1992, vol. 1, p. 267.

40 See 1906 Paris, for further assessment of individual pieces.

41 Although there is no published catalogue of the Japanese collection in Hamburg, a close consultation of the inventory books does provide ample evidence as to when specific pieces officially entered the collection. For further information, see Hempel 1981, p. 160.

42 See inv. no. 418–6.

43 See inv. no. 418–3.

44 The earliest copies were most likely made by Monka in 1556 for the Seiganji Temple (Nakajima, Akimoto, Kazusa province), and these were recopied in 1881. See also Gonse 1883, vol. 1, pp. 175–6.

45 By way of comparison, in 1881 the British Museum (London) bought the entire Anderson collection of about two thousand paintings collected in Japan for the equivalent of 75,000 francs.

46 Prints, inv. nos. EO 183–206; casket, inv. no. EO 30; kakemono scroll, *Eagle on a Rock*, inv. no. EO 26; fan with crayfish decoration by Hokusai, inv. no. EO 28. Now in the Musée Guimet, Paris.

47 Sculpture, 1906 Paris, no. 9, inv. no. EO 821; screen, 1906 Paris, no. 862, inv. no. EO 2141; scroll, 1906 Paris, no. 913, inv. no. EO 2145; bottle, 1906 Paris, no. 237, inv. no. EO 3418. Now in the Musée Guimet, Paris.

48 Inv. no. EO 2622, Musée Guimet, Paris.

49 Mask, 1906 Paris, no. 40 (?), inv. no. EO 2165; statue, inv. no. EO 2066; Musée Guimet, Paris.

50 Inv. no. EO 827, Musée Guimet, Paris.

51 Inv. nos. EO 2535, 2536 (the latter acquired from Baron Takahashi), Musée Guimet, Paris.

52 Inv. no. EO 3011, Musée Guimet, Paris; reproduced in Gonse 1883, vol. 2, p. 269.

53 The exhibition *Le Japon à travers les siècles*, which examined many issues in Japanese art, took place at the Musée d'Art moderne, Paris, in 1958.

THE CREATION OF JAPONISME

1 For an overview of literature on Japonisme, see Weisberg 1975; Weisberg 1990; and exhib. cat. *Le Japonisme*, Paris (Grand Palais) 1988. On Edmond de Goncourt as a Japoniste and collector of Japanese art, see Michel Beurdeley and Michèle Maubeuge, *Edmond de Goncourt chez lui*, Nancy 1991, especially chapters 1 and 6. See also Koyama-Richard 2001.

2 On Philippe Burty, see Weisberg 1993. Burty's first article on Japonisme appeared in *La Renaissance Littéraire et Artistique* in May 1872.

3 On early shops in Paris selling Japanese material, see Lacambre 1980; and Gabriel P.Weisberg, 'Japonisme: Early Sources and the French Printmaker, 1854–1882', in Weisberg 1975, pp. 1–19.

4 Weisberg 1986b.

5 Ibid., p. 8. Burty called his journal *Le Japon Artiste*; the only issue that appeared contained etchings by Burty of Japanese objects in his collection. Some of the etchings are known, but no copy of the journal itself has been found. See Weisberg 1993, pp. 242, 251 n. 67.

6 Staff at the Museum für Kunsthandwerk Leipzig/Grassi Museum, in discussion with the author, commented on the Leipzig firm that had printed *Le Japon Artistique* in Germany. They also noted that the archives of this firm were destroyed in World War II.

7 Brinckmann and Bing were extremely close colleagues in the dissemination of Japanese art in Germany. The first documented ties between Hamburg's Museum für Kunst und Gewerbe and S. Bing date from 1883. At that time Brinckmann purchased Japanese wooden items and *inrô* from Bing's shop; see *Museum Record Book*, 1884, nos. 239, 277–185. Brinckmann remained a supporter of both

Japanese objects and *art nouveau* pieces; he was also staunchly supportive of the *Japon Artistique* venture.

8 Weisberg 1986b, p. 9.

9 On the South Kensington Museum's early contacts with Japan and art dealers, see Faulkner and Jackson 1995. The first contacts with Bing began in 1875. Some of the Japanese pieces sold by Bing to South Kensington emphasised educational qualities.

10 Weisberg 1986b, p. 9. Huish became one of the directors of the Fine Art Society in 1876. Information supplied by Peyton Skipwith, Fine Art Society, London.

11 The Fine Art Society hosted Japanese art exhibitions in 1888–90, including one in November/December 1890 on 'Hokusai, Drawings and Engravings' (Fine Art Society, Minute Book, 20 December 1888, p. 294). Bing may have provided objects for the exhibition, although the text for the catalogue was written by Huish (see n. 31).

12 Weisberg 1987, p. 67 n. 19.

13 See *The Complete Letters of Vincent van Gogh*, vol. 2, Greenwich & Boston 1978, pp. 600–1; and Weisberg 1986, pp. 28, 270 n. 51.

14 *Catalogue of the Van Gogh Museum's Collection of Japanese Prints*, Zwolle & Amsterdam 1991; see especially the preface by Ronald de Leeuw and the essay 'Van Gogh's Utopian Japonism' by Tsukasa Kôdera, both of which mention the artist's fascination with Japanese prints and the fact that he built a large portion of the collection that is now in the Van Gogh Museum.

15 The magazine was printed by Charles Gillot at 79, rue Madame; it was distributed by C.Marpon and E. Flammarion at 26, rue Racine. Charles Gillot was the son of Firmin Gillot, who had invented a non-photomechanical system that could transform line drawing and lithographic and etched images into relief zinc plates that could be economically printed. Charles Gillot added to his father's invention by including the photographic process. Whether documentation exists in the Flammarion archives on ties with Bing is open to conjecture; each monthly edition of the French version carried references to these ties.

16 George Auriol, 'Le Japon Artistique', *Le Chat Noir*, 26 May 1888, p. 1128.

17 *Japan Weekly Mail*, 8 June 1889, p. 538.

18 See Shimizu in this catalogue, p. 44; and *Exposition de la Gravure Japonaise, à l'Ecole Nationale des Beaux-Arts*, April-May 1890. The introduction to the catalogue was written by Bing; it also contained advertisements for *Le Japon Artistique* and reproduced pages of reproductions from the journal, thereby reinforcing interest.

19 *Japan Weekly Mail*, 7 September 1889, p. 211.

20 *The Academy*, 30 June 1888, p. 454.

21 'Fine Art, Art Books', *The Academy*, 12 October 1889, p. 242.

22 'The Fine Arts, Art Notes', *The Critic*, 4 December 1889, p. 302.

23 On the relationship between the South Kensington Museum and dealers in Asian art, see Faulkner and Jackson 1995, pp. 176, 178, 180–2. See also the letter from S. Bing (at 19, rue Chauchat) to the Director of the South Kensington Museum, 27 January 1876, noting that he was offering thirty Nô-masks to the museum at a price of 1,800 francs. On the Victoria and Albert Museum masks collection and S. Bing, see Gregory Irvine, 'Collecting a Tradition: The Japanese Mask Collection of the Victoria & Albert Museum', *Oriental Art* 41, no. 3 (Autumn 1995), pp. 2–9.

24 See A. Lequeux, 'The Theatre in Japan', *Artistic Japan* 4, no. 24 (May 1890), pp. 303–12.

25 See 'Report on Objects Received from Monsieur S. Bing [of 19, rue Chauchat], Bristol Hotel, Burlington Gardens, London', 14 December 1887 (Victoria and Albert Museum, General Stores). This document states that the museum received 150 Japanese combs from Bing, noting also that a few combs were slightly damaged. Significantly, Bing had come over to London with the merchandise to meet members of the Museum curatorial staff.

26 See Théodore Duret, 'On Combs', *Artistic Japan* 5, no. 26 (July 1890), pp. 335–41.

27 Weisberg 1986a, p. 37.

28 This is especially noted in Goncourt's attack on Bing's Salon de L'Art Nouveau in 1895. See Edmond and Jules de Goncourt, *Journal: Mémoires de la Vie Littéraire*, Paris 1959, vol. 4, Monday 30 December 1895, pp. 893–4. Edmond de Goncourt accused Bing of an internationalism that undermined the French national effort. Goncourt had begun to see Japanese objects at Bing's in July 1875, a fact that attests to the long relationship between the two men.

29 See Weisberg 1993, pp. 271–5.

30 Weisberg 1986b, p. 13. See also Gonse 1886.

31 See Ary Renan, 'Hokusai's Man-gwa', *Artistic Japan* 2, no. 8 (December 1888), pp. 83–90, and no. 9 (January 1889), pp. 99–104. See also *Exposition de la Gravure Japonaise* (April-May 1890). See also *Catalogue of the collection of drawings and engravings by Hokusai exhibited at the Fine Art Society*, London 1890; 204 works were shown; the introduction written by Marcus B. Huish stated that it was 'through the aid of Mons. Bing [...] [that] the present collection has been assembled'.

32 S. Bing, 'Hokusai: A Study, In Two Parts: Part 1', *Magazine of Art* 14 (December 1890-November 1891), pp. 242–8, 264–8, 307–9. Bing was establishing his credentials as an art critic with these English-language articles. Bing's ties with England were strengthened when he was elected to membership of the Japan Society, based in London, on March 31, 1892. Information kindly supplied by Annette Beaulieu and Sebastian Dobson, Honorary Librarian, Japan Society, London.

33 Victor Champier, 'Japanese Architecture', *Artistic Japan* 1, no. 3 (July 1888), pp. 19–25, and no. 4 (August 1888), pp. 31–7.

34. Lucien Falize, 'Jeweller's Work', *Artistic Japan* 1, no. 5 (September 1888), pp. 43–50.

35 William Anderson, 'Hiroshige', *Artistic Japan* 3, no. 15 (July 1889), pp. 183–9, and no. 16 (August 1889), pp. 195–201.

36 Justus Brinckmann, 'The Poetic Tradition in Japanese Art', *Artistic Japan* 4, no. 19 (December 1889), pp. 239–45, and no. 20 (January 1890), pp. 251–8.

37 Arthur Lasenby Liberty, 'The Industrial Arts and Manufacturers of Japan', *Artistic Japan* 6, no. 34 (March 1891), pp. 431–43. On Liberty, see Ashmore 2001.

38 Weisberg 1986b, p. 17.

39 Marcus B. Huish, 'Hints Upon the Formation of a Collection of Japanese Art', *Artistic Japan* 6, no. 35 (April 1891), pp. 447–55. As a director of the Fine Art Society Huish was a perfect individual to provide advice on the ways in which an art collection could be started and appropriate objects secured. Huish stressed working carefully with art dealers.

40 Roger Marx, 'On the Role and Influence of the Arts of the Far East and of Japan', *Artistic Japan* 6, no. 36 (May 1891), pp. 459–66. Marx suggests that there was always a specific goal for the magazine even when the periodical had first appeared. He wrote: 'As to the success of the review, the honour thereof lies with the erudite editor, whose supreme ability and energetic enthusiasm are borne witness to in the few farewell pages which follow, pages written without his knowledge and despite his express prohibition.'

41 See G. Pennetier, 'Collection J. Adeline', in *La Collection Japonaise (Legs Adeline)*, Rouen *(Actes du Museum de Rouen)* 1910, pp. 17–22. Jules Adeline was born in Rouen and trained as an architect-designer; he was also a printmaker and an art critic. He willed his collection of Japanese curios to the Museum d'Histoire Naturelle, Ethnographie et Préhistoire in Rouen. Information on Adeline and his collection provided by Monique Fouray, Curator, Museum d'Histoire Naturelle, Rouen.

42 Ibid, p. 22, where it is stated that, 'Parmi les japonaiseries, le grand dessin donné par S.Bing, mérite d'être regardé. C'est une immense aquarelle gouachée – sur plusieurs feuilles – représentant les différentes scènes d'un drame populaire. C'est une affiche de théâtre.'

43 S. Bing to Jules Adeline, 17 August 1896, from Berck-sur-Mer (Bibliothèque d'Etude, Bibliothèques Municipales, Rouen). The author is grateful to Marie-Dominique Nobécourt

Mutarelli, Librarian, for her help in finding the documentation on Jules Adeline and Eugène Brieux.

44 The dedication of the print reads: 'A S. Bing / bien cordialement / J. Adeline / Rouen / 8 Nov. 90', thus referring to their friendship. As noted in the short notice that accompanies the image in Weisberg 1986a, p. 28, the work is in the Library of the Musée des Arts décoratifs. What that notice does not specify is that it is pasted down in one of the volumes of the Maciet collection (vol. 180, Costumes: Japon, no. 5: Artistes Troyon – Z). The author is grateful to Annette Beaulieu for rediscovering this image, which had been out of sight during the rebuilding of library, and for providing added information about the nature of the work.

45 *Mikika. Japonaiserie Rouennaise rimée par Eugène Brieux. Avec un bois publié dans la Revue Illustrée* (1893) d'après le portrait gravé à l'eau-forte (Deuxième Exposition des Peintres-Graveurs) (1890) par Jules Adeline (Le Havre: Imprimerie Lemalle et Cie., n.d.). The poem is dedicated to 'Madame Jules Adeline'. Copy in Bibliothèque d'Etude, Bibliothèques Municipales, Rouen.

46 Weisberg 1986a, p. 37.

47 Ibid., p. 39.

48 Ibid., p. 40.

49 Ibid., p. 40 n. 80.

50 See *Catalogue d'une collection d'arbres nains du Japon, cultivés et dressés Yamanaka et Co. d'Osaka*, Paris, 30 November 1903.

51 See *Collection Ch. Gillot, Objets d'art et peintures d'Extrême Orient*, Sale, Paris (Galeries Durand-Ruel), 8–13 February 1904.

52 See *Catalogue Objets d'Art de la Chine et du Japon, Collections de Sir J.C. Robinson and Feu M. Ernest Hart*, Sale, Paris (Hôtel Drouot), 9–10 June 1904.

53 Weisberg 1986a, pp. 40–1. Marie Nordlinger, born in Manchester, studied painting at the Manchester School of Art and then in Paris in the atelier of Gustave Courtois. Later, realising that painting was not her forte, she went to Hamburg – where her grandmother lived – probably to study design. She went back to Paris in 1903 to work in Bing's jewellery ateliers (information in a letter from Pauline Green, Nordlinger's daughter, 17 October 1982, to the author). See also G.D. Painter, *Proust: The Early Years*, Boston 1959–65; and Philip Kolb, *Marcel Proust: Correspondance*, Paris 1970–98, 4 vols. Nordlinger was mentioned prominently in Marcel Bing's will as one of the primary legatees.

54 Weisberg 1986a, p. 41. See also Charles Lang Freer Papers, Vouchers III, 1903–1904, and Vouchers IV, 1905–1906 (Freer Gallery of Art, Washington, D.C.). There are also letters between Freer and Marcel Bing dated 1916.

55 The sale and location of Bing's Japanese print collection, essentially those pieces he kept in his Paris apartment, remains mysterious. Some were sold to Sir Alfred Beit in Ireland, although the number and whereabouts are unspecified.

ARTS AMBASSADOR FOR EUROPE AND AMERICA

1 Weisberg 1987, p. 51. Letter from Bing to L.P. di Cesnola, 2 October 1882 (Archives, The Metropolitan Museum of Art, New York, correspondence files, 1870–1950).

2 Ibid. In his letter to the Metropolitan, Bing wrote: 'I have intended to make some contribution to the collection of the Museum [...] watching with interest the efforts of your liberal citizens to establish a museum of art.'

3 As in March 1896, when his nephew Enrique Baer was sent to the Metropolitan. Letter from S. Bing to the Metropolitan Museum of Art, 13 March 1896 (ibid.).

4 Weisberg 1987, p. 54. See *Throw's New York City Directory*, vol. 101, for the year ending 1 May 1888. Both S. Bing and John Getz are listed on p. 155 at 220 Fifth Avenue; there is no listing for either Bing or Getz for the year ending on 1 May 1887. However, Bing is listed in the *Murphy's New York Business Directory*, 1887 edition, p. 27, under the subject heading 'Antiquities and Bric-a-Brac'.

5 Getz's trip back to the United States aboard the *Normandy* is documented in 'Courrier des Etats-Unis' (National Archives, Washington, D.C.: M 237-Roll 501).

6 Montague Marks, 'My Note-Book', *Art Amateur* 34, no. 6 (May 1896), p. 128, notes that Getz became the 'American representative of the house of Bing, of Paris'.

7 Weisberg 1987, p. 54.

8 Montezuma, 'My Notebook', *The Art Amateur* 17, no. 1 (June 1887), p. 3.

9 See *Catalogue of rare and valuable art objects comprising Chinese and Japanese porcelains, faiences [...] Including many specimens for collectors and amateurs to be sold by auction under the direction of the firm of S. Bing, 220 Fifth Avenue, New York at Davis and Harvey's Art Galleries, no. 1212 Chestnut Street*, 16–20 April 1888.

10 *Catalogue of bronzes and other works of art comprising antique Chinese and Japanese porcelains [...] To be sold at auction under the direction of the firm of S. Bing at their art rooms, nos 220 and 222 Fifth Avenue, New York*, 21 November 1888. It is likely that the magazine was sold on these premises.

11 For the period between 1889 and 1900, see Gabriel P. Weisberg 'The Republican Style in the Age of the Eiffel Tower' in exhib. cat. *When the Eiffel Tower Was New, French Visions of Progress at the Centennial of the Revolution*, ed. Miriam R. Levin, South Hadley, Mass. (Mount Holyoke College Art Museum), 1989, pp. 2–10.

12 See 'Une mission en Amérique' (National Archives, Washington, D.C.: Consular Dispatches from Paris, 1790–1906, T 1–27, January 2, 1890-December 29, 1893, Enclosure no. 2 with Dispatch no. 22). The nature of special 'missions' to the United States needs further examination.

13 Passenger List, New York, 12 February 1894–16 March 1894 (National Archives, Washington, D.C.: Microfilm. M 237, R 623 no. 172). Bing arrived on *La Champagne* as a first-class passenger, listing his occupation as 'art critic'.

14 Weisberg 1987a, p. 56.

15 See *Catalogue of antique Chinese and Japanese porcelains, pottery, enamels [...] To be sold at public sale by order of S. Bing, Paris*, Friday, 23 February 1894, at The American Art Galleries, Madison Square South, New York.

16 *Japanese engravings, old prints in color collected by S. Bing, Paris*, The American Art Galleries, Madison Square South, New York 1894.

17 'Art Notes', *The Critic*, 17 March 1894.

18 'Art News', *New York Evening Post*, Saturday, 17 March 1894; 'The Chronicle of the Arts, Exhibitions and Other Topics', *New York Daily Tribune*, Sunday, 18 March 1894, p. 14.

19 'The Fine Arts, Events in the Museum', *Boston Herald*, Sunday, 1 April 1894, p. 13. The article specifically emphasised Bing's coming to Boston to study the Japanese collections in the museum. On the significance of Morse and Fenollosa as American propagators of Japanese art, see Meech and Weisberg 1990, pp. 45–7.

20 Ibid., and 'The Fine Arts', *Boston Herald*, Sunday, 8 April 1894, p. 13.

21 Ibid., p. 14.

22 Ibid., 15 April 1894, p. 22. The newspaper commented on Chinese clasps and buckles on display without ever mentioning Japanese objects in metal.

23 Weisberg 1986a, p. 34.

24 In 1894 the collection was loaned to the museum by S. Bing; S.P. Avery asked for clarification as to what Bing had left on loan to see how the textiles related to objects already owned by the Havemeyers (Archives, The Metropolitan Museum of Art, Mr. and Mrs. H.O. Havemeyer File H 2983). See Frances Little, 'Japanese Textiles from the Bing Collection', *Bulletin of the Metropolitan Museum of Art* 27 (January 1932), pp. 14–16.

25 Robert Koch, in his introduction to the translation of Bing's *La Culture Artistique en Amérique*, writes that Bing, after 'visiting New York, Boston, Albany, Chicago, Cincinnati, Pittsburgh, and Washington, D.C., [...] returned home.' See Bing 1970, p. 6. See also 'Bing on American Art. The French expert praises American architecture and industrial arts', *New York Sun*, Sunday, 23 February 1897, which states that

Bing 'traveled as far west as Chicago and south as Richmond.' It has been established beyond doubt that Bing was in New York and Boston; however, no mention in the local press has been found about Bing's visit to other cities. Yet, Bing's own writings about Rookwood in Cincinnati or Henry H.Richardson, especially Richardson's Pittsburgh Courthouse, lead us to believe that Bing did, indeed, travel to these cities.

26 On Tiffany, see Koch 1964; Joppien 1999; and Loring 2002.

27 Weisberg 1986a, p. 49, citing a letter from Edouard Vuillard to Maurice Denis, 30 May 1894 (Archives familiales de Maurice Denis, Musée départemental Maurice Denis 'Le Prieuré', Saint-Germain-en-Laye). A study for Vuillard's stained-glass window is reproduced in Cogeval 2003, fig. 125. It is presumed that the window itself is lost.

28 Weisberg 1986a, pp. 49–51.

29 Ibid., pp. 46–52. Cogeval 2003, p. 184, notes that there were 13 windows executed by 11 artists. Only the windows by Roussel, Bonnard and Toulouse-Lautrec have been found.

30 Weisberg 1986a, p. 51.

31 'Le Home', *La Revue Franco-Américaine* 1 (July 1895), p. 93.

32 Ibid. The Salon of the Société Nationale des Beaux-Arts was held at the Champ-de-Mars.

33 'Objets d'Art – L'Exposition de la Société Nationale des Beaux-Arts au Champs de Mars', *Journal des Arts*, 26 June 1895.

34 B.F., 'The Salon of the Champs-de-Mars', *Art Amateur* 33, no. 1 (June 1895), p. 6.

35 See Becker in this catalogue, p. 126.

36 On the reception of *La Culture artistique en Amérique*, see Bing 1970. See also Weisberg 1987b.

37 See S. Bing, 'L'Architecture et les arts décoratifs en Amérique', *Revue Encyclopédique*, 11 December 1897, pp. 1029–36. There were numerous illustrations of Tiffany's works included with the article.

38 '"Literature: Books on Art", *La Culture artistique en Amérique* par S. Bing, Paris: 22, rue de Provence, New York: Drysen and Pfeiffer, 1896', *New York Evening Post*, 21 March 1896, p. 16. The utilisation of what would appear to be a direct quotation from Bing's pamphlet strongly supports the existence of an English language version, even though the sentence structure and syntax were not of the best. Drysen and Pfeiffer in New York are listed on the masthead of the review, which further reinforces the likely availability of an English edition. This edition has not been located.

39 Ibid. The pamphlet was dedicated to Henri Roujon, Directeur des Beaux-Arts, who had asked Bing, at the time of his departure for the United States, to return with a report on the development of the arts in America. The dedication is dated Paris, November 1895.

40 Ibid.

41 *New York Sun*, 23 February 1897, p. 7.

42 Weisberg 1987b, p. 63. Robert Koch and subsequent writers on Tiffany have documented Bing's visit to the Tiffany workshops in New York.

43 Koch 1964, pp. 74–5, confuses the time that Bing and Tiffany spent together in New York City; his account has been repeated by almost all subsequent writers examining Tiffany's early glasswork. Recent discussion with the Tiffany Archives in Winter Park, Florida, have not yielded any further new detailed information on ties between Tiffany and Bing.

44 'La Culture Artistique en Amérique', *The Nation*, 19 March 1896, p. 240.

45 Weisberg 1987b, p. 63.

46 Following Tiffany's success with Bing in 1895, both men worked on the organisation of an independent exhibition in Bing's gallery in June 1897. This was part of the series of exhibitions Bing organised in his gallery from March 1896 to 1905 (see Becker in this catalogue, pp. 262–3, n. 47).

47 Letter from S. Bing to Hofrath de Scala [sic], 4 August 1897 (Österreichisches Museum für angewandte Kunst, Vienna, Permanent Collection and Research Archives). The author is grateful to Ms. Kathrin Pokorny-Nagel, Leiterin der Bibliothek und Kunstblättersammlung, for her help in finding the letters pertaining to the relationship between the Museum and Bing.

48 Bing did not produce an elaborate catalogue for this show. As with other shows Bing organised between 1896 and 1905, it was a small pamphlet of a few pages with no illustrations. This was not the first time that Bing had shown Tiffany Favrile glass pieces in his gallery, as he had exhibited twenty in 1895–6 at his first Salon de l'Art Nouveau, in addition to the stained-glass windows executed after designs by the Nabis. Loring 2000 does not mention the 1897 exhibition at Bing's, but lists an exhibition in1898–9 for which this author has found no specific reference. The number of pieces exhibited in 1897 is not known, but it is possible to surmise that it is close to the seventy pieces Bing sent on tour to several European cities.

49 Letter from Bing to Scala, 4 August 1897 (see n. 47). For earlier texts on Tiffany and Europe, see Schaeffer 1962; Weisberg 1986a, pp. 135–7; and especially Rüdiger Joppien, 'Tiffany und Europa', in Joppien 1999, pp. 22–9.

50 For reference to glass in Reichenberg, see *Die Gläsersammlung des Nordböhmischen Gewerbe-Museums in Reichenberg*, Leipzig 1902. There was a movement at the time to develop a collection of glass from the region that would also use Tiffany pieces as models for designers there.

51 Letter from S. Bing to Jenö Radisics (Director of the Országos Magyar Iparmüvészeti Muzeum, Budapest), 6 October 1897.

52 Letter from Bing to Scala, 31 January 1898 (see n. 47).

53 S. Bing, 'Die Kunstgläser von Louis C.Tiffany', *Kunst und Kunsthandwerk* 1 (1898), pp. 105–11.

54 Schaeffer 1962, p. 317.

55 Extract of a letter originally sent from Jenö Radisics to S. Bing, Paris, in 1897 (Országos Magyar Iparmüvészeti Muzeum, Budapest, Extract book, document no. 452, 1897). The original letter has most likely not survived.

56 Letter from Bing to Radisics, 19 December 1897.

57 Ibid., 20 January 1898.

58 Ibid., 28 March 1898.

59 Ibid., 3 May 1898.

60 Invoice from Bing's gallery L'Art Nouveau to the Budapest Museum for twelve works by Louis Comfort Tiffany, 20 July 1898. Prices for the pieces ranged from 50 francs to 225 francs; most of the pieces sold for 100 francs or more.

61 Invoice from L'Art Nouveau to M. Jens Thiis, Director of the Nordenfjeldske Kunstindustrimuseum, Trondheim, 27 July 1900. A letter from S. Bing to Thiis, 9 October 1900, noted a reduction of 10% on the purchase of the Tiffany white lamp. Thiis, on behalf of his museum, not only became an important client for Bing but also wrote a lengthy report on Bing in 1900; see *Arborg, 1898–1901*, Trondheim (Nordenfjeldske Kunstindustrimuseum) 1901.

62 Peck 1962, pp. 66–7, 72.

63 Weisberg 1999, pp. 157, 163.

64 'Les récompenses de l'Exposition. Classe LXXI–Céramique', *L'Evénement*, 4 October 1900, p. 3, cited in Weisberg 1999, p. 216 n. 44.

65 Weisberg 1999, p. 163.

66 Peck 1962, p. 66.

67 Ibid., p. 67.

68 Order of payment to L'Art Nouveau, Paris, 29 May 1900, including no. 3510 Vase Rookwood by Shirayamadani (1900.192), purchased for 750 francs, and no. 3512 Vase Rookwood by Albert R. Valentien (1900.193), purchased for 625 francs (Archiv, Museum für Kunst und Gewerbe, Hamburg, Document no. 1443).

69 Letter from Alena Adlerová (Curator at Umeleckoprumyslové Museum v Praze), 5 August 1983, confirming the purchase of two Rookwood pieces.

70 Inv. nos. Ke 4373, 4374, 4372 (Permanent Collection and Research Archives, Österreichisches Museum für angewandte Kunst, Vienna).

71 See Montgomery 1993, pp. 31ff.

72 Exhib. cat., *Inspiring Reform. Boston's Arts and Crafts Movement*, Wellesley, Mass. (Wellesley College / Davis Museum and Cultural Center), 1997, pp. 59ff.

73 Montgomery 1993, p. 37.

74 Ibid., p. 39.

75 Ibid., chapter 3, n. 42.

76 Ibid., p. 39.
77 Bing sold Vienna the vase, which he had shown at the 1900 World's Fair, for 190 francs, and it entered the museum (inv. no. Ke 4460) on 22 March 1901 (Permanent Collection and Research Archives, Österreichisches Museum für angewandte Kunst, Vienna).
78 Montgomery 1993, pp. 44–5, 101 n. 12.
79 Mary Ann Smith, *Gustav Stickley. The Craftsman*, Syracuse, New York, 1983, p. 19.
80 Bing 1903, p. 8. See also Weisberg 1986a, pp. 190, 278 n. 17; and Weisberg, 'Bing porcelain in America', *The Connoisseur* 178 (November 1971), pp. 200–3. In this article, the author rightly stated that Stickley purchased the complete table service, but in Weisberg 1986 mistakenly noted that it was used in the Craftsman restaurants while, in reality, it was only used by Stickley in the model dining room in the 1903 Arts and Crafts exhibition held in the Craftsman Building in Syracuse, New York. For this latest information see Cathers 2003, pp. 72 and 77, where Cathers writes: 'The dining room table was set with the champagne glasses and Colonna-designed porcelain that Stickley had bought from Bing, arrayed on pale yellow embroidered table runners.'
81 Coy L. Ludwig, *The Arts and Crafts Movement in New York State 1890s–1920s*, Hamilton, New York, 1983, p. 57.

THE OPENING OF LA MAISON DE L'ART NOUVEAU

1 'Petite chronique', *L'Art Moderne*, 2 June 1895, p. 175.
2 *L'Art Moderne*, 5 January 1896, p. 7.
3 Ibid., 19 January 1896, p. 22.
4 Ibid.
5 Hippolyte Fierens-Gevaert, 'A propos de l'inauguration de la Maison de l'Art Nouveau de M. Bing', *L'Indépendance Belge*, 10 January 1896. Note that at Libre Esthétique exhibitions objects on display were marked with their price.
6 Outraged by the reactions of certain French art critics to the inauguration of L'Art Nouveau, *L'Art Moderne* declared (5 January 1896): 'We have taken up arms so often against the petty-minded snobbery that results from nationalism of this sort that it is useless to pursue the point. Let us content ourselves with rejoicing to see the avant-garde once more fighting the good fight, and on a new battleground. We should congratulate M. Bing for his outstanding courage in provoking this outcry.'
7 Jane Block, 'La Maison d'Art. Edmond Picard's Asylum of Beauty', in *Irréalisme et Art Moderne. Les voies de l'imaginaire dans l'art des* XVIIIe, XIXe, *and* XXe *siècles. Mélanges Philippe Robert-Jones*, ed. Michel Draguet, Brussels 1991.
8 Such instances of generosity were not infrequent among patrons of *art nouveau*. Fritz Wärndorfer, a prosperous textile merchant, sank his fortune into the running of the Wiener Werkstätte, in the foundation of which he had also been involved.
9 *L'Art Moderne*, 16 December 1894, p. 395. Though unsigned, this statement of the Maison d'Art's philosophy is by Picard himself.
10 Other institutions admittedly attempted this on a more spectacular and ambitious scale, for example, the Künstlerkolonie in Darmstadt, established in 1898–9 through the determination of a single man, Ernst Ludwig, last Grand Duke of Hessen.
11 Van de Velde 1992, vol. 1, pp. 263, 265.
12 Krahmer 1992–4, pp. 149–52.
13 Bing 1902; and Bing 1903.
14 The public were required to pay an entrance fee of 1 franc, whereas entry to the Maison d'Art was free.
15 See Signac's Journal, 8 and 12 January 1896 (private archives). For Signac's relationship with L'Art Nouveau, see Philippe Thiébaut, 'Art nouveau et néo-impressionnisme', *Revue de l'Art* 92 (1991), pp. 72–8.
16 Letter from Signac to Angrand, Paris, 30 December 1896 (private archives).
17 Letter from Van Rysselberghe to Signac, Brussels, summer 1895 (private archives).
18 Letter from Van Rysselberghe to Signac, Brussels, 10 October 1895 (private archives).
19 Eidelberg and Henrion-Giele 1977, pp. 747–52.
20 See Gabriel P. Weisberg, 'Siegfried Bing, Louis Bonnier et la Maison de l'Art nouveau en 1895', *Bulletin de la Société de l'Histoire de l'Art français* (1983), pp. 241–9.
21 By systematically omitting Horta's name from all his writings, Van de Velde appears to have been encouraging a conspiracy of silence.
22 See, in particular, the documents assembled by Cécile Dulière in her edition of Victor Horta's *Mémoires*, Brussels 1985, pp. 296–303.
23 Private archives.
24 'I saw Bing [...] who has employed one of my friends (Jaeger, Congo) on pretty good terms.' Letter to Signac (private archives). Later, Van Rysselberghe advised Signac, who was clearly irritated by Bing's procrastination, 'In any case, friend Jaeger will keep an eye open for squalls – and by autumn I'll try and sort things out with Bing.' (Private archives.) Further, on 9 December 1895, Van de Velde wrote to his wife Maria: '[...] Otherwise, everything is in a crazy mess. Apart from Jaeger, who is the real organiser, they're all running round in circles.' (Brussels, Bibliothèque Royale, Archives et Musée de la Littérature, FS X 784/1895/5).
25 'In the morning we leave Passy, where Jaeger has a very modest but very cheerful and very artistic apartment on the fifth floor, a stone's throw from the station ...' (Letter from Henry Van de Velde to Maria Van de Velde, 9 December 1895, ibid.)
26 In their remarkable and exemplary edition of Van de Velde's memoirs, Anne van Loo and Fabrice van de Kerckhove cite a passage from the first edition of Meier-Graefe's *Entwicklungsgeschichte der Modernen Kunst* (1904), which contains a highly sympathetic appreciation of Jaeger's character (Van de Velde 1992, vol. 1, p. 317). It was most probably Jaeger who suggested to Bing the idea of displaying African pottery alongside traditional Flemish artefacts.
27 Brussels, Bibliothèque Royale, Archives et Musée de la Littérature, FS X 784. See also Philippe Thiébaut, 'La Ligne «belge» et la création française: Tout cela sent le belge roublard...', in exhib. cat. *Paris–Bruxelles. Bruxelles–Paris*, Paris (Grand Palais) & Ghent (Museum of Fine Arts) 1997, pp. 390–6.
28 Letter of 23 December 1895 (Brussels, Bibliothèque Royale, Archives et Musée de la Littérature, FS X 784/1895/14). The subject of dispute is the mural decoration for the dining room that Van de Velde had himself designed.
29 Letter from Paul Signac to Henri Edmond Cross, undated (private archives).
30 Van de Velde 1992, vol.1, pp. 273–5.
31 Ibid., p. 275.
32 Ibid.

LES SALONS DE L'ART NOUVEAU

I am grateful to Gabriel and Yvonne Weisberg for allowing me to make use of their comprehensive archives in writing this article.

1 Anonymous, 'Le Home échos' and 'L'Art échos', *La Revue Franco-Américaine* 1 (July 1895), pp. 95 and 99.
2 *L'Art Moderne*, 5 January 1896, p. 7.
3 Gabriel Weisberg, 'Siegfried Bing and Frank Brangwyn. The Gallery L'Art Nouveau in Paris in 1895', *Jaarboek Stad Brugge, Stedelijke Musea*, Bruges 1985–6, pp. 277–86.
4 Boileau 1896.
5 Alexandre 1895, p. 1.
6 With many thanks to Libby Horner for giving me permission to use this detailed information about Frank Brangwyn; she is at the moment writing a catalogue raisonné and preparing an exhibition of his work.
7 Originally Bing asked the Brussels architect Victor Horta for a design (fig. 103), but this proved to be too expensive and too time-consuming to carry out. See Thiébaut in this catalogue, pp. 105–7.
8 Herbert Furst, *The Decorative Art of Frank Brangwyn*, London 1924, p. 51.

9 Dominique Marechal, exhib. cat., *Collectie Frank Brangwyn*, Bruges (Municipal Museum) 1987, pp. 93 ff.

10 Emile Bosquet, *L'Art Nouveau? Lettre ouverte adressée à l'auteur de la notice Le Style dans les Arts décoratifs, appliqués à la reliure des livres*, Paris 1896, pp. 10–11.

11 Julius Meier-Graefe, 'L'Art Nouveau Die Salons', *Das Atelier* 6 (1896), p. 3.

12 Exhib. cat. *Beyond the easel: decorative painting by Bonnard, Vuillard, Denis, and Roussel, 1880–1930*, Chicago (The Art Institute of Chicago) & New York (The Metropolitan Museum of Art) 2001.

13 Letter from Siegfried Bing to Maurice Denis, 30 April 1895 (Archives familiales de Maurice Denis, Musée Départemental Maurice Denis 'Le Prieuré', Saint-Germain-en-Laye).

14 André Halays, 'Au jour le jour', *Journal des Débats*, 12 January 1896, p. 1.

15 Camille Mauclair, 'L'Art décorative de M.Albert Besnard', in *L'Art en Silence*, Paris 1901, pp. 289–307.

16. Bailly-Herzberg 1989, vol. 4, pp. 147–8.

17. Annette Leduc Beaulieu and Brooks Beaulieu, 'The Thadée Natanson Panels: A Vuillard Decoration for S. Bing's Maison de L'Art Nouveau', *Nineteenth-Century Art Worldwide*, www.19thc-artworldwide.org, vol. 1, issue 2 (Autumn 2002).

18 Ibid. for the criticism by Camille Mauclair, Edmond Cousturier and Octave Mirbeau.

19 Félix Fénéon, entries in the auction catalogue *Collection Thadée Natanson*, Paris, 13 June 1908, cited from Félix Fénéon, *Œuvres plus que complètes*, ed. Joan U. Halperin, Geneva & Paris 1970, vol. 1, p. 258.

20 *Tableaux modernes collection Bing*, Sale, Paris (Hôtel Drouot), 17 May 1900, no. 115. There was another drawing by Van Gogh recorded in the auction catalogue as no. 114 ('Femme à genoux, dessin, 43,5 x 54,5 cm'), which cannot however be located.

21 *The Complete Letters of Vincent van Gogh*, Greenwich & Boston 1958, vol. 2, pp. 600–1, 611–5.

22 Meier-Graefe 1896.

23 Ibid.

24 *Salon de L'Art Nouveau*, premier catalogue, December 1895, no. 662. *Salon de L'Art Nouveau*, deuxième catalogue, January 1896, no. 187.

25 Piotr Michalowski *et al.*, *Galeria Rogalinska Edwarda Raczynskiego*, Poznán 1997–8, no. 28 (Paul-Albert Besnard, fig. 135), no. 63 (Charles Cottet, fig. 131) and no. 91 (Charles Doudelet, fig. 133).

26 Exposition internationale du livre, June 1896, no. 1134. The books illustrated by Beardsley are no. 86: Sir Thomas Malory, *Le Morte d'Arthur* (J.M. Dent & Co.); no. 905 (cover); no. 306: Sidney Smith and R.B. Sheridan, *Bon-Mots* (J.M. Dent & Co.); no. 310: Charles Lamb and Douglas Jerrold, *Bon-Mots* (J.M. Dent & Co.); no. 311: Theodore Hook and Samuel Foote, *Bon-Mots* (J.M. Dent & Co.); no. 350: Oscar Wilde, *Salomé* (E. Mathews and J. Lane); no. 378: Alexander Pope, *The Rape of the Lock* (L. Smithers); no 957: Henry Harland, *Grey Roses* (J. Lane); no. 959: H. de Vere Stacpoole, *Pierrot* (J. Lane); no. 964: Grant Allen, *The British Barbarian* (J. Lane); no. 965: Florence Farr, *The Dancing Faun* (J.Lane); no. 969: F. Dostoevsky, *Poor Folk* (Elken [sic] Mathews).

27 Colleen Denney, 'English Book designers and the role of the modern book at l'Art Nouveau; Part one: Modern merriment and morality in the art of Walter Crane', *Arts Magazine* 61, no. 9 (May 1987), pp. 76–83. Colleen Denney, 'English book designers and the role of the modern book at l'Art Nouveau; Part two: Relations between England and the Continent', *Arts Magazine* 61, no. 10 (June 1987), pp. 49–57. Rowan Watson, Bing, 'Art Nouveau and the book in the late nineteenth century', *Apollo* 151, no. 459 (May 2000), pp. 32–40.

28 Meier-Graefe 1896, p. 4.

29 Léon Abry, 'Les Salons d'Art. Leurs Locaux et le placement des oeuvres', *L'Art Moderne*, 12 January 1899, p. 54.

30 Edwin Becker, 'White, Blue and Gold: In Search of New Harmony', in exhib. cat. *In Perfect harmony: picture + frame*, ed. Eva Mendgen, Amsterdam (Van Gogh Museum) & Vienna (Kunstforum) 1995, p. 263 n. 36.

31 This was probably Henri Jaeger, 'a very intelligent young man, and second [Theo] van Gogh, who was head of the firm', according to a letter from Camille to Georges Pissarro, 15 July 1895 (Archives Félix Pissarro), in Bailly-Herberg 1989, vol. 4, p. 80. See Thiébaut in this catalogue, p. 261 nn. 24–26.

32 Boileau 1896, p. 15. Boileau was, among other things, the architect of the large department store Au Bon Marché (1869–72).

33 *Tableaux modernes collection Bing*, Sale, Paris (Hôtel Drouot), 17 May 1900; annotated version in the Koninklijke Bibliotheek, The Hague (Lugt 58199).

34 Exhib. cat., *Theo van Gogh 1857–1891: art dealer, collector and brother of Vincent*, ed. Chris Stolwijk and Richard Thomson, Amsterdam (Van Gogh Museum) 1999 & Paris (Musée d'Orsay) 2000, pp. 210–17.

35 Claire Leblanc, 'Les verreries Art Nouveau des frères Daum conservés aux Musées royaux d'Art et d'Histoire', *Bulletin des Musées royaux d'Art et d'Histoire* 7 [2000], Brussels 2003, pp. 187–212.

36 Georges Lecomte, foreword in exhib. cat. *Salon de L'Art Nouveau. Exposition Constantin Meunier*, Paris, 16 February–15 March 1896.

37 Anonymous, 'Constantin Meunier à Paris', *L'Art Moderne*, 23 February 1896, p. 62.

38 Unfortunately for those invited, the invitation card with the original engraving by Legrand had to be handed in at the entrance! Léon de Saint-Valéry, 'Exposition de M. Legrand, à «L'Art Nouveau»', *Revue des Beaux-Arts et des Lettres*, 15 April 1896, p. 110.

39 Ernest Jaubert, 'L'Exposition de Louis Legrand', *L'Artiste* 66 (May 1896), p. 356.

40 Eugène Carrière, introduction in exhib. cat. *Salon de L'Art Nouveau. Exposition Eugène Carrière*, Paris, 18 April 1896.

41 Frances Keyzer, 'Eugène Carrière', *The Studio* 8, no. 41 (August 1896), p. 141.

42 Meier-Graefe 2002, pp. 19–20.

43 Jan Kneher, *Edvard Munch, in seinen Ausstellungen zwischen 1892–1912*, Worms 1994, pp. 92–7.

44 Camille Mauclair, 'Edvard Munch, galerie de l'Art Nouveau', *Mercure de France* 21 (July 1896), p. 187.

45 August Strindberg, 'L'Exposition d'Edward Munch', *La Revue Blanche* (June 1896), p. 525.

46 Frantz Jourdain, [review of Munch exhibition, Salon de L'Art Nouveau], *La Patrie*, 30 May 1896.

47 The special exhibitions at Bing's gallery were (in chronological order):

December 1895	1st Salon de L'Art Nouveau
February 1896	2nd Salon de L'Art Nouveau
16 February-15 March 1896	Constantin Meunier
2–15 April 1896	Louis Legrand
18 April-13 May 1896	Eugène Carrière
May 1896	Edvard Munch
June 1896	International Modern Book Exhibition
August 1896	Simon Moulijn
November 1896	Charles Cottet
May-June 1897	József Rippl-Rónai
December 1897	Charles Pepper (watercolours)
March 1898	Alphonse Legros
April 1898	Daniel Vierge
November-December 1898	Jean-François Raffaelli, (colour) etchings
April 1899	Gaston Prunier (watercolours)
October-November 1899	Santiago Rusiñol
March-April 1901	Japanese Artists Association Nihon-Gwakai (Tokyo)
March 1902	Marie Bermond
April 1902	Felix Borchardt
May 1902	Japanese dwarf trees
June 1902	Meta Warrick
June 1902	Paul Signac
November 1902	William Degouve de Nuncques and Juliette Massin
January 1903	Adolphe Dervaux
March 1903	Georges de Feure
March 1903	Ernest Baillet
May 1903	Hiroshige, Hokusai and Kuniyoshi
March 1905	Paul Jouve

48 Alexandre 1895, p. 1.
49 Ibid.
50 Thadée Natanson, '«Art Nouveau»', *La Revue Blanche* 10 (1896), p. 115.
51 Bing 1902.

BING AND ENGLAND

1 A photograph of glassware by James Powell and Sons occurs on p. 28 of the *Album de références*; the Album contains 37 pages of photos in all.
2 Morot 1938. Marcel Morot appears as the representative of the gallery L'Art Nouveau with the administration of the Dessins et Modèles déposés.
3 Jens Thiis was at the time director of a new museum of decorative arts in Trondheim, Norway, the Nordenfjeldske Kunstindustrimuseum. Weisberg 1986a, pp. 100 ff.
4 Photos in the Archives Louis Bonnier (Paris, Institut Français d'Architecture). The designs are to be found in the *Album de références* (nos. 7/82 and 83: 'Coin Hall, 90 f, Banquette Hall, 200 f').
5 Edmond Cousturier, 'Galeries S. Bing. Le mobilier', *La Revue Blanche* 10 (1896), pp. 92–5. This article provides the most detailed description of the various rooms decorated for the opening of the gallery in December 1895.
6 The two circular salons by Besnard and Isaac, the dining room with accompanying rest room by Van de Velde and another room with hangings by Ranson and decorated with English drawings and furniture. See Meier-Graefe 1898, p. 205.
7 The dining room was reproduced for publicity purposes in *Le Gaulois du dimanche* (44), 16–17 April 1898, p. 4; also in Meier-Graefe 1898, p. 9. Isaac's salon appeared on a publicity insert in the supplement of *Art et Décoration* 4, no. 2 (August 1898), p. 6.
8 A. de Bussières, 'L'Art nouveau. S. Bing. Paris', *Revue internationale des expositions, Moniteur général de l'Exposition 1900* 2 (16–31 January 1899), p. 8.
9 S. Bing, 'Wohin Treiben Wir?', *Dekorative Kunst* 1, no. 2 (October 1897), pp. 68–71; Bing 1903.
10 Numerous links have been established with British specialists, which will, in the long run, make possible a number of identifications. I would like to thank my British colleagues, Mrs Judy Rudoe (British Museum, London), Mr Richard Edgecumbe (Victoria and Albert Museum, London) – and particularly Mrs Sarah Medlam of the furniture department of the Victoria and Albert Museum – for their kindness in sharing with me their expertise in this area and introducing me to their numerous contacts specialising in English furniture of the period.
11 A large quantity of these objects was purchased by the Trondheim Museum in 1896: two lamps, firedogs, ewer, plate-warmer, teapot, dish. A design for firedogs, different from the Trondheim example, appears in the *Album de références* with the notice: '100 f. No. 293, Chenets mod. Germain' (no. 25/293).
12 Walter Shaw Sparrow, *Flats, Urban Houses and Cottage Homes*, London 1906, p. 72. My especial thanks to Mr Peter Rose, the Benson specialist, for his kind co-operation, and hoping that our joint researches will lead to further identifications.
13 Saint-Cloud buffet (no. 4/46); 'Lily' (nos. 6/77 and 78) or 'Deauville' (nos. 8/99 and 100) chairs. Research into the English archives has not so far yielded any written traces of Bing's orders to Morris and Co., but the evidence is of a fragmentary nature. Documents are also dispersed between various storage centres, and not all the many catalogues have survived.
14 The Liberty Registers, including those of the store opened in Paris in 1889, are preserved in the Westminster Archives Centre, London,
15 Particularly the Valfin item (no. 2/13).
16 My gratitude to John Jesse and Peter Rose for their invaluable assistance. A study of the J.S. Henry firm is at present in progress and may permit identification of other items from Bing's reference book.
17 Weisberg 1996.
18 Weisberg 1985–6; Eidelberg and Henrion-Giele 1977. See also Becker in this catalogue, pp. 119–21.
19 My heartfelt thanks to Mrs Libby Horner, who is preparing the catalogue raisonné of Brangwyn's work, for her generosity in sharing some of her conclusions on the artist's commissions from Bing.
20 In a sketchbook (private collection) we find: 'sent to S. Bing [...] 2 designs for carpets/ 1 large design for carpet/ one large carpet £100.0.0/ 1 small carpet 20.0.0' (Information supplied by Mrs Libby Horner).
21 Morot 1938.
22 Camille Mauclair, *Servitude et Grandeur littéraires*, Paris 1922, pp. 177–8.
23 Weisberg 1986a, pp. 195–6. Catalogue of the collection, vol. 6: *Modern art of metalwork*, Berlin (Bröhan-Museum) 2001.
24 See Weisberg, 'A Family Affair' in this catalogue, pp. 16–26.
25 Bing was an important supplier of fine arts museums in France. He provided the Louvre with showcases from 1897 (Bibliothèque des Musées nationaux, série MN: comptabilité des musées nationaux), as well as office chairs and armchairs ('Beaux-Arts' design, no. 23/260) inspired by items in the 1898 English dining room but sold for 35 or 50 francs. One of these armchairs, formerly in the Louvre, is now in the collections of the Musée des Arts décoratifs (Inv. 998.86.1). That museum also possesses a cane *banquette* purchased from Bing in 1902 as a functional item. In correspondence preserved in the Union centrale des Arts décoratifs archives, Bing offers the museum a reduced price, for its inauguration in 1905, on benches, chairs and armchairs he had hired out for an exhibition at the Grand and Petit Palais. He even points out the prices to the Ministry of Fine Arts, proving that he was a regular provider to French museums of certain functional furniture, particularly the attendants' seats still found today in the Musée national du château de Compiègne or in the Service de restauration des musées nationaux. My thanks to Mme Béatrice Lauwick, Archivist with the Service de restauration des musées nationaux and Mme Caude, Curator at the Musée national du château de Compiègne, for advising me of the existence of these items.

REDESIGNING THE HOME

1 Weisberg 1986, pp. 66–71. See also Debora L. Silverman, 'National initiative to international awakening: The Maison de l'Art nouveau Bing', in Silverman, *Art Nouveau in Fin-de-Siècle France, Politics, Psychology, and Style*, Berkeley & Los Angeles 1989, pp. 274–7; and Nancy J. Troy, 'Art Nouveau in Paris: from an eclectic movement to a national style', in Troy, *Modernism and the Decorative Arts in France. Art Nouveau to Le Corbusier*, New York & London 1991, pp. 23–7.
2 Dresden 1897, p. 83. The exhibition did not take place in an art museum, but probably in an exhibition hall.
3 See Meier-Graefe 1898; and 'Van de Velde', *L'Art Décoratif* 1 (October 1898), pp. 1–44.
4 Dresden 1897, pp. 84–6. On Adrien Dalpayrat and Lesbros, see Horst Makus *et al.*, *Adrien Dalpayrat, 1844–1910, Französische Jugendstil-Keramik/Céramique française de l'Art Nouveau*, Stuttgart 1998.
5 *Führer durch die Internationale Kunst-Ausstellung Dresden 1897, Eine Auswahl aus den darüber erschienenen Besprechungen, zusammengestellt im Auftrage der Ausstellungs-Commission*, Dresden-Blasewitz 1897, pp. 8–14; and Meier-Graefe 1897, pp. 201–6.
6 *Führer durch die Internationale Kunst-Ausstellung Dresden 1897* (see n. 5), pp. 11–12.
7 See Possémé, 'Bing and England', in this catalogue: pp. 154–62.
8 Weisberg 1996, pp. 184–93.
9 Letter from S. Bing to Jenö Radisics dated 3 February 1898, in which Bing states that, 'Quant à Isaac, il est mon ami intime; il a imaginé pour la première fois de teindre les étoffes

de si jolie façon pour décorer une de mes expositions japonaises, et depuis lors il s'adonne à cet art de préférence à celui de la peinture qu'il cultivait autrefois.'

10 Ibid., 'J'ai fait faire à des peintres de mes amis des cartons de tapis que je fais exécuter à Aubusson (rien que des dessins largement décoratifs).' Despite several attempts, the author has not been able to obtain any pertinent information about the relationship between Bing and Aubusson from the Aubusson archives.

11 G. [Georges] Lemmen, 'Moderne Teppiche von G. Lemmen', *Dekorative Kunst* 1, no. 3 (December 1897), pp. 97–105.

12 The third-floor addition is recorded in the Archives de Paris; see Weisberg 1983.

13 Letter from Friedrich Deneken to S. Bing, dated February 1898 (Museum archives, Kaiser Wilhelm Museum, Krefeld). All the letters in this correspondence were transcribed and translated by Walter O. Michael; without his help much would have been lost on the relationship between Bing and Deneken.

14 Letter from Bing to Deneken, 2 April 1898.

15 Ibid., 3 May 1898.

16 See *Album de références.*

17 See *Cadastre 1876*, D P 4 C 251, 19, rue Chauchat, where the construction of the new space is noted as 'addition en 1899 – au 2e et au 3e étages de deux ateliers pour ébenistes et bijoutiers – en briques, fer et vitrages'.

18 Bing's letter, addressed to 'Monsieur le Préfet de la Seine', requesting the permission to build is dated 17 May 1899, and the document from the 'architecte voyer' (inspecting architect) granting the request is dated 3 June 1899 (Archives de Paris, Quote VO 11 643, 19, rue Chauchat).

19 Julius Meier-Graefe, *L'Art Décoratif* 2, no. 1 (October 1899), pp. 14–15, and 2, no. 2 (December 1899), pp. 112–113; Viviane, 'L'Art Nouveau et les bijoux', *La Revue Illustrée* 28, no. 24 (1 December 1899).

20 Ashmore 2001.

21 *Grafton Galleries: Exhibition of L'Art Nouveau: S. Bing, Paris*, London (Grafton Galleries) 1899. In a letter to the Board of Education, Secondary Branch, dated 22 June 1901, the artist and designer Walter Crane wrote that 'if these pieces of furniture, tapestries, posters, etc., were offered to art students and furniture designers as patterns of work to be studied or imitated, it would do nothing but harm.' (Archives, Victoria and Albert Museum, Donaldson Bequest – called 'New Art Collection'.)

22 In a letter from Bing to Deneken dated 13 August 1899, Bing writes that he has decided to re-open the exhibit at the Grafton Galleries in October, and that if Deneken wants the paintings exhibited in London for his museum, Bing will have to know in advance and will need them back by 1 October (Museum archives, Kaiser Wilhelm Museum, Krefeld).

23 'Minor Art Exhibition', *The Times*, 9 June 1899.

24 'The Grafton Gallery', *Westminster Gazette*, 8 June 1899.

25 'Art Notes – "L'Art Nouveau" in Grafton Street', unknown journal (in Victoria and Albert Museum Library, *Archives / Newspaper Cuttings / Paintings Index*, April 1899–July 1903, p. 9/1899).

26 *The Grafton Galleries – Exhibition of Modern French Art in Conjunction with a Representative Collection of the Artistic Work of Louis Tiffany of New York*, London 1899, nos. 144–184. The exhibition was held from October to December. In addition to all the decorative arts objects shown, Bing, as he had done in the first exhibition, included paintings by contemporary artists such as Fritz Thaulow, Albert Besnard, Charles Cottet, Eugène Carrière, etc., and many more whose works Bing collected.

27 Horace Townsend, 'American and French applied art at the Grafton Galleries', *The Studio* 17, no. 75 (June 1899), pp. 39–46.

28 Viviane, 'L'Art Nouveau', *La Revue Illustrée* 30, no. 14 (1 July 1900). The cabinetmakers' workshop was located on the second floor of the building on rue Chauchat; it measured 6 m by 5 m, for a surface of 30 m^{2}. The jewellery workshop was located on the added third floor, and measured 5 m by 5 m, or a surface of 25 m^{2}. See *Cadastre 1876*, D P 4 1876 C 251.

29 *Cadastre 1876*, ibid. In an addition to the same document, p. 2, column 17, under 'annotations diverses', two notations appear: 1) 'un atelier d'ébénisterie pour la fabrication des modèles qu'il fait ensuite copier au dehors'. 2) '(...) un atelier de bijoutiers – ne fabrique que des commandes par le magasin. Les modèles sont exposés dans une vitrine du hall.'

30 Jallot was interviewed in 1968 by the art historian Mrs Hilda Benichou, while she was conducting research for her dissertation, which was never completed (communication from Mrs Benichou to the author at a meeting in Paris soon after the publication of the first Bing book in 1986, and again on 30 June 2002). The notes about the meeting with Jallot are handwritten and follow no clear order of historical events that Jallot either knew about or participated in.

31 Ibid.

32 See Millman 1992; Amsterdam 1993–4; and Saint-Germain-en-Laye & Gingins 1995.

33 Interview with Mrs Benichou (see n. 30).

34 Ibid. See also *Didot-Bottin* 1899, 1900. Colinot was listed in 1899 on p. 337 as 'menuisier', 86, rue Truffault, and again in 1900 at the same address. J.P. Niederkorn was listed in 1899 on p. 697, as 'ébéniste', 9, rue des Immeubles Industriels, and again in 1900 (p. 1326).

35 Ibid. See also *Didot-Bottin* 1899, 1900. Laforêt was listed in 1899 on p. 565 under the heading 'Ciseleurs sur métaux', at 20, rue Thorigny, with the same listing in 1900. Pigeon was listed in 1899 on p. 1054 under 'Bijoutiers' (jewellers) as selling 'Colliers, dormeuses et épingles de cravates en perles et similidiamant' [necklaces, stud ear-rings, tie-pins made of pearls and imitation diamonds] at 74, rue de Bondy. Alfred Daguet contributed to the Salons of the Société Nationale des Beaux-Arts, giving for his address 22, rue de Provence.

36 Archives Léon Jallot in the possession of Maître Hervé Poulain, Paris. Maître Poulain kindly gave the author access to his archives in 1982, and again in 2002, and also gave him the photographs in question.

37 Weisberg 1988.

38 See Lacquemant in this catalogue, pp. 197–221.

39 Ibid. On the history of the Société Prelle et Cie., see Florence Charpigny, 'Mémoire d'histoire', Université de Lyon II, 1979–81. In a letter to the author, 13 March 1987, Madame de Bellay states that between 1899 and 1901 Prelle (at the time Lamy et Bornet) worked for L'Art Nouveau, and two designs for silk fabric, by Edward Colonna (Model 649 in silk damask) and Georges de Feure (Model 6502, in silk damask), were manufactured. On 18 December 1899 Bing ordered 30 m of the Colonna fabric in blue and 30 m in rose-colour at 32.50 francs per metre. He again placed orders on 26 January, 30 July and 28 November 1900.He first ordered 30 m of the de Feure fabric 'of a certain colour' (sic) and, on 24 April 1900, 30 m in sky-blue.

40 Weisberg 1978. Apart from Edward Colonna, Georges de Feure, Adrien Delovincourt and Pierre-Paul Jouve, Léopold Lelée (1872–1947) also designed Limoges porcelains for Bing's L'Art Nouveau; see auction cat. 'Angewandte Kunst', I, Munich (Quittenbaum), 11.5.1998, no. 331.

41 See 'Porcelaines G.D.A. Société anonyme au capital de 1,500,000 francs divisé en 90 actions de 16,666.6666 chacune – Siège Social: à Limoges (Haute-Vienne) Faubourg des Casseaux, no. 27. Statuts dressés suivant acte reçu par Me Merle, Notaire à Saint-Junien (Haute-Vienne) et Me Bouquillard, Notaire à Limoges le 26 Décembre 1900.'

42 Registre des procès-verbaux de dépôt des dessins et modèles déposés au Conseil de Prudhomme du Bâtiment, document no. 868, dated 7 March 1900 (Archives de Paris: Register for 1900).

43 Ibid., document no. 908, 16 July 1900.

44 Ibid., document no. 914, 7 September 1900.

45 *Art Nouveau Bing* 1904. See also 'Réquisition afin de vente de meubles et objets d'art (art nouveau) appartenant à Mr. Bing' (Archives de Paris, D 42 E 3 111, no. 375). Bing was authorised to dispose of his business stock

because he had ceased operation. The sale netted 30,971 francs.

46 'Vente de marchandises neuves "Art Nouveau" en vertu du jugement, Requête de M. Bing du 15 Juin, 1909' (Archives de Paris, D 42 E 3 111, no. 880). The sale netted 11,920 francs.

THE BING ART NOUVEAU PAVILION AT THE WORLD'S FAIR OF 1900

1 Louis Hautecœur, *Histoire de l'architecture classique en France*, Paris 1957, vol. 7, p. 459.

2 The Esplanade des Invalides was devoted largely to Group XII (decoration and furnishings of public buildings and private dwellings).

3 Siegfried Bing, jury member, Group XII, Class 72: Ceramics (reserve juror, Japanese section).

4 The precise date of the opening of the pavilion is unknown. According to Octave Maus, in an article dated 1 July 1900: 'It was only last week that M. Bing was able to open – or half open, as not everything was finished!' (Maus 1900).

5 See the documentation relating to the construction of Henri Sauvage's Loïe Fuller Theatre. Exhib. cat. *Loïe Fuller, danseuse de l'Art nouveau*, Nancy (Musée de l'École de Nancy) 2002.

6 André Arfvidson, born in Boulogne-sur-Seine, is remembered for his collaboration with the potter Bigot on the studio building in the rue Campagne-Première, Paris. He also designed several large private houses and inexpensive housing.

7 Alfred Picard, *Rapport général administratif et technique*, Paris 1902, p. 293.

8 Morot 1938.

9 Meier-Graefe 1900.

10 According to Verneuil: 'On his return from military service in 1899, Jallot went to work for Bing, who, at the time, was making his brave attempts at modern art in the rue de Provence. Jallot took charge of all the furniture making, working in collaboration with Gaillard, de Feure, and Colonna.' M.P. Verneuil, 'Les Meubles de Jallot', *Art et Décoration* 25 (January-June 1909), p. 130.

11 'M. Gaillard was the first artist used by M.Bing to design the furniture sold by his establishment.' Gustave Soulier, 'Quelques meubles d'Eugène Gaillard', *Art et Décoration* 11 (January-June 1902), p. 22. As is pointed out in Eidelberg 1983, p. 77, no. 116, the design for a 'lady's desk, Mod. G', signed and dated E.G., June 97 is preserved as no. 4/49 in the *Album de références*.

12 Julius Meier-Graefe, 'Französisches Mobiliar', *Dekorative Kunst* 2 (1898), p. 108.

13 According to Ian Millman, the date and method of Georges de Feure's recruitment by Bing remain shrouded in mystery. We know through Meier-Graefe, writing under the pseudonym of 'G.M. Jacques' (Meier-Graefe 1900, p. 95), that 'M. Georges de Feure is amongst the many recruits drawn into the Bing group's circle over the last few months.'

14 Soulier 1900, p. 43.

15 Meier-Graefe 1900, p. 97.

16 Mourey 1900a, p. 262. See also Weisberg, 'Redesigning the Home', in this catalogue, pp. 182–7.

17 Swiss by birth, Robert Forrer was both a historian (specialising in early printing) and a graphic designer. He rubbed shoulders with the world of L'Art Nouveau, producing designs for wallpaper, posters and invitation cards. We owe this valuable information to M. Bernard Jacqué of the Musée du Papier Peint, Mulhouse.

18 Alberto del Castillo, *José Maria Sert, su vida y su obra*, Barcelona 1949.

19 According to Jacques-Emile Blanche, the theme chosen by Sert for Gaillard's dining room was the Grape Harvest. Jacques-Emile Blanche, *Propos de peintre II*, Paris 1921.

20 Maus 1900, p. 210.

21 O. Gerdeil, 'Le Meuble', *L'Art Décoratif*, no. 7 (January 1901), p. 173.

22 Soulier 1900, p. 45.

23 Notably, the museums of applied arts in Budapest, Helsinki, Hamburg, Copenhagen and Frankfurt.

24 Jean-Paul Bouillon, *Journal de l'Art nouveau 1870–1914*, Geneva 1985–6, p. 144.

25 Viviane, 'L'Art Nouveau', *La Revue Illustrée* 30, no. 17 (15 August 1900).

26 The *portière* featured in the pattern book as no. 351 was sold for 750 francs.

27 Mourey 1900a, p. 264.

28 Soulier 1900, p. 44.

29 Mourey 1900a, p. 257.

30 Ibid.

31 Mourey 1900b, p. 283.

32 The journals *L'Art Moderne* (Belgian), *The Studio* and *The Cabinet Maker* (English), *Brush and Pencil* (American) and *Deutsche Kunst und Dekoration* (German) helped greatly in spreading the fame of the display.

33 Mourey 1900b, p. 279.

34 Meier-Graefe 1900, p. 96.

35 Soulier 1900, p. 43.

36 Viviane, 'L'Art Nouveau', *La Revue Illustrée* 30, no. 17 (15 August 1900).

37 Mourey 1900b, p. 263.

38 Maus 1900, pp. 209–10.

39 Soulier 1900, p. 44.

40 Meier-Graefe 1900, p. 96.

41 This was not Princess Maria Tenicheva, who owned an important collection of decorative art. (Letter of 11 October 2003, Fine Arts Museum, Smolensk, Russia.)

42 Viviane, 'L'Art Nouveau', *La Revue Illustrée* 30, no. 17 (15 August 1900).

43 Meier-Graefe 1901, p. 23.

44 Morot 1938.

45 The description of the 92 items of furniture listed in the sale catalogue suggests that Bing had attempted to edit those featured in the 1900 pavilion, particularly Colonna's inlaid work and the giltwood items by Georges de Feure – with varying degrees of success, given the considerable stock remaining in his possession. See *Art Nouveau Bing* 1904.

BING AND INTERIOR DECORATION

1 G.M. Jacques [Julius Meier-Graefe], 'L'Art décoratif. L'intérieur rénové', *L'Art Décoratif* 2, no. 24 (September 1900), p. 228.

2 *Le Gaulois du dimanche* (44), 16–17 April 1898, p. 4, advertising insert.

3 *Album de références*, p. 5/35–40.

4 Camille Gardelle, 'Moderne Kunst in der Französischen Architektur', *Dekorative Kunst* 2, no. 5 (February 1898), pp. 215–21, repr. p. 217.

5 In the meantime they had created the English dining room shown in 1898 in place of the one by Henry Van de Velde, which was dismantled from 22, rue de Provence so that it could be shown at the Dresden Exhibition in 1897.

6 Meier-Graefe 1901, p. 30.

7 *Galerie l'Art Nouveau Bing, Œuvres de Georges de Feure*, March 1903. Incidentally, the other two designers, Colonna and Gaillard, were offended by this exclusiveness and almost certainly left Bing at this time. See Saint-Germain-en-Laye & Gingins 1995, p. 25.

8 Morot 1938.

9 James Montjarret de Kerjégu was born at the Château de Trévarez on 27 February 1846. He married Laure de Habert, the daughter of a banker's family from Frankfurt and widow of Octave de Béhague, by whom she had had two daughters, Berthe and Martine de Béhague. She died giving birth to Kerjégu's daughter, Françoise, who married Henri Ferron de la Ferronnays and inherited the castle after her father's death. Françoise's heirs were the sons of her elder sister Berthe, the Marquise de Ganay. Le Goffe 1989; Laure Stasi, 'Le mécénat de Martine de Béhague, comtesse de Béarn (1870–1939): du symbolisme au théâtre d'avant-garde', *Bulletin de la Société de l'Histoire de l'Art français* (1999), pp. 337–66.

10 The estate and the castle were bought from the heirs in 1968 by the Finistère Regional Council. Since opening it to the public in 1971, the Council has gone to great lengths to maintain the park and restore the castle, which was bombed during the last war. My grateful thanks go to Catherine Kerouanton, acting for the Regional Council, for having brought the existence of this castle and Bing's decorations to our attention.

11 The total bill for the Bing installation, dated 31 October 1903, amounted to 37,100 francs. By way of comparison, the price of a comfortable suburban house in 1910 was around 12,000 francs (comparison made by Catherine Kerouanton in a report on the furniture for Trévarez commissioned by the Finistère Regional Council in January 2003: 'Plis de serviette, feuilles d'acanthe et tiges de roseau, éléments de connaissance du mobilier et du décor de château de Trévarez', in-house study, January 2003; 'L'eau confortable, étude du système technique et de confort du château de Trévarez', in-house study, July 2002.)

12 Quimper, Archives départementales du Finistère, 109 J 40.

13 Dry rot is the decay of timber caused by the fungus *merulius lacrymans*, which feeds on wood cellulose. Our thanks to M.Benoît Jenn, head of the museums' restoration workshop.

14 Le Goffe 1989, p. 283. Our thanks to Monsieur Inizan for kindly making the photographs he had taken before the panelling was dismantled available to us. The restoration, agreed by the Finistère Regional Council, was carried out by the Ateliers de la Chapelle under the direction of Isabelle Gargadennec, Curator of Antiquities and Objets d'Art for Finistère.

15 O. Gerdeil, 'Un atelier d'artiste', *L'Art Décoratif*, no. 9/10 (January 1902), p. 146. The author wishes to thank Mr Ian Millman for kindly passing on the photographs taken for this 1902 article, some of which were not published at the time.

16 Quimper, Archives départementales du Finistère.

17 Luc 1903, p. 3.

18 Quimper, Archives départementales du Finistère.

19 *Album de références*, nos. 37/521 and 522. Designs: Inv. CD 2690.

20 The bedside table, kept in the home of Madame de la Ferronnays's heirs, is decorated with panels of parquetry veneering that can also be made out on the bed and the wardrobe, which have legs and feet characteristic of furniture by Gaillard. The solid mahogany and veneered bed, with a decoration of sagittaria leaves, is similar to some of the models in the *Album de références*. The restoration of this furniture would make it possible to carry out further research, identify the woods, and make more detailed identifications through the castle archives.

21 Apart from those of the 1900 World's Fair, the only interior reproductions are photographs nos. 37/516–520 and drawings reproduced as nos. 35/494 and 35/495, which also seem to be by Georges de Feure.

22 Luc 1903, p. 8.

23 Siegfried Bing sold his firm to the company of Majorelle Frères in December 1904 and organised a sale of his stock on 19 and 20 December 1904 (92 items of furniture). He died in Vaucresson on 6 September 1905 after an illness lasting several months.

BING'S INFLUENCE AND PLACE IN THE ART OF HIS TIME

1 Max Osborn, 'La Maison Moderne', *Deutsche Kunst und Dekoration* 4, no. 2 (October-March 1900–1), p. 99. On La Maison Moderne, see Bettina John-Willeke, 'Die Galerie "La Maison Moderne" in Paris' in Ulmer 1999, pp. 148–57.

2 On Bing's work as a gallery owner, see Weisberg 1986a; supplementary to this and following on from Weisberg, Rüdiger Joppien, 'Siegfried Bings Kunsthaus "L'Art Nouveau"' in Ulmer 1999, pp. 116–27. See also Becker in this catalogue, pp. 115–49.

3 On Meier-Graefe, see Catherine Krahmer, 'Meier-Graefes Weg zur Kunst', *Hofmannsthal Jahrbuch zur europäischen Moderne* 4 (1996), pp. 169–226, especially pp. 169–78; also Krahmer 1992–4, pp. 148–64.

4 Weisberg 1986a; also Joppien 1999.

5 'Avis aux Artistes et Artisans...' (copy in Hamburg Museum für Kunst und Gewerbe, Collection of Graphics).

6 Otto Feld, 'Bings L'Art Nouveau', *Kunstchronik* 7, no. 28 (4 June 1895–6), column 441–7. Meier-Graefe also commented on the diminishing supply of Japanese works of art; see Meier-Graefe 1896, p. 2.

7 For these projects, see also excerpts from letters in Meier-Graefe 2002.

8 A letter from Meier-Graefe to Julius Levin of 31 October 1895 refers to his plan to set up a salon 'à la Bing' with Pächter ('You know I am an expert on the Salon idea'); Meier-Graefe 2002, no. 94, pp. 146–8. Meier-Graefe had already purchased a large number of objects for the art gallery that he was planning to set up with the help of *Pan* and incurred considerable costs in doing so. After his departure from *Pan*, he lacked the necessary means to fund the project. He arrived in Paris at the beginning of November 1895, and it is thought that he brought these objects with him and sold them to Bing or gave them to him to sell on commission. The author is grateful to Catherine Krahmer, Paris, for an enlightening discussion on this subject.

9 *The Studio* 10, no. 48 (March 1897), p. 124, states that Bing had commissioned a large number of orders 'in connection with Art Nouveau' from Brangwyn, Van de Velde, Ranson and Mme Thaulow (relating to the design and manufacture of decorative leather goods for the dining room being produced by the 'Art Nouveau associates' and, it should be added, due to be exhibited in Dresden in 1897).

10 See Philippe Thiébaut, 'Das Pariser Kunsthandwerk. Wachstum und Krise', in exhib. cat. *Paris. Belle Epoque 1880–1914*, Essen 1999, p. 215. See also *The Studio* 10, no. 48 (March 1897), pp. 119–124.

11 *Dekorative Kunst* 2, no. 9 (June 1898), pp. 104, 106.

12 *Dekorative Kunst* 1, no. 2 (November 1897), p. 93.

13 *Art et Décoration* 3 (April 1898), advertisement section. The text reads: 'Installations Modernes. Ameublements d'art. Tapis – Tentures – Papiers peints – Vitraux – Ferronerie – Céramique – Verreries – Bronzes – Etains, Appareils d'Eclairage (Suspensions – Lampes de Parquet, etc.) Electricité – Pétrole – Gaz. Modèles exclusifs'. The same picture appears again in *Art et Décoration* 4 (July 1898), advertisement section. A selection of different kinds of lamps is also offered in *Art et Décoration* 3 (February 1898), advertisement section. Bing would not have been able to manufacture in his own workshops all the works advertised for sale. He had to rely on a number of other suppliers. It is realistic to assume that Bing maintained a furnishing firm for everyday commissions and had exclusive individual pieces created for art exhibitions. Weisberg's conclusion, therefore, that Bing devoted himself solely to exclusive luxury items (Weisberg 1988, pp. 326–9, 379) can only partly be accepted.

14 *Dekorative Kunst* 2, no. 9 (June 1898), p. 135, advertising 'Carpets, textiles, etc. All kinds of decorative works of art, manufactured exclusively for L'Art Nouveau'.

15 *Dekorative Kunst* 2, no. 6 (March 1899), advertisement section.

16 Foreword of exhib. cat. *Japanische Holzschnitte, 17.-19. Jahrhundert*, Dresden (Ernst Arnold, Königlich Sächsische Hofkunsthandlung) May-June 1895.

17 Official catalogue of the Dresden International Art Exhibition, 3rd ed., Dresden, 1 June 1897, p. 83.

18 Meier-Graefe 1898, pp. 202–6.

19 Ibid., p. 205.

20 Paul Schumann in *Deutsche Kunst und Dekoration* 1, no. 1 (October 1897), pp. 12–22; Wilhelm Bode in *Pan* 3, no. 1 (July 1897), p. 46, and no. 2 (September 1897), pp. 117–18, where he states, 'This uniform character, this strong statement in form and colour, demonstrates the great importance of Bing's interiors as achievements of modern interior design.'

21 Several photographs of room interiors, largely overlooked in previous literature, are published in Klaus-Peter Arnold, 'Van de Veldes Zimmerausstattung auf der internationalen Kunstausstellung, Dresden 1897', *Dresdner Kunstblätter* 26, no. 5 (1982), pp. 168–73.

22 Joppien 1999, pp. 22–9.

23 Correspondence between Bing and Deneken (Museum archives, Kaiser Wilhelm Museum, Krefeld).

24 *Dekorative Kunst* 1, nos. 1, 2 and 4 (October, November 1897, January 1898), pp. 1–3, 68–71, 160–77.

25 *Kunst und Kunsthandwerk* 1 (1898), pp. 105–11.

26 This aspect is discussed at length in the Bing-Deneken correspondence (Museum archives, Kaiser Wilhelm Museum, Krefeld).

27 Joppien 1999, pp. 22–9.

28 *Dekorative Kunst* 3, no. 1 (October 1899), p. 7. For Colonna, see also Julius Meier-Graefe, *Dekorative Kunst* 2, no. 9 (June 1898), p. 108 and Eidelberg 1983, p. 40.

29 *Dekorative Kunst* 1, no. 3 (December 1897), p. 105; also *The Studio* 16, no. 72 (March 1899), p. 138.

30 *Deutsche Kunst und Dekoration* 3, no. 3 (December 1898), pp. 130–1.

31 For the history of the Hohenzollern Kunstgewerbehaus, see John Heskett, *Design in Germany 1870–1918*, London 1986, pp. 24–5; and Thomas Föhl, 'Henry van de Velde und Eberhard von Bodenhausen. Wirtschaftliche Grundlagen der gemeinsamen Arbeit' in Hagen etc. 1992–4, pp. 169–205, especially pp. 197, 199 and notes; see also Becker 1993, pp. 43–5.

32 Ludwig Pietsch, 'Das Hohenzollern-Kunstgewerbehaus–Berlin', *Deutsche Kunst und Dekoration* 8, no. 3 (October 1904-March 1905), p. 172.

33 Ibid., p. 173.

34 *Deutsche Kunst und Dekoration* 3, no. 3 (December 1898), p. 134, see also *Dekorative Kunst* 2, no. 7 (April 1899) p. 6.

35 Alfred Lichtwark, *Briefe 1898*, Hamburg 1899, vol. 6, pp. 210 ff; see also Becker 1993, p. 38.

36 *Dekorative Kunst* 3, no. 6 (March 1900), advertisement section.

37 For Brinckmann's Japanese collection, see Hempel 1981.

38 Letter of 20 January 1902 from Ch. Been of the Danske Kunstindustrimuseum, Copenhagen (Archiv, Museum für Kunst und Gewerbe, Hamburg). See also Justus Brinckmann's obituary for Bing in the *Hamburger Nachrichten*, 3 May 1906, which illustrates how close they were, when, for example, Brinckmann describes how, often, after a lively dinner in Bing's private apartment his Japanese treasures were 'covetously admired or eruditely discussed over a good cigar'. In 1883 Bing had entertained Brinckmann and Lichtwark in his country villa; see Klemm 2004, p. 225.

39 Letters from Brinckmann (in Paris) to Deneken (Hamburg), 26 January, 28 January, 30 January, 2 February 1896, with reports on *objets d'art* and references to Karl Engelbrecht and August Kähler, whom Brinckmann recommended to Bing (Archive, Museum für Kunst und Gewerbe, Hamburg).

40 Inv. nos. 1896, 66; 1896, 90; 1896, 91. Earlier in the year of 1895, Julius Lessing had purchased Tiffany glassware from Bing for the Berlin Kunstgewerbemuseum as the first German museum director to do so; see Joppien 1999, p. 23.

41 Letter of 27 February 1896, see Klemm 2004, p. 225. Grateful thanks are extended to Herr David Klemm for this valuable reference.

42 In conclusion, it is worth noting that no study on the applied art trade around 1900 appears to have been published to date that examines the network of contacts between international art houses and galleries. Such a study would be highly desirable.

LIST OF WORKS

DOCUMENTATION

Advertisement 'Dwarf Trees'
1902, paper, 13.4 x 17.5 cm
Album Maciet, vol. 268, no. 3
Bibliothèque des Arts décoratifs, Paris
fig. 65

Advertisement 'Price list for Japanese and Chinese papers'
c. 1881, paper, 33 x 24 cm
Album Maciet, vol. 256, no. 6
Bibliothèque des Arts décoratifs, Paris
fig. 22

Poster 'Le Japon Artistique' (Artistic Japan)
c. 1888, lithography on paper, 33 x 25 cm
Musée de la Publicité, Paris
inv. no. 9813
fig. 57

Album de références (Pattern book)
album with photographs, 74 x 56 cm
Bibliothèque des Arts décoratifs, Paris
inv. no. LL 53
Gift of Marcel Bing, 5.5.1919
figs. 161, 162, 174–80, 180, 211, 219, 223, 231, 235, 243, 251, 258, 267, 268, 273, 276
This collection bears on its endpaper the inscription: 'Album de références de l'Art Nouveau / 381 Photographies d'après des meubles de Colonna, de Feure et Gaillard, vers 1900 / Don de M. Bing 5 mai 1919 / Enreg: 23787' (Art Nouveau Pattern book / 381 Photographs of furniture by Colonna, de Feure and Gaillard, circa 1900 / Gift of M.Bing 5 May 1919 / Reg: 23787). In fact, this book contains five hundred and twenty-four photographs of furniture and a few room environments produced by the gallery L'Art Nouveau. Donated by Marcel Bing, son of Siegfried, a couple of months before his death, it is made up of thirty-seven pages on each of which are stuck twelve reproductions of furniture, sometimes fewer, numbered sequentially from 1 to 524, and three last pages at the end that reproduce the stamps (modèles d'applique) found on the furniture depicted. Each item of furniture carries a number, the name of the model, sometimes the initials of the creator, rarely the complete name, and occasionally the selling price. The study of this album raises many questions as to the date it was put together and its use, not to mention, of course, the identification of the models, which alone requires a long period of research.

Siegfried Bing, 'La Culture artistique en Amérique' (Artistic Culture in America)
Paris, 1896, book, 25.5 x 18 cm
Bibliothèque des Arts décoratifs, Paris
inv. no. HY 746

Exposition Internationale du Livre Moderne (International Exhibition of the Modern Book)
May-June 1896, exhibition catalogue, L'Art Nouveau, paper, 26 x 21.5 cm
Bibliothèque des Arts décoratifs, Paris
inv. no. Y 650

Le Japon Artistique (Artistic Japan)
1888–1891, journal, 3 vols., 33 x 25 cm
Van Gogh Museum (Library), Amsterdam
inv. nos. 8 E 5–7/BVG 5372–4
figs. 20, 48, 293

WESTERN ART & DESIGN

For designers and factories, short biographies or histories of the firms have been incorporated; biographies of other artists can be found in standard reference works such as Thieme-Becker.

JULES ADELINE

Japanese Doll (Mikika)
1883, etching on paper, 33.5 x 25.5 cm
Bibliothèque d'Etude, Bibliothèques municipales de Rouen
inv. no. Rés Ng 90 (2)

Japanese Doll (Mikika)
1890, etching on paper, hand-coloured, dedicated to Bing, 29.2 x 23.7 cm
Album Maciet, vol. 180, no. 5
Bibliothèque des Arts décoratifs, Paris
fig. 63

Illustrations for Mikika. Japonaiserie Rouennaise (Rouen Japonaiserie) by Eugène Brieux
after 1893, book, 10 x 8 cm
Bibliothèque d'Etude, Bibliothèques municipales de Rouen
inv. no. Petite Rés. p 2841

PAUL WAYLAND BARTLETT

Sculpin fish
1895, bronze, 11.2 x 26.2 x 14.4 cm
Musée d'Orsay, Paris
inv. no. RF 3157
Exhibited at the first Salon de L'Art Nouveau, 1895, no. 303

WILLIAM ARTHUR SMITH BENSON

The English architect and interior decorator William Benson (1854–1924) opened his first factory making metal objects in Fulham in 1880. As the success of his business grew, he set up workshops in Hammersmith. A representative of the Arts and Crafts movement and founding member of the Arts and Crafts Exhibition Society in 1886, he took over the chairmanship of Morris & Co when William Morris died in 1896. During his time at Morris & Co. he produced designs for furniture and wallpaper for the firm. He also created pieces for the firm of John Sollie Henry. William Benson is remembered above all for his utilitarian objects, particularly lighting fixtures, widely advertised in the journals of the period. He exhibited light fittings and items in copper and brass at the first Salon de l'Art Nouveau in 1895. These items, as well as a few pieces of furniture, were sold by Siegfried Bing in his gallery on the rue de Provence (until at least 1899).

Tea pot
c. 1895, copper and brass, h: 15 cm; diam: 6.4 cm
Nordenfjeldske Kunstindustrimuseum, Trondheim
inv. no. NK 4747
Purchased (45 francs) from S. Bing, 1896
fig. 181

Pitcher
c. 1895, copper and brass, h: 11 cm; diam: 5.6 cm
Nordenfjeldske Kunstindustrimuseum, Trondheim
inv. no. NK 4748
Purchased (22 francs) from S. Bing, 1896
fig. 170

Paraffin lamp
c. 1895, copper, brass and glass, h: 63.5 cm
Nordenfjeldske Kunstindustrimuseum, Trondheim
inv. no. NK 4752
Purchased (60 francs) from S. Bing, 1896
fig. 169

Foodwarmer
c. 1895, copper and brass, 12.7 x 57.6 x 28.6 cm
Nordenfjeldske Kunstindustrimuseum, Trondheim

inv. no. NK 4753
Purchased (75 francs) from S. Bing, 1896

Table
c. 1895, wood, with ceramic tiles by Alexandre Bigot, h: 71 cm
Nordenfjeldske Kunstindustrimuseum, Trondheim
inv. no. NK 4768
Purchased (60 francs) from S. Bing, 1896

PAUL-ALBERT BESNARD

Decorative panels
c. 1895, oil on canvas, 306.2 x 67.3 cm/ 289.4 x 131.4 cm/ 306.2 x 71.7 cm
Telfair Academy, Savannah
inv. no. 1984.3.1
Exhibited at the first Salon de L'Art Nouveau, 1895, no. 20
fig. 129

Woman with Blue Drapery
c. 1900, oil on canvas, 46 x 61.5 cm
Rogalin Gallery, Poznán
inv. no. MNP FR 173
Purchased (4,200 francs) at the Sale of the Bing Collection, Hôtel Drouot, Paris, 1900, no. 5
fig. 135

ALEXANDRE BIGOT

A highly accomplished ceramic technician, Bigot (1862–1927) taught physics and chemistry at the Ecole des Mines (Mining School). He experimented with different kinds of clay – porcelain, stoneware, earthenware – fired at a high temperature. After working briefly with the ceramicist Paul Beyer in Switzerland, he built himself a studio at Mer (Loir-et-Cher) in his native village. He worked for a time alongside Jean Carriès and helped Ernest Chaplet to perfect certain glazes. In 1894, at the Salon of the Société Nationale des Beaux-Arts, he exhibited stoneware in simple shapes, then in December 1895 he took part in the inaugural Salon de l'Art Nouveau. At the Paris World's Fair of 1900 he obtained the Grand Prix for his frieze of ceramic animals, after drawings by the animal sculptor Pierre-Paul Jouve, which decorated the monumental door by René Binet. Shortly afterwards, Bigot returned to Paris, opened a shop at 13, rue des Petites-Ecuries and – like his colleague Emile Müller – devoted himself to architectural ceramics.

Jar
1890s, stoneware, with silver-gilt mount by Bies, h: 7.6 cm; diam. 6.7 cm
Victoria and Albert Museum, London
inv. no. 1701–1900
Purchased (£4.8.0) from S. Bing, 1900

Vase
1895, ceramic, h: 18.5; diam: 17 cm
Kaiser Wilhelm Museum, Krefeld
inv. no. 1898/53
Purchased (109.27 francs) from S. Bing, 1898

Bowl
1895, stoneware, with silver-gilt mount by Edward Colonna, h: 8 cm; diam. 16.5 cm
Victoria and Albert Museum, London
inv. no. 1700–1900
Purchased (£16.2.0) from S. Bing, 1900
fig. 296

Pitcher
c. 1895, stoneware, with metal mount by Edward Colonna, h: 20.5 cm; diam: 6 cm
Musée des Arts décoratifs, Paris
inv. no. 15227
Gift of Marcel Bing, 26.10.1908

Sugar pot
c. 1896, ceramic, 9.7 x 14.4 cm
Collection Marc Lambrechts
(with original Art Nouveau label)

Creamer
c. 1899, stoneware, with silver-gilt mount by Edward Colonna, h: 8 cm
Musée des Arts décoratifs, Paris
inv. no. 9079
Purchased (175 francs) from S. Bing, 5.7.1899
fig. 295

Small Bowl
c. 1899, stoneware, with silver-gilt mount by Edward Colonna, h: 7 cm
Musée des Arts décoratifs, Paris
inv. no. 15228
Gift of Marcel Bing, 26.10.1908

MARCEL BING

A goldsmith and jeweller, Marcel Bing (1875–1920) was the fourth child of Siegfried Bing and Johanna Baer. After studying at the Ecole du Louvre and training as a jeweller, he assisted his father in running the gallery L'Art Nouveau. He designed jewellery and metal mounts for the gallery, which were exhibited at the Paris World's Fair in 1900 and at the Salon of the Société Nationale des Beaux-Arts from 1901. After his father's death in 1905, Marcel Bing opened a small shop at 10, rue Saint-Georges, specialising in the sale of oriental and medieval objects. Here, he organised numerous exhibitions accompanied by catalogues.
In 1908, Marcel Bing gave to the Musée des Arts décoratifs in Paris a large portion of the Art Nouveau objects commissioned by his father, notably works by Georges de Feure, Edward Colonna and Eugène Gaillard.

Pendant
1900, copper, enamel and gold, 5 x 4 cm
Musée des Arts décoratifs, Paris
inv. no. 15280 B
Gift of Marcel Bing, 26.10.1908
fig. 204

Pendant
1900, gold and mother of pearl, 5 x 3.5 cm
Musée des Arts décoratifs, Paris
inv. no. 15280 C
Gift of Marcel Bing, 26.10.1908
fig. 205

Tie pin
1900, gold and pearl, length: 9 cm
Musée des Arts décoratifs, Paris
inv. no. 15280 D
Gift of Marcel Bing, 26.10.1908

JACQUES-EMILE BLANCHE

The Painter Thaulow and his Children
1895, oil on canvas, 180 x 200 cm
Musée d'Orsay, Paris
inv. no. RF 1325
Exhibited at the first Salon de L'Art Nouveau, 1895, no. 31
fig. 137

Portrait of Aubrey Beardsley
1895, oil on canvas, 90 x 72 cm
National Portrait Gallery, London
inv. no. NPG 1991
Exhibited at the first Salon de L'Art Nouveau, 1895, no. 32
fig. 136

LOUIS BONNIER

A student at the Ecole des Beaux-Arts, Louis Bonnier (1856–1946) became architect-surveyor of the City of Paris before qualifying in 1886. His personal approach became apparent very early on – rational, economical use of materials and somewhat rustic. The Flé house (built in 1895) demonstrates his intellectual affinities with both Viollet-le-Duc and the Arts & Crafts movement. In 1895 Siegfried Bing turned to him for the façades and interior decoration of the gallery L'Art Nouveau. Bonnier used cut-out metal sheets for the entrance, and glass bricks for the ceilings. He executed several projects for the Paris World's Fair of 1900, including the Schneider pavilion.

Plan of 22, rue de Provence and 19, rue Chauchat, façades
3 July 1895, tracing paper
Les Archives de Paris
inv. no. V.O.11
fig. 100

Plan of 22, rue de Provence and 19, rue Chauchat, central floor
3 July 1895, tracing paper
Les Archives de Paris
inv. no. V.O.11
fig. 101

Project for the doorway at 19, rue Chauchat
c. 1895, pen and ink on paper, 50 x 42 cm
Fonds Louis Bonnier, Institut français d'architecture, Paris
inv. no. 35/35/14
fig. 106

Project for the balustrade in Bing's L'Art Nouveau
c. 1895, pen and ink on paper, 135.5 x 73 cm
Fonds Louis Bonnier, Institut français d'architecture, Paris
inv. no. 35/35/16
fig. 105

Plan of the jewellery and cabinetmakers' workshops
3 June 1899, tracing paper
Les Archives de Paris
inv. no. V.O.11
fig. 187

Preliminary sketch for L'Art Nouveau Bing pavilion at the Paris World's Fair
1900, pen and ink on paper, 48 x 63 cm
Fonds Louis Bonnier, Institut français d'architecture, Paris
inv. no. 35/43/01
fig. 212

Preliminary sketch for L'Art Nouveau Bing pavilion at the Paris World's Fair
1900, pen and ink on paper, 35 x 55 cm
Fonds Louis Bonnier, Institut français d'architecture, Paris
inv. no. 35/43/02

EMILE BOURDELLE

Kiss (Baiser aux nattes)
c. 1891, bronze, 19.4 x 25.5 x 21 cm
Musée Bourdelle, Paris
inv. no. MBR 402
Exhibited at the first Salon de L'Art Nouveau, 1895, no. 316

Sleeping child (mask)
c. 1893, bronze, 18.5 x 21.5 x 13 cm
Musée Bourdelle, Paris
inv. no. MBR 999
Exhibited at the first Salon de L'Art Nouveau, 1895, no. 310

FRANK BRANGWYN

Stencil design for the exterior of Bing's gallery
c. 1895, stencil, 37 x 53 cm
Fonds Louis Bonnier, Institut français d'architecture, Paris
inv. no. 35/35/18
fig. 107

Music
1895, oil on canvas, 188.1 x 143.8 cm
William Morris Gallery, Walthamstow
Gift of Frank Brangwyn, 1935
inv. no. 1/1935 (144)
Exhibited at the first Salon de L'Art Nouveau, 1895, no. 38
fig. 125

Dance
1895, oil on canvas, 255 x 155 cm
Collection Sir Angus and Lady Grossart
Exhibited at the first Salon de L'Art Nouveau, 1895, no. 38
fig. 124

'Japanese Vine' carpet
1896–97, wool, 361 x 261 cm
Stedelijke Musea, Brugge
inv. no. 66.72. XVII
Exhibited in the English dining room at L'Art Nouveau, 1898
fig. 160

Bedside carpet
c. 1898, wool, 185 x 95 cm
Musée des Arts décoratifs, Paris
inv. no. 15284
Gift of Marcel Bing, 26.10.1908
fig. 173

Poster for L'Art Nouveau's exhibition at the Grafton Galleries, London
1899, colour lithograph on paper, 79.5 x 57 cm
Musée de la Publicité, Paris
inv. no. 9416
fig. 194

LEONETTO CAPPIELLO

Siegfried Bing at an auction
c. 1903–04, pencil on paper, 39 x 33.4 cm
Collection Rémy Le Fur
fig. 5

EUGENE CARRIERE

Portrait of Gustave Geffroy
1890, oil on canvas, 50 x 61 cm
Musée d'Orsay, Paris
inv. no. RF 2627
Exhibited at the Eugène Carrière exhibition, L'Art Nouveau, April-May 1896, no. 10
fig. 158

Gabriel Séailles and his Daughter
1893, oil on canvas, 114 x 89.5 cm
Musée d'Art moderne et contemporain, Strasbourg
inv. no. 55 974 0 631
Exhibited at the Eugène Carrière exhibition, L'Art Nouveau, April-May 1896, no. 8
fig. 157

ALEXANDRE CHARPENTIER

Painting
c. 1897, bronze plaque, 8.1 x 15.9 x 5 cm
Victoria and Albert Museum, London
inv. no. 328
Purchased from S. Bing, 1901

Sculpture
c. 1897, bronze plaque, 8.1 x 14.8 x 5 cm
Victoria and Albert Museum, London
inv. no. 327
Purchased from S. Bing, 1901

JULES CHERET

Poster 'Exhibition of Japanese Prints'
1890, lithography on paper, 88 x 124.5 cm
Musée de la Publicité, Paris
inv. no. 10834
fig. 21

CAMILLE CLAUDEL

The Waltz
1896, ceramic (executed by Emile Müller), 40.5 x 37.5 x 18 cm
Private collection
Exhibited at the first Salon de L'Art Nouveau, 1895, no. 326
fig. 150

The Little Châtelaine
1896, marble, 44 x 36 x 29 cm
Musée d'Art et d'Industrie, Roubaix
inv. no. 996–5–1
Exhibited at the second Salon de L'Art Nouveau, 1896, no. 788
fig. 149

EDWARD COLONNA

Born near Cologne, Edward Colonna (1862–1948) studied architecture in Brussels before travelling to the United States in 1882. After a brief stay in New York, where he worked for Louis Comfort Tiffany, he settled in Dayton, Ohio, where he designed railway carriages for the Barney & Smith Manufacturing Company. In 1887 he prepared a manuscript, "Essay on Broom-Corn", which featured his whole ornamental repertoire. Following a brief period in Canada, Edward Colonna moved to Paris and became a pattern-designer for Siegfried Bing in 1898. He drew patterns of furniture, and also designed frames for mirrors, mounted leather objects and furnishing fabrics, as well as the famous Canton Service, produced c. 1899–1900 by the GDA factory (Gérard, Dufraisseix et Abbott) in Limoges. His style was clearly defined, often characterised by a whiplash line ending in an abstract scroll, as seen in his jewellery designs, with their flowing, rounded lines, and in his vase mounts for Tiffany, Bigot and Dalpayrat. Colonna participated, together with Georges de Feure and Eugène Gaillard, in the design of the many of the objects created for the pavilion of L'Art Nouveau Bing at the 1900 Paris World's Fair.

Drawing for a bookcase
1895–1905, watercolour and pencil on paper, 26.2 x 21 cm
Musée des Arts décoratifs, Paris
inv. no. CD 2682
Gift of Marcel Bing, 1919

Drawing for a glazed bookcase
1895–1905, watercolour and pencil on paper, 26.4 x 20.7 cm
Musée des Arts décoratifs, Paris
inv. no. CD 2683
Gift of Marcel Bing, 1919

Plate
1895–1905, porcelain (Limoges, GDA), diam: 21.5 cm
Musée des Arts décoratifs, Paris
inv. no. 9619
Purchased (10 francs) from the Atelier Art Nouveau, 18.5.1901

Cup and saucer
1895–1905, porcelain (Limoges, GDA), cup, diam: 5.5 cm; saucer. diam: 13.6 cm
Musée des Arts décoratifs, Paris
inv. no. 9622 A/B
Purchased (15 francs) from the Atelier Art Nouveau, 18.5.1901

Card case
1898–99, leather, silver gilt, silk lining, 12 x 6.8 cm
Musée des Arts décoratifs, Paris
inv. no. 15276
Gift of Marcel Bing, 26.10.1908
fig. 196

Knotted rug
c. 1899, wool and cotton, 186 x 108 cm
Österreichisches Museum für angewandte Kunst, Vienna
inv. no. T 5177/1899
Purchased (125 francs) from S. Bing, 20.9.1899

Knotted rug
c. 1899, wool and cotton, 169 x 100 cm
Österreichisches Museum für angewandte Kunst, Vienna
inv. no. T 5178/1899
Purchased (125 francs) from S. Bing, 20.9.1899
fig. 241

Fabric 'Orchids'
c. 1899, silk and cotton, 198 x 131 cm;150 x 131 cm
Museum für Kunst und Gewerbe, Hamburg
inv. no. 1900.361/1900.365
Purchased from S. Bing at the Paris World's Fair, 1900
fig. 239

Fabric 'Orchids'
c. 1900, silk, 102 x 130 cm
Musée des Arts décoratifs, Paris
inv. no. 12924
Purchased (71.50 francs) from Marcel Bing, 26.7.1906

Display cabinet
c. 1899–1900, lemon wood, 180 x 117 x 53 cm
Museum für Kunst und Gewerbe, Hamburg
inv. no. 1900.366
Purchased from S. Bing at the Paris World's Fair, 1900
fig. 238

Stand
c. 1899–1900, lemon wood, h: 117 cm; depth: 36.5 cm
Museum für Kunst und Gewerbe, Hamburg
inv. no. 1900.367
Purchased from S. Bing at the Paris World's Fair, 1900

Round table
c. 1899–1900, lemon wood, height: h: 70 cm; diam: 63 cm
Museum für Kunst und Gewerbe, Hamburg
inv. no. 1900.368
Purchased from S. Bing at the Paris World's Fair, 1900
fig. 237

Armchair
c. 1899–1900, lemon wood, 98 x 62.5 x 45 cm
Museum für Kunst und Gewerbe, Hamburg
inv. no. 1900.369
Purchased from S. Bing at the Paris World's Fair, 1900

Table
c. 1900, Brazilian rosewood, 100 x 72 x 60 cm
Musée des Arts décoratifs, Paris
inv. no. 27977
Raymond Koechlin Bequest, 10.12.1931
fig. 236

Coffee pot
1899–1900, porcelain (Limoges, GDA), 22.5 x 6.5 cm
Musée des Arts décoratifs, Paris
inv. no. 15269
Gift of Marcel Bing, 26.10.1908

Plate
1900, porcelain (Limoges, GDA), diam: 21.5 cm
Musée des Arts décoratifs, Paris
inv. no. 9621
Purchased (10 francs) from the Atelier Art Nouveau, 18.5.1901

Notebook
(attributed to Edward Colonna)
c. 1900, leather, 20.5 x 15.7 x 1.5 cm
Bernische Stiftung für angewandte Kunst und Gestaltung, Bern
inv. no. 1777
Purchased (50 Swiss francs) from S. Bing, 1900

Purse
c. 1900, morocco leather and metal, 11 x 5 cm
Musée des Arts décoratifs, Paris
inv. no. 15278
Gift of Marcel Bing, 26.10.1908

Belt buckle
c. 1900, gilded silver, mother of pearl, 6 x 4.5 cm
Museum für Kunst und Gewerbe, Hamburg
inv. no. 1987.245

Pendant
c. 1900, gold, enamel and pearl, length: 5 cm; diam: 3.5 cm
Musée des Arts décoratifs, Paris
inv. no. 15280 A
Gift of Marcel Bing, 26.10.1908

Tie pin
c. 1900, gold and opal, length: 8 cm
Musée des Arts décoratifs, Paris
inv. no. 15280 E
Gift of Marcel Bing, 26.10.1908

Ring
1899–1900, gold and emerald, diam: 2 cm
Musée des Arts décoratifs, Paris
inv. no. 15280 F
Gift of Marcel Bing, 26.10.1908
fig. 203

Scarf ring
c. 1900, gold and pearl, diam: 3 cm
Musée des Arts décoratifs, Paris
inv. no. 15280 G
Gift of Marcel Bing, 26.10.1908

Fastener or clasp
c. 1900, gold, green enamel and baroque pearl, length: 13 cm
Musée des Arts décoratifs, Paris
inv. no. 15280 I
Gift of Marcel Bing, 26.10.1908
fig. 195

Pendant brooch
c. 1900, gold and mother of pearl, 3.5 x 4 cm
Musée des Arts décoratifs, Paris
inv. no. 15280 J
Gift of Marcel Bing, 26.10.1908
fig. 202

Ring
c. 1900, gold, length: 2.5 cm
Musée des Arts décoratifs, Paris
inv. no. 15280 K
Gift of Marcel Bing, 26.10.1908

Belt buckle
c. 1900, mother of pearl, enamel, gilt metal, 8.1 x 7 cm
Musée des Arts décoratifs, Paris
inv. no. 15281
Gift of Marcel Bing, 26.10.1908
fig. 7

Large dish for the Canton Service in pink
c. 1900, porcelain (Limoges, GDA), 47 x 29.5 cm
Porcelaines GDA, Limoges

Canton Service in green
c. 1900, porcelain (Limoges, GDA)
Musée national Adrien Dubouché, Limoges
inv. no. ADL 4337, 4342–4344
fig. 95

Vase
c. 1900, porcelain (Limoges, GDA), h: 30 cm
Musée national Adrien Dubouché, Limoges
inv. no. ADL 10572
fig. 234

Vase
c. 1900–01, porcelain (Limoges, GDA), h: 10.5 cm; diam: 15 cm
Musée des Arts décoratifs, Paris
inv. no. 15266
Gift of Marcel Bing, 26.10.1908

Wine carafe
c. 1900, glass, 27 x 21.7 x 7 cm
Nordenfjeldske Kunstindustrimuseum, Trondheim
inv. no. NK 181–1900
Purchased (20 francs) from S. Bing at the Paris World's Fair, 1900
fig. 240

Water glass
c. 1900, h: 11.2 cm; diam: 6.8 cm
Nordenfjeldske Kunstindustrimuseum, Trondheim
inv. no. NK 182–1900
Purchased (3.50 francs) from S. Bing at the Paris World's Fair, 1900

Wine glass
c. 1900, h: 11.2; diam: 5.5 cm
Nordenfjeldske Kunstindustrimuseum, Trondheim
inv. no. NK 183–1900
Purchased (5 francs) from S. Bing at the Paris World's Fair, 1900

Spoon for caster sugar
1900, silver-gilt metal, 14.5 x 5 cm
Musée des Arts décoratifs, Paris
inv. no. 15282
Gift of Marcel Bing, 26.10.1908

Tapering vase, abstract flower design
c. 1900–02, porcelain (Limoges, GDA), h: 31 cm; diam: 4 cm
Musée des Arts décoratifs, Paris
inv. no. 15232
Gift of Marcel Bing, 26.10.1908

Plate
c. 1900–02, porcelain, diam: 22.7 cm
Musée des Arts décoratifs, Paris
inv. no. 10283 B
Purchased (15 francs) from Marcel Bing at the Société Nationale des Beaux-Arts, Paris, 1.7.1902

Tapering vase
c. 1900–02, porcelain (Limoges, GDA), h: 31.5 cm; diam: 10 cm
Musée des Arts décoratifs, Paris
inv. no. 15253
Gift of Marcel Bing, 26.10.1908

Covered vase
1902, porcelain (Limoges, GDA), h: 30 cm; diam: 6.5 cm
Musée des Arts décoratifs, Paris
inv. no. 15236
Gift of Marcel Bing, 26.10.1908
fig. 233

CHARLES COTTET

Fine Evening in Brittany
c. 1896, oil on board, 55.8 x 70 cm
Rogalin Gallery, Poznán
inv. no. MNP FR 190
Purchased (2,600 francs) at the Sale of the Bing Collection, Hôtel Drouot, Paris, 1900, no. 31
fig. 131

HENRI-EDMOND CROSS

Mediterranean Shores
1895, oil on canvas, 65 x 92 cm
Walter F. Brown Collection
Exhibited at the first Salon de L'Art Nouveau, 1895, no. 61
fig. 143

ALFRED DAGUET

Daguet executed numerous raised metal objects for Bing's L'Art Nouveau, ranging from small boxes, mirrors and book covers to complete clocks. Often these objects were set with multi-coloured stones, emphasising the elaborate hammered metal surfaces. Many of Alfred Daguet's works are illustrated in *Der Moderne Stil*, vols. 5–7.

Clock
1902, gilded and silvered copper, oak, glass cabochons, 41 x 22.5 cm
Museum für Kunst und Gewerbe, Hamburg
inv. no. 2000.832

ADRIEN DALPAYRAT

A native of Limoges, Adrien Dalpayrat (1844–1910) learned the techniques of drawing and painting on porcelain from an early age at the Ecole Pratique. He worked in several factories: in Bordeaux (Jules Vieillard & Cie.), Toulouse, Monaco and Menton. At Limoges he worked with Léon Sazerat and became interested in stoneware. In 1889, he settled in Bourg-la-Reine, where he embarked on an independent career. His collaboration with the sculptor Alphonse Voisin-Delacroix started in 1892 and proved fruitful, despite the latter's premature death in 1893.
In 1894 Dalpayrat formed a partnership with Adèle Lesbros in Bourg-la-Reine, and the company took the name Dalpayrat et Lesbros until around 1905. It executed the forms designed by Maurice Dufrêne for the Maison Moderne, and by a number of sculptors, including Constantin Meunier. After working for a short period on the manufacture of glazed earthenware (imitating pieces from Nevers and Rouen), from 1902 Dalpayrat concentrated on stoneware and porcelain. His finest technical achievement is found in the celebrated Dalpayrat red glaze. In 1906, his workshop closed, and he retired to his native village. Adrien Dalpayrat participated in two Salons de L'Art Nouveau, in December 1895 and February 1896, and a number of his pieces were also exhibited in the L'Art Nouveau Bing pavilion at the 1900 Paris World's Fair.

Small covered vase
c. 1897, stoneware, with metal mount, h: 10.8 cm
Österreichisches Museum für angewandte Kunst, Vienna
inv. no. Ke 4059
Purchased from S. Bing, 17.4.1899

Vase with leaves in relief
1897, stoneware, h: 16.5 cm; diam: 20 cm
Kaiser Wilhelm Museum, Krefeld
inv. no. 1898/50
Purchased (100 francs) from S. Bing, 1898

Gourd flask
1897, stoneware, height: h: 25.5 cm; diam: 11 cm
Kaiser Wilhelm Museum, Krefeld
inv. no. 1898/51
Purchased (137.39 marks) from S. Bing, 1898

Cup
c. 1898, stoneware, with silver mount by Edward Colonna, h: 9.9 cm; diam: 9.5 cm
Museum für Kunst und Gewerbe, Hamburg
inv. no. 1900.245
Purchased from S. Bing at the Paris World's Fair, 1900

Inkwell
1898–1903, stoneware, with bronze mount by Edward Colonna, h: 9.7 cm
(with original Art Nouveau label)
Design Museum, Ghent
inv. no. 2003/101
fig. 93

Vase in the shape of fruit
c. 1903, glazed stoneware, h: 20.5 cm; diam: 16.5 cm
Musée des Arts décoratifs, Paris
inv. no. 15224
Gift of Marcel Bing, 26.10.1908

Vase in the shape of fruit
c. 1903, glazed earthenware, h: 21 cm
Musée des Arts décoratifs, Paris
inv. no. 15225
Gift of Marcel Bing, 26.10.1908

Ewer
c. 1903, glazed earthenware, h: 17 cm
Musée des Arts décoratifs, Paris
inv. no. 15226
Gift of Marcel Bing, 26.10.1908

ALBERT-LOUIS DAMMOUSE

Albert Dammouse's background was in ceramics; he studied at the Paris Ecole des Arts Décoratifs, then at the Ecole des Beaux-Arts, where he worked in the studio of the sculptor François Jouffroy. He exhibited at public exhibitions from 1869 onwards and at the World's Fairs of 1878 and 1889. He joined the workshop of Charles Haviland in Auteuil, where he and Ernest Chaplet learned to work in stoneware. During the 1890s, with the help of his brother Edouard, he set up his own workshop in Sèvres, where he manufactured porcelain, earthenware and stoneware. His shapes were simple, influenced by Chinese and Japanese ceramics, and his decoration was often monochromatic or punctuated by restrained motifs. He exhibited works in stoneware and porcelain at the first Salon de l'Art Nouveau in 1895. From 1898 onward, Dammouse worked in pâte de verre with naturalistic plant decoration in relief. A number of his pieces were distributed by the gallery L'Art Nouveau.

Vase with vine decoration
1897, stoneware, h: 30.5 cm; diam: 16 cm
Kaiser Wilhelm Museum, Krefeld
inv. no. 1898/62
Purchased (200 francs) from S. Bing, 1898
fig. 94

Bowl
c. 1897, pâte de verre, h: 6.5 cm
Musée des Arts décoratifs, Paris
inv. no. 15268
Gift of Marcel Bing, 26.10.1908

Vase
c. 1900, stoneware, h: 62.5 cm; diam: 33 cm
Kunstgewerbemuseum, Berlin
inv. no. 1900/689
Stamped: L'Art Nouveau/22 Rue de Provence
Purchased (589.43 marks) from S. Bing, 24.7.1900
fig. 89

DAUM FRERES

The Daum glass and crystal works was founded in 1875 in Nancy by Jean Daum (1825–1885). Following the example of Emile Gallé, the brothers Auguste (1853–1909) and Antonin (1864–1930) Daum embarked on their artistic production from 1890 onwards. Eugène Damman was put in charge of the decorative workshop that was set up at the heart of the factory. Artists in glass and designers who were engaged to work there included Jacques Gruber, Emile Wirtz, Charles Schneider and Henri Bergé.
Preference was given to naturalistic decoration, employing various techniques: blowing and moulding, layering, enamelling, engraving, cameo and pâte de verre. Daum won numerous prizes at the World's Fairs. He worked regularly with a number of designers, notably Louis Majorelle, who in 1900 produced mounts in wrought iron for Daum glassware. Exceptional pieces from the Daum workshops were exhibited at the second Salon de L'Art Nouveau in February 1896.

The Violet Mourning of the Colchicum
1893, layered crystal, h: 46.7 cm; diam: 25 cm
Musée d'Orsay, Paris
inv. no. OAO 292
Exhibited at the second Salon de L'Art Nouveau, 1896, no. 805
fig. 145

Calm Hour/Twilight Incantation, designed by Jacques Gruber
1895, blown and triple-layered glass, wooden plinth, h: 46.1 cm
Musées royaux d'Art et d'Histoire, Brussels
inv. no. 6846
Exhibited at the second Salon de L'Art Nouveau, 1896, no. 804
fig. 144

WILLIAM DEGOUVE DE NUNCQUES

Child with Owl
1892, pastel on paper, 41 x 35 cm
Private collection, courtesy Van Herck, Antwerp
Exhibited at the first Salon de L'Art Nouveau, 1895, no. 66
fig. 130

Lemon Trees in Majorca
c. 1901, oil on canvas, 61 x 90 cm
Private collection
Exhibited at the William Degouve de Nuncques exhibition, L'Art Nouveau, November 1902, no. 4
fig. 138

ADRIEN DELOVINCOURT

Adrien Delovincourt, who worked with Siegfried Bing for his gallery L'Art Nouveau, is an underrated artist. He designed several patterns for furniture, including a twin bed *(lit jumeaux)* exhibited at the Société Nationale des Beaux-Arts in 1901 and featured in the *Album de références* with the number 28/342, and an 'Inverted Delovincourt armchair' (*Album de références* no. 8/106).
The Paris Musée des Arts décoratifs also has a white porcelain bonbonnière by Delovincourt that came from L'Art Nouveau.

Bonbonnière
c. 1900–02, porcelain (Limoges, GDA), h: 10 cm; diam: 11.5 cm
Musée des Arts décoratifs, Paris
inv. no. 15257
Gift of Marcel Bing, 26.10.1908

MAURICE DENIS

Women at the Stream
1894, gouache on paper, 134 x 87 cm
Musée départemental Maurice Denis 'Le Prieuré', Saint-Germain-en-Laye
inv. no. PMD 976.1.97 (Donation Family Denis)
fig. 72

The Boat
1894, gouache on paper, 132 x 81 cm
Musée départemental Maurice Denis 'Le Prieuré', Saint-Germain-en-Laye
inv. no. PMD 976.1.99 (Donation Family Denis)

GERRIT WILLEM DIJSSELHOF

Illustrations for Jan Veth, Kunst en Samenleving
1894, book, 22.6 x 18.2 cm
Museum van het Boek, Meermanno-Westreenianum, The Hague
inv. no. K 096 F 061
A copy exhibited at the International Modern Book exhibition, L'Art Nouveau, June 1896, no. 241 (990)

CHARLES DOUDELET

Devotion
c. 1894, oil on panel, 15.7 x 22 cm
Rogalin Gallery, Poznán
inv. no. MNP FR 199
Exhibited at the first Salon de L'Art Nouveau, 1895, no. 84
Purchased (18 francs) at the Sale of the Bing Collection, Hôtel Drouot, Paris, 1900, no. 59
fig. 133

GEORGES DE FEURE

(pseudonym of Georges Joseph Van Sluÿters)
After modest beginnings as a caricaturist in 1890, de Feure (1868–1943) continued his artistic career as a printmaker and poster artist for café-concerts. During the early 1890s, he exhibited his symbolist compositions at the Salons de la Rose+Croix and Le Barc de Bouteville's Expositions des Peintres impressionnistes et symbolistes. By 1895, he had built a reputation as a fashionable poster designer and exhibited his oils as works of art at the Salon de la Société Nationale des Beaux-Arts. His interest in the applied arts led to his collaboration with André Marty's Artisan moderne before Bing recruited him for his pavilion at the 1900 Paris World's Fair. Bing also held an independent exhibition for de Feure at his gallery in 1903. After having exhibited furniture (for Maison Krieger) at the Salon du Mobilier in 1908, de Feure diversified into the fields of aviation and the theatre. He re-established his reputation as an interior designer with the decoration of the Madeleine Vionnet fashion house in 1923 and the design of the Roubaix-Tourcoing pavilion at the 1925 Art Déco exhibition.

Drawing for a dining room
1895–1905, ink, heightened with white, on paper, 37.5 x 50 cm
Musée des Arts décoratifs, Paris
inv. no. CD 2671
Gift of Marcel Bing, 1919
fig. 217

Drawing for a boudoir
1895–1903, pencil, heightened with white, on paper, 38 x 47 cm
Musée des Arts décoratifs, Paris
inv. no. CD 2672
Gift of Marcel Bing, 1919
fig. 218

Drawing for chairs in a drawing room
1895–1903, pen and ink and watercolour on paper, 17.7 x 33.3 cm
Musée des Arts décoratifs, Paris
inv. no. CD 2673
Gift of Marcel Bing, 1919
fig. 186

Drawing for a desk
1895–1903, pen and ink and watercolour on paper, 15 x 19 cm
Musée des Arts décoratifs, Paris
inv. no. CD 2678
Gift of Marcel Bing, 1919

Six drawings for carpets
1895–1903, gouache on paper, 25 x 15 cm
Musée des Arts décoratifs, Paris
inv. nos. CD 2697 A-F
Gift of Marcel Bing, 1919

Drawing for a lady's desk
c. 1900, pen and ink and watercolour on paper, 20.7 x 29.4 cm
Musée des Arts décoratifs, Paris
inv. no. CD 2677
Gift of Marcel Bing, 1919

Damned Women
1897–98, watercolour on paper, 34.5 x 25 cm
Victor and Gretha Arwas Collection, London
Sold at the Sale of the Bing Collection, Hôtel Drouot, Paris, 1900, no. 89
fig. 192

Elegant Women on the Beach
1900–02, watercolour on paper, 55 x 41 cm
Collection Jane Abdy, London
Exhibited at the Georges de Feure exhibition, L'Art Nouveau, March 1903
fig. 193

Fabric with peonies
c. 1899, silk, 147.5 x 127 cm
Museum für Kunst und Gewerbe, Hamburg
inv. no. 1900.363
Purchased from S. Bing at the Paris World's Fair, 1900

Fabric with birds among vines
c. 1899–1900, velveteen, 152.5 x 85 cm
Museum für Kunst und Gewerbe, Hamburg
inv. no. 1900.364
Purchased from S. Bing at the Paris World's Fair, 1900
fig. 256

Fabric with birds among vines
c. 1899–1900, velveteen, 205 x 84 cm
Musée des Arts décoratifs, Paris
inv. no. 12927
Purchased from M. Majorelle, 26.7.1906

Fabric 'Cytisus' (Scotch broom)
c. 1899–1900, silk, 149 x 126 cm
Museum für Kunst und Gewerbe, Hamburg
inv. no. 1900.362
Purchased from S. Bing at the Paris World's Fair, 1900

Fabric 'Cytisus' (Scotch broom)
c. 1899–1900, silk, 289 x 127.5 cm
Österreichisches Museum für angewandte Kunst, Vienna
inv. no. 5422/1901
Purchased (105 francs) from S. Bing, 12.4.1901

Fabric 'Cytisus' (Scotch broom)
c. 1899–1900, silk, 163 x 128 cm
Musée des Arts décoratifs, Paris
inv. no. 12926
Raymond Koechlin Bequest, 9.4.1934
Purchased (56 francs) from M. Majorelle, 26.7.1906,

Fabric
c. 1899–1900, silk, 290 x 89 cm
Österreichisches Museum für Angewandte Kunst, Vienna
inv. no. 5423/1901
Purchased (31.50 francs) from S. Bing, 12.4.1901

Wall hanging from the boudoir
c. 1900, silk, pattern: 45 x 31.5 cm
Det Danske Kunstindustrimuseum, Copenhagen
inv. no. 1044
Purchased (320.50 francs) from S. Bing at the Paris World's Fair, 1900
fig. 255

Rug
c. 1900, silk (plush) and wool, 193 x 120 cm
Det Danske Kunstindustrimuseum, Copenhagen
inv. no. 1041
Purchased (500 francs) from S. Bing at the Paris World's Fair, 1900

Embroidered seat cover
1900, silk, 55 x 43 cm
Musée des Arts décoratifs, Paris
inv. no. 19844 A
Gift of Marcel Bing, 25.7.1914

Invitation to L'Art Nouveau
1900, paper, 12 x 18.1 cm
Museum für Kunst und Gewerbe, Hamburg
inv. no. E 1983.57
fig. 214

Glass
c. 1900, painting for the pavilion L'Art Nouveau Bing
oil on canvas, 280 x 103 cm
Galerie Tonon, Geneva
fig. 242

Display cabinet
c. 1900, carved and gilt wood, 190 x 118 x 76 cm
Musée des Arts décoratifs, Paris
inv. no. 24731
Gift of René Haase, 11.4.1925
fig. 253

Table from the boudoir
c. 1900, gilt beechwood, green leather, 70.5 x 70 x 50 cm
Det Danske Kunstindustrimuseum, Copenhagen
inv. no. 1042
Purchased (750 francs) from S. Bing at the Paris World's Fair, 1900
fig. 255

Sofa from the boudoir
c. 1900, gilt beechwood, embroidery, 90 x 117 x 40 cm
Det Danske Kunstindustrimuseum, Copenhagen
inv. no. 1042
Purchased (2,500 francs) from S. Bing at the Paris World's Fair, 1900
fig. 255

Chair from the boudoir
c. 1900, gilt beechwood, embroidery, 99.4 x 40.1 x 39.8 cm
Det Danske Kunstindustrimuseum, Copenhagen
inv. no. 1042
Purchased (750 francs) from S. Bing at the Paris World's Fair, 1900
fig. 255

Vitrine
c. 1900, gilt beechwood, 101,6 x 76,2 x 27,9 cm
Det Danske Kunstindustrimuseum, Copenhagen
inv. no. 1042
Purchased (1,500 francs) from S. Bing at the Paris World's Fair, 1900

Screen
1900, gilt beechwood, 120 x 103 cm
Musée des Arts décoratifs, Paris
inv. no. 12846
Gift of Marcel Bing, 30.5.1906
fig. 254

Console table
1900, carved and gilt beechwood and alabaster, 99 x 47.5 x 41 cm
Musée des Arts décoratifs, Paris
inv. no. 21493
Gift of Marcel Bing, 16.5.1919
fig. 252

Dressing room chair
1900, American ash, h: 88.5; seat, h: 42 cm
Nordenfjeldske Kunstindustrimuseum, Trondheim
inv. no. NK 140–1900
Purchased (195.75 francs) from S. Bing at the Paris World's Fair, 1900
fig. 257

Display cabinet
1902, sycamore wood, 182 x 101 cm
Musée des Arts décoratifs, Paris
inv. no. 10279
Purchased (15 francs) from Marcel Bing at the Société Nationale des Beaux-Arts, 1.7.1902

Vase
c. 1900, porcelain (Limoges, GDA), h: 28 cm; diam: 8 cm
Musée des Arts décoratifs, Paris
inv. no. 15235
Gift of Marcel Bing, 26.10.1908

Bonbonnière
c. 1900, porcelain (Limoges, GDA), 17.5 x 13 cm
Musée des Arts décoratifs, Paris
inv. no. 15241
Gift of Marcel Bing, 26.10.1908
fig. 249

Cup and saucer, abstract flower design
c. 1900, porcelain (Limoges, GDA), cup, h: 4.7 cm; saucer, diam: 13.7 cm
Musée des Arts décoratifs, Paris
inv. no. 15255
Gift of Marcel Bing, 26.10.1908
fig. 246

Vase
c. 1900, porcelain (Limoges, GDA), h: 21 cm
Porcelaines GDA, Limoges

Vase
c. 1900, porcelain (Limoges, GDA), h: 20.5 cm
Porcelaines GDA, Limoges

Plate
c. 1900, porcelain (Limoges, GDA), diam: 21.5 cm
Musée des Arts décoratifs, Paris
inv. no. 9616
Purchased (10 francs) from the Atelier de L'Art Nouveau, 18.5.1901

Plate
c. 1900, porcelain (Limoges, GDA), diam: 21.5 cm
Musée des Arts décoratifs, Paris

inv. no. 9617
Purchased (10 francs) from the Atelier de L'Art Nouveau, 18.5.1901
Plate, seaweed design
c. 1900–01, porcelain (Limoges, GDA), diam: 21.8 cm
Musée des Arts décoratifs, Paris
inv. no. 9618
Purchased (10 francs) from the Atelier de L'Art Nouveau, 18.5.1901
Plate
c. 1900–02, porcelain (Limoges, GDA), diam: 21.8 cm
Musée des Arts décoratifs, Paris
inv. no. 10283 A
Purchased (15 francs) from Marcel Bing at the Société Nationale des Beaux-Arts, 1.7.1902
Inkwell
1900, porcelain (Limoges, GDA), h: 8 cm
Musée des Arts décoratifs, Paris
inv. no. 15231
Gift of Marcel Bing, 26.10.1908
Small teapot
1900–01, porcelain (Limoges, GDA), h: 11.5 cm; diam: 6.5 cm
Musée des Arts décoratifs, Paris
inv. no. 15245
Gift of Marcel Bing, 26.10.1908
Vase
1900–01, porcelain (Limoges, GDA), h: 21.5 cm; diam: 7.5 cm
Musée des Arts décoratifs, Paris
inv. no. 15234
Gift of Marcel Bing, 26.10.1908
Sugar bowl
c. 1900–01, porcelain (Limoges, GDA), h: 13.5 cm; diam: 10 cm
Musée des Arts décoratifs, Paris
inv. no. 15265
Gift of Marcel Bing, 26.10.1908
fig. 248
Statuette of a woman
c. 1900, painted plaster, h: 24 cm
Musée des Arts décoratifs, Paris
inv. no. 15250
Gift of Marcel Bing, 26.10.1908
fig. 208
Statuette of a woman
c. 1900–01, porcelain (Limoges, GDA), h: 25.5 cm; diam: 13 cm
Porcelaines GDA, Limoges
Statuette of a woman
c. 1903, porcelain (Limoges, GDA), h: 25.5 cm
Victor and Gretha Arwas Collection, London
fig. 209
Clock with figure of a woman
c. 1900–01, porcelain (Limoges, GDA), h: 22.9 x 20.3 x 12.7 cm
Porcelaines GDA, Limoges
fig. 207
Planter
c. 1901–02, porcelain (Limoges, GDA), 12.5 x 35 x 21 cm
Porcelaines GDA, Limoges
Vase 'Woman in Snow Scene'
c. 1901–02, porcelain (Limoges, GDA), h: 21 cm
Porcelaines GDA, Limoges
fig. 247
Chocolate pot
c. 1902, porcelain (Limoges, GDA), h: 27.5 cm
Porcelaines GDA, Limoges
fig. 245
Ice bucket
c. 1902, porcelain (Limoges, GDA), h: 20 cm; diam: 13 cm
Musée des Arts décoratifs, Paris
inv. no. 10282
Purchased (75 francs) from Marcel Bing at the Société Nationale des Beaux-Arts, 1.7.1902
Pitcher
c. 1900–02, porcelain (Limoges, GDA), h: 15 cm; diam: 9 cm
Musée des Arts décoratifs, Paris
inv. no. 10281
Purchased (40 francs) from Marcel Bing at the Société Nationale des Beaux-Arts, 1.7.1902
Bonbonnière
c. 1900–02, porcelain (Limoges, GDA), h: 8 cm; diam: 9.5 cm
Musée des Arts décoratifs, Paris
inv. no. 15247
Gift of Marcel Bing, 26.10.1908
Bonbonnière
c. 1900–02, porcelain (Limoges, GDA), h: 7 cm; diam. 7.8 cm
Musée des Arts décoratifs, Paris
inv. no. 15249
Gift of Marcel Bing, 26.10.1908
Rectangular vase
1903, porcelain, h: 21.5 cm
Musée national Adrien Dubouché, Limoges
inv. no. 10760
Three glasses
c. 1900, glass, h: 13.5 cm; diam: 9.1 cm/ h: 18 cm; diam: 5 cm/ h: 12 cm; diam: 7 cm
Musée des Arts décoratifs, Paris
inv. nos. 15267 A/B/C
Gift of Marcel Bing, 26.10.1908
Candelabra
1900, silvered bronze, h: 26; width: 35 cm
Musée des Arts décoratifs, Paris
inv. no. 15220
Gift of Marcel Bing, 26.10.1908
Cutlery, dessert spoon and fork
1900, silver, length: 19.5 cm
Germanisches Nationalmuseum, Nürnberg
inv. no. LGA 8.533/ 1 & 2
Purchased (75 francs) from S. Bing, 5.11.1900
fig. 244
Comb
c. 1900, carved horn, 7.5 x 10 cm
Musée des Arts décoratifs, Paris
inv. no. 15279 A
Gift of Marcel Bing, 26.10.1908
Fan
c. 1900, tortoise-shell and ivory, h: 20.5 cm
Musée des Arts décoratifs, Paris
inv. no. 12871
Gift of Marcel Bing, 28.6.1906
Fan
c. 1900, wood and silk, h: 20.5 cm
Musée des Arts décoratifs, Paris
inv. no. 12872
Gift of Marcel Bing, 28.6.1906
fig. 206
Wallet (made by Ribe-Roy)
c. 1902, leather, 21.2 x 15 cm
Musée des Arts décoratifs, Paris
inv. no. 15274
Gift of Marcel Bing, 26.10.1908
Seal
1900–04, plated metal, h: 10.3 cm; diam: 2.5 cm
Musée des Arts décoratifs, Paris
inv. no. 15283
Gift of Marcel Bing, 26.10.1908
Advertisement for de Feure
1901, paper, 12 x 18 cm
Album Maciet, vol. 256, no. 12
Bibliothèque des Arts décoratifs, Paris
Invitation for the de Feure exhibition
1903, paper, 12 x 18 cm
Album Maciet, vol. 268, no. 2
Bibliothèque des Arts décoratifs, Paris

EUGENE GAILLARD

In his collaboration with Siegfried Bing's L'Art Nouveau, Eugène Gaillard (1862–1933) specialised in furniture and textile design. Together with Georges de Feure and Edward Colonna, he was a principal contributor to Bing's L'Art Nouveau pavilion at the Paris World's Fair in 1900. Gaillard was inspired by the Louis XV style in the contours of the large items of furniture in the dining room and bedroom at Bing's pavilion. He rejected straight lines and angles in favour of curves and lines, in order to make the decoration integral to the body of the piece. His famous chair (fig. 230), a great commercial success, made use of the cantilever advocated by Viollet-le-Duc, which had already been used by Grasset in 1880 and Guimard around 1889; the chair was acquired by all the principal European museums of the decorative arts.
Gaillard ended his collaboration with Bing in 1903 and established his own firm, which produced furniture of similar design, although this gradually became lighter with less emphatic decoration.
In 1906 Gaillard wrote a theoretical essay on furniture: 'A propos du mobilier: Opinions d'avant-garde, technique fondamentale, l'évolution', based upon five rules: a piece of furniture should express its function as far as possible; the nature of the material must be respected; no unnecessary structural elements ought to be included; in wood the arch can only to be regarded as a decorative element; and ornament should be abstract.

Fabric with floral design
c. 1899–1900, velvet, 192 x 85 cm
Musée des Arts décoratifs, Paris
inv. no. 12928
Purchased from M. Majorelle, 26.7.1906

Fabric with floral design
c. 1899, velveteen, 149 x 81 cm
Museum für Kunst und Gewerbe, Hamburg
inv. no. 1900.359
Purchased from S. Bing at the Paris World's Fair, 1900
fig. 220

Fabric with floral design
c. 1899, velveteen, 151 x 84 cm
Museum für Kunst und Gewerbe, Hamburg
inv. no. 1900.360
Purchased from S. Bing at the Paris World's Fair, 1900

Chair
c. 1899, mahogany and leather, 93.5 x 42 x 41 cm
Musée des Arts décoratifs, Paris
inv. no. 31483
Eugène Gaillard Bequest, 9.2.1934
fig. 221

Sideboard
c. 1899, Italian walnut, 210 x 226 x 54 cm
Museum für Kunst und Gewerbe, Hamburg
inv. no. 1900.378
Purchased from S. Bing at the Paris World's Fair, 1900
fig. 222

Chair
c. 1899, Italian walnut and leather, 91.5 x 44.5 x 43.5 cm
Museum für Kunst und Gewerbe, Hamburg
inv. no. 1901.220
Purchased from S. Bing at the Paris World's Fair, 1900
fig. 230

Dado
1900, walnut, 99 x 193,6 x 1,9 cm
Det Danske Kunstindustrimuseum, Copenhagen
inv. no. 1007
Purchased from S. Bing at the Paris World's Fair, 1900

Bedroom suite
c. 1899–1900, wood, wardrobe: 251 x 183 x 71 cm, bed: 150 x 72 x 195 cm, bedside table: 105 x 40 x 34 cm
Private collection
Exhibited at L'Art Nouveau Bing, Paris World's Fair, 1900
fig. 224–229, 232

GRUEBY POTTERY, BOSTON (MASSACHUSETTS)

The business was founded by William Henry Grueby (1867–1925) to produce industrial ceramics and art pottery. In 1890 he set up a factory at Revere, Massachusetts, and in 1894 he founded the Grueby-Faience Company. Among the firm's pattern designers were Georges Prentiss Kendrick and Addison Le Boutillier.
In 1899, 'Grueby Pottery' became the trademark for the art ceramics, and 'Grueby Faience' for the architectural ceramics. In 1909 the business failed. Grueby is known for the use of three dominant colours: crackled yellow, bluish grey and green. The shapes are sober, and the decorations, which are in low relief, were inspired by the leaves of the lilac, the plane tree and the mullein. Examples were regularly exhibited at the Société Nationale des Beaux-Arts and sold by Siegfried Bing in his gallery L'Art Nouveau.

Jar
1898–99, earthenware with semi-matt glaze, h: 33.2 cm; diam. 15 cm
Victoria and Albert Museum, London
inv. no. 1685–1900
Purchased (£7.12.9) from S. Bing, 1900

Vase
1900, earthenware, h: 48 cm; diam: 23 cm
Kunstgewerbemuseum, Berlin
inv. no. 1900/583
Purchased (221.04 marks) from S. Bing, 24.7.1900

Vase
c. 1900, enamelled earthenware, h: 25 cm; diam: 17 cm
Musée des Arts décoratifs, Paris
inv. no. 9352
Purchased (270 francs) from S. Bing, 1.11.1900

Vase
c. 1900, earthenware, h: 28.6 cm; diam: 12.7 cm
Det Danske Kunstindustrimuseum, Copenhagen
inv. no. 933
Purchased (189 francs) from S. Bing at the Paris World's Fair, 1900
fig. 86

HENRI GUERARD

Fan with cat
1895, watercolour on paper, 31,5 x 59 cm
Private collection
Exhibited at the first Salon de L'Art Nouveau, 1895, no. 99

CLEMENT JOHN HEATON

The English painter and interior decorator Clément Heaton (1861–1940) was the son of the founder of the firm of Heaton, Butler & Bayle, one of the most important manufacturers of stained glass established in England in the 19th century. He spent his youth in London before settling in Neuchâtel (1893–1914), where he opened a workshop.
Clément Heaton devoted himself principally to monumental decoration, and played an important part in decorating the Musée d'Art et d'Histoire in Neuchâtel, a project for which he used the processes of cloisonné metalwork and papier repoussé. At the same time, he produced a large number of vases, dishes and other cloisonné items, which established his reputation in London and Paris, where his work was on display at the gallery L'Art Nouveau.

Large Jardinière
1898, enamel and copper, h: 34 cm; diam: 45 cm
Österreichisches Museum für angewandte Kunst, Vienna
inv. no. EM 254/1898
Purchased from S. Bing, 29.7.1898

Large round dish
1898, cloisonné enamel and copper, diam: 65 cm
Musée des Arts décoratifs, Paris
inv. no. 8722
Purchased (250 francs) from S. Bing, 25.5.1898
fig. 172

THOMAS THEODOR HEINE

Jealousy
1894, oil on canvas, 26 x 42 cm
Private collection
Exhibited at the second Salon de L'Art Nouveau, 1896, no. 678
fig. 141

VICTOR HORTA

Horta (1861–1947) was a brilliant student in the school of architecture at the Académie des Beaux-Arts in Brussels. After starting his career with the architect Alphonse Balat, Victor Horta came to notice in 1893 when he built the Hôtel Tassel, one of the very first examples of *art nouveau* in Europe. Around the same time, Horta was approached by Siegfried Bing to carry out work to enlarge his shop at 22, rue de Provence in Paris. Horta's next important works were the Hôtel Solvay and the celebrated Maison du Peuple, opened in 1899, both in Brussels, and he moved on to an official career. Between the two World Wars, he built the Palais des Beaux-Arts in Brussels and taught at the Free University there, as well as at the Fine Art Institute in Antwerp. In 1927 he became director of the Académie des Beaux-Arts in Brussels, where he trained an entire generation of architects.

Drawing for the façade of Bing's L'Art Nouveau
1895, pen and ink and watercolour on paper, 41.8 x 41.8 cm
Musée Horta, Brussels
inv. no. Do/Bing/A1/o (Fondation Delhaye)
fig. 103

CHARLES HOUDARD

Frogs
1893, aquatint on paper, 26.2 x 39.5 cm
Van Gogh Museum, Amsterdam
inv. no. p 1050 v/2000

Exhibited at the first Salon de L'Art Nouveau, 1895, no. 244

P.A. ISAAC

Wall hanging
c. 1895, cotton, 290 x 133 cm
Österreichisches Museum für angewandte Kunst, Vienna
inv. no. 5424/1901
Purchased (55 francs) from S. Bing, 12.4.1901

JEANNE ITASSE

Mask of Richard Wagner
c. 1895, ceramic by Emile Müller, 29 x 28 x 18 cm
Private collection
Exhibited at the first Salon de L'Art Nouveau, 1895, no. 425

LEON JALLOT

Vase
c. 1900, porcelain (Sèvres) with crystalline glazes by Millet, with silver mount by Jallot, h: 18.8 cm; diam. 12.3 cm
Victoria and Albert Museum, London
inv. no. 1699–1900
Purchased from S. Bing, 1900
fig. 198

PIERRE-PAUL JOUVE

Pierre-Paul Jouve (1880–1975), who specialised in paintings and sculptures of animals, was born at Marlotte, near Barbizon. He grew up in an artistic environment, as his father was himself a portrait and landscape painter. Although he enrolled at the Ecole des Arts Décoratifs in Paris, he preferred to draw from nature and became a familiar figure in the Jardin des Plantes. At his father's side, he learned how to model, began to make engravings, and from the age of fifteen exhibited several drawings of animals at the Salon des Artistes Français. He collaborated with the architect René Binet on the decoration of the monumental door on the Place de la Concorde for the 1900 Paris World's Fair; Jouve produced a long frieze of wild animals, which was realised in stoneware by the ceramic artist Alexandre Bigot. This brought him to the attention of Siegfried and Marcel Bing, who decided to support his work. Paul Jouve carried out several projects for the Bings, including designs and animal sculptures, some of which were realised in porcelain by the GDA factories in Limoges. His friendship with the Bings enabled him to visit the zoos in Antwerp and Hamburg, and, in 1905, his first retrospective exhibition was organised at Marcel Bing's premises in rue Saint-Georges, bringing him to the attention of a wider public.

Baboon
1905, bronze, 14 x 33 x 34 cm
Collection Dominique Suisse
Exhibited at the Paul Jouve exhibition, L'Art Nouveau, March 1905, no. 3

Plaque with tiger
1905, bronze, 20 x 49 cm
Collection Dominique Suisse
Exhibited at the Paul Jouve exhibition, L'Art Nouveau, March 1905, no. 8

Monkeys
c. 1905, bronze, h: 16 cm
Musée des Arts décoratifs, Paris
inv. no. 15223
Gift of Marcel Bing, 26.10.1908

Card case with pencil holder (made by Ribe-Roy)
c. 1900–05, morocco leather, 14 x 9.5 cm
Musée des Arts décoratifs, Paris
inv. no. 15273
Gift of Marcel Bing, 26.10.1908

Blotter in embossed leather (made by Ribe-Roy)
c. 1900–05, leather, 44 x 32 cm
Musée des Arts décoratifs, Paris
inv. no. 15270
Gift of Marcel Bing, 26.10.1908

Cat and snail
c. 1900–05, porcelain (Limoges, GDA), 13.9 x 19.8 cm
Musée national Adrien Dubouché, Limoges
inv. no. ADL 4390

Bear lying down
c. 1900–05, porcelain (Limoges, GDA), length: 19 cm
Musée des Arts décoratifs, Paris
inv. no. 15259
Gift of Marcel Bing, 26.10.1908

HERMANN AUGUST KÄHLER

The Danish ceramic artist Hermann August Kähler (1846–1917) started his career in his father's workshop. In 1864–65 he underwent training in the studio of the sculptor Hermann Bissen in Copenhagen, and he then worked at ceramic factories in Berlin and Zürich. He took over his father's workshop in Næstved in 1872. His ceramics, with copper-lustre reduction glazes, were influenced by Islamic art and received great acclaim at the World's Fairs in Paris, 1889, and Chicago, 1893. His bold forms and decorations had a major influence on Danish ceramic artists such as Thorvald Bindesbøll.

Vase
c. 1896, stoneware, h: 11 cm
Musée des Arts décoratifs, Paris
inv. no. 8424
Purchased (70 francs) from S. Bing at the Salon du Champ de Mars, 7.7.1896

FERNAND KHNOPFF

At Fosset/Under the Fir Trees
1894, oil and mixed media on paper mounted on canvas, 66.5 x 45.2 cm
Musées royaux des Beaux-Arts de Belgique, Brussels
inv. no. 12086
Exhibited at the first Salon de L'Art Nouveau, 1895, no. 118
fig. 142

MAX KLINGER

Illustrations for Reinhold Jachmann, Amor und Psyche
1880, book, 36.7 x 27 cm
Museum van het Boek, Meermanno-Westreenianum, The Hague
inv. no. K 083 A 018
A copy exhibited at the International Modern Book exhibition, L'Art Nouveau, June 1896, no. 218

KARL KOEPPING

Painter and engraver Karl Koepping (1848–1914) is regarded as one of the masters of contemporary German engraving. In 1895 he abandoned engraving to work in glass, specialising in producing art items reminiscent of old Venetian glassware. His association with Friedrich Zitzmann, who had previously worked in Murano, was perhaps not unconnected with this relationship. Their collaboration ended in 1897. Karl Koepping used the blown glass technique, producing extremely fragile chalices, cups and decanters that recall the nuances of agate and the most delicate metallic iridescences. He exhibited his flower vases at Siegfried Bing's premises from 1895 and in the various Paris salons between 1896 and 1900.

Two wine glasses
c. 1896–99, h: 12 cm; diam: 6.3 cm
Nordenfjeldske Kunstindustrimuseum, Trondheim
inv. no. NKY 187
Purchased (653 Noorse kronen) from S. Bing, 1900

Glass
c. 1896, h: 17.5 cm
Musée des Arts décoratifs, Paris
inv. no. 8428
Purchased (80 francs) from S. Bing, 7.7.1896
fig. 287

Glass
c. 1899, h: 28 cm
Musée des Arts décoratifs, Paris
inv. no. 9085
Purchased (110 francs) from S. Bing, 5.7.1899

GEORGES LACOMBE

Return of the Sardine Fishers
1895, oil on canvas, 81 x 60 cm
Private collection
Exhibited at the first Salon de L'Art Nouveau, 1895, no. 121
fig. 140

MAX LAEUGER

The painter and interior designer Max Laeuger (1864–1952) studied painting and interior decoration at the School of Applied Arts in Karlsruhe, where he subsequently taught. He executed his first ceramic works at the Mayer factory in Karlsruhe in 1886. At the time of the 1889 Paris World's Fair, his interest was drawn to ancient ceramics. He travelled to Italy and, on his return, completed his training at the Académie Julian in Paris. Back in Germany, he taught interior design in the architecture section of the Karlsruhe School of Applied Arts. At the same time, he was appointed artistic director (1895–1914) at a factory in the Grand Duchy of Baden-Württemberg: Tonwerke Kandern AG, in the Black Forest. He exhibited his own ceramic designs for the first time in Munich and Berlin in 1897. He was awarded gold medals at the World's Fairs in Paris, 1900, and St Louis, 1904, and his works were sold by the Paris galleries L'Art Nouveau and La Maison Moderne.

Vase
c. 1898, earthenware, h: 21.5 cm
Musée des Arts décoratifs, Paris
inv. no. 8767
Purchased (22 francs) from S. Bing, 19.11.1898
Pitcher
c. 1898, earthenware, h: 21 cm
Musée des Arts décoratifs, Paris
inv. no. 8768
Purchased (14 francs) from S. Bing, 19.11.1898
fig. 294
Vase
c. 1898, earthenware, h: 44.5 cm
Musée des Arts décoratifs, Paris
inv. no. 8766
Purchased (58 francs) from S. Bing, 25.5.1898

M. LE CHATELIER

Vase (Glatigny workshop)
c. 1898, porcelain, h: 19 cm
Musée des Arts décoratifs, Paris
inv. no. 8719
Purchased (20 francs) from S. Bing, 25.5.1898

LOUIS LEGRAND

Invitation for Legrand's exhibition at Bing's
April 1897, engraving on paper, 22.4 x 11.2 cm
Museum für Kunst und Gewerbe, Hamburg
inv. no. 1897.804
fig. 146

ALPHONSE LEGROS

Mask of a young girl (Miss Swainson)
c. 1890–91, bronze, 31.6 x 19.3 x 17.1 cm
Musée d'Orsay, Paris
inv. no. RF 1279
Exhibited at the Alphonse Legros exhibition, L'Art Nouveau, March 1898, no. 164

GEORGES LEMMEN

The Belgian painter, poster artist and engraver Georges Lemmen (1865–1913) joined the group Les XX in 1888. His talent for graphic design became evident early in the 1890s, and he produced several catalogue covers for Les XX as well as vignettes for *L'Art moderne*. He was an accomplished journalist and also contributed articles to *L'Art moderne* and *L'Art décoratif*.
Lemmen was a friend of Van de Velde, and they collaborated on the smoking room designed for the inauguration of the gallery L'Art Nouveau in December 1895. He also designed several posters and invitation cards for Siegfried Bing, while the art critic Julius Meier-Graefe put him in charge of publicity for his gallery, La Maison Moderne. He also produced designs for wallpaper, fabrics, tiles and carpets.

Invitation card for the opening of the gallery L'Art Nouveau
1895, lithography on paper, 12 x 16.9 cm
Museum für Kunst und Gewerbe, Hamburg
inv. no. E 1897.803
fig. 102
Programme for L'Art Nouveau
1895, lithography on paper, in relief, 22.2 x 20.1 cm
Museum für Kunst und Gewerbe, Hamburg
inv. no. E 1897.802
Placard for L'Art Nouveau
1895, lithography on paper, in relief, 66.5 x 92 cm
Museum für Kunst und Gewerbe, Hamburg
inv. no. DFP II, no. 1055
fig. 108
Notice to artists
1895, lithography on paper, 23.7 x 19.2 cm
Museum für Kunst und Gewerbe, Hamburg
inv. no. E 1897.801
fig. 120

LEULLIER ET BING

Table service
1867, Paris hard-paste porcelain
Musée national Adrien Dubouché, Limoges
inv. no. 3509–3511
Gift of Leullier et Bing, 1867 and 1868
fig. 8

LIBERTY & CO.

Interior decoration business founded by Arthur Lasenby Liberty (1843–1917).
After the 1862 Universal Exhibition in South Kensington, where Japanese art and crafts made a strong impression, Farmer and Rogers decided to open an oriental shop, appointing Liberty to manage it in 1864. In 1875, Liberty opened his own shop in Regent Street, importing a great variety of wallpapers, silks and art objects, and in 1883 he established a furniture and decoration workshop. The firm also commissioned textiles and furnishing fabrics from the best English designers, including Voysey and Arthur Silver. In 1889, Liberty opened a branch in Paris.
At the turn of the century, Liberty, who imported a great many items from Europe, decided to create his own product line. The firm amalgamated with a Birmingham goldsmith, W.H. Haseler, and became Liberty & Co. Its products were very strongly influenced by the Celtic designs of Archibald Knox, Rex Silver and others, but the designers' names never appeared; the items were sold anonymously under the brand name. Liberty also distributed glassware from the Glasgow factory of James Cooper & Sons.

'Thebes' stool, designed by Laget
1884, wood, h: 35.5 cm; depth: 28 cm
Nordenfjeldske Kunstindustrimuseum, Trondheim
inv. no. NK 4770
Purchased (28 francs) from S. Bing, 1896
fig. 182
Fabric, abstract plant design, designed by Arthur Silver
c. 1896, printed cotton, 95 x 80.5 cm
Nordenfjeldske Kunstindustrimuseum, Trondheim
inv. no. NK 93–1897
Purchased from S. Bing, 6.2.1897
fig. 171
Fabric, abstract plant design, by Silver Studio
c. 1896, printed cotton, 94 x 81 cm
Nordenfjeldske Kunstindustrimuseum, Trondheim
inv. no. NK 92–1897
Purchased from S. Bing, 6.2.1897
fig. 279

HENRI MARTIN

Orpheus
c. 1894, oil on canvas, 54.2 x 64 cm
Musée des Beaux-Arts, Dijon
inv. no. 2053
Sold (410 francs) at the Sale of the Bing Collection, Hôtel Drouot, Paris, 1900, no. 65

JOSEPH MENDES DA COSTA

Monkeys
c. 1895, bronze, h: 16 cm
Musée des Arts décoratifs, Paris
inv. no. 15222
Gift of Marcel Bing, 26.10.1908

CONSTANTIN MEUNIER

The Metalworker
1886, bronze, h: 48,5 cm
Musée Constantin Meunier, Bruxelles
inv. no. 10.000/90
A cast exhibited at the Constantin Meunier exhibition, L'Art Nouveau, February-March 1896, no. 11, and at the Grafton Galleries, London, 1899, no. 24
fig. 151

Woman Coalminer with Shovel
1888, bronze, 49.6 x 14.5 x 11.5 cm
Museum für Kunst und Gewerbe, Hamburg
inv. no. 1900.458
Purchased from S. Bing at the Paris World's Fair, 1900
fig. 152

Glassblower
1889, bronze, 54.5 x 18.3 x 14.2 cm
Musée Constantin Meunier, Brussels
inv. no. 10.000/94
A cast exhibited at the Constantin Meunier exhibition, L'Art Nouveau, February-March 1896, no. 7, and at the Grafton Galleries, London, 1899, no. 31
fig. 285

Ecce Homo
1890, bronze, 57 x 23 x 31 cm
Museum Mesdag, The Hague
inv. no. HWM 465
A cast exhibited at the Constantin Meunier exhibition, L'Art Nouveau, February-March 1896, no. 3, and at the Grafton Galleries, London, 1899, no. 35

Motherhood
1893, bronze, h: 63.3 cm
Van Gogh Museum, Amsterdam
inv. no. V 0099 S/1995
A cast exhibited at the Grafton Galleries, London, 1899, no. 13

The Dockworker
1893, bronze, 118.2 x 58.8 x 47.3 cm
Musée Constantin Meunier, Brussels
inv. no. 10.000/17
A cast exhibited at the Constantin Meunier exhibition, L'Art Nouveau, February-March 1896, no. 13, and at the Grafton Galleries, London, 1899, no. 32
fig. 153

The Pardon (The Prodigal Son)
1895, bronze, h: 45 cm
Victoria and Albert Museum, London
inv. no. 764–1899
Purchased (£60) at the Grafton Galleries, London, 1899, no. 36

GEORGES MORREN

Inkwell
1895, bronze, 10 x 18 x 12.3 cm
Private collection
Exhibited at the first Salon de L'Art Nouveau, 1895, no. 646
fig. 110

WILLIAM MORRIS

The English interior designer, craftsman and theorist William Morris (1834–1896) was one of the representative figures of the Arts and Crafts movement, founded in response to the way the creative process was seen to have been debased as a consequence of the Industrial Revolution. Morris's activities spanned many fields, from furniture to publishing. His designs were inspired by nature, and his medieval-style furniture espoused the principles of traditional, handcrafted production.
The famous Red House, built for him by the architect and interior designer Philip Webb and completed in 1860, was the meeting-place for a group of friends, who designed the furniture there and decided to form an association of interior designers under the name of Morris, Marshall, Faulkner and Co. In 1875, William Morris assumed the leadership of this group, which, as Morris and Co., produced wallpapers with floral motifs as well as numerous patterns for fabrics. Morris founded his own factory for fabric-printing at Merton Abbey, as well as a small publishing house, Kelmscott Press, in 1891. A number of Morris and Co. wallpapers and fabrics were distributed by Siegfried Bing in his gallery L'Art Nouveau.

Fabric 'Tulip'
1875, printed cotton, 131 x 95 cm
Nordenfjeldske Kunstindustrimuseum, Trondheim
inv. no. NK 97–1897
Purchased from S. Bing, 6.2.1897
fig. 166

Fabric 'Brer Rabbit'
1883, printed cotton, 140 x 92 cm
Nordenfjeldske Kunstindustrimuseum, Trondheim
inv. no. NK 88–1897
Purchased from S. Bing, 6.2.1897
fig. 167

Fabric 'Roses and Trellis'
1885, printed cotton, 95 x 80 cm
Nordenfjeldske Kunstindustrimuseum, Trondheim
inv. no. NK 91–1897
Purchased from S. Bing, 6.2.1897
fig. 168

Fabric, abstract leaf design
printed cotton, 134 x 97 cm
Nordenfjeldske Kunstindustrimuseum, Trondheim
inv. no. NK 96–1897
Purchased from S. Bing, 6.2.1897

The Works of Geoffrey Chaucer (William Morris & Edward Burne-Jones)
1896, book, 42.5 x 29.2 cm
Museum van het Boek, Meermanno-Westreenianum, The Hague
inv. no. 309 B 001 (D 040 A 001)
A copy exhibited at the International Modern Book exhibition, L'Art Nouveau, June 1896, no. 723–4

EDVARD MUNCH

Self-portrait with a skeleton arm
1895, lithograph on paper, 45.4 x 31.8 cm
Hamburger Kunsthalle, Hamburg
inv. no. 34597
An example exhibited at the Edvard Munch exhibition, L'Art Nouveau, May 1896, no. 48

The Kiss
1895, etching and drypoint on paper, 35.6 x 31.8 cm
Hamburger Kunsthalle, Hamburg
inv. no. 1914–151
An example exhibited at the Edvard Munch exhibition, L'Art Nouveau, May 1896, no. 31

Madonna
1895, colour lithograph with lithographic crayon on paper, 60.5 x 44.2 cm
Albertina, Vienna
inv. no. DG 1946/47
An example exhibited at the Edvard Munch exhibition, L'Art Nouveau, May 1896, no. 36
fig. 156

MANUEL ORAZI

Illustrations for Austin de Croze, 'The Magic Calendar', published by L'Art Nouveau
1895, book, 54.6 x 18.7 cm
Collection Jacques et Rolande van der Heyde
A copy exhibited at the second Salon de L'Art Nouveau, 1896, no. 739 bis
fig. 134

JAMES PITCAIRN-KNOWLES

Illustrations for Georges Rodenbach, 'Les tombeaux', published by L'Art Nouveau
1895, book, 26 x 17.5 cm
Van Gogh Museum, Amsterdam
inv. no. P 1793 V/2000
A copy exhibited at the first Salon de L'Art Nouveau, 1895, no. 632, and the International Modern Book exhibition, L'Art Nouveau, June 1896, no. 44

PAUL-ELIE RANSON

Four Women at the Fountain
1895, oil on canvas, 134 x 225 cm
Musée départemental Maurice Denis 'Le Prieuré', Saint-Germain-en-Laye
inv. no. PMD 978.9.1
Exhibited at the first Salon de L'Art Nouveau, 1895, no. 163
fig. 113

PAUL RENOUARD

Portrait of Siegfried Bing
c. 1890, pencil on paper, 14 x 10.5 cm
Musée des Arts décoratifs (Cabinet des dessins), Paris
inv. no. 56921
fig. 2

Portrait of Siegfried Bing
c. 1890, pencil on paper, 14 x 10.5 cm
Musée des Arts décoratifs (Cabinet des dessins), Paris
inv. no. 56922
fig. 3

Portrait of Siegfried Bing
c. 1890, pencil on paper, 14 x 10.5 cm
Musée des Arts décoratifs (Cabinet des dessins), Paris
inv. no. 56923
fig. 4

CHARLES RICKETTS

Illustrations for Oscar Wilde, 'The Sphinx'
1894, book, 22 x 17 cm
Museum van het Boek, Meermanno-Westreenianum, The Hague
inv. no. K 097 D 018
A copy exhibited at the International Modern Book exhibition, L'Art Nouveau, June 1896, no. 102

JOZSEF RIPPL-RONAI

Woman with Birdcage
1892, oil on canvas, 185.5 x 130 cm
Magyar Nemzeti Galéria, Budapest
inv. no. 1385
Exhibited at the first Salon de L'Art Nouveau, 1895, no. 169, and the József Rippl-Rónai exhibition, L'Art Nouveau, June 1897, no. 4
fig. 155

Illustrations for Georges Rodenbach, 'Les Vierges' (Virgins), published by L'Art Nouveau
1895, book, lithograph on paper, 26 x 17.5 cm
Van Gogh Museum, Amsterdam
inv. no. p 1794 v/2000
A copy exhibited at the first Salon de L'Art Nouveau, 1895, no. 633, and the International Modern Book exhibition, June 1896, no. 123

Pale woman
1896, oil on canvas, 99.7 x 80 cm
Magyar Nemzeti Galéria, Budapest
inv. no. 2314
Exhibited at the József Rippl-Rónai exhibition, L'Art Nouveau, June 1897, no. 124
fig. 154

AUGUSTE RODIN

Head of St John the Baptist
1887, bronze, 21 x 14 x 27 cm
Musée Rodin, Paris
inv. no. S 519
Marble version exhibited at the first Salon de L'Art Nouveau, 1895, no. 361
fig. 147 (marble version)

ROOKWOOD POTTERY

The Rookwood Pottery, founded in 1880 by Marie Longworth Nichols (1847–1939) at Cincinnati, Ohio, was active from 1880 to 1941. From its inception, the firm produced ceramics that were both commercial and artistic. At the turn of the century, Rookwood developed decorative motifs influenced by Japanese art: the designs, executed principally under glaze, were asymmetrical and drew on forms from nature for their decoration.

Rookwood was awarded the Grand Prix at the 1900 Paris World's Fair. Several items were acquired by European museums through Siegfried Bing. The Boston Fine Arts Museum possesses a substantial collection bequeathed by Marie Longworth Nichols. Even more so, the objects in the Cincinnati Art Museum demonstrate the range of the Rookwood decorators and designers who made Rookwood internationally famous.

Vase, decorated by Sara Sax
1896, earthenware, h: 19.5 cm
Museum für Kunst und Gewerbe, Hamburg
inv. no. 1900.302
Purchased from S. Bing at the Paris World's Fair, 1900

Vase, decorated by Kataro Shirayamadani
1897, earthenware, h: 29 cm
Germanisches Nationalmuseum, Nürnberg
inv. no. LGA 8.530
Purchased (400 francs) from S. Bing, 5.11.1900
fig. 91

Vase, decorated by Albert R. Valentien
1899, earthenware, h: 44.8 cm; diam: 18.5 cm
Museum für Kunst und Gewerbe, Hamburg
inv. no. 1900.193
Purchased (625 francs) from S. Bing at the Paris World's Fair, 1900

Vase, decorated by Anna Maria Valentien
1899, earthenware, h: 27 cm
Germanisches Nationalmuseum, Nürnberg
inv. no. LGA 8.529
Purchased (300 francs) from S. Bing, 5.11.1900
fig. 92

Vase, decorated by Amalia B. Sprague
1899, earthenware, h: 25.7 cm; diam: 12 cm
Kunstgewerbemuseum, Berlin
inv. no. 1900/579
Purchased (110.52 marks) from S. Bing, 7.7.1900
fig. 87

Vase, decorated by Harriet E. Wilcox
1899, earthenware, h: 19.5 cm; diam: 8.8 cm
Kunstgewerbemuseum, Berlin
inv. no. 1900/582
Purchased (73.68 marks) from S. Bing, 24.7.1900

Vase, decorated by Olga Geneva Reed
1900, earthenware, h: 22 cm
Germanisches Nationalmuseum, Nürnberg
inv. no. LGA 8.532
Purchased (125 francs) from S. Bing, 5.11.1900

Vase, decorated by Harriet E. Wilcox
1899, earthenware and silver, h: 20.7 cm; diam: 14.5 cm
Kunstgewerbemuseum, Berlin
inv. no. 1900/578
Purchased (276.30 marks) from S. Bing, 24.7.1900
fig. 88

'Freesias' Vase, decorated by Harriet E. Wilcox
1900, earthenware, h: 26.3 cm; diam. 14 cm
Victoria and Albert Museum, London
inv. no. 1686–1900
Purchased (£10.0.9) from S. Bing, 1900
fig. 85

'Poppies' Vase, decorated by Constance A. Baker
1900, earthenware, h: 21; diam. 9.5 cm
Victoria and Albert Museum, London
inv. no. 1688–1900
Purchased (£5.0.9) from S. Bing, 1900

'Wisteria' Vase, decorated by Olga Geneva Reed
c. 1900, earthenware, h: 31.1 cm; diam. 11.8 cm
Victoria and Albert Museum, London
inv. no. 1689–1900
Purchased (£12.0.7) from S. Bing, 1900

RÖRSTRAND

This Swedish factory, founded in 1726, is one of the oldest ceramic factories in Europe. The early years of the Rörstrand factory were troubled until it merged with the competing Marieberg factory in 1782. During the second half of the 18th century, the two factories produced glazed earthenware. From 1850, Rörstrand perfected its skills and designs and became extremely successful.

In 1900, the factory diversified its techniques, producing majolica, hard- and soft-paste porcelain and biscuit.

The decoration, in low relief, was inspired by the world of plants and animals, using pastel tones obtained by high-temperature firing.

The factory also employed painters and sculptors, notably Alf Wallander, E.H. Tryggelin, Algot Eriksson, Nils Lundström and Karl Lindström.

Rörstrand was awarded a Grand Prix at the 1900 Paris World's Fair. There are many examples in the collections of European museums of the decorative arts that were acquired through Siegfried Bing or La Maison Moderne.

Vase with celandine flowers
1890s, porcelain, h: 16.8 cm; diam. 8.3 cm
Victoria and Albert Museum, London
inv. no. 1695–1900
Purchased (£1.17.0) from S. Bing, 1900

Vase
c. 1898, porcelain, h: 15.5 cm
Musée des Arts décoratifs, Paris
inv. no. 8718
Purchased (35 francs) from S. Bing, 25.5.1898
fig. 290

Vase 'Red Clover', designed by Alf Wallander
c. 1899, porcelain, h: 12.3; diam. 7.5 cm
Museum für Kunst und Gewerbe, Hamburg
inv. no. 1900.294
Purchased from S. Bing at the Paris World's Fair, 1900

Vase 'Arrowhead', designed by Alf Wallander
c. 1899, porcelain, h: 22.6; diam. 11 cm
Museum für Kunst und Gewerbe, Hamburg
inv. no. 1900.293
Purchased from S. Bing at the Paris World's Fair, 1900

Vase 'Bellflowers'
c. 1899, porcelain, h: 16 cm; diam. 10 cm
Museum für Kunst und Gewerbe, Hamburg
inv. no. 1900.312
Purchased from S. Bing at the Paris World's Fair, 1900

Vase with fish
c. 1899, porcelain, h: 29.9 cm
Österreichisches Museum für angewandte Kunst, Vienna
inv. no. 344/Ke 4054
Purchased (176 francs) from S. Bing, 17.4.1899
fig. 289

Black floral vase
c. 1899, porcelain, h: 27.1 cm
Österreichisches Museum für angewandte Kunst, Vienna
inv. no. 313/Ke 4055
Purchased (176 francs) from S. Bing, 17.4.1899

Vase with pansies
c. 1900, porcelain, h: 21.3 cm; diam. 10.2 cm
Victoria and Albert Museum, London
inv. no. 1694–1900
Purchased (£2.16.0) from S. Bing, 1900

Fruit dish
c. 1900, porcelain, diam: 23.3 cm
Musée des Arts décoratifs, Paris
inv. no. 9620
Purchased (35 francs) from the Atelier Art Nouveau, 18.5.1901

Vase
c. 1900, porcelain, h: 18.5 cm
Österreichisches Museum für angewandte Kunst, Vienna
inv. no. 345/Ke 4052
Purchased (76 francs) from S. Bing, 16.8.1900

VICTOR ROUSSEAU

Happiness
1894, marble, 57 x 57 x 28 cm
Musée des Beaux-Arts, Tournai
inv. no. Sc/71.85
Exhibited at the first Salon de L'Art Nouveau, 1895, no. 365
fig. 148

KER-XAVIER ROUSSEL

The Garden
1894, oil on board, mounted on canvas, 121 x 91.4 cm
Carnegie Museum of Art, Pittsburgh
inv. no. 69.27
Gift of Mr. and Mrs. John F. Walter
fig. 70

ROYAL COPENHAGEN

Originally founded in 1775 by the chemist Frantz Heinrich Müller, the factory was taken over in 1779 by King Christian VII as sole proprietor and named the Royal Danish Porcelain Factory. In 1868, the government decided that the factory was too expensive and handed it over to an entrepreneur, Mr Falck, who was permitted to retain the company name and use the trade mark – three horizontal wavy lines that symbolise the three Danish waterways.

Business improved and in 1882 Falck sold the factory to the Alumina company, which had been a successful manufacturer of glazed earthenware since 1872. This company was headed by Philipp Schou, an engineer by training.

With the intention of creating a 'national style', he appointed the young architect and painter Arnold Krog (1856–1931) as the factory's artistic director in 1885. Krog immediately gave up the imitations of Persian faience, Delft and majolica and devoted himself to inventing an entirely new style. A palette of colours obtained from high-temperature firing was perfected: cobalt blue, chromium green, and a red derived from gold. The ornamental vocabulary was at first influenced by Japanese art and later inspired by Danish fauna and flora.

The Factory's efforts were rewarded with a Grand Prix at the 1889 Paris World's Fair. The gallery L'Art Nouveau was one of the Paris shops where the public could buy Copenhagen porcelain.

Fish, designed by M. Andresen
c. 1888, porcelain, length: 17 cm
Musée des Arts décoratifs, Paris
inv. no. 5012
Purchased (10 francs) from S. Bing, 8.12.1888

Platter
c. 1888, porcelain, diam: 40 cm
Musée des Arts décoratifs, Paris
inv. no. 5010
Purchased (350 francs) from S. Bing, 8.12.1888

Vase
c. 1888, porcelain, h: 22 cm
Musée des Arts décoratifs, Paris
inv. no. 5001
Purchased (75 francs) from S. Bing, 1.12.1888
fig. 291

Platter
c. 1888, porcelain, diam: 25 cm
Musée des Arts décoratifs, Paris
inv. no. 5002
Purchased (45 francs) from S. Bing, 1.12.1888
fig. 292

TONY SELMERSHEIM

The architect and interior designer Tony Selmersheim (1871–1971) studied at the Ecole des Arts décoratifs and completed his training by taking the classes taught by the painter and interior designer Eugène Grasset at the Ecole Guérin. He exhibited suites of furniture from 1896 onwards and participated in the 1900 Paris World's Fair. At that time his name was often linked with those of the architect Charles Plumet (between 1896 and 1904) and his brother Pierre Selmersheim. Tony Selmersheim is best known for having designed an important suite of furniture for the French Embassy in Vienna and for his collaboration with Maurice Dufrêne in furnishing the liner *Paris*. His style, associated with the *art nouveau* movement, grew progressively more restrained and, influenced by the revival of the French tradition, turned towards classical models.

Fabric
c. 1900, silk, 133 x 63 cm
Musée des Arts décoratifs, Paris
inv. no. 12925
Purchased (48.60 francs) from Majorelle, 26.7.1906

PAUL SERUSIER

The Pilgrimage to Notre-Dame des Portes
1894–95, oil on canvas, 92 x 73 cm
Musée des Beaux-Arts, Quimper
inv. no. E 1073
Exhibited at the first Salon de L'Art Nouveau, 1895, no. 175
fig. 139

HENRY SOMM

Fantaisies Japonaises
c. 1879, etching on paper, 8.1 x 11.9 cm
Van Gogh Museum, Amsterdam
inv. no. p 0825 M/1994
fig. 13

Japonisme
1881, etching on paper, 24.2 x 31.9 cm
Van Gogh Museum, Amsterdam
inv. no. p 1796 s/2000
fig. 14

ALEXANDRA THAULOW

The second wife of the painter Fritz Thaulow (see fig. 137), Alexandra Thaulow (1862–1955) designed a number of bookbindings and leather items.

Wallet
c. 1905, leather, 16 x 11.5 cm
Musée des Arts décoratifs, Paris
inv. no. 15275
Gift of Marcel Bing, 26.10.1908

LOUIS COMFORT TIFFANY

Charles Louis Tiffany founded Tiffany & Co in New York in 1837. At that time, the shop specialised in fancy goods and stationery. His son, Louis Comfort Tiffany (1848–1933), who took over the family business, travelled to North Africa, where he discovered the Roman and Spanish-Moorish glassware that influenced his work.
In 1877, Tiffany, Colman Innes and John La Farge founded an artists' cooperative, the Society of American Artists, which led to the formation of Louis C. Tiffany & Associated Artists in 1878. During these same years, Tiffany began producing remarkable stained glass. In 1885 he created Tiffany Glass and, at the instigation of Siegfried Bing, he produced a series of stained-glass panels for the gallery L'Art Nouveau designed by Toulouse-Lautrec, Paul Sérusier, Edouard Vuillard and Pierre Bonnard in 1895. Influenced by oriental objects and his numerous contacts with Europe, Louis Comfort Tiffany also produced objects in blown glass inspired by Gallé. In 1894, he registered the Favrile trademark (for iridescent glass).
In Paris, the gallery L'Art Nouveau had exclusive rights to Tiffany items. In 1890, Tiffany Studio was founded to produce bronzes and lamps and, in 1900, Tiffany also began producing jewellery and objects in gold and silver. This development was further extended to the design of furniture, textiles, and artistic wrought iron.

Vase
c. 1893, favrile glass, h: 16 cm
Musée des Arts décoratifs, Paris
inv. no. 7971
Purchased (125 francs) from S. Bing, 2.6.1894
Stained-glass window
1894, 110 x 70 cm
Musée des Arts décoratifs, Paris
inv. no. 7972
Purchased (450 francs) from S. Bing, 2.6.1894
fig. 73
Vase
c. 1894–95, favrile glass, h: 18 cm
Musée des Arts décoratifs, Paris
inv. no. 8202
Purchased (150 francs) from S. Bing, 5.7.1895
Vase
c. 1894–95, favrile glass, h: 9 cm; diam: 9 cm
Musée des Arts décoratifs, Paris
inv. no. 8203
Purchased (50 francs) from S. Bing, 5.7.1895
Spherical vase
c. 1895, favrile glass, h: 11.5 cm
Museum für Kunst und Gewerbe, Hamburg
inv. no. 1896.090
Purchased from S. Bing at the first Salon de L'Art Nouveau, 1895
Bottle
c. 1895, favrile glass, h: 15 cm
Musée des Arts décoratifs, Paris
inv. no. 8425
Purchased (160 francs) from S. Bing, 7.7.1896
Bowl
c. 1895, favrile glass, h: 12.2 cm
Germanisches Nationalmuseum, Nürnberg
inv. no. LGA 8.334
Purchased from S. Bing, 1898
Gourd vase
c. 1895, favrile glass, h: 15 cm
Musée des Arts décoratifs, Paris
inv. no. 8426
Purchased (100 francs) from S. Bing at the Salon du Champ de Mars, 7.7.1896
Gourd vase
c. 1895–96, favrile glass, h: 34.5 cm
Österreichisches Museum für angewandte Kunst, Vienna
inv. no. Gl. 1988
Purchased (100 francs) from S. Bing, 21.3.1898
fig. 286
Vase
c. 1896, favrile glass, h: 32 cm
Musée des Arts décoratifs, Paris
inv. no. 8554
Purchased (150 francs) from S. Bing, 2.7.1897
fig. 84
Glass
c. 1896, favrile glass, h: 30 cm
Österreichisches Museum für angewandte Kunst, Vienna
inv. no. Gl. 1984
Purchased (156 francs) from S. Bing, 21.3.1898
fig. 78 (right)
Vase
c. 1896, favrile glass, h: 27.2 cm
Österreichisches Museum für angewandte Kunst, Vienna
inv. no. Gl. 1986
Purchased from S. Bing, 21.3.1898
fig. 82
Vase
c. 1896, favrile glass, h: 38.5 cm
Österreichisches Museum für angewandte Kunst, Vienna
inv. no. Gl. 1989
Purchased (180 francs) from S. Bing, 21.3.1898
fig. 90
Vase
c. 1897, favrile glass, h: 21.2 cm
Österreichisches Museum für angewandte Kunst, Vienna
inv. no. Gl. 1987
Purchased (120 francs) from S. Bing, 21.3.1898
fig. 81
Vase
c. 1897, favrile glass, h: 22 cm
Musée des Arts décoratifs, Paris
inv. no. 8552
Purchased (350 francs) from S. Bing, 2.7.1897
Vase
c. 1897, favrile glass, h: 10 cm
Musée des Arts décoratifs, Paris
inv. no. 8553
Purchased (175 francs) from S. Bing, 2.7.1897
fig. 80
Double gourd vase
c. 1897, favrile glass, h: 26.5 cm
Museum für Kunst und Gewerbe, Hamburg
inv. no. 1900.334
Purchased from S. Bing at the Paris World's Fair, 1900
fig. 83
Vase
c. 1897, favrile glass, h: 7 cm
Museum für Kunst und Gewerbe, Hamburg
inv. no. 1900.338
Purchased (50 francs) from S. Bing, 22.11.1900
Vase
c. 1898–99, favrile glass, h: 11 cm
Musée des Arts décoratifs, Paris
inv. no. 9084
Purchased (350 francs) from S. Bing, 5.7.1899
fig. 79
Onion flower vase
c. 1899–1900, favrile glass, h: 34.8 cm
Museum für Kunst und Gewerbe, Hamburg
inv. no. 1900.337
Purchased from S. Bing at the Paris World's Fair, 1900
fig. 278
Covered box
c. 1900, metal, copper, enamel, h: 8.3 cm; diam: 9 cm
Kunstgewerbemuseum, Berlin
inv. no. 1900/598
Purchased (204.66 marks) from S. Bing at the Paris World's Fair, 24.7.1900
fig. 280
Lamp
c. 1900, glass and bronze, 46 x 31 cm
Nordenfjeldske Kunstindustrimuseum, Trondheim
inv. no. NK 8793
Purchased from S. Bing at the Paris World's Fair, 1900
fig. 298

HENRI DE TOULOUSE-LAUTREC

At the Nouveau Cirque: The Female Clown and the Five Penguins (Papa Chrysanthème)
c. 1894, oil and mixed media on paper,
59.5 x 40.5 cm
Museum of Fine Arts, Philadelphia
inv. no. 1939–8–1
Purchased with the John D. McIlhenny Fund
fig. 75

Theatre Box with Gold Mascaron (mask)
1894, lithograph on paper, 37.2 x 23.7 cm
Van Gogh Museum, Amsterdam
inv. no. P 1330 V/2000
An example sold (15 francs) at the Sale of the Bing Collection, Hôtel Drouot, Paris, 1900, no. 125
fig. 126

VICTOR VALLGREN

Vase with figure (Pain)
1894, bronze, 25 x 14 x 14 cm
Ateneum, Helsinki
inv. no. B 168:1
Exhibited at the first Salon de L'Art Nouveau, 1895, no. 375
fig. 288

Vase (Red poppy)
c. 1894, bronze, 17.5 x 8.5 x 8 cm
Ateneum, Helsinki
inv. no. B 168:2
Exhibited at the first Salon de L'Art Nouveau, 1895, no. 377

Vase
1895, bronze, 15 x 10.5 x 8.5 cm
Ateneum, Helsinki
inv. no. B 293
Exhibited at the first Salon de L'Art Nouveau, 1895, no. 379

FELIX VALLOTTON

The Burial
1891, woodcut on paper, 25.7 x 35.2 cm
Van Gogh Museum, Amsterdam
inv. no. P 1297 V/2000
An example exhibited at the second Salon de L'Art Nouveau, 1896, no. 777

Swans
1892, woodcut on paper, 13.5 x 17.7 cm
Van Gogh Museum, Amsterdam
inv. no. P 1480 V/2000
An example exhibited at the second Salon de L'Art Nouveau, 1896, no. 783

The Murder
1893, woodcut on paper, 14.7 x 24.5 cm
Van Gogh Museum, Amsterdam
inv. no. P 1486 V/2000
An example exhibited at the second Salon de L'Art Nouveau, 1896, no. 762

The Bath
1894, woodcut on paper, 18.1 x 22.5 cm
Van Gogh Museum, Amsterdam
inv. no. P 1099 V/2000
An example exhibited at the second Salon de L'Art Nouveau, 1896, no. 765
fig. 127

Parisian Women, cartoon for a stained-glass window
1894, oil on canvas, 128.5 x 60 cm
Private collection
fig. 77

Business card for L'Art Nouveau
1895, paper, 14 x 9 cm
Museum für Kunst und Gewerbe, Hamburg
inv. no. Vallotton (10)

Poster for L'Art Nouveau
1895, lithography on paper, 62 x 45 cm
Musée de la Publicité, Paris
inv. no. 14548
fig. 117

Illustrations for the Prospectus for the Exposition Internationale du Livre Moderne
1896, paper, 28 x 40.7 cm
Museum für Kunst und Gewerbe, Hamburg
inv. no. 1897.805

VINCENT VAN GOGH

Woman Bending Down
1885, black chalk, washes on paper, 52.5 x 43.5 cm
Kröller-Müller Museum, Otterlo
inv. no. KM 119.134
Sold (200 francs) at the Sale of the Bing Collection, Hôtel Drouot, Paris, 1900, no. 115
fig. 132

Pear Tree in Blossom
1888, oil on canvas, 73 x 46 cm
Van Gogh Museum, Amsterdam (Vincent van Gogh Foundation)
inv. no. S 0039 V/1962
fig. 49

THEO VAN RYSSELBERGHE

The Canal in Flanders
1894, oil on canvas, 60 x 80 cm
Private collection
Exhibited at the first Salon de L'Art Nouveau, 1895, no. 201
fig. 115

Illustrations for Emile Verhaeren, Almanach
1895, book, 21 x 19.5 cm
Collection A. and L. F.
A copy exhibited at the International Modern Book exhibition, L'Art Nouveau, June 1896, no. 384

HENRY VAN DE VELDE

Architect and interior designer. After taking painting classes at the Antwerp Academy and studying in Paris under Carolus-Duran, Van de Velde (1863–1957) began his career as a painter in 1889 as a member of the Brussels avant-garde group Les XX. However, his social convictions and his admiration for William Morris inclined him towards the decorative arts, and *La veillée des anges* (The angels' vigil, 1892–93), inspired by the example of painter Emile Bernard, marked the beginning of his work in the applied arts. Van de Velde produced his first furniture in 1894, and he built and decorated his own house, Bloemenwerf at Uccle near Brussels, in 1895. His meeting with Siegfried Bing was to be decisive: Bing commissioned him to furnish three rooms (a dining room, a smoking room and an art-collector's study) for the opening of his gallery L'Art Nouveau in December 1895. In 1899, the art critic Julius Meier-Graefe asked him to decorate his new shop, La Maison Moderne. While continuing his theoretical work, he moved to Berlin, where he received several commissions and was appointed to construct the Werkbund theatre for the 1914 Cologne exhibition. Van de Velde later spent time in Switzerland and Holland, where he designed the plans for the Kröller-Müller Museum, before returning to Belgium, where he founded the Brussels Institut Supérieur des Arts Décoratifs, which he ran for ten years. Towards the end of his life he settled in Switzerland, devoting his last years to writing his memoirs.

Chair
1895–1902, wood/textile, 87.8 x 64 x 53 cm
Nordenfjeldske Kunstindustrimuseum, Trondheim
inv. no. NK 44–1900
An example exhibited at the first Salon de L'Art Nouveau, 1895, no. 527
fig. 109

Two tiles
c. 1900, coloured glass with glazed decoration, 20.25 x 20.2 x 0.5 cm
Bernische Stiftung für angewandte Kunst und Gestaltung, Bern
inv. no. 8–20 a+b
Purchased (10 francs the two) from S. Bing, 1900
fig. 111

Tile
c. 1900, opal glass with enamelled colours, 19.75 x 19.8 x 0.6 cm
Bernische Stiftung für angewandte Kunst und Gestaltung, Bern
inv. no. 8–19
Purchased (5 francs) from S. Bing, 1900
fig. 111

Door handle with key hole
c. 1900, brass, h: 30 cm
Nordenfjeldske Kunstindustrimuseum, Trondheim
inv. no. NK 10–1901
Purchased (60 francs) from S. Bing, 22.2.1901
fig. 112

EDOUARD VUILLARD
Chestnut Trees, cartoon for a stained-glass window
c. 1894–95, oil on board mounted on canvas, 110 x 70 cm
Private collection
fig. 71
Three plates
c. 1895, porcelain, diam: 24.5 cm
Private collection
Exhibited at the first Salon de L'Art Nouveau, 1895
fig. 123
Woman in a Striped Dress
1895, oil on canvas, 65.7 x 58.7 cm
National Gallery of Art, Washington
Collection of Mr. and Mrs. Paul Mellon
inv. no. 1983.1.38
Exhibited at the first Salon de L'Art Nouveau, 1895, no. 210
fig. 128

LUDWIG VON ZUMBUSCH
Cover for the journal 'Jugend'
1896, journal, 30 x 24 cm
Van Gogh Museum (Library), Amsterdam
inv. no. BVG 16303
Copies of the journal exhibited at the International Modern Book exhibition, L'Art Nouveau, June 1896, no. 263

ORIENTAL ART & DESIGN

Please note that all items are Japanese unless otherwise stated

Paintings and drawings

ANONYMOUS
Still Life with Cat (two-leafed screen)
beginning of the 17th century
ink and colours on paper, 86 x 98.5 cm
Musée national des Arts asiatiques-Guimet, Paris
inv. no. EO 827
Gift of Marcel Bing, 1906
figs. 27, 45

KITAGAWA UTAMARO (1754–1806)
Fan 'Courtesan playing the Koto'
ink and colours on silk, 52.8 x 20.8 cm
Mr. John C. Weber Collection
Sold (400 francs) at the Sale of the Bing Collection, Paris, 12.5.1906, no. 702
fig. 51

KATSUSHIKA HOKUSAI (1760–1849)
Fan 'Crayfish'
c. 1807–10, ink and colours on paper, 16 x 43 cm
Musée national des Arts asiatiques-Guimet, Paris
inv. no. EO 28
Gift of S. Bing, 1893

MATSUMURA KEIBUN (1779–1843)
Iris, Shijô school
ink and colours on silk, 197 x 62 cm
Museum für Kunst und Gewerbe, Hamburg
inv. no. 1897–374
Purchased (75 francs) from S. Bing, 1897

SHIBATA ZESHIN (1807–1891)
Diptych, Eagles near a waterfall
c. 1880, ink and colours on silk, 92 x 34 cm
Museum für Kunst und Gewerbe, Hamburg
inv. no. 1901–743 a/b
Purchased at the Sale of the Bing Collection, Paris, 12.5.1906
fig. 37

ANONYMOUS
Album of botanical drawings
1827, pen and ink and watercolour on paper, 40.5 x 27.7 cm
Victoria and Albert Museum, London
inv. no. D 975–1002–1889
Purchased from S. Bing, 1889
Album of drawings
19th century, pen and ink and colours on paper, 60.2 x 32.8 cm
Victoria and Albert Museum, London
inv. no. D 1003–1008–1889
Purchased from S. Bing, 1889
fig. 41

UTAGAWA KUNIYOSHI (1797–1861)
Album of sketches
pen and ink on paper, 22.7 x 32.2 cm
Victoria and Albert Museum, London
inv. no. D 1194–1210–1889
Purchased from S. Bing, 1889

Woodblock prints

KAIGETSUDÔ ANCHI (ACTIVE EARLY 18TH CENTURY)
Courtesan with a Cat
c. 1700–16, woodblock print (sumizuri-e), 56 x 30.5 cm
Musée national des Arts asiatiques-Guimet, Paris
inv. no. EO 185
Gift of S. Bing, 1893

TORII KIYONAGA (1752–1815)
The Iris Pond, right print from a diptych
colour woodblock print (nishiki-e), 36.7 x 94.7 cm
Musée des Arts décoratifs, Paris
inv. no. 3857
Purchased (20 francs) from S. Bing, 15.11.1887
fig. 53

UTAGAWA TOYOKUNI (1769–1825)
The Fifth Month from the 'Twelve Months' series
c. 1801, colour woodblock print (nishiki-e), 37 x 74.8 cm
Musée des Arts décoratifs, Paris
inv. no. 7197
Purchased (350 francs) from S. Bing, 14.5.1892

UTAGAWA HIROSHIGE (1797–1858)
Red-headed Crane on a Wave, from the 'Flowers and Birds' series
1830–44, colour woodblock print (nishiki-e), 36.5 x 17 cm
Musée national des Arts asiatiques-Guimet, Paris
inv. no. EO 196
Gift of S. Bing, 1893

KATSUSHIKA HOKUSAI (1760–1849)
The Ghost of Kohada Koheiji, from the series 'One Hundred Tales'
c. 1831, colour woodblock print (nishiki-e), 25.8 x 18.5 cm
Musée national des Arts asiatiques-Guimet, Paris
inv. no. EO 190
Gif of S. Bing, 1893
fig. 38

UTAGAWA KUNIYOSHI (1797–1861)
Tsukudajima from the series 'Famous Views of Tokyo'
1833–35, colour woodblock print (nishiki-e), 24.7 x 35.8 cm
Musée des Arts décoratifs, Paris
inv. no. 3873
Purchased (20 francs) from S. Bing, 15.11.1887
fig. 60

Ceramic

ANONYMOUS
Bottle
early 19th century, unglazed stoneware with slip decoration, Hagi ware, Fukawa kilns, h: 18.3 cm
Musée des Arts et Métiers, Paris
inv. no. 11365
Gift of S. Bing, 1888

Gourd bottle
19th century, porcelain with design in overglaze enamels, Kutani ware, Yoshidaya kilns, h: 21 cm; diam. 10.5 cm
Musée des Arts décoratifs, Paris
inv. no. 651
fig. 31

Bowl with design of a bird on a branch of plum tree
19th century, ceramic with underglaze painting, possibly Fujina ware, 9.3 x 17.4 cm
Museum für Kunst und Gewerbe, Hamburg
inv. no. 1890–80
Gift from Alfred Beit to Justus Brinckmann. Originally purchased from S. Bing, 1890

Brazier in form of fabulous lion's head
19th century, stoneware, Bizen ware, h: 32 cm; diam. 33 cm
Musée des Arts décoratifs, Paris
inv. no. 2207
Purchased (350 francs) from S. Bing, 27.1.1886
fig. 36

Furnace
19th century, unglazed ceramic, possibly Kyoto
Musée national de Céramique, Sèvres
inv. no. MNC 7046
Purchased from S. Bing, 1874

OGATA KENZAN (1663–1743)

Incense burner
stoneware with overglaze enamels, Kyoto ware, 10.4 x 11.7 cm
Museum für Kunst und Gewerbe, Hamburg
inv. no. 1896–88
Purchased from S. Bing, 1896

KÛCHÛSAI

Incense burner in the form of the Chinese monk Fenggan resting on his tiger
18th century, ceramic with iron oxide glaze, h: 8.7 cm
Museum für Kunst und Gewerbe, Hamburg
inv. no. 1905–37 a,b
Purchased from Marcel Bing (Hayashi Sale, no. 752), 1905

ANONYMOUS

Jar
end of the 18th century, stoneware with designs in underglaze iron in the Sonkoroku style, Satsuma ware, 31.1 x 25.5 cm
Victoria and Albert Museum, London
inv. no. 1120–75
Purchased (£16) from S. Bing, 1876

Jar
19th century, stoneware with multiple layers of glaze, north Kyûshû (possibly Takatori), h: 28 cm
Musée des Arts décoratifs, Paris
inv. no. 4605
Purchased (125 francs) from S. Bing, 25.2.1899

Plate
17th century, porcelain, suisaka style, Arita ware, h: 26 cm; diam. 14.8 cm
Musée des Arts décoratifs, Paris
inv. no. 2204
Purchased (35 francs) from S. Bing, 27.1.1886

Bowl
end of the 17th century, enamelled Kyoto ware, Iwakurasan kilns, 14.3 x 7 cm
Musée des Arts décoratifs, Paris
inv. no. 2183
Purchased (35 francs) from S. Bing, 27.1.1886
fig. 34

Plate, style of Ogata Kenzan
first half of the 18th century, ceramic, Kyoto ware, 18.7 x 19.4 cm
Museum für Kunst und Gewerbe, Hamburg
inv. no. 1897–92
Purchased from S. Bing, 1897

Plate
early 19th century, pottery with moulded design and green glaze, Gennai ware
Musée des Arts décoratifs, Paris
inv. no. 2212
Purchased (35 francs) from S. Bing, 27.1.1886

Sake bottle
19th century, enamelled stoneware with engraved decoration, Agano ware, Hoshô kilns
Musée des Arts décoratifs, Paris
inv. no. 2211
Purchased (140 francs) from S. Bing, 27.1.1886
fig. 35

Sake bottle in a gourd form
19th century, ceramic with a slip design of a horse and shark-style glaze, Soma-Ohori ware, h: 20 cm
Musée des Arts et Métiers, Paris
inv. no. 11392
Purchased from S. Bing, 1888

RAKU ICHIGEN

Tea bowl
18th century, pottery with raku glaze, Kyoto, Tamamizu ware, 6.9 x 10.8 cm
Museum für Kunst und Gewerbe, Hamburg
inv. no. 1901–143
Purchased from S. Bing, 1901

OKUDA KIBAI (1799–1871)

Tea bowl
pottery with design of Mount Fuji, Akahada ware, 8 x 10 cm
Museum für Kunst und Gewerbe, Hamburg
inv. no. 1895–230
Purchased from S. Bing, 1895

ANONYMOUS

Tea bowl
19th century, ceramic with moulded design of a horse, Soma-Ohori ware, h: 7.8 cm
Musée national de Céramique, Sèvres
inv. no. MNC 7103
Purchased from S. Bing, 1875
fig. 32

Tea bowl
19th century, stoneware with coloured glaze, Agano ware, h: 7 cm
Musée des Arts et Métiers, Paris
inv. no. 11395
Gift of S. Bing, 1888

ISENIN HÔIN

Tea caddy (cha-ire)
late 18th, early 19th century, pottery with raku glaze, 8.5 x 6.5 cm
Museum für Kunst und Gewerbe, Hamburg
inv. no. 1901–17 a,b
Purchased from S. Bing, 1901

ANONYMOUS

Water jar (mizusashi)
early 19th century, pottery with a design of crows in black and gold, ancient gold lacquer restoration, Kyoto ware, h: 16.5 cm
Musée des Arts et Métiers, Paris
inv. no. 11356
Purchased from S. Bing, 1888
fig. 9

Water jar (mizusashi)
early 19th century, stoneware with underglaze iron painting of a landscape, h: 11.5 cm
Musée des Arts et Métiers, Paris
inv. no. 11358
Purchased from S. Bing, 1888
fig. 33

Water jar (mizusashi)
19th century, stoneware with multiple layers of glaze, Takatori ware, 17.3 x 18.5 cm
Musée des Arts et Métiers, Paris
inv. no. 11357
Purchased from S. Bing, 1888

Lacquerware

ANONYMOUS

Comb
19th-century, wood, gold lacquer, length: 13.7 cm
Victoria and Albert Museum, London
inv. no. 42–1888
Purchased from S. Bing, 1888

Comb
19th century, wood, gilt metal, applied silver and bronze, length: 11.1 cm
Victoria and Albert Museum, London
inv. no. 45–1888
Purchased from S. Bing, 1888

Comb
19th century, wood, gold lacquer, length: 13.7 cm
Victoria and Albert Museum, London
inv. no. 46–1888
Purchased from S. Bing, 1888

Comb
19th century, wood, gold and white lacquer, length: 13.7 cm
Victoria and Albert Museum, London
inv. no. 48–1888
Purchased from S. Bing, 1888

Comb
19th century, wood, red and gold lacquer, mother-of-pearl, length: 12.7 cm
Victoria and Albert Museum, London
inv. no. 54–1888
Purchased from S. Bing, 1888
fig. 10

Comb
19th century, wood, gold lacquer, length: 11.7 cm
Victoria and Albert Museum, London
inv. no. 65–1888
Purchased from S. Bing, 1888
fig. 11

Comb
19th century, wood, black lacquer, mother-of-pearl, length: 14 cm
Victoria and Albert Museum, London
inv. no. 72–1888
Purhased from S. Bing, 1888
fig. 54

Comb
19th century, wood, gold lacquer, mother-of-pearl, length: 14 cm
Victoria and Albert Museum, London
inv. no. 82–1888
Purchased from S. Bing, 1888

Comb
19th century, wood, red and gold lacquer, length: 12.7 cm
Victoria and Albert Museum, London
inv. no. 86–1888
Purchased from S. Bing, 1888

Comb
19th century, wood, lacquer, length: 11.4 cm
Victoria and Albert Museum, London
inv. no. 87–1888
Purchased from S. Bing, 1888

Fabrics

ANONYMOUS

Fabric with cranes in circular forms (tsurumaru)
18th century, embroidery on silk, 98.5 x 83 cm
Musée des Arts décoratifs, Paris
inv. no. 12813
Purchased (1,100 francs) at the Sale of the Bing Collection, Paris, 12.5.1906, no. 724

Fabric with cranes flying over the waves
18th century, embroidery on silk, 98.5 x 83 cm
Musée des Arts décoratifs, Paris
inv. no. 12825
Purchased (550 francs) at the Sale of the Bing Collection, Paris, 12.5.1906, no. 773

Fabric with foliage and butterflies
19th century, silk and velvet, 46 x 29 cm
Musée des Arts décoratifs, Paris
inv. no. 4539
Purchased (10 francs) from S. Bing, 10.1.1888
fig. 42

Fabric with noren (shop curtain) pattern
19th century, embroidery on silk, 38.7 x 50.8 cm
Musée des Arts décoratifs, Paris
inv. no. 7363 A
Purchased from S. Bing, 12.11.1892

Fabric with peonies and butterflies
19th century, silk, 45 x 24 cm
Musée de la Mode et du Textile, Paris
inv. no. 7383 A
Purchased from S. Bing, 12.11.1892

Fabric with a carp swimming against the current
19th century, embroidery on silk, 76 x 68.5 cm
Musée des Arts décoratifs, Paris
inv. no. 9008
Purchased (75 francs) from S. Bing, 23.05.1899
fig. 23

Fabric with puppies playing
19th century, silk, 37 x 19.5 cm
Musée de la Mode et du Textile, Paris
inv. no. 12805
Gift of Marcel Bing, 12.5.1906
fig. 15

Fabric with rabbits in the snow
19th century, satin and embroidery, 57 x 52 cm
Musée des Arts décoratifs, Paris
inv. no. 12814
Purchased (66 francs) at the Sale of the Bing Collection, Paris, 12.5.1906

Fabric with three cranes flying over the waves
19th century, embroidery on silk, 81.5 x 75.5 cm
Musée des Arts décoratifs, Paris
inv. no. 12826 (12815)
Purchased (198 francs) at the Sale of the Bing Collection, Paris, 12.5.1906
fig. 43

Obi (belt) with a pattern of wisterias on a wooden fence
18th century, embroidery on silk, 170 x 40 cm
Musée des Arts décoratifs, Paris
inv. no. 12818
Purchased (330 francs) at the Sale of the Bing Collection, Paris, 12.5.1906

Undergarment
18th century, silk, satin and patchwork, 112 x 136 cm
Musée des Arts décoratifs, Paris
inv. no. 19534
Purchased (350 francs) from Marcel Bing, 3.11.1914

Metalware

ANONYMOUS

Cylindrical vase
19th century, bronze, h: 28.7 cm
Victoria and Albert Museum, London
inv. no. 85–1876
Purchased (£7) from S. Bing, 6.11.1875
fig. 30

Incense burner in the form of a goose
19th century, patinated bronze, h: 69 cm
Victoria and Albert Museum, London
inv. no. 1904–76
Purchased (£108) from S. Bing, 26.5.1876

Jardinière
18th century, bronze, 15.1 x 22.6 cm
Nordenfjeldske Kunstindustrimuseum, Trondheim
inv. no. NK 4793
Purchased (750 francs) from S. Bing, 1896
fig. 28

Sake kettle
18th century, mottled and chased iron, silver inlay and lacquered lid, h: 20 cm; diam: 17.5 cm
Victoria and Albert Museum, London
inv. no. 1874–76
Purchased (£7.10.0) from S. Bing, 26.5.1876

Sake kettle
19th century, mottled and chased iron, white metal, 14.5 x 24 cm
Victoria and Albert Museum, London
inv. no. 1877–76
Purchased (£5.10.0) from S. Bing, 26.5.1876

Sword guard (tsuba)
Momoyama period (1568-1600)
iron, pierced and carved with bridge and waves, Kamakura-bori style, diam. 6.8 cm
Museum für Kunst und Gewerbe, Hamburg
inv. no. 1904–52
Purchased from S. Bing, 1904 (Gillot Sale)

UMETADA SHIGEYOSHI

Sword guard (tsuba)
1662, copper, inlaid gold, pierced and carved with designs of decorated fans, 8.4 x 8 cm
Museum für Kunst und Gewerbe, Hamburg
inv. no. 1885–1105
Purchased from S. Bing, 1885

UMETADA TACHIBANA SHIGEYOSHI

Sword guard (tsuba)
Kyoto, c. 1700, copper, inlaid gold, with a design of the Tatsuta river in autumn, 7.1 x 6.6 cm
Museum für Kunst und Gewerbe, Hamburg
inv. no. 1885–617
Purchased from S. Bing, 1885

NAKAI ZENSUKE TOMOTSUNE I (1706–1780)

Sword guard (tsuba)
iron and inlaid gold, pierced and carved with a design of swallows, 8.3 x 0.3 cm
Museum für Kunst und Gewerbe, Hamburg
inv. no. 1893–382
Purchased from S. Bing, 1893
fig. 19

CHÔSHÛ (SCHOOL OF)

Sword guard (tsuba)
18th century, iron, pierced and carved with a design of facing sprouts of the *myôga* plant, diam: 8.4 cm
Museum für Kunst und Gewerbe, Hamburg
inv. no. 1885–650
Purchased from S. Bing, 1885
fig. 18

TETSUGENDÔ SHÔRAKU

Sword guard (tsuba)
Kyoto, 18th century, iron, inlaid gold, with dragon motif, 7.2 x 6.8 cm
Museum für Kunst und Gewerbe, Hamburg
inv. no. 1897–280
Purchased (240 francs) from S. Bing, 1897 (Goncourt Sale, no. 807)

BUSHÛ (SCHOOL OF)

Sword guard (tsuba)
19th century, iron and copper, pierced and carved with a design of flying cranes in the rain, 7.5 x 6.9 cm
Museum für Kunst und Gewerbe, Hamburg
inv. no. 1885–846
Purchased from S. Bing, 1885
fig. 17

SUNAGAWA MASAYOSHI

Sword guard (tsuba)
19th century, copper with inlaid gold, pierced and carved with a design of peonies, 7.9 x 7.5 cm
Museum für Kunst und Gewerbe, Hamburg
inv. no. 1892-471
Purchased from S. Bing, 1892

ANONYMOUS

Vase
19th century (Chinese), bronze, h: 24 cm
Musée des Arts décoratifs, Paris
inv. no. 7195
Purchased from S. Bing, 14.5.1892
Vase
19th century (Chinese), bronze, h: 22 cm
Musée des Arts décoratifs, Paris
inv. no. 7196
Purchased (40 francs) from S. Bing, 14.5.1892

Carving

ANONYMOUS

Nô-mask of the female demon Hannya
18th century, carved and painted wood, 23.5 x 16.7 cm
Victoria and Albert Museum, London
inv. no. 578J–1886
Purchased from S. Bing, 1876
fig. 55
Nô-mask of the old woman Uba
18th century (signed Himi Saku), carved and painted wood, 20.9 x 14.1 cm
Victoria and Albert Museum, London
inv. no. 578K–1886
Purchased from S. Bing, 1876
fig. 56
Nô-mask of the old woman Uba
18th century, carved and painted wood
Musée national des Arts asiatiques-Guimet, Paris
inv. no. EO 2165
Donation Marteau (1916), previously purchased at the Bing Sale

SELECT BIBLIOGRAPHY

1906 Paris
Collection S. Bing, Objets d'art et peintures du Japon et de la Chine, Sale, Paris (Galerie Durand-Ruel), 7–10 May 1906.

Album de références
Album de références de l'Art Nouveau, Bibliothèque des Arts décoratifs, Paris.

Alexandre 1895
Arsène Alexandre, 'L'Art Nouveau', *Le Figaro*, 28 December 1895, p. 1.

Amsterdam 1993–4
Ian Millman, exhib. cat. *Georges de Feure. The Crucial Years 1895–1905*, Amsterdam (Van Gogh Museum) 1993–4.

Art Nouveau Bing 1904
Art Nouveau Bing. Meubles artistiques, tapis, bronzes, céramiques, appareils d'éclairage, bijoux enrichis de pierreries et d'émaux, Sale, Paris (Hôtel Drouot), 19–20 December 1904.

Arwas 2002
Victor Arwas, *Art Nouveau: The French Aesthetic*, London 2002.

Ashmore 2001
Sonia Ashmore, *Liberty's Orient: Taste in late Victorian and Edwardian Britain, 1875–1917*, Ph.D., Camberwell College of Arts, The London Institute, 2001.

Bailly-Herzberg 1975
Janine Bailly-Herzberg, 'Essai de reconstitution grâce à une correspondance inédite du peintre Pissarro du magasin que le fameux marchand Samuel Bing ouvrit en 1895 à Paris pour lancer l'Art Nouveau', *Connaissance des Arts*, no. 283 (September 1975), pp. 72–82.

Bailly-Herzberg 1989
Janine Bailly-Herzberg, *Correspondance de Camille Pissarro*, Paris 1989, 4 vols.

Becker 1993
Ingeborg Becker, exhib. cat. *Henry van de Velde in Berlin*, Berlin (Bröhan Museum) 1993.

Bing 1902
Siegfried Bing, 'L'Art Nouveau', *The Architectural Record* 12 (August 1902), pp. 279–85.

Bing 1903
Siegfried Bing, 'L'Art Nouveau', trans. from the French by Irene Sargent, *The Craftsman* 5, no. 1 (October 1903), pp. 1–15.

Bing 1970
Artistic America, Tiffany Glass, and Art Nouveau. Samuel Bing, trans. Robert Koch, Cambridge, Mass., & London 1970.

Boileau 1896
Louis-Charles Boileau, 'La Maison de L'«Art Nouveau»', *L'Architecture* 2 (11 January 1896), pp. 9ff.

Cadastre 1876
Ville de Paris. Cadastre de 1876 (Archives de Paris).

Cathers 2003
David Cathers, *Gustav Stickley*, London & New York 2003.

Chalmers Johnson 1979
Diane Chalmers Johnson, *American Art Nouveau*, New York 1979.

Chesneau 1878a
Ernest Chesneau, 'Le Japon à Paris–1', *Gazette des Beaux-Arts* 8 (September 1878), pp. 385–97.

Chesneau 1878b
Ernest Chesneau, 'Le Japon à Paris–2', *Gazette des Beaux-Arts* 8 (November 1878), pp. 841–56.

Cogeval 2003
Guy Cogeval *et. al.*, exhib. cat. *Edouard Vuillard*, Washington, D.C. (National Gallery of Art), Montreal (Museum of Fine Arts), Paris (Galeries Nationales du Grand Palais) & London (Royal Academy of Arts) 2003–4.

Didot-Bottin 1854 etc. (to 1900)
Didot-Bottin, *Annuaire-Almanach du Commerce et de l'Industrie*, Paris 1854 etc. (to 1900).

Dresden 1897
Führer durch die Internationale Kunst-Ausstellung, Dresden 1897, 2nd ed., 4 May 1897, Dresden-Blasewitz 1897.

Eidelberg and Henrion-Giele 1977
Martin Eidelberg and Suzanne Henrion-Giele, 'Horta and Bing: An Unwritten Episode of l'Art Nouveau', *Burlington Magazine* 119, no. 896 (November 1977), pp. 747–52.

Eidelberg 1983
Martin Eidelberg (ed.), exhib. cat. *E. Colonna*, Dayton (Dayton Art Institute) 1983.

Faulkner and Jackson 1995
Rupert Faulkner and Anna Jackson, 'The Meiji Period in South Kensington, The Representation of Japan in the Victoria and Albert Museum, 1852–1912', in *Meiji No Tarara: Treasures of Imperial Japan (The Nassar D. Khalili Collection of Japanese Art)*, ed. Oliver Impey and Malcolm Fairley, vol. 1, London 1995, pp. 152–94.

Gonse 1883
Louis Gonse, *L'Art Japonais*, 2 vols. Paris 1883.

Gonse 1886
Louis Gonse, *L'Art Japonais*, new ed., Paris 1886.

Guérrand 1965
Roger H. Guérrand, *L'Art Nouveau en Europe*, Paris 1965.

Hagen etc. 1992–4
Exhib. cat. *Henry van de Velde – Ein Europaïscher Künstler in seiner Zeit*, ed. Klaus-Jürgen Sembach and Birgit Schulte, Hagen (Karl Ernst Osthaus Museum), Weimar (Kunstsammlungen zu Weimar), Berlin (Bauhaus-Archiv, Museum für Gestaltung), Ghent (Design Museum), Zürich (Museum für Gestaltung) & Nuremberg (Germanisches Nationalmuseum) 1992–4.

Hempel 1981
Rose Hempel, 'Die Japansammlungen des Museums für Kunst und Gewerbe Hamburg' in 'Japan-Sammlungen in Museen Mitteleuropas', *Bonner Zeitschrift für Japanologie* 3 (1981), pp. 159–66.

Joppien 1999
Rüdiger Joppien, exhib. cat. *Louis C. Tiffany. Meisterwerke des amerikanischen Jugendstils*, Hamburg (Museum für Kunst und Gewerbe) 1999.

Klemm 2004
David Klemm, *Das Museum für Kunst und Gewerbe Hamburg. Von den Anfängen bis 1945*, Hamburg 2004.

Koch 1964
Robert Koch, *Louis C. Tiffany, Rebel in Glass*, New York 1964.

Koechlin 1930
Raymond Koechlin, *Souvenirs d'un vieil amateur d'art de l'Extrême-Orient*, Chalon-sur-Saône 1930.

Koyama-Richard 2001
Brigitte Koyama-Richard, *Japon Rêvé, Edmond de Goncourt et Hayashi Tadamasa*, Paris 2001.

Krahmer 1992–4
Catherine Krahmer, 'Über die Anfänge des Neuen Stils. Henry van de Velde – Siegfried Bing – Julius Meier-Graefe', in Hagen etc. 1992–4, pp. 148–64.

Lacambre 1980
Geneviève Lacambre, 'Les milieux japonisants à Paris, 1860–1880', in *Japonisme in Art. An International Symposium*, Tokyo (Committee for the Year 2001) 1980, pp. 43–55.

Le Goffe 1989
Michèle Le Goffe, *Sites, signes, vies au centre de la vallée de l'Aulne*, Châteauneuf-du-Faou 1989.

London & Washington 2000–1
Exhib. cat. *Art Nouveau 1890–1914*, London, ed. Paul Greenhalgh (Victoria and Albert Museum) & Washington (National Gallery of Art) 2000–1.

Loring 2002
John Loring, *Louis Comfort Tiffany at Tiffany*

and Co., New York 2002.

Luc 1903
Luc, 'Le château de Trévarez', *Le Figaro*, 15 October 1903, p. 3.

Maus 1900
Octave Maus, 'Le Pavillon de l'Art nouveau à l'Exposition Universelle', *L'Art Moderne*, no. 26, 1 July 1900, pp. 209–10.

Meech and Weisberg 1990
Julia Meech and Gabriel P. Weisberg, *Japonisme Comes to America, The Japanese Impact on the Graphic Arts, 1876–1925*, New York 1990.

Meier-Graefe 1896
Julius Meier-Graefe, 'L'Art Nouveau. Das Prinzip', *Das Atelier* 6, no. 5 (1896), pp. 2–4.

Meier-Graefe 1898
Y [Julius Meier-Graefe], 'Belgische Innendekoration', *Dekorative Kunst* 1, vol. 1, no. 5 (February 1898), pp. 199–206.

Meier-Graefe 1900
G.M. Jacques [Julius Meier-Graefe], 'L'Exposition Universelle. L'Art nouveau Bing', *L'Art Décoratif* 6, no. 21 (June 1900), pp. 88–97.

Meier-Graefe 1901
G.M. Jacques [Julius Meier-Graefe], 'Un petit salon', *L'Art Décoratif* 7, no. 31 (April 1901), pp. 23–30.

Meier-Graefe 2002
Julius Meier-Graefe, *Kunst ist nicht für Kunstgeschichte da. Briefe und Dokumente*, ed. Catherine Krahmer with Ingrid Grüninger, Göttingen 2002.

Midant 1999
Jean-Paul Midant, *L'Art Nouveau en France*, Paris 1999.

Millman 1992
Ian Millman, *Georges de Feure. Maître du Symbolisme et de l'Art Nouveau*, Paris 1992.

Moffett 1973
Kenworth Moffett, *Meier-Graefe as art critic*, Munich 1973.

Montgomery 1993
Susan J. Montgomery, *The Ceramics of William H. Grueby. The Spirit of the New Idea in Artistic Handicraft*, Lambertville, New Jersey, 1993.

Morot 1938
Manuscrit Morot, *Notes sur l'Art nouveau. Entreprise de S. Bing à la fin du XIXe siècle, par son fidèle collaborateur de 1888 à 1904*, March 1938, Archives Louis Bonnier, Institut français d'architecture, Paris.

Mourey 1900a
Gabriel Mourey, 'L'Art nouveau de M. Bing à l'Exposition Universelle', *Revue des Arts Décoratifs* 20 (1900), pp. 257–68.

Mourey 1900b
Gabriel Mourey, 'L'Art nouveau de M. Bing à l'Exposition Universelle' (2nd article), *Revue des Arts Décoratifs* 20, (1900), pp. 278–84.

Owen 2001
Nancy E. Owen, *Rookwood and the Industry of Art: Women, Culture, and Commerce, 1880–1913*, Athens, Ohio, 2001.

Paris 1988
Exhib. cat. *Le Japonisme*, Paris (Galeries nationales du Grand Palais) 1988.

Peck 1968
Herbert Peck, *The Book of Rookwood Pottery*, New York 1968.

Saint-Germain-en-Laye & Gingins 1995
Exhib. cat. *Georges de Feure. Du symbolisme à l'art nouveau, 1890–1905*, ed. Ian Millman, Saint-Germain-en-Laye (Musée départemental Maurice Denis, 'Le Prieuré') & Gingins (Fondation Neumann) 1995.

Schaeffer 1962
Herwin Schaeffer, 'Tiffany's Fame in Europe', *The Art Bulletin* 44, no. 4 (December 1962), pp. 309–28.

Shimizu 2001
Christine Shimizu, *Le Grès japonais*, Paris 2001.

Sichel 1883
Philippe Sichel, *Notes d'un Bibeloteur au Japon*, avec une préface de M. Edmond de Goncourt, Paris 1883.

Silverman 1989
Deborah L. Silverman, *Art Nouveau in fin-de-siècle France. Politics, Psychology, and Style*, Berkeley, Los Angeles & London 1989.

Soulier 1900
Gustave Soulier, 'L'Ameublement à l'Exposition', *Art et Décoration* 8 (August 1900), pp. 34–45.

Spielmann 2003
Heinz Spielmann, *Justus Brinckmann*, Hamburg 2003.

Troy 1991
Nancy Troy, *Modernism and the decorative arts in France. Art Nouveau to Le Corbusier*, New Haven & London 1991.

Turin 1994
Torino 1902. *Le Arti Decorative Internazionali del Nuovo Secolo*, Turin 1994.

Ulmer 1999
Renate Ulmer (ed.), exhib. cat. *Art Nouveau. Symbolismus und Jugendstil in Frankreich*, ed. Darmstadt (Institut Mathildenhöhe) 1999.

Van de Velde 1992
Henry Van de Velde, *Récit de ma vie*, ed. with commentary by Anne Van Loo in collaboration with Fabrice van de Kerckhove, Brussels 1992.

Weisberg 1975
Gabriel P. Weisberg *et al.*, *Japonisme, Japanese Influence on French Art, 1854–1910*, exhib. cat. Cleveland (The Cleveland Museum of Art), New Brunswick, New Jersey (The Rutgers University Art Gallery) & Baltimore (The Walters Art Gallery) 1975.

Weisberg 1978
Gabriel P. Weisberg, 'Gérard, Dufraisseix and Abbott: The Manufactory of Bing Porcelains in Limoges, France', *The Connoisseur* 197, no. 792 (February 1978), pp. 125–9.

Weisberg 1983
Gabriel P. Weisberg, 'A note on S. Bing's Early Years in France, 1854–1876', *Arts Magazine* 57, no. 5 (January 1983), pp. 84–5.

Weisberg 1985–6
Gabriel Weisberg, 'Siegfried Bing and Frank Brangwyn. The Gallery L'Art Nouveau in Paris in 1895', *Jaarboek Stad Brugge* Bruges (Stedelijke Musea) 1985–6, pp. 277–86.

Weisberg 1986a
Gabriel P. Weisberg, exh. cat. *Art Nouveau Bing: Paris Style 1900*, Richmond, Virginia (The Virginia Museum of Fine Arts), Omaha, Nebraska (The Joslyn Art Museum), Sarasota, Florida (John and Mable Ringling Museum of Art) & New York (The Cooper-Hewitt Museum) 1986–7.

Weisberg 1986b
Gabriel P. Weisberg, 'On Understanding Artistic Japan', *The Journal of Decorative and Propaganda Arts* (Spring 1986), pp. 6–19.

Weisberg 1987a
Gabriel P. Weisberg, 'S. Bing in America', in Gabriel P. Weisberg and Laurinda Dixon (eds.), *The Documented Image, Visions in Art History*, Syracuse 1987, pp. 51–68.

Weisberg 1987b
Gabriel P. Weisberg, 'S. Bing and "La Culture Artistique en Amérique": A Public Report Reexamined', *Arts Magazine* 61, no. 7 (March 1987), pp. 59–63.

Weisberg 1988
Gabriel P. Weisberg, 'Siegfried Bing and Industry. The Hidden Side of L'Art Nouveau', *Apollo* 128, no. 321 (November 1988), pp. 326–9, 379.

Weisberg 1990
Gabriel P. Weisberg and Yvonne Weisberg, *Japonisme. An Annotated Bibliography*, New York, London & New Brunswick, New Jersey 1990.

Weisberg 1993
Gabriel P. Weisberg, *The Independent Critic, Philippe Burty and the Visual Arts of Mid-Nineteenth Century France*, New York & Bern 1993.

Weisberg 1996
Gabriel P. Weisberg, 'Clement Heaton, Siegfried Bing, and Art Nouveau, Paris: 1895–1902' in *Clement Heaton 1861–1940, Londres – Neuchâtel – New York*, Hauterive 1996, pp. 184–93.

Weisberg 1999
Gabriel P. Weisberg, 'The French Reception of American Art at the Universal Exposition of 1900' in exhib. cat. *Paris 1900. The 'American School' at the Universal Exposition*, ed. Diane P. Fisher, Montclair (Montclair Art Museum) 1999, pp. 145–80.

INDEX

ACKNOWLEDGEMENTS

We would like to express our heartfelt gratitude to all public and private lenders for their most generous support of this project, especially the following persons and institutions:

Austria

Albertina, Vienna
Dr. Klaus-Albrecht Schröder, Director
Österreichisches Museum für angewandte Kunst, Vienna
Kathrin Pokorny-Nagel, Head of the MAK Library and Collection of Works on Paper
Dr. Johannes Wieninger, Curator Far Eastern and Islamic Art
Dr. Christian Witt Dörring, Curator Furniture and Woodwork
Dr. Jan Van Nimmen, Vienna

Belgium

Design Museum Gent
Musée des Beaux-Arts, Tournai
Musée Constantin Meunier, Brussels
Musée Horta, Brussels
Françoise Aubry, Curator
Musées royaux d'Art et d'Histoire, Brussels
Werner Adriaenssens, Arts Décoratifs et Industries d'Art du XXe siècle
Claire Leblanc, Attaché scientifique
Musées royaux des Beaux-Arts de Belgique, Brussels
Véronique Coomans-Cardon, The Contemporary Art Archives
Frederik Leen, Head of the Department of Modern Art
Dominique Marechal, Curator 19th-Century Paintings
Francisca Vandepitte, Curator Modern Prints & Sculpture
Stedelijke Musea, Bruges
Laurence van Kerkhoven, Adjunct-conservator
Tony Calabrese
Patrick Derom, Brussels
Jan Eykelberg, Van Herck BVBA, Antwerp
Adrienne Fontainas
Jacques et Rolande van der Heyde
Marc Lambrechts
Librairie Fl. Tulkens, Brussels
Jean Warmoes

Czech Republic

Michaela Hajková, Curator, Jewish Museum, Prague
Dr. Karel Holesovsky

Denmark

Det Danske Kunstindustrimuseum, Copenhagen
Bodil Busk Laursen, Director
Marianne Ertberg, Curator
Jørgen Schou-Christensen, Curator
Freddy Jensen
Erik Lassen
Steen Vedel

Finland

Ateneum Art Museum, Helsinki
Leena Ahtola-Moorhouse, Curator
Ebba Bränback, Design Museum, Helsinki
Laura Gutman-Hanhivaara, Helsinki
Marjatta Levanto, Helsinki
Marja Supinen, Helsinki
Marketa Tamminen, Porvoo

France

Archives d'architecture du XXe siècle (Institut français d'architecture), Paris
Guillaume Marchand, conservateur
Les Archives de Paris
Brigitte l'Aîné, conservateur
Marie-Andrée Corcuff, conservateur en chef
Christiane Filloles, documentaliste
Archives des Musées nationaux, Paris
Archives du Ministère des affaires étrangères, Paris
Archives nationales de France, Paris
Bibliothèque administrative de la Ville de Paris
Bibliothèque d'Art et d'Archéologie-Bibliothèque Doucet, Paris
Bibliothèque des Arts décoratifs, Paris
Josiane Sartre, conservateur général
Guillemette Delaporte, bibliothécaire
Bibliothèque d'Etude, Bibliothèques municipales de Rouen
Marie-Dominique Nobécourt Mutarelli, responsable du fonds ancien
Bibliothèque Forney, Paris
Bibliothèque historique de la Ville de Paris
Bibliothèque de la manufacture de Céramiques, Sèvres
Bibliothèque des musées nationaux, Paris
Bibliothèque nationale de France, Paris (Cabinet des Estampes, Département des Imprimés, Département des Manuscrits)
Conseil général du Finistère
Annick Barré
Daniel Créoff
Isabelle Gargadennec
Pierre Jouvenel
Catherine Kerouanton
Mme Martin-Thoméré
Institut français d'architecture, Fonds Louis Bonnier, Paris
Mairie de Paris
Manufacture nationale de Sèvres
Tamara Préaud, conservateur, bibliothèque
Musée d'Art et d'Industrie, Roubaix
Musée d'Art moderne et contemporain, Strasbourg
Musée des Arts décoratifs, Paris
Cabinet des dessins, Chantal Bouchon, conservateur
Musée de la Mode et du Textile, Jean-Paul Leclerc, conservateur
Musée de la Mode et du Textile, Véronique Belloir, assistant à la conservation
Département Art Nouveau, Art Déco, Bijoux anciens, Hélène Andrieux
Département des Papiers peints, Véronique de la Hougue, conservateur
Musée des Arts et Métiers, Paris
Musée des Beaux-Arts, Dijon
Sophie Barthélémy, conservateur
Emmanuel Starcky, directeur
Musée des Beaux-Arts, Quimper
André Cariou, conservateur en chef
Musée Bouilhet-Christofle, Saint-Denis
Musée Bourdelle, Paris
Musée départemental Maurice Denis 'Le Prieuré', Saint-Germain-en-Laye
Agnès Delannoy, conservateur
Muséum d'Histoire naturelle, Rouen
Monique Fouray, conservateur en chef
Musée d'Orsay, Paris
Serge Lemoine, directeur
Musée d'Orsay, Service de Documentation, Paris
Dominique Lohenstein, directeur
Musée du Petit Palais
Musée de la Publicité, Paris
Réjane Bargiel, conservateur
Musée le Vergeur, Société des Amis du Vieux Reims, Reims
Liliane Chatillon, assistante de l'archiviste
Colette Cortet, archiviste
Dominique Néouze, président

Musée national Adrien Dubouché, Limoges
Laure Chabanne, conservateur
Chantal Meslin-Perrier, conservateur en chef
Musée national des Arts asiatiques-Guimet, Paris
Jacques Gies, conservateur en chef
Musée national de Céramique, Sèvres
Antoinette Fay-Halle
Christine Shimizu
Musée Rodin, Paris
Porcelaines GDA, Limoges
Raymond Clappier, directeur
Royal Limoges
Lionel Delaygue, directeur
Tribunal de Commerce, Paris
The late Jean Adhémar
Jean d'Albis, Limoges
Laurens and Yolande d'Albis, Paris
Cymbeline Audouy
Lucile Audouy
Françoise Aujogue, conservateur, section des fonds d'origine privée, Centre historique des Archives nationales, Paris
Gabriel Badéa Päun
Thérèse Barruel
Marc Bascou, ancien conservateur, Musée d'Orsay, Paris
Brooks and Annette Beaulieu, Saint-Germain-en-Laye
Chantal Beauvalot, Paris
Hilda and Gabriel Bénichou, Paris
The late Bernard Bonnier
Geneviève Bonté, Paris
Jean-Paul Bouillon, Paris
Yvonne Brunhammer, Paris
Anne Burdin-Hellebranth
Françoise Cachin, Paris
Mrs. M. Cappiello, Paris
Elisabeth Caude, conservateur, Musée National du Château de Compiègne
The late Jean-Loup Charmet
Marie-Cécile Comerre, Drouot documentation, Paris
Marie-Claude Coudert, conservateur, Musée des Beaux-Arts, Rouen
Gérard Daydé
Dominique and Claire Denis
Jacqueline Derbanne
Mr. and Mrs. Patrick Destrez, Nancy
Hervé Doucet
Christiane Douyère-Demeulenaere, conservateur, Section du XIXe siècle, Centre historique des Archives nationales, Paris
Jean-François Dreyfus
Véronique Dumas
The late Andrée Duizend
Henri Duizend
The late Charles Durand-Ruel
Yann Farinaux-Le Sidaner
Isabel Fonseca, Paris
Yves Gibbert, les ateliers de La Chapelle
Maître Rémy Le Fur, Paris
Marie-Noël de Gary, conservateur en chef,
Musée Nissim de Camondo, Paris
Nadine Gasc, Paris
The late Renée Genay
Geneviève Gille
Afsaneh Girardot, documentation, Espace Landowski, Boulogne-Billancourt
The late Renée Haase
Jean-Yves Inizan
Bernard Jacqué, directeur, Musée du Papier Peint de Rixheim
The late Mme Pierre-Paul Jouve
Jean-David Jumeau-Lafond, Paris
Catherine Krahmer
Geneviève Lacambre, Saint-Denis
Béatrice Lauwick, documentaliste, Service de Restauration, Les Musées Nationaux
Michèle Le Goffe, Brest
Jean-Marc Leri, directeur, Musée Carnavalet, Paris
David Liot, directeur, Musée des Beaux-Arts, Reims
Sylvie Le Ray, conservateur des Bibliothèques, des archives et de la Documentation générale, Direction des Musées de France, Paris
Patrick Locqueneux
The late Jacqueline Lordonnois
Georges Maldan, Les Amis de Georges Lacombe
Guillaume Marchand, conservateur, Institut français d'architecture, Archives d'Architecture du XXe siècle, Paris
Félix Marcilhac, Paris
Bernard Marrey, Paris
Nicole Maritch-Haviland
Ian Millman, Paris
Susanne Nagy, Paris
Monique Nonne, Aix-en-Provence
Christine Nougaret, conservateur général, responsable de la section des Archives privées, Centre historique des Archives nationales, Paris
Reine Marie, Paris
Roberto Polo
Maître Hervé Poulain, Paris
Prelle et Cie, Lyon
Anne Rivière
Dominique Suisse, Paris
Suzanne Tise-Isoré, Paris
Valérie Thomas, conservateur, Musée de l'Ecole de Nancy
Lynne Thornton, Paris
Bertrand de Viviés, conservateur, Musée des Beaux-Arts, Gaillac
Marie Watteau, Paris

Germany

Germanisches Nationalmuseum, Nürnberg
Hamburger Kunsthalle, Hamburg
Kaiser Wilhelm Museum, Krefeld
Dr. Sabine Röder, Curator
Kunstgewerbemuseum, Berlin (Staatliche Museen zu Berlin, Preußischer Kulturbesitz)
Dr. Susanne Netzer, Director
Museum für Kunst und Gewerbe, Hamburg
Dr. Nora von Achenbach, Curator of Oriental and Far Eastern Art
Dr. Jürgen Döring, Curator, Posters, Prints and Drawings
Prof. Dr. Wilhelm Hornbostel, Director
Dr. Rüdiger Joppien, Curator, Art Nouveau and Modernism
Helmut Sander, Managing Director
Dr. Margrit Bauer
Ms. E. Bornfleth, Nürnberg
Michael Buhrs, Deputy Director, Museum Villa Stuck, Munich
Ute Camphausen, Curator of Exhibitions, Museum für Kunsthandwerk, Leipzig
Dr. F.A. Dreier
Dr. Volkmar Enderlein, Museum for Islamic Art, Berlin
Dr. Gisela Fiedler
Fritz Fischer
Ms. Götze, Museums Zentral Archiv, Staatliche Museen zu Berlin
The late Dr. Rose Hempel, Hamburg
Dr. Julian Heynen
Dr. Kötzsch, Hamburg
Vera Leuschner
Dr. Ursula Lienert, Hamburg
The late Dr. Ruth Malhotra, Hamburg
Eberhard Patzig, Librarian, Museum für Kunsthandwerk, Leipzig
Jürgen Sielemann, Staatarchiv, Hamburg
Dr. Heinz Spielman, Hamburg
Dr. Andreas Stolzenburg, Hamburger Kunsthalle (Kupferstichkabinett)
Dr. Paul Tauchner, München

Great Britain

The Fine Art Society PLC, London
Simon Edsor, Director
William Morris Gallery, Walthamstow
Norah C. Gillow, Director
National Portrait Gallery, London
Victoria and Albert Museum, London
Richard Edgecumbe, Curator, Metalwork Department
Gregory Irvine, Curator of Japanese Art, Asian Department
Anna Jackson, Curator of Japanese Art, Asian Department
Sarah Medlam, Deputy Curator of Furniture and Woodwork
Lady Jane Abdy, London
Sir Angus and Lady Grossart
Victor and Gretha Arwas, London
Sonia Ashmore, London
Graham S. Gadd
Elizabeth Horner, London
David Hugues and Adrian Mibus, Whitford and Hugues, London
John Jesse
Peter Rose
Judy Rudoe, Curator 19th and 20th Century

Collections, Department of Prehistory and Europe, British Museum

Hungary
Iparmúveszeti Múzeum, Budapest
Hilda Horváth, Departemental Head
Dr. Pál Miklós, General Director
Magyar Nemzeti Galéria, Budapest
Dr. Anna Jávor, Director of the Collections
Veronika Kaposy, Budapest

Japan
Masayoshi Homma
Dr. Shigemi Inaga
Brigitte Koyama-Richard, Tokyo
Akiko Mabuchi, Curator, Museum of Western Art, Tokyo
Hisao Miyajima
Chisaburoh F. Yamada

The Netherlands
Kröller-Müller Museum, Otterlo
Museum van het Boek, Meermanno-Westreenianum, The Hague
Museum Mesdag, The Hague
Maartje de Haan, Curator-Manager
Van Gogh Museum (Library), Amsterdam
Anita Vriend, Librarian
Van Gogh Museum (Vincent van Gogh Foundation), Amsterdam
Andreas Blühm, Head of Exhibitions and Display
Sjraar van Heugten, Head of Collections
Aly Noordermeer, Senior Registrar
Fieke Pabst, Documentalist
Louis van Tilborgh, Curator of Paintings
Marije Vellekoop, Curator of Prints and Drawings
Sara Verboven, Registrar
Peter van Dam
Prof. Dr. Matthi Forrer, Curator of Japanese Arts, National Museum of Ethnology, Leiden
Ursula de Goede, RKD, Den Haag
Willem O. Russell

New Zealand
Prof. Dov Bing, University of Waikato

Norway
Nordenfjeldske Kunstindustrimuseum, Trondheim
Knut Astrup Bull, Curator
Jan I. Opstad, Director

Poland
Rogalin Gallery, Poznán
Piotr M. Michalowski, Curator

Spain
Fundación 'la Caixa', CaixaForum, Barcelona
Imma Casas, Director, Exhibitions Department
Marta Ponsa, Coordinator, Exhibitions Department
Mireia Gubern, Exhibitions Coordinator
Jordi Penas, Exhibitions Coordinator
Anna Font, Assistent Coordinator

Sweden
Elisabet Hidemark, Stockholm
The late Dr. and Mrs Dag Knutson, Granna
Dr. Helena Dahlback Lutteman, National-museum, Stockholm

Switzerland
Bernische Stiftung für angewandte Kunst und Gestaltung, Bern
Sara Stocker
Galerie Tonon, Geneva
Musée Barbier-Müller, Geneva
Marina Ducrey, Lausanne
Samuel Josefowitz
Dr. Hans Lüthy, Zurich
Alain Tarica
Claude, Donald, and Philippe Vallotton, Lausanne
Dr. Max Werren, Bern

United States
Carnegie Museum of Art, Pittsburgh
Museum of Fine Arts, Philadelphia
National Gallery, Washington
Telfair Museum of Art, Savannah
Holly Koons McCullough, Curator of Fine Arts and Exhibitions
Patricia Boyer
Janet Brown Barnes
Walter F. Brown
Dr. Doreen Burke, Director, The Baltimore Museum of Art
Dennis Cate, Curator, The Jane Voorhees Zimmerli Museum, Rutgers University
Dr. Petra Chu, Seton Hall University, South Orange
Dr. Helen Conant, New York
Louise Cort, Curator, The Freer Gallery of Art, Washington, D.C.
The late Henri Dorra
Dr. Martin Eidelberg, New York
Sarah G. Epstein, Washington, D.C.
Jane M. Farmer
Anne Gossett, SITES, Washington, D.C.
Gloria Groom, David and Mary Winton Green Curator of European Painting, The Art Institute of Chicago
Sylvia Herschede
Kathryn B. Hiesinger
The late Elizabeth G. Holt
Anthony Janson
The late Dora Jane Janson
The late H.W. Janson
William R. Johnston, Associate Director and Senior Curator of 18th and 19th Century Art, The Walters Art Museum, Baltimore
The late Robert Koch
Rebecca Lawton
Peggy Loar, Director, The American Centre for Wine, Food & The Arts, Nappa Valley
Mr. and Mrs Lloyd Macklowe, New York
Dr. Henry Millon
The late Lilian Nassau
Paul N. Perrot
David Ryan, Adjunct Curator of Design, Department of Decorative Arts, The Minneapolis Institute of Arts
Kenneth Trapp, Curator, The Renwick Gallery, Smithsonian American Art Museum, Washington, D.C.
Mr. John C. Weber, New York
Liz S. Ziegler, Assistant Curator of Art, Springfield Library and Museums

In addition, several other individuals have played a significant role during the long gestation of the Bing investigation, first in the preparation of the first Bing exhibition which took place in the United States in 1986 and, the present exhibition, organised by the Van Gogh Museum in concert with the Musée des Arts décoratifs in Paris: the late Professor Christopher Gray at Johns Hopkins University who introduced Gabriel P. Weisberg to the importance of S. Bing for the development of nineteenth-century art, the late H.W. Janson who understood the value of the project and helped in its fruition. Last, but not least, a very special word of thanks is due to Walter O. Michael and Carola Michael. Without their help we would have been unable to clarify the Bing family relationships or decipher the enormous business correspondence that is still extent between Bing and German and Scandinavian Museums. Walter Michael spent many hours translating documents that, in the absence of Bing's personal archive, made it possible for us to understand his vast business enterprise.

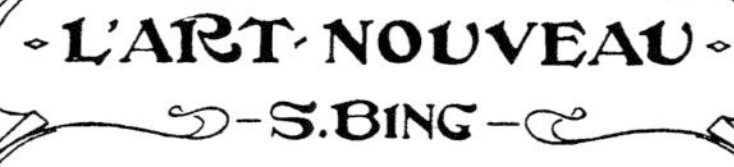
L'ART NOUVEAU
S. BING
22, RUE DE PROVENCE, PARIS
Objets d'art & d'ameublement
Bronzes · Etains · Poteries d'art
Bijoux d'art de style moderne
Verrerie d'art de Tiffany